BRINGING CARTHAGE HOME

UNIVERSITY OF BRITISH COLUMBIA
STUDIES IN THE ANCIENT WORLD
VOLUME 2

BRINGING CARTHAGE HOME

The Excavations of Nathan Davis, 1856–1859

JOANN FREED

With a Foreword by R. J. A. Wilson

Oxbow Books
Oxford and Oakville

for the Department of Classical, Near Eastern and Religious Studies
University of British Columbia

comitatui meo

UBC Studies in the Ancient World: Volume 2
Series editor: R. J. A. Wilson

First published in 2011
by Oxbow Books, Oxford, UK
for the Department of Classical, Near Eastern & Religious Studies,
University of British Columbia,
Vancouver V6T 1Z1

ISBN 978-1-84217-992-5

A CIP record for this book is available from the British Library

Library of Congress Cataloging-in-Publication Data
Freed, Joann, 1943–
Bringing Carthage home : the excavations of Nathan Davis, 1856-1859 / Joann Freed; with a foreword by R. J. A. Wilson.
p. cm. – (University of British Columbia studies in the ancient world ; v. 2)
Includes bibliographical references and index.
ISBN 978-1-84217-992-5
1. Davis, N. (Nathan), 1812–1882. 2. Carthage (Extinct city) 3. Excavations (Archaeology)–Tunisia–Carthage (Extinct city) 4. Punic antiquities. 5. Tunisia–Antiquities, Roman. 6. Romans–Tunisia–Carthage (Extinct city) 7. Pavements, Mosaic–Tunisia–Carthage (Extinct city) I. Title. II. Series: University of British Columbia studies in the ancient world ; v. 2.
DT269.C33F74 2011
939'.7303–dc23
2011032122

Cover photographs by R. J. A. Wilson, courtesy of the Trustees of the British Museum
Front cover: Carthage, detail of the Mosaic of the Months and Seasons, bust of Summer, excavated by Davis in 1857; last quarter of the fourth century AD
Back cover: another detail of the same mosaic, bust of Spring, and panel showing the month of April

This book is available direct from

Oxbow Books, Oxford, UK
(Phone: 01865-241249; fax: 01865-794449)

www.oxbowbooks.com

and

The David Brown Book Company
PO Box 511, Oakville, CT 06779, USA
(Phone: 860-945-9329; fax: 860-945-9468)

Designed by Charlotte Westbrook Wilson

Printed in Great Britain at Short Run Press, Exeter

Contents

NOTE TO READER

Two maps are referred to constantly throughout this book, those of Falbe and of Davis, and details of these are to be found respectively as Fig. 3.2 on p. 40 and Fig. 4.4 on p. 54 (with the whole map of the latter shown in Fig. 4.3). Reference is also made at several points to Davis' hitherto unpublished sketch-maps, which are Fig. 4.13 on p. 66 and Fig. 4.14 on p. 67. A Table of Concordance between the numbers on all four maps can be found on p. 82. A map showing the author's conclusions about precisely where mosaics found by Davis were located on the ground appears as Fig. 14.2 on p. 210. Fig. 14.2 also provides the detailed numbering of Carthage's Roman street-grid, frequently referred to throughout this book. A glossary of Arab place names often mentioned in the text can be found on p. 260. In the captions, all of the objects illustrated are in the British Museum in London (although not all are currently on display), unless otherwise indicated.

Foreword

by R. J. A. Wilson

Every day hundreds of visitors make their way up and down the north-west staircase in the British Museum on their way to other galleries. If they look up they will see the walls almost entirely covered by lavish polychrome mosaics. Any who care to stop and read the labels will learn that a majority of them come from Carthage in north Africa, one of the great metropolises in the ancient world; furthermore, if they decipher the Museum's cataloguing system, they will learn that all arrived in the Museum between 1857 and 1860. Two or three of these colourful pavements have received their share of discussion in modern academic works on ancient mosaic, most notably the Mosaic of the Muses, the Vandal Hunting Mosaic and especially the Mosaic of the Months and Seasons; but the story of their discovery, and of the man who excavated them, has never been told in detail.

That man was Nathan Davis, clergyman, adventurer and snake-handler extraordinaire; he was also widely-read and fluent in several languages. His qualifications to excavate at Carthage, however, rested on little more than that he 'knew' Tunisia, was on good terms with the Bey, and had already in the 1840s published books about the country. It seems extraordinary today that not only did he propose himself to the British Museum that he should acquire 'Punic' antiquities for its collections, but also that he persuaded the Foreign Office to fund him; he lived of course in a very different world. Energetic and resourceful, he was also chaotic, and the 'popular' account that he himself published in 1861, *Carthage and Her Remains*, has infuriated scholars who have tried to use it ever since. His brief to discover things Punic led him to make huge blunders: the most spectacular was perhaps his insistence that a fourth-century-AD mosaic, that of the Months and Seasons, belonged to a Punic temple. But it is greatly to Joann Freed's credit that she has persevered, and through painstaking research in archives, in London, Tunis, Paris and Rome, she has pieced together Nathan Davis' story and his pioneering achievements. In the course of it she has unearthed remarkable, hitherto unpublished, documents, presented in *Bringing Carthage Home* for the first time. They include magnificent watercolour paintings of The Mosaic of the Months and Seasons, a sketch of the Vandal Hunting Mosaic while still *in situ* (so allowing an appreciation of its overall composition which has not been possible before), and two sketch maps of the location of Davis' excavations, which have been crucial to the author's placing of them for the first time within the topography of ancient Carthage. The quality of the evidence available to do this with even approximate accuracy obviously varies from one find to another, but the author has argued the case for each with perseverance and determination, and the results (so far as the mosaics are concerned) are presented in Fig. 14.2.

The author has also performed signal service to scholarship by indicating the entire range of Davis' discoveries, so far as they can now be ascertained, for the first time. Only a fraction what he found was even briefly reported by him in *Carthage and Her Remains*, and he did not see it as his responsibility to provide a scholarly publication of his discoveries. The majority of the mosaics that he brought to London, for example, were not published until 1933, and those appeared in a British Museum catalogue which itself is now scarce and not to be found in many libraries around the world. As a result many of the floors that Davis found are little known, especially those in store which have never been on public display. Publishing or republishing images of them in *Bringing Carthage Home* will help make them accessible to a wider audience.

This book is, however, not only about Davis. By discussing in detail the antiquaries who worked at Carthage before him – and here the name of Christian Falbe and the magnificent map that he published in 1833 stand out – as well as those who followed later in the nineteenth century, the author has set Davis in the wider context of our knowledge of Carthage in the early stages of its exploration. At such she has made a major contribution to our knowledge of the history of archaeological exploration in north Africa. In addition, through a rich series of colourful vignettes, her book also provides us with a varied and fascinating glimpse of social and political intrigue in mid-nineteenth-century Tunisia.

Joann Freed has, in short, achieved the difficult task of extracting meaning out of the disorganized records left behind by Nathan Davis, and has decisively and impressively set the man and his achievements in the context of his age. In particular, she finds, with good reason, that Davis deserves especial credit for safely bringing over thirty mosaics to England, perfecting a lifting technique which represented a vast improvement on what had gone before. That some of his finds can still be seen and enjoyed in the British Museum is fitting testimony in itself to his energy and skill.

If I may be permitted a personal note, it is appropriate to record what a pleasure it has been to work on this book with the author and the designer. It was satisfying to have had the chance to take photographs specially for this book, in London, Karlsruhe and Tunisia, in 2009 and 2010, and throughout the editorial process my own personal copy of the 1861 edition of Nathan Davis' *Carthage and Her Remains* (longer pagination) has been constantly at my side. Still bound in its original blue cloth, with embossed gold lettering, it is one of only two archaeological books in my maternal grandmother's collection which has come down to me – it has been in my family's possession, as an ancestor's inscription on the inside front cover makes clear, since 1863. Davis' maps and drawings reproduced in *Bringing Carthage Home* have all been taken from this copy. There is even a connection, albeit a tenuous one, between *Bringing Carthage Home* and British Columbia. Of the colourful cast of characters which inhabits this book, one of the more intriguing is Captain Edwin Porcher, who assisted Davis at Utica, and whose map of the site, and the plan of a structure which yielded two mosaics, are included here (Figs 11.8 and 11.12). Combining his artistic skills with a naval career, Porcher later put the former to good use both in Cyrene and subsequently in British Columbia, where he was to command HMS *Sparrowhawk* between 1865 and 1868. We have included here as Fig. 1.2 a self-portrait of himself in his cabin on the latter expedition. There is even to this day an island in British Columbia, Porcher Island near Prince Rupert, named after him. I rather like what I know about Captain (later Commander) Porcher. His humanity, or at the very least his love of nature, is demonstrated on his plan of Utica (Fig. 11.8). In addition to the expected labels of 'ruins', 'cisterns', 'remains of temples' etc., he also chose to mark at one point, in the same size of lettering and no doubt of equal importance in his eyes, 'tortoises found here very tame'.

A final observation, and then I will leave the reader to turn the page and enjoy the fascinating story that here unfolds. By coincidence rather than design, *Bringing Carthage Home* is being published in the 150th anniversary year of the publication of Davis' *Carthage and Her Remains*. It brings a fresh and sympathetic assessment of his contribution to our knowledge of ancient Tunisia – a contribution that has hitherto been largely ignored. How Nathan Davis would have glowed with pride!

R. J. A. Wilson
University of British Columbia, Vancouver
August 2011

Preface and acknowledgements

This book recounts the earliest excavations at Carthage in the period from 1817 to 1859, although my focus is Nathan Davis and his excavations from 1856 to 1859. The book began as a footnote in which I attempted to summarize the sites and mosaics which Davis had excavated at Carthage, for a paper on the Mosaic of the Months and Seasons read at the Conference of the Classical Association of the Canadian West in March 2001.

While researching the early history of archaeology at Carthage, I had read Nathan Davis' *Carthage and Her Remains*. I was struck by his detailed discussion of the circumstances of the find of the Mosaic of the Months and Seasons, as well as his wrong-headed interpretation of the mosaic. I had proposed a paper on the excavation of the mosaic and its early scholarly publication, but the project almost immediately expanded beyond the boundaries of a conference paper. Since then I have given papers on the subject of this book at the Annual Meeting of the Archaeological Institute of America (January 2003), for the Archaeology Society at Wilfrid Laurier University, at Hartwick College in Oneonta, New York (October 2003), and at a conference, 'Building New Bridges/Batîr de nouveaux ponts' at the University of Ottawa in May 2004. In February 2006, I gave a paper at the North American conference of AIEMA, held at the Getty Villa in Santa Monica, on Davis' technique of lifting mosaics.

While Nathan Davis did not publish his excavations in a scholarly format, and provided hardly any dates for his excavations in *Carthage and Her Remains*, he sent his finds to the British Museum on ships of the British navy according to an agreement between himself, various staff members of the British Museum, including the Head Librarian, Antonio Panizzi, and the British Foreign Office, particularly the Earl of Clarendon. The practicalities were documented in Davis' book and in a number of letters and committee reports that survive in the Archives of the British Museum. When the finds were received, they were immediately recorded in a more or less cursory accession list now in the Department of Greek and Roman Antiquities. Some of the original documents and copies of documents relating to the excavations of Nathan Davis are held in the Department of Greek and Roman Antiquities in the Museum.

I was helped in my first inquiries by curator Paul Roberts and researcher Kate Cooper of the British Museum's Department of Greek and Roman Antiquities, and by Chris Entwistle, of the Department of Medieval and Modern Europe. Kate Cooper put copies of Davis' letters and sketch-maps into my hands, and answered my early queries with dispatch. Kenneth Uprichard, Head of Stone Conservation, answered questions on the conservation and display of Nathan Davis's mosaics. Ian Jenkins encouraged me to contact Christopher Date of the Central Archives of the Museum, where I was subsequently helped by Archives Assistant Gary Thorn. I owe a special debt of gratitude to Susan Walker, then Deputy Keeper in the Department of Greek and Roman Antiquities, for her enthusiasm and support for this project. To all of these and to all the other members of the staff of the Museum whom I contacted in my research on Davis and his excavations, I am very grateful.

In the summer of 2002, I consulted the correspondence between Davis and the Foreign Office, most of which has been gathered into one large volume held in the British National Archives (formerly the Public Record Office) at Kew. When it was impossible for me to go myself, Meg Armstrong went to the Scott Polar Research Institute in Cambridge, and took notes for me from the unpublished letters and journal of Sophia Cracroft. I warmly thank her for her kindness. I also thank Mr R. K. Headland, the archivist there, for his assistance to both of us. In the summer of 2004, I spent a day looking at papers related to Davis in the Archives of the Royal Geographical Society, where I was kindly aided by archivist Sarah Strong. I would also like to thank Julia Bolton Holloway and Akita Bright-Holloway, who created the wonderful website on the Protestant cemeteries at Florence, which I discovered in the summer of 2004.

This book benefits from nearly twenty years of work at Carthage under the aegis of Abdelmajid Ennabli, who for most of that time was Director of the National Museum of Carthage and Curator of the Site of Carthage, and from the kindness and scholarly guidance of both himself and his wife Liliane. Many scholars at Carthage have had the same generous treatment that I enjoyed from these wonderful friends of the archaeology of Carthage, and it is impossible to express my gratitude to them adequately. The book would also never have been born without hundreds of conversations about Carthage with the late Colin Wells, and much practical help from him, for whose deep knowledge and encouragement I am constantly grateful. Ron Ross has listened for many hours to my ideas about Davis and Carthage's early archaeology, and has offered many useful suggestions in the face of my difficulties with the knotty skein of evidence.

I have studied the history of archaeology at Carthage in many libraries; these include the library of the National Museum of Carthage; the Ashmolean (now Sackler) and Bodleian libraries at Oxford; the British Library and the Bibliothèque Nationale de France; the library of the Institut des Belles-Lettres Arabes in Tunis; the New York Public Library, and the Toronto Reference Library. The libraries of the University of Toronto have been a constant resource. In Rome I have worked in the library of the American Academy, where I was a Visiting Scholar in the fall of 2001, in the Vatican Library, and in the library of the French School at Rome. On a number of visits to Rome, I have worked at the library and archives of the White Fathers (Missionari d'Africa), where I have been greatly helped by archivist, Father Ivan Page, who has my warmest gratitude. I have also had much help from the interlibrary loan system at my home university and from TRELLIS, which combines the library resources of Wilfrid Laurier University, Waterloo University and the University of Guelph. I owe a special thanks to reference librarian Karen Peters at the University of Guelph, and to Reverend Bill Musk of St George's Anglican Church, Tunis.

Drafts of this book or parts of it have been read by Tana Allen, Paul Dion, Ronald Ross, Jeremy Rossiter and the late Colin Wells, whom I thank for their interest and suggestions. Following my father's suggestion that I could benefit from the views of a much younger person, I turned to Erika Nitsch, my outstanding undergraduate research assistant, whom I warmly thank for her reading of the text and her comments. Colin Wells supplied me with a copy of the Bordy map and of Gauckler's annual reports. Jennifer Moore told me about Carol Mendleson's catalogue of the Punic stelae in the British Museum. Paul Dion meticulously checked my references to French culture, and Chris Hebert suggested the chapter on Beulé.

Many other colleagues at Carthage, of whom many are personal friends and acquaintances, have helped increase my understanding of the ancient city. I am particularly grateful to scholars and friends such as the late Margaret Alexander, and to Tana Allen, Michel Bonifay, Beaudouin Caron, Jean Deneauve, Simon Ellis, Mylène Francescon, Mark Garrison, Roger Hanoune, John Hayes, John Humphrey, Angela Kalinowski, the late Serge Lancel, Hélène Leclerc, John Lund, Stefanie Martin-Kilcher, Guy Métraux, Jean-Paul Morel, Jihan Nacef, Lucinda Neuru, Naomi Norman, the late Friedrich Rakob, Jim Richerson and Judy Lee, Jeremy Rossiter, Pierre Senay, Susan Stevens, Sebastian Storz, Pol Trousset, Mercedes Vegas, the late Colin Wells and Christine Zitrides, who have all helped and influenced me in various ways.

I have taken small groups of students from Laurier to Carthage with me a number of times. I have spent many days trekking across the monuments of Carthage with students, among whom I would particularly like to recognize and thank Tracey Eckersley and Jennifer Moore; at least twenty other students and assistants at Carthage also deserve my gratitude.

I owe an enormous debt to the many nineteenth-century archaeologists and academics who explored the ruins of Carthage and interpreted the evidence, not only Nathan Davis himself, but also Christian Falbe, Sir Grenville Temple, Charles Beulé, Evariste Pricot de Sainte-Marie, Gustav Wilmanns, Father Alfred-Louis Delattre, René Cagnat, Salomon Reinach and Ernest Babelon, Paul Gauckler and Auguste Audollent. They are all members of the supporting group to whom this book is dedicated.

A research grant from the Social Sciences and Humanities Research Council of Canada supported two of my early seasons at Carthage. Many of the ideas in this book could never have been born without years of financial support from internal grants at Wilfrid Laurier University, a program backed by SSHRCC funding. Research for this book was funded by internal short-term research grants received in 1999 and 2002; I also received a book-preparation grant in 2007. I am very grateful for this support. I would also like to thank Anna Marguerite McCann and Robert Taggart for the financial support that allowed me to study in Rome in the fall of 2001, and for their friendship. The McCann-Taggart Foundation also made a grant towards the publication of this book. Thanks also to Meg and Mike Armstrong, Tana Allen and Jeremy Rossiter, Debra Foran, Betty Leventhal and Barry Kay, Kristin Lord and Christopher Small, for strategic help with housing.

My heartfelt thanks also go to Roger Wilson, who championed the book's publication, offered it a home in his UBC series, provided a subsidy, and has been a sympathetic and involved editor throughout. He also had the vision of a much more highly illustrated book than I had dared hope for, and has provided many of the additional illustrations from his own archive, as well as drafting all the additional captions. Thanks are also due to Charlotte Wilson for her elegant design of this book. Finally, for much personal support I thank my husband Ron Ross, my friend Janet Wason, and all four generations of my amazing extended family.

Joann Freed

1

Nathan Davis at Carthage

Friends at dinner

In the spring of 1858 the Reverend Nathan Davis hosted a distinguished group to Sunday dinner. Two of his guests were to achieve lasting renown, but Davis himself is almost unknown, although he, too, was a remarkable person. Born in London, Davis was a Jewish convert to Christianity, a former Protestant missionary at Tunis, an expert on Tunisia with complete fluency in Arabic, and the personal friend of the Bey. He had at this moment been funded by the British Foreign Office for more than a year to excavate at Carthage. He had already shipped home the remains of a fine Roman mosaic and had packaged up many other mosaics and finds for transport. Davis' dinner was held just over ten miles north-east of Tunis at a villa in the isolated and tiny oasis village of Gammarth on the shores of the Mediterranean. Davis had recently moved his family there to be closer to his new excavations north of Carthage, in the ancient necropolis of Gammarth and at Roman villas along the coast.

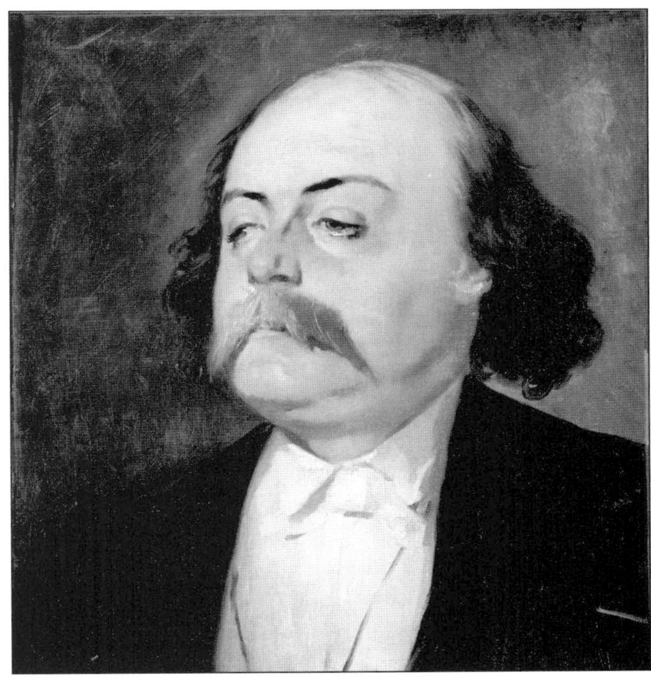

Fig. 1.1 Gustave Flaubert (1821–1880), oil portrait by Eugène Giraud, about 1856, in the Musée National du Château de Versailles et du Trianon

Among those Davis had invited to dinner was the novelist Gustave Flaubert, who had ridden out from Tunis for the occasion (Fig. 1.1). Flaubert had recently arrived from France to absorb impressions for the novel he was planning on Punic Carthage. This would be a significant day for Flaubert's novel-to-be. Feeling excluded from the English conversation, he used the occasion to observe Mrs Davis' young lady companion, Nelly Rosenberg, who would become the physical model for his Punic heroine, Salammbô. The elderly Lady Franklin, the former first lady of Van Diemen's Land and wife of Sir John Franklin, leader of a lost Arctic expedition, was also present, accompanied by her niece and devoted companion, Sophia Cracroft. The two women had been rescued from an unsuitable hotel in Tunis by the Davises, and invited to stay with them at Gammarth.

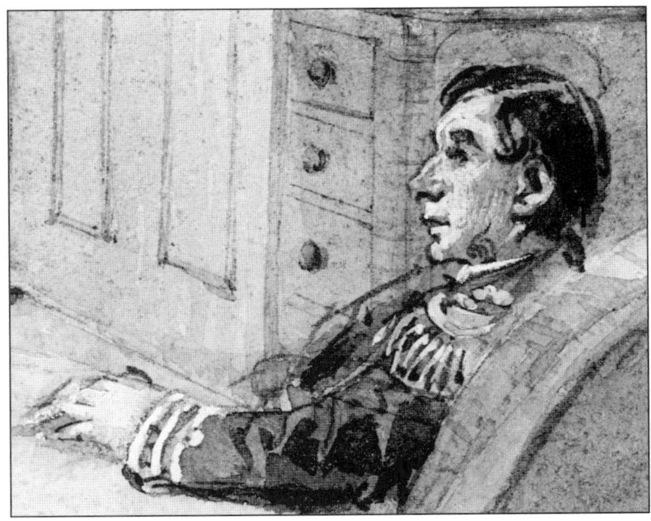

Fig. 1.2 Lieutenant Edwin Augustus Porcher (1825–1878), water-colour self-portrait of himself in his cabin on HMS Sparrowhawk *between 1865 and 1868, during his tour of duty in the Pacific North-West*

The intelligent and outspoken Lady Franklin would have taken a leading role in the conversation. Her listeners included Captain Edwin Porcher (Fig. 1.2), who had instructions to put his ship HMS *Harpy* at the service of Reverend Davis. Before the recent arrival of Captain Porcher, Davis had been planning to investigate archaeological sites on Cap Bon, and it may have been this day's conversation that turned Davis' interest in a completely different direction, to the nearby Roman city of Utica, where much of this group proceeded a few days later. The meeting of Davis and

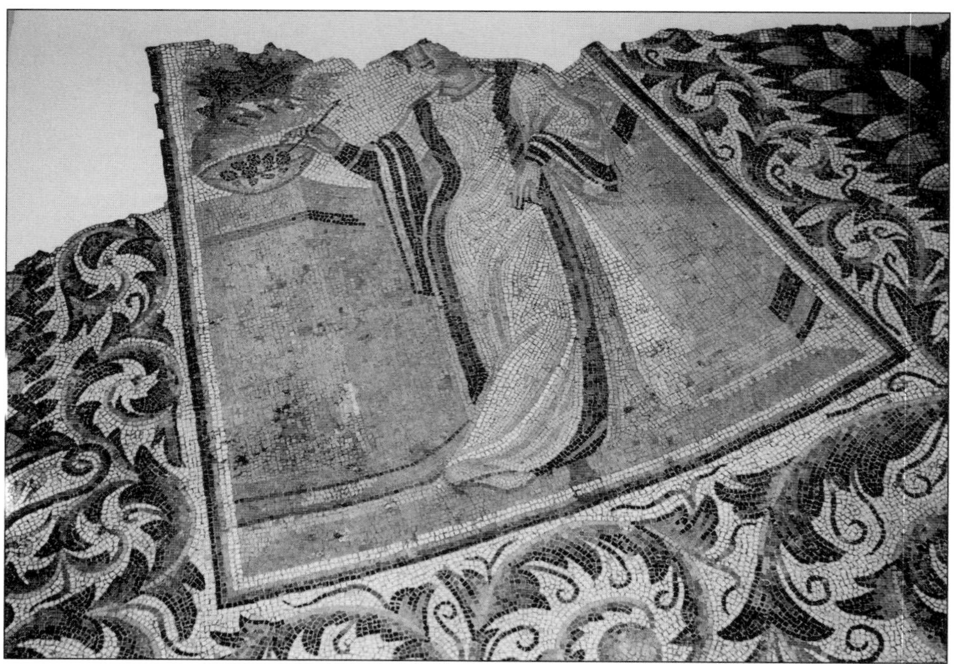

Fig. 1.3 Detail of the Mosaic of Months and Seasons, the first mosaic found by Davis. This fragment shows the Month of July: a figure in a long robe uses a thin instrument to take black berries from a glass bowl.

Porcher had a further significance for Mediterranean archaeology, for Porcher was soon involved in his own excavations at Cyrene.

David Porter Heap, a young American medical doctor who was the son of the former long-time U.S. consul at Tunis, was also present with his wife Elizabeth. Heap was positioning himself for a future consular posting, but in the meantime Davis had recruited the young doctor to work with him on his excavations. The Heap family occupied the Davises' former home and workshed on the ruins of Carthage, about four miles to the south. The Davises and the Heaps had a total of six or seven young children, and some of them were certainly running about the scene.

Davis' archaeological excavations at Carthage were arousing widespread interest, and he had had European visitors before. Nevertheless the guests at this dinner, with their various roles and preoccupations, formed a microcosm of the colonialist enterprise. Today we see Davis primarily as an archaeologist, and identify him with the intellectual and 'scientific' side of his venture. Certainly his status in this group was at least partly determined by what his contemporaries saw as his scientific role, but Davis was also an energetic and enterprising man with heavy financial obligations and a family to support, who had found a field for his many talents in Tunisia. Davis and his European contemporaries led their lives in a context in which exploiting, reforming and eventually governing the colonial world was closely linked to the appropriation of its art and culture. This was as true for Davis' archaeological forerunners and contemporaries as it was for Davis, and the question of who benefits economically, politically and culturally from archaeology is still relevant today.

A mystery in the British Museum

Today visitors to the British Museum can see a spectacular collection of Roman polychrome mosaics in the north-west stairwell, many of which were lifted at Carthage by Davis between 1856 and 1859. In a three-year campaign funded by the British Foreign Office, Davis excavated twenty-eight individual Roman mosaics at Carthage, lifted twenty-six (plus five more from Utica) and sent them to the Museum on British naval vessels. These mosaics date from the late first to the mid-sixth century AD. The most important for the history of Roman art is the first mosaic Davis lifted, the Mosaic of the Months and Seasons (Fig. 1.3), but the group as a whole has great value as a representative sample of Roman mosaics at Carthage.

When I first saw these mosaics, I was taken aback by the disparity between the impressiveness and number of these finds, and the fact that Davis' excavations at Carthage were almost unknown to the many archaeologists, including myself, who worked at Carthage in the later twentieth century. I had read and enjoyed Davis' book on his excavations at Carthage, but Davis hardly gave the impression in that account that he had sent the British Museum significant archaeological finds. I found myself asking questions that had no obvious answers. How did it happen that so many once permanently installed and essentially fragile Roman mosaic floors were lifted and shipped to England, despite the fact that they were large, extremely heavy, and generally impractical to manage? What were the motivations behind these exploits? How did this happen at a time when archaeology as a science was as yet unborn? What were the original contexts of these mosaics? Was there contemporary documentation of the excavations and the objects discovered? I realized that if the Museum had these mosaics on display, they must also have records of their acquisition, and I began research on Davis and his finds. As I followed up very disparate clues, I was eventually able to reconstruct an account of Davis' excavations. This book is the result. It is Davis' story, but it is also the story of his colleagues and rivals in the earliest archaeological excavations at Carthage.

Carthage in its Mediterranean context

Today Tunisia is a small country with a long Mediterranean coastline. It lies in the middle of the north coast of Africa, opposite Sicily and Italy. Here the Phoenicians founded the trading settlement of Carthage, according to tradition in 814 BC. The port city of Carthage eventually controlled an empire in the western Mediterranean, but the jealousy of Rome led to three Punic Wars and the destruction of Carthage in 146 BC. Because Carthage was an ideal port site, it was re-founded as a Roman colony by 29 BC, if not a little earlier. The city again became rich, with high points of prosperity in the second and fourth centuries AD. In AD 439, Carthage was captured by the Vandals, a Germanic tribe that controlled large areas of North Africa until the Byzantine reconquest of North Africa under Justinian in 534. Carthage then had another century as a Byzantine city before it was taken by the Arabs and finally sacked in 698. Gradually Tunis, which lay fifteen kilometers to the west, inland from the Mediterranean on the west side of the Lake of Tunis, became an important population centre. Particularly after Tunis became the Arab capital in 894, the site of Carthage was used as a quarry for Arab and European building projects, and these depredations continued for a thousand years.

In the nineteenth century, Carthage was part of the territory of Tunis. The Bey of Tunis, theoretically the regent of the Ottoman Sultan, ruled the area that today forms the country of Tunisia. The earliest attempts at archaeology in Carthage lie between two crucial dates: the first was the British Lord Exmouth's bombardment of Algiers in 1816 and the second the French occupation of Tunisia in 1881. In this period European interference with the 'Barbary States' of North Africa rapidly progressed to conquest. The Regency of Tunis was tiny when compared to the territory of Algiers to the west and Tripoli to the east. It was also a poor and poorly-governed land, with a drastically falling population and a declining economy, but the brief reign of Mohammed Bey, Davis' personal friend, would seem bright in contrast to the series of economic and political disasters that overtook Tunisia from the 1860s.

The Crimean war had ended in March of 1856. Britain and France had supported the Ottoman Empire against Russia and in return wanted liberalization and guarantees of human rights, to facilitate European commercial ventures. The French, who had controlled neighbouring Algeria since 1830, saw Tunisia as a potential colony, while the British Foreign Secretary, Lord Clarendon, aimed to stabilize the regime of Mohammed Bey, who was not a strong personality, by urging him to honour his ties to the Ottoman Sultan. Clarendon also hoped to strengthen British prestige in Tunis in relation to the French.

By the time Davis began to dig at Carthage, the site had already suffered the depredations of centuries, and all the great buildings of cut stone had been, one by one, dismantled and removed. Yet the desolation apparent on the surface (Fig. 1.4) was not so different from many untouched ancient sites (compare Fig. 1.5, today). For his part, the Danish consul, Christian Falbe, who drew a plan in the early 1830s that provided more knowledge of the ancient city than many years of archaeological exploration (Fig. 3.2), did not see or map intact structures, but only the core of concrete and rubble walls left behind when the stone facing had been removed.

In the course of his generally frustrating first months of excavation, Davis discovered that the poor raped site of Carthage still had one intact treasure to offer: its mosaics. Roman mosaics were almost certainly not what the British Museum was looking for. Nevertheless, Davis' agreement with the Foreign Office required him to bring home artefacts, and therefore he devised a method to lift mosaics, and sent them to the Museum on ships of the British navy.

Archaeology at Carthage in its wider historical perspective

Archaeologists working at Carthage have only rarely had a strong historical understanding of previous work. There is no unified overview of what is now nearly two centuries of excavation. Furthermore, at a number of historical moments the work of earlier archaeologists has been ignored or discounted. The establishment of the French Protectorate in 1881 put an end to the first period of international adventure (the subject of this book) and privileged the work of French scholars, whether missionaries or part of the professional establishment. After the death in 1932 of Father Alfred-Louis Delattre, his fifty years of archaeological work at Carthage were often disregarded, largely because of his perceived lack of professional status. Tunisian independence in 1956 brought a break in the French traditions and staffing of the archaeological service. Finally, the beginning of the UNESCO 'Save Carthage' campaign in 1972 introduced a period of comparatively sophisticated methodology, but the European and North American scholars and students who came to Carthage in great numbers in the last quarter of the twentieth century often knew little or nothing of its long archaeological history.

Before the Danish consul, Christian Falbe, created an accurate topographical plan of the peninsula (Fig. 3.2),[1] the site of Carthage was essentially incomprehensible. Because ancient Carthage is actually two superimposed cities with a history between them of more than fifteen hundred years, nineteenth-century archaeologists faced a three-dimensional puzzle. The site was enormous, covering a minimum of a square mile (260 ha) and with a typical depth of twenty-five feet (7.60 m) of soil. Furthermore, there was little guidance as to a best starting point. The plan of Falbe was published in 1833 and galvanized the French scholar Dureau de la Malle,[2] because it revealed the outline of the circus, the amphitheatre and two enormous cisterns, typical remains of a Roman city. Falbe's topographical map has the same fundamental importance for archaeology at Carthage as survey has for archaeological sites today.

Dureau de la Malle immediately interpreted the structures of Falbe's plan in terms of Punic and Roman structures mentioned in the ancient texts. Most obviously, the low-lying 'lagoons' which Falbe identified as the ports agreed with the ancient description of the Punic circular naval harbour and the rectangular merchant harbour at Carthage during the Third Punic War. Falbe and Dureau de la Malle agreed that the highest hill in the centre of the city was therefore the Byrsa, the traditional name for the Punic acropolis, and that the Punic *forum* (generally regarded as a Roman rather than a Punic concept – an open public area including markets and civic buildings) lay between the ports and the Byrsa. Their identification of the location of the ports and the Byrsa has stood the test of time, but their propositions have been tested hard, because later scholars have repeatedly interpreted the site in a very different way.

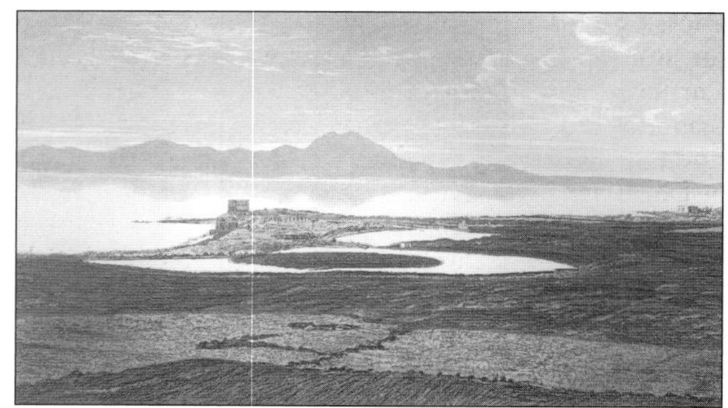

Fig. 1.4 (above right) *Carthage, the Punic harbours in the 1850s, looking south, as recorded in* Carthage and Her Remains *(compare Fig. 1.5)*

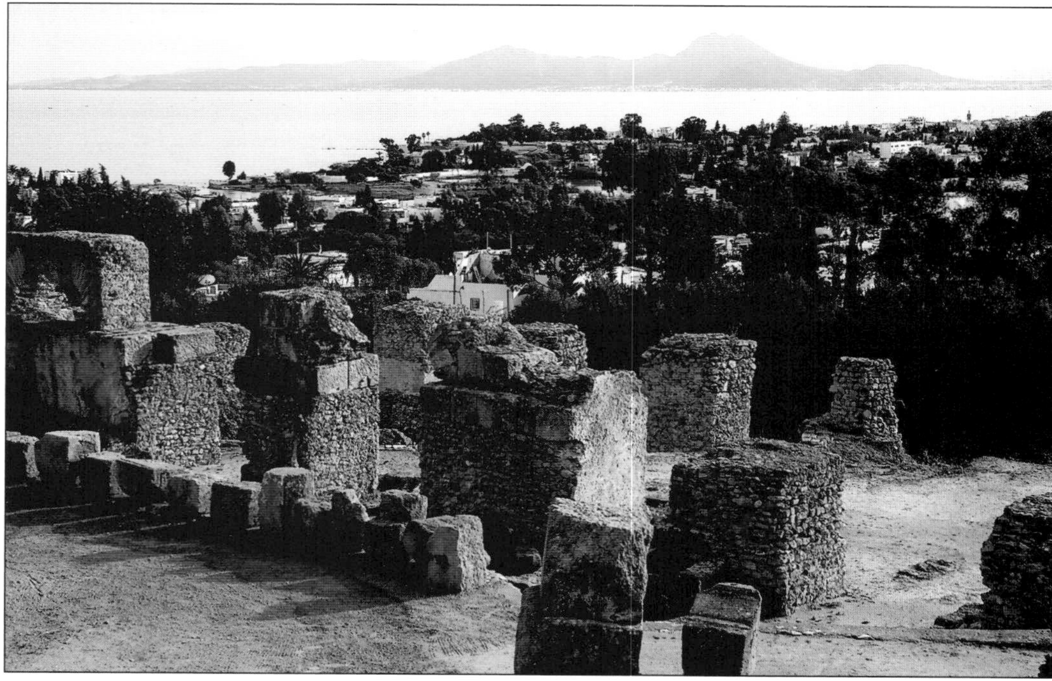

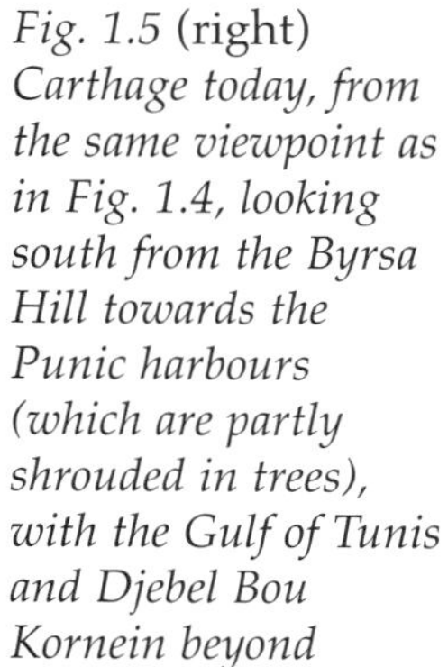

Fig. 1.5 (right) *Carthage today, from the same viewpoint as in Fig. 1.4, looking south from the Byrsa Hill towards the Punic harbours (which are partly shrouded in trees), with the Gulf of Tunis and Djebel Bou Kornein beyond*

The earliest period of archaeology at Carthage provided the underpinnings for everything that we know today about the material culture of the Punic and Roman cities. The beginnings of archaeology at Carthage date to the first tentative excavations of the Dutch engineer Jean Emile Humbert in 1817, followed by his excavations for the Museum of Leiden in 1822 and 1824. A limited and abortive personal effort of Danish consul Falbe in 1824 was followed by excavations funded by the Paris-based Society for the Exploration of Carthage, and was carried out by Falbe and his British colleague Sir Grenville Temple in 1838. Falbe and Temple based their work directly on Falbe's experiences in preparing his plan. In open competition with Falbe and Temple, the British consul Sir Thomas Reade sponsored brief excavations at the same time. All these men were essentially amateur archaeologists.

After these earliest pioneers, the British Foreign Office unexpectedly funded Nathan Davis' excavations, giving him the mandate to bring home finds for the British Museum. Davis dug extensively at Carthage from 1856 to 1859, and, as already noted it was mosaics which formed by far the bulk of Davis' finds which were shipped to the Museum.[3] The extent of Davis' achievement in sending a total of thirty-one mosaics to London can be measured against the fact that in 1860 Augustus Franks, a curator at the British Museum who was the first to publish the results of Davis' excavations, found evidence in the museum collections for only three mosaics previously recovered from Carthage.[4] In fact, the known mosaics excavated before Davis came from only two sites, and all three were heavily damaged in the lifting process.

Davis' excavations were a political coup for the British, but from the French point of view Davis was an interloper, a 'cuckoo in the nest'. Galvanized by Davis' excavations, the French archaeologist Charles Beulé arrived in 1859 to demonstrate an approach to excavation based on informed hypotheses and professional expertise. Despite Beulé's indignation at Davis' role at Carthage, Davis and Beulé were at least equally important there in terms of their actual accomplishments. Those who followed immediately after them in the early 1860s (the Frenchmen Daux, Flaux and Gouvet) have sunk into the deepest obscurity, not always undeservedly.

Davis therefore stands at the culminating point of the first generation of archaeologists in Tunisia, the men who dug at Carthage in the mid-nineteenth century (it was unthinkable that women would excavate until well into the twentieth century, although Beulé's wife accompanied him and drew his finds). At this time archaeology was not yet defined as a scientific discipline. At least in theory, today's archaeologist reconstructs past cultures by meticulously integrating the physical evidence of context and artefacts; both provide essential clues. Davis, although he excavated extensively, was one of a number of men of his time who are rightly called antiquarians, because their interest was purely in artefacts rather than their context.

Davis was judged harshly by the archaeologists of his own day for reasons that were largely political, but his actual performance was not out of line with the British conception of archaeology as formulated by his distinguished contemporary, C. T. Newton. In a lecture given at Oxford in 1850, Newton described archaeology in terms of an anthropological and museological approach to ancient culture. As Mary Beard has noted, his views illuminate the subject areas of the degree course in classical archaeology introduced at Cambridge in the 1880s as 'the history of classical culture in its broadest sense'.[5]

Davis' contemporary and rival, Charles Beulé, was a conscientious professional. To Beulé the task of the archaeologist was first and foremost to uncover ancient architecture, and he greatly underestimated the value of both context and artefacts.[6] Both Davis and Beulé were pioneers who boldly and often rashly threw themselves up against an immensely large problem. The archaeologists of the mid-nineteenth century made direct contributions to our present understanding of Carthage, but they rarely understood the significance of their discoveries. One of the purposes of this book is to explain what they achieved in terms of today's accumulated knowledge.

Colonialist aspects of the early archaeology of Carthage

In the mid-nineteenth century, archaeological acquisitions aroused intense interest among ordinary citizens and aggrandized national prestige: the European colonial powers took a mutually competitive interest in the great civilizations of the past. In the Regency of Tunis the Bey and his ministers controlled access to archaeological sites, but the rules of procedure were still *ad hoc*. Consuls and other representatives of European governments had the best claim to access, and did the lion's share of excavation in Tunisia as in other countries of the Mediterranean. The purpose of such excavation was unabashedly the acquisition of museum-quality objects, although there were also fledgling and sometimes unconscious contributions to science and methodology. Acquiring artefacts for the public at home was a political contribution, and this was what Davis was paid by the Foreign Office to do.

The model of licensed plunder provided by Lord Elgin's acquisition of the Parthenon frieze at the beginning of the nineteenth century was still generally accepted by the colonial powers. Strong objections had been voiced, however, in some countries that were the objects of such expeditions, particularly in Greece and Italy. A Greek law of 1827, the year in which Greece threw off the domination of the Turks, already prohibited the export of antiquities, and the Greek archaeological service was first organized in 1834.[7] Yet when Newton passed through Athens in 1856, he noted with some indignation that what was prohibited there was not prevented.[8]

Beulé, who was to dig at Carthage in 1859 while Davis was still on the scene, was the first to excavate on the Acropolis of Athens, under the aegis of the French School in 1852 to 1853. In keeping with his association with the French School, Beulé made it a principle to reject the appropriation of finds.[9] By contrast, when Davis planned his excavation project at Carthage, there were no prickings of conscience among Europeans in regard to countries without a direct claim to a classical heritage. No one suggested that an artefact should be preserved where it was found so that its associations would not be lost, much less that an archaeological find was part of the national heritage of the country in which it was found. Newton himself was to excavate at Halicarnassos and Cnidos (in Ottoman territory) between 1856 and 1859, sending the British Museum quantities of late Classical Greek sculpture and architecture at the very same time that Davis was struggling to discover Punic finds at Carthage. In 1858 Henry Dunant, a young Swiss gentleman traveler, wrote that people kept anything they liked from excavations in Tunisia, in contrast to his experience at Pompeii and Herculaneum.[10] Beulé was the first to suggest that objects found at Carthage should stay on the site 'for visitors',[11] but Beulé was essentially indifferent to archaeological artefacts.

At the time of Davis' initiative, a number of Near Eastern excavations, most notably that of Layard at Nimrud, were being funded by the British government. The title of Layard's popular publication, *Nineveh and Its Remains* (1849), clearly provided a model for Davis.[12] Even the Crimean War was seen as an archaeological opportunity. A medical doctor, Duncan MacPherson, assigned to organize the hospital system at Kertch (ancient Panticapaeum) on the northern shore of the Black Sea, also received authorization to bring home archaeological finds from the front. William Vaux, a curator at the British Museum who was also to advise Davis, provided MacPherson with 'a practical and useful paper of instructions' on excavation methodology. MacPherson did not just collect antiquities, but also mounted full-scale excavations of burial mounds. MacPherson had tremendous practical difficulties not only with his excavations, but also with safeguarding the finds for the British Museum, as colleagues, fellow-soldiers and workmen appropriated everything which they were able to lay their hands on. Elegant drawings clarify his work to some extent, but like Davis, MacPherson was an amateur and his attempts at identification and analysis are far from convincing.[13]

Who was Nathan Davis?

No significant biography of Davis exists,[14] and I have not attempted to produce one, but I have found enough evidence to create a portrait of him and his milieu during the years in which he was excavating at Carthage. Davis was a prolific writer, the eventual author of a number of books on his travel and adventures in Tunisia. His later books, *Evenings in My Tent* (1854),[15] *Carthage and Her Remains* (1861) (Fig. 1.6), and *Ruined Cities* (1862),[16] although they were written for

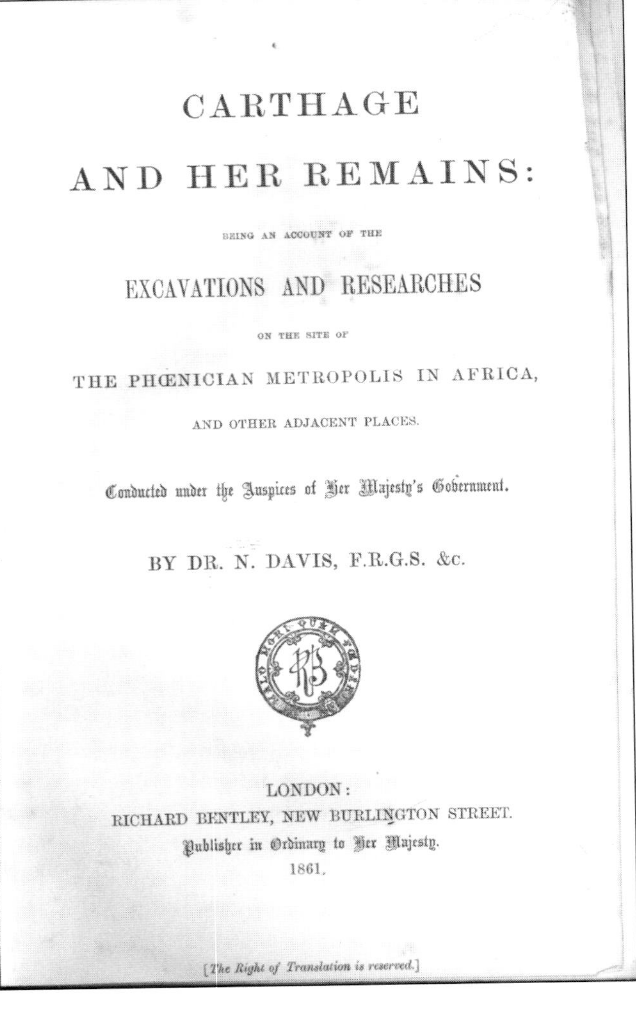

CARTHAGE

AND HER REMAINS:

BEING AN ACCOUNT OF THE

EXCAVATIONS AND RESEARCHES

ON THE SITE OF

THE PHŒNICIAN METROPOLIS IN AFRICA,

AND OTHER ADJACENT PLACES.

Conducted under the Auspices of Her Majesty's Government.

BY DR. N. DAVIS, F.R.G.S. &c.

LONDON:

RICHARD BENTLEY, NEW BURLINGTON STREET.

Publisher in Ordinary to Her Majesty.

1861.

[*The Right of Translation is reserved.*]

Fig. 1.6 Carthage and Her Remains, *the title page of the revised 1861 edition (see 'Note to reader' on p. 221)*

the general public and ignored scholarly standards, established him as an expert on the culture and geography of Tunisia. Outside the cities North Africa in the nineteenth century was a rough and tough frontier,[17] in many ways reminiscent of the American wild west. Despite his clerical identity, his extensive reading, and the fact that he had reached early middle age (he was in his mid-forties in 1856), Davis was an adventurer, fond of riding, rough travel, guiding and guns. Outgoing, cheerful and optimistic, when he liked he could be rowdy, and he was always happy to show off his masculine prowess. He was confident to the point of recklessness, as an unwise demonstration of his snake-handling ability demonstrated.[18] At Utica, in the last period of his archaeological endeavors in Tunisia, but no doubt also earlier, he carried a Colt revolver in a hidden holster. The revolver was a piece of new technology at the time, and Davis' demonstration of its qualities to an inquisitive group of villagers is an example of his occasionally boisterous behaviour. He startled them by pulling the gun and firing into the air, then galloped away firing until it was completely discharged.[19]

Obviously, Davis did not emphasize his rougher side when he was at home in Britain. After Antonio Panizzi, the Principal Librarian (and head) at the British Museum, had made enquiries, he wrote to Lord Clarendon that Davis was a converted German or Polish Jew, now a minister of the church of Scotland, who was at present employed by the Society for the Conversion of the Jews. Despite the fact that Panizzi knew that Davis was a Protestant missionary, he described him as 'a German or Polish Jew'; to quote Todd Endelman, 'Jewishness obviously could not be obliterated by a splash of water from the baptismal font'.[20] Although Panizzi, who may have already met Davis when he wrote this letter, made it clear that Davis was not a scholar, he was confident of Davis' competence and his status as a gentleman.[21]

Davis' personality may have been culturally determined, since, at least by comparison with the English, the Jews of London were known for exuberant behaviour and unselfconsciousness.[22] In one of the few glimpses which he allowed of his personal views, Davis wrote: 'nothing can be more disagreeable than a monotonous life'.[23] One source even described him as an American by birth,[24] a detail not supported by other evidence, but in keeping with his extroverted personality and his consistent friendships with the American consuls at Tunis.

The only evidence that I have found for Davis' personal appearance is an illustration of a 'Workmen's Encampment' from *Carthage and Her Remains* (Fig. 1.7). I take the man standing by his horse in the centre of the picture as Davis. Inasmuch as the tiny figure and the technique of engraving allow accurate delineation, he seems to have trim hair, a full beard and quite a prominent nose. Panizzi's comment might suggest that Davis looked like an Eastern European Jew, but that leaves great room for variation in colouring as well as feature. The hipshot posture of the man in the engraving is casual, yet the left arm is firmly in control of the reins. He is wearing a kind of high peaked captain's hat and a rather ordinary gentleman's daytime outfit. The image fits Davis and his situation very well.[25]

The forthright nature which Davis revealed in his books contrasts with his discretion about his personal life. One could not guess his background or family situation from his books, where he revealed only the occasional scrap of personal information. In fact, he deliberately obscured his personal history. Davis had a number of different sides to his personality, which made him something of a chameleon. Nevertheless, while he knew how to present information selectively, I have found no evidence to justify the negative views of Davis' character that can be traced back to his contemporary French critics and which are now accepted without question. As recently as 1974, historian L. Carl Brown noted British Consul Thomas Reade's negative opinion of Davis, and Davis' 'flamboyant role as a missionary to the Jews of Tunis'. Evaluating Davis as a source for the reign of Ahmed Bey, Brown wrote: 'Something of a maverick with perhaps a touch of the charlatan, Davis is neither reliable nor especially significant . . .'.[26] I believe that although Davis had many faults, he was in fact honest, as well as conscientious and effective as an archaeologist. The flaw that did him the most harm was his political naïveté. Davis was blind to the offense he caused in some quarters simply because he did not belong to the establishment to whose prerogatives he assumed an equal right. Seeing his position as secure, with the Bey, the British Foreign Office, and the British Museum all behind him, Davis did not guess that he could lose all this support within a relatively short period of time. Because he was overconfident, he failed actively to cultivate potentially powerful friends and to do everything possible to protect himself from ill-will.

Even more relevant to the eventual wreck of his reputation as an archaeologist was the fact that Davis' excavations at Carthage were not just a *coup* for him, but also a *coup* for Britain. Davis rightly saw himself as a crucial team member successfully advancing the interests of the political and cultural aristocrats of British society, and he seems to have been oblivious to just how much the situation would rankle with the French. With foresight Davis might have realized that his newly-eminent position in itself made him vulner-

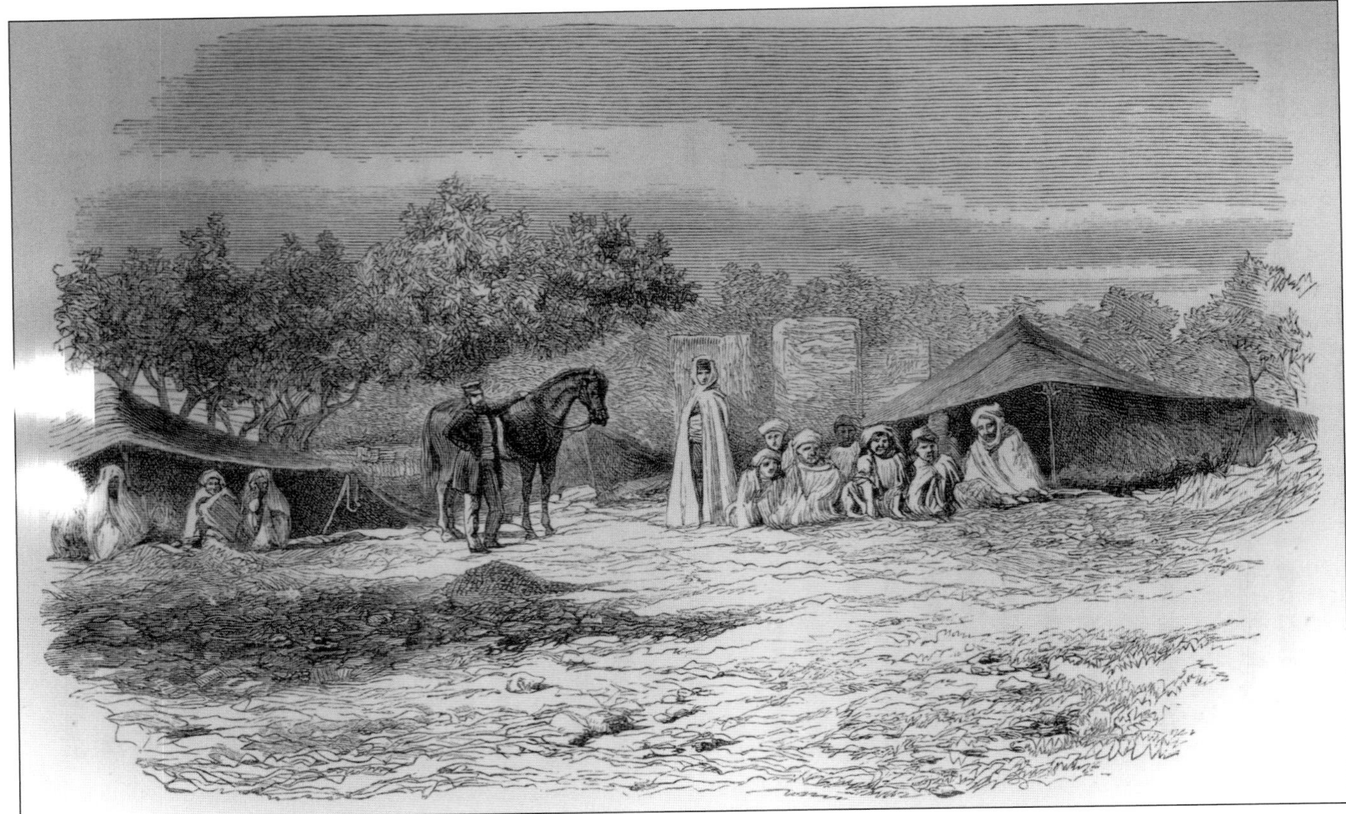

Fig. 1.7 'Workmen's Encampment', an engraving from Davis' Carthage and Her Remains, *perhaps showing Davis himself in the centre (with the horse)*

able, and that a violent backlash from the French against the weakest and most accessible link, himself, could be expected.

According to the record on Nathan Davis at the Modern Protestant Cemetery in Florence, where he was buried, Davis was a British citizen, born in London.[27] He was a native speaker of English and was accepted without question as a British citizen in later life. Various difficulties made it practically impossible for Jews to be naturalized in Britain before the middle of the nineteenth century. If Davis' father was the immigrant, he came to London in an era when an average of 150 Jews arrived each year, most of them destitute, and most coming from Holland, Germany and Poland.[28]

The name Nathan was popular in the early nineteenth century, largely because of Gotthold Lessing's poem *Nathan der Weise* ('Nathan the Wise'), written in 1779. The Nathan of Lessing's story lives by the idea that Judaism, Islam and Christianity share the same God, and that members of these religions are brothers. The choice of their son's name suggests that Davis' parents were well disposed towards assimilation with English Christian culture. Perhaps Davis himself was influenced by the story behind his name to avoid sectarianism and to embrace the Arabic world.[29]

Davis had an excellent Hebrew education and was also acquainted with classical texts. If he was brought up in London, where the great majority of British Jews resided in the early nineteenth century, he could have attended very good Jewish schools. There were no expectations of advanced education in the Jewish community, however, since education for boys, even in middle-class business families, usually ended at eleven or twelve.[30] His Hebrew later gave him an advantage in learning Arabic and in making sense of Punic texts. He also acquired varying levels of competence in Latin and Greek, as well as in French, Italian and German, as is shown by his liberal use of these languages in his writing.

Davis was monumentally well-read. His romanticism and his inability to deal critically with the enormous amounts of information at his disposal are, however, evident on nearly every page that he wrote, and betray that he was not university-educated. Oxford and Cambridge were closed to Jews at the age when he might have gone to university.[31] He never signed himself 'Esquire,' a poorly-defined but common appellation in the nineteenth century, which claimed gentlemanly status on the basis of education or property. On the other hand, one of Davis' letters from Tunis was closed with a small red wax seal portraying a nude classical goddess;[32] with this seal Davis demonstrated his sympathy with the ancient classical world.

Davis was certainly not a scholar of Greek or Latin. He did not have an adequate grasp of the Latin inscriptions which he collected during his travels around western Tunisia, and for which he gave rather feeble transcriptions.[33] In *Ruined Cities*, Davis inaccurately transcribed Latin inscriptions that had already been published, earning him the scorn of the great German scholar Theodor Mommsen. Mommsen rudely labeled Davis' *Ruined Cities* as a *pessimum opus* ('a terrible work').[34] He was objecting to Davis' poor grasp of Latin and of Latin epigraphy. This was a period when inscriptions offered far more compelling interest than other classical remains to the most authoritative scholars, who were primarily philologists.

In *Carthage and Her Remains* Davis said that he had first visited Carthage as a young man of seventeen or eighteen;[35] this is a tantalizing piece of the puzzle. If true Davis would have arrived in Tunisia for the first time in 1830, at about the time when the French were taking Algiers. It is likely that this trip coincided with his first study of Arabic; possibly his family intended him to train as a merchant in the Arab world. If so, Davis seems to have soon abandoned any involvement with business.

From at least his late twenties, Davis was employed as a Protestant missionary by the London Society for Promoting Christianity among the Jews. There is plenty of evidence to confirm that he was primarily identified as a Protestant minister among the society of Tunis. According to Amos Perry, who was to be the American consul at Tunis from 1862 to 1867, the Protestant missionary to the Jews was also styled chaplain to the British consulate, perhaps because the British consuls had for some time been Catholics.[36] It is impossible to know exactly when Davis converted to Christianity, since his father may have led the family to convert when Nathan was still quite young. Identification with British culture and sensitivity to rampant prejudice were among the influences encouraging conversion, especially for Jews who, economically and socially, were upwardly mobile.[37] As Davis later styled himself 'Doctor' and 'Reverend,' and as he was clearly trained to preach rather than to construct an academic argument, it is likely that he had attended seminary; it may be that the London Society sponsored his seminary education. Although the Society, which had been founded in 1809, was ineffective in making converts, it was an arm of the Anglican Church, and had very distinguished patrons and a wide support-base in Britain as a whole.[38] The Society had a missionary outpost in the Regency of Tunis before Davis arrived, and he seems to have immediately found himself at home.

Nathan Davis published *Tunis; or Selections from a Journal during a Residence in that Regency* in 1841,[39] when he was not quite thirty years old. This is the earliest book inspired by his experiences in North Africa that I have found, but he was already described on the title page as the author of *Elements of Arabic*. The book was dedicated to S. D. Heap, the American consul at Tunis, and to Ahmed, then Bey of Tunis. Davis' book was elegantly bound, with marbled end-papers and pages edged with gold leaf. The brief volume is a mixed bag of cautionary stories which Davis had collected about individual Christian converts to Islam, observations on Tunisian culture, and a history of the Aghlabid dynasty, translated from Arabic.[40] Some main themes of Davis' life were already established, including his lively interest in the Jewish culture of Tunis, the situation of slaves in the Regency, and the work of the Protestant mission to the Jews. Arabic was necessary for Davis' work with the Jewish community, for, although their books were in Hebrew, Arabic was their spoken language. Still a young man, Davis made no pretence of adapting himself to the local folkways; when invited to a large ladies' party, he was glad to be given a spoon for his *couscous* and found the local music annoying; one can sense the suppressed outrage in his report of being hit with a stick by an Arab 'saint' of the demented kind. Davis also commented on Ahmed Bey's newly-constituted army of 20,000 men, suggesting that a thousand would have been enough to keep the country in good order.[41]

Another of Davis' early books, similarly disorganized, was *A Voice from North Africa*, published in 1844. This book gave an Edinburgh address for Davis, although he described himself at this time as having lived in North Africa for nearly four years. Tunis was his home-base there, as he again dedicated his book to the American consul, Dr Heap, and to Ahmed Bey.[42] Davis was married by this time or soon after, for his daughter Margaret was born at Tunis on October 23rd, 1846.[43] Although I have found evidence of his wife's personality, I have not discovered her name. In this book Davis wrote that a Mr Ewald headed the London Society in Tunis and acted as the minister for the small group of Protestants with which Davis was affiliated, but he himself was involved in the Society's project of selling Bibles among the Muslim population.[44]

Davis later ascribed the closeness of his acquaintance with Mohammed Bey to a two-month tour which he had made with him through Tunisia while Mohammed was still heir-apparent.[45] The two men were very nearly of the same age, Mohammed being the elder by only a year,[46] and they became personal friends. The tour, an epic progress in which Mohammed was accompanied by the country's entire army, took place twice a year as a duty of the heir to the throne. The tour was a demonstration of the Bey's authority and a method of tax collection.[47] Davis had his own tent and a bevy of servants supplied by the prince. The tour took place in March and April at some [illegible] between 1846 and 1850, although Davis' account [illegible] volumes, *Evenings in my Tent*, was not published until 1854.[48] In this book Davis first found his mature voice. While at Neftah during this tour, he [illegible]oned gathering together some Jews, speaking to them about religion, and giving them copies of the Bible.[49] Evidently the prince was not opposed to Davis' proselytizing, as his hospitality resulted in his implicit support.

In 1852 Davis lived in London and produced a monthly journal, the *Hebrew Christian Magazine*. Davis' writing for this showed that he was completely comfortable quoting in Hebrew from Hebrew religious literature.[50] This may have been another initiative sponsored by the London Society, but the journal was a financial failure, and Davis was forced to give it up and turn his pen to other subjects. In addition to *Evenings in My Tent*, he published a brief text-book, *Arabic Reading Lessons*, with a collaborator in 1854.[51]

William Gregory, the Irish MP, read Davis' *Evenings in My Tent* before making his own tour of Tunisia in 1858.[52] The first volume of this book is devoted to Davis' travels through the country with the prince Mohammed and his army. Perhaps this work, published in 1854, helped Davis to gain his status as a Fellow of the Royal Geographical Society. Davis was proposed as a Fellow and elected in the summer of 1855; his Certificate of Election described him as a 'Missionary and Traveller in Northern Africa'.[53] He was listed as a member in the society's journal for six years, but was removed in 1861. As he was probably no less useful to geography than most other members, I suspect he was removed for non-payment of dues. Alphabetical order determined that Davis' name appeared near that of Charles Darwin, and this is probably how it happened that Darwin listed Davis at Tunis among persons to whom he had written in December 1855. Darwin was asking colleagues to send him skins of domesticated pigeons and poultry, but there is no evidence that Davis followed up on this opportunity to aid Darwin's research.[54]

Although Davis did not abandon his Christian faith, he began to have doubts about his role as a missionary, and was searching for another occupation at the time of his proposal as a Fellow of the Royal Geographical Society. He did not hesitate to enlist the aid of his wife; in December 1855 and January 1856, a correspondence took place between Mrs Davis and several members of the Society. Mrs Davis, who was in London, wrote that her husband was planning an expedition in the Regency of Tunis and hoped for financial support from the Society. She had interviews with several members of the Society, but was unable to deal with their requests for a budget, nor to provide a clear statement of how Davis' travels would advance the science of geography. Mrs Davis did her best to establish her husband's professional competence, writing '. . . it strikes me that. . . an individual speaking the language – furnished with proper instruments for ascertaining & fixing localities, and a good photographing machine for taking views, cannot fail to be of use to modern geography. . . '.

The members of the Royal Geographical Society were not unfriendly, but were perhaps dubious about Davis' ability to identify the sites of Caesar's campaign and Jugurtha's adventures. It is clear that as late as the beginning of 1856 Davis had not yet realized that Carthage was the site which he was perfectly placed to exploit. Davis had given his wife an assignment that was beyond her powers, but these letters reveal her as an intelligent and self-assured lady, a credit to her husband, and useful to him as well.[55]

Glimpses of Davis' personal milieu suggest that his social status at Tunis, if not his financial position, was higher, more solidly established, and more conventional than could be guessed from his own account. By the mid-1850s Davis was married to a woman of some competence, and was father to a number of children. He was a member of the highest society at Tunis due to his position as a 'man of the cloth,' as well as to the close social relationship between his family and that of the Bey. Living in the Regency of Tunis with its tiny English-speaking community gave Davis the subject matter, social contacts and expert status that allowed him to re-invent himself as director of the first major excavations at Carthage. Moving between different cultures and languages had also made him a relatively sophisticated man of the world.

Although many a nineteenth-century gentleman wrote and published copiously on his travel adventures, the evidence suggests that Davis wrote about his experiences in North Africa mainly to increase his income, while he kept his eyes open for other opportunities that it might pay him to pursue. In the late 1850s Davis' perceived importance and financial status were much enhanced by the support of the Foreign Office for his excavations at Carthage; for example, Dunant, the young Swiss traveler, described him among scientists at work at Tunis at this time.[56] Although it was less secure, excavating for the Foreign Office and British Museum offered far better pay and higher status than the missionary post that he had held previously, and was in many ways a challenge better suited to his personal strengths. Nevertheless, Davis did not have the unexceptional middle-class family background, the classical education and the social connections which might have best fitted him for a career as an archaeologist in the Mediterranean world. The careers of Antonio Panizzi, who headed the British Museum, and of Richard Wood, the British consul at Tunis, who were Davis' contemporaries, show that Victorian Britain was more than willing to make use of the creative energies of a person whose background did not fit the accepted mould.

Davis' *Carthage and Her Remains*

Davis described his excavations in a verbose, eclectic, disorganized, yet highly entertaining text, *Carthage and Her Remains*. Only about a fifth of the book was directly relevant to his excavations. He wrote for a popular audience and in the same random way in which he had dug, giving no clear chronological or systematic account of the various sites, and constantly lighting on a different topic. Although Davis described his travels and adventures in a straightforward and attractive style, he became distressingly bombastic on any subject where he meant to display intellectual authority. Accuracy was certainly not the aim of his writing style, with the result that he misled scholars and his misguided interpretations invited their scorn. The voluminous puffery of Davis' writing style made his achievements incomprehensible to scholars, and particularly to the French, who were to control excavation and the interpretation of archaeology at Carthage subsequently.

Although Davis may have kept proper records, such as a daily journal, plans of individual sites and trenches, and drawings of finds, I have not found them, and he did not refer to them. Davis saw and often objectively reported evidence which he then interpreted through a haze of wildly romantic misapprehension, but he also provided his readers with information that has not been properly appreciated. His accounts of the conditions under which he worked were both frank and lively. He was, moreover, a near genius in practical matters, as shown by the ease with which he managed his men, and the speed with which he formulated and implemented a new method to lift his mosaics. Finally, it is evident that Davis was open and honest in whatever he chose to recount, although he did not always succeed in being clear.

For example, although I know the site of Roman Carthage very well, I found that Davis' descriptions of topography can be extremely confusing. Davis had his own designation for each of his sites, which often appropriated other scholars' names for something completely different. His reasons for such designations often seemed arbitrary, if not ignorant, to his academic critics. Finally, his carelessness with grammatical structure was particularly misleading when he described location. A quote from Charles Tissot published in 1884 expressed the opinion of the academic community: '. . . [Davis'] critical sense errs so regularly, in all questions having to do with the topography of Carthage, that his conclusions, and even, to a certain extent, his indications, should be regarded with extreme reserve'.[57] This severe and magisterial comment came from a scholar with his own flaws. Nevertheless, in subsequent discussions of Davis' work, practically no weight was given to the topographical opinions of the excavator.

In *Carthage and Her Remains* Davis was angrily dismissive of Beulé's claim to have excavated Punic fortifications on the Byrsa in 1859, and his competitive attitude towards Beulé decisively turned the French academic establishment against him. In 1878, Sainte-Marie, who had read Davis carefully and outlined the contents of *Carthage and Her Remains* chapter by chapter, saw almost no academic value in the work, irritably noting that Davis only first presented some useful material in his ninth chapter, 'after 170 pages of digressions and repetitions'. Sainte-Marie was particularly annoyed that Davis attacked Beulé's results at Carthage, which in Sainte-Marie's opinion were conclusive.[58]

Auguste Audollent, who in 1901 published an academic tome on Roman Carthage which has not yet been replaced, went further, pouring abuse on Davis' text and his work at Carthage. Audollent literally had nothing good to say, describing Davis' writing style as 'unbearable blabber', his book as 'empty', and his map as 'absolutely fantasist'. His opinion sealed Davis' academic reputation as an incompetent. While conceding that Davis' book included important information, Audollent groaned at the labour required to winnow it out. Audollent resented the fact that Davis had been ideally supplied with permissions and funding, yet his discoveries, which Audollent dismissed in a phrase, were impressive neither in number or quality. Audollent had clearly failed to pursue his research on Davis' finds to the British Museum, where half of Davis' mosaics were already on display and museum accession records documented the rest of his finds.

While I have found enlightening the glimpses of political background which Davis gives, Audollent complained, 'Why are these personages of any interest? How do they concern archaeology?'. In conclusion, Audollent wrote: 'The result of his excavations was to devalue and even destroy the treasures, which, received by more able hands, would have enriched the common patrimony of science'. This critique is so harsh as to deny Davis any achievement whatsoever. It is motivated by a passionate prejudice in favour of Beulé and French archaeology; as Audollent said, in a direct comparison between the two men, neither of whom he could have known personally, 'I know that Beulé had failings, but he at least was a learned and intelligent man'.[59]

Audollent's deployment of the French term *patrimoine* shows that there was a far deeper issue at stake than who was the more competent archaeologist. In French culture the *patrimoine* is the cultural inheritance of the [French] fatherland. By Audollent's day, it was accepted by the French that Tunisia was part of France, and that what originated in Tunisia belonged to France. From this point of view, the mosaics that Davis had sent to the British Museum were indeed 'lost.' Audollent quoted Flaux,[60] Sainte-Marie,[61] and Salomon Reinach[62] in support of his judgment that Davis was incompetent; these men were of course all French. Of these authorities, Reinach would use methodology which compared very favorably to that of other archaeologists of his day, which, on the other hand, was a quarter of a century after Davis; Sainte-Marie, who was to excavate at Carthage in 1874 and 1875, was on much the same level as Davis in terms of method;[63] but Audollent undermined his own credibility by citing the incompetent Armand de Flaux, whose expedition to Carthage in the early 1860s was a ludicrous failure.

Of scholars named by Audollent, only the German von Maltzan, who also criticized Davis' work, took the latter's accomplishments seriously. Von Maltzan had visited Davis' excavation of the Circular Monument (Falbe no. 70), which Davis called the 'Temple of Saturn', when the excavation was in progress in the late fall of 1857 (Fig. 10.16). Von Maltzan said that Davis uncritically named sites after temples, but the ancient sources could not be used topographically; he also said that Davis was wrong to consider his mosaics Punic as most must certainly be Roman. Nevertheless, to the incredulity of Audollent, von Maltzan regarded Davis and Beulé as nearly equal in their contribution to archaeology at Carthage.[64]

Davis' early English critics were clear-sighted enough to see his deplorable deficiencies, but they were not burdened by the deep resentment shown by the French. In his 1870 history of the British Museum, Edwards, who was aware of the museum acquisitions for which Davis was responsible, summed up Davis' book and his achievement as follows:[65]

> No index; no summary; no marginal dates; conflicting and obscure dates, when any dates appear anywhere; no introduction, which introduces anything; scarcely any divarification of personal knowledge and experiences, from borrowed knowledge and experiences; such are some of the difficulties which await the student of *Carthage and her Remains*. Yet the book is full of deep interest; its author is, none the less, a benefactor to Britain, and to the world.

My study of Davis has taken this more positive approach, as I have ploughed through the undeniable difficulties in order to find the nuggets of information that Davis' text and letters preserve. Because Audollent's negativism was so convincing, I was well into this project before I realized how useful Davis' topographical descriptions could be when they are checked against his maps. I have come to the conclusion that Audollent's flat accusation, that Davis' expensive project accomplished nothing, made it almost impossible for a serious scholar to evaluate Davis' contribution objectively.

Davis' archaeological goals

When Davis volunteered his services as an archaeologist of the site of Carthage to the British Museum and the British Foreign Office, his stated aim was 'only to dig for such antiquities as I was able to remove', beautiful and portable objects with which to enrich the Museum's collections.[66] Davis was looking for Punic finds and betrayed his preference for Punic culture in his stubborn interpretation of the Mosaic of the Months and Seasons, his first great find, as Punic. Once he had learned by hard experience exactly how difficult it was to unearth portable Punic objects, he cited the story of the unfortunate Roman Caesellius Bassus, who convinced the emperor Nero to fund a fruitless search for Punic treasure at Carthage. Davis said that he himself never found any objects of precious metal at Carthage, and he explained this by the fact that both the Punic and Roman cities were pillaged and then abandoned, allowing looters every opportunity to remove valuables. Although he certainly found coins, he found no coins that were certainly Punic.[67] Furthermore, he had undoubtedly hoped for more easily portable finds from his excavations than the practically immovable mosaics that were repeatedly his most visually impressive finds. Courageous, resourceful, strong-willed and self-confident, Davis did not accept defeat, but, by devising a method to lift the mosaics, turned them into an admirable haul of antiquities for the museum.

Although there is no doubt that Davis had serious flaws as an archaeologist, his great merits were his energy and his resourcefulness. Accepted procedure allowed him to delve through unimaginably countless cubic yards of soil without regard to their significance. He revealed by the scope of his efforts the gargantuan scale of operations required to achieve results at Carthage. Yet the finds themselves and the descriptions he gave of their contexts suggest that he never reached Punic levels. By far the greater part of his effort was spent in levels which were Roman, and often late Roman, Vandal or Byzantine. Even his Punic *stelae* were discovered in a late Roman or early Christian context, according to his own observations. His finds, especially of mosaics, represent a broad sample from the contexts of the Roman, Vandal and Byzantine city.

Davis was not a scholar in any academic sense, nor was he always brilliantly intelligent. There is no hint that he thought of himself as an early practitioner of a new science. At the same time Davis had a formidable array of the skills needed to run a major excavation: he had the vision to see the opportunity, spoke and read the necessary languages, was politically and socially well connected, was well read, a published author, self-confident, energetic, an able manager of men, and a good administrator. Davis also had a wide acquaintance with the ancient literary sources on Punic and Roman culture, if not an educated critical judgment. Davis knew that there was a context of European knowledge about Carthage which had been gathered on the ground by travellers, antiquarians and cartographers, and he made conscientious efforts to acquaint himself with this previous work. Yet Davis did not dig in order to gain a better knowledge of any aspect of ancient Carthage; he gladly went elsewhere in the hope of better finds, and he stated forthrightly that architecture, Beulé's passion, did not interest him.

In his own day, no one discouraged Davis from his archaeological pursuits because he did not have a suitable academic background. Only Beulé made Davis aware that there was ground for criticism. It is not true, on the other hand, that Davis was not 'vetted' in any way. Antonio Panizzi, who directed the British Museum, and the Trustees, took responsibility for deciding if Davis' work was valuable, and Davis had sought their intellectual sponsorship at the inception of his project. Davis depended on the curators at the British Museum to publish his finds, and they did so. Although a complete catalogue of the mosaics did not appear until 1933,[68] Augustus Franks wrote a magisterial article on Davis' early mosaic finds before Davis' own book was published, and William Vaux published a definitive account of the Punic *stelae* in 1863.[69] In the final analysis, Davis was stopped because the political situation had changed, and because his finds did not seem important enough to Panizzi to justify the expense.

2

Davis in his social context

The Bey Mohammed and his court

Davis' friend and patron, the Bey Mohammed, was elected to succeed on May 30th, 1855, the day after the death of his cousin, Ahmed Bey,[1] and was succeeded by Mohammed es-Sadok on September 23rd, 1859.[2] His reign coincides very closely with the period during which Davis excavated at Carthage. Davis had some value as a British pawn in the political game at the time of the succession of Mohammed Bey, but the necessity of continuing to support his excavations was being questioned at the Foreign Office after a year, and more concertedly after two years. This was partly because of doubts about the importance of Davis' finds, which were not the Punic finds he had promised, but more because of a change in the political situation. Davis' position in the political scheme of things became less important as events made it easy for Britain and France to pressure the Bey directly.

Up to the early nineteenth century, the 'Barbary States' had acted entirely independently of the European world, and Arab corsairs had made the Mediterranean Sea unsafe for Europeans. After the French took Algiers in 1830, they made a treaty directly with the Bey of Tunis that both recognized his autonomy relative to the Ottoman Empire, and demonstrated that France expected to influence decisions at Tunis. Mohammed Bey's cousin and predecessor, Ahmed Bey, ruled from 1837 to 1855 and was the first Bey to promote westernization.[3] The construction of the Chapel of Saint Louis on the Byrsa Hill in the 1840s was a symbol of French intentions (Fig. 2.1).[4] It was a significant concession for the Regency of Tunis, and Davis, who was already in Tunis at the time of the Chapel's construction,[5] would have understood its political meaning.

The situation in North Africa was therefore 'interesting' to the French, but unstable from the British point of view. William Gregory, a lively and observant Irish MP, traveled in the interior of Tunisia in 1857, and reported a great deal of suspicion of the French among ordinary Tunisians, and a corresponding liking for the English.[6] Gregory himself was clearly suspicious of the French. In his autobiography he re-published notes he had made in 1858 in which he stated that the Bey Mohammed was 'perfectly alive to the fact that France is only waiting for the propitious moment to extend her African frontier to the borders of Tripoli. . . The possession of Tunis is essential for this project'.[7]

Travelling in the interior of Tunisia in the mid-nineteenth century was an adventure. Gregory and his companion, Sir Sandford Graham, whom Davis admired as a sportsman,[8] had come to Tunisia largely for the hunting. Hunting was important in the Regency and attracted British sporting men. Gregory and Graham followed an itinerary that Davis inspired them to take, and it may have been partly through Davis' influence that they found the Bey Mohammed so well disposed to their travel plans.[9] This kindness on the part of the Bey was part of a larger political situation, for Mohammed was being pressured by both the French and the British just at this time to show a more cosmopolitan and humane face to the world.

During the reign of Ahmed Bey, a lively contest for influence at Tunis had arisen between the French and the British; both nations saw Tunisia as a field poten-

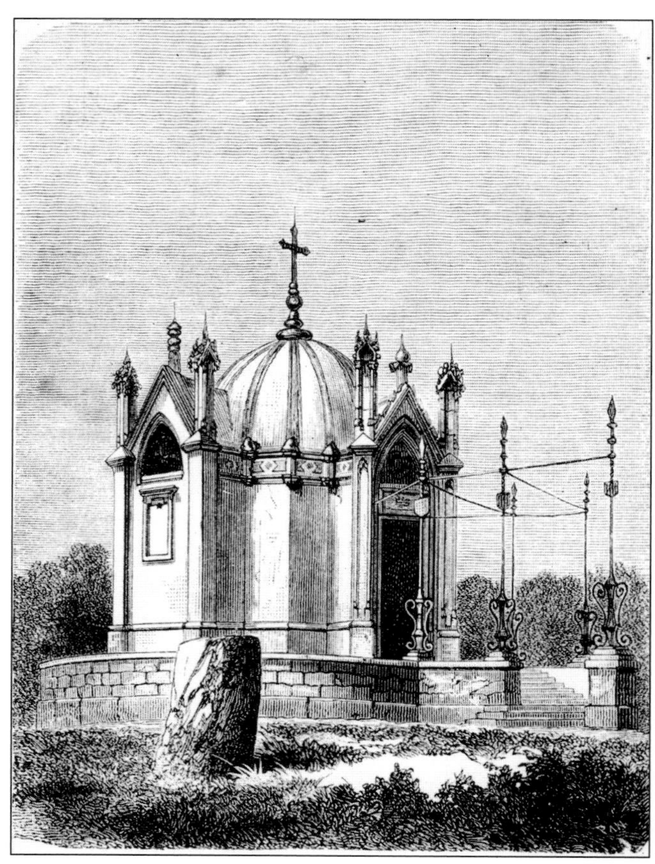

Fig. 2.1 Carthage, Byrsa Hill, the Chapel of St. Louis, commenced in 1841 and consecrated in 1845

tially open to commercial development; but the issue of human rights was still unsettled in Tunisia, and European nationals needed guarantees of their personal security. The internal political situation in Tunisia was complicated, however, and although the Beys were theoretically absolute rulers inside their own country, it was difficult to be sure where influence could best be applied.

The Husainid dynasty of the Beys did not identify with the people of Tunisia, but had originally established themselves as viceroys of the Ottoman Empire. Husain, the first member of the dynasty and a Greek by birth, came to power in 1705. Although the tie with the Ottoman Empire had never been completely abandoned, the dynasty had guarded a certain degree of autonomy.[10] The succession was determined by the age of descendants more or less in the direct line; a genealogical chart of the family documents only males.[11] The family maintained its separate identity from upper-class Tunisians by drawing administrators from the Mamelukes, who typically married into the family. Furthermore, the ladies of the harem, the mothers of princes and Beys, included slave women, who were at least occasionally European Christians by birth.[12] The Husainids were Muslims, but mixed-blood Europeans rather than Arab princes.

The Mamelukes were a class formed of individuals of non-Muslim birth who had been bought as boys on the slave markets of the Turkish empire. In Tunisia they were raised with the boys of the Husainid family and freed when they converted to Islam.[13] Slavery had been brought to an end in Tunisia only under Ahmed Bey in the mid 1840s, still the very recent past. The British consul, Thomas Reade, was credited with convincing Ahmed Bey to abolish slavery in Tunisia.[14] For his part, Davis gave himself a great deal of the credit for influencing Ahmed Bey. Although slavery had since been illegal, it did not immediately disappear, and Davis said that slaves and traffic in slaves still existed, especially in the interior.[15] At first, the abolition of slavery in Tunisia was most effective in safeguarding Europeans, who had been no less liable to enslavement than black Africans. For example, the Mameluke Mustapha Khaznadar, who in his first long tenure of power was prime minister of Tunisia from 1837 to 1873, was Greek by birth. He had been brought to Tunisia after being captured at Chios as a four-year-old.[16] The Khaznadar had married into the Husainid family, and predictably served the family and his own self-interest rather than the popular welfare.[17]

The succession of Mohammed Bey might have been seen by both the British and French as a mini-crisis, as Mohammed was regarded at best as gentle and well-intentioned, and at worst as debauched and controlled by unscrupulous ministers. Davis himself reported that Mohammed's character was gentle and mild; furthermore, 'his courtesy and affability to Christians were proverbial'.[18] According to Henry Dunant, the young Swiss gentleman who visited Tunis in 1857, Mohammed was an artist who loved painting and sculpture and conscientiously carried out his duties as Bey, although he had never wanted this distinction.[19] Among other duties Mohammed held court, hearing legal cases two days a week.[20] On the other hand, Davis did not hesitate to describe Mohammed's education and culture as limited.[21]

Mohammed Bey did not lead an immured life, but was, relatively speaking, socially accessible. Glimpses of his character appear in the travel writings of several Europeans. William Gregory joined a hunting party in which Mohammed Bey, dressed in striking Arab costume and mounted on a fine grey horse, killed a boar with one shot to the heart.[22] His skill was not as unlikely as it might seem, since beaters were employed to drive the boars out of the forest and funnel them towards the hunters. The Anglican Rev. E. W. L. Davies described such a hunt near Algiers in 1858, and an illustration of another, which required 300 beaters and resulted in the deaths of twenty boar, appeared in the *Illustrated London News* in 1861.[23]

William Gregory also met the Bey at his palace at La Marsa, and described him as a well-bred-looking middle-aged man, courteous, and with a particularly kind face.[24] Sophia Cracroft, the niece and travelling companion of Lady Franklin, the widow of the Arctic explorer,[25] met the Bey when she visited his summer palace at La Marsa with Mrs Davis, and displayed her characteristic interest in dress: 'He is a tall, fair man with grey reddish hair and rather prominent features, and was in the Arab dress, a beautiful grey burnous'. Miss Cracroft was kindly disposed, since she had had the good luck to meet the Bey in his harem, and later saw him listening to musicians with his little boy in his lap: 'Here he was *en famille* (a pretty large family party!), and we spoke to him face to face'.[26]

The novelist Gustave Flaubert's impressions were more melodramatic. He described the Bairam he attended in the spring of 1858, a celebration at the end of Ramadan in which Mohammed Bey received the salutations of the community. Those attending kissed the palm of Mohammed's hand, which he offered with his elbow supported on a pillow. To the eye of the novelist, who was more interested in the person than in his social status or attire, Mohammed appeared 'lost under his gilt and medals' and 'tired to death, greying, with heavy eyelids and an inebriated eye'.[27] Possibly the Bey was more bored and sleepy than intoxicated, but at any rate his energy was not up to two or three days of ceremonial salutations.

Nor was it up to controlling the misgovernment of his ministers. While travelling in the interior of Tunisia, William Gregory met an Arab who told him that Mohammed Bey was 'a mild well-meaning man', but was 'surrounded by a set of robbers and extortioners'.[28] Davis had repeated problems with a particular member of the Bey's court, whom he avoided naming directly, but who by innuendo was Count Guiseppino Raffo, a Genoese who had been granted his title by the King of Sardinia in 1851.[29] Raffo had been Ahmed Bey's Minister for Foreign Affairs, a post he continued to hold under the Bey Mohammed. Gossip said that Raffo gained this position after his sister-in-law married a Tunisian prince, although his own father had been a clock-maker.[30] Ahmed Bey's loyalty to Raffo was based on long habit and family feeling.[31] According to Davis, Raffo was not a man of principle, and was 'either coaxed, bullied or coerced, as the case required' by the French and British consuls.[32] Evidently Raffo found Davis' position a threat to himself. At one point Davis criticized the difficult minister without mentioning his name, but placed his complaints in close juxtaposition with a description of Raffo's bad character. Later in his book he even described the minister in question as a 'moral pestilence'.[33]

While Davis despised Raffo, he was evidently on good terms with the rest of the court and willing to overlook their flaws. He particularly relied on his friendship with Sidy Mustapha, another important and consummately loyal figure in the family of the Bey.[34] Sidy Mustapha was the 'Sahab Ettaba' or Lord Keeper of the Seal, a Georgian Mameluke, and brother-in-law to the previous Bey. Although significantly younger, Mustapha Khaznadar had pushed the Lord Keeper of the Seal into the background, but Sidy Mustapha had held his position, the highest administrative office in the country, since 1837.[35] The European community casually referred to this personage as the 'Saptap';[36] possibly they were amused by the similarity of the nickname to 'Satrap.' The European attitude suggests that members of the Bey's court could be taken less than seriously.

The foreign consuls at Tunis

Davis worked closely with the British consul at Tunis and his friendship with the Bey cemented his status in the same social milieu as the diplomatic community. Under Ahmed Bey the foreign diplomatic community at Tunis had had two very long serving members: one was the coolly aristocratic British consul, Sir Thomas Reade, who held his post from 1824 to 1849;[37] the other the American consul, Dr Samuel Davies Heap,[38] consul at Tunis four times from 1824 until his death in 1853. Dr Heap's portrait suggests that he was a bookish and gentle man, despite the profusion of gold braid on his jacket, while his wife Margaret was a sweet and thoughtful-looking lady. The Heaps ran a happy home for their seven children, and also made visitors, who certainly included Nathan Davis, welcome.[39]

Consul Heap had concluded a favorable treaty with Tunis in 1825; among other provisions, he won the right to refuse to return escaped slaves who sought sanctuary on American ships. On May 6th, 1842, the British consul, Thomas Reade, wrote to Heap on one of the occasions in which Heap was removed from office because of political events at home. Belying his reputation for coldness and arrogance, Reade wrote that 'his Highness the Bey . . . added that your separation from him was a matter of deep public concern and had created in his breast emotions of real grief'.[40] Amid rivalry between the French and British, the respect accorded to Reade and Heap helped to create a workable balance and consensus, but fate took both men from the field by the mid-1850s.

In contrast to the long service of the British and American consuls, the French consuls seldom served more than two or three years, although Charles de Lagau had held the post from 1838 to 1848. Alphonse Rousseau was the French acting consul from 1855 to 1857;[41] he remained in Tunis until at least May of 1858.[42] Léon Roches then served as French consul from 1857 to 1863.[43] Roches had deserted from the French army in Algeria as a young man in the 1830s, and then collaborated with the great Algerian resistance fighter Abd el-Khader and converted to Islam.[44] Davis said that the Tunisians called Roches 'Hadj Amor';[45] this was a not very well disguised attack on Roches's dignity. The title 'Hadj' referred to Roches's purported pilgrimage to Mecca. While the significance of the Arabic name 'Amor,' 'Omar' or 'Umar' is multi-faceted, the overtones in Italian, the *lingua franca* of Tunis, are not. Roches had constructed a romantic past for himself. His account does not agree with more objective sources and is at least partly plagiarized; furthermore, he probably never went to Mecca. Historical documents reveal Roches as an unstable young man, filled with romantic and heroic dreams that he was not able to carry out in the real world. Nevertheless his knowledge of Arabic was genuine and provided the basis for his later successful diplomatic career.[46] Armand de Flaux, a Frenchman who came to Tunisia on an abortive archaeological mission in 1862, was impressed by the intelligence and affability of Roches, as well as his consummate ability to make a dramatic impression.[47]

A new British Consul, Richard Wood, had been appointed on August 30th, 1855. Wood had thirty years of British government service in the Levant behind him, and proved to be remarkably competent in strengthening the British position in Tunis. A portrait of him shows a strong-featured man with a dark complexion, thinning hair, and an open and intelligent expression (Fig. 2.2).[48] Wood was of Syrian Jewish descent, but his family had converted to Catholicism and he had changed his name from 'Rhattab' to 'Wood' to fit his adopted English identity.[49] Sophia Cracroft, who resented his indifference to the wishes of her aunt, Lady Franklin, said, 'We did not like his appearance or manner – both are those of a foreigner and he even speaks English with a foreign accent. Certainly he did not give us the impression of being a proper representative of England'.[50] While Wood may not have been deferential or British-seeming enough to please these ladies, he spoke Arabic with native-born fluency,[51] so much so that the Tunisian historian, Ibn abi Dhiaf, spoke warmly of Wood's intelligence, dignity, eloquence and respect for Arab learning.[52] He also spoke and wrote Italian and French, both of which were crucial to his diplomatic role in Tunis. A strong and even ruthless personality, Wood chose to work closely with the powerful Khaznadar, even to the point of living next door to him;[53] by contrast, Léon Roches, who was the more polished and flexible of these two powerful consuls, courted the good opinion of the Bey.[54] These men's characters demonstrate that in the mid-nineteenth century both Britain and France felt the necessity of appointing representatives distinguished by long experience of Muslim political systems, rather than by correct pedigree and affiliation.

Davis was placed under Wood's direct supervision, and occasional conflicts arose. Not surprisingly, after Davis' earlier career as a missionary, there were weaknesses in his personal financial position. A letter from Malmesbury, in answer to a letter from Wood, reveals that late in 1857 Davis was being sued for 300 pounds by an Englishman, a Mr Squires, who had taken his case to Tunis in pursuit of Davis.[55] This was not a small sum; the amount paid to Davis by the Foreign Office as his annual salary during his excavations at Carthage was 365 guineas. The lawsuit suggests that Davis' financial affairs were in precarious disorder, and Wood's letter to Malmesbury seemed aimed at exposing Davis rather than protecting him.

Although Wood and Davis reached a *modus vivendi* based on their mutual usefulness to each other, there were occasional signs of strain. For example, an officious letter from Wood to Davis complaining that Davis' accounts were not signed and that he could not therefore approve them, was answered by a sharp

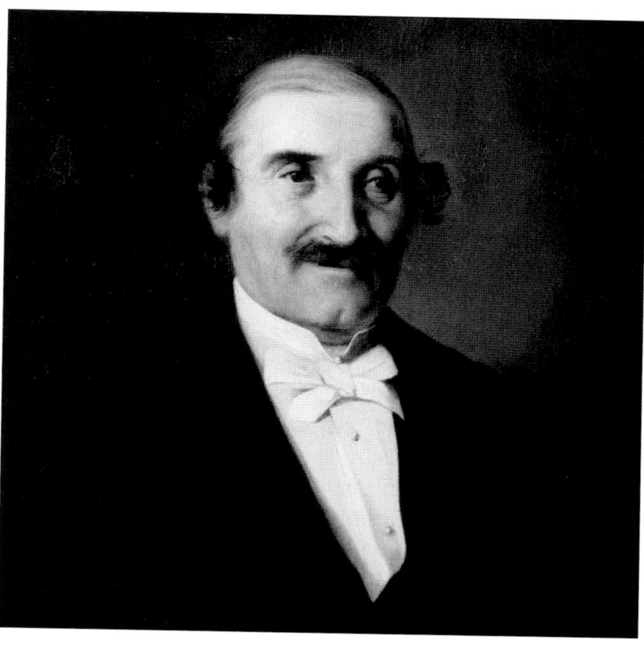

Fig. 2.2 Sir Richard Wood (1806–1900), Consul-General to Tunisia from 1855 to 1879, oil portrait (1877) by Lieron Mayer. It now hangs in the British embassy in Tunis.

riposte from Davis to Wood, saying that he would sign the receipts but that the Foreign Office had already approved them.[56] When Davis was arranging his expedition to Utica in May 1858, he depended on Wood to acquire various permissions for him. According to Sophia Cracroft, who was certainly repeating Davis' own opinions, Wood had put many difficulties in his way, although these were eventually overcome.[57]

The European social scene

At the end of the 1850s, Tunis was a city of about 90,000 people, of whom 60,000 were Muslims, 20,000 Jews, and 10,000 Christians.[58] For the time it was a very large city, described by a French observer in 1854 as a queenly city uniting Africa, Europe and the Orient, and much larger than Algiers.[59] Thirty years later, Guy de Maupassant was to describe Tunis as a Jewish city, remarking at length on the colourful costumes and odd marriage customs of the Jewish population.[60] Brown would describe the Jews of Tunisia in Bey Ahmed's times as a 'despised if useful minority'.[61] Of the Christian population, which formed a large minority group, more than half was Maltese. The Maltese, who were often impoverished laborers, were under the protection of the British consul, and Armand de Flaux pointed out that it was therefore appropriate that Consul Wood was Catholic.[62] After the Maltese the European population was made up of about 3,000 Italians, plus a total of about 1,500 French, Spanish,

Germans and British. The British were the smallest group among the European nationalities.[63] There were at most only a couple of hundred British citizens in Tunis, and the Americans would have formed a much smaller group.

While Tunis could be described as large and cosmopolitan, it was not modern. Seen across the Lake of Tunis from the port of La Goulette, Tunis was a 'white city surrounded by a wall bristling with guns',[64] and its gates were closed at sunset, which could at times be very inconvenient.[65] Tunis had no police force and no postal system. Europeans left mail at their consulates and received it hand-delivered by a dragoman, a high-level consular official whose skills included knowledge of Arabic.[66] All water in the city was supplied from cisterns.[67] The city had open sewers and no garbage collection; the resulting stench was nearly unbearable to European sensibilities.[68] In addition, the streets were not paved, and rain turned the whole terrain into a sea of mud; Davis ruefully described the results of being splashed by a camel under these conditions.[69] Davis had mentioned in 1841 that there were no street signs,[70] and at the end of the 1850s there was still no street lighting; anyone venturing out at night required a lantern. On the other hand, many of these problems were being addressed. Victor Guérin, who came to Tunisia in 1860 to search out Roman inscriptions, reported plans to bring covered sewers, paved streets, and a system of street lighting, at least to the French sector of the city. A plan to restore the ancient Roman aqueduct and bring piped-in water to the city was also underway.[71]

Tunis had an established European social life, in contrast to Algiers, and the society was at least superficially morally conservative and correct.[72] Henry Dunant published his impressions of the regency of Tunis in 1858. He wrote that there were two social systems among the wealthier European families; the families that frequented the consular set were self-consciously the best people, well educated and wealthy, rigorously distinguishing themselves from the society of the merchant class.[73] Dunant found the consular circle 'very select and elegant, hospitable and friendly' and the winter of 1856–1857 had been particularly socially brilliant.[74] Dunant's account shows that Davis had an integral place in a sophisticated, if small, European social circle.

The leading lights in this society were Count and Countess Raffo, the Léon Roches, the Richard Woods; then Lewis Ferriere, who had formerly been British vice-consul; Père Anselme, a learned and well-mannered Parisian and a Capuchin monk who served as secretary to Monsignor Sutter (as Apostolic Vicar, Sutter was the head of the Catholic church at Tunis);[75] and Alphonse Rousseau, a distinguished Orientalist who had acted as French consul until the appointment of Roches. It was said that Madame Roches took the social lead, to which Mrs Wood would produce a carefully measured equal response.[77] The key people in this social circle were therefore largely French and Catholic.

The European social amenities at Tunis included a club, a philharmonic society, and a theatre with presentations in Italian. Dunant also mentioned the Catholic school run by Abbé Bourgade, which was attended by about sixty boys of good family. The shared pleasures of the European community included hunting parties that ended in picnics.[77] The picture Dunant presented was almost certainly idealized, but suggests that the small size of the European community encouraged a disparate group to form a well-integrated little society. In fact, although the best society among the foreign contingent at Tunis in these years was very mixed, marriage between the families was not uncommon. For example, British consul Richard Wood's daughter, Féridah, married Joseph Raffo,[78] the grandson of the Genoese Foreign Minister who was Davis' enemy.

Dunant mentioned a number of other families of foreign origin as belonging to the charmed circle, including the Heaps, the Davises, the Cubisols, and the Tulins (the family of the Swedish consul). Other than the Cubisols, whose religious affiliation is uncertain, these families were all Protestant. The religious interests of the Protestants were looked after by the American and Swedish consuls; the Heap family had had Protestant services held in English at the American consulate until the death of the pastor from cholera.[79] This Protestant congregation, of which Davis was a part, numbered only about fifteen souls in 1841.[80] In 1865 Flaux noted that although the Protestant community had no church, religious services were held in the home of a pastor sent by a religious society in London.[81] By now proliferation of the Protestant families might have doubled the size of the congregation.[82]

Henry Dunant himself, though a visitor, implicitly illustrates the mentality of these upper class Protestant families. Davis had worked to end slavery in Tunisia, while Dunant was an admirer of Harriet Beecher Stowe, and his book on Tunis included an attack on slavery in America. Dunant was also an enthusiastic evangelical, who, like Davis, saw his time in North Africa as an opportunity to distribute Bibles.[83] Such concerns would have set them apart from the French families with whom they socialized, but made the Protestants very comfortable companions for Davis, as they were likely to be both English-speaking and in sympathy with his missionary work.

Davis' close acquaintances always included the American consuls. In Tunisia in the late 1850s the American consuls were relative nonentities politically, especially since Dr Heap was followed by a string of consuls whose terms were very short. John Howard Payne, the composer of 'Home, Sweet Home,' as Davis reminded his readers, was consul for a brief period in 1851 or 1852, but Payne died not long after his arrival in Tunis.[84] On the death of Dr Heap, Mr William Penn Chandler served from 1854 to 1858. A letter of Wood to the Foreign Office in March 1857 reported an irregular arrival of Mr Chandler, who had hitched a ride from Malta on HMS *Miranda*, a steam frigate of the British navy.[85] Sophia Cracroft and Lady Franklin called on the Chandlers in May 1858 and noted that both seemed quite unwell; the Tunisian climate did not always agree with foreign diplomatic personnel.[86] John Merritt, who served only for the first six months of 1859, succeeded Chandler. The American consuls evidently considered Davis a reliable man; Merritt left Davis in charge and Davis would serve as acting U.S. consul at Tunis from June 27th to October 8th, 1859, although a British subject. In April of 1860, after his excavations at Carthage were brought to a close, Davis travelled in the interior of Tunisia with Mr George W. S. Nicholson from Delaware, the U.S. consul who replaced him.[87]

The Heaps, the family of the long-serving American consul, remained in Tunisia for some years after his death. Dr Heap and his wife Margaret had married in 1810, and four of their seven children were still living in the 1850s; the older children were Davis' near contemporaries. Their eldest daughter, also named Margaret, married the Swedish consul at Tunis, Gustavus Augustus Tulin, who had succeeded to the post on the death of his father and would be succeeded by their son, Charles.[88] The Heaps' youngest son was thirty-two in 1858, when Davis hired him to assist in his excavations. David Porter Heap was named after his uncle, Commodore David Porter, who had been American consul at Constantinople. In his early teens, David Porter Heap had served on his testy uncle's staff.[89] Fluent in Arabic from childhood, the young man also had the Turkish he had learned in Constantinople. American political realities made foreign service an insecure lifestyle; following in his father's footsteps, he returned to the United States and trained as a medical doctor. In 1854 he married a girl from Virginia. Shortly thereafter the young couple arrived in Tunis and by 1859 they had three little children, all born there.[90]

The younger Dr Heap served as a consul-in-training and acting U.S. consul for short periods in 1854 and 1858,[91] but Heap was aiming for the consulship at Constantinople, and avoided accepting the consulate at Tunis. Despite his birth and schooling abroad, David Porter Heap was a patriotic American who was to become a hero of the American Civil War. In 1855 he responded to a call for tribute stones for the Washington Monument by sending a decorative block made of 'marble taken from the ruins of Carthage'.[92] According to Dunant, Dr Heap supplied medical treatment to the poor of Tunis without charging a fee,[93] but his medical practice did not prevent him from assisting Davis with his excavations in 1858 and 1859. His preparation and ambitions paid off when he was appointed Consul General at Constantinople in 1861, but the Civil War and a change of government took him home to serve in the Union Army instead.[94]

Antiquaries and scholars

European scholars scorned the level of culture at the Tunisian court, and took for granted that ancient objects could not be properly appreciated in that country. It is true that there was no obvious link between Punic or Roman culture and that of the Muslim Beys of Tunis. Nevertheless, the European prejudice was blatant; for example, in 1881, Wilmanns, then a young German epigrapher collecting inscriptions in Tunisia, described how Mohammed, the son of the Prime Minister Mustapha Khaznadar, although 'a completely barbarous man', had picked up the idea of collecting ancient objects from the European example (the comment was expressed in Latin). A good proportion of Mohammed's collection was to be sent to an exhibition in Paris in 1867 and then to an exhibition in Vienna in 1873, where, after the Khaznadar's fall from power, they remained.[95] These finds included two small fragments of a mosaic pavement, which, like most mosaics in Tunisia before the establishment of the French antiquities service, were clearly lifted without the benefit of Davis' method.[96]

Nevertheless, already in 1838 Falbe, the former Danish consul at Tunis (Fig. 3.3), had mentioned the support of Ahmed Bey for the excavations of the British consul, Thomas Reade, as well as for the excavations of Falbe and Sir Grenville Temple, which was given at least partly because excavation provided employment for Tunisian workmen.[97] Likewise the Bey Mohammed, Davis' patron and friend, gave official permission for Davis' excavations,[98] and he would take as great, if uninformed, an interest in the excavations as many a modern statesman would.

Certain members of the French community at Tunis were highly educated intellectuals with antiquarian interests. The French consular official, Alphonse Rousseau, carried on a scholarly correspondence with Adrien Berbrugger at the Museum of Algiers, and scholars Wilmanns and Mommsen recorded that Rousseau sent three inscriptions from Carthage to Berbrugger for the museum there.[99] Rousseau himself published a number of scholarly works.[100] He had taken a great interest in a mosaic discovered by stone robbers in Carthage in 1844 (Fig. 6.3); he not only sketched the mosaic, but also excavated briefly beneath it after it was lifted and sent off a description to *Revue archéologique* that was published in 1850.[101]

Abbé François Bourgade was the heavyweight among intellectuals at Tunis, but he left Tunis in 1858 to spend his remaining years in France.[102] Bourgade was an intelligent, well-educated and distinguished gentleman[103] who used much of his personal fortune to benefit the Catholic church in Tunis, where he had arrived as the chaplain of an order of nuns in 1841; the founder of the order, Emilie de Vialar, was later sainted.[104] The French government approved his appointment as chaplain of the Chapel of Saint Louis at Carthage in 1843, although the Abbé chose to live in Tunis. Bourgade was regarded with affection and respect by the European community, with the exception of his spiritual superior, Monsignor Sutter, an Italian from Ferrara, who strongly disapproved of Bourgade's French patrotism.[105]

Abbé Bourgade had published several books, including one on his collection of forty-one Punic and neo-Punic *stelae*, with translations of their inscriptions.[106] In the 1840s Bourgade was unable to find any French scholar at the Academy who could advise him on the interpretation and significance of the neo-Punic *stelae* which he had collected. Although it is clear that they are not from Carthage, they are still imperfectly understood today (see below, Chapter 9).[107] He brought his pupils from the College of Saint Louis in Tunis on excursions to Carthage, where he set them to search for antiquities for his collection. He established a small museum of antiquities in the school, where his collection included examples of Roman amphorae,[108] and another in the residence which had been constructed for him in the enclosure of the chapel at Carthage.[109] Flaubert visited at least one of these during his visit to Tunisia in the spring of 1858.[110] Both of these museum collections were dismantled after Bourgade left Tunisia. Davis was acquainted with Bourgade when the Abbé was still resident in Tunis, and repeatedly, but unsuccessfully, offered to buy Bourgade's collection for the British Museum.[111] Davis later succeeded in acquiring nine examples of Bourgade's neo-Punic *stelae*, but he was evidently not aware that they had already been published by Bourgade.

Charles Tissot, later an academic and ambassador to Constantinople and Athens,[112] was posted to Tunis from 1852 to 1858 as a young diplomat-in-training. His contemporaries did not mention him, so he may have been too junior or too socially backward to attract attention. At Tunis the young Tissot, who had a classical education, became a friend of Abbé Bourgade, and through him developed an interest in antiquarian pursuits. During his posting in Tunisia, Tissot explored much of the country, concentrating particularly on the

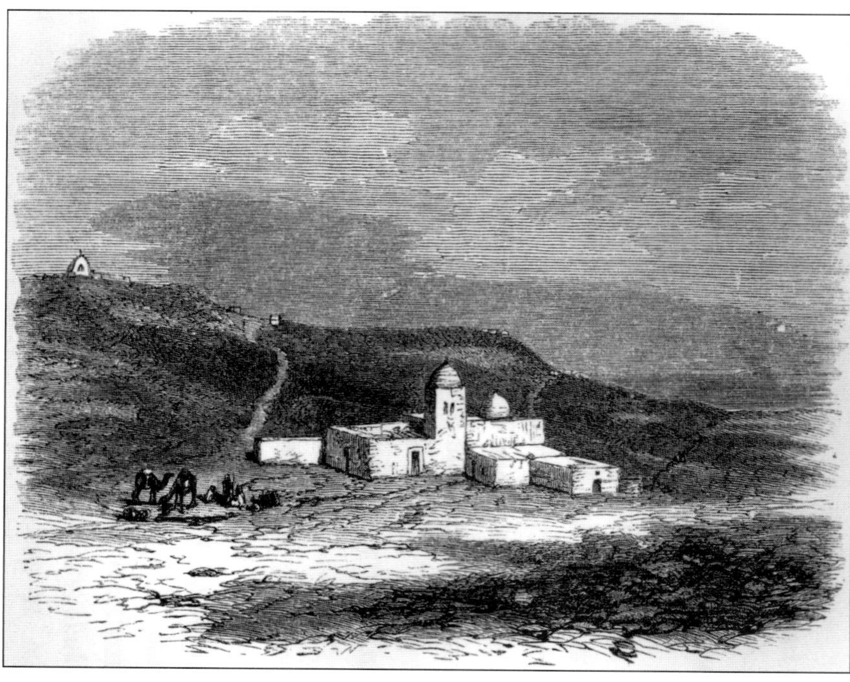

Fig. 2.3 Davis' first house in Tunisia, at Douar ech-Chott, as it appears in his Carthage and Her Remains

Roman road system and epigraphy, and actively published his finds.[113] Tissot is of interest because as a young scholar he was a contemporary of Davis, although the two volumes of his major work were not published until a quarter of a century later. Since Davis lived in Tunis during much of the 1850s, he and Tissot must have been acquainted; in fact Tissot accurately described Davis as 'an English missionary'.[114] Rousseau, Bourgade and Tissot were undoubtedly well aware that they had a level of education to which Davis would never have been able to aspire.

Charles Cubisol, who acted as vice-consul at La Goulette, the port of Tunis, for all the European nations, also had antiquarian interests, forming a collection of Punic and neo-Punic *stelae,* which he published.[115] In addition, Wilmanns recorded Latin inscriptions from Cubisol's collection, including a neo-Punic *stele* with a Latin inscription, a number of Roman inscriptions and a Christian epitaph.[116] Sophia Cracroft and her aunt, Lady Franklin, visited the home of the Cubisols on their arrival at La Goulette, and were given some useful practical help by the vice-consul. Miss Cracroft, although she was unable to spell the family name correctly, noted that Cubisol and his wife were both native-born Tunisians who had never left the country. 'They both speak French and seem kindly unpretending people'.[117] Charles Cubisol often acted in the service of the other European consulships; he was acting U.S. consul for two months in the fall of 1867.[118] The Cubisols were not as socially humble as Miss Cracroft implied, but at least she did not find them worthy of her disdain.

Davis observed

Several people who were guests of the Davis family recounted their experiences at Tunis or Carthage, and gave a vivid impression of Davis in his social milieu. In May 1858, Lady Franklin, the widow of the Arctic explorer, and her niece Sophia Cracroft, who was an indefatigable letter-writer and also kept a journal, stayed with the Davis family in their home at Gammarth for more than a week. On Sunday, Mr Davis, like many another Victorian household head, read the morning service, while Mrs Davis provided the music on the family piano; the eldest girl sang along with her mother. This was Davis' daughter Margaret ('Margherita'), who was twelve years old in 1858. Margaret was so impressed by these visitors that she later named her youngest son Franklin.[119] Miss Cracroft wrote, 'Mr Davis reads well and devoutly and the service was a great comfort'.[120]

Sophia Cracroft was favourably impressed by Davis, and wrote, clearly echoing his own words, that he was too broad-minded and too much like Dr Livingstone (the African explorer) to conform to the demands of his church. He had explained to his synod that he did not want to convert Muslims, but rather to meet them 'on their own ground'. She implied that he had given up his missionary posting because of the demands of his conscience.[121] This may well have been true. Davis clearly did not understand his religious affiliation as demanding any pious religious pose. Revealing himself slightly more than was his wont, Davis praised a Muslim religious leader for his broad-minded pleasure in life. Davis wrote: 'I liked this man, . . . attached to his creed without being fanatical, . . . religious without canting, . . . pious and devout without being gloomy and morose'.[122]

When Davis began his excavations in 1856 he at first had to come out from Tunis every day. The Reverend Joseph Blakesley, a Cambridge-educated Anglican vicar touring Tunis in 1858, said, with evident approval, that the ride from Tunis to Carthage in a one-horse cabriolet took less than two hours,[123] and the ride on horseback was probably not significantly faster. Davis soon arranged to rent an isolated house in the village of Douar ech-Chott, on the site of Carthage. Dunant later described Davis as living with his family in 'a charming cottage built over the very ruins of Carthage';[124] Dunant's description suggests the little house which was Davis' original excavation headquarters at Douar ech-Chott (Fig. 2.3), in which case Dunant probably visited the Davis family in 1857, after Mrs Davis had returned from a stay in London.

In the autumn of 1858, a story in the *Illustrated London News* described the adventures of a party of British travellers who had ridden the fifty miles from Tunis to Zaghouan, the mountain source of the Carthage aqueduct, returning by way of Oudna and along the line of the aqueduct's arcades (Fig. 2.4). The party included two ladies, and was guided by a couple identified only as living at Carthage; clearly this was Davis and his wife. The extravagant dress of the females, the fact that all were comfortable on horseback, and that the men were at home with guns, suggests that the party was made up of self-assured ladies and gentlemen. The participants in this adventure were not only hardy and adventurous, but also intellectually sophisticated, as their interest was in the ancient remains. Since Arabs at Zaghouan told the party a garbled version of the execution at Tunis that took place in July of 1857, the outing must have taken place not long afterward.[125] Davis mentioned that Admiral Lord Lyons was accompanied by his niece on a visit in the fall of 1857;[126] I think it is likely that the party included Lyons, commander of the British fleet in the Mediterranean, his niece Miss Pearson, her female companion, and a select entourage of naval

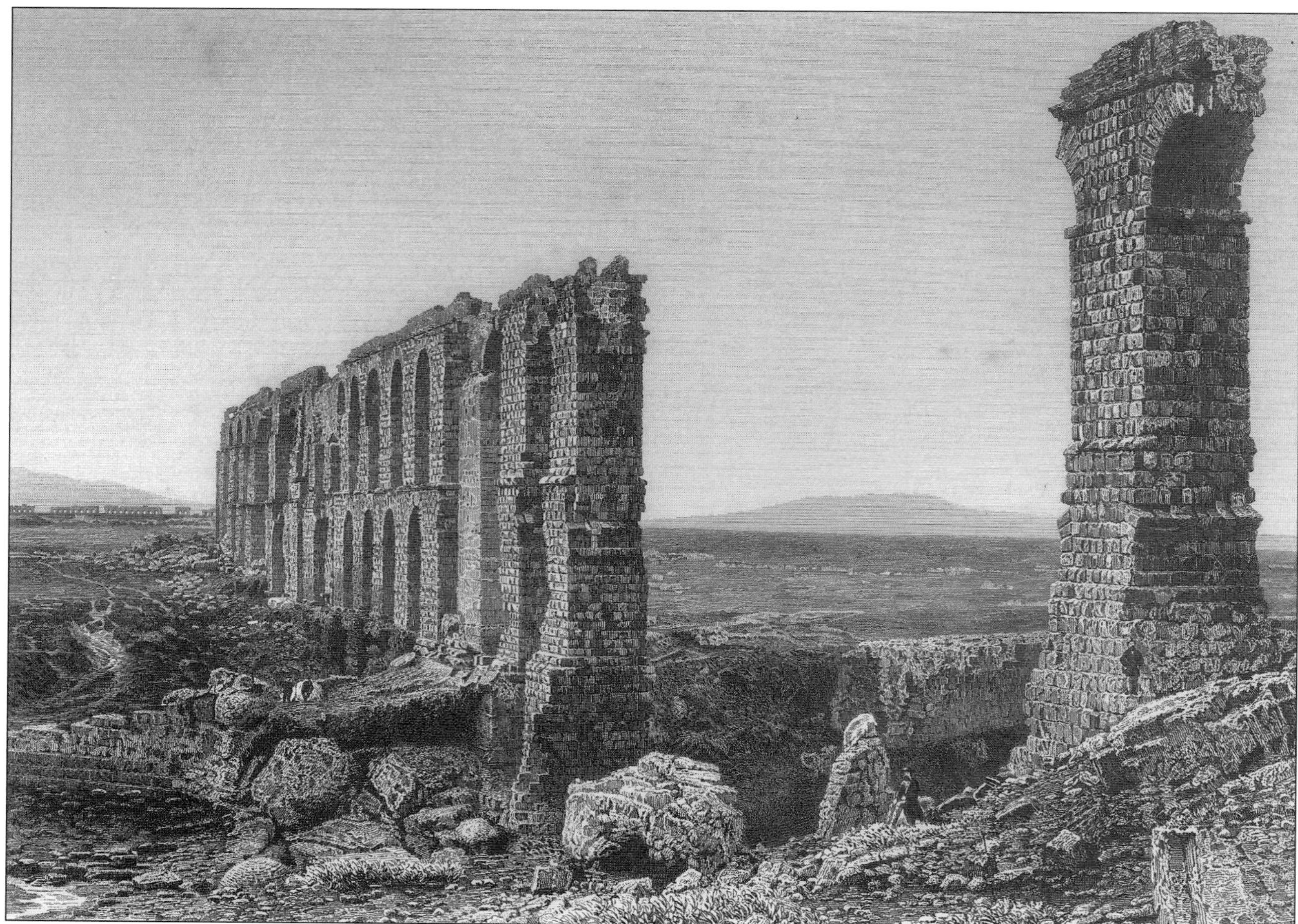

Fig. 2.4 The arches of the Zaghouan aqueduct south of Carthage, as recorded in the frontispiece of Davis' Carthage and Her Remains

officers. The young ladies' behaviour was unconventional; it would have been ungentlemanly for Davis to mention the excursion, and it makes excellent sense that Mrs Davis was required as a chaperone. The story is typical of Davis' many travel adventures in the Regency, but also gives an insight into the character of Davis' wife and their marital partnership.

Davis and his family circumstances were observed by Flaubert in May 1858. Flaubert's first published novel, *Madame Bovary*, had appeared a year earlier, when the author was thirty-five. The subject of this novel, the adultery of a bourgeois provincial lady, led to a public trial for indecency, but Flaubert was acquitted, and the sensation caused by the trial guaranteed his novel's success and brought him fame. Flaubert, however, immediately turned to research on something completely different, a historical novel on Punic Carthage, which he decided to title *Salammbô*.[127] As Flaubert had found that *Madame Bovary* was known to a minor French official and his dinner guests, whom he had met in Algeria,[128] it is likely that Davis, who was a member of a society very largely French, knew very well who Flaubert was.

This was the very same moment when Davis and his family were hosting Lady Franklin and her niece Sophia Cracroft. These two ladies had arrived unexpectedly in the port of La Goulette just before mid-May 1858 (Fig. 2.5). They were met there by consular representatives, evidently including the British consul Wood, and, having heard from them of Davis' excavations, expressed a desire to meet him, although it was in fact a surprise to them that Carthage was so close by. They noted a British ship in port, the HMS *Harpy*, which they were told had been dispatched to La Goulette by Admiral Lord Lyons to aid Mr Davis in his excavations. The ladies were disappointed that both Consul and Mrs Wood were unwilling to get them invitations for the Bairam, at which they might have been presented to the Bey. The reason given was that they were in mourning, and black was inappropriate dress for the occasion.

On their second day in Tunis, Mr Davis and a small party were announced at their hotel. It is unlikely that this hotel was suitable for British ladies, since Blakesley, who had arrived in Tunis two weeks earlier, said there was only one hotel in Tunis (the Hôtel de France) that had doors on its bedrooms and fastenings on its doors. Furthermore, hot weather had begun early, and the hotel was stifling.[129] Davis' entourage included his wife and the commander of the *Harpy*, Lieutenant Porcher. The Davises, whom Lady Franklin and her niece found 'heartily kind', invited the ladies to stay with them at Gammarth.

Hosting Jane Franklin must have been a social *coup* for the Davises, as, due to her personal genius for publicity, she was one of the great celebrities of the mid-nineteenth century. In May 1858, she was not yet a widow in her own eyes, but a wife single-mindedly fighting for the rescue and vindication of her husband. Of course, not every sixty-six-year-old female of means would have undertaken a Mediterranean tour for mental and physical respite in this situation.[130] Her niece Sophia, now forty-two years old, was to spend her life as her aunt's companion, and supported her interests in every way. Sir John Franklin had headed a British naval expedition to find the North-west Passage, leaving England with two ships and 134 men in May 1845. After nearly three years with no news, the search for the expedition began. An enormous amount of energy, money and ink was spent in the effort to discover Franklin's fate; this outpouring was largely driven by an unremitting barrage of letters from Lady Franklin, who contributed to the funding of three rescue expeditions. A huge area of the Canadian Arctic was explored due to her persistence, and she became an expert on its geography and climate.[131]

Since Lady Franklin and her niece knew that the Davises were long established in the country, they reiterated their wish to see the Bey. Mrs Davis proposed that they accompany her to his country palace at La Marsa, where she would go herself to pay her respects to his two wives. Lady Franklin and Miss Cracroft therefore left Tunis early on Saturday morning, May 15th, 1858, and met Mrs Davis, her four (or five) children,[132] and her young woman companion, Nelly Rosenberg, at La Marsa. On their arrival at the palace of the Bey, they saw the Bey and Mustapha Khaznadar, the Prime Minister, in the courtyard. The Khaznadar bowed to Mrs Davis, with whom he was acquainted. Inside, Mrs Davis was met with kisses by one of the Bey's daughters, who led her to the Bey's elder wife, the Lilla Kabira. The visit was eased by the fact that Mrs Davis spoke Arabic. Next they visited the apartments of the favorite wife, the Lilla Jenina, which Mrs Davis told them was always a lively and cheerful place.

They found this lady sitting in conversation with the Khaznadar. 'Our notions of the seclusion of the harem were being strangely dissipated', wrote Miss Cracroft. The English ladies recognized the Khaznadar to be an intelligent and cultured gentleman. He questioned Mrs Davis in Arabic and Italian about Franklin

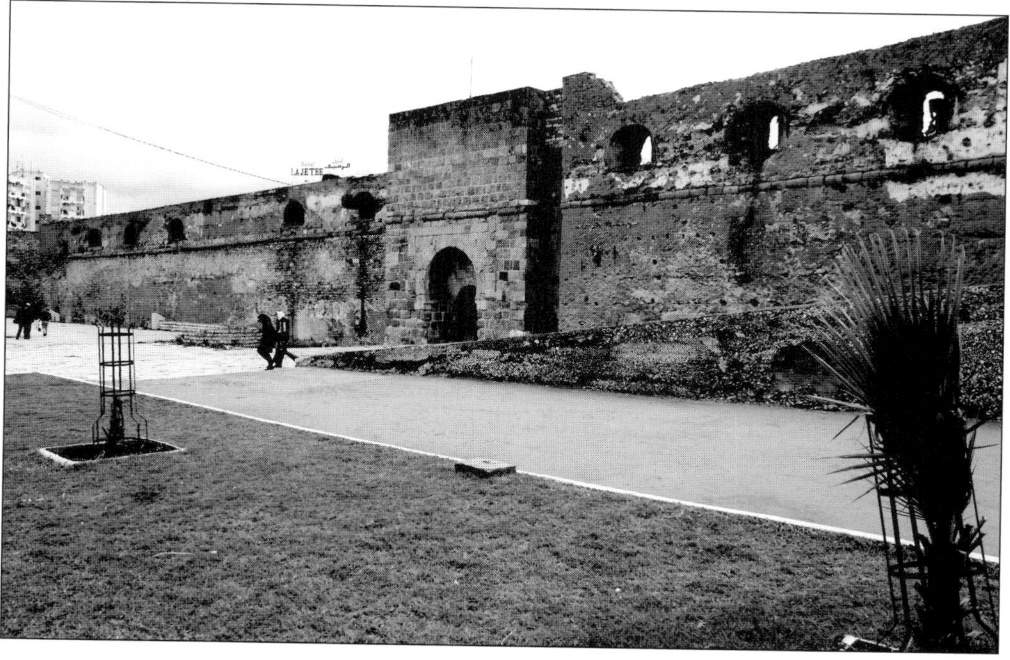

Fig. 2.5 La Goulette, the Kasba as it appears today. It was built by Charles V (Charles I of Spain) in 1535; despite its strengthening by Don Juan of Austria in 1573, it fell to the Turks the following year. By the mid-nineteenth century, when Davis would have seen it, it was used as a prison.

and his expedition. The conversation was not all serious, for he also teased Miss Rosenberg about her dark Arabic looks and said she should marry a Mameluke; she objected that as an English girl she liked her liberty too much to do so. The Bey then joined the party and was interested to hear of Lady Franklin's plight. Later that day, Lady Franklin and Sophia were driven to the house of the Davises at Gammarth, and stayed there for nine very happy days, leaving on Monday, May 24th for Malta.[133]

Mrs Davis was a lively and intelligent woman and an important social asset to her husband. William Gregory, the Irish MP, dined with the Davis family, and recounted that Mrs Davis provided medical services to the Arabic villagers of La Malga.[134] She was a great success with Sophia Cracroft, and was clearly not intimidated by Jane Franklin, who was an extremely strong-minded woman of the world. Mrs Davis easily convinced Sophia and Lady Franklin to disguise their mourning black with light-coloured shawls and scarves in order not to offend during their visit to the harem. Throughout the visit, which could have become tedious due to the language barrier, Mrs Davis provided an amusing running pantomime of what was being said. Mrs Davis was clearly not a typical non-conformist minister's wife: she caused delighted consternation among all the ladies when she showed how her hoop underskirt was constructed so they could understand why she took up so much room.[135]

Miss Cracroft's account illuminates the relationship between the Davis family and the family of the Bey Mohammed as one between neighbors and friends. This relationship was certainly facilitated by the fluency in Arabic shown by both husband and wife. Davis stated flatly that it was forbidden for a Jew or Christian to study Arabic in Tunisia,[136] yet he himself not only spoke Arabic, as many recorded exchanges prove, but he also had written two textbooks on reading Arabic, so his knowledge of the language was of a higher order than simple conversation.

Although Davis was pleased to record his acquaintance with the socially correct Lady Franklin, he never mentioned meeting Flaubert, yet he invited Flaubert to his home several times. It is no surprise, however, that Davis did not mention meeting Flaubert in *Carthage and Her Remains*, a book that was meant for family audiences. Flaubert, on the other hand, made several notes on his encounters with Davis and his household in his private journal.

Flaubert visited Tunis and Carthage in April and May 1858, noting local colour in the most literal sense, with numerous colour-coded drawings. After riding along the Sebkha, the shallow salt lake west of Gammarth, Flaubert evoked the dramatic intensity of his surroundings. 'Between the sand dunes of Gammart the sea appeared with an incredible brutality, like a slab of indigo; in comparison the blue of the sky seemed pale, the sand white'.[137] He came to Carthage to absorb the landscape, and he was satisfied with his success, but it required him to abandon everything he had already written.

Flaubert said that he arrived at Carthage on the same boat as a Russian gentleman, the Baron Alexandre de Krafft, who went on from Tunis to Tripoli and the Sudan.[138] Davis also met Baron de Krafft, for on May 15th, 1858, he wrote on his behalf to Dr Norton Shaw, editor of the *Journal of the Royal Geographical Society*, asking for introductions for him to British Consuls and consular agents in Central Africa.[139] Although the dates do not agree perfectly, it is possible that this was the Russian gentleman to whom Davis was to refer as seeking artefacts for Russian museums.[140]

Before his trip Flaubert had acknowledged news from a friend on Davis' discovery of a mosaic at Carthage, but he wrote back that this did not interest him if the mosaic was not Punic.[141] Nevertheless, on May 6th, Flaubert visited Dr Heap at Douar ech-Chott. Flaubert noted, without further comment, that there were mosaics stored in the courtyard.[142] Later on the same day, Flaubert also visited Davis at his house at Gammarth, several miles to the north of the Roman site of Carthage. This house was an old Moorish palace, 'ten miles north of Tunis', where Davis is reported to have lived for many years and offered his hospitality to many guests.[143] From Davis' own account he only acquired the house at Gammarth at the end of 1857, once he had started to concentrate on excavation beyond the Roman city, but the family may have stayed on there in later years.

The house, a luxury summer residence, which was 'partly in ruins, but still exhibited traces of its former splendour', had had a long history. Davis said that it had belonged to Haj Yonas, a minister of Hamoda Basha[144] and had been built by Christian slaves. Lord Exmouth had been entertained there in 1817; in 1816, Exmouth, at the head of the British fleet, had bombarded Algiers to punish the Bey for corsair activity, and to compel him to free European prisoners.[145] The house was at some distance from La Marsa[146] in an oasis near the desert of Gammarth. Davis said of it 'we denominated this residence "Our Desert Home".'[147] Davis clearly felt that this house allowed him to entertain in a fitting way, and Admiral Lord Lyons, whom he was particularly pleased to recall, had been his guest here.[148]

Gammarth was a very small village, and a long way from the markets of Tunis, but the Davises evidently had no worries about provisions for family and guests. In 1819, Mordecai Noah, the former U.S. consul to Tunis, had praised the gardens of nearby La Marsa as producing every vegetable and fruit that could be desired, with game extremely common and easily procured.[149] William Gregory, the Irish MP, and his friend Sir Sandford Graham, who dined with the Davises in November 1857, were astonished by the size of Tunisian prawns and radishes.[150] According to the Anglican Reverend Blakesley, who was Davis' guest in May of 1858, Davis' fluency in Arabic allowed him to mobilize the support of his neighbours, who brought him quail in exchange for small amounts of gunpowder.[151]

Both Flaubert and Sophia Cracroft were favorably struck by the house. Sophia wrote: 'This is indeed a charming house, purely Moorish, and so beautiful, the rooms are entered from a large open quadrangle, in which is a large tank; the effect by moonlight was beyond description charming. From my window at the back I looked down upon the garden of an adjoining Moorish house, with beautiful palm trees, and a well from which a camel drew water by working a wheel; beyond are the sand hills which conceal a part of the ruins of Carthage, and the blue sea beyond that, such blue!'.[152]

Flaubert described the house in very similar terms and also recorded his reactions, not to Davis, but, characteristically for him, to Davis' wife. In the telegraphic style of his travel journal, Flaubert described Mrs Davis' physical endowments – 'thin, graceful, small eyes, bony' – and her manner, '. . . ready, I think, to accept an invitation to the waltz'. A rapturous description of Miss Nelly Rosemberg (Rosenberg), 'a real gypsy type', followed. On Sunday May 16th, Flaubert paid a second visit to the home of Mr Davis at Gammarth. Flaubert took dinner there at 3 pm with an assembled company which included the ship captain who was to accompany Davis to Cap Bon (Lieutenant Porcher, captain of the *Harpy*), as well as Lady Franklin, Miss Cracroft and Miss Rosenberg, whom Flaubert mistook for Lady Franklin's companion.[153] The party also included Dr Heap and his wife Elizabeth.

Flaubert was unflatteringly described by Sophia Cracroft: 'He is not young, very coarse looking, red faced and tall, dressed in huge boots with a large sash around his waist'. In his favour, Flaubert was most deferential to Lady Franklin as an older lady, although he may not have understood who she was.[154] In a letter home, Flaubert complained to his little niece Caroline that conversation with the Davises was entirely in English, since 'neither he nor anyone in his family speaks a word of French';[155] in fact the Davises certainly knew French, as did Lady Franklin and her niece, so the complete dominance of English was a choice, and somewhat rude to their French guest.

On the other hand, choosing to speak French to accommodate Flaubert would have been very artificial. Italian was the *lingua franca* at Tunis, so common that even the French used it, and sometimes even at home.[156] Wherever in his text Davis recounts an exchange with a European verbatim, the language used is Italian. In a sketch of Tunis written by Guy de Maupassant in 1889, nearly a decade after the establishment of the French protectorate, he observed that whereas hardly anyone had spoken French at Tunis ten years earlier, Italian was now disappearing, and the Italians felt they were being pushed out.[157]

Given that Flaubert had recently been in court on charges of writing a scandalous book, it is perhaps just as well that he did not freely join in the conversation.[158] Under these circumstances, Flaubert had eyes only for Nelly, whom he found attractive to a degree that would have shocked his dinner companions. He made exact and detailed notes of her fine features of face and figure, and she was to supply the physical model for his heroine, Salammbô. At 7 pm Flaubert left the party to return to Tunis 'on a terrible horse'.[159]

On the same day several members of the party drove to the house at Douar ech-Chott to see the mosaics. Miss Cracroft wrote:[160]

> The mosaics are lying in a sort of enclosure behind the house, in various stages of renovation. Mr Davis has invented a perfectly successful method of removing the mosaics. Without this, the cement in which they are embedded w[oul]d crumble away and break up the pattern. We saw some most beautiful patterns upon the larger surfaces – some geometrical, some with heads, animals, fish, flowers. In a covered shed were the slabs of inscriptions and other small objects – a collection of earthenware lamps of the Punic, the Roman and the Christian era. Mr Davis has already sent some very fine specimens to the British Museum and is preparing another cargo.

These accounts show that Davis' excavations at Carthage took place in a context that was more intellectually and socially supportive than one might have guessed. He was not forced by his interests in the ancient world to leave home and comforts for any prolonged length of time, but found his field of exploration close by. This was undoubtedly one of the factors that made it possible for him to manage so many different excavations in a relatively brief period of time.

3

Davis becomes an archaeologist

Davis applies to the Foreign Office for funding

In the summer of 1856, Nathan Davis wrote to Lord Clarendon, then the British Foreign Secretary (Fig. 3.1), offering to excavate at Carthage and return the finds to the British Museum at a cost of 1,000 pounds sterling per annum. Although Davis was not the first person to dig at Carthage, Davis' initiative was the first large-scale and long-term official foreign archaeological excavation at Carthage. Davis cited his credentials as his long acquaintance with Tunisia, which he had left only one month previously; his travels through the country a few years earlier with the present Bey Mohammed, from whom he now had permission to carry on archaeological excavation; his active stand against slavery in Tunisia in the years 1841 to 1845, and his friendship with Sidy Mustapha, the Lord Keeper of the Seal.[1] Clearly Davis' only real qualifications as an archaeologist at Carthage were his enterprising personality, his personal standing with the Bey and other members of his family, and the fact that he had the Bey's permission to undertake excavation.

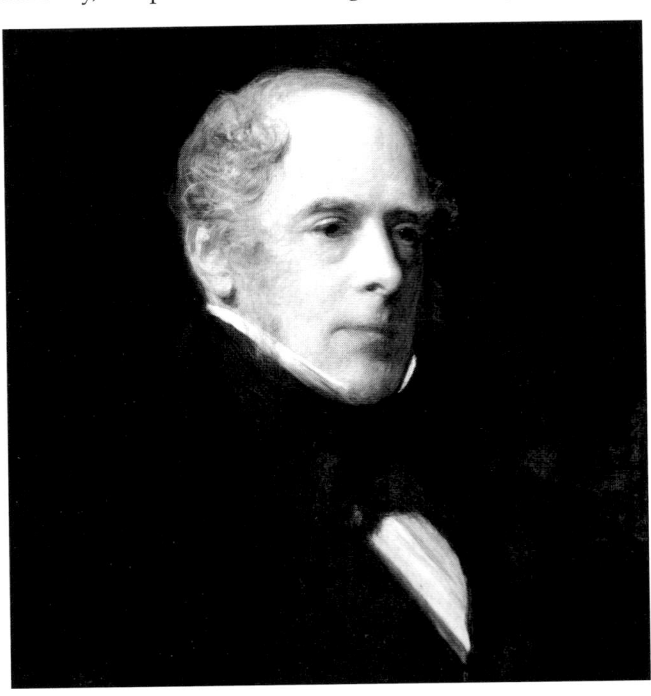

Fig. 3.1 George William Frederick Villiers, 4th Earl of Clarendon (1800–1870), British Foreign Minister from 1853 to 1858 (and twice again later between 1865 and 1870), oil painting by James Sant. It now hangs in the British embassy in Madrid, where Lord Clarendon served as ambassador between 1833 and 1839.

The fourth Earl of Clarendon had been responsible for the management of the Crimean War, which had just ended in the spring of 1856.[2] Clarendon was evidently struck by Davis' proposal. Clarendon, not alone among British parliamentarians and aristocrats at this time, was a patron of the British Museum,[3] and saw Davis' proposal as a chance to benefit the Museum as well as to create closer British ties to Mohammed Bey. Finds for the Museum aggrandized the cultural prestige of the British, especially vis-à-vis the French, and this was certainly another consideration.

As we have seen, Clarendon immediately sent an inquiry to Antonio Panizzi, head of the British Museum,[4] as to Davis' character and abilities. After making enquiries, Panizzi confirmed that Davis had lived several years in Tunis and knew Arabic. In Panizzi's opinion, Davis was 'a man of quick parts, but not a learned man, nor a good antiquarian'. Summing up, Panizzi thought he was nevetheless qualified to undertake the excavations he had proposed, particularly since it was certain that he had the permission of the Bey.[5]

Panizzi himself was an Italian and a man described as having 'the face and something of the manners of a bandit';[6] he was an outsider who had earned his distinguished position by his personal competence. Panizzi may at first have felt some personal sympathy with Davis; this seems to have evaporated later, but Panizzi's judgments, as represented in reports of meetings of the Trustees, were always distinguished by an open-minded fairness.

The fact that Davis was paid directly by the Foreign Office suggests that the Foreign Office wished to proceed with special delicacy in Tunisia. It was irregular for the Foreign Office to support an archaeologist directly; the contemporary excavations of C. T. Newton were supported by the Treasury through a decision of Parliament. Newton, a former assistant at the British Museum, had been appointed British Vice-Consul at Mytilene. While there he carried on excavations at Halicarnassos and Cnidos from 1856 to 1859. Newton kept up an indefatigable correspondence with the Trustees during this time. He was later to become Keeper of Greek and Roman Antiquities at the Museum, a post he held from 1861 to 1886.[7] In a volume of letters written during his excavations, Newton recounted the details of his finds of the Mausoleum of Halicarnassos and the Sanctuary of Demeter at Cnidos. While he included many details of his experiences that are not strictly relevant to the archaeology, his style is straightforward and his content is far more to the point than most of what Davis wrote in *Carthage and Her Remains*.[8]

There are other indications of the sensitivity of Davis' role. On February 6th, 1857, the Foreign Office alerted the Admiralty that transport would be wanted for Davis' mosaic finds; at that time the Admiralty was advised to deal directly with the Consul at Tunis and to keep the matter quiet. In fact, the American Consul Chandler believed that Davis' expedition disguised a British intention to acquire a defensible site at Carthage equivalent to the French Chapel of Saint Louis on the Byrsa Hill.[9] Edmund Hammond, the Under Secretary of State for Foreign Affairs, managed relations between Davis and the Foreign Office, and was liberally thanked by Davis in his preface.[10] A note, probably by Hammond, who was certainly not always Davis' warmest supporter, commenting unofficially in September 1859, when Davis was being pushed to close his excavations, said that the Treasury should also pay for Davis as there was no longer 'any occasion for secrecy'.[11]

Davis' project is approved

After addressing Lord Clarendon, Davis also wrote to the Trustees of the Museum in August 1856, requesting their support for his excavations in North Africa.[12] The question was deferred; at the next meeting, which did not take place until October, Panizzi informed the committee that the government had already taken action.[13] Although I have found no other record of this, Davis himself said that he had appeared before the trustees and received a communication from them approving his plan.[14]

Davis named his backers at the Museum as Mr Vaux, Mr Carpenter,[15] both distinguished Keepers, and Mr Panizzi.[16] William Vaux, who was originally an assistant in the Department of Antiquities and later Keeper of the Department of Coins and Medals, was ranked with Augustus Franks among distinguished scholars on the staff of the Museum at this time; Vaux subsequently produced a catalogue of the Punic inscriptions found by Davis.[17] Of these men only Panizzi sat on the Trustees' Committee. Panizzi was the head of the museum hierarchy and by far the most powerful person among Davis' supporters at the Museum. Although Panizzi's mildly favorable opinion had secured Davis his funding, it was Panizzi's later judgment, that more of Davis' finds were not needed and would not be worth the expense to the Foreign Office, that told most strongly against Davis and eventually brought his excavations to an end.

Meanwhile, however, Clarendon's consultation with the British consular office at Tunis in the person of Lewis Ferriere, the British Vice-Consul, was positive, and on August 4th, 1856, Clarendon approved the expenditure of £1,000 for the venture for one year.[18] Davis did not hear from the Foreign Office immediately, and visited Panizzi on August 18th to find out how matters stood.[19] He received a letter with his instructions in early September, however, only about six weeks after he had first sent his proposal to Clarendon. Davis was asked to proceed with as little publicity as possible to avoid any problems with the French or Tunisians.[20] He was to have a guinea a day personally, a salary which indicates that he was regarded as a gentleman, and would be reimbursed for labourers' wages and tools, but was asked to maintain a reasonable budget. It was agreed that he would report his expenses quarterly, enclosing receipts.[21] The funding was generous, as Davis appreciated.[22] Reports from Wood to the Foreign Office for 1857 show that the money was regularly paid out, with Davis receiving an annual total of £600 for expenses beyond his quarterly salary.[23]

As soon as he received permission and funding from the Foreign Office, Davis, who was then in England, arranged to buy the needed excavation tools and have them sent to Tunis.[24] He then set out for Carthage, stopping in Paris where he bought plans of Carthage, including the plan of Falbe.[25] He continued from Paris overland to Genoa and then travelled by boat, first to Sardinia and then to La Goulette.[26] Having arrived at the port of La Goulette on October 14th, 1856, Davis proceeded with dispatch; he renewed his acquaintances at Tunis, including all the necessary political ones. Davis visited Consul Richard Wood on the day after his arrival, and Wood accompanied him on a visit to the Bey on October 18th. Davis reported that the Bey was delighted at the opportunity to gratify the British government by supporting the excavations.[27]

Davis was well aware of the long-established rivalry between the French and British consuls for influence at the court of the Bey.[28] Both Wood and Roches were highly accomplished if somewhat unscrupulous; of the two, Wood was the more politically competent. Davis relied heavily on his somewhat problematic friendship with Wood, and would not be successful in his request to Roches for permission to dig on the Hill of Saint Louis.[29] Nevertheless, he got along well with some French individuals, including Charles Cubisol, the Tunisian-born French vice-consul at the port of La Goulette, who often also served in this position for the other European powers.

Having dealt with his crucial political contacts, Davis next turned to the practical side, assembling a corps of Arab workmen eventually numbering between twenty-five and fifty men, and acquiring beasts of burden. Actual work began on November 11th, 1856.[30] The lively interest of the Bey in Davis' work can be judged from the fact that he and his entourage visited the excavation site on November 19th; this visit gave Davis the recognition he needed to get cooperation from the villagers.[31]

The railway had not yet come to Carthage in the 1850s; Davis travelled back and forth to Tunis when necessary either on horseback or by carriage. In early December Davis rented a little house in the village of Douar ech-Chott from a Maltese family, as noted above (p. 31), so that he was able to live directly on the site of the ancient city while he excavated (Fig. 2.3).[32] Douar ech-Chott was one of the two tiny Arab villages directly on the site of the Roman city of Carthage; it was located on the low-lying ground in the southern half of the Roman site, at the eastern end of the Roman circus. The other village was La Malga, built into the cisterns near the amphitheatre.[33] Davis lived on site partly to save travel time, but also to spare himself his friends' comments when the excavations were unproductive.[34]

Excavation began in mid-November, plowing and seeding time; Davis said that this necessitated choosing ruins for excavation, as they could not be sown. Davis' first few months of excavation were frustrating; as Davis said, 'I toiled most assiduously, with from forty to fifty men, for nearly three months, without realizing any thing worth the labour of a single day'.[35] This was one of the few times when Davis exaggerated; he had worked for somewhat less than two months with a corps of about twenty-five workmen before he came upon the Mosaic of the Months and Seasons, his first major find. His first report noted finds only of fragmentary statues and reliefs, with 'domestic implements', probably of pottery, and mostly of late date.

During the first year, Davis wrote regular reports of his excavations and his most important finds to Lord Clarendon. By contrast, Davis did not write directly to Panizzi. After his find of the Mosaic of the Months and Seasons in January 1857, Davis sent his wife to visit Panizzi and read him Davis' account of the find. Evidently Mrs Davis had remained in England up to this point, and Davis must have counted on her to make a good impression. Panizzi subsequently wrote to Lord Clarendon to ask for a copy of Davis' letter, which was duly sent.[36] Edmund Hammond then wrote to Davis encouraging him to communicate freely with Panizzi.[37] This Davis completely failed to do; the fact that he did not send detailed reports of his excavations and finds to Panizzi was a mistake that would later cost him a continued diplomatic and archaeological career.

Those of Davis' letters that were copied at the British Museum are concentrated in the first year of his project, and this incorrectly suggests that the letters and the work fell off sharply in the subsequent two years. In fact, Davis worked consistently until the summer of 1858; as excavation was impossible in July, August and even September, he put in two years' work before falling victim to personal problems and illness, and returned to excavation briefly after his recovery in December 1858. Davis later complained to Panizzi in a letter of January 15th, 1859 that his letters to the Earl of Malmesbury, Clarendon's successor, had been ignored,[38] and they were not passed on to the museum. Only one letter to Malmesbury survives at the museum in this series, also dated January 15th, 1859, in which Davis reported having been unwell.[39]

The length of Davis' illness indicates that it was serious. The control of contagious diseases and the availability of European-trained doctors were important concerns to Europeans visiting or living in Tunisia in the nineteenth century. For example, a relatively minor epidemic of cholera had killed 200 people among the Christian community of Tunis in August and September 1856, just before Davis' return from London to start his excavation project. Henry Dunant was therefore particularly interested in assuring his readers of the level of medical care available at Tunis; this led him to list twenty doctors of medicine by name, including the young Dr Heap.[40] In September 1858, Sophia Cracroft wrote to her family that she and Lady Franklin would return from Trebizond on the Black Sea via the Danube because an outbreak of something very like plague at Tripoli was imposing quarantine at Constantinople and other Mediterranean ports.[41] Nevertheless, the autumn of 1858 was not a year of epidemic at Tunis.[42] While cholera, typhoid, typhus and smallpox were all endemic there in the nineteenth century, it seems most likely that Davis had contracted malaria during his excavations at Utica in the spring of 1858.

From April 1858, Davis had a paid assistant in Dr Heap,[43] who took over the excavations in Carthage proper while Davis worked at Gammarth.[44] While Dr Heap was both well-educated and personally involved in Davis' project, there is no evidence that he made any archaeological discoveries while employed by Davis. Davis also noted Heap's services during his illness;[45] given Dunant's praise of Heap's medical competence, it is likely that these services were not strictly archaeological, but also included medical attention.

The significance of the plan of Falbe

Many earlier explorers and academics had written about the site of Carthage, although some, even such an important commentator as Dureau de la Malle, had never visited it. Davis was aware of and used some of the most important books and maps that had appeared previously. While working at Carthage, Davis was armed with several manuals:[46] among other aids, he mentioned Falbe's topographic map of the peninsula, a map by a man named Dedreux;[47] Dureau de la Malle's treatise of 1835, which associated the sites on Falbe's plan with sites which were attested in the ancient sources;[48] a map by a man named Dusegate (Davis' spelling for Dusgate);[49] and Sir Grenville Temple's account of his earlier travels in the regency.[50] Although some of the works he mentioned might not have been with him at Carthage, Dureau de la Malle, Falbe, Dusgate and Temple certainly were.

Davis was the most influenced by Falbe and Dureau de la Malle. They would be the most important scholars in the eyes of Evariste Pricot de Sainte-Marie, an aristocrat attached to the French consulate at Tunis as a translator in the early 1870s. Trained as a scholar, Sainte-Marie would use his leisure to excavate Punic *stelae* at Carthage. At the same time, he wrote a bibliography of previous research on Carthage, which he published in 1875.[51] When Sainte-Marie's bibliography received a scathing review in a German academic journal,[52] he revised it, producing a second version that was more accurate and twice as long.[53] In Sainte-Marie's opinon, Falbe, Dureau de la Malle and Beulé were the three great forerunners in terms of an understanding of the topography of Carthage.[54] Davis' dependence on the first two of these suggests that Davis had sought and taken advice on the sources considered most reliable by the academic community in his day. Beulé's work at Carthage was contemporary with Davis' own, although Davis read and acerbically criticized Beulé's *Fouilles* before finishing *Carthage and Her Remains*.

It is extremely important that Davis was armed with a copy of the plan of Falbe (Fig. 3.2), which had been published with a brief companion volume in 1833. During Falbe's service as Danish consul at Tunis, he had spent two years making the first scientifically surveyed and topographically accurate map of the whole peninsula.[55] Davis worked directly from the plan of Falbe, and eventually had the person who drafted his own published map follow it more or less exactly. Davis' work at Carthage was based not only on the best available topographic map, but also on one that still meets our standards today. Since Davis' own published map directly copied the plan of Falbe, Falbe's cartographic achievements are preserved in relation to Davis' own finds. Although Davis' plan is not as scrupulously accurate as Falbe's, it can be used to locate the sites of his excavations with an accuracy to within thirty to fifty meters.

Many subsequent archaeologists would pay lip service to the accuracy of Falbe's plan, but few have either seen or used the 1833 original of this crucial map, of which I personally have seen only two copies. In 1881, Count d'Hérisson, then owner of the site of Utica and a man with pretensions as an archaeologist, described Falbe's map as 'very rare and hard to find today'.[56] Comments from as early as the 1870s explicitly reveal that Falbe's original plan was not in general circulation.

Because the original was difficult to acquire, later scholars made versions of Falbe's plan which they had a tendency to think were as good as the original, ignoring the fact that the strength of the original was its topographical accuracy. For example, Sainte-Marie was to include a map of Carthage with his article on the ancient structures under the house of Mustafa Ben Ismaïl at Falbe no. 68. Sainte-Marie's map was inspired by the plan of Falbe and the observations of Dureau de la Malle, but it did not reproduce Falbe's numbers.[57] A somewhat more faithful reproduction of the plan of Falbe, drawn by the French engineer Philippe Caillat, and including Falbe's site numbers, appeared in Sainte-Marie's *Mission à Carthage* in 1884.[58] Charles Tissot also used Falbe's numbers on a plan of Carthage, which appeared with his discussion of Carthage in 1884,[59] but Tissot combined the impeccable work of Falbe with his friend Auguste Daux's detailed but fantasist reconstruction of the triple outer fortifications of the Punic city.[60] Daux was an engineer who had been employed by the emperor Napoleon III to provide topographical maps of North Africa to illustrate the emperor's life of Julius Caesar.[61]

In a paper given at the Sorbonne on January 30th, 1886, Salomon Reinach was to note the difficulty of consulting an original copy of the plan of Falbe. He was reporting on the excavations he and Ernest Babelon had carried out at Carthage in 1884. Reinach referred his audience to Sainte-Marie's map in *Mission à Carthage*, because it reproduced Falbe's site numbers.[62] Despite Reinach's recommendation, Sainte-Marie's map is a far cry from the intentions and accuracy of Falbe's original, which outlined the ruins themselves.

Falbe marked all ancient structures visible on the ground, accurately outlining those of any significant size. Falbe's plan, with its delineation of all the significant visible ruins of the ancient city, including the harbors, circus, amphitheatre and the great cisterns of La Malga and Bordj-Djedid, served as an implicit proof of

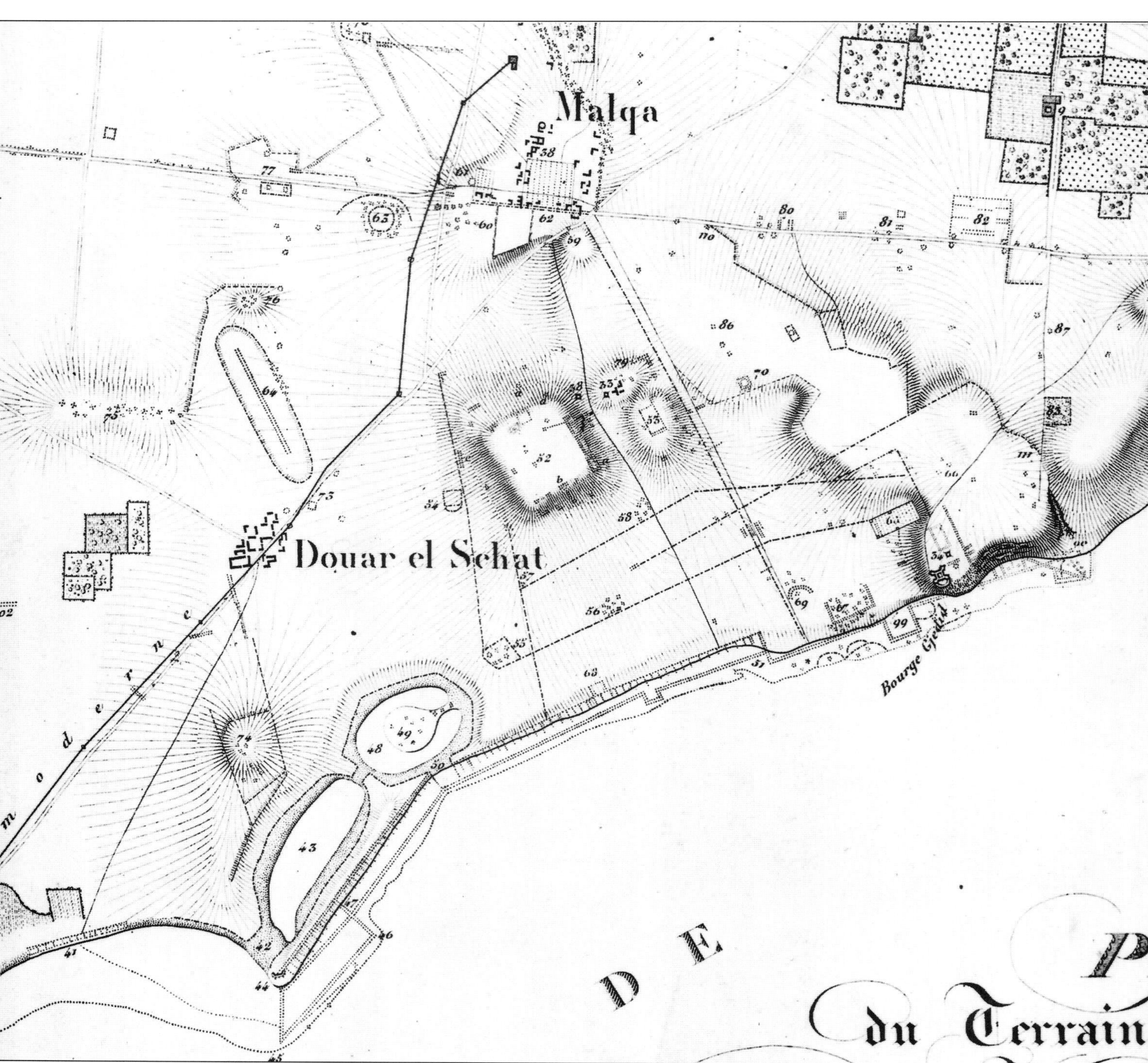

Fig. 3.2 The urban area of Carthage, a detail from the map drawn by Captain C. T. Falbe in 1831 and 1832, and published in 1833. North lies in the direction towards the top right-hand corner of this map. Prominent landmarks indicated here include the Byrsa hill (no. 52), the Punic circular harbour and its central island (nos 48–9), the rectangular harbour (no. 43), the Roman amphitheatre (no. 63), the Roman circus (no. 64), the La Malga cisterns (north of no. 62), and what were later to be recognized as the Antonine Baths (no. 67). The following site numbers marked on this part of Falbe's map are also referred to in this book: nos 34 (structure on the summit of Bordj Djedid), 53 ('temples and large buildings' on the summit of the 'hill of Juno'), 54 (where the 'carpet mosaic' was to be found in 1844), 55, 56, 58, 65 (the Bordj-Djedid cisterns), 66 (small building with vaulted roofs), 68, 69 ('temple', what is now known to be the south-west latrine of the Antonine baths), 70 (now known as the 'Circular Monument'), 72, 73, 74, 79, 80–83 ('Vandal defences'), 86 and 87. The number 90 (an extramural seaside villa, where the mosaics shown in Fig. 6.1–6.2 and Figs 8.3–8.6 were found) is not clearly legible: it is the number on the coastline nearest to the right-hand edge of this illustration. Nos 92 and 93 lie off this portion of Falbe's map: both refer to suburban sites at Gammarth, north of Carthage itself.

the location of the Roman city of Carthage. Falbe's plan had an immediate and tremendous impact on the aristocratic French academic Dureau de la Malle, who used it to identify various sites mentioned in the ancient sources with the ruins marked on Falbe's map. After studying Falbe's map, Dureau de la Malle regarded the position of the ports as established, saying 'Falbe's plan leaves no doubt'.

The position of the ports had not been obvious earlier, and the persons who took an interest in the question had no adequate support for their theories. There were numerous options, but the possibilities had to be reconciled with the dangers of the prevailing northwest winds. Furthermore, the ancient historian Appian had described an artificially excavated double harbour in some detail.[63] In 1807, Jean Emile Humbert, a Dutch engineer in the service of the Bey, had shown Chateaubriand the site of Carthage. The aristocratic author of the subsequently famous *Itinéraire de Paris à Jérusalem* published Humbert's theory about the location of the ports on the site of the two 'lagoons' as his own. Within a few years, Humbert was considering a very different theory. Mordecai Noah, American consul at Tunis from about 1813 to 1815, also visited 'Carthage' with Humbert. They actually toured Sidi bou-Said, a village a few kilometers north of the site of Carthage. This village is located on a very steep hill that descends precipitously to the sea. If Humbert suggested the location of the harbour, or *cothon*, at this time, Noah was not convinced.[64]

According to Debergh, Humbert vacillated in his identification of the site of the ports over the thirty years that he lived in La Goulette. He first placed them on the sea-front before what we now recognize as the site of the ancient city, then on the site of the two lagoons, which is the accepted site today. Humbert was later convinced by Count Camillo Borgia, who was in Tunis after being exiled from Naples, that the ports lay to the north near the village of La Marsa; Borgia was influenced by Thomas Shaw, an English traveller in the eighteenth century. By 1818 Humbert had returned to the theory that the two lagoons marked the site.[65] This now proven location was to be accepted by Falbe, Dureau de la Malle and Beulé. Davis, who accepted Falbe's placement of the harbours without giving him credit for it, argued vigorously against the alternative theories proposed by Estrup and Mannert, but their cases were already definitively lost.[66]

Once the location of the ports was established, the Punic forum and the Punic Temple of Apollo could also be located, as ancient sources put them between the ports and the Byrsa. The Byrsa was certainly the highest point in the centre of the city, which was easy to ascertain from Falbe's map and text, and the location of the Byrsa determined the general location of the Punic temple of Aesculapius, which according to reliable ancient sources was on that summit, as well as the approximate location of the sixty-step stairway which led up to the temple.[67] These basic certainties that Dureau de la Malle reached about the topography of Punic Carthage from his study of Falbe's map have remained fundamental; even Davis, who equated the Byrsa with the hill of Bordj-Djedid, did not question the placement of the ports. The influence of Dureau de la Malle on Davis, on the other hand, was largely negative. Although Davis accepted few of the identifications suggested by Dureau de la Malle, he implicitly adopted the same model, as for example when Davis defined his own 'Temple of Astarte' and 'Temple of Apollo.' As Audollent complained, 'This is Dureau de la Malle's system, aggravated by all the ignorance of an amateur'.[68]

Humbert's excavations in the early 1820s

Davis was not the first archaeologist to excavate at Carthage. Indeed, there was a long history of antiquarian research at Carthage through the eighteenth century and even earlier.[69] In the seventeenth, eighteenth and much of the nineteenth century, antiquarians were particularly interested in inscriptions, and this usually involved surface collecting and copying, rather than excavation. Most of these men were not archaeologists in the modern sense, and they often spent very little time on the site of Carthage.[70] The Dutch engineer Jean Emile Humbert, who first came to Carthage in 1796, was an exception.

Humbert spent many years in the service of the Bey of Tunis and, although he was not classically educated, he collected antiquities from Carthage. According to the American consul Mordecai Noah, Humbert was a sociable man with a weakness for presents, who had lived for twenty years in a house at La Goulette, the port of Tunis. Humbert was married to the sister of the Dutch consul, Mr Nyssen, and had a fine coin collection.[71] Humbert's portrait reveals a mild-looking man with dark hair, blue eyes and extravagant sideburns.[72] Humbert's archaeological achievements, which were significant, were later completely eclipsed by his very brief association with the famous traveler Chateaubriand.[73] Davis knew of Humbert only in that context, noting that 'Humberg' had shown Chateaubriand the site of Carthage in little more than half an hour.[74]

From 1817, the Bey permitted Humbert to excavate at Carthage. In his first excavation Humbert discovered four inscribed Punic *stelae* between the amphitheatre and the village of La Malga.[75] Humbert undertook a total of six campaigns over a period of thirty-seven days, returning to excavate in 1822 and 1824 on a mission sponsored by the Museum of Leiden, which now holds both his finds and his papers.[76] These were the first deliberate archaeological excavations at Carthage; like Davis' excavations, they were carried on for the sake of potential finds, particularly inscriptions, but they were relatively well-documented by Humbert's notes.

Humbert's most sustained effort by far, over two seasons and for a total of twenty-eight days, with a crew of thirty workmen, was on the same site that produced the Punic *stelae* which he published in 1821.[77] He also worked for four days with sixteen men at a site 475 meters from the village of La Malga, in the direction of Sidi bou-Said.[78] Although his description does not locate this excavation exactly, the approximate site (within a twenty-five meter radius) is along the easternmost line of the rural grid, just outside the street-grid of the north-western quarter of Roman Carthage. The site was very close to Davis' Site 26, where Davis was to excavate Roman tombs.[79] The evidence suggests that Humbert dug mainly within an extent of about three-quarters of a mile (1.2 km) along the north-west limit of the street-grid of Roman Carthage. His sites follow the last line of the rural grid, which is indicated both on the plan of Falbe and on Davis' published map (see below, pp. 62–3). It may be that Humbert was deliberately following the line of this ancient road, which was flanked by the amphitheatre, the La Malga cisterns and a long succession of tombs.

A century after Humbert and his work sank into obscurity, his pottery finds were published by Holwerda with the Roman Mediterranean pottery from the Rijksmuseum. Although Holwerda did not ascribe the vessels to individual excavations, making it impossible to ascribe specific pieces to Humbert, at least fifteen pieces of Italian *terra sigillata*, most with potter's stamps, dating from the late first century BC to the first half of the first century AD, are described as coming from Tunis, Carthage or La Malga. At least fifty pieces of fine and coarse pottery produced in North Africa came from Carthage or Tunis; the relevant forms belong to between the second and the fourth centuries AD.[80] The fact that these pieces were complete or could be completely restored suggests that they came from tombs; in this period Roman graves at Carthage would have included pottery as grave gifts. Hayes subsequently drew a number of Humbert's complete vessels to illustrate a typology of Roman pottery manufactured in Tunisia.[81]

Humbert mentioned two Christian epitaphs and two other inscriptions in his notes on these excavations.[82] Wilmanns documented eighteen other Latin inscriptions from Carthage, mostly pagan epitaphs, as 'Humbertiana'. A museum inventory of Humbert's finds exists at Leiden[83] as well as a catalogue of the antiquities he contributed to the museum.[84] His papers have formed the basis for a modern account of this early archaeologist,[85] who, like Davis, may better be described as a 'dirt antiquarian.'

Humbert had a maximum of thirty men working over a period of thirty-seven days for just under 1000 working man-days, and Humbert's excavations were therefore no small undertaking. As we shall see below, this investment of man-hours was roughly comparable to the excavations of Falbe and Grenville Temple at Carthage in 1838. Davis dug far more; Davis had an average of twenty-five men working eight months of the year for two and a half years (with the exception of the period of his illness in the autumn of 1858), probably six days a week, for an estimated total of 12,000 working days. It seems that, relatively speaking, Davis also recorded far less; at least he did not take care to archive his drawings and notes as Humbert did. On the other hand, Davis wrote and published an account of his excavations, a valuable exercise in that it forced Davis to express and defend his opinions and actions in a summary overview. A complete re-evaluation of Humbert's excavations and finds would be necessary in order to judge Humbert's work fairly, but he seems to have been well ahead of his times in the conscientiousness of his documentation. His accomplishments compare favorably with those of Davis, particularly since Humbert worked thirty-five years earlier.

The excavations of Falbe and Temple in 1838

The most important of Davis' archaeological predecessors at Carthage were the Danish consul, Captain Falbe, and the long-serving and strong-minded British consul, Sir Thomas Reade. Although I believe it is not unjust to call these men archaeologists, because they used excavation to explore ancient sites, there is almost no discernible line between their archaeological activities and licensed plunder. They did not record their excavations properly, they did not publish their results, and it is largely by chance that some of their finds eventually were acquired by museums.

Christian Tuxen Falbe was trained in the Danish navy and reached the rank of captain, but accepted the post of Danish consul general in Tunis in 1820, and served there until 1833. While he was consul, antiquarian and topographical studies occupied much of his time. In addition to creating the first accurate topographical map of Carthage, he was also a serious numismatist[86] and was to become curator of the royal collection in the National Museum of Denmark in Copenhagen from 1840.[87] A portrait reveals a clean-shaven, intelligent-looking gentleman with an expression both humorous and austere (Fig. 3.3). Captain Falbe had unearthed a mosaic in Carthage at a seaside villa in 1824, but Humbert immediately and wilfully had this destroyed. Falbe created his map of Carthage in 1831 and 1832 (on which the site of the mosaic was designated as site no. 90), and he returned in 1838 with a British gentleman, Sir Grenville Temple, as his colleague to excavate for the Parisian Society for the Excavation of Carthage.[88] Grenville Temple was a former Lieutenant-Colonel of the 15th Hussars, who in 1835 had published an account of his travels in the Mediterranean, particularly in Algeria and Tunisia, which Guérin later described as knowledgeable and accurate.[89]

Thomas Reade, the English consul, regarded the archaeological sites of Carthage as his personal domain. Reade was not just possessive of Tunisian archaeological remains; during the reign of Ahmed Bey, Reade was the dominant force among the foreign consuls who were vying for political influence with the Bey. A German traveller later recounted that in the days of Ahmed Bey nothing happened without the consent of Sir Thomas Reade.[90] As we have seen, Reade had a warm working relationship with Dr Heap, the American consul. In 1827, when Reade was newly appointed at Tunis, Heap wrote that Reade had distinguished himself in his previous post as Lieutenant Governor of Saint Helena during Napoleon's imprisonment 'by the suavity of his manners, and the delicacy with which he performed the painful duty assigned him', so that 'he was much less obnoxious than his superior'.[91] This is faint praise, but clearly an indication that Reade was a conscious gentleman. Reade was nevertheless seen as unlikeable by the French, as well as militantly English. Alexandre Dumas, the author of the *Three Musketeers*, who attended a ball at Tunis in 1846, noted that 'Sir Thomas Ride' was known as a cold man who held himself aloof from the other diplomatic personnel.[92]

Reade had a hospitable side, however; he was more than friendly to Sir Grenville Temple and Temple's entourage of family and friends, who made a Mediterranean tour in a chartered brig in the early 1830s. Reade hosted them all in his pretty villa, a 'spacious summer palace' called Abdeallah, at La Marsa, a few miles north of Carthage, where Sir Grenville Temple said the first families of Tunisia as well as the foreign consuls had their homes.[93] Temple spent a good deal of time with Reade during this visit, and there is no sign that he found him difficult; in this case perhaps shared social status and archaeological interests drew them together. Reade was the probable source of Temple's story, no doubt true, that Ali Bey

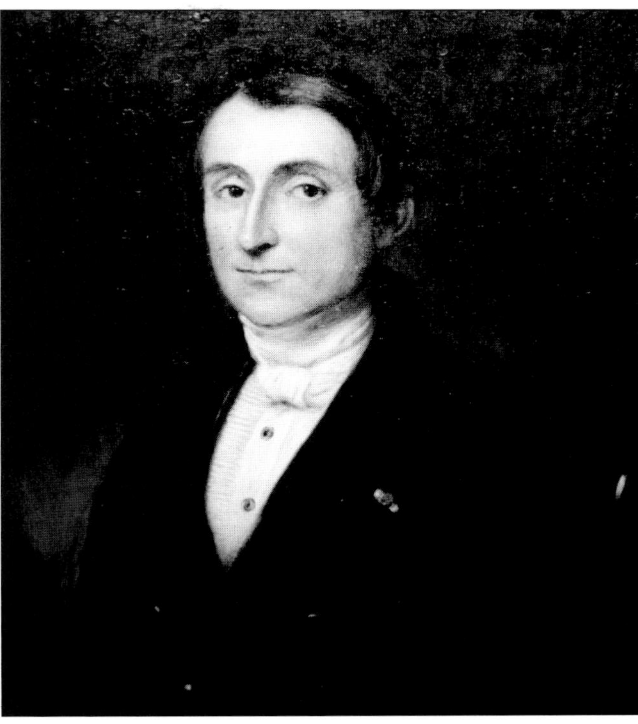

Fig. 3.3 Portrait of Christian Tuxen Falbe (1791–1849), Danish Consul-General in Tunis between 1820 and 1831, private collection

had resided in this house, and smoked his pipe while he watched decapitations there.[94]

Grenville Temple, who was well-educated as well as being personable and unaffected, wrote a voluminous description of his Mediterranean travels. He gives pause when he described the sudden illness and death of one of his two little boys, an event which he did not allow to darken his delight in the voyage.[95] This death in the family, a dramatic encounter with pirates between Tabarka and Bizerte,[96] and his casual purchase of a slave, 'an ugly boy',[97] are reminders that the Mediterranean in the early nineteenth century was a different world. Grenville Temple's description of Carthage emphasized accurate measurements of the cisterns and the aqueduct; he also briefly noted the very extensive ruins on the summit of Bordj-Djedid, which he interpreted as the remains of the 'Temple of Ceres,' and the substructures of a monumental stairway that had once climbed the face of the cliff.[98]

In 1837 Falbe and Dureau de la Malle united to create a private consortium, the 'Society for the Exploration of Carthage,' since both men agreed that only archaeological excavation could provide a definitive answer to topographical questions at Carthage. The Society was made up of eighteen learned and wealthy men, who raised 23,600 francs for the project, with the understanding that they would share the finds.[99] The plan of the Society was to fund long-term archaeological excavation by selling finds to museums and collectors, although the original plan for raising new funding was subsequently given up.[100] The articles of the Society were set out in a legal document notarized at Paris on August 21st, 1837, which promised potential subscribers that the still-virgin soil of Carthage would furnish a great number of objects of Punic and Roman art.[101] Sir Grenville Temple was one of the subscribers of this Society.

The excavations of Falbe and Temple for the Society took place between January and June of 1838. The sites of their five excavations have been described in some detail by Lund, using letters and papers of Falbe in collections in Denmark.[102] Although Falbe and Temple had permission to excavate, granted by the Bey, they were to respect the claims to precedence of the English consul, Thomas Reade.[103] Falbe made no secret of his dislike for Reade, but this did not prevent Falbe and Sir Grenville Temple from working together in 1838 on an archaeological project that Reade characteristically tried to disrupt.[104]

Falbe noted that Reade had begun excavations at the Antonine Baths, then described as the 'Basilica of Thrasamund' (Falbe no. 67), in March 1838,[105] at exactly the same moment as Falbe and Grenville Temple went to work (Fig. 3.4). According to Davis, while the expenses of excavation at the Antonine Baths were assumed by Reade, the actual work was supervised by a Mr Honegger, 'a clever German architect'. Reade's excavations exposed the ruins of an extensive building, as well as of a 'small theatre facing the sea':[106] the latter was actually the south-western latrine of the Antonine Baths, which was later excavated, equally blindly, by Davis (Fig. 5.6).

According to the French archaeologist Charles Beulé, the Antonine Baths was the only site at Carthage that Reade excavated (Fig. 3.5). Beulé referred to the Antonine Baths, not then yet identified by inscriptional evidence, as the 'basilica of

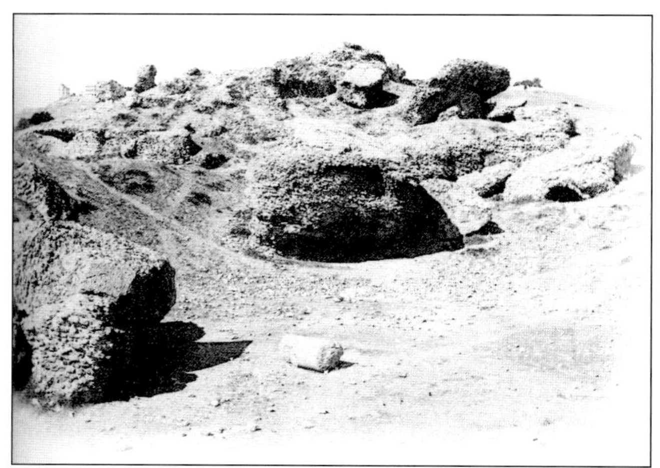

Fig. 3.4 (right) *The ruins of the Antonine Baths as they appeared in 1898, not very different from how they were in Davis' day (compare Fig. 5.5)*

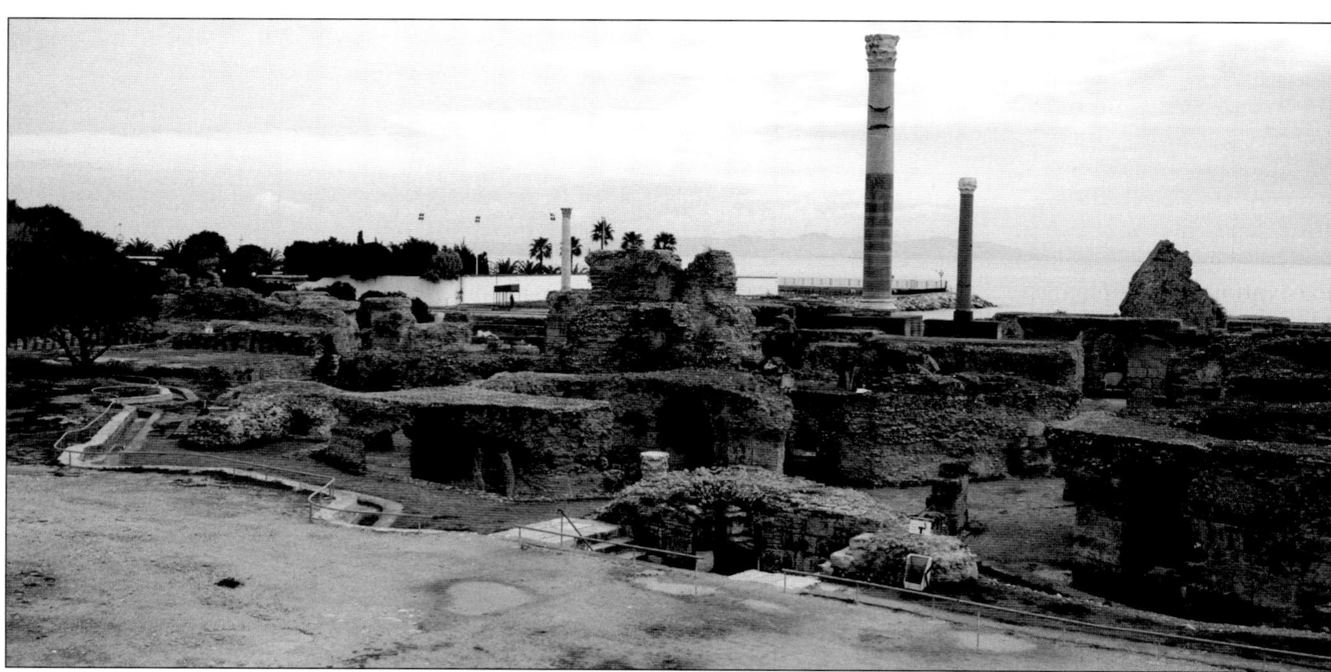

Fig. 3.5 (below) *The Antonine Baths as they appear today, looking east towards the sea*

Thrasamund'.[107] Reade was notorious among both the French and native Tunisians for having removed fifty columns of the Antonine Baths and sending them to England on ships of the British navy. In October of 1848, Monsignor Pavie, bishop of Algiers, visited Carthage with Abbé Bourgade and Count Raffo, and observed the columns lined up on the beach waiting for the English ships that were to take them away.[108] Delattre said that in the early 1880s there were still Arabs who remembered seeing the columns embarked on British warships.[109] What was the ultimate fate of these columns? It is possible that six of them may now adorn 'Eagle's Nest,' once the estate of William K. Vanderbilt, in Centerport, New York. The columns of *cipollino* there ('Carystian marble' from the Greek island of Euboea, characterized by green and white streaks) are said to be from Carthage. They are fourteen feet (6.6 m) high and fifty-nine inches (1.5 m) in circumference and they are now topped by a variety of capitals.[110]

Clark Kennedy, a visiting British traveller, reported that Reade found a mutilated statue of Jupiter in the Antonine Baths[111] and also chanced upon mosaics there, which, according to Gauckler, were not lifted.[112] Reade never published any account of his excavations, although according to Sainte-Marie he sent finds to the British Museum between 1830 and 1849.[113] A pagan Roman funerary epitaph which was retrieved, but perhaps not excavated, by Reade was recorded in the corpus of Latin inscriptions.[114]

As mentioned above (p. 44), Grenville Temple undertook actual excavation at Carthage in 1838, together with Falbe, in the Society's first and only season of work.[115] Temple had earlier tried archaeology elsewhere on the model of purely private enterprise; he dug at Nisoua on the north-western tip of Cap Bon in 1831 or 1832, finding many small artefacts, following the model of Consul Reade who had dug there the previous year.[116] The excavations at Carthage, by contrast, involved a much greater commitment of time and energy. It is unlikely, however, that the actual excavation techniques were scientific in any sense; Davis referred scathingly to the fact that Temple did not dig trenches, but irregular pits.[117] Thirty-one crates of finds from four months of excavation as well as a number of maps and plans were subsequently sent off to France.[118] The Society's report included colour illustrations of a mosaic and a fresco. The mosaic, from the seaside villa at no. 90 on the plan of Falbe, was of a Nereid on a hippocamp (Fig. 6.2); the fresco, from a building at no. 87 on the plan of Falbe ('the house of the daughters of the sultan') was of limited aesthetic interest.[119] The book is a hodge-podge of documents: it includes the articles of incorporation of the Society, a report by Temple and Falbe on their travels with the French army at the capture of Constantine in Algeria, and notes on their archaeological finds there and on two desultory excavations at Carthage.

Excerpts from Falbe's letters to the Danish Crown Prince add more information. Between January and July 1838, Grenville Temple excavated at four sites identified by Falbe. Falbe did not actively excavate, but was responsible for a number of ground-plans of sites explored during the project. Five places were explored: the eastern cisterns (Falbe no. 65), which were not excavated; then, a small building, fifteen meters square with vaulted rooms (Falbe no. 66: Fig. 3.6); third, the Circular Monument (Falbe no. 70); then walls at Falbe no. 79, on the west side of the Hill of Juno; and, finally, a seaside villa at the foot of a ravine just beyond the northern extent of the Roman city street-grid (Falbe no. 90: Fig. 3.7).

The eastern (Bordj-Djedid) cisterns at Falbe no. 65 are inaccessible today within the grounds of the Presidential Palace, but they attracted a great deal of interest in the nineteenth century because of their admirable state of preservation (Fig. 5.4). It would eventually become clear that these cisterns occupied exactly one whole city-block of the street-grid of the Roman city. Grenville Temple described them as made of concrete and measuring 449 feet by 116 feet (35 m by 138 m, very close to the dimensions of one Roman city-block at Carthage, 35 m by 140 m). He counted eighteen compartments, each able to hold seventeen feet (5.2 m) of water. Temple asserted that the cisterns were supplied only by rainwater, which was conducted from the roof by terracotta pipes that could still be seen,[120] and many scholars, including Falbe and Davis, repeated this idea.

Grenville Temple's accurate description is generally in good agreement with a plan drawn by Falbe in 1838, although Falbe only drew seventeen compartments.[121] Falbe drew the ground-plan of the eastern cisterns with just as extensive detail at the north end as at the south (Falbe had also published a plan of the cisterns in 1833 with his plan of Carthage).[122] On Falbe's plan, the outer dimensions of the cistern are approximately 36 m by 132.6 m, correct for the width, but about eight meters short of the length of one Roman city-block at Carthage; the missing compartment would have made up the required length.

Falbe said the cisterns at no. 65 were thirty-six feet (11 m) below the surface. The top of the cistern at its north end is at most ten meters underground, as can be seen from a drawing of a lengthwise section of the cisterns later published by Babelon and Cagnat.[123] Recent maps of Carthage with elevations show that the top of the south-eastern corner of the cisterns lies at 25

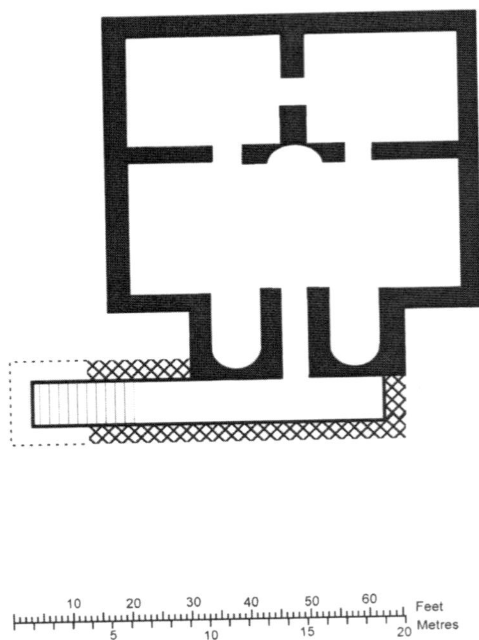

Fig. 3.6 Plan by C. T. Falbe of a small underground 'baths', at his point no. 66

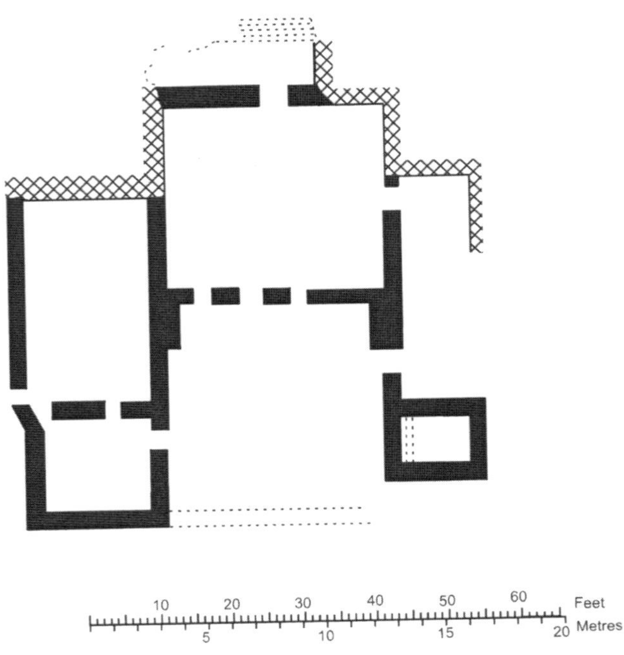

Fig. 3.7 Plan by C. T. Falbe of the building at his point no. 90

meters above sea-level, modern ground-level, and the ground rises over the cisterns to 35 meters above sea-level on the north side. Even in Roman times, the cistern complex was partly built into and supported by the hill.

At least four of the curved vaults and one of the cupolas covering the cistern were visible above ground in Davis' day.[124] Davis published an almost unintelligible drawing of the impression given by 'The Rain-water Cisterns,' evidently while looking across them to the southwest (Fig. 5.3).[125] A somewhat clearer drawing looking along the underside of a line of curved vaulting was published in the *Illustrated London News* in 1857; the drawing was from the sketchbook of a tourist who had visited Douar ech-Chott and was aware of Davis' excavations.[126] Falbe and Temple did not excavate the cisterns. Falbe simply entered them at the south end, where the upper part of the wall as well as the top of the vaults and cupolas were exposed, and drew his plan from an exploration of the interior. Falbe wrote, 'I had to repeat the boarding exercise from my naval cadet days in order to enter the well, A, and the cistern, B, . . .'. Unfortunately, these points were not marked on his plan.[127]

Meanwhile Grenville Temple excavated a building he reported as fifteen meters square at no. 66 on the plan of Falbe, which Falbe had identified as the 'ruins of a bath';[128] Falbe drew a simple plan of this fairly small symmetrical building showing two projections with apsed ends and a shallow semicircular fountain basin opposite the entrance in July 1838 (Fig. 3.6).[129] Falbe had described it as '. . . a subterranean building divided into several small vaulted rooms, which can have functioned as baths. The walls of one room still preserve feeble remains of a fresco painting similar to those, which adorn the Baths of Titus at Rome'.[130] This same building was completely excavated by Storz during the UNESCO 'Save Carthage' campaign.[131] According to him it was 17.03 m wide, and occupied half the width of the short side of a Roman city-block at Carthage.[132] Storz was drawn to study this building because of the construction method of the roof over its central space, which used vaulting tubes (hollow ceramic tubes which can be joined to form a light-weight vault or dome). The building, which was intended as an underground complex from the beginning, has a large central room which was added to a pre-existing long double cistern; the cistern spaces were renovated as two small rooms on the west side of the complex. Traces of painted decoration were found as well as a well-preserved geometric mosaic floor in the northern half of the former cistern. An irregular fragment of mosaic had been taken up from the middle of this floor, certainly by Falbe and Temple, as I will show. The first phase of this building dates to *c.* AD 320 to 340, while the mosaic floor belongs to a second phase, from the end of the fourth or the early fifth century. This underground complex does not fit the common architectural profile of a Roman house, and Storz suggested that it might have been the meeting place of an intellectual sodality.[133]

Temple next excavated to a depth of twenty feet at the Circular Monument without reaching the foundation. Falbe and Temple identified the site as a 'house',[134] but the site has nothing in common with Roman housing of any period. Except for two Greek 'phials', the reported finds were medieval, Byzantine and Roman. One of their workmen, Ali, was later headman for Davis; the site had been disappointing, but Ali thought Temple should have dug deeper.[135] Davis was also to dig at this site, his twenty-third, in the fall of 1857. Falbe drew a ground plan of it with the caveat that it had not been completely excavated.[136] Temple then moved to the ruins at Falbe no. 79, walls that lie just west of the Hill of Juno and which Dureau de la Malle had considered to be remains of the 'Temple of Saturn,' but nothing further was reported from this site.[137]

Temple's most extensive excavation took place at the seaside site, Falbe no. 90, just to the north of the street-grid of the Roman city. Falbe had discovered a mosaic here in 1824, which was destroyed through the machinations of Humbert.[138] Temple excavated a marine mosaic here in 1838, at which time Falbe drew a plan of the rooms which he had excavated (Fig. 3.7). Mr Hudson Gurney, one of the Society's members, later gave the central section, the Mosaic of the Mask of Ocean, to the British Museum (Fig. 6.1),[139] while Falbe got the pieces of the Mosaic of a Nereid on a Hippocamp (Fig. 6.2). The latter were restored in Paris and given by Falbe to the King of Denmark, who in turn presented the mosaic to the National Museum of Copenhagen. Davis was to dig at this site, his thirteenth, in the spring of 1857.

Despite the fact that the legal clauses of the Society required a daily log of finds, the planned excavation report was never published and the consortium fell into abeyance.[140] Only chance has preserved a further record of the existence of many of the artefacts: Wilmanns and Mommsen recorded six Latin inscriptions which were sent to France by the Society, of which two are early Christian funerary inscriptions;[141] and several mosaic fragments exist in the National Museum of Denmark where Falbe was later curator. Audollent was later to comment that the skills of Falbe as an engineer complemented those of Dureau de la Malle as an academic.[142] He also noted that Falbe was a fine engineer and Temple a well-educated adventurer rather than a scholar; while the two had enormous enthusiasm, Audollent found it unsurprising that no scholarly report of these excavations was subsequently forthcoming.[143] Since Falbe later became curator at the National Museum of Denmark and also collaborated in the publication of his numismatic collection, this is estimating Falbe's competence too lightly.

Davis was inadequately informed about previous foreign work at Carthage. He had first resided at Tunis from about 1840, a couple of years too late to have known Humbert or to have met Falbe and Temple at work on their excavations. In fact, Davis knew nothing of the excavations of Humbert, who must have been a shy or even deliberately secretive man for his work to have made so little impression on his contemporaries. Davis was, however, well aware of the excavations of Falbe and Temple. Although their work had taken place two decades earlier, he had not only their publications, but also first-hand information on their sites from his headman, Ali. On the other hand, Davis had evidently never heard of Alphonse Rousseau's brief exploration beneath the carpet mosaic discovered at Falbe no. 54 in 1844 (see below, pp. 88–9); yet Rousseau was French consul at Tunis when Davis began his excavations late in 1856. This suggests that his lines of communication within the European social world at Tunis were partly blocked. Although the French would later think of Falbe, who wrote in French, as their man, Davis probably did not think of the French as having any particular interest in archaeological exploration at Carthage.

Finds during the construction of the Chapel of Saint Louis

Construction at Carthage, which was still rare in the early nineteenth century, required digging foundations; although this is not excavation in the archaeological sense, any digging at Carthage regularly resulted in ancient finds, which fell into the hands of antiquarians. An important case was the construction of the French Chapel of Saint Louis on the summit of the Byrsa Hill in the early 1840s (Fig. 2.1). The stones used to build the chapel were recovered from Roman buildings at Carthage. Jourdain, the French architect of the chapel, had to dig a foundation, and he must have been aware that the chapel lay over an ancient structure, but he had no particular interest in the archaeology of the site.

A Punic votive *stele*, supposedly recovered here in 1841 during construction, was acquired by the Louvre before 1860. The site of the find was questioned by Franks, however, who believed that all seventeen of the Punic *stelae* from Carthage known by that time were from Falbe no. 58,[144] an extensive ruin that lay just to the north-east of the summit of the Hill of Saint Louis or Byrsa.[145] This idea, almost certainly mistaken, seems to have come from Guérin, who explored Tunisia for inscriptions in 1860; Guérin identified Falbe no. 58 as the 'Temple of Saturn,' because Punic *stelae* were found on this site.[146]

Davis, who was living in Tunis at the time of the find, wrote that a colossal marble bust he identified as 'Samian Juno' (he was thinking of an important sanctuary of Hera on Samos) had been found in the 'Forum' near the ports. According to the more authoritative sources of Augustus Franks, however, the bust was discovered in the 1840s during excavations for the foundation of the Chapel of Saint Louis. The bust was acquired from Ahmed Bey by the French consul and presented to the Louvre.[147] Much later Gros would argue that this colossal bust was found on the median axis of the great Antonine basilica which the French excavations of the UNESCO campaign have shown lay along the east face of the Byrsa (where Beulé, working in 1859, was to think that he had discovered the Palace of the Proconsul). Gros identified the subject as the empress Faustina the Younger, the wife of Marcus Aurelius,[148] but others identify her daughter Lucilla, the wife of Marcus's co-emperor Lucius Verus. The bust in either case dates to the second half of the second century AD, and probably to the 160s (Fig. 3.8).[149]

Other finds in the construction of the chapel of Saint Louis included inscriptions and architectural fragments.[150] The objects found were used to decorate the chapel garden. Capitals that once surmounted the pilasters of the principal gate of the octagonal enclosure around the Chapel came from the excavation, as did two lengths of column that later flanked the gate on the eastern side of the enclosure. Beulé mentioned the find of columns under the chapel.[151] All of these architectural finds became part of the small museum collection on the grounds of the Chapel of Saint Louis. After Abbé Bourgade returned to France in 1858, they became the basis of the collection of artefacts for sale to wealthy tourists by the guardian of the chapel. Davis was struck by the fact that the fragments on display in the walls were entirely Roman rather than Punic.[152] Although his observation was correct, he jumped to the conclusion that the Hill of Saint Louis was therefore not possibly the Punic Byrsa; subsequent deep

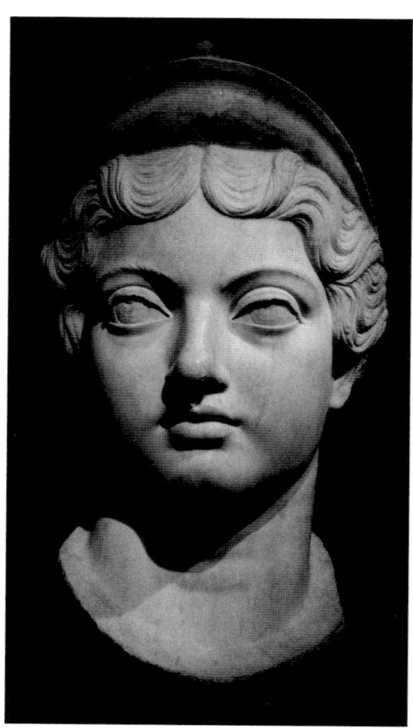

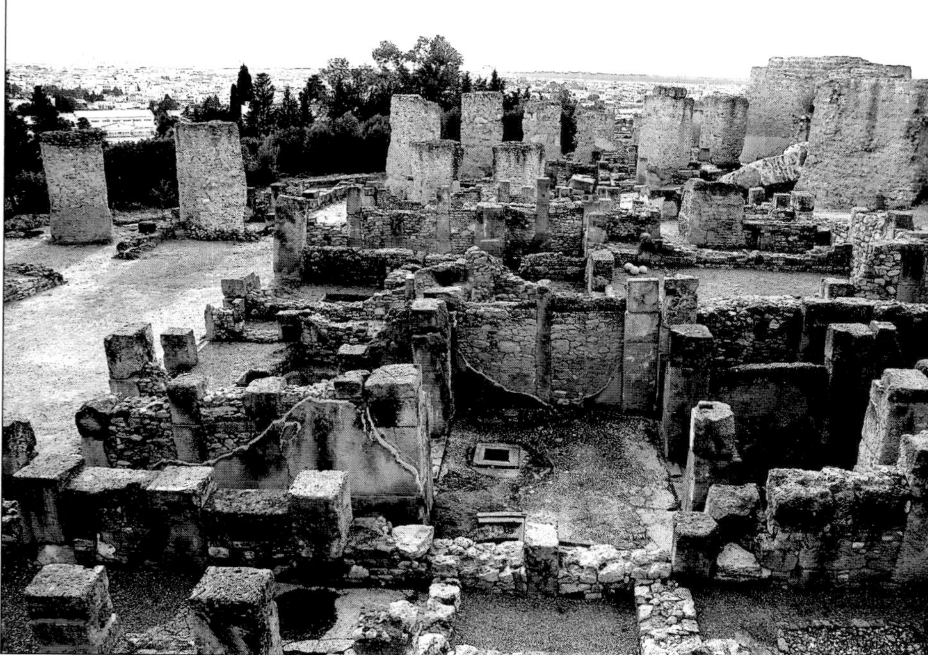

Fig. 3.8 (above left) *Colossal female bust discovered on the Byrsa in the early 1840s during excavations for the Chapel of St Louis (Fig. 2.1); it most probably adorned the Antonine basilica on the site. The hairstyle indicates that the bust portrays either Faustina the Younger, wife of Marcus Aurelius, or her daughter, Annia Lucilla. It is 1.60 m high, so the statue to which it belonged (unlikely itself to have been of marble) is estimated to have stood nearly 8 m high (if a standing figure) or between 6 m and 7 m (if seated). It is now in the Musée du Louvre, Paris.*

Fig. 3.9 (above right) *Punic houses of the first half of the second century BC on the southern slopes of the Byrsa Hill, excavated by a French team since 1974* excavation by the French on the south corner of the platform has shown that remains of late Punic housing lay deep below (Fig. 3.9).[153]

By the 1850s the groundwork had been laid for scientific excavation at Carthage. Falbe's plan clearly indicated the location of the Roman city. The architectural remains and finds of sculpture, mosaic, coins and pottery from previous excavations, while sparse, included Punic as well as Roman objects. These results strengthened the conviction that Punic Carthage was waiting to be discovered beneath the Roman city. Surely a heavy investment of time and effort would produce exciting finds. Now it was Davis' turn to excavate at Carthage and, as he must have hoped, to improve in every way on the achievements of his predecessors.

4

The site of Carthage

The hills of Carthage

The site of the Punic and Roman city of Carthage (which is now overlain by the modern suburb of the same name) lies immediately on the shore of the Mediterranean. It lay along a glowing turquoise sea with, to the east across the Gulf of Tunis, the majestic double peak of Bou Kornein at the beginning of the Cap Bon peninsula. Although Davis seems to have been somewhat oblivious to the beauty of the setting, Delattre, the missionary archaeologist who devoted his entire adult life to Carthage, was later to write: 'On certain days, especially in summer towards sunset, the water and the mountains reflect a fairyland variety of colours . . . In the beautiful evenings, the spectacle is not less ravishing'.[1]

Despite its loveliness the site was almost entirely deserted in 1856 except for the tiny villages of La Malga and Douar ech-Chott, and the summer villas of two of the Bey's ministers. This desolation was still largely unchanged in 1875, when a great admirer of the site noted 'the great silence of its solitude'.[2] Evidence for the ancient city was also hard to discern. During his first visit to Carthage in 1831 or 1832, Sir Grenville Temple wrote, 'my heart sank within me when . . . I beheld nothing more than a few scattered and shapeless masses of masonry'.[3] Delattre was to find the soil ashy-grey and marked with the debris of the lost city, but he said that when he arrived in 1875 even the ruins were largely gone.[4]

Davis therefore set to work on a beautiful but barren site. In the absence of other landmarks, he oriented himself with reference to the hills in the centre and northern half of the city (Fig. 4.1). The southern half of the ancient city is on relatively low-lying ground, rising from sea-level to a maximum elevation of 60.5 m (slightly higher than Falbe's measurement) on the

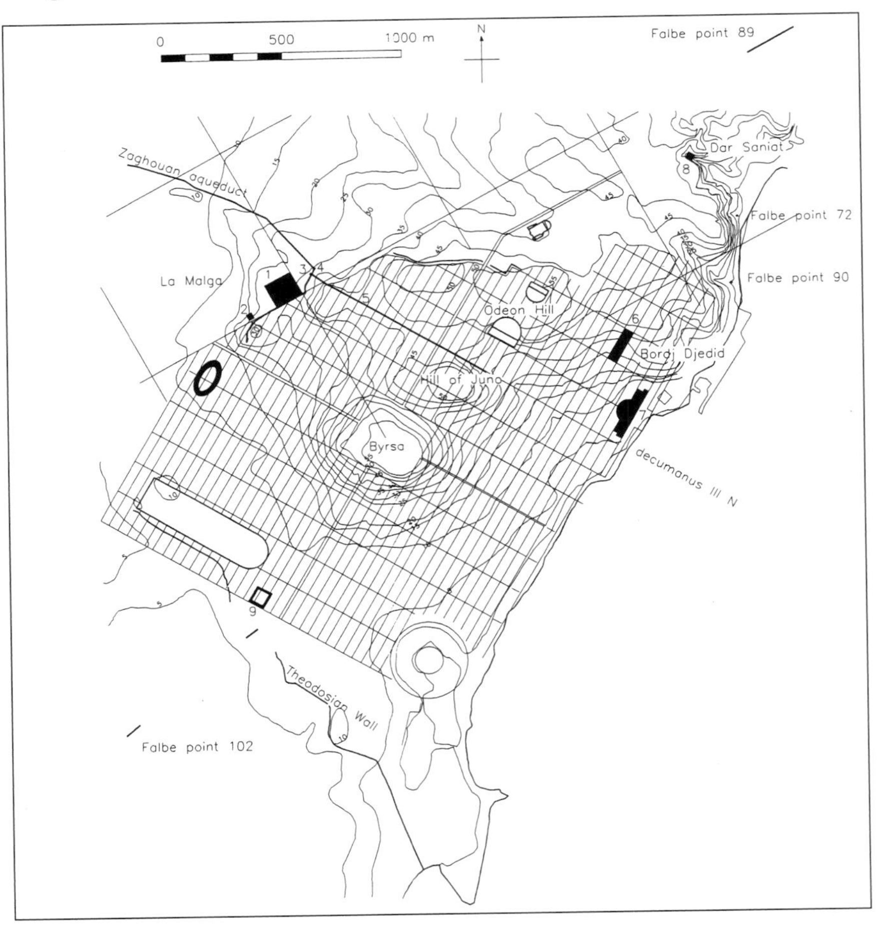

Fig. 4.1 Carthage, plan of the Roman city (1998), showing the street-grid; the position of the Byrsa, the Hill of Juno and the Odeon Hill are indicated, as are Falbe's points 72, 90 and 102. The contours are at 5 m intervals, rising to 55 m (the Byrsa and Odeon Hills) and 50 m (the Hill of Juno). The outline of the circus is indicated in the south-west part of the city, and that of the circular harbour on the south (both unlabelled). The numbers on this map refer to aspects of Carthage's water-supply: **1** *La Malga cisterns;* **2** *Small cisterns at La Malga;* **3**, **4** *and* **9** *Water installations;* **5** *Aqueduct branch;* **6** *Bordj-Djedid cisterns;* **7** *Antonine Baths;* **8** *Dar Saniat cisterns.*

highest hill, which lies in the centre of the city. This hill was known as the Hill of Saint Louis in Davis' day. It was topped by the little stone Chapel of Saint Louis (Fig. 2.1), which the French had built in the 1840s according to the terms of a treaty made with Ahmed Bey at the time of the French invasion of Algeria in 1830, and which was to be demolished in 1955.[5] Dureau de la Malle identified this hill as the Byrsa, the citadel of the Punic city, and scholars since him have generally agreed.

The northern half of the site of Carthage lay on relatively high ground, distinguished by a succession of three summits, the highest and most central of which is the Byrsa (Fig. 13.6, background). The second of these, immediately north of the Byrsa, is the Hill of Juno, which also received its designation from Dureau de la Malle: he judged it an appropriate site for the temple of Tanit or Astarte, known as Juno Caelestis (or 'Coelestis' in nineteenth-century parlance) in Roman times, although direct archaeological confirmation was lacking. Audollent later said that Guérin, Beulé, Tissot and Sainte-Marie shared this opinion, and incorrectly added Davis, who in fact did not use this designation, to his list.[6] The name continues to be used at Carthage today even though the idea behind it has long been rejected. The Hill of Juno is slightly smaller and lower than the Byrsa, rising to about fifty meters.

Beyond the Hill of Juno to the north is the longer and wider rise of the Odeon Hill, which has a maximum elevation of fifty-five meters and continues to the northern edge of the Roman city. Davis, however, had no name for the Odeon Hill, as the Roman theatre and odeon that give it its present designation were not then known. The Odeon was to be discovered by chance in 1901 by Paul Gauckler, the director of the French antiquities service. The hill was already called the Odeon Hill at that time, however, because the hollow on the south side of the hill that betrays the *cavea* (seating area) of the theatre (Fig. 4.2) had been incorrectly identified as the remains of the Odeon.[7]

In his day Davis saw the Odeon Hill as simply a higher continuation of the hill still known as Bordj-Djedid, which rises steeply from the seashore. Davis at times used the name Bordj-Djedid for the whole extent of rising ground in the northern part of the ancient city; the hill is also shown as a single unit on the plan of Falbe. 'Bordj-Djedid' means 'New Fort', and a somewhat derelict small Turkish fort overlooked the sea from the hill of Bordj-Djedid in Davis' day; Davis described it as manned by five or six ragged soldiers.[8] William Gregory, the Irish MP, thought that the fort had only two soldiers, one of whom worked on Davis' excavations.[9] The condition of the fort and its few soldiers would be no better in 1885.[10] The hill that now answers to the name rises to about thirty meters above sea level immediately above the shoreline, but seems higher, as it rises very steeply. The hill continues to rise away from the shore, reaching up to about fifty meters farther inland.

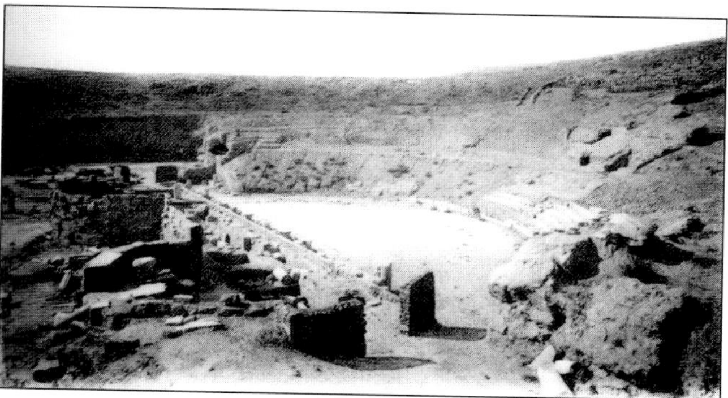

Fig. 4.2 Carthage, the Roman theatre as it appeared in 1907 (note the unexcavated slope of the hill behind), before its extensive restoration

The site of Carthage as Davis saw it owed some features of its topography to Roman intervention. The Romans had cut down the Byrsa Hill to its present maximum height of 60.5 m and used infill to form a wide flat plateau, supported by a great circuit wall of contiguous vaults. On the south-western corner, as we now know, the plateau covered late Punic houses (Fig. 3.9).[11] The artificial nature of the rectangular shape of the Byrsa hill was first commented on by Barth, a German traveller who had published a meticulous account of observations at Carthage made during his travels in 1845 to 1847,[12] which Davis does not seem to have known. Of Davis' contemporaries, Guérin, who came to Tunisia to search out inscriptions in 1860, was not convinced by Barth's theory that the form of the Byrsa Hill was artificial, while Beulé accepted Barth's observations, but with some reservations.[13] The Romans also widened the Hill of Juno by vaulting on at least its north side, and its summit was also a flat plateau.[14] Recent work on the Odeon Hill indicates that the summit was at least slightly cut down to form a level base for the construction of the Roman Odeon.[15] The flattening of the summits of these hills gives the city of Carthage a slightly unnatural topography, very evident when the site is approached from the sea.[16]

The topography shown by the plan of Falbe

As mentioned above (p. 39), Davis took a copy of the plan of Falbe (Fig. 3.2) with him to Carthage. Falbe is far more important to archaeology at Carthage for his accurate topographical plan than for his archaeogical investigations. He spent 1831 and 1832 surveying the entire ancient peninsula, and his plan covers the area from La Goulette to Gammarth, an area much larger than the Roman city. Falbe's map in fact covers a zone measuring about twelve kilometers (seven and a half miles) north–south and about ten kilometers (six miles) east–west. In the brief but valuable book that accompanied the plan, Falbe wrote that earlier visitors had not had the time, money or permission to do extensive research at Carthage, with the result that the scholar in his library had nothing precise with which to work.[17]

While Falbe had the time to prepare a properly measured and drafted plan, he did not have the permission of the government of Ahmed Bey. Although Falbe sometimes referred to elevations in feet and distances in paces, the ground measurements for this map were taken in meters. To be as discreet as possible, Falbe used a sextant with a mere three-inch (7.6 cm) radius, and chose deserted spots as his fixed points. He freely used the summer homes of the other European consuls as bases, except for the home of the British consul (Thomas Reade), to which he was not given access. The only work that could not be done with near-complete discretion was taking the measurements between his various points. For this he had the help of a French military officer, Saint-Georges, and Ferdinand de Lesseps, whose father Mathieu de Lesseps held the French consulship at Tunis; they took the necessary measurements with a twenty-meter chain. Ferdinand de Lesseps later organized the financing for, and oversaw the construction of, the Suez Canal.[18] Falbe's completed plan was drawn at a scale of 1:16,000. He was perhaps exaggeratedly confident of its accuracy; he said that someone working in a library could advise someone at Carthage of where to work accurately enough that the person on the site would be within eight to ten paces (approximately eight to ten meters) of the exact spot wanted.[19]

Carthage lay on what in the Punic era had been a wide peninsula jutting into the sea. To the north where the Sebkha de la Soukra or salt lake of Ariana lies today was once open sea. To the south, the Lake of Tunis covered a much larger area than now, extending inland perhaps as far as today's five-meter contour line. This explains the name of the village of Douar ech-Chott, which means 'village on the salt lake.' Douar ech-Chott lies two kilometers from the Lake of Tunis today, but Arab settlers may have first occupied the village not long after the destruction of Byzantine Carthage.[20]

The plan of Falbe designated points of interest by numbers, and outlined standing structures over this immense area; Sainte-Marie was inaccurate in reporting that Falbe's plan 'only indicates the elevations of the modern ground and does not mark the position of the ancient structures'.[21] In fact, Falbe did not show elevations on his plan, and he not only marked the position of ancient structures, but also outlined many of them. While he said that his map showed elevations at thirty-foot (9 m) intervals,[22] his map does not in fact have contour lines as such, nor can I see elevations marked anywhere. Falbe certainly took elevations in the course of surveying the territory, and the fact that they do not appear on the published map suggests that the information was lost, or left out when the map was sent to the printer. Falbe mentioned elevations in his text a few times, in particular estimating the height of the Byrsa as 188 feet (57.3 m) and the height of Bordj-Djedid as 120 feet (36.6 m) above sea-level.[23] The map of Carthage made by the army engineer Bordy in 1897, long after Falbe's or Davis' researches, was to be the first map to use elevations and contour lines systematically at Carthage.[24] Elevation lines are marked on the map of Carthage in the *Atlas archéologique* of 1893, but they are very inaccurate.

Although Falbe recorded the location of a large number of monuments, one of the most immediately noticeable characteristics of his plan is how relatively empty this great area was. When Davis began his excavations, what we recognize today as the site of Carthage was practically a trackless waste. Davis' published map (Fig. 4.3; cf. also Fig. 4.4) echoes the same story, and implicitly shows that there had been few significant changes since Falbe. Falbe indicated a total of 117 points with architecture or standing remains on his plan. Nos 1–40 were modern buildings mostly to the north of the site of the Roman city. Nos 41–117 designated the ancient remains of Carthage itself. The numbers on the plan are often barely legible, but this difficulty is offset by a list of the sites and their identifications in Falbe's text.[25]

Many of these points are inside the Roman street-grid as we know it today. The remains of the Roman city are concentrated between the easternmost road of the rural grid and the sea, and between the harbours to the south and a steep ravine running down to the sea on the north. The rural grid is oriented north-east–south-west and its easternmost road passed immediately along the eastern side of the La Malga cisterns. In the northern half of the city, the two major sets of cisterns, one at La Malga, and the eastern cisterns on the Bordj-Djedid hill, were nearly a mile apart, with only the Circular Monument, Falbe no. 70, identifiable about halfway between them. While the ancient landmarks were sparsely laid out across the terrain, they were grouped in a limited area and provided unarguable evidence for the presence of an ancient Roman city, as Beulé was explicitly to state.[26]

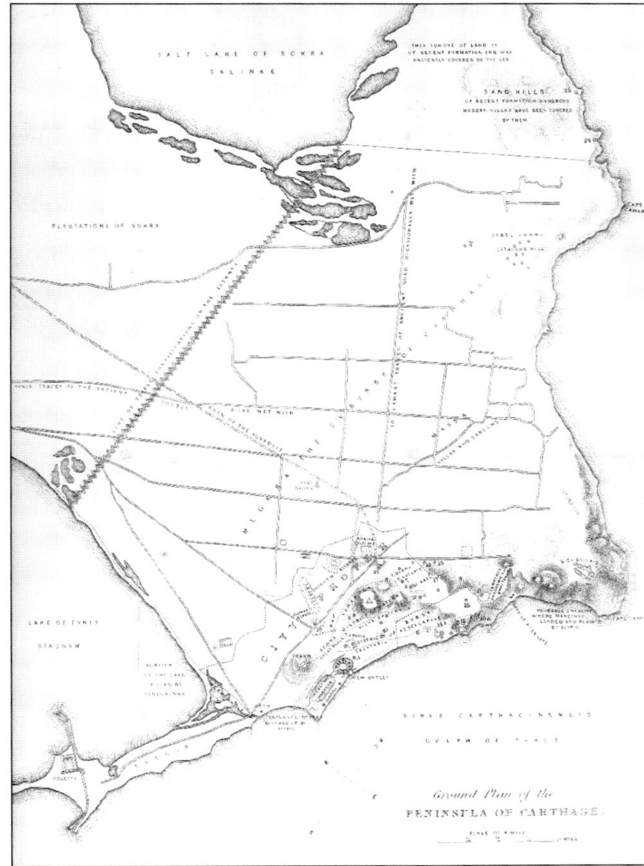

Fig. 4.3 Davis' published ground-plan of the Carthage peninsula, as it appears in his Carthage and her Remains. *Davis' map covers the same area as Falbe's (of which a detail appears in Fig. 3.2), at the same orientation, and copies some details. See also Fig. 4.4.*

Falbe noted that the area in the south part of the peninsula, which we now know is that occupied by the Roman urban street-grid, was covered by a burned layer of grey black earth, which was not present in the north at La Marsa and Sidi bou-Said; he therefore took the latter to have lain outside the central area of the ancient city. The burnt layer that Falbe saw did not belong to the Punic city, as he may have thought, because it lay over the mosaic at Falbe no. 90,[27] a mosaic dated by its style to no earlier than the mid-second century AD.

A great virtue of Falbe's map is the timelessness of its information. Falbe did not let it be contaminated by labels that reflected mere opinion, but allowed the bare evidence to speak for itself. With only common sense to guide the user, the area actually occupied by the Roman city of Carthage is identifiable by the two harbours (Falbe nos 43 and 48) with the port island (no. 49), the circus (no. 64), the amphitheatre (no. 63) and the cisterns of La Malga (marked but not numbered). The Bordj-Djedid or eastern cisterns (no. 65) and the great complex of ruins on the shore (no. 67), with its dependent hemicycle (no. 69), also clearly belong to an ancient Roman city. The great square terraced summit in the centre of the city (no. 52) was identified by Falbe as the Byrsa, the acropolis of the Punic city of Carthage. The area with identifiable urban monuments is quite limited, covering a little more than one square mile.

Falbe did not try to cite the ancient sources exhaustively, but he noted that the topographical facts of the area of the harbours agreed closely with the accounts in Appian and Strabo.[28] Appian wrote a Roman history in Greek in the second century AD, which included a detailed account of the Third Punic War (149–146 BC), and followed the eyewitness account of Polybius; Strabo, a Greek geographer, wrote a compendium on the cities of the Roman world during the reign of the emperor Augustus.[29] Neither author gave much explicit information on the topography of Carthage, although Appian's account of the ports does agree with the facts on the ground. On the other hand, nineteenth-century scholars made maximum use of the least shred of textual evidence. Appian's account of the Third Punic War was repeatedly quoted at length, not only by Davis, but also by reputable scholars; the vividness of Appian's description evidently convinced men who had been excited by the story as schoolboys that it had more topographical content than was in fact the case.

In Falbe's day the two basins of the ports each held only about a foot of water, while the elevation of the island in the Circular Harbour was about twelve feet (3.7 m). The ruins of the circus and amphitheatre were distinctly visible. The amphitheatre (Falbe no. 63), which Falbe thought should be excavated (Fig. 4.5), was identified by its interior hollow, only about fifteen feet deep (4.6 m), but 240 feet (73 m) in the longest direction. Falbe observed that the ruins of the amphitheatre included *opus reticulatum* (a diagonally-set facing of small squared blocks on the exterior of the concrete), a method of construction which was common at Rome (Fig. 4.6). Falbe suggested that an aqueduct channel at no. 62 might have been carrying water to the amphitheatre.[30] According to Falbe, the circus (no. 64) was 1,600 feet long (487.7 m) and 330 feet wide (100.6 m) at the mid-point, its form resembling the interior of a ship's hull. Part of the *euripus* (the barrier which divided the two sides of the track) could still be seen (Fig. 4.7); it was about 1000 feet long (304.8 m). On the narrow east side, towards the sea, the entrance to the circus was visible, between the foundations of two walls. In alignment with the *euripus*, across the modern

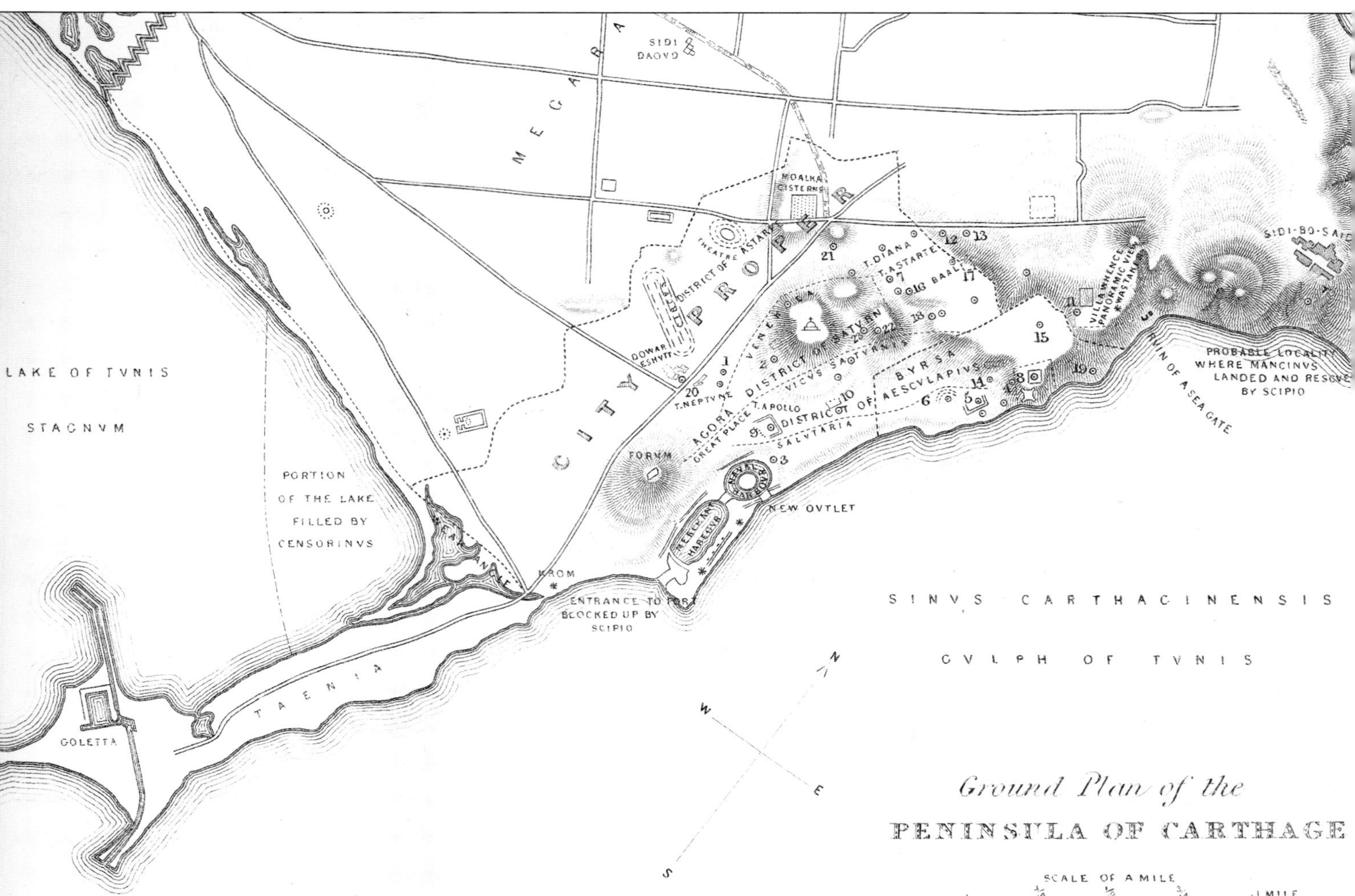

Fig. 4.4 Davis' plan of the area of the city of Carthage, a detail taken from the larger map shown in Fig. 4.3 Davis correctly noted the location of the harbours, the circus and the La Malga ('Moalka') cisterns, but for 'theatre,' read 'amphitheatre'. His placement of the 'forum' is totally idiosyncratic and wrong, as are his 'districts' and marked streets. Except for no. 11, the twenty-five numbers on Davis' map designate excavation sites, as follows: ***1*** *vaulting south-east of the circus (Site 1);* ***2*** *massive bath-house at Falbe no. 54 (Site 2);* ***3*** *north side of the Circular Harbour (Site 9);* ***4*** *the slope and monumental stair below Bordj-Djedid (Site 5);* ***5*** *the Antonine Baths (Site 12);* ***6*** *latrine of the Antonine Baths (Site 4);* ***7*** *Mosaic of the Months and Seasons, Davis' 'Temple of Astarte' (Site 8);* ***8*** *large enclosure on the summit of Bordj-Djedid (Site 11);* ***9*** *the 'Temple of Apollo' north of the Circular Harbour (Site 10);* ***10*** *probably one of Davis' unproductive sites (Sites 17–20);* ***11*** *'villa whence panoramic view was taken';* ***12*** *and* ***13*** *Roman tombs (Sites 26 and 27);* ***14*** *excavations around the Bordj-Djedid cisterns (Site 3);* ***15*** *small underground house, probably one of Davis' unproductive sites (Sites 17–20);* ***16*** *'Circular Monument' (Site 23);* ***17*** *Late Roman 'Carthaginian house' (Site 16);* ***18a*** *Roman house east of the theatre (Site 21);* ***18b*** *Mosaic of Two Gazelles (Site 22);* ***19*** *Vandal Mosaic of Victory (Site 13);* ***20*** *Second Mosaic of Nereids and Tritons (Site 35);* ***21*** *hill near La Malga cisterns; one of Davis' unproductive sites (Sites 17–20);* ***22*** *Mosaic of Baskets of Fish and Fruit (Site 14);* ***23*** *Punic votive* stelae *(Site 15). Nos* ***24*** *and* ***25****, the Roman seaside villas at Gammarth (Sites 28 and 29), lie off this map to the north of Carthage; they are marked on the coast near the top of Fig. 4.3. In addition, Davis excavated a further nine sites not marked on his map: the summit of the Hill of Juno (Site 6); the structure known as 'Gate of the Wind' (Bab-el-Rih, Site 7); the house with the prostrate column, re-excavated in the 1990s (Site 24); debris on the south slope of the Byrsa hill (Site 25); catacombs dug into the hill of Gammarth (Site 30); the Byzantine mausoleum at Gammarth (Site 31); a site near the Bey's palace at La Marsa (Site 32); the Mosaic of the Sirens (Site 33); and the Vandal Hunting Mosaic (Site 34).*

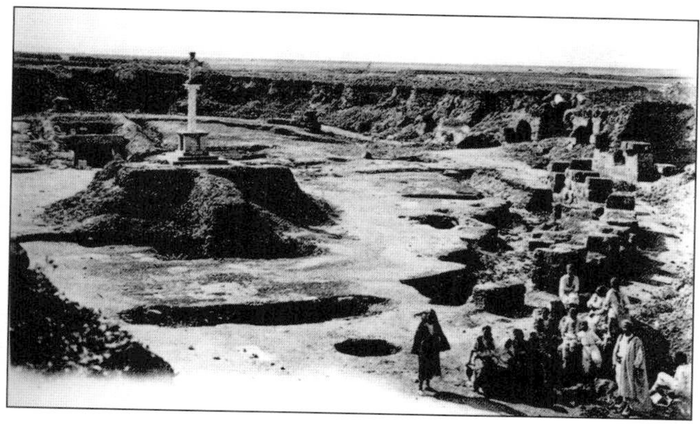

Fig. 4.5 The amphitheatre at Carthage as it appeared in 1902, during an early stage in its excavation. The cross to commemorate the Christian martyrs who died there was erected on modern ground level before the start of the excavation, and demonstrates incidentally the depth of soil around it that was removed to reveal the ancient structure.

road, ruin no. 73 dominated the whole circus. On the long north-east side of the circus, there were remains in concrete, but excavation here (Falbe does not say by whom), down to about ten feet (3.0 m), had not discovered anything.

Falbe calculated the elevation of the La Malga cisterns at seventy feet (21.3 m; very low in relation to the major hills of the city). He noted that they had the same construction as the cisterns at no. 65. Although few nineteenth-century scholars agreed with him, Falbe thought the La Malga cisterns were Roman, as was the aqueduct from Zaghouan to Carthage. With his numismatic interests, he used the find of a coin of Septimius Severus and Caracalla, dated to AD 203, to support his argument.[31]

The largest ruin of the entire city (Falbe no. 67), which lay immediately on the seashore in the north-eastern quarter of the city, included both concrete and remains in ashlar masonry (rectangular cut stone blocks); a great mass of concrete, cement and small stone blocks covered the area (Figs 3.4–3.5). Beulé later identified the edifice as 'the basilica of Thrasamund,' the great baths praised in Vandal poetry. Falbe and Davis did not use that designation, and Davis was not convinced that it was a bath building. Reade and Beulé recognized it as an immense bath building (the site was later identified as the Antonine Baths), and Beulé, who knew the poetry, mentioned the Vandal poet Felix as the source for the designation 'the basilica of Thrasamund' (Fig. 5.5).[32] To Falbe, the adjoining ruin at no. 69 was certainly a temple, as the building was 160 feet long (48.8 m), with a chord of 120 feet (36.6 m) joining two points along its hemicyclic exterior;[33] in fact, the structure is the south-west latrine of the Antonine Baths (Fig. 5.6). Falbe also described great ashlar blocks that he thought must once have formed the revetment of moles in the water on the seashore in front of this huge complex.[34]

As noted above (p. 41), the hill in the centre of the city was identified as the Byrsa. Falbe thought this area

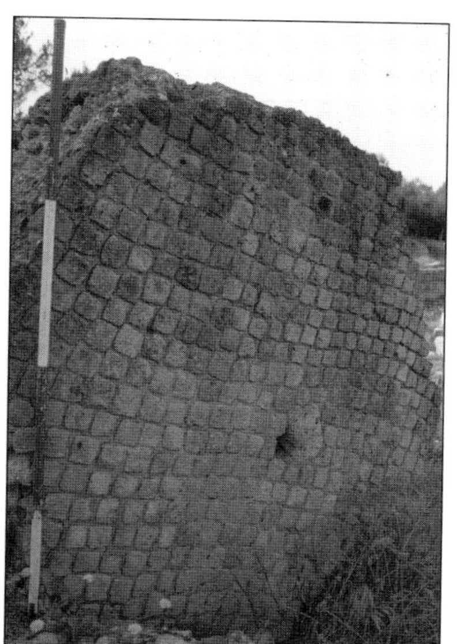

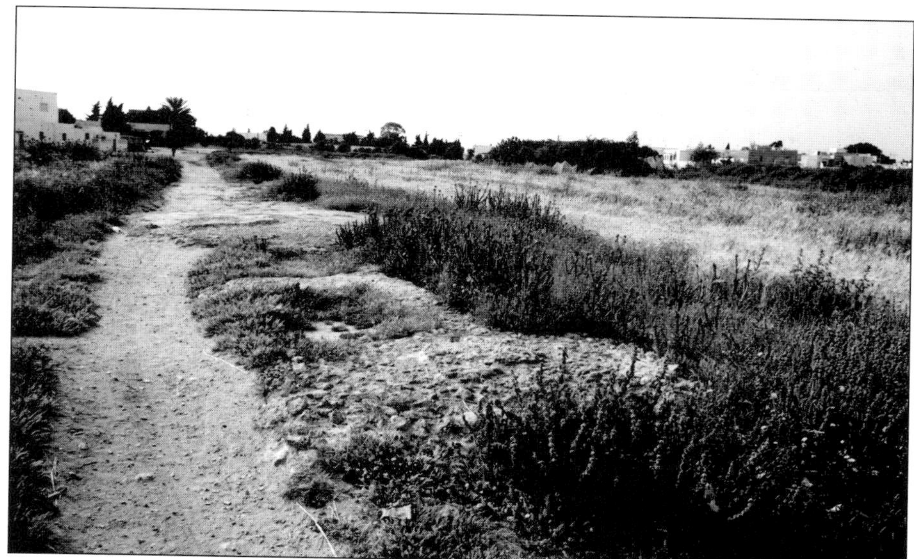

Fig. 4.6 (above left) *A fragment of surviving* opus reticulatum *walling in the amphitheatre at Carthage; the scale is marked in components of 50 cm.*

Fig. 4.7 (above right) *The circus at Carthage as it appeared in 1991; the concrete line in the foreground represents the unexcavated central barrier of the circus (the* euripus*).*

clearly demanded excavation. Lines of vaulting at different heights were visible, and some of these vaults were between twenty and thirty feet wide (about 6–9 m), although he could not measure their depth because of fallen debris. To Falbe, the ranges of debris at different levels around this hill suggested the triple wall that he believed surrounded the Punic Byrsa, or acropolis. Beulé also took this view, but Davis, who was correct, declared that Appian described a triple wall surrounding the Punic city as a whole, arguing heatedly that Beulé had been led astray on this question by the opinions of Falbe and Temple.[35]

Falbe's plan showed that the top of the Byrsa plateau formed a level square with remains of walls on three sides; his plan did not show walls on the south side, but there were considerable remains of walls on the north. Falbe drew and described a relatively small paved area of 80 by 100 feet (24.4 m by 30.5 m) at the centre of the west side (that is, away from the sea), which was built over vaults, but otherwise left the top of the hill undefined. Falbe also said that the relation of this hill to the circus, amphitheatre and cisterns of La Malga confirmed that it was the Byrsa.[36] Other minor sites also interested him. Ruin no. 66 was on the hill above the smaller cisterns. Falbe returned to Carthage with Temple in 1838, at which time he explored and drew the building,[37] while Temple removed at least one fragment of mosaic. Of sites that seemed to him to have certainly been temples, Falbe no. 70 is particularly important for Davis. Falbe wrote that this ruin, now known as the Circular Monument (Figs 10.15–10.18), was only sixty-five feet in diameter (19.8 m), including its square base,[38] but this estimate is much too small; I estimate the size of the building at 38 m by 36.8 meters according to Hallier's plan.[39] Falbe also outlined a very large monument, 400 meters north of the city street-grid and on the seashore (Falbe no. 72). Falbe thought it was a city gate, and Davis also referred to it as the 'Sea Gate,' but it was far too large to be a gate, with ground dimensions of about eighty by sixty meters, as Falbe's plan showed.

Falbe's plan galvanized Dureau de la Malle to write his influential work on the topography of Punic and Roman Carthage. He combined Falbe's evidence of the standing remains with a minute knowledge of the ancient sources, suggesting identifications for many of the sites.[40] Davis later complained and Beulé confirmed that Dureau de la Malle never visited Carthage in person, but made his observations exclusively from the plan of Falbe.[41] Audollent observed that Dureau de la Malle expressed his opinions with more certainty than could be felt by an observer of the actual terrain.[42] While some of his identifications were certainly wrong, Dureau de la Malle is one of the few early scholars to distinguish rigorously between arguments applicable to Punic, as opposed to Roman, Carthage.

Although Davis' excavations began twenty-five years after Falbe had produced his plan, no significant archaeological work had been done since the excavations of Falbe and Grenville Temple in 1838. The great monuments of the city had been continually plundered by stone robbers, who treated the site of Carthage as a quarry. Falbe had noted the heavy losses of architectural remains at Carthage during the eleven years he had lived at Tunis during the 1820s and 1830s; his point was that if this much could be removed in eleven years, how much more could have been removed over the same number of centuries! On the other hand, Falbe said that most of what he had seen taken away was Vandal and Byzantine, and implicitly suggested that there must be much remaining of earlier date.[43]

Nevertheless much of the site was largely as Falbe had seen it, even in the 1870s. Sainte-Marie, who was to excavate Punic *stelae* at Carthage in 1874, said of the circus, which had not yet been touched by further archaeological excavation, that its outline was still perfectly recognizable. One can compare Falbe's measurements of the circus with those personally taken by Sainte-Marie more than forty years later; Sainte-Marie said that the circus was 675 meters (2,214 feet) long by 90 meters (295 feet) wide, and that the central barrier (*euripus*) was 5.5 m (18 ft) wide. Sainte-Marie conceded that the length he gave, 600 feet longer than Falbe's measurement, could be incorrect. His measurements suggest, however, that there had been no significant loss of the outline of the circus in the intervening years. On the other hand, the *euripus* had been reduced to ground level and the terracing of the stadium had been removed to construct houses at the port of La Goulette, so that the raised outline of the seating area was by then only about two meters in height.[44] Sainte-Marie also published an illustration of the plowed hollow field which marked the amphitheatre, and said that while the entrances and exits were not visible, there were large blocks of masonry on the ground, and these massive remains of the structure form a ring around the central hollow in his illustration. Sainte-Marie himself had found a fine Corinthian capital there, which he sent to the Museum of Algiers.[45]

Davis' idiosyncratic views on the topography of Carthage

Davis depended heavily on Falbe and Dureau de la Malle, but he was more aware of the shortcomings of his predecessors than of their contributions. Having noted that it was 'preposterous' to assign specific sites to the 'Villa of Galerius,' the 'Baths of Gargilius' or the

'House of Hannibal,' Davis himself also did this freely. Since he did not agree with the correlations of Dureau de la Malle, he gave him no credit for his thinking, but was clearly inspired to do the same thing, and thus named different sites, even more fancifully, as the 'Temple of Astarte' or 'Temple of Saturn'.[46]

Because Davis had little success when he dug at ruins indicated by Falbe, he ignored the latter's site numbers and used his own numbering system exclusively. This has made it unnecessarily difficult to correlate Davis' work with that of his predecessor. While some of Davis' sites clearly are the same as some of Falbe's sites, the majority of the former's excavations are not at places marked on Falbe's plan. Nevertheless, the location of Davis' sites which are on Falbe's plan can be taken at face value and correlated with the street-grid, because Falbe's sites were surveyed in, while many of the places which are marked on Davis' plan alone were undoubtedly set by eye. Those of Davis' excavations that correlate with Falbe's sites form a pattern which can be checked against the rest of Davis' sites to fix them with reasonable accuracy.

Davis was confident of the location of both Punic and Roman Carthage. He believed, correctly, that the Roman city of Carthage lay directly over its destroyed Punic predecessor, and he marshalled the ancient literary evidence to support his opinion. His explicit argument, however, was that since Punic Carthage covered the whole peninsula, Roman Carthage *must* have been built over it; this argument was confirmed for him by the fact that he found Punic and Roman remains together.[47] While Falbe's plan reveals the Roman city, defined by its typical monuments, as within a limited and relatively small part of the whole peninsula, Davis seemed unconscious of what Falbe's topographic landmarks revealed. At the same time Davis' excavation sites were concentrated inside the city street-grid, which indicates that he implicitly recognized the outlines of the Roman city and generally chose to stay within its limits.

The location of the 'Cothon', or Circular Harbour (Figs 13.5–13.9), Davis considered certain, agreeing with Falbe, Dureau de la Malle, 'Dusegate' and Temple,[48] and rejecting the arguments of the majority of earlier topographers at Carthage. As Beulé pointed out, Shaw, Anville and Estrup put the harbours on the north side of the city, and Mannert linked the harbours to the Bay of Tunis, but Humbert, Chateaubriand, Falbe and Dedreux got the location right.[49] Although Davis used the term 'Cothon' only for the Circular Harbour, he understood the term to refer more generally to an excavated harbour that communicates with the sea by a channel.[50] Beulé, who excavated at both harbours in the autumn of 1859, found the ancient sources unclear as to whether 'Cothon' specifically referred to the circular military harbour, but was in agreement that the word indicates that the harbours were excavated and therefore artificial.[51] In a letter written from Carthage in December 1859, Beulé said that visitors scoffed at the site. The merchant harbour was three-quarters dry, and it was easy to wade across the military harbour in summer.[52] Guérin, who visited Carthage in 1860, said that the commercial harbour was filled in and planted with vines and figs.[53] Both the Khaznadar and Khereddine, Mameluke ministers at the court of the Bey, had summer homes by the ports.[54] The harbours as we see them today were to be dug out in the 1870s by the son of the Prime Minister and at the instance of Madame Elias Masulli, a lady of influence at the court of the next Bey, Mohammed-es-Sadok.[55]

Davis also recognized remnants of the city wall and ditch to the south, near the village of Le Kram; to the west, behind the village of Douar ech-Chott and continuing to the La Malga cisterns, and again not far from the house belonging to the Lord Keeper of the Seal (Sidy Mustapha), on high land just north of the city street-grid, and continuing from there east to the 'sea gate' (Falbe's no. 72). According to Davis, the wall had forts 'near many of its angles'.[56] Davis did not explicitly state that he thought that this was the Punic city wall; in fact, the structures Davis saw belonged to the late Roman city, which was not walled until AD 425 in the reign of the emperor Theodosius II.[57]

Having struggled with his maps, Davis turned to the ancient literary sources for topographical insights, and found evidence in Strabo and Appian for the placement of the Temple of Apollo at the 'great place' or Forum, which lay between the circular harbour and the Byrsa; on the latter stood the Temple of Aesculapius.[58] Unfortunately, Davis found that being on the actual spot did not resolve the difficulties of these texts. For example, he strongly objected to the view, generally accepted by scholars even in his day, that the Hill of Saint Louis was to be identified with the Punic Byrsa. The Byrsa was the site of the Temple of Aesculapius, the Roman equivalent of the Punic Eshmoun, god of medicine according to ancient sources. In Davis' opinion, the topography of the Saint Louis hill was not consistent with the sources that described the Byrsa, and no Punic remains whatsoever had been recovered from the Saint Louis hill: here he was specifically attacking the arguments of Beulé.[59] Furthermore, he had found a Punic inscription of Eshmoun on the slope of Bordj-Djedid.[60] Davis thought that the hill of Bordj-Djedid was the Punic Byrsa, and the Temple of Aesculapius was therefore on Bordj-Djedid (at point 8 within a square on his published map, Fig. 4.4). Contemporary and later scholars regarded Davis' arguments with a mixture of horror and outrage, and rejected them without further consideration. Guérin described Davis' idea that the temple of Aesculapius was on the Bordj-Djedid hill as 'ignorant';[61] Delattre was later to note that Davis had confused the topography of Carthage by identifying the Punic Byrsa with the Bordj-Djedid hill instead of with the hill of Saint Louis.[62]

Other idiosyncratic placements on Davis' published map (Fig. 4.4) are the 'district of Astarte,' across the west side of the city; the 'district of Saturn,' across the centre of the city, and the 'district of Aesculapius,' across the eastern (seaward) side of the city. He placed the 'Agora,' or 'Great Place,' between the Circular Harbour and the circus, although he had also considered the Antonine Baths as a possible site of the Punic forum. His published map shows the three streets mentioned in the *Acta Proconsularia*, which recounted the death of Saint Cyprian in AD 258:[63] these were the 'Salutaria,' the 'Vicus Saturni' and the 'Veneria.' Davis thought it reasonable that the 'Via Salutaria' would run to the 'Temple of Aesculapius;' the 'Vicus Saturni' to the 'Temple of Baal,' and the 'Via Veneria' along the 'district of Astarte,' leading to the 'Temple of Diana' and the 'Temple of Astarte.' Davis went drastically wrong here by trying to integrate evidence for the topography of Punic Carthage with that of Roman Carthage, and adding in his own fanciful identifications of temples, which he was evidently thinking of as Punic. The result is sheer fantasy. His published map also marks the 'portion of lake filled by Censorinus', the 'entrance to port blocked up by Scipio', and the 'probable locality where Mancinus landed and [was] rescued by Scipio'; all these can be taken with a grain of salt, although they are more justifiable efforts to link recognizable topography on the ground with Appian's account of Roman strategy in the Third Punic War.

The Roman urban street-grid and the Roman rural grid

Confirmation of the layout of the street-grid of Roman Carthage is one of the most important outcomes of the UNESCO projects.[64] An understanding of the street-grid combined with information from excavation has brought the pattern of use for different areas of the city into clear focus, as the aerial view of Roman Carthage recently drawn and published by Golvin brilliantly illustrates (Fig. 4.8).[65] Knowledge of the street-grid allows relative distances and the relative position of different sites to be understood easily. Knowledge of the street-grid also makes it possible to visualize traffic through the city and to understand the Roman city as a system of neighbourhoods. For example, the port district was also an industrial district. The amphitheatre and circus are along the south-west edge of the city, forming a kind of rough entertainment district on reclaimed low ground. Urban Romans buried their dead immediately outside the city walls, or in the case of Carthage, which was unwalled until the fifth century AD, outside the defined habitation area. The whole extent of the road that defines the easternmost line of the rural grid was lined with cemeteries and tombs. The Byrsa Hill is the centre of Roman Carthage, where the main grid-lines cross. It is also its highest point and was dedicated to civic buildings, both religious and administrative. The northern half of the city is on high ground and includes elegant housing as well as the more refined entertainment district of the theatre and Odeon. With an estimated maximum of 400 habitable city-blocks, the population of the Roman city within the area covered by the street-grid itself seems unlikely to have been higher than 100,000. The estimated seating of the circus at Carthage provides a relevant comparison: the circus may have held 60–63,000 people, or perhaps as many as 75,000.[66]

Falbe did not completely understand the layout of the street-grid, but he recognized a good deal of evidence for it. His accurate plan led to observations that could not be made on the ground; Falbe himself made many of these by comparing what his own map showed him with his knowledge of the site. For example, his plan shows a good number of intermittent straight lines; his map legend describes them as 'the prolongation of ruins just visible'. While those on the northern side of the city generally relate to the Theodosian Wall, Falbe also saw continuous straight lines within the area of the Roman street-grid. He described one of these as the line of a main street with ruins on either side. This particular line runs east–west straight across the whole city, starting from the seashore, then along the south side of Falbe no. 69 (the south-west latrine of the Antonine Baths), and passing along the north side of no. 53 (the Hill of Juno); it ends just north-east of the cisterns at La Malga. Today scholars designate the streets that run north–south as *cardines* [singular *cardo*] and the streets that run east–west as *decumani* [singular *decumanus*]. We can now recognize that the line which Falbe described follows a particular street, *decumanus* 3 north, all the way across the city.

Falbe thought he could pick out ancient streets by the alignment of ruins, especially near the Byrsa, and around the two major cisterns,[67] but not all his examples faithfully follow the Roman street-grid. A line that he drew as heading south from the Bordj-Djedid or

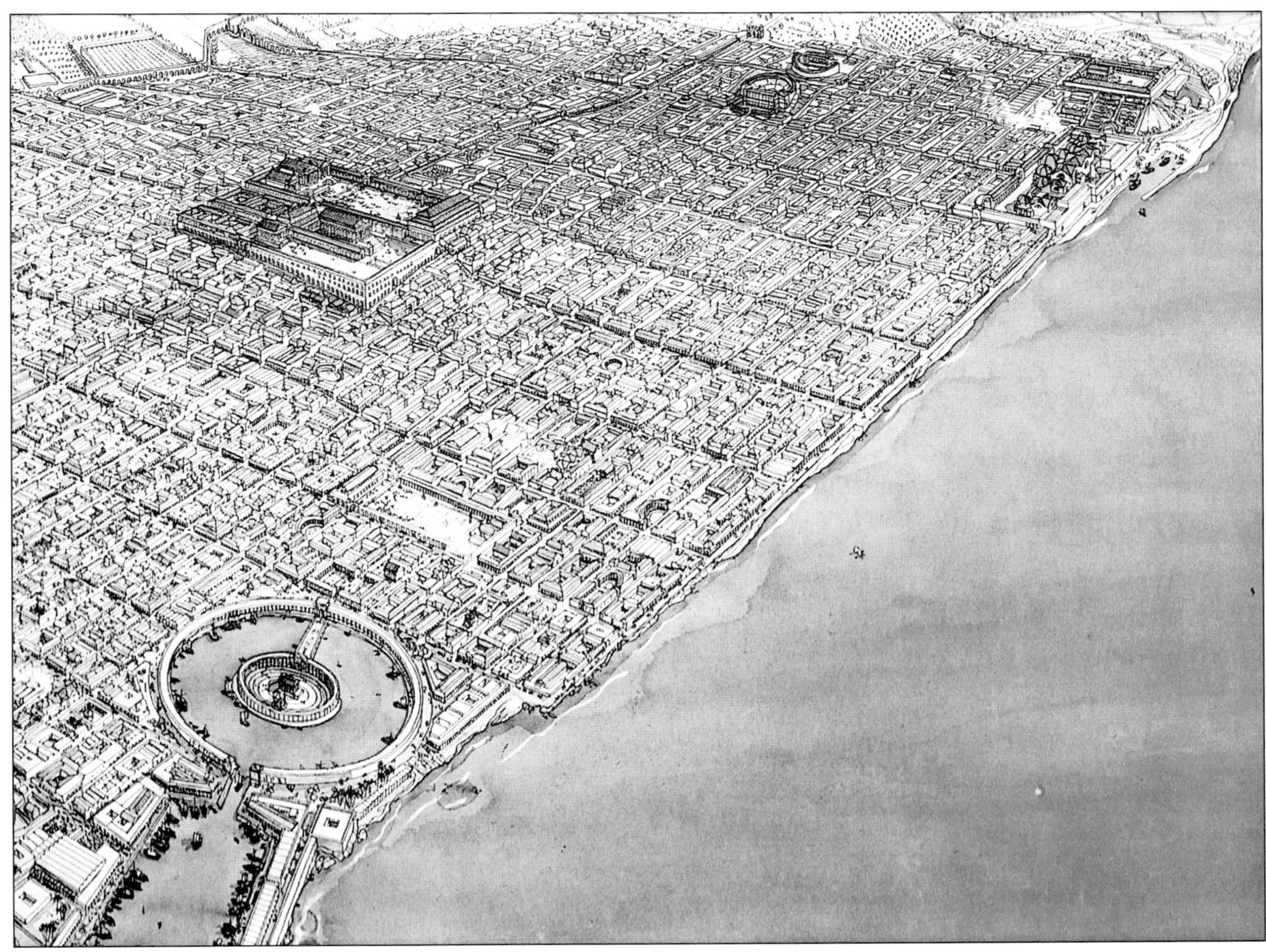

Fig. 4.8 Carthage in the third century AD, from the south, as envisaged in a painting by Jean-Claude Golvin. This shows the central and northern parts of the city, including the huge forum and basilica complex on the Byrsa hill, visible at upper left, the theatre and odeon *(top, right of centre), the Antonine Baths (upper right), and the harbours (lower left). More uncertain is the nature of the complex on top of the hill above the Baths (shown here, probably correctly, as a temple), and the position of a second earlier forum (we know Roman Carthage possessed a 'maritime forum'), shown here close to the circular harbour.*

eastern cisterns (Falbe no. 65) turns after 300 meters to follow the orientation of the *cardines*. This line, more or less parallel to the sea-front, follows *cardo* 13 east from *decumanus* 3 north to *decumanus* 3 south, just north of the circular harbour; this is a distance of more than 840 m, or 1140 m in total (more than a kilometer). After skirting an unidentified major edifice (Falbe no. 55), it continued another 850 m to the west. It is possible that this line marked the remains of Byzantine defensive walls that would have been standing very late in the history of the city. At its farthest northern extent where it met the eastern cisterns, such a line of wall would have reached the easily-defended high ground in the north of the city.

Other evidence supports this hypothesis. Although the Byzantine army approached Gelimer's forces from the landward side, there is no evidence that the Theodosian Wall had ever been carried across the sea-front of the city,[68] in which case Byzantine Carthage would have been vulnerable to attack from the sea. Pringle has shown that the Byzantine walls of North Africa usually enclosed an area much smaller than the inhabited area of the city, even where the pre-Vandal walls survived.[69] Typically the plan of such walls was sub-rectangular, with straight lines of curtain wall between towers. Furthermore, Byzantine walls were usually very well built, in ashlar stone blocks facing a rubble core, and had a standard height of twenty cubits (9.37 m).[70] The masonry style was imported from the Greek east;[71] the facing would have been particularly attractive to later stone robbers, but the core might have survived to Falbe's day.

On the other hand, Falbe was not just hypothesizing a street running across the width of the city at *decumanus* 3 north, for he wrote to the Danish Crown Prince in a letter of March 23rd, 1838:[72]

> At the places indicated by me between the ruins 52 [the summit of the Hill of Saint Louis or Byrsa], 53 [the Hill of Juno] and 70 [the Circular Monument] on my plan of Carthage we have inspected three of the main roads of Carthage by means of the sewers running along them. I have been through one of them, from Malqah [La Malga] to below the hill no. 53 [the Hill of Juno] and had nearly been frightened back by a hedgehog . . . This underground journey gave us knowledge of the existence of five side drains, which stand for an equal number of streets as well as of conduits built immediately above the sewers and, finally, we also found the pavement of the street, which leads from La Malqah between no. 53 and no. 70 [this is the paving of *decumanus* 3 north, probably between *cardines* 2 and 3 east]. It consists of ashlars laid diagonally to the direction of the street, [each] measuring a couple of feet in length and six inches in thickness.

Falbe's letter implies that he had ascertained the existence of drains under the *decumanus maximus* on the Byrsa, under *decumanus* 2 north on the hill of Juno, and under *decumanus* 4 north near the Circular Monument, as well as paving on *decumanus* 3 north, the line of Roman street running from the La Malga cisterns to the sea. Falbe's description implies that fresh water conduits generally lay above the drains. The long underground line that he explored, from La Malga to the Hill of Juno, was later to be explored again by Delattre and Vernaz.[73] Falbe here identified five cross streets (*cardines*) from the presence of their drains, over an extent where he might have expected to have met fifteen or so.

None of this evidence for the regular grid of Roman streets seems to have been known to Davis, although he was aware of the matter, and mentioned 'the evident remains of lines of ruins, which clearly indicate streets'.[74] The streets which Davis perceived and had drawn on his published map, however, bear no relationship to the Roman grid-system. Nevertheless, one can sympathize with Davis' general inability to see much that Falbe could see.

One of the most informative early clues to the street-grid was the plan of the eastern cisterns on Bordj-Djedid (now, as already noted [p. 45], inaccessible in the grounds of the Presidential Palace), because they occupy exactly one Roman city-block. The cisterns both indicate the dimensions of a block and the orientation of the street-grid; on the other hand, these cisterns lay almost entirely underground, and their significance for the street-grid could only be guessed from study of a map as accurate as the plan of Falbe.

On his map of 1897 (Fig. 4.9) the engineer Bordy was to indicate many lines of the Roman urban street-grid, especially in the north-eastern quarter of the city (*decumani* 3, 4 and 5 north, and sections of *cardines* 4, 6–8, 10, and 12–17 east). The lines are clearly indicated, but not labelled, because the present designations of *decumani* and *cardines* had not yet been applied. Bordy was advised by both Gauckler, who headed the French antiquities service in Tunisia from 1892 to 1905,[75] and by Delattre, who in 1897 had been excavating at Carthage for two decades. Gauckler, in particular, established the pattern of the street-grid on the basis of his excavations among the houses on the Odeon Hill.[76]

The layout of the street-grid was first to be explicitly discussed by Paul Gauckler in 1903 in his annual report for the antiquities service.[77] In 1913, Haverfield was to publish a map of the street-grid of the north-eastern quarter of Carthage, which he had derived from Bordy's map.[78] A detailed analysis with the numbering used today was published by Charles Saumagne only in 1924 (Fig. 4.10),[79] with refinements by Davin in 1930.[80] Saumagne's 1924 hypothesis that the individual blocks measured 480 by 120 Roman feet, with the *groma* (the device with which the cardinal points were laid out) set up on the summit of the Byrsa hill, the highest point in the city, has been consistently confirmed, although Hurst was later to attack the idea that the theoretical street-grid illustrated by Saumagne was laid out to this complete extent at the foundation of the Roman city.[81] Davin noted that the regular width of the streets was twenty-four Roman feet with the exception of the *cardo maximus* and *decumanus maximus*, which were forty Roman feet wide. This street-grid was certainly laid out by the Romans, since the area within the blocks corresponded exactly to two *iugera*, the *heredium* defined by the old Roman colonial laws as the lot of each male citizen colonist.[82]

The ideas of Saumagne and Davin have since been found essentially reliable by excavators at Carthage,[83] and excavations at Carthage, particularly since the beginnings of the UNESCO 'Save Carthage' project in the early 1970s, are described in relation to their position on accurately developed plans of the street-grid of Roman Carthage (Fig. 4.11). Edith Wightman calculated the size of the blocks at 141.20 m by 35.30 m, noting that the Italian excavation used a slightly different equivalence: 141.60 m by 35.40 m. Since this variation gives a margin of error of only about three/tenths of

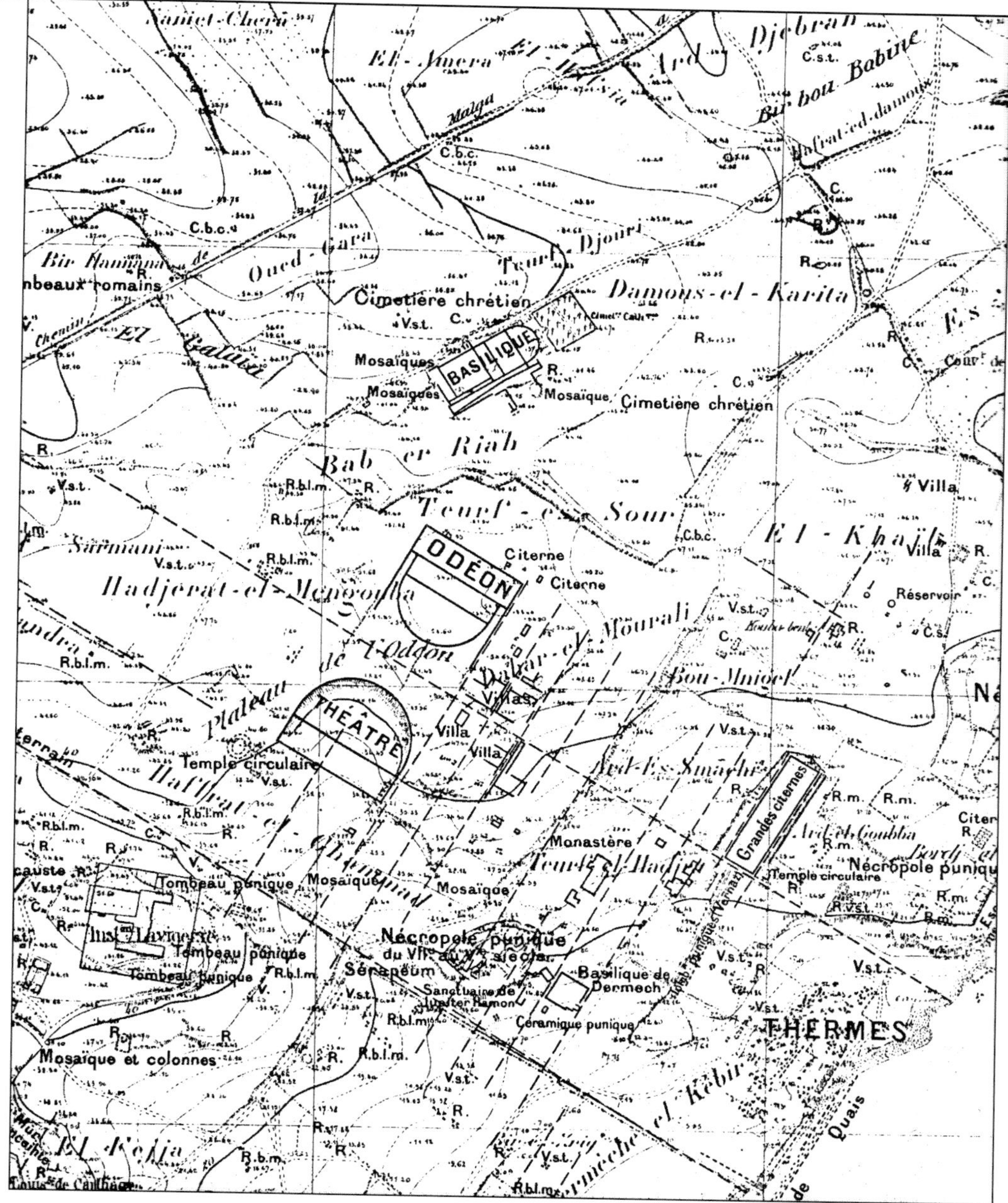

Fig. 4.9 A detail from engineer Bordy's map, showing the ancient remains around the 'Hill of Juno' (lower left), the Odeon Hill (centre), and the Antonine Baths (lower right) at Carthage, together with part of the street-grid. The map was completed in 1897 and exhibited at the Exposition Universelle in Paris in 1900.

one percent, it is not surprising that all the UNESCO teams were able to predict the placement of intersections with very good accuracy, despite the fact that there is certainly some variation in street-widths, especially over time. Wightman allowed 7 m for the width of the ordinary streets; the two main streets would have measured 11.67 m across.

We know today that the street-grid of Roman Carthage covers an area of a little more than one square mile. The *decumanus maximus*, the major east–west street, rises from the sea at sea-level and runs in a straight line across the Byrsa hill, reaching a maximum elevation of about sixty meters, and falling again on the west side of the city to about fifteen meters above sea-level. In the original layout of the city street-grid, there were six *decumani* south of the *decumanus maximus* and six *decumani* to the north. The *cardo maximus*, the major north–south street, also crosses the Byrsa in a straight line. There were originally twenty *cardines* to the west of the *cardo maximus*, and twenty *cardines* to the east of it. This layout resulted in blocks that were very long, 140 meters between *decumani*, and quite narrow, 35 meters between *cardines*. There were therefore many more streets running north–south than east–west, and the street widths, which were figured separately from the area inside the blocks, helped to increase the east–west width of the city. Even so, the original grid covered a square significantly less than two kilometers per side (approximately 1,765 m by 1,685 m, or 5,790 ft

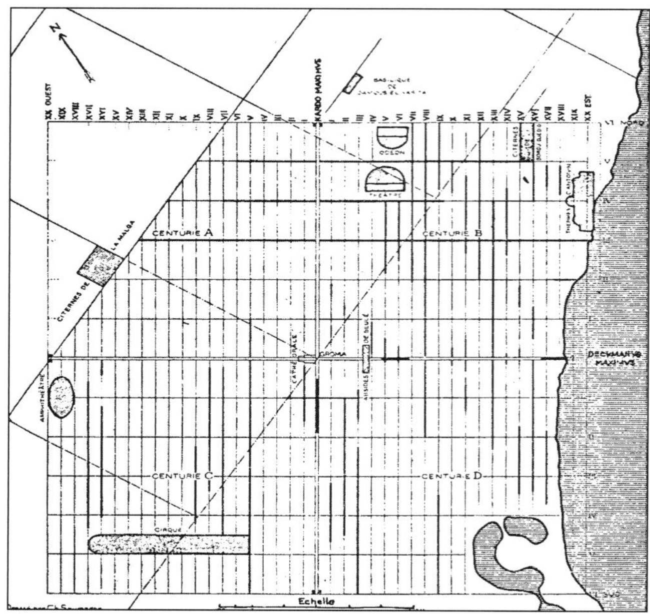

by 5,528 ft). One might say that the city was in modern terms relatively small, but as an archaeological site this is an enormous area.

Not all the area within this theoretical grid was developed. On the north-west side, the cisterns of La Malga were on the west side of the rural grid-line and that line, which cut across the north-western quarter of the urban grid, defined the limit of development of the north-west side of the city. On the other hand, a tiny stretch of *decumanus* 6 north, just behind the portico of the Odeon, on the north-eastern side of the city, was excavated in 1996 and showed a sequence of deliberately-laid hard street-layers which begin in the early first century AD; this indicates that the majority of the grid was functional, with streets marked out on the ground and maintained in use from the early life of the Roman colony.[84]

Falbe was the first to map the evidence for, and understand the existence of, the rural grid that covered the territory to the west of the Roman city, the side

Fig. 4.10 (above) *Plan of the urban and rural grid at Carthage and nearby, as reconstructed by Charles Saumagne in 1924*

Fig. 4.11 (right) *The street-grid of Roman Carthage (1999), showing the position of the Byrsa forum at the centre, the theatre and* odeon *in adjacent* insulae *(top), the Antonine Baths (top right), the circus (bottom left) and the Punic harbours (bottom centre)*

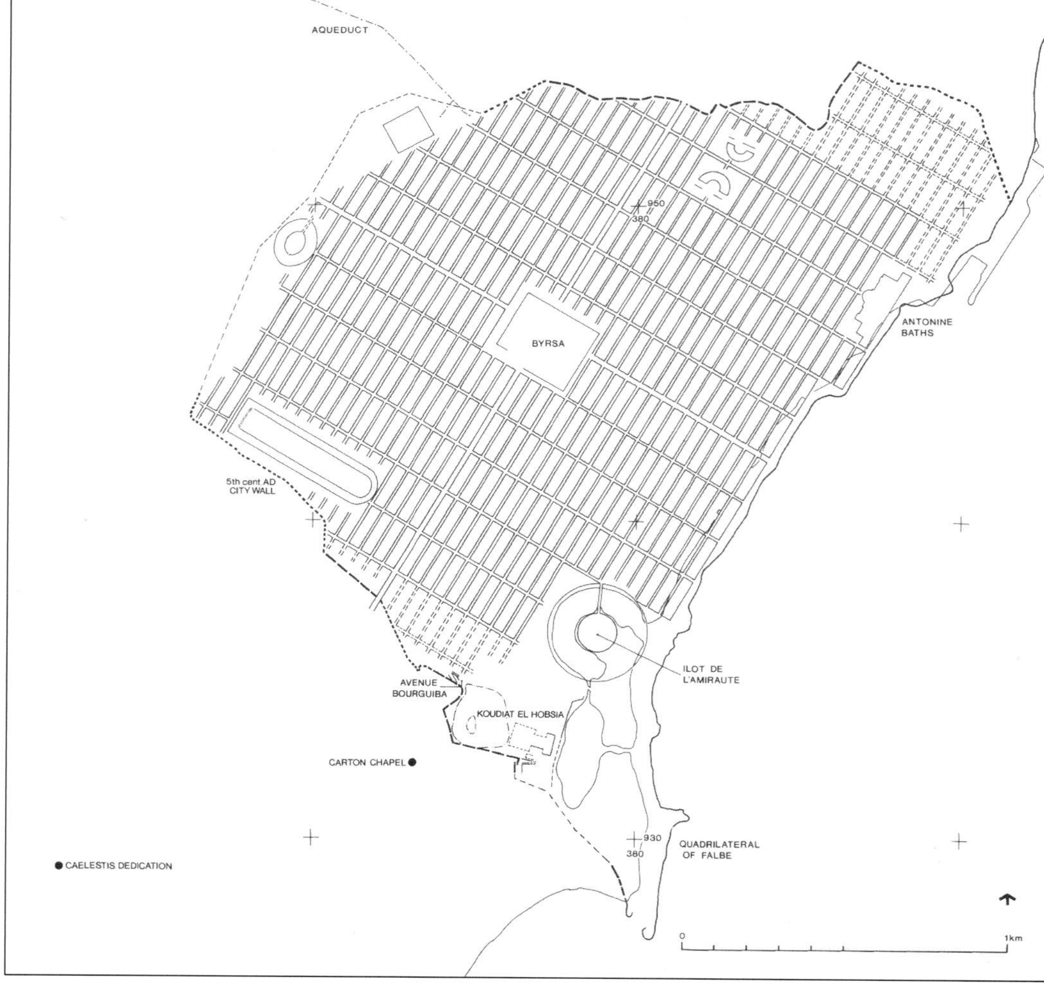

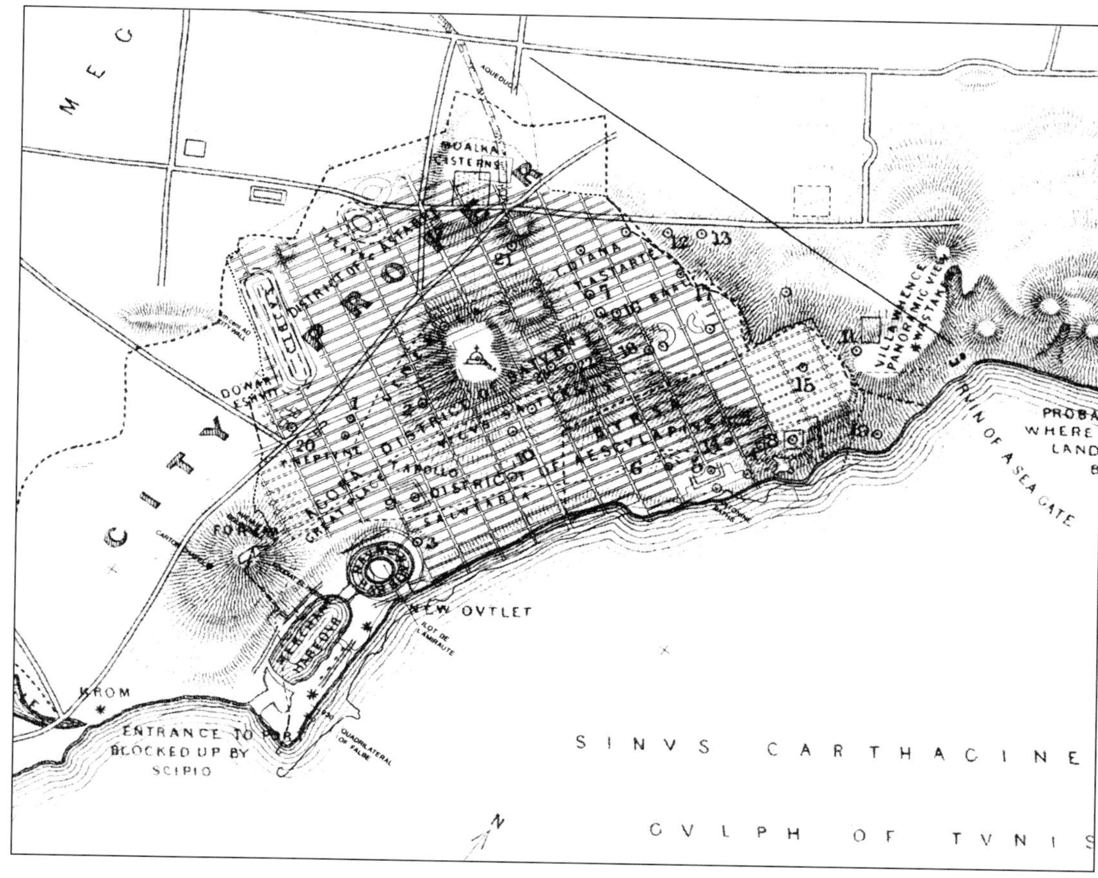

Fig. 4.12 Davis' published map of the area of Roman Carthage, with the street-grid of the city as presently understood superimposed on it at the same scale

away from the sea. The grid preserved the lines of the Roman centuriation, which laid out parcels of agricultural land for the Roman colony. Falbe had noted that the whole plain of La Marsa was divided by roads and paths into squares, and said that he noticed this not on the ground, but only as he mapped his topographical observations. His first pertinent observation was the straight line of the road on the south-east side of the La Malga cisterns. He then noted squares of regular size, which agreed with the Roman definition of a 'century,' or 100 *heredia*, a square 2400 Roman feet per side (708 m). For Augustus' 3,000 colonists, there should have been 3000 *heredia* or 30 centuries; and Falbe was able to pick out twenty-eight squares, with plenty of room for two more.[85] Davis generally preserved the evidence for the rural grid on his published map and confirmed Falbe's observations with two of his own: he marked the road to Tunis 'traces of the ancient double road met with', and the road to Gammarth 'traces of ancient road occasionally met with', but he did not state anything relevant to the rural grid in his text.

In 1924 Charles Saumagne was to demonstrate that the rural and urban grids were most likely surveyed at the same time, because the four lines of the two grids intersect at a point on the summit of the Byrsa. This demonstrates that the latter was the original point of reference for both. This is easiest to see on Saumagne's plan, as he continued the lines of the rural grid across the city in order to show the intersection of the two grid-plans on the summit of the Byrsa (Fig. 4.10).[86] As mentioned above (p. 60), the layout of the urban grid also conforms to Roman land allocations. These facts confirm that the rural and urban grids are both due to deliberate and contemporary decisions by Roman land surveyors (*agrimensores*), who acted within the religious context of the proper foundation of a city. I prefer the hypothesis that both grids were laid out for the Augustan colony of 29 BC. It may be argued, however, that the rural survey took place in an earlier Gracchan or Caesarian foundation, especially because the entire northern half of Tunisia shows evidence for Roman land survey on the same plan and orientation as the rural grid at Carthage.[87]

The orientation of the grid-lines

Orienting oneself correctly to the compass directions is difficult at Carthage. The psychological impulse is to orient oneself by the sea, which is generally to the east. In fact, the urban street-grid of Roman Carthage is thirty degrees off alignment with true north; the *car-*

dines ran, not north, but north-north-east, while the *decumani* ran east-south-east to the sea. The Roman surveyors determined true north (as opposed to magnetic north) by setting up a central point within a circle and sighting from the centre across the circle to the horizon for sunrise and sunset. Once the angle formed by these sightings was determined, the angle was bisected, and the resulting line was oriented north–south. This process could theoretically be done on any day of the year. Once a south or north point was determined, the Romans used a simple sighting device on which two lines crossed at a perpendicular (the *groma*) to sight to the cardinal points. It is certain that Roman surveyors set up the rural and urban grids at Carthage, but neither grid lies on the primary north–south axis. North–south orientation was adopted by the Romans from the Etruscans and had a religious meaning, and it is likely that the different orientation of the Roman city of Carthage also had religious significance.

Despite the common belief that Punic Carthage was obliterated and the Roman foundation was made *de novo*, Rakob's excavations have shown that the Roman urban grid at Carthage overlies and follows exactly the same orientation as a pre-existing Punic orthogonal grid on the eastern, seaward side of the city. In 1887 Vernaz had noted that the early Punic tombs he found were aligned along the Roman aqueduct and the line of a Roman street which we now identify as *cardo* 16 east, but he believed that this was simply chance.[88] In fact, the Punic grid used a base line running down from the Byrsa, which is more or less identical to the line of the *decumanus maximus*. This Punic grid is Greek in inspiration (a 'Hippodamian grid'), and therefore does not pre-date the sixth or more probably the fifth century BC. The Punic street-grid at Carthage had blocks that are only slightly longer but significantly wider than the blocks of the Roman grid: the Punic blocks were approximately 150 m by 50 m while the Roman blocks were about 140 m by 35 m.[89]

Rakob has shown that the orientation of the Roman urban grid exactly followed the alignment of the Punic urban grid, so exactly as to suggest deliberate choice. In the case of the urban grid, the remains of the Punic city were perhaps significant enough to make this orientation the path of least resistance for the Roman founders of Carthage. For example, Rakob's excavations revealed the line of the Punic sea-wall of the city, made of huge ashlar blocks, and along the same line as the Roman street *cardo* 18 east.

Falbe's map is rotated slightly from a north–south orientation to make the best use of space; the resulting orientation is closer to the orientation of the Roman rural grid than the Roman city-grid. The 'north–south' axis of the rural grid is rotated to 30 degrees west of north (330 degrees east of north). The 'east–west' axis of the rural grid (from La Malga to Bordj-Djedid) is therefore on a line 60 degrees east of north. At the summer solstice, the sun rises at approximately 60 degrees east of north,[90] more or less exactly on the 'east–west' axis of the rural grid.[91] Trousset has therefore argued that the rural grid was deliberately oriented to sunrise at the summer solstice. He suggested that the orientation of the rural grid was chosen out of respect for the power of the Punic goddess Tanit or Astarte in her Roman guise as Juno Caelestis.[92] This would be interesting, because it is clear that the rural grid was laid out by Roman, rather than Punic, land-surveyors.

The orientation of the urban street-grid, on the other hand, was first laid out in the Punic era, and might more easily be argued to reflect Punic religious concerns. The 'north–south' axis of the urban grid (on the orientation of the *cardines*) is rotated to 30 degrees east of north. The 'east/west' axis of the urban grid (on the orientation of the *decumani*) is 60 degrees west of north (300 degrees east of north). At the summer solstice, the sun sets at 60 degrees west of north, on the axis of the *decumani*. Delattre long ago recorded that from 6.00 pm on the summer solstice (sunset takes place at 7.30 pm), the sun shone straight down the nave of the cathedral[93] (the cathedral shares the orientation of the Roman city street-grid and its main doors open towards the west-north-west). Trousset has argued that this alignment cannot be a matter of deliberate choice, because the Romans regarded the orientation of the sunset to be the most dangerous orientation possible.[94] Perhaps, however, the orientation of both the rural and urban grids of Roman Carthage had a Punic religious significance, and the orientation of these grids were deliberately taken from the angles of sunrise and sunset at the summer solstice.

Davis' sites in relation to the street-grid of Roman Carthage

Carthage and Her Remains included a quite accurate topographic map of the peninsula of Carthage (Fig. 4.3). Although Davis' map was later derided by Audollent as fantasist and useless,[95] Audollent was not criticizing the map's topography, but rather Davis' highly idiosyncratic identifications of ancient sites. The map is actually very useful for locating the sites of his excavations. Davis must have worked with a professional draftsman to place the sites on his published map. It is also very likely that Davis and his illustrator worked directly from his own plan of Falbe, which he had with him in Carthage and may have marked up while on the site. This hypothesis would explain the accuracy with which Davis' published map follows the topography of the plan of Falbe, as well as the relative accuracy of the location of his own sites.

I used a map of the Roman street-grid of the entire Roman city, developed by the British mission (Fig. 4.11), as an overlay at the same scale as Davis' map,[96] lined up as accurately as possible with the shoreline, the north declivity of the city, and the two harbours. Davis' map fits the modern map very closely in the eastern half of the city (Fig. 4.12). On the western side, although the outlines of both the amphitheatre and the La Malga cisterns are only partly contiguous on the two plans, the general placement is correct. The agreement between those of Davis' sites that can be located exactly by independent evidence and the street-grid is very close; many are no more than the short side of one block (thirty-five meters) east of the point he indicated. This suggests that the other sites indicated on Davis' map can also be located with a similar small margin of error. The result is that the majority of Davis' major finds have specific provenances.

The Department of Greek and Roman Antiquities at the British Museum possesses copies of two sketch-maps of Davis' excavations with copies of a selection of his letters to the Foreign Office. These maps are good copies of maps made by Davis, of which the originals can be found in the British National Archives (Figs 4.13 and 4.14). The sketch-maps are clear and detailed, and contain useful information, but neither the originals nor the copies were topographically accurate or drawn to scale; the sites were represented by numbers, and there was no attempt to represent surveyed-in points.

The map published in *Carthage and Her Remains* documents twenty-five numbered sites (Fig. 4.4), but the numbering differs from that of the sketch-maps. The sketch-map sites and numbers have theoretical equivalents to the points on Davis' published map and text, although some sketch-map sites are missing and some new sites are added (see Table 1). Furthermore, Davis did not refer to these published map numbers until three-quarters of the way through his book, probably at the point where he first had the finished map beside him as he wrote, when he mentioned the 'Temple of Saturn' (Site 23) as (published) map-site no. 16.[97] Davis then mentioned only ten of the published map-site numbers in his text, which creates difficulties in identifying those sites not mentioned in the text or not labelled on the map. The site numbers from the published map are therefore noted in a very restricted section of *Carthage and Her Remains*, over only about fifty or sixty pages of his text: pp. 315–74 (pp. 394–443 of the revised edition). Unfortunately Davis did not edit his earlier manuscript to correlate more site descriptions with his published map numbers.

The ten sites which Davis discussed with the numbers that appear on the published map are site 7 (the Mosaic of the Months and Seasons); sites 12 and 13 (the Roman tombs outside the walls on the northern side of the city); site 16 (the 'Circular Monument'); site 17 (the 'Carthaginian House'); site 18 (the Roman house east of the theatre); site 19 (the seaside structures with mosaics at Falbe no. 90); site 23 (the 'Punic Mine') and sites 24 and 25 (seaside villas at Gammarth). Only four of the numbered sites on the published map are also labelled. The labels demonstrate Davis' fond belief that he was digging at the sites of Punic or Roman temples: 7 ('Temple of Astarte'); 9 ('Temple of Apollo'); 16 ('[Temple of] Baal') and 20 ('Temple of Neptune').

The numbers on Davis' published map suggest that they reflect the chronological order in which the sites were excavated, but this is not correct. The order of excavated sites on the two sketch-maps sent to the Foreign Office, which are earlier and correlate with information in dated letters, is slightly different and must be preferred. For example, the 'Temple of Astarte' is site 7 on the published map, but in his letters and on the sketch-maps it is the eighth site which Davis excavated. I follow the numbering of the sketch-maps in my account of his excavations.

Davis' letters to the Foreign Office provide more data and a chronological structure, and allow many other sites as well to be tied into the overall picture. Furthermore, his published map uses points as well as numbers and labelling to define the sites which he discussed; this fact allows the spot designated to be located much more accurately than on the sketch-maps, where a number or site designation stands alone. In some cases, the equivalency of sites on the different maps can be demonstrated indisputably by their relative position.

Eight sites on Davis' map and also within the street-grid can be correlated with specific monuments and located exactly and independently today; this is crucial, as the location of these sites confirms the general topographical accuracy of his map. The most obvious of these sites is the Circular Monument. Davis published both a plan and a drawing of the site which he called the 'Temple of Baal' or 'Temple of Saturn' (Figs 10.15–10.16),[98] which reveal it to be identical with the structure that was to be re-excavated by Pierre Senay of the Université du Québec à Trois-Rivières in the UNESCO excavations of the 1970s and 1980s.[99] While Senay identified the 'Circular Monument' with a site mentioned in ancient sources as the *Aedes Memoriae* (the 'Temple of Memory'), other scholars prefer to consider the building the fourth-century Christian *memoria* of an unidentified saint (Fig. 10.18).[100]

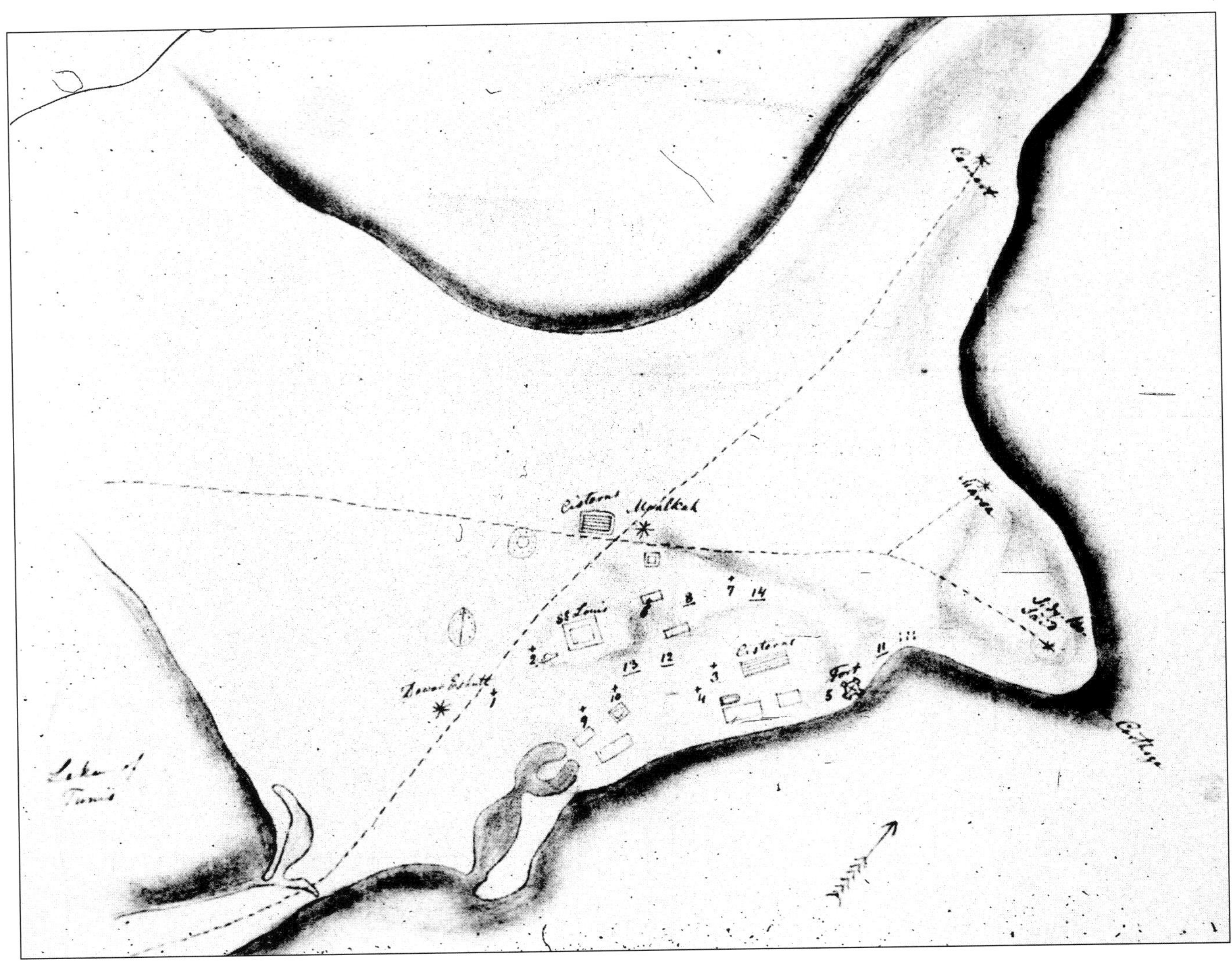

Fig. 4.13 (above) *Davis' first sketch-map of his excavations, hitherto unpublished, now preserved in the British National Archives, Kew (UK). For a key to the numbers, see the Table on p. 82.*

Fig. 4.14 (opposite) *Davis' second sketch-map; kept like that shown in Fig. 4.13 in the British National Archives at Kew, it is also published here for the first time.*

The Circular Monument is site no. 70 on the plan of Falbe, accurately marked as a circle within a square. In his text, Falbe identified the structure only as a 'temple'.[101] He himself was to excavate extensively at the Circular Monument with Grenville Temple in 1838,[102] and in the nineteenth century the concrete core of this structure was among the few immediately visible ancient buildings at Carthage. The patent identity of Davis' 'Temple of Baal/Saturn' (Falbe no. 70) and Senay's Circular Monument, combined with the general topographical accuracy of Davis' map, provide a secure point from which to check the accuracy of Davis' map and its correlation with the street-grid.

Seven other sites excavated by Davis can be located more or less exactly on the ground from physical evidence independent of his map. They include the site with high walls at the south-eastern foot of the Saint Louis Hill (Falbe no. 54); the Bordj-Djedid or eastern cisterns (Falbe no. 65); the south-west latrine of the Antonine Baths (Falbe no. 69); walls to the north of the Turkish fort, near Falbe no. 34; the north-west enclosure wall of the Antonine Baths (Falbe no. 67); the northern gate on the *cardo maximus*, Bab el-Rih (the site in question is actually a Roman triumphal arch rather than a gate; it is marked on the plan of Falbe as a rectangle around a circle); and the site with prostrate column to the west of the Circular Monument.

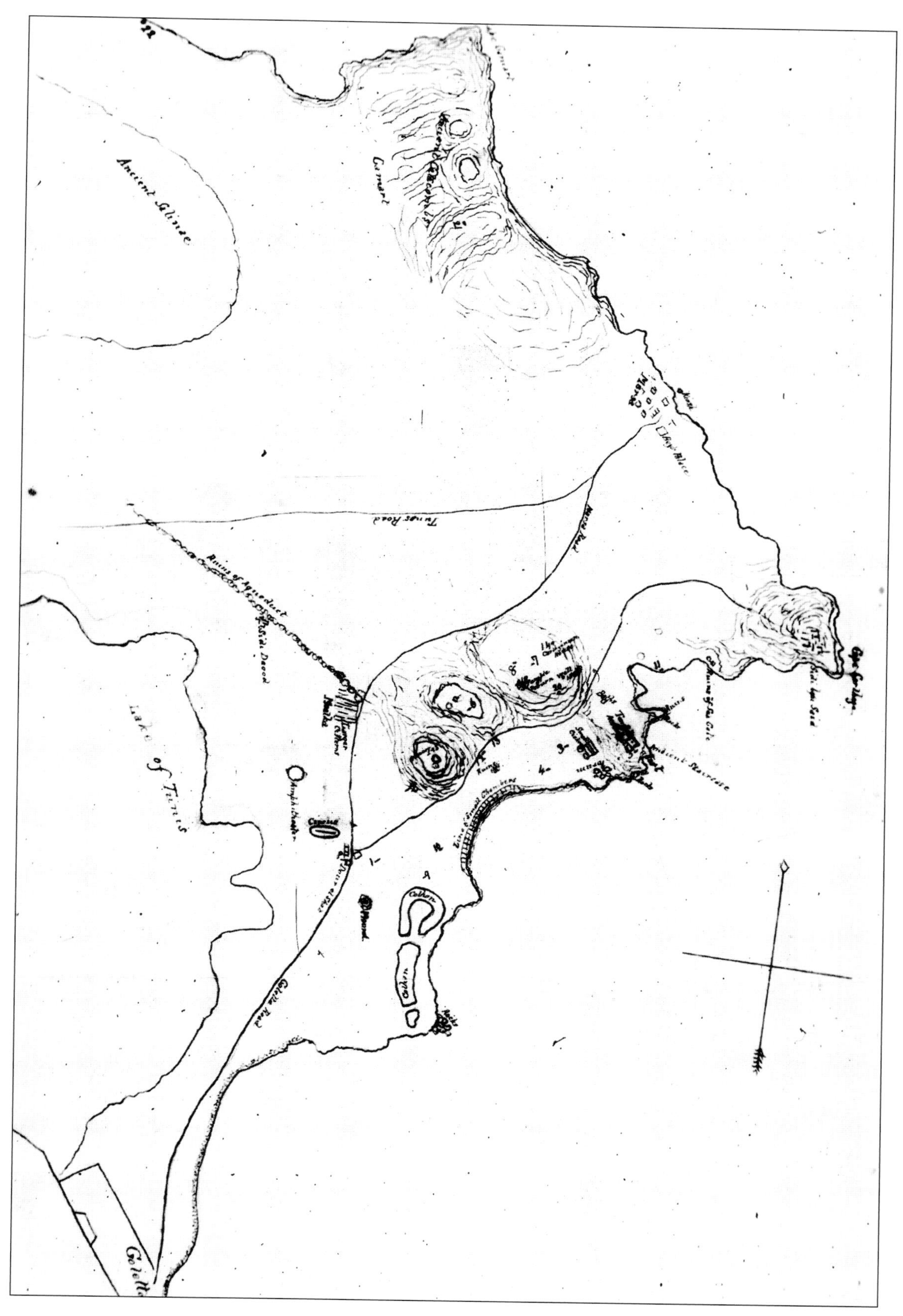
Tunis Road
Ruins of Aqueduct
Lake of Tunis
Amphitheatre
Goletta Road
Ancient Staircase

At least twenty-six and probably thirty of Davis' thirty-five excavation sites at Carthage were within the area defined by the Roman street-grid. Study of his excavation sites shows that while he dug in all the quadrants of the street-grid he preferred the north-eastern quadrant. This area is illustrated on a plan drawn by Lézine in the 1960s (Fig. 8.2). Davis' preference is lucky in terms of identifying the sites today, because he had four hills there by which to orient himself. The north-eastern quadrant of the city also had five visible ancient monuments which were the sites of excavations by Davis and were discussed by him at least briefly: the Circular Monument (Falbe no. 70), the eastern cisterns (Falbe no. 65), the Antonine Baths (Falbe no. 67) with its south-west latrine (Falbe no. 69), and 'Bab el-Rih' (the arch that was marked but not numbered on the plan of Falbe). In addition, Davis oriented himself by the Turkish fort on the summit of Bordj-Djedid, which is also marked on Davis' plan as well as on the plan of Falbe.

Eighteen of twenty-six sites which Davis certainly dug in the Roman city proper are in the north-eastern quadrant of the city or just outside it. The combined evidence of Davis' map, his sketch-maps and his written descriptions allow the addition of thirteen sites in this quarter to the five already mentioned above. In other words, eighteen sites can be located within an area just under one kilometer square. He dug a site, probably of Roman housing, near the Turkish fort; a site that cannot be located exactly on the summit of the Hill of Juno; the site of the Mosaic of the Months and Seasons; the massively-walled double enclosure to the north of the Turkish fort; a sea-side site with four mosaics at Falbe no. 90; the site of the Mosaic with Baskets of Fish and Fruit; the 'Punic mine' of Punic votive *stelae*; the 'Carthaginian House' near Bab el-Rih; the house on the Odeon Hill east of the theatre; another house forty yards away and higher on the slope; the site of the prostrate column near the Circular Monument; and two sites with Roman tombs on the east side of the road following the rural grid. With an understanding of how Davis tends to err in the placement of the sites on his map, these sites can be placed within specific blocks. Furthermore, three of the four mosaics from Gammarth, six to seven kilometers north of the city proper, are from one sea-side villa, and can be located within less than a hundred meters by relating Davis' map to the coastline.

Davis' sites were of Roman, not Punic, date, so relating them to the Roman street-grid is highly relevant. Correlation with the street-grid locates his sites within thirty-five meters. This is nothing like the accuracy which we require in archaeology today, but it places the sites and finds in relation to known structures and within neighbourhoods of the ancient city, and gives each of his finds a meaningful context. In turn, Davis' discoveries illuminate the function of particular areas of Roman Carthage. Only one of the twenty-six mosaics that were certainly sent by Davis from Carthage to London has no accompanying evidence for its original location. The accurate placing of Davis' sites allows for a revolutionary re-evaluation of his work (Fig. 14.2), and simply ignoring his achievements can no longer be justified.

5

Davis gets to work

Davis' strategy and methods

It is likely that Davis was not fully prepared for his success with the Foreign Office and had no detailed plan of action when he arrived at Carthage. His early choice of excavation sites implies that his original strategy was to dig at places marked on the plan of Falbe. He moved from one to another in quick succession, which suggests that he expected quick results, although he did not get them. Riding on horseback over the site of the ancient city, armed with the maps and texts of earlier explorers, he looked for locations which he considered likely to produce results. During his entire excavation career at Carthage, Davis was constantly disappointed by his finds and as a result 'butterflied' from site to site. He described his written sources as useless; unfortunately, random digging was even less rewarding.[1] A few days or at most a few weeks were sufficient for his workmen to reach startling depths, remove tons of earth and find 'nothing', by which Davis meant nothing Punic, nothing in silver or gold, nothing of museum quality.

In his first months of work, his excavations were in the eastern half of the city-grid, the side of the city towards the sea. He avoided the harbours and the cisterns at La Malga, although he thought of both these sites as Punic. His headman had warned him away from the high water table of the harbours, but it is also possible that he thought them unlikely sources of the finds he was looking for. On the other hand, he dug near the Bordj-Djedid cisterns, which he also thought were Punic. He avoided the circus and amphitheatre, possibly because they were clearly Roman public monuments.

Of a total of twenty-six excavation sites within or just outside the Roman street-grid, Davis dug six sites in the southern half of the city compared to twenty sites in the northern half, showing a distinct preference for sites on elevated ground, particularly on Bordj-Djedid and the Odeon Hill. Permission and land rights had some influence on his choices; the Mosaic with Baskets of Fish and Fruit was on the site of a bean field, and Davis had to pay for the lost crop. Once he learned how to retrieve mosaics, he dug the area on the south-western summit of the Odeon Hill because he thought its wide view made it a natural site for luxury housing.[2] This was a great advance, as it was the first time Davis' own experience led to an independent and reasoned approach to the problem of choosing excavation sites at Carthage. He kept some kind of recording system, perhaps even a daily log (he described his trip to Sardinia by referring to his log, but perhaps he meant specifically the record of a sea voyage).[3] In general, dates and accurate chronology seem to have meant nothing to him. He kept accounts of his expenses in order to be reimbursed, and these, made up every three months, appear among the papers Davis sent to the Foreign Office. He also regularly produced lists of the names of his Arab workmen, as Consul Wood had requested.[4] On the other hand, he does not seem to have kept a running list of individual finds, which Wood had asked for as well.[5]

There is no evidence to suggest that drawings of the layout of Davis' trenches were ever made, except for the ground-plan of the soil over the Mosaic of the Months and Seasons.[6] He published drawings of the Mosaic of the Months and Seasons, two Punic votive *stelae*, the Punic inscription on sacrifices, a plan of an apsed room with mosaic floors at Utica, and the ground-plan of the Circular Monument. In addition, I have found large coloured stone-by-stone drawings of the Mosaic of the Months and Seasons (Colour Plates 1 and 2), and a drawing of the ground-plan of the 'Carthaginian House' from published map site 14 among papers in the Foreign Office (Fig. 10.1), while a detailed sketch in coloured pencils of the Vandal Hunting Mosaic (Colour Plate 8) was enclosed with a letter of Davis in the archives of the British Museum.

Davis mentioned Henry Ferriere as a man 'to whose artistic taste I am indebted for several illustrations'. Ferriere was the son of Lewis Ferriere, the former British vice-consul and sometime acting consul general at Tunis, who had given Clarendon a positive recommendation of Davis.[7] Davis published Ferriere's drawings of the site of the Circular Monument, of the 'Carthaginian House' during excavation, of the vaults of the eastern cisterns and the La Malga cisterns, as well as essentially indecipherable illustrations of the ruins of the staircase to the 'Temple of Aesculapius,' the Antonine Baths, and the 'Sea-Gate'.[8] Davis promised 'upwards of one hundred illustrations, executed in the best style' for a volume, *Carthaginian Remains Illustrated*, noting that 'the mosaics are all to be coloured and the bas-reliefs and inscriptions reduced . . .'. The volume, which he was aware would be expensive to produce, never appeared, and the drawings have evidently been lost.[9]

Davis was concerned about the need to make a photographic record and had acquired photographic equipment early,[10] but he never found the time to use it. Photography in the field was a new technology at the time.[11] Engravings from photographs were included in Davis' text, but they suggest that photography was unwieldy and slow, better suited to capturing scenic views than recording excavation and finds. Nevertheless, his exact contemporary and implicit rival, Charles Newton, took a photographer with him to his excavations at Halicarnassos,[12] and Newton presented copies of his photographs and drawings to the German Archaeological Institute.[13] Davis made a trip to Cagliari in Sardinia with HMS *Curaçoa* in the summer of 1857 and brought back a professional photographer,[14] but there is no evidence that finds were photographed.

In short, Davis' recording seems to have been minimal, and he was content to report what he had found after the fact in his letters to the Foreign Office. This was particularly long after the fact in the case of his 'Statement explanatory of the contents of fifty-one cases of antiquities embarked on board the HMS *Supply*' of December 21st, 1858, which included a summary of everything found since the second departure of the *Curaçoa* in July 1857. When the finds were picked up by the *Supply* in October 1858, Davis was too ill to write. If he had not survived the illness, we would know almost nothing about the circumstances of the finds made in that year-long period.

Davis, at least at times, used trenches that were laid out before excavation began, and was disdainful of earlier excavators, like Sir Grenville Temple, who had dug formless pits. He said, 'My plan of operations was to mark out a certain number of narrow trenches, and set my men to work'.[15] When he began digging at published site 17 (Site 16, the 'Carthaginian House'), he laid out three oblique trenches, each four feet wide by twenty feet long (1.2 m by 6.0 m), spaced twenty-five feet (7.6 m) apart. Twenty yards away he put in three more trenches, evidently following the same scheme, for a total excavated area equivalent to about 120 one-meter square trenches.[16] Since I cannot know what he means by 'oblique', I can only observe that the complex of trenches seems to have covered an extent of forty yards (36.6 m) in the longest direction, which was a little longer than the short side of a Roman city block. The 'Carthaginian House' was found on this site, with mosaics, including the Mosaic Imitating Green Marble, appearing at a depth of between ten and twelve feet (3.0 m to 3.7 m) (Fig. 10.2). Once Davis had unearthed a mosaic, he cleared the entire room rather than continue to observe the boundaries of his trenches. The trenches he described at or near the 'Punic mine' are more bizarre; here Davis laid out radiating trenches that looked like a spider's web. The technique was nevertheless an effective sampling strategy, given that Davis was involved in a blind search for archaeological remains.[17] The trenches described had an aggregate length of 300 feet (91.4 m), and were mostly four feet wide (1.2 m) and dug to a depth of between six and fifteen feet (1.8 m to 4.6 m).[18] Clearly these schemes were fairly arbitrary and had administrative as well as scientific significance; they defined areas for the workmen to attack. Unlike many other early excavators at Carthage, Davis also conscientiously backfilled his trenches when his excavations were over, fulfilling the agreements he had made with various landowners.[19]

Davis had a nascent concept of stratigraphy, but he did not record or apply stratigraphic evidence consistently. Like most archaeologists of his day, he did not rigorously distinguish between evidence for Punic and Roman Carthage. Earlier in his book he stated that Punic and Roman Carthage were still to be found under a great deposit of gradually accumulating soil, and that ruins which predated the final Punic war were nearly twenty feet below the surface, which to him suggested an average accumulation of a foot per century, although he expected deeper cover over low ground and shallower over exposed or high sites.[20] Later he implied that the relative depth of earlier periods was more or less absolute; Roman pavements occurred at a depth of between two and five or six feet, while Punic ones appeared at a depth of ten feet or more.[21] The second Mosaic of Nereids and Tritons, found in the 'Temple of Neptune' at Davis' thirty-fifth site, lay below eighteen feet of earth,[22] which Davis would have taken as evidence that this structure was also Punic. Davis opined that ruins which appeared above the surface were usually Roman,[23] but then argued that the great cisterns of La Malga and Bordj-Djedid and perhaps the Circular Monument, which met that criterion, were Punic.[24] In his day, construction in concrete was not yet clearly associated with the Romans; even Beulé never explicitly stated that concrete construction was Roman, although he recognized the fact in specific cases.[25]

Davis and his workmen

Davis worked with an Arab headman, Ali Karema, whom he had chosen from the group that surrounded him on an early organizational visit to Carthage; the man's qualifications were his intelligence, energy and roguishness.[26] Ali Karema was nevertheless an ignorant man, and Davis was amused to find that Ali was ready to believe that Davis could fly, on the one hand, and that the man had no idea of the correct order of the months, on the other.[27] Given Ali's excavation experience, Davis often, but not always, took his advice; he had plenty of chance to hear it at the beginning of his excavations, since Ali spent the evenings with him at Douar ech-Chott, discussing plans for the next day, and then locked Davis safely in before going off for the night.[28] When Davis considered digging at the 'Cothon,' he took Ali Karema's advice against it; Ali had dug there for stone for the Khaznadar's house throughout an entire summer, and knew by experience that they would meet the water-table at seven or eight feet. The French archaeologist, Charles Beulé, was to dig there in the autumn of 1859, but could go down only about eleven feet, which was already well below the water-table; Davis implied that Beulé had wasted his time.[29]

During the early excavations, Ali and his men began to lose confidence in Davis when the sites chosen were unproductive, despite the fact that the latter based his decisions on information from books, to which his illiterate men gave great authority.[30] Nevertheless Davis provided his readers with many impressive examples of his masterful management of his workmen. He often derided his ignorant and gullible men, and revelled in the ease with which he was able to command their obedience. In an early letter, he said, '. . . I find the Arabs extremely docile and, though not very active, yet steady labourers'.[31] The story as understood by an anonymous correspondent to the *Illustrated London News* was a little harsher: 'The Arabs are a thoroughly lazy sort of fellows . . . Three or four pounds of soil is considered a load . . . Two English navigators would do the work of eight or ten of these lazy Mahometans'. An illustration of eight of Davis' men at work shows them passing small baskets along to the spoil heap; it is not clear that any one of them is actually digging, but the irregularly-shaped trench, which has neat vertical sides, seems to be about five feet deep (Fig. 5.1). The men were clearing a chamber, and the artist has represented a wall of stone

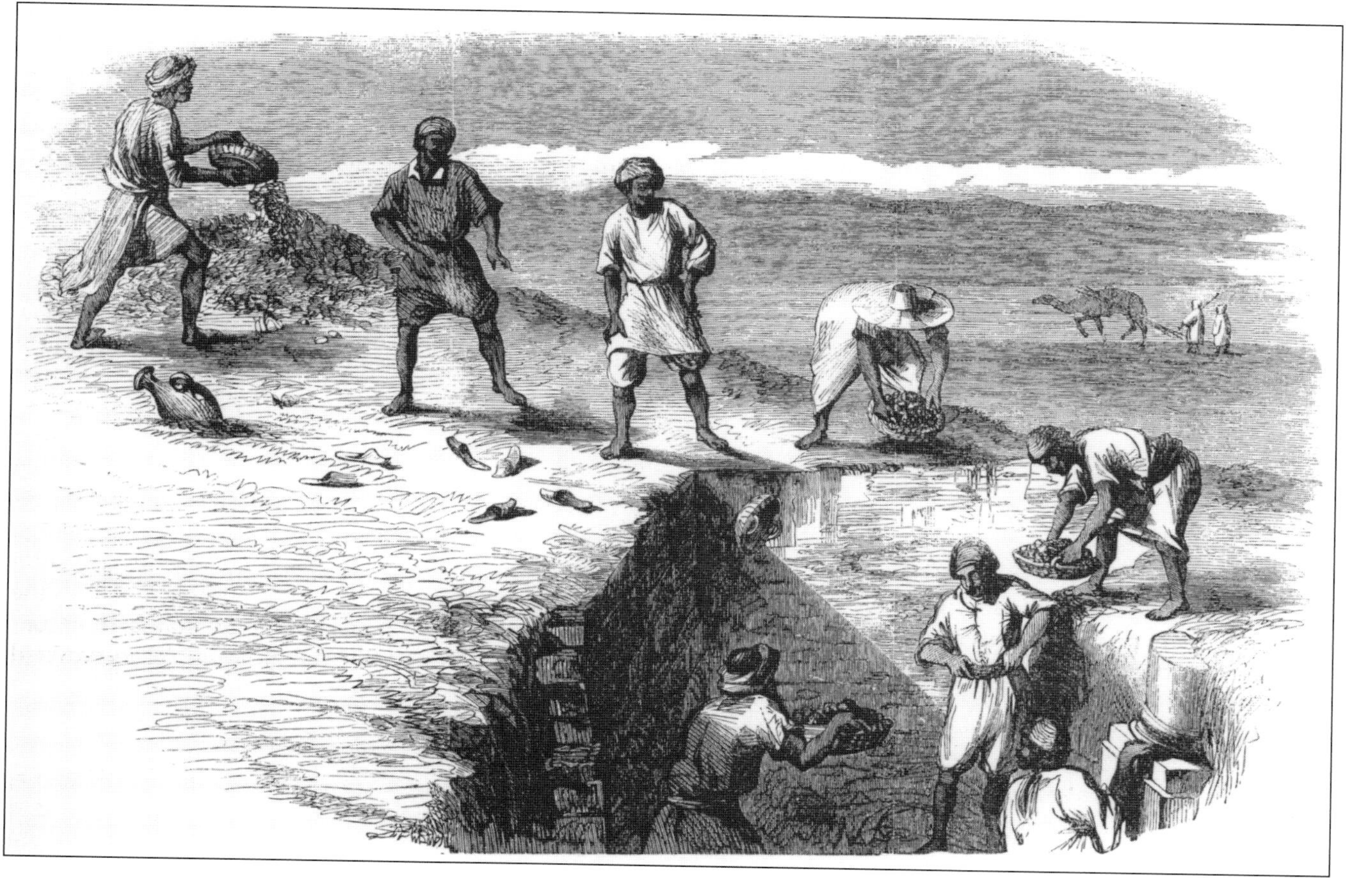

Fig. 5.1. Davis' men at work, as shown in The Illustrated London News *on May 15th, 1858. The accompanying text observes: 'The Arabs are most difficult to manage. Sometimes in the middle of the day they will strike and go away altogether. Our sketch represents one party excavating a chamber, and, just at the time this sketch was being made, the base of the column on the right-hand side was being cleared away.'*

masonry along one side of the trench, while a pilaster and column base *in situ* was being cleared while the drawing was in progress.[32]

Matters were not always so serene. At one point, Davis jumped into the trench and personally assaulted a workman who accused him of cursing Islam; his remaining workmen applauded this reaction, and even the victim of the assault, who lost his job, later apologized.[33] The situation was potentially a dangerous one for Davis, as it happened in the aftermath of an international incident in the summer of 1857 caused by the execution in Tunis of a Jew who had cursed Islam. The incident led to united pressure from Britain and France for human rights reform in Tunisia.[34]

The morale of his men seems to have been relatively high, however, and Davis never accused them of robbing him or the excavation. The rarity with which coins were found suggests that Davis was systematically deceived with regard to coins and similarly to small finds. His attitude to his men was very different from that of a later archaeologist at Carthage, however, who spoke of excavating a workman's mouth at the end of the day.[35] In the one case where Davis dealt with a clear case of theft, at Utica, he believed that a European had commissioned it.[36]

European visitors

Davis gave the impression that he ran his excavation at Carthage single-handedly, but he was seldom without the companionship of Europeans and Americans for long. Consul Richard Wood kept a close eye on him and expected monthly reports from him. Wood obtained the Tunisian permits for Davis' excavation at Utica, which took place in June 1858, and for which Davis had the co-operation of Captain Porcher and the officers and men of HMS *Harpy*, who provided the workforce.[37] Their participation had been approved by the Admiral of the British fleet in the Mediterranean, Lord Lyons, who enthusiastically supported Davis' excavations.[38]

Davis also received reporters and tourists. Although visits to Carthage by tourists were not yet common, people distinguished by their wealth and education were already coming to Carthage as one of a range of broadening travel experiences. The visitors were intellectually stimulating for Davis; at the same time each of these encounters increased public awareness of his endeavours and raised his social standing.[39] An American travel writer, George Leighton Ditson, published an article on Davis' excavations in the *New York Tribune*, which must have appeared sometime after the spring of 1857.[40]

From the beginning of his researches, Davis was regularly joined by amateur photographers. He thanked Alfred Cox, W. J. C. Moens, the Marquis de Noailles, Henry Ferriere and Lieutenant Porcher for illustrations.[41] The first three were photographers. Davis published a view of the ports photographed by the Marquis de Noailles, whom he met during the latter's travels in North Africa.[42] A photograph of the 'sea gate' (Falbe no. 72) was taken by Alfred Cox, and Davis also published a panoramic photograph of Carthage taken from the house of Sidy Mustapha by photographers Alfred Cox and W. J. C. Moens, whom Davis described only as friends. The house of Sidy Mustapha, Davis' friend the 'Lord Keeper of the Seal,' was between Carthage and Sidi bou-Said. It is labelled 'Villa whence panoramic view was taken' on Davis' published map. The camera was aimed to the west and away from the sea and from the split peak of Bou Kornein – an unusual choice, with the chapel of Saint Louis only barely discernible on the left side of the photograph.[43]

The *Illustrated London News* ran a number of articles mentioning Davis' excavations; not surprisingly, they varied in their accuracy. The article published in mid-May, 1858, which showed Davis' men at work (Fig. 5.1), also explained that the Reverend N. Davis was carrying on excavations at Carthage for the British Museum, and added 'permission to dig was granted entirely through the influence which Mr Davis has with the Bey of Tunis, and perhaps few men besides Mr Davis would have been able to overcome the religious and political difficulties. . .'.[44] So far, so good, but in an article two weeks later the anonymous correspondent (perhaps not the same person who wrote the earlier article), ascribed the excavation of the Mosaic Imitating Green Marble to the 'Rev. W. Davies' (Fig. 10.2). The editor confused Davis the excavator at Carthage with an Anglican curate who had recently published a book about his three-month stay in Algiers in the company of his ill wife.[45] A drawing by Arthur Hall of the scene with the 'Mosaic Pavement, Discovered at Carthage' accompanied the article. This drawing is so similar to one that appears in *Carthage and Her Remains* as to suggest that both were made from the same vantage point and perhaps on the very same day.[46]

Another important article appeared in March 1859, near the end of Davis' excavations at Carthage. The writer noted that Mr Davis, previously alone in the field, had recently been joined by M. Beulé, a professor of archaeology at Paris. This correspondent wrote that the excavations at Carthage, 'the results of very limited and economical expenditures', were now attracting so many tourists, 'literary, scientific and fashionable', that 'every steamer brings fresh visitors'. Despite the fact that Mr Davis was named correctly at the beginning of the article, he appeared as the Rev. Mr Davies near the end, which suggests that a careless editor compiled the story from more than one source. Sketches by Arthur Hall again accompanied the story, one of the Circular Monument at Carthage, and the other of the Roman shrine at Zaghouan, the mountain source of the Carthage aqueduct.[47]

Singling out his most distinguished visitors, Davis mentioned the visits of Admiral Lord Lyons, of Lady Franklin, who accompanied him to Utica in May 1858, and of Prince Alfred, whom he guided to the sites of Carthage and Oudna in January 1859.[48] Others who visited Davis and his excavations included the German scholar von Maltzan in the fall of 1857, the Irish MP William Gregory in November 1857, and the French novelist Flaubert in May 1858.

Another visitor was the Reverend Joseph Blakesley, an Anglican vicar with a Cambridge degree, who visited Carthage very briefly at the beginning of May 1858.[49] Blakesley had been compelled to winter in North Africa because of poor health.[50] He recorded meeting Davis, who invited him to dinner at his home at Gammarth. Blakesley described Davis as busy removing a mosaic with the help of half a dozen Arab workmen, but said not a word to describe the mosaic or record where it was found. In return for Davis' hospitality, Blakesley criticized his project; he found it dubious that the government should pay Davis to send home 'objects of amusement to holiday folk in England'.[51] His reference to the excavations gave Davis some useful publicity, but his observation that Davis put the Byrsa on Bordj-Djedid came to the attention of Beulé, the distinguished young French archaeologist, and almost certainly played a part in motivating Beulé to come to Carthage.[52]

Davis' first site: vaulting south-east of the circus

Davis began excavation on November 11th, 1856, and dug at seven sites in the two months before he came upon his first major find in January 1857. This was the Mosaic of the Months and Seasons, which was found at the eighth site he excavated. The first seven sites were indicated on his first and second sketch-maps, and are scattered across the eastern half of the street-grid of Roman Carthage. The location of these sites shows that Davis was making serious efforts to excavate at potentially productive sites, and was no doubt perplexed by his repeated failures to find objects of any interest.

The numbers given to Davis' sketch-map sites are the best indicators of the real order of excavation (see the Table on p. 82 for correlations of Davis' site numbers on his published map, Fig. 4.4, and the sketch-maps, Figs 4.13 and 4.14). At least the first few of these was dug during the autumn plowing and seeding time, and Davis chose archaeological sites with ruins, avoiding land that could be used for agriculture. Falbe's plan, from which Davis was working, marked and even outlined such sites.

Davis described excavation at his first two sites in an early chapter of *Carthage and Her Remains*.[53] His first site (Site 1) was in the south-eastern quarter of the Roman city, near the Arab village of Douar ech-Chott, where Davis had signed a contract to rent a house in early December. The present elevation in the area is very low, about seven to eight meters above sea-level, and the ground may have still been part of the shallow Lake of Tunis in the early Punic era. Davis came back to the near neighbourhood in 1859 to dig his last site, Site 35, and discovered a second-century mosaic 18 feet (5.5 meters) below the surface, demonstrating that almost the entire depth of soil had built up since the Roman colonization of the city.

Excavation here uncovered vaulting east of the eastern end of the circus. Although it was not evident to nineteenth-century archaeologists, the eastern end of the circus is the oval end, with the starting gates at the western end.[54] On his first sketch-map (Fig. 4.13), Davis used the convention of marking the numbers of sites that had ruins with a plus, and underlining the number if there were significant finds. His first site had ruins but no finds. His second sketch-map (Fig. 4.14) shows the site just on the east side of the then existing road to La Marsa. Falbe's plan had shown the same road, and Falbe no. 73, the closest numbered ruin on the plan of Falbe (Fig. 3.2), is also on the east side of the road; but the location of no. 73 does not agree with the placement of Davis' site. Falbe no. 73, which Falbe described as 'a building dependent on the circus', is about fifty meters beyond the eastern end of the circus and aligns with its central barrier.

Davis' first site is about one long Roman city block (100–150 m) north-east of Falbe no. 73. The site is located where *decumanus* 4 south crossed the *cardo maximus*. Although he did not know it, Davis' site was very close to the main north–south street of the Roman city. Falbe noted a small unnumbered ruin between his no. 73 and no. 54 that is very close to the point Davis indicated. If this is the site which the latter excavated, he chose a quite insignificant site on Falbe's plan for his first investigation.

A fragment of ruin was visible above the ground at this first site; as noted above (p. 70), Davis said that according to his later experience ruins above ground indicated remains of Roman date. He cleared a line of three vaulted chambers, each measuring twenty-two by ten feet (*c.* 7 m by 3 m), which 'communicated with each other by lofty doors'. Davis had no interest in architecture for its own sake and did not describe the structure adequately, but he did say that the walls, of massive squared blocks, were fourteen feet high (4.3 m) up to the beginning of the vaults, while the vaults were constructed of concrete ('cement') which was as solid as the stone walls. Davis set his men to clearing one of these chambers, over which most of the vault had collapsed, leaving only a half-arch. They cleared the unroofed area, leaving the soil standing under the surviving vault. When Davis returned, his men had reached the floor of the chamber, fifteen or sixteen feet (4.6 m to 4.9 m) down. Seeing the danger, he ordered them to come up out of the trench, into which the unexcavated soil immediately collapsed, although the surviving structure stood firm.

The individual chambers of this vaulted structure were relatively small. The structure sounds too finely constructed to be a cistern, and the vaulted chambers were similar in size to the supporting vaults which Davis later found on the south-west side of the Hill of Saint Louis (Site 25). On the other hand, Saumagne's later excavation of hydraulic installations, including cisterns and a water tower, to the south-west of Douar ech-Chott – nearby, but closer to Davis' latest site – supports the possibility that Davis' structure was a cistern complex. Saumagne described a line of cisterns with the features Davis described, including communicating doors and walls made of stone blocks; the dimensions of the individual chambers are not the same but they are on the same large scale.[55] No matter what their specific purpose, rows of vaulted chambers were a characteristic component of the Roman architecture of Carthage, providing a potential platform for structures at a higher level. They were of no interest to Davis, who noted that his only finds here consisted of 'a marble hand, and a few terracotta lamps'.[56]

In 1884, a quarter of a century after Davis' excavations, Salomon Reinach and Ernest Babelon came to Carthage to test the ideas of Charles Tissot on Punic Carthage by excavation.[57] Although one of their trenches, Dar Fedriani, was one long city-block (150 m) south of Davis' first trench, their account of their excavation and finds here provide comparable evidence of Roman construction. The trench of Reinach and Babelon was far bigger than any Davis dug, but no deeper. Reinach and Babelon did not publish plans of their work at Douar ech-Chott, because there were no Punic remains. As noted above (p. 52), Punic finds from this area are intrinsically unlikely. In their publication Reinach and Babelon briefly catalogued eighteen Roman lamps specifically from the trench at Douar ech-Chott. Five of these are certainly late Roman by form or by Christian motif, while two belong to the early empire.[58] No doubt Davis did not discover Punic finds or contexts in this area either, and the range of his lamp finds was probably similar.

Davis' second site: a massive bath-house at Falbe no. 54

Davis' second site (Site 2) lay in the centre of the Roman city at the foot of the south-west slope of the Hill of Saint Louis or Byrsa. Although still just within the south-eastern quarter, Davis had moved to a higher elevation, between twenty and twenty-five meters above sea-level. This site correlates with Falbe no. 54, where some fragments of ancient concrete wall are still standing today. Davis mentioned two walls standing to a height of thirty feet (9 m) among a 'ponderous mass of shapeless masonry'. Davis found the structure itself incomprehensible, the means of its destruction even more so, and never formulated a hypothesis on the identity of the site. He merely noted this as another site with ruins where nothing was found. In fact, he mentioned a leg and thigh in dark marble, part of a statue for which, to his puzzlement, no joins could be found. Davis did not see the clear signs that he was digging in an area that had been previously disturbed. Roman architectural finds from a depth of twelve feet (3.7 m) in other trenches at this site included marble and granite columns and a fine Corinthian capital.[59] Davis said that he dug here for nearly two weeks, in which time he sank one trench to a depth of thirty feet. An excavation nine meters deep might well have taken him down to Punic levels, which Davis elsewhere said he expected to find at a depth of twenty feet (6 m) of soil; but there is no evidence that he found anything of Punic date in the trench.

In Falbe's day, nearly twenty-five years before Davis' excavation, massive standing ruins at the site of no. 54 were clear enough to outline. The large enclosure marked by Falbe takes up an area equivalent to about half a Roman city-block at Carthage, but it is significantly wider than the short side of a Roman city-block. According to Falbe's plan, the main axis of the building lay on a north-west alignment and obliquely across *decumanus* 2 south and *cardo* 1 east on the Roman street-grid. The nearly square outer wall of the structure was about sixty-two meters across, judging from Falbe's scale, with a wide but shallow hemicycle on the eastern side. Falbe also saw evidence for an entrance on the eastern side, that is, facing the sea.[60] He classed no. 54 with a group of ruins he described as 'temples and large buildings', and implied that it might be the Temple of Apollo, which ancient sources said lay between the ports and the Byrsa.

In this same area, on the south-west side of the plateau of the Byrsa and down the slope near no. 54,

Falbe had noted evidence for different periods of construction, in that the walls (including those of Falbe no. 54) were not parallel to those to the north-east; in modern terms, they were not aligned with the Roman street-grid. The orientation of the building provides a clue to its date, as the basic integrity of the Roman street-grid was observed in construction at Carthage from the Augustan foundation down to at least the Vandal conquest in the fifth century.

Davis' site is indicated by a point on his map and falls at the intersection of *decumanus* 2 south and *cardo* 1 east, while the outline of Falbe no. 54 is on the same *decumanus* and between the *cardo maximus* and *cardo* 2 east, less than twenty meters off Davis' point and certainly indicating the same large building. The plan of the building, as well as its concrete construction, suggests a large public bath rather than a temple. Judging from ancient literary sources and Falbe's plan, Dureau de la Malle had tentatively identified the site as the 'Baths of Gargilius,' which Saint Augustine described as a cool place in the centre of the city where an important church council was held in AD 411;[61] however, this identification is too early to agree with the building's orientation and the suggested dating of the important carpet mosaic that was found on the site before Davis worked there, and of which he seemed to be unaware. A mosaic with medallions depicting a personified Carthage, the Seasons, charioteers and hunting scenes had been found at this site in 1844 by Tunisian workmen who were robbing out stone for the canal at the port of La Goulette. The mosaic was first published in 1850 by Alphonse Rousseau, who was French acting consul when Davis began his excavations in the autumn of 1856. Rousseau both drew the mosaic (Fig. 6.3) and sent information about the site to *Revue Archéologique*.[62]

Rousseau went back to the site after the mosaic had been lifted and excavated briefly in the area that the mosaic had covered. There in the ruins of older structures, he found a mutilated marble head which he believed would have belonged to a life-sized statue of Juno. This, together with a fragmentary block of mosaic which he believed to be Punic, led him to suppose that the building in which the mosaic lay was from the 'last era of Roman Carthage', and that it had been built over an imposing building of earlier date. Aware of the scholarly theories of Falbe and Dureau de la Malle, Rousseau neatly but no doubt incorrectly hypothesized that the later building was the Baths of Gargilius, built over the earlier Temple of Apollo. Gauckler was later to suggest that the site was a large public bath,[63] and Davis' description corroborates this interpretation. The massive size and concrete construction of the building make it unlikely that the carpet mosaic excavated there in 1844 belonged to a private residence, as was suggested by Frank Clover.[64]

The mosaic discovered by Rousseau has received a good deal of scholarly attention. Gauckler identified the lady in the middle of the first row of medallions as a personification of Carthage.[65] Most recently, Clover has made a convincing case that the mosaic should be dated to the middle of the Vandal period, *c.* AD 500. This might suggest that the building itself was from the mid-Vandal era; if so, the irregular orientation of such a massive public building would confirm the hypothesis that the Vandals did not necessarily respect the Roman street-grid. Perhaps Falbe no. 54 was actually the Basilica of Thrasamund, baths which Frank Clover has argued were built by the Vandal king *c.* AD 500 (see further p. 89 below).[66]

Davis returned to the site at a later but unspecified date and recovered a small Mosaic of Birds in Square Frames (Fig. 5.2). The mosaic consisted of three contiguous square compartments, each two feet six inches (0.76 m) square, framed by discontinuous lines of single cable, with a different bird in each (two ducks and a quail), as well as a scrap of vegetal decoration.[67]

Davis' third site: excavations around the Bordj-Djedid cisterns

After his first two excavations, Davis moved to the north-eastern quadrant of the city, continuing to choose relatively high ground. The point marking his third site on his published map was on the south side

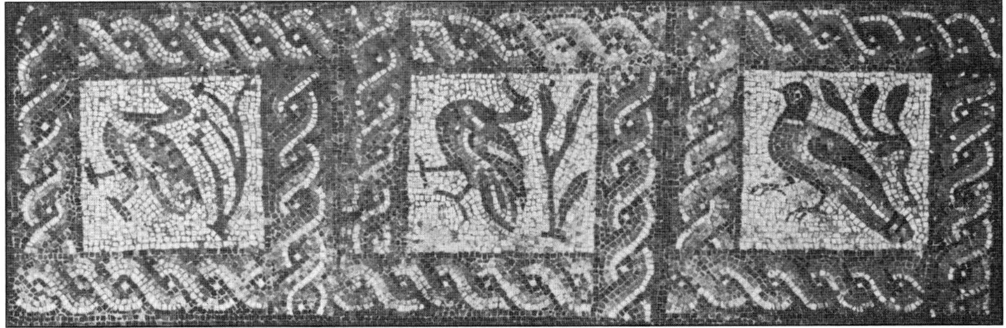

Fig. 5.2 Carthage, the Mosaic of Birds in Square Frames, of uncertain date (fifth/sixth century AD?)

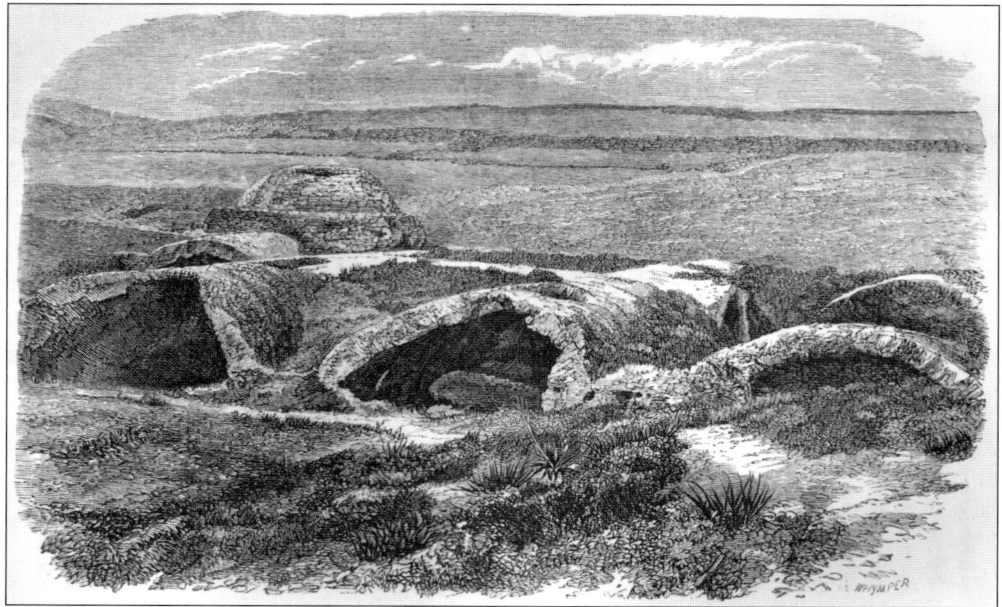

Fig. 5.3 (left) *The Bordj-Djedid cisterns, as recorded by Davis in his* Carthage and Her Remains

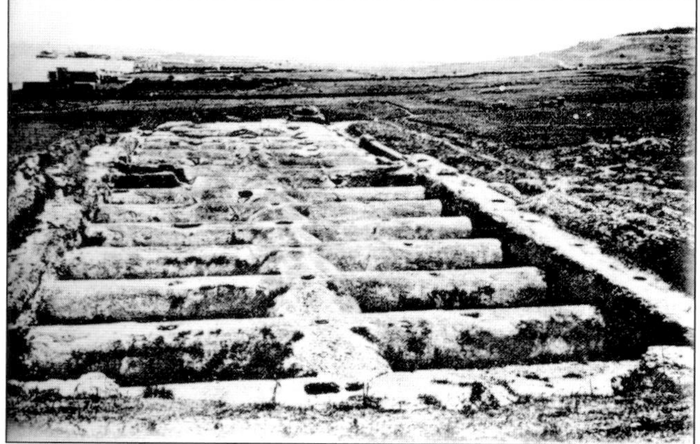

Fig. 5.4 (below) *The Bordj-Djedid cisterns in a photograph taken by J. André Garrigues in 1885, before their restoration. Known locally as the Doumès ech-Chiatinn ('The Devil's underground'), they comprised 16 contiguous reservoirs, each 30 m long and 7.50 m wide; total water capacity is estimated at about 20,000 cu. m.*

of the cisterns on Bordj-Djedid (Site 3); the brief and exasperated description of his excavations here came late in his book.[68] This was another site with ruins where Davis found nothing significant. On the second sketch-map, the site was placed south-west of the cisterns, which were inaccurately outlined and misaligned. On the published map, the point is east of the south end of the cisterns, which again are slightly misaligned. The cisterns themselves are accurately outlined on Falbe's plan as no. 65.

By correlation with the street-grid, Davis' third site, on the south-eastern corner of the cisterns, falls at the intersection of *decumanus* 5 north and *cardo* 16 east. His site was more probably thirty to fifty meters to the east, since his map shows the point slightly to the east of the cisterns. Davis said that he dug more than one unsuccessful trench in this area, which may explain why the placement of the point varies slightly on his maps. The vaulting of the cisterns was partly above ground on the south side, and he certainly did not dig inside the cisterns, which still held some water and had not been completely filled in (Fig. 5.3 and cf. Fig. 5.4). The surrounding area was the site of good housing in Roman times, although nothing specific is known of this particular block.[69] For Davis it provided nothing but frustration, and he refused to bore his readers with a description of his efforts here.

As mentioned earlier (pp. 45–6), the cisterns themselves lie inside a steeply rising slope, with just the upper part of the southern end of the cisterns visible above ground. The elevation of the ground at the south end of the cisterns is between twenty and twenty-five meters above sea-level, but it is between thirty-five and forty meters at the north end.[70] Davis had almost nothing to say about the eastern cisterns,[71] but visitors like Temple and Falbe had been quite taken by them. In the spring of 1858, the same cisterns struck Flaubert far more romantically. Flaubert described visiting the interior, noting the surviving dome with its top open, the light, the dusty silence, the plants hanging down from above and the water in some of the basins. His visit inspired a vivid, if unhistorical, passage in the fourth chapter of *Salammbô*, Flaubert's novel of Punic Carthage.[72]

Davis did not say whether the trenches he had dug in the area of the Bordj-Djedid cisterns were extensive or deep, and it is not clear that he dug to the south of the cisterns or only there, but subsequent excavations by Gouvet and Vernaz showed interesting contexts in areas which Davis obviously missed. In 1862, only five years after Davis' excavations in the area, Gouvet, a

French engineer in the service of the Bey, was commissioned to clean out and restore the Bordj-Djedid cisterns. In one of the cylindrical reservoirs, Gouvet found a large bronze tap fastened to the end of a piece of lead pipe; this characteristically Roman object was exhibited at the Universal Exposition at Paris.[73] Daux wrote that Gouvet also dug a trench ten meters deep on the south side of the cisterns. Vernaz later reported that Gouvet's trench was perpendicular to the south facade of the Bordj-Djedid cisterns and followed a drain.[74]

In 1884 Vernaz said that along the drain Gouvet had found Christian tombs; one of them was covered by a re-used tile with a stamp of Perellius Hedulus.[75] Perellius Hedulus was a wealthy citizen of early Roman Carthage and priest of the cult of Augustus. It is likely that the same man also erected the altar of Augustus near the 'Temple of the Magna Mater' on the eastern slope of the Hill of Saint Louis.[76] In this same trench and already at a 'great depth', Gouvet found a burnt layer. The finds from below it show that the burnt layer was Roman, although the excavator did not explicitly recognize this. Below the burnt layer was the cross-road of a paved street, which overlaid a well-made sewer, a characteristically Roman ensemble, which would have dated to the second century AD.[77] Gouvet was therefore the second investigator, after Falbe, to uncover a Roman street at Carthage, perhaps *decumanus* 5 north, which lay immediately on the south side of the cisterns. The fact that the street was found at a great depth suggests that the whole south face of the Bordj-Djedid cisterns was originally above ground. Gouvet identified Roman housing in the same area, and beneath that, groups of very early [Punic] tombs, oriented north-west by south-east, all already robbed. With his characteristic tendency to fantasy, Daux was to comment that as these tombs were found at the depth of ten meters, they must have preceded the Phoenician settlement.[78]

In 1884 Vernaz, like Gouvet a French engineer, again excavated in the block lying to the south of the Bordj-Djedid cisterns.[79] The French had occupied Tunisia in 1881, and Vernaz had a government commission to make the cisterns reusable. The excavations of both Gouvet and Vernaz revealed Roman houses, streets and tombs and early Punic tombs in the area immediately to the south of the Bordj-Djedid cisterns; they also showed that intact Punic finds could be excavated from tombs, sometimes very near the sites which Davis chose to explore.

Davis' fourth site: the latrine of the Antonine Baths

The huge complex of ruins on the shore (Fig. 5.5) at Falbe nos 69 and 67 tempted Davis to dig at a lower elevation. His fourth site (Site 4) is also in the north-eastern quarter of the Roman city, but lies only between five and ten meters above sea-level. Here Davis excavated the earliest mosaic he found, but he did not attempt to lift it. The site was equivalent to Falbe no. 69, where Falbe showed a roughly semicircular line of wall; in his accompanying text, Falbe said that this wall had a chord of 120 ft (36.6 m), and that its portico was 160 ft (48.8 m) across.[80] Falbe no. 69 was on

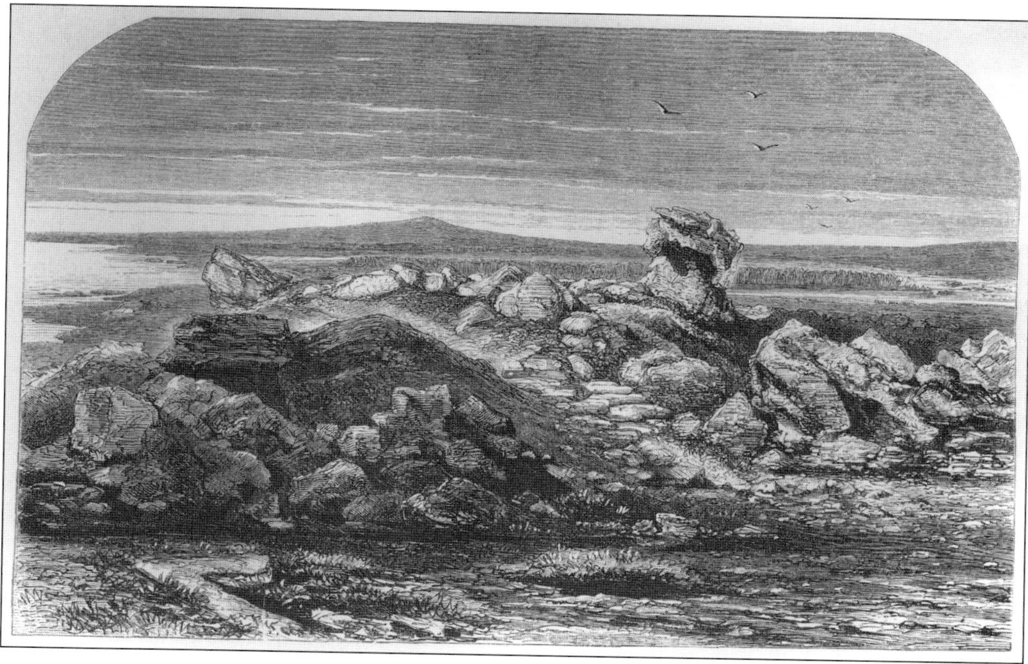

Fig. 5.5 The Antonine Baths as recorded by Davis in his Carthage and Her Remains *(compare Fig. 3.4 on p. 44)*

the south-west side of the great ruin marked no. 67 on Falbe's plan (where the number is nearly illegible).

Falbe identified this huge building as 'the most impressive among ruins of a bath' (Fig. 5.5) and the subsidiary structure at Falbe no. 69 as a 'temple'.[81] In 1835, Grenville Temple had described the massive concrete building by the sea, and noted the 'small theatre adjoining, facing the sea'.[82] The massive ruins of Falbe no. 67 were to be identified as the 'Antonine Baths' by an inscription of the Roman emperor Antoninus Pius in 1887.[83] Sainte-Marie would also believe that the very solidly-built subsidiary site (Falbe no. 69), which he described as circular, was a theatre. In Sainte-Marie's day, it was being used as a stone quarry; he said that its rose and black granite columns had been shipped off to Europe, and that only one or two large fragments were left.[84]

Davis' first sketch-map indicated the semicircular subsidiary structure as an oval, flattened on one side, contiguous to the large rectangular enclosure of the Antonine Baths. On his second sketch-map the large area of ruins is designated the 'Forum,' indicating that Davis did not accept Falbe's identification of the site as a bath. On his published map, his smaller site is designated a semicircular ruin to the south-west of the enclosure on the site of the main baths. Correlating Davis' map with the street-grid locates his site as being on the north side of *decumanus* 3 north and between *cardines* 16 and 17 east.

Davis said the oval building had earlier been identified as a theatre, but he thought it was a church from finds of a marble cross and lamps with Christian symbols. He presented arguments, which he himself found unconvincing, that it was the site of the burial of Saint Cyprian.[85] The site is not a temple, theatre, or church, but the huge south-west hemicycle latrine of the Antonine Baths (Fig. 5.6). It is not surprising that the grandiosity of the decoration of this building misled early explorers and archaeologists as to its identity. The latrine is immediately north of the line of *decumanus* 3 north, between *cardo* 17 and the line of *cardo* 18 east;[86] its true location is one short side of a Roman city-block (*c.* 35 m) to the east of its placement on Davis' map.

The excavation of its mosaic as recorded in Davis is important because comparison with modern documentation of the same mosaic, which is intact and *in situ* today, confirms the general reliability of his description, and indicates that his published map is here accurate to within thirty-five meters. Davis found the Mosaic of Monochrome Scales three feet (0.9 m) below the surface, and said that the mosaic was 'of

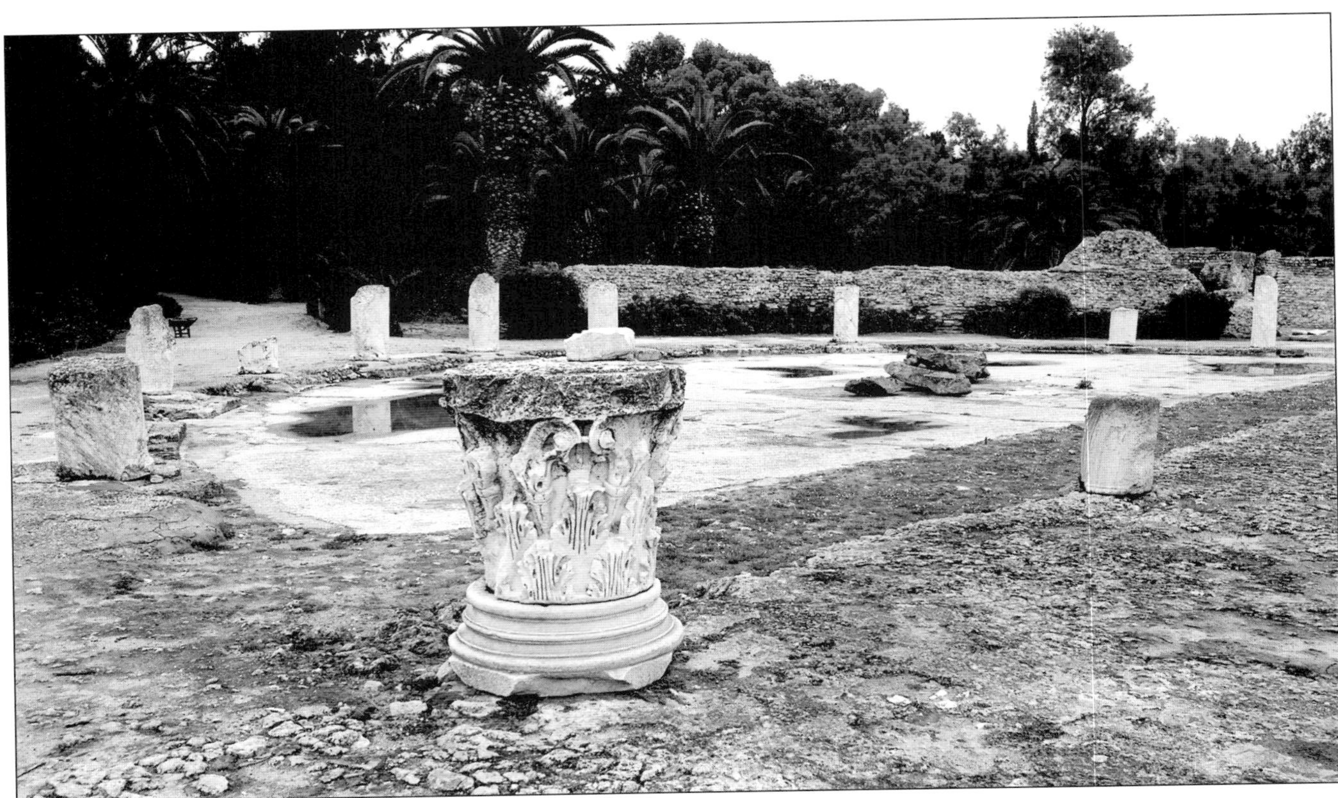

Fig. 5.6 The south-west latrine of the Antonine Baths, as it appears today, from the south

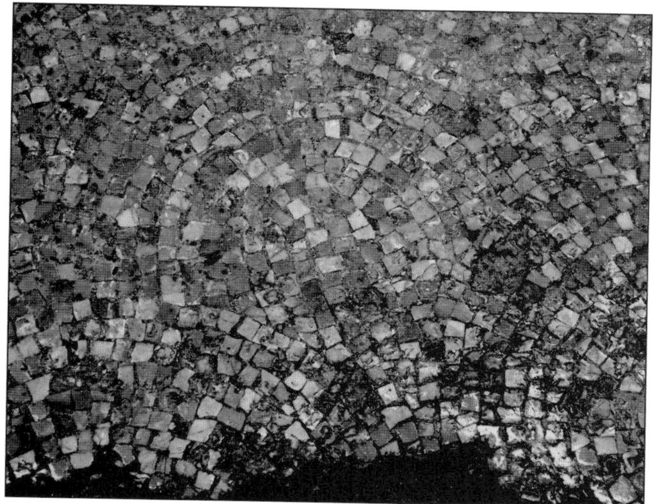

Fig. 5.7 A portion of the tessellated pavement excavated by Davis in the semicircular courtyard of the latrine building; the plain tesserae *are made mostly of yellow and some of purplish-pink marble, both from Chemtou in north-west Tunisia, laid in a pattern of adjacent scales.*

extraordinary solidity',[87] a feature in agreement with the enormous size of the baths. Davis described a plain mosaic with an unchanging pattern.[88] In fact, the mosaic has a subtle pattern of large overlapping scales laid in *tesserae* (small, squared cut stones) of pale Chemtou marble, naturally variegated cream and orange to red (Fig. 5.7). In a recent study of the mosaics from the Antonine Baths, the floor is dated to the original Antonine construction of the building.[89] None of this huge mosaic (it measures 28.8 m by 14.3 m) was lifted by Davis, who had not yet considered the problems involved.

On the curving north-east side where the wall was missing Davis found two red 'Africana' marble column bases, which had once supported columns three feet (0.9 meters) in diameter. A recent plan of the south-west latrine shows that the two columns and column bases on the north-east side are indeed missing, and their dimensions generally agree with Davis' description.[90] Davis gave these bases to Consul Wood, who had them cut into slabs and polished.[91]

Davis' fifth site: the slope and monumental stair below Bordj-Djedid

Davis next dug farther up the steep southern slope of Bordj-Djedid (Site 5), but he confused matters by marking two very different points in this area on his published map. His fifth site falls in the north-eastern quarter of the city grid, either in the middle of the block north of the Antonine Baths on *cardo* 20 east, or, much farther up the slope, at the intersection of *decumanus* 6 north and *cardo* 18 east. The elevation of the first site is about ten meters above sea-level,[92] while the elevation of the second is between thirty and thirty-five meters above sea-level. Falbe had indicated a steep slope in this area but no ruins. The Bordy map was to suggest a thirty percent grade for the lower section of the slope, too steep to stand comfortably.

The placement of Davis' points is questionable and his reasons for digging in this area are not immediately obvious. The lower of the two sites which he marked was below the Turkish fort, which is shown on his first sketch-map as a generally square outline with projecting gun emplacements. The general area, to the south-west of the fort, is marked on the first sketch-map to indicate no ruins, and nothing found. On the second sketch-map Davis labelled the immediate area 'Fort,' placing this label next to his label 'Ancient Staircase.'

If Davis had dug in the exact area which he marked for the lower point, it is unlikely that he would have found anything, as the area was downwash from the summit of Bordj-Djedid to the north. If on the other hand he had been far enough down the slope and had dug down deep enough, he would have come down on the east side of the northern latrine of the Antonine Baths.[93] If this had been the case, however, he would surely have noted that its plan and decoration was identical to the south-western latrine, which he had very recently excavated. If, however, I correct the lower point to thirty-five meters east of the point marked by Davis, it is possible that he was investigating the lower end of the ancient monumental staircase to the summit of Bordj-Djedid. Grenville Temple had visited Bordj-Djedid and wrote, 'The supports of a long and wide flight of stairs leading down to the sea are still extant'.[94] Davis himself published a view of the site, unfortunately incomprehensible.[95]

In 1859 Beulé was to describe this grandiose staircase in detail. Beulé said that it was supported over its immense width by six evenly-spaced walls, each 1.2 m to 1.9 m thick. Each step was 48 m (150 ft) wide, significantly wider than the short side of a regular city-block (35 m) at Carthage. Two landings and three ramps were still visible. The ramps progressively diminished in height, from twelve to ten to eight meters, for a total height of thirty meters, thus requiring 120 to 130 steps up from the sea.[96] The equivalent 'Monumental Staircase' was to be outlined on the Bordy map of 1896, aligned with the north–south *cardines* of the Roman street-grid and along Bordy's 25-m elevation line. Correlations with Lézine's plan of this area[97] show that Bordy placed the stair approximately along *cardo* 21 east (an extension of the original street-grid on the north-eastern seashore), and that it reached the summit at the line of *decumanus* 6 north, that is, on the same alignment as the northern end of the Bordj-Djedid cisterns.

This stairway, which rises from the beach-front of the city at sea-level to the summit of Bordj-Djedid thirty meters above, could comfortably have held five hundred to a thousand pedestrians. It is unimaginable that such a grandiose and inviting access to the upper city could have been built except in conditions of perfect peace in the Mediterranean; this and the materials of its construction dictate that the staircase belonged to the Roman city and possibly to the same period in the second half of the second century AD in which the city gained the monumental basilica and temples on the Byrsa, and the Odeon on the Odeon Hill.

By the time Bordy made his map, the materials of the staircase had been removed. In his commentary on the *Atlas archéologique* of 1893, Babelon was to identify his site CX (110) as the *Platea Nova* ('New Square'), as there were ruins of a monumental staircase rising to the plaza that Babelon thought Victor of Vita, writing in the Vandal era, had described. According to Babelon, who saw the actual remains, the plaza at the summit of the stairs was paved. He also said that the ramps for this staircase still existed in 1881 and that he himself had seen it destroyed by stone robbers in 1884. According to Delattre, whom Babelon cited, the Italian workmen who dismantled the stair had taken away 100 cubic meters of *cipollino* marble.[98] If Davis excavated at this site he was combining clues from Falbe and Temple with the visible evidence for the monumental stairway. Given the nature of the site, it is not surprising that Davis' investigations here were not repaid by the type of finds he was looking for.

The higher point Davis marked correlates with an area of excavated Roman housing about which Davis said nothing. During Flaubert's exploration of the site of Carthage in the spring of 1858, only slightly more than a year after Davis was excavating here, he noted an area on the regular shallow slope above the eastern cisterns, with 'ordinary' Roman mosaics and walls covered with white plaster, decorated with wide, raised, chocolate-coloured bands.[99] It is likely that this was the higher area excavated by Davis on this slope, but Flaubert's description of the location is only approximate. The same area was to be noted by Gauckler, who described the terraced ruins of a number of Roman houses, with mosaic pavements showing through the soil here and there; perhaps because Gauckler saw the site thirty years later, he did not seem to realize that he was looking at an abandoned excavation. Gauckler said that the mosaics were made of marble *tesserae* and had geometric motifs on a white ground. He described the location as north of the cisterns on Bordj-Djedid, on the slopes of the hill with the Turkish fort.[100] My guess is that these houses were immediately beyond the northern end of the cisterns and slightly to the east, which requires them to be at least five meters higher than the Turkish fort and slightly to its west. They should lie between *decumani* 6 and 7 north, and between *cardines* 16 and 18 east, which correlates well with Davis' second point.

Davis' sixth site: the summit of the Hill of Juno

The next excavation site in Davis' early months at Carthage was on the summit of the Hill of Juno, Falbe no. 53 (Site 6). Falbe had marked no. 53 on a large rectangular enclosure running parallel to the *decumani*; this was one of several points that Falbe considered to be 'temples and large buildings'.[101] Falbe described the ruins at his site no. 53 as comparable to those of the Antonine Baths; together they were 'the most extensive ruins at Carthage'.[102] There is no reason to doubt Falbe's veracity and accuracy in any other case, yet later excavators found nothing of the sort at this site. The common name of the site preserves Dureau de la Malle's suggestion that this summit was the site of the Temple of the Punic goddess Astarte, or Tanit, who was known to the Romans as Juno Caelestis. It falls within the northern half of the city grid and near the *cardo maximus*; the site marked by Falbe is between *decumani* 1 and 2 north. The elevation is between forty-five and fifty meters above sea-level,[103] and the location is clearly suitable for an important Roman public building.

The site was evidently a complete disappointment to Davis, however, and he said nothing about excavations on the Hill of Juno in his book or his letters. On the first sketch-map, he marked the site as ruins where nothing was found. The map shows a long rectangular enclosure running north–south, on the same alignment but smaller than the square double enclosure which he indicated on the Saint Louis hill. On Davis' second sketch-map he marked the site on the summit of the Hill of Juno, which he surrounded by crude lines meant to indicate elevation. He did not mark an equivalent point on his published map, however, which means that it is impossible to propose exactly where Davis excavated here. Furthermore, while his published map is usually topographically accurate, the western summit of the Hill of Juno is drawn two blocks too far to the west.

Beulé, who was to discuss Davis' sites with him in 1859, was more forthcoming. He wrote that Davis had found nothing but cisterns and coarse mosaics on the Hill of Juno. Beulé pointed out that the emperor Constantius had ordered the Temple of Caelestis to be razed in AD 421, and Beulé therefore believed that

Vandal and Byzantine houses were built on the summit in the later fifth or sixth century.[104] He did not address the question of how a major temple complex could be 'lost without trace.' Delattre was also to put in trenches on the summit of the Hill of Juno, in 1878, but he found nothing other than Roman mosaics and, at a very great depth, early Punic tombs. Delattre never found any evidence to confirm the presence of a major public building of either the Punic or the Roman era on the summit of the hill.[105] Since Falbe had reported significant ruins here, remains on the summit of the Hill of Juno may have been dismantled by stone robbers in the twenty-five years between Falbe's map and Davis' excavations.

The excavations of Jules Renault and Baron Byron Khun de Prorok in the early 1920s were to uncover extensive Roman mosaics, of which the most impressive was certainly not earlier than the end of the fourth century AD. Khun de Prorok, who was an adventurer rather than a scholar, dated this mosaic to circa 50 BC (pre-dating the Roman refoundation), but a photograph of it argues otherwise.[106] Renault and Khun de Prorok demonstrated that the northern side of the Hill of Juno is partly built up on lofty Roman vaulting, still visible today, which may in fact have originally supported a Roman temple or other public building. Khun de Prorok's description of the vaults was: 'our garage is an old Roman cistern, our Ford sits inside'.[107]

Davis' seventh site: the 'Gate of the Wind'

Davis next moved to high ground on the northern side of the city; the elevation is between forty-five and fifty meters above sea-level.[108] This site was in the area which Davis knew as Bab el-Rih (Site 7). The site would be roughly equivalent to point LXXX (80) on the map of Carthage prepared by Babelon, Cagnat and Reinach for the *Atlas archéologique* in 1893. It was there also described as Bab-er-Rih, a site known as the 'Gate of the Wind' to the Arabs, which Babelon further noted was 'a gate now destroyed'.[109] On Davis' first sketch map, this site is marked as ruins where nothing was found, with no indication of a structure. It is not indicated on his published map, no doubt because the excavation was not productive, nor did he mention it in his book or his letters. The site lies between the Mosaic of the Months and Seasons and the 'Carthaginian House' (see below). On the second sketch-map, the site is shown as lying well back from the slope formed by the city wall and between the same two excavations.

A line drawn from the location of the Mosaic of the Months and Seasons to the 'Carthaginian House' would cross the *cardo maximus* north very near an unlabelled enclosure that was clearly outlined on the plan of Falbe. I believe that this was Davis' seventh site. This relatively small rectangular structure covers an area of about ten by thirty meters. An overlay of Falbe's plan with the Roman street-grid shows that it lay across the *cardo maximus*, about 100 m south of the northern limit of the street-grid and about ten to twenty meters north of *decumanus* 5 north. *Decumanus* 5 is the last cross-street on the *cardo maximus* north, as *decumanus* 6 north never continued west to this point.[110] Falbe's structure is not the gate that must have lain across the *cardo maximus* after the much later construction of the Theodosian Wall, because the structure indicated by Falbe was too small, and also lay well inside the line of the later Theodosian Wall.

The plan, size, alignment and placement of Falbe's structure might suggest that it was a city gate, as it distinguished the main northern entrance and exit of the Roman city; but since it was built for an unwalled city, it no doubt took the form of a Roman triumphal arch. Although it certainly belonged to the Roman as opposed to the later city, there is no further evidence for its date; it might belong with the monumental embellishment of the city in the second century AD. The placement of the arch suggests that when it was built it was not expected that the Roman city would expand to fill the north-western quarter of the street-grid. The *cardo maximus* with its arch led out into the countryside and gave access to the suburbs north of the ancient city, as far as the sites now known as La Marsa and Gammarth. Marshy land along the coast north of Gammarth meant that Roman travellers to destinations farther north, such as Castra Cornelia, Utica and Hippo Diarrhytus, either went by sea, or left Carthage on the western side of the city.[111]

The relatively unproductive excavation of these seven sites demonstrates Davis' determination and energy in the first two months of his excavations. The places he chose were on Falbe's plan or closely related to sites which Falbe had marked on his plan. In the course of these excavations Davis must have learned a great deal about what he could expect from excavation at Carthage, and although he did not formulate how his orientation changed, his subsequent choices show that he had come to some fundamental conclusions about what he could retrieve and how to place his sites in terms, not of Falbe's map, but of his own understanding of the topography of the city. He would soon be rewarded by the discovery of the Mosaic of the Months and Seasons.

TABLE: Davis' thirty-five sites – a concordance of site numbers

Davis' first fourteen sites were numbered on his first sketch-map (Fig. 4.13). Davis explained that the numbers with underlining denoted places where something had been found, and that numbers accompanied by a cross indicated Roman ruins still standing above ground. His second sketch-map (Fig. 4.14) indicates numbers for twenty-two sites (several numbers are missing), when by my count he had already excavated at thirty-two sites. Davis' published map (Figs 4.3–4) indicates numbers for twenty-five sites: points, labels and outlines on the map, correlated with locations as described in his text, identify others. The numbers for the same sites on Falbe's map, of which a detail appears in Fig. 3.2, are added below for convenience.

Site No.	Site Name	Davis' First Sketch-Map No.	Davis' Second Sketch-Map No.	Davis' Published Map No.	Falbe's Map No.
1	Vaulting south-east of the circus	1+	1	1	near 73
2	Bath-house at Falbe no. 54	2+	2	2	54
3	Bordj-Djedid cisterns	3+	3	14	65
4	Latrine of Antonine Baths	4+	4	6	69
5	Stair at Bordj-Djedid	5	-	4	-
6	Summit of the Hill of Juno	6+	6	-	53
7	'Gate of the Wind'	7+	7	-	-
8	Mosaic of the Months and Seasons	8	8	7	-
9	North side of the circular harbour	9+	9	3	-
10	'Temple of Apollo'	10+	10	9	near 55
11	Enclosure on Bordj-Djedid	-	-	8	near 34
12	Antonine Baths	-	-	5	67
13	Mosaic of Victory	11	11	19	90
14	Mosaic of Baskets of Fish and Fruit	12	13	22	-
15	'Punic Mine'	13	12	23	-
16	'Carthaginian House'	14	14	17	-
17–20	unproductive		-	-	one site is near 66
21	House east of the theatre		20	18	-
22	Mosaic of Two Gazelles		-	18	-
23	'Circular Monument'		-	16	70
24	Prostrate column		-	-	-
25	South-west slope of Saint Louis		-	-	-
26	Roman tomb		-	12	80
27	Roman tomb		-	13	-
28	Roman seaside villa		-	24	-
29	Roman seaside villa		22	25	near 98
30	Catacombs at Gammarth		21	-	-
31	Mausoleum at Gammarth		21	-	-
32	La Marsa		-	-	-
33	Mosaic of the Sirens			-	79
34	Vandal Hunting Mosaic			-	-
35	Second Mosaic of Nereids and Tritons			20	-

6

Mosaics discovered at Carthage before Davis' excavations

How mosaics were lifted before Davis' invention of his method

Davis did not originally imagine that mosaics would form his major category of finds, and was minimally prepared for such a turn of events. Yet ancient mosaics were being discovered and removed from their contexts long before Davis found them at Carthage and invented his method of lifting them. Antiquarian interest in ancient mosaics was born in Italy in the seventeenth and eighteenth centuries.[1] To the general disgust of the citizenry of Palestrina, the Nile Mosaic was lifted in large pieces between 1624 and 1626 and taken to Rome. The scenes on the individual fragments were only subsequently drawn, so that the drawings did not provide information for the correct restoration of the mosaic as a whole. Giovanni Battista Calandra of Vercelli, 'a most excellent worker in mosaic', restored the Nile Mosaic, which soon suffered further damage in transportation and was restored again.[2] Werner's case-studies of the restoration and use of ancient mosaics in the decoration of the Vatican Museum in the eighteenth and nineteenth centuries have also shown that total preservation of the mosaic in lifting and even replication of the original design in restoration were by no means a priority at that time.[3]

The method of lifting mosaics that was ordinarily used in the mid-nineteenth century was described by C. T. Newton. The British Museum received a group of mosaics from Newton at Halicarnassos at the same time and even on the same ship as many of those they received from Davis at Carthage. Although Newton successfully retrieved these mosaics, they needed extensive restoration before their exhibition[4] (a number of Newton's mosaics from Halicarnassos are in fact displayed on the same north-west stairwell of the British Museum where Davis' mosaics from Carthage are also exhibited).[5] As a former assistant at the British Museum, Newton had the expert's view on how the job was done. He described the method as follows:[6]

> The usual method of taking up a mosaic pavement is to glaze canvas on the upper surface, and to lay a bed of plaster of Paris upon this. When the bond of the tessellae [diminutive of *tesserae*] has thus been strengthened by this applied surface, the pavement can be safely detached from the ground on which it rests. This is usually done by driving a gallery in the earth below, and then cutting away the lower and heavier part of the bed of the pavement. This bed commonly consists of three strata –a coarse rubble foundation, a layer of mortar, and a layer of fine cement, in which the tessellae themselves are fixed. When the bed is in a sound state, and can be got at from below, nearly the whole thickness of its layers may be detached with safety. The pavement may then be taken up in large squares, and being held together by its original cement and partly by the canvas and plaster of Paris applied to its upper surface, will bear transport if carefully packed. The pavement in Hadji Captan's field being laid on the native rock instead of upon earth, it was found impossible to cut it away from below. It was, moreover, in many places, in a very unsound state. However, I succeeded in taking up one entire room, by dividing it into very small squares, and then lifting them up by a gentle application of leverage at the sides.

Clearly the 'usual method' described by Newton would not work if the bedding was unsound or could not be tunnelled under from below. Davis' account of the lifting of the Mosaic of the Months and Seasons shows that he knew this method, but that it did not work for him or the 'experts' to whom he turned (see below, Chapter 7).

The history of mosaics lifted at Carthage before Davis reveals that they were retrieved very incompetently. Generally only relatively small pieces were lifted intact on their mortar bed, with heavy losses - that necessitated heavy restoration. In fact, only if drawings of the whole pavement had been made while the mosaic was still *in situ*, which was seldom the case, could the design of the floor be restored with confidence and understood in terms of its original meaning.

Mosaics known at Carthage in 1860

In 1860 Augustus Franks noted three mosaics that had been discovered at Carthage before Davis' finds. Of these, only two were retrieved. As a museum curator and scholar at the British Museum, Franks was naturally thinking of published mosaics in museum collections. He listed two pavements excavated at Falbe no. 90 and one at Falbe no. 54.[7] Falbe no. 90 is a villa site on the sea-shore immediately north of the Roman street-grid, which Davis was later to excavate (Site 13). The earliest mosaic find to be documented at Carthage in any way was excavated by Falbe in 1824 at Falbe no. 90, and immediately destroyed. The second, a Mosaic of the Mask of Ocean, in the collection of the British Museum since 1844 (Fig. 6.1), was excavated at the same site by Falbe and Temple in 1838. The third mosaic noted by Franks was a chance discovery in 1844 of a Vandal carpet mosaic by workmen collecting stone at Falbe no. 54.[8] I have already described Falbe no. 54 as the second site excavated by Davis, a large bath-house probably of Vandal date in the centre of the Roman city, just south of the Byrsa Hill.

Franks's list was not complete. Since the mosaics lifted before Davis were the objects of purely private enterprise, only chance has preserved their documentation. Furthermore, Franks evidently did not know the report of the Parisian Society for the Exploration of Carthage, in which Falbe and Grenville Temple had published a drawing of the Mosaic of a Nereid on a Hippocamp, also discovered by them at Falbe no. 90 in 1838 (Fig. 6.2).[9] On the other hand, Franks was correct in his understanding that the first mosaics to be discovered at Carthage were excavated by Falbe in 1824 and by Falbe and Temple in 1838.

The research of Lund among the museum documentation and papers of Falbe at the National Museum of Denmark, where Falbe was conservator of the royal collection from 1840,[10] has revealed that the Mosaic of the Mask of Ocean was in fact the central motif of a Marine Mosaic which included the Mosaic of a Nereid on a Hippocamp; restored, the latter has been in the collection of the National Museum of Denmark since 1842. Moreover, two other fragments of the same mosaic exist – a small piece of the fish border in the Louvre, and a fragment, in which the border joins the partially framed bust of a young Triton, in the municipal library of Versailles.[11] Chance brought these two further fragments, once in private hands, to public ownership and subsequent publication.

The third mosaic known to Franks was discovered in 1844 at Falbe no. 54; it was granted by the Bey to the French consul, and was more or less completely destroyed in the lifting process. Fortunately, before the pavement was disturbed, Alphonse Rousseau made a drawing of it and also wrote a brief description of the circumstances of the find.[12] Rousseau was selective in his representation of detail, but the drawing shows a carpet mosaic, probably of Vandal date, with rows and columns of medallions which include a personification of the city of Carthage, the four Seasons, and four named charioteers; a variety of hunting scenes in medallions cover the majority of the floor (Fig. 6.3).[13] The mosaic is busy, unified only by its layout. Three small fragments of this mosaic are preserved in the Louvre.[14]

Although Franks did not note it in this context, a 'Mosaic of the Months with Latin Inscriptions' was also found at Carthage at the time of Davis' excavations, most probably in 1857 or 1858. Franks did mention the mosaic later in the same article together with his discussion of Beulé's discoveries in 1859.[15] This mosaic was found in a house at the south-west corner of the summit of the Byrsa Hill by the guardian of the Chapel of Saint Louis. It was evidently of late date, and Davis derided its coarse quality.[16] Although Davis said that the lifting of this mosaic had been bungled by the guardian of the Chapel, who thought he could emulate Davis' methods but failed, at least the part of the floor containing the months of May and June were lifted, and were subsequently for some time kept in the grounds of the Chapel.

Of these three mosaics, the carpet mosaic from Falbe no. 54 is the best understood, because, while only three small fragments survive, the entire mosaic was drawn as a unit before it was broken up. Sources contemporary with its discovery have improved our understanding of the layout of the Marine Mosaic from Falbe no. 90, but the overall design of the Mosaic of the Months from the south-west corner of the summit of Saint Louis can only be surmised, because no eye-witness described or sketched the layout of the original pavement.

The history of these pavements shows that all of them were broken up during the lifting process. In each case good intentions were accompanied by complete and reprehensible technical ignorance. At best only restored fragments survive today. The fragments of the Marine Mosaic from Falbe no. 90 are scattered, and a proper interpretation of the mosaic was impossible until the history of the excavation was recovered.[17] The fragment of the personification of 'Carthage' from Falbe no. 54 has undergone restoration affecting its interpretation.[18] The lost, dispersed and often pitifully-damaged and freely-restored fragments of these mosaics can be compared with the many small mosaics as well as large sections of large mosaics which were retrieved intact by Davis. If Davis had been permitted to lift the five 'Months' that were extant when the Mosaic of the Months with Latin Inscriptions was found, that mosaic would probably have survived in a complete enough condition to reconstruct its original design.

The mosaic excavated by Falbe in 1824

In Falbe's description of his plan of Carthage, he mentioned mosaics in three contexts. One of these was the pavement which was destroyed at his site no. 90 in 1824,[19] and another the coarse Roman mosaic on the floor of the circular tower, Falbe no. 61, near the cisterns of La Malga.[20] Falbe also knew of mosaics at no. 1 on his plan, a modern house at La Marsa, more than a kilometer north of the street-grid of Roman Carthage.[21] Falbe's plan shows house no. 1 built around two courtyards.[22] Falbe probably lived in this large house, since one of the pencil sketches among Falbe's plates is of 'Falbe's house in La Marsa',[23] and the house was Falbe's base-point in mapping the whole area of Carthage.[24]

The most important site for Falbe's mosaics is his point no. 90, on the sea-shore just north of the enlarged city grid. Falbe wrote that the mosaic found in 1824 was discovered near the end of the piers on the sea-shore; the mosaic was therefore very near the sea.[25] Falbe no. 90 is at the foot of a steep and narrow ravine, under a cliff that rises to fifty meters above sea level. The mosaic, about thirty feet (9.14 m) square, was found eight to ten feet below the surface. Falbe did not describe the design (and, so far as I know, no description has survived elsewhere). Falbe also wrote that this pavement was covered with a layer of ashes, evidence that the building had perished in a fire.[26] The mosaic itself was destroyed three days after its discovery by henchmen of the Bey, because of the machinations of a jealous European, who said there would be a lead box filled with gold and silver coins below it.[27] The jealous European, who Falbe said had never published any of his own finds, was Jean Emile Humbert.[28] Davis later implied that Sir Thomas Reade ('a minister of this enlightened government') was responsible for the destruction of the mosaic.[29] Falbe and Sir Grenville Temple returned to the same site in 1838, and only the fact that Falbe described the mosaic of 1824 as destroyed clearly indicates that the Marine Mosaic found in 1838 with the mask of Ocean and the Nereid on a hippocamp, was a different floor to the equally large mosaic pavement which Falbe discovered in 1824.

The Marine Mosaic excavated by Sir Grenville Temple in 1838

The Mosaic of the Mask of Ocean (Fig. 6.1) known to Franks, therefore, came from the same large pavement as the Mosaic of a Nereid on a Hippocamp; both were excavated by Sir Grenville Temple in 1838. Falbe directed Temple to the site where the former had found the floor destroyed in 1824, and set him to work to find more mosaics.[30] As noted above (pp. 43–4), the excavation was funded by the Society for the Exploration of Carthage; Falbe and Temple were among the subscribers. The members of the society had agreed that they would divide the finds among themselves, and subsequent evidence indicates that they did so.

The marine mosaic floor was excavated by Temple between March 20th and 23rd, 1838.[31] Falbe subsequently drew a plan of the 'house' in which the pavement was found, but did not indicate the points of the compass, nor in which specific room the mosaic was located (Fig. 3.7). The plan does not show a recognizable or complete Roman house, but rather four or possibly five rectangular rooms of varying size set around a rectangular area that is open on one side. The size of the structure as drawn is 19 m square; the largest enclosed room is a rectangle with an interior measurement of 9.0 m by 7.8 m, comparable in size to the adjacent rectangular area open on one side. These measurements are roughly comparable with Falbe's description of the dimensions of the mosaic he found in 1824, which he described as thirty feet on each side. Either of these two areas provides enough space for a very large mosaic pavement,[32] and it may well be that one of these rooms was actually the location of the mosaic destroyed in 1824. In this building in 1838 the excavators found paintings 'in the Pompeian style', and 'mosaics representing men and animals'.[33]

The fragment of floor depicting a Nereid on a hippocamp was originally a subsidiary part of a large Marine Mosaic with the mask of Ocean[34] in which the head of the god was central. The Danish museum inventory entry, which was probably written by Falbe himself, notes: 'Four figures, of which the above-mentioned Nymph was one, and a fisherman in a boat another, were placed around Oceanus, and surrounding these was a broad border with different fishes, one of which has been transported to Paris and restored there'.[35] The mask of Ocean was described as 'an old man with rushes and corals in his hair'.[36] A mosaic fragment depicting two fish, now in the Louvre, evidently comes from the border of the same floor.[37] A fourth fragment, now in the municipal library at Versailles, also belongs to the same pavement; this piece shows at least two more fish and a squid from the border, while the head and upper body of a young Triton, which has been restored, appears in a partial rectangular frame.[38]

Temple had made a colour drawing of the Nereid on a hippocamp while it was still *in situ*,[39] and a drawing of the scene, framed within a rectangle, was published in Falbe and Temple's report to their excavation society (Fig. 6.2).[40] There is no evidence that the mosaic as a whole was ever drawn, which might suggest that it was already partly destroyed when found. In fact Falbe's notes commented that the floor had several layers and had been repeatedly repaired.[41] The section with the Nereid was lifted by Grenville Temple's workmen in his absence. It was done so incompetently that it was broken up into a hundred pieces, to Falbe's chagrin, as he considered this the best piece of mosaic found.[42]

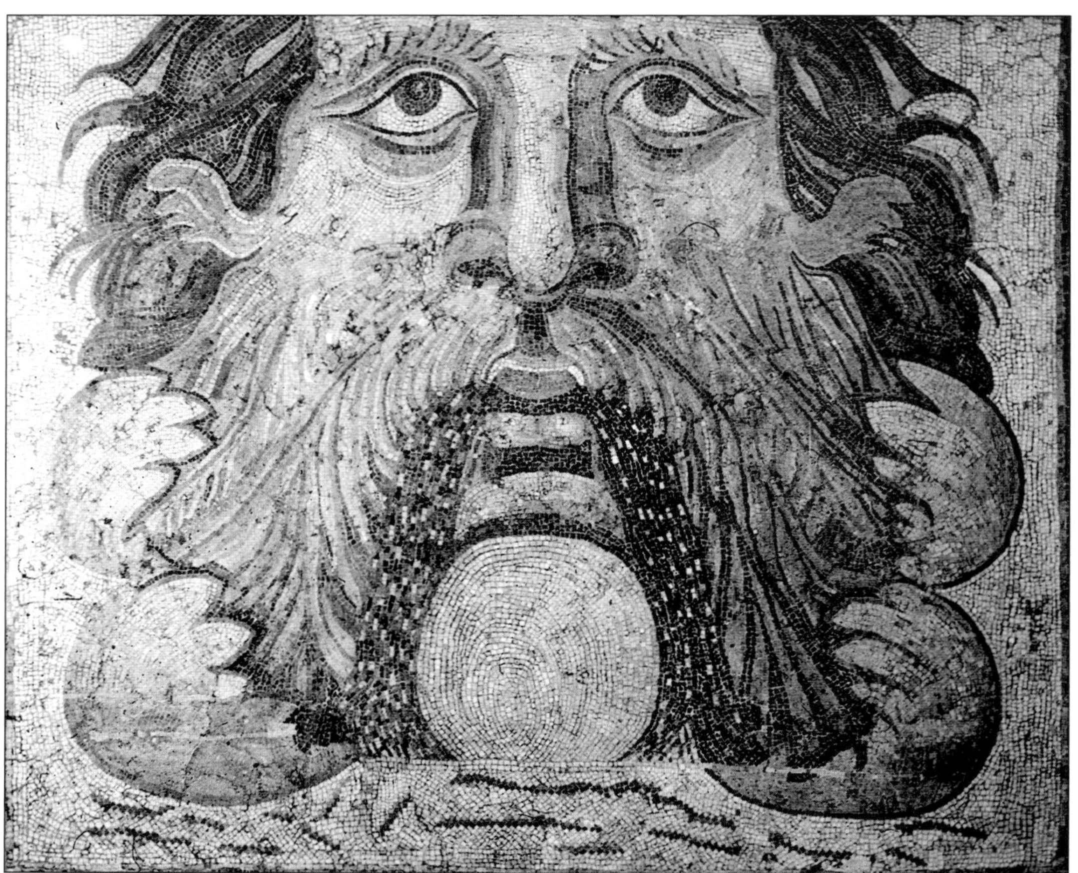

Fig. 6.1 Mosaic showing a head of Oceanus (the 'Mosaic of the Mask of Ocean') in the British Museum, part of a larger marine mosaic uncovered in 1838; third century AD (?). This vast portion alone measures 1.75 m high and 2.11 m across.

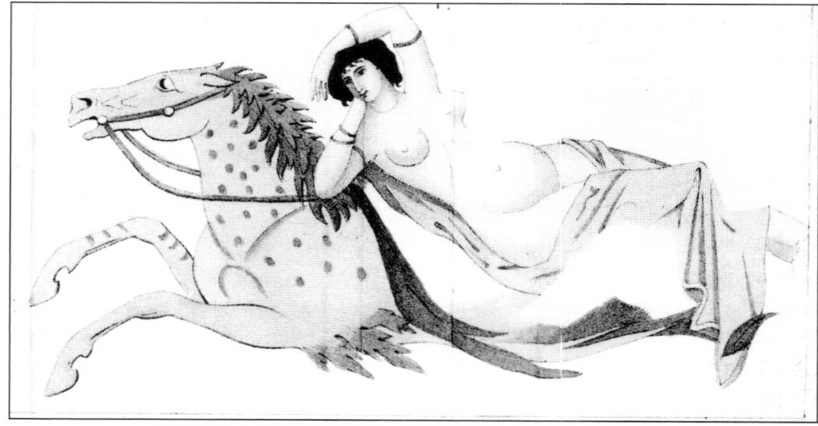

Fig. 6.2 Drawing of the Mosaic of the Nereid on a Hippocamp, which formed part of the same mosaic to which Oceanus (Fig. 6.1) also belonged; this illustration of it was published by Falbe and Temple, who found it, in 1838. The mosaic fragment itself, considerably restored, is on display in the National Museum of Denmark, Copenhagen.

The Mosaic of the Nereid on a Hippocamp as it now exists was restored by the firm of C. Giuli in Paris.[43] I believe that it was most probably restored from the drawing and these broken pieces. The mosaic as it exists today shows the hippocamp swimming left; it follows the drawing published in the excavation report exactly.[44] Working from a drawing and the original *tesserae* was the standard method of the best nineteenth-century restorers of mosaics. The alternative, which I think much less likely, is that a second identical scene of a Nereid and hippocamp was found, which was lifted more successfully without breaking up.[45] The Mosaic of the Nereid on a Hippocamp was subsequently in Falbe's possession, and he presented it to the King of Denmark in 1842;[46] today it forms part of the collections of the Department of Classical and Near Eastern Antiquities in the National Museum of Denmark.[47]

Since Falbe did not mention it with his original description of the Nereid, the mask of Ocean was evidently lifted subsequently and sent to Paris as a separate piece. Only the lower half of the head[48] (the lower third according to Gauckler, who exaggerated the loss[49]), survived the lifting process and was returned to Paris among the finds of the Society. While the mask of Ocean may have been damaged by the lifting process, it is equally possible that the upper part of the head was already seriously damaged when found. The restored dimensions of the head, 2.11 m by 1.75 m,[50] suggest the great size of the original pavement of which it formed the central focus.

Hudson Gurney, a British gentleman who was also a subscriber to the Society for the Exploration of Carthage, presented the restored Mosaic of the Mask of Ocean to the British Museum in 1844, at which time Gurney was a Vice-President of the British Museum Society. Gurney must have received it with his share of the finds from the Society. According to a brief note with an engraving of the mosaic in the *Illustrated London News*, the mosaic was restored by Sir Richard Westmacott.[51] The elder Sir Richard Westmacott was a sculptor who was in charge of all displays of sculpture at the British Museum for fifty years.[52] The upper third of the head was restored, on what basis is uncertain, and the round water outlet in the bearded chin below the mouth was stopped with white mosaic *tesserae*. As the chin of the mask of Ocean seems to have been formed by a circular fountain opening, the entire mosaic may have been designed to line a shallow pool or to be awash with water.

The mosaic fragment was restored to a neat rectangle, the upper edge of which cuts the mask of Ocean at mid-forehead. The upper third shows stylistic signs of restoration.[53] Much of the mouth, beard and vegetal tendrils (described by Hinks as 'pink scrolls of seaweed',[54] but by Dunbabin as truncated acanthus scrolls from an earlier use of the design)[55] on either side of the chin and beard look original, but the nose, eyes and hair do not. The restored Mosaic of the Mask of Ocean is now on display in the Roman Empire Gallery (Room 70) in the British Museum.

A circular composition around a mask of Ocean is a well-attested mosaic design,[56] which was already popular at the end of the second century. In her discussion of the type, Dunbabin noted two mosaic panels from Bougie (Bejaia) in Algeria with a mask of Ocean flanked by two Nereids reclining on hippocamps; these are badly drawn and may date to the early third century.[57] Another 'immensely impressive head', which reminded Dunbabin of the Mosaic of the Mask of Ocean in the British Museum, was found in the *frigidarium* (cold room) of baths at Themetra in the region of Sousse. On this mosaic, for which Dunbabin suggested a date of *c.* AD 200/210, a huge mask of Ocean was surrounded by a marine scene with fish, boats and fishermen on a much smaller scale.[58] Dunbabin also noted two further North African mosaics with a central mask of Ocean, of probable fourth-century date, with Latin inscriptions that express the apotropaic meaning of the head.[59] In her discussion of the motif, she observed that the eyes of comparable masks of Ocean were sometimes defaced, perhaps in response to their intended power,[60] raising the question of whether serious damage to the upper part of the mask of Ocean in the British Museum may in fact have occurred in ancient times.

Because Dunbabin was not aware of the history of the Mask of Ocean discovered by Falbe in 1838, she believed that this particular floor might have come from a semicircular fountain basin,[61] which the shape of the head and mosaic as restored certainly suggests. This is not the case, however, given the early description of the complete floor, and Falbe's plan of the consistently rectangular rooms in the building from which the mosaic came. On the other hand, Dunbabin's collection of parallels suggests that the building excavated by Falbe and Temple, with its two very large rooms, one evidently open on one side, may have been a bath-building with public access, rather than a private suburban villa. The huge Antonine Baths, which date to the mid-second century, lie a half kilometer away to the south-west and also immediately on the sea-shore.

The Louvre has a small fragment of mosaic with two fish, which formed part of the wide border of the complete pavement. The fragment, which forms a suspiciously neat rectangle, measures 0.59 m by 0.49 m and is in good condition. A rather small fish is accompanied by part of a larger unidentifiable fish; both swim in a sea formed of pale *tesserae* laid on the diagonal, with waves defined by one gray and one black line of *tesserae* on the diagonal. Two lines of black *tesserae* delimit the bottom of the scene.[62] This portion of mosaic was presented to the Louvre by the heirs of Massieu de Clerval, who in 1838 was Major General of the Place Maritime at Toulon. Since the shipment of the Society's finds went by way of Toulon, it has been suggested that the fragment was given to Clerval by E. F. Jomard, who was also a member of the Society for the Exploration of Carthage. Jomard's share of the booty included another piece of the border, but in this case contiguous to the framed head and upper body of a young Triton. The fragment is now preserved in the municipal library of Versailles, which received the mosaic from Jomard's daughter.[63]

In his note on this fragment, Lavagne suggested that the figure of the Triton was completely modern, but copied from an ancient model. In the following discussion, Picard asked if the little wings on the head of the Triton were not in fact the claws of a crustacean which the restorer did not understand. In fact, complete uncertainty as to the authenticity of specific parts of such a mosaic is unavoidable, because there is no original record of the fragment. The piece was heavily restored in the nineteenth century, and it is possible that the scene has been reorganized.[64] The fish of the border swim in a sea produced by a mosaic technique exactly comparable with that in the fragment in the Louvre. By contrast, the framed Triton lies against a clear field of white *tesserae*, like the empty white field around the Nereid on a Hippocamp in the National Museum of Denmark. The fate of this important marine mosaic, now in four widely separated and highly restored pieces, makes it clear that Falbe and Grenville Temple knew of no reliable method to lift mosaics in the course of their excavations in 1838.

The Carpet Mosaic excavated at Falbe no. 54 in 1844

Only small fragments of the second mosaic to be lifted at Carthage are extant today. This was excavated at Falbe no. 54, the site of an extensive building in concrete on the south-west side of the Byrsa Hill. The mosaic was found in 1844 by workmen hired by the Tunisian government in search of stone to build the canal at the port of La Goulette. The floor was essentially complete, although damaged, when found, and

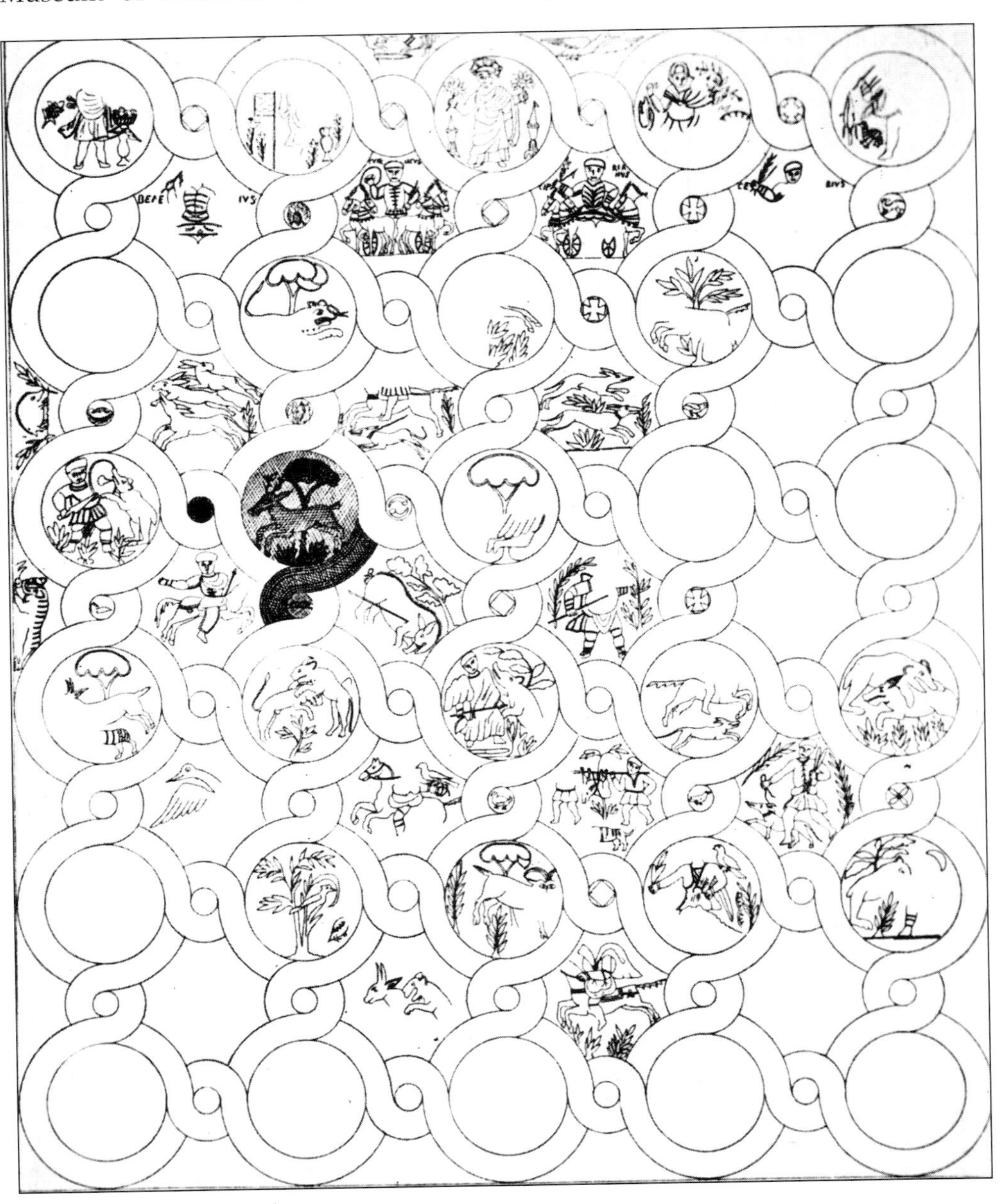

Fig. 6.3 Drawing of the 'Carpet Mosaic' found at Carthage in 1844, showing the Four Seasons and four charioteers; later fifth century or early sixth century AD. Only fragments now survive, in the Musée du Louvre, Paris.

a detailed drawing of the mosaic *in situ*, made by Alphonse Rousseau, was published in *Revue archéologique* in 1850 (Fig. 6.3). The pavement was quite large, at twenty-six by sixteen feet (8.0 m by 5.0 m).[65] A carpet mosaic, it was organized into rows and columns of figural medallions, alternately circular and lozenge-shaped, among which figures of the four Seasons flanking a personification of the city of Carthage and four named charioteers formed the 'top' two rows, while varied hunting scenes were arranged in the medallions over the rest of the floor. The format necessarily deprived the hunting theme of any narrative impact.[66] The bibliography on this mosaic published by Gauckler showed that the mosaic attracted a great deal of scholarly attention in the second half of the nineteenth century. As only fragments survived the lifting process, the interpretations were largely based on the drawing published by Rousseau.

The style in which the hunters are drawn indicates that the mosaic is unlikely to be earlier than the Vandal period, while the frontality of many of the figures and Byzantine crosses in four of the small circular medallions suggest that the mosaic may actually date after the Byzantine reconquest.[67] On the other hand, Frank Clover has, as noted above (p. 75), argued strongly for a Vandal date, at the end of the fifth century. He has pointed out that the figure of Carthage is broadly comparable to a personification of Carthage on the coins of the Vandal King Hildiric (AD 523–530) and on earlier Vandal coins of the later fifth century. In addition, one of the charioteers is named Quiriacus; this was the name of a famous charioteer mentioned by Luxorius in a poem which forms part of a collection of Vandal poetry of the late fifth century preserved in the *Anthologia Latina*. Clover also pointed out that the style and pose of the horseman in the third fragment echoes a horseman in the Vandal Hunting Mosaic excavated by Davis in 1859.[68] In my opinion Clover's arguments for a date *c.* AD 500 are convincing.

The mosaic was given by the Bey to the French Consul, Monsieur de Lagau.[69] It was later lifted in separate blocks. It seems to have been catastrophically broken up in the lifting process, after which some parts were taken to France, while others remained at the little museum of Abbé Bourgade at the Chapel of Saint Louis.[70] Wilmanns evidently saw some pieces still at Saint Louis in 1873.[71] The Louvre has three small catalogued fragments of this mosaic today. According to Parrish, the figure of 'Carthage' was heavily restored; he illustrated the figure in a circle framed by a single line of dark *tesserae*. 'Carthage' originally had a mural crown, which was restored as a radiate nimbus, so that the figure has been incorrectly described by scholars as an *orans* (an early Christian figure with hands outspread in prayer). The figure of the charioteer Quiriacus has ragged edges, and may be relatively free from restoration, but the third figure, a fragmented horse and rider, each without his head, was also heavily restored; interestingly, the head of the rider survives in the drawing published in 1850.[72] The mosaic shows an abundant use of glass *tesserae*.

The Mosaic of Months with Latin Inscriptions, excavated in 1857

As mentioned above (p. 84), another Mosaic of the Months, this one with Latin inscriptions naming the figures inscribed above their heads, was discovered at Carthage during the same period as Davis' excavations. Neither Davis nor Beulé took credit for the discovery of this pavement, but both mentioned it. It was discovered in a house off the Roman alignment at the south-west corner of the summit of the Saint Louis Hill; Beulé indicated the spot on his plan.[73] Davis said that he had offered to lift it on condition that it be presented to a museum, but, according to him, the person who discovered it insisted on imitating Davis' method of lifting mosaics, but without success. The mosaic was therefore discovered after Davis had invented and tested his new process, in or after the spring of 1857.

This mosaic was laid out in framed squares, perhaps in a checkerboard pattern, and showed children, both boys and girls, in 'Byzantine costume', as the Months, with the names of the individual months labelled in Latin above the head of the corresponding figure. There were five Months extant when Davis first saw the mosaic. He regarded its execution with scorn: May was 'a turgid boy with a brick-red face, dressed in a short tunic, and bearing a basket of flowers . . . A little girl, of equal dimensions in deformity, and bearing a basket of fruit, personated June'. Davis also said that Beulé saw the figure of May, which was the only one extant when the latter was excavating at Carthage in 1859. According to Davis, the guardian had only succeeded in retrieving the Month of May, which, Davis said, 'has since crumbled to pieces'.[74]

In a letter to Malmesbury written in April 1858, Davis mentioned a Russian at Carthage trolling for finds for museums in Russia;[75] this was probably Baron Alexander de Krafft, who arrived from Algiers on the same boat as Flaubert. This would have been nearly a year before Beulé saw the figure of May. Today there is a mosaic pavement in the Hermitage, transferred there in 1925 from the St Petersburg Winter Palace, which depicts a blond boy with medium-length hair wearing a short tunic with two stripes.[76] The boy carries a platter with eight round fruits on his left arm and a basket with some kind of vegetable in his right hand. He wears a gold torque and 'IUNIVS' is inscribed directly over his head. To the left there is a pedestal with a squid, while on the right a lower pedestal has two fish, with a larger fish at its base. The mosaic is a half meter square, and has many glass *tesserae*. Saverkina ascribed the mosaic to Rome, but there seems to be no evidence for its actual provenance. The ascription of this pavement to Rome is likely based on its Latin inscription, which implies only that the mosaic belongs to the western Roman Empire.[77] Parrish reviewed the dates suggested for this mosaic by earlier scholars and found the latest date suggested, the early third century, the most likely.

Might it be possible that this was a portion of the mosaic Davis saw? If so, both his and Beulé's memory of it would have been very faulty, as both described figures in Byzantine costume. Furthermore, the mortar of the Mosaic of the Months that Davis saw agreed with his theories about Punic versus Roman mortar; it was thin but very hard[78] and therefore of Roman date. His observations on the mortar may in fact suggest that the mosaic was datable to the late fourth century or later, and this would agree with his description of figures in Byzantine costume. Furthermore the fact that the house in which the mosaic was found was evidently off the Roman alignment suggests that the structure was Vandal or later. Doro Levi was later to suggest a fifth-century date for the Carthage Mosaic of the Months with Latin Inscriptions on the basis of the mosaic's description, and this is the date which Parrish accepted in his survey of mosaics of the Months.[79]

A mosaic of May in a similar layout and style exists in the Capitoline Museum in Rome. A young man in a capacious wide-sleeved tunic stares upward; his eyes are exaggeratedly large. He holds a bud to his nose with his right hand, and lifts up a basket with his left hand. There are two cross-hatched windows behind him, a container wreathed with ivy on a pedestal to the left, and a basket with flowers on the right. The piece is very damaged, but the squat proportions of the figure and the simple lettering of 'MAIVS' at the top right are reminiscent of the IVNIVS mosaic in the Hermitage. The design is also a square framed by a band of dentils.[80] This mosaic, which is closer to Davis' description of the figures in the Mosaic of the Months with Latin Inscriptions, was dated to the second half of the fourth century by Parrish, but may be somewhat later. Its provenance is not in question; it came from the Gardens of Maecenas on the Esquiline Hill and is now in the Antiquarium Comunale at Rome.

I do not believe that the IVNIVS mosaic in the Hermitage is a fragment of the mosaic which Davis and Beulé saw at Carthage in 1858 and 1859, but it is certainly a relevant parallel. While Davis did not regret the loss of the guardian's mosaic on aesthetic grounds, it is significant in terms of the Empire-wide corpus of mosaics depicting the Months. The location of the guardian's mosaic at Carthage and the description of the figures suggest a date for it in the Vandal or Byzantine period.

Other mosaics lifted at Carthage before Davis' excavations

A number of other mosaics were discovered at Carthage, but in general their histories are inadequately known. Sir Grenville Temple, who as we have seen (p. 43), made a lengthy stay with the British consul, Sir Thomas Reade, while at Tunis in the early 1830s, mentioned the mosaic pavements visible on the site now known as the Antonine Baths.[81] Mosaics were certainly exposed at the Antonine Baths during excavations by Reade in the mid-nineteenth century, but they were evidently not lifted. Sophia Cracroft mentioned seeing remains of mosaics during her visit to the site in 1858, while Gauckler also noted their existence in 1910, citing Clark Kennedy's *Algeria and Tunis in 1845* as a source for Reade's involvement.[82] The few mosaics from the area of the Antonine Baths still *in situ* have now been published by the team led by Ben Khader.[83]

Although he thought that they were possibly lost in transit, Gauckler noted that fifteen boxes of mosaics, frescoes and vases were sent to France by the Society for the Exploration of Carthage, citing Audollent.[84] In fact, the preface to the publication of the society mentioned these fifteen boxes and an additional sixteen that had just arrived at Marseilles. Since, however, Audollent had found no further trace of these finds or their publication, he precipitately judged the whole enterprise of the society worthless.[85] In fact, the researches of Falbe and Temple produced at least two other surviving mosaics besides those noted above. Falbe said that he showed Grenville Temple two sites where mosaics had been found, of which site no. 90 was one.[86] Another mosaic was certainly from site Falbe no. 66, as I will show. Falbe also knew of a coarse mosaic floor from near the La Malga cisterns (his site no. 61),[87] as well as another mosaic at his site no. 1, a modern house at La Marsa.[88]

Neira Jiménez has discussed two relevant mosaics now in the National Museum of Denmark. A figural mosaic shows four groups of dwarf riders and miniature performing horses on wheeled platforms; the figures are worked in much smaller *tesserae* than the white mosaic background (Fig. 6.4). Above the figures a line of cable on a dark background ends abruptly at either end of the panel,[89] an indication that the mosaic as it now exists is a restoration. The pavement was given to the museum by Falbe in 1846.[90] It is therefore almost certain that this mosaic, too, comes from his

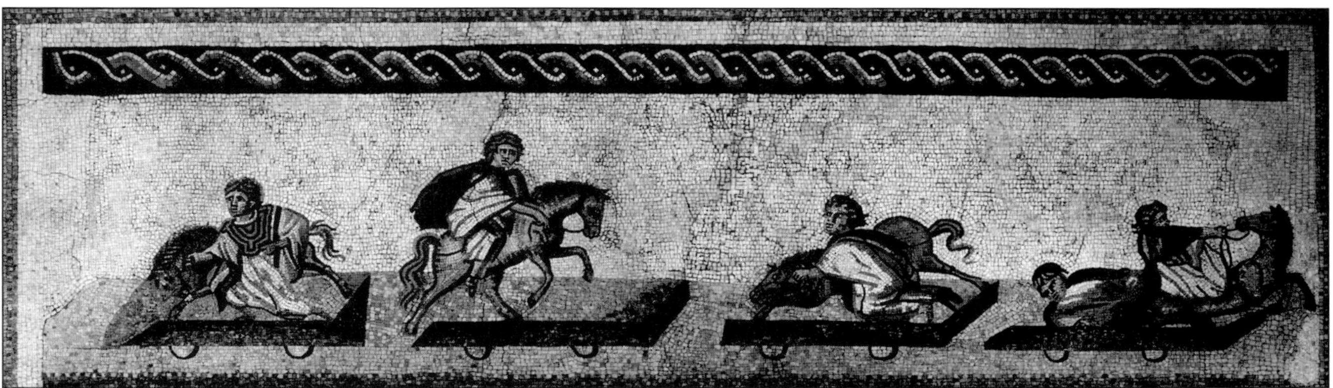

Fig. 6.4 Carthage, detail from the iconographically enigmatic mosaic depicting horses and riders on top of wheeled platforms (equestrian performers?); second/third century AD (?). The mosaic is on display in the National Museum of Denmark, Copenhagen.

excavations at Carthage, and was given to the museum after extensive restoration. The second mosaic is a fragment of a large-scale floral carpet pattern; the preserved piece is a rectangle that appears to be slightly less than a meter across its shorter side, with coarse *tesserae* evidently about a centimeter square.[91] The style is characteristic of Carthage. The fragment was never catalogued, and the museum has no direct evidence that it was a gift of Falbe. Parlasca argued that this fragment of floral carpet mosaic in the National Museum of Copenhagen is from the floor excavated by Falbe in 1824,[92] but this is incorrect.

I see this fragment as the oval area robbed out of an otherwise complete mosaic floor from the northern room of the 'Kobbat bent el Rey,' the small 'bathhouse' at Falbe no. 66 which was drawn by Falbe and explored by Sir Grenville Temple, and which (as noted above, p. 46) has now been excavated and studied in detail by Storz.[93] The northern room and its floor measure 4.25 m by 3.28 m.[94] Storz dated the damaged mosaic remaining *in situ* to the late fourth or early fifth century AD on the basis of the building history of the site. The triple border of the floor survives on all four sides. The plan of the room compared with the photograph of the existing floor suggests that the oval area of missing mosaic opens onto the entrance of the room.[95] The robbed-out area measures approximately one meter wide by two meters long, almost exactly the size of the piece in Copenhagen, which, however, has been restored along the edges to form a neat rectangle.

I have no doubt that this piece was removed in the excavations of Falbe and Grenville Temple; the tell-tale irregular shape of the hole in the remaining floor suggests that they cleared a small area of the pavement and then lifted it, leaving the rest of the room unexcavated. According to Storz, the bedding layers under the mosaics in the northern and southern rooms of this building were single, unlike the double layer of make-up in the central room, and the mortar of the corresponding bedding layer that survives in the southern room was extremely resistant.[96] The properties of the mortar suggest that the outline of the mosaic fragment which was lifted was cut, and the whole piece levered up without necessarily stabilizing the top surface first. Furthermore, since the excavators worked from the doorway, they might have chosen to tunnel under the mosaic as well in order to ease its removal. The central room of this structure was paved with a combination of *opus sectile* (cut marble laid in a pattern) and mosaic, nearly all of which is lost. It is possible that Temple's men also retrieved or tried to retrieve the mosaics in the central room. The Mosaic of Performing Horses may have come from this room, although I think it is more likely that it came from Falbe's house no. 1 at La Marsa. The existence of these two mosaics in Copenhagen is a reminder that there are many unprovenanced mosaics and mosaic fragments in museum and personal collections, of which others may also have been lifted at Carthage before Davis' day.

Other mosaics that were broken up or destroyed

It is therefore clear that a few mosaics of some importance were being excavated and lifted at Carthage before Davis' excavations. Such finds were mutilated and largely or entirely destroyed by persons who had the temerity, but not the competence, to lift them. As Davis' method was not known or not mastered by the French, mosaics at Carthage continued to be lost to incompetent lifting for some time after Davis' day. For example, two small fragments from one mosaic that are now in Vienna were excavated at Carthage for Mohammed, the son of the Khaznadar. M'Charek has suggested that Mohammed's collection was formed around 1858 to 1860,[97] which puts them in a period in which Davis' method might have been used, but was clearly not. A third small fragment from the same mosaic exists in the Bardo Museum in Tunis and a fourth was noted by Balmelle from the museum of Tarbes in the province of Aquitaine in France, where it was first recorded in 1907.[98] The mosaic, which features birds in concave frames, has an all-over floral carpet pattern of interlocking circles. Gozlan proposed a reconstruction of the original design, noting that floral carpet patterns appeared in Italy in the second century and were commonly adopted in the North African provinces in the third century. Only chance and persevering research has linked these scattered and pitifully incomplete fragments, and restored the appearance of this mosaic.[99] Its provenance at Carthage is unknown.

Sainte-Marie was quite justifiably to pass up the opportunity to lift a fine geometric mosaic, a more elegant version of the pattern of the Mosaic of Interlaced Green and Red Circles excavated by Davis at the 'Carthaginian House'. Sainte-Marie discovered this geometric mosaic in 1874 in the area to the south of the Bordj-Djedid cisterns,[100] an area of Roman housing. He described leaving the mosaic *in situ*, because he did not consider it worth the effort of laying it on canvas (*mise en toile*) and the cost of transport. His turn of phrase implies that he was aware of the method of lifting mosaics described by Newton. Sainte-Marie in fact witnessed the partial destruction of a Mosaic of the Grooming of Pegasus by his workmen in 1875.[101] According to Gauckler, this mosaic depicted the winged horse being groomed by three life-sized human figures. The mosaic was discovered in 1874 on the north-west side of gardens belonging to the house of Sidi Ismaïl at Falbe no. 68; that is, between the *decumanus maximus* and *decumanus* 1 north, about three Roman city-blocks from the sea. According to Gauckler, an attempt was made to lift this important figural mosaic by Sainte-Marie's workmen, but it was severely damaged. The only surviving fragment was kept in the house of Mustapha ben-Ismaïl, but was no longer extant when Gauckler arrived at Carthage.[102]

The history of mosaic fragments there which survived the incompetence of early researchers and antiquarians may sometimes be reconstructed by scholars, but a unified index of museums and private collections and a search of records on the original acquisition of artifacts would be required to make confident claims of completeness for the early history of the excavation of Roman-period mosaics at Carthage.

7

The late Roman Mosaic of the Months and Seasons

Davis' eighth site: the Mosaic of the Months and Seasons

Davis' first major find (much delayed from his point of view, as it was discovered only in the January of 1857) was an extraordinarily elegant large polychrome figural mosaic, the Mosaic of the Months and Seasons (part is shown in Fig. 7.1).[1] The mosaic was found at the eighth site that he dug (Site 8); it was also the first he explored which was not marked on Falbe's plan. In Davis' eyes, all the guides and maps with which he had armed himself had proved a useless guide to excavation. Oblivious to how dependent he actually was on the information that they contained and the interpretive views that they embodied, he summarily rejected them, saying: 'Repeated disappointments compelled me to throw aside those published productions which profess to treat upon the topography of Carthage, and I was forced to fall back upon my own resources'.[2]

In the excitement of this first very important find, Davis recorded and published far more information than was his usual wont. He gave a detailed account of the discovery, description and interpretation of this mosaic in about forty pages of more or less relevant text, with two color plates and a plan of the reconstructed mosaic. In addition, the site was marked as 'T[emple of] Astarte' on the map of Carthage included with his text (Fig. 4.4, no. 7).[3] Davis also sent a very large coloured, composite, stone-by-stone drawing of the two main surviving sections of this mosaic to the Foreign Office; they were being completed in May of 1857 and were sent at the end of June (see Colour Plates 1–2).[4]

He eventually lifted the surviving sections of this first pavement, the Mosaic of the Months and Seasons, by an original method invented and carried out by himself. Thanks to the cooperation of the Foreign Office, he sent it off to the British Museum on the frigate HMS *Curaçoa,* which left Carthage with nineteen pieces of this mosaic and one fragment of another in May 1857; the ship returned in July to load more cases on board.[5] The pieces of the Mosaic of the

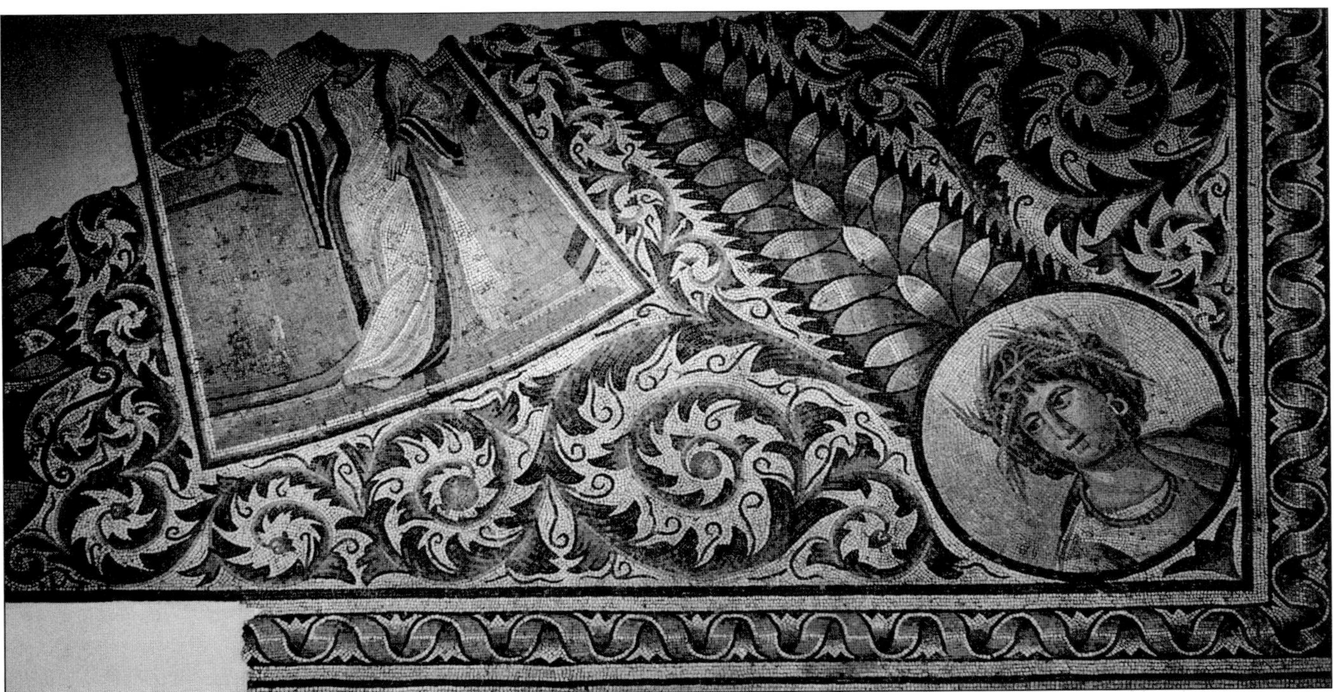

Fig. 7.1 Carthage, Mosaic of the Months and Seasons, last quarter of the fourth century AD, detail of the part showing the bust of Summer (right) and the Month of July (left); compare also Fig. 1.3, colour plate 1 and the front cover of this book. Other parts of the same mosaic are illustrated on the back cover, in colour plates 2 and 3, in Figs 7.4–7.8 and 7.14–15.

Months and Seasons arrived in London in good condition in August[6] and were registered in December; they are now on display in several reconstituted sections on the walls of the north-west stairs in the British Museum.[7] The mosaic was the subject of its first scholarly treatment in an article by Augustus Franks of the British Museum in 1860,[8] which appeared before Davis' own publication of *Carthage and Her Remains*.

The restless Davis often left his men unsupervised as he rode over the site of Carthage looking for possible excavation sites. He had looked over and considered this particular site, but not seriously, as it had minimal ruins above ground. The very next day he discovered that the guardian of the Chapel of Saint Louis, inspired by Davis' own interest, had begun to excavate at a wall which Davis had been inspecting. The wall was located in a large area that had been diligently worked over by Arab stone-robbers. Only this one wall of relatively poor materials was visible above the ground.[9] The long-serving guardian of the chapel, identified as 'Touzon' by most sources, was a rifle-toting former officer of a French North African military unit, the Zouaves.[10] Touzon had regularly been involved in clandestine excavation and the vending of antiquities.[11] This man was a font of false information for the unwary. When the Reverend Joseph Blakesley visited Tunis in 1858, for example, the guardian of Saint Louis assured him that an inscription in his possession of some interest to Blakesley, which referred to Thysdrus (El Djem), came from Carthage itself. Later that morning Davis set him straight, and Blakesley was shocked by the gratuitous lie.[12]

Undoubtedly there were many others who had no way of judging Touzon's veracity or competence. The guardian was much appreciated by Armand de Flaux, who called him 'Dalmas' (possibly his first name). Flaux came to Carthage in the early 1860s on a research mission sponsored by Count Walewski. Flaux was possibly the least effective and least focused among mid-nineteenth-century archaeologists at Carthage. He summarized his expedition as follows: 'I found the famous field to have been traversed by so many able gleaners that there remained not one single ear of grain'. His report to Count Walewski is included in a book he wrote on his impressions of Tunisia; the report is less than twenty brief pages, and half of it was devoted to criticizing Davis and Beulé.[13]

Flaux said that Touzon was originally from Toulon, but had served as guardian of the chapel of Saint Louis for twenty years. In Touzon's own opinion, he was not paid enough to live on. In the opinion of Flaux, however, the guardian was worth more on topographical questions than Falbe, Dureau de la Malle, Davis or Beulé, and he hired him to supervise his excavations. Despite the supposed acumen of his site supervisor, however, all that Flaux recovered from a month's labour were a few mutilated statuettes and sherds of pottery.[14]

Having opened a trench in the area which Davis had inspected the previous day, the enterprising guardian had immediately come down on a four-foot by two-and-a-half-foot (1.2 m by 0.8 m) section of a very fine mosaic. Touzon, who communicated with Davis in Italian, poured water over the mosaic so that Davis could see its elegant polychrome figural design, and added insult to injury by refusing to sell it to him. What he had uncovered was the section of a figure carrying a *sistrum* (the rattle usually associated with the cult of Isis), of which at least twice as large a piece was originally found as survives now. Today the subject is identified as the Month of November (Colour Plate 3). The fragment was subsequently damaged when Touzon tried to lift it, but Davis was eventually able to buy the best remnant from him.[15]

In his published account, Davis freely confessed his extreme mortification that the guardian had beaten him to 'a gem of ancient art'.[16] Touzon pointed out that he had found the mosaic immediately against a wall that was flanked by deep robber pits, and therefore had recovered all that had survived. But Davis saw that the wall post-dated the mosaic, since it cut through it. Beyond the wall and to the right, where he thought that the mosaic must have continued, there was a very high mound of soil, evidently thrown up from a deep trench which ran perpendicular to the wall. The trench was undoubtedly relatively recent, and dug by Arabs looking for building materials. This was Franks' interpretation, and it is certainly correct, given the known endemic presence of Arab quarriers for building materials at Carthage.[17] Ignoring the guardian's ridicule, Davis at once set his men to dig through this fourteen-foot-high (4.3 m) depth of soil.

A sketch-plan of the disturbed ground immediately above the mosaic (Fig. 7.2) was published in *Carthage and Her Remains*. In the original edition, the plan was incorrectly and inexplicably labelled 'The northern portion of the regency of Tunis'. This was corrected to 'Ground Plan of the First Discovery' in the edition with longer pagination; the plan has no scale or indication of direction. Letters of the alphabet related the topography above the ground to the mosaic finds below;[18] the plan shows heaps of soil thrown up by the local stone-robbers on either side of a line of deep trenching. On this plan, 'H' marks the guardian's first find, against a wall of irregularly-placed stones; 'D' the placement of the colossal corner bust on the large section of mosaic first found by Davis; and 'I' the corner bust on the second large section found by Davis.

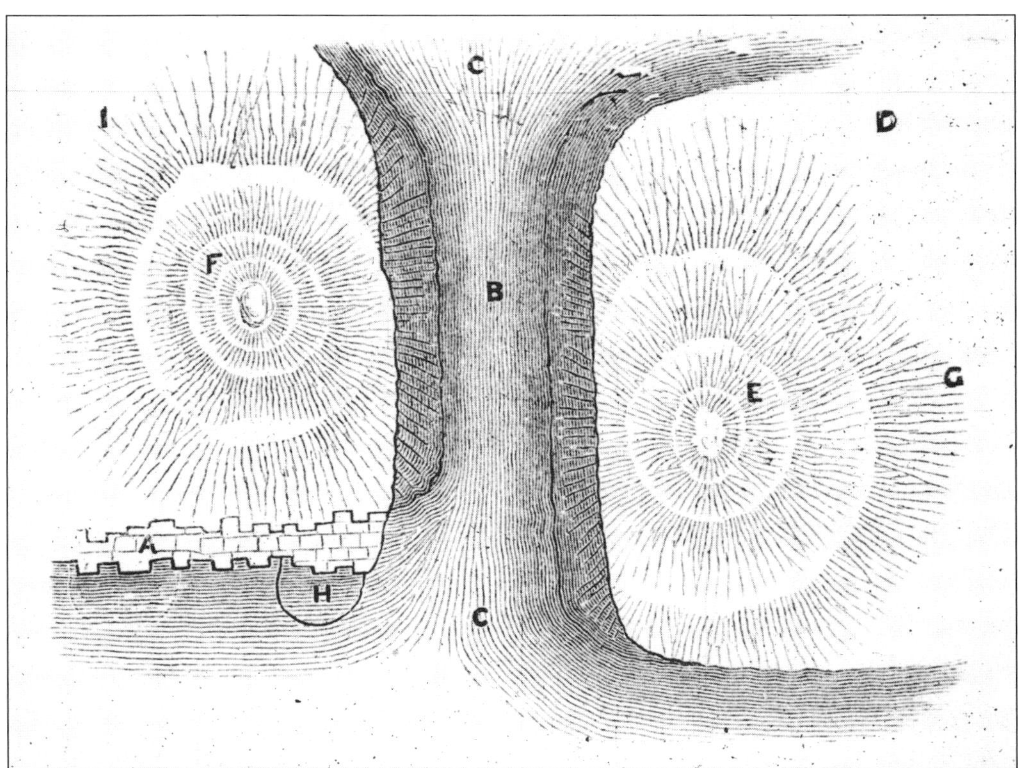

Fig. 7.2 Davis' drawing of the ground plan of the area above the Mosaic of the Months and Seasons

Davis and his men dug in the area on the other side of the wall for the rest of the day, with no pause for meals until after darkness had fallen. Before the day was over, they had revealed and then began to clear a large section of the mosaic, described by Davis as about fifteen by nine feet (4.6 m by 2.7 m).[19] This section was found under the mound labelled 'E' on the ground plan. Against a background of acanthus scrolls, two framed sections of a wide circular band were preserved, with full-length figures, just under life-size and modestly robed. A colossal bust filled a circular medallion in the corner of the mosaic.[20] The figures in this panel are now identified as the Months of March and April; the corner bust is Spring (see photograph on back cover and Figs 7.14–15).

After a troubled night, Davis woke to the realization that the mosaic must have originally continued on the other side of the robber trench, immediately on the other side of the wall, where there was another high mound of soil ('F' on his ground plan); so he set his men to work again. A second large section of the mosaic was found here; this section had another full-length framed female figure and a colossal corner bust, this time of a person crowned by ears of wheat.[21] The figure in this framed panel is now identified as July; the corner bust is Summer. Davis had the pieces cleared, cleaned and drawn *in situ*. Since both large segments had corners and borders, his artist, Henry Ferriere, was able to reconstruct the plan of the whole floor. The reconstruction showed the figures as having occupied eight symmetrically-placed, framed sections of a wide circular band (Fig. 7.3).[22]

On three sides of the original room there are stretches where the mosaic is complete; the fourth side is entirely missing. Two opposite sides of the room have identical symmetrical borders, with large, classical, footed craters at either end, from which rise curving acanthus garlands (Fig. 7.4). In the middle of these two symmetrical borders there was a large rosette formed of acanthus leaves, slightly larger than the corner medallions of the main floor. It seems most likely that the mosaic ran up to the walls of the room on these two sides.

The border of the third preserved side is completely different. It is made up of rectangular panels, and the surviving layout is symmetrical. According to Davis' plan of the floor, the rectangular panel with two dolphins facing each other that survives in this border would have been just to the right of the centre point of this side of the room (Fig. 7.5; compare Colour Plate 1). There is more than enough room for a second identical dolphin panel to the left, but this area of the mosaic was lost to the robber trench, leaving room in the centre of the border for a small square panel, with no good basis for its suggested restoration. Two different geometric panels with lozenges survived at either end of

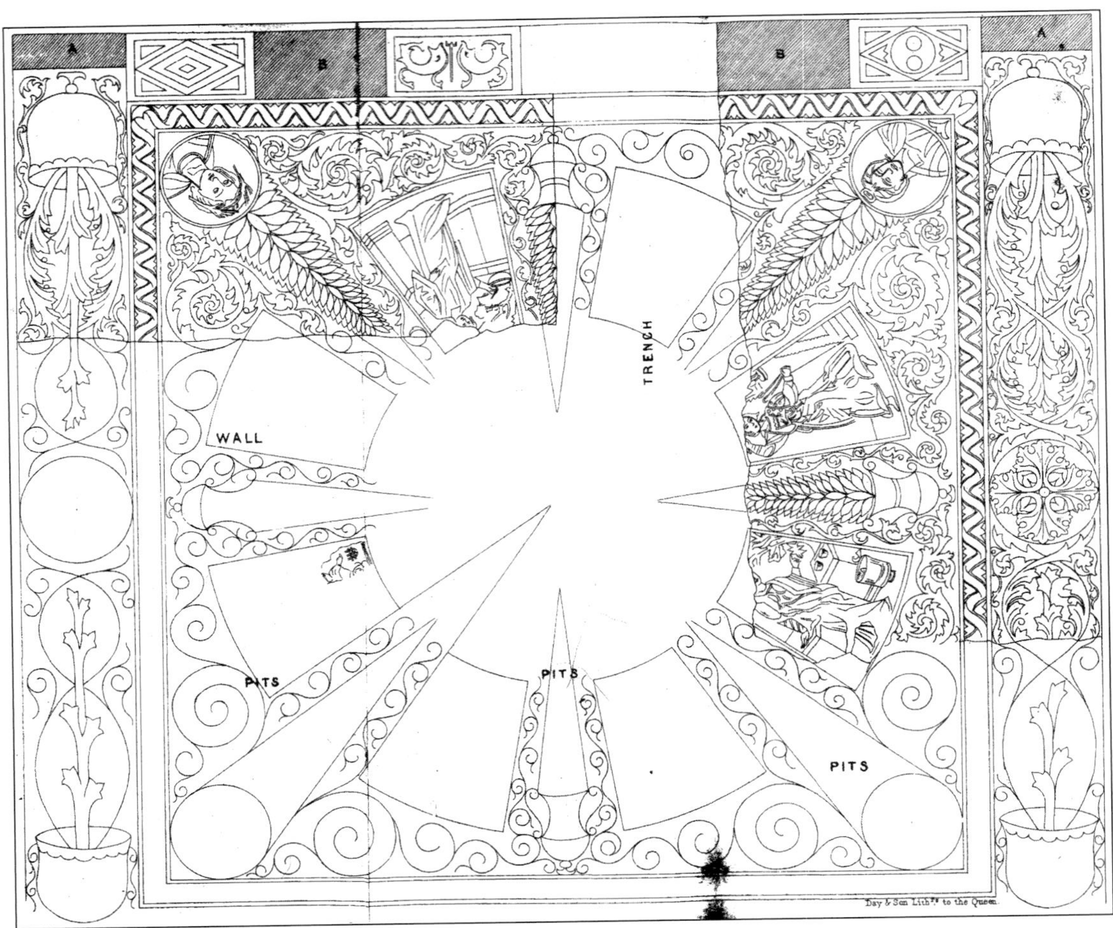

Fig. 7.3 Davis' reconstruction of the Mosaic of the Months and Seasons, drawn by Henry Ferriere

this border, and are still extant (one is Fig. 7.6). Two alternating rectangular panels which appear hatched on Davis' drawing of the mosaic were marked 'found broken' in a sketch-plan of which a copy survives, while narrower rectangles at the extreme ends of the border were labelled 'plain white & broken'.[23] This information shows that Franks' suggestion that the missing panels were the bases of half-columns and pilasters cannot be correct.[24] Franks suggested that this side of the room was a threshold, as themes having to do with the sea were commonly used for thresholds. Davis eventually retrieved all the surviving mosaic in nineteen pieces,[25] except for a piece of the border lost in the first experiment at lifting (see below). Davis published two colour plates of details of the mosaic, including one of April, which he entitled 'Priestess dancing before an idol' (Fig. 7.7), and the other of 'Ceres' (see below).

Davis' interpretation of the mosaic

Although Davis had read very widely in the ancient texts and used them as a basis for his interpretation of the mosaic, he gave them all the same weight and did not apply any serious critical tests to his theories. He was of the opinion that his first big find was Punic, its subject dancing priestesses, while the bust crowned with ears of wheat he called a 'Head of Ceres' (Fig. 7.8; compare photograph on front cover). According to Davis, the mosaic was part of a Punic chapel in the immediate environs of the 'Temple of Astarte.' He implicitly understood the 'Hill of Juno' as the location of the Temple. It was his belief that this subsidiary chapel was dedicated to four female divinities, shown in the corner medallions; he identified the four as Dido and Anna, Ceres and Proserpina.[26] In Davis' opinion, the two surviving medallions were therefore of Dido (the bust subsequently identified as 'Spring') and Ceres (now identified as 'Summer').

The ancient texts which Davis used for this interpretation of the floor had been cited in Dureau de la Malle.[27] Most influential on Davis was a description written in the early fifth century AD, and ascribed in his day to Prosper of Aquitaine. According to this, the 'Temple of Coelestis' at Carthage was huge, surrounded by temples of all the gods, the whole occupying nearly two miles in extent. The temple was gorgeous-

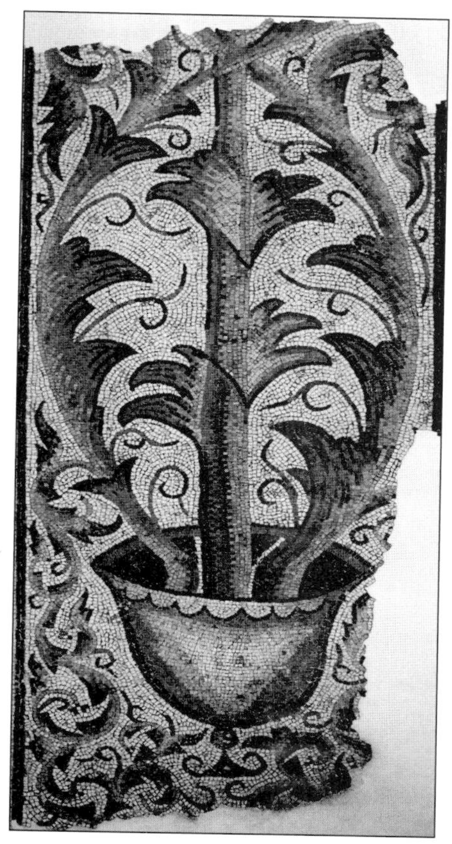

Fig. 7.4 An acanthus scroll, detail of part of the border from the Mosaic of the Months and Seasons; it comes from the part adjacent to the roundel containing the bust of Summer (see Colour Plate 2, right)

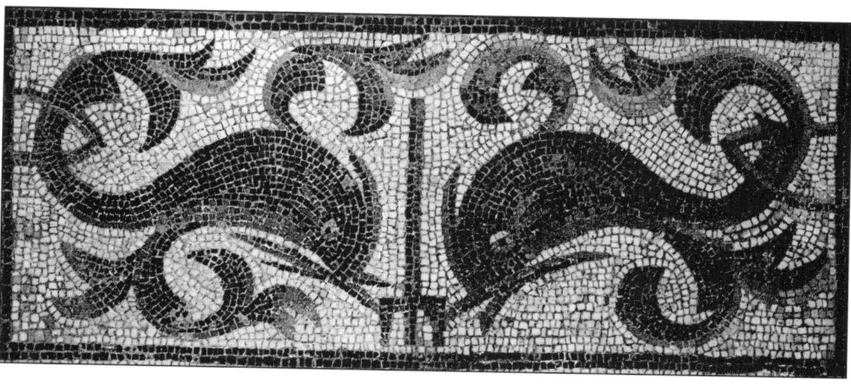

Fig. 7.5 (above) *A panel depicting decorative dolphins, symmetrically confronting one another either side of a trident, a detail from the Mosaic of the Months and Seasons. Fig. 7.6* (below) *A geometric panel from the same mosaic; for the position of both panels on the floor, see Fig. 7.13 and Colour Plates 1 and 2.*

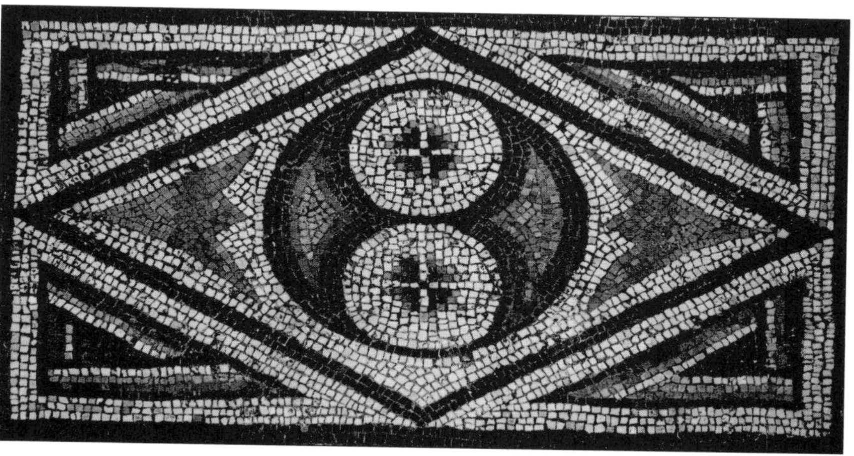

ly decorated, and although the Latin is somewhat obscure, the text made a point of the elegance of its pavements.[28] The writer was an eye-witness when the site was consecrated by Bishop Aurelius as a Christian church, perhaps in AD 399,[29] so he was not describing the Punic arrangements, but the state of the Temple of 'Coelestis' (Caelestis) in the late Roman era. A precinct occupying nearly two miles (3.2 km) in extent does not square easily with the actual size of the Hill of Juno, or even with the entire extent of the street-grid of Roman Carthage, which is just under two kilometers from north to south.[30] Davis' published map shows that he dealt with the space problem by running the 'District of Astarte' in a curving line along the western (where it is marked) and north-western side of the city (where he placed the 'Temple of Diana' and the 'Temple of Astarte'), all of which he saw as belonging to the precinct described by Prosper (Fig. 4.4, no. 7).

He then argued that Dido and her sister Anna were worshipped at Carthage. For Dido, Davis cited Justin, who said that the Carthaginians worshipped Dido as a goddess as long as the city stood unconquered.[31] As for Anna, Davis argued that a visit of Anna to Italy was recorded in Vergil's *Aeneid*, after which she was considered a goddess in Rome and elsewhere under the name Anna Perenna.[32] Ovid had told the story of Dido's sister Anna in Italy and her subsequent metamorphosis into the Italian goddess Anna Perenna, whose festival was celebrated on the Ides of March.[33] Silius Italicus also recounted the story of Anna in his epic poem on the Second Punic War, and had Hannibal vow a temple to her at Carthage.[34] Davis was correct that the Romans conflated Dido's sister with the Roman year goddess, Anna Perenna, but when he took these sources as evidence for a Punic cult of Anna at Carthage, he was not thinking critically.

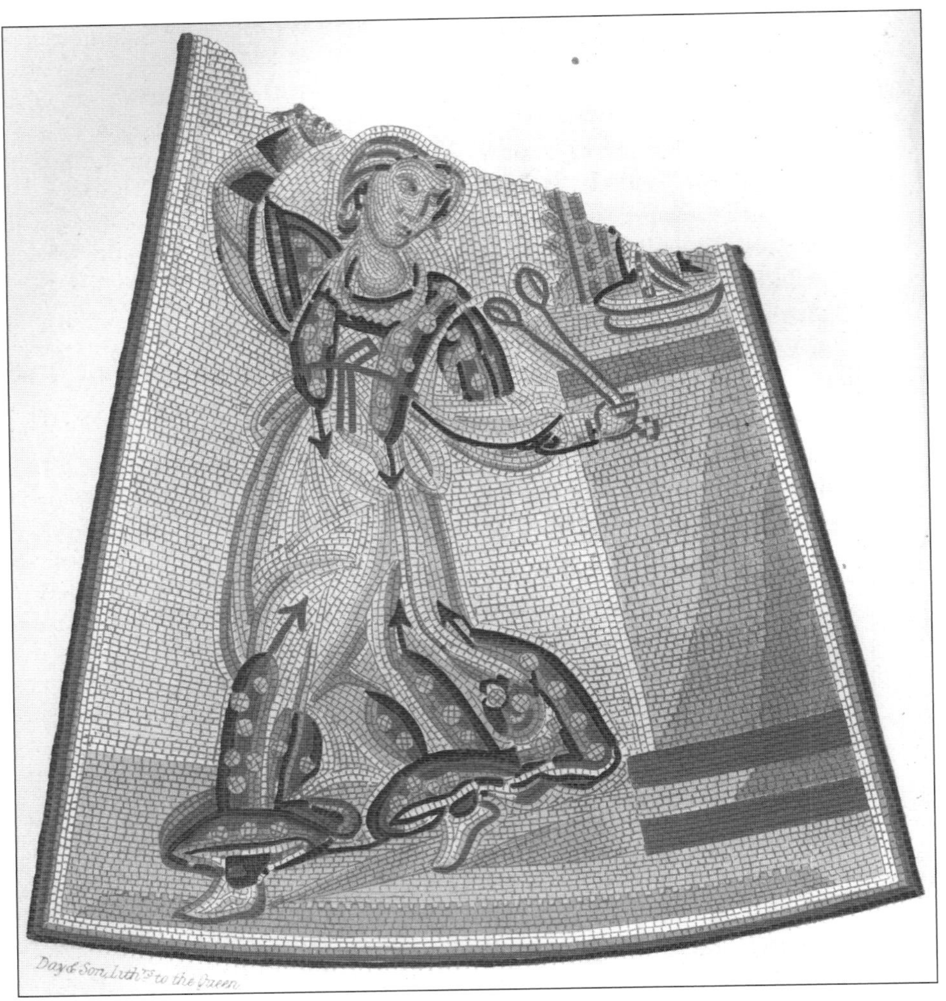

7.7 (left) *Davis' (coloured) lithograph of the Month of April, which he called 'priestess dancing before an idol'*

Fig. 7.8 (below) *Davis' (coloured) lithograph of the bust of Summer, which he called 'head of Ceres from the Temple of Astarte'*

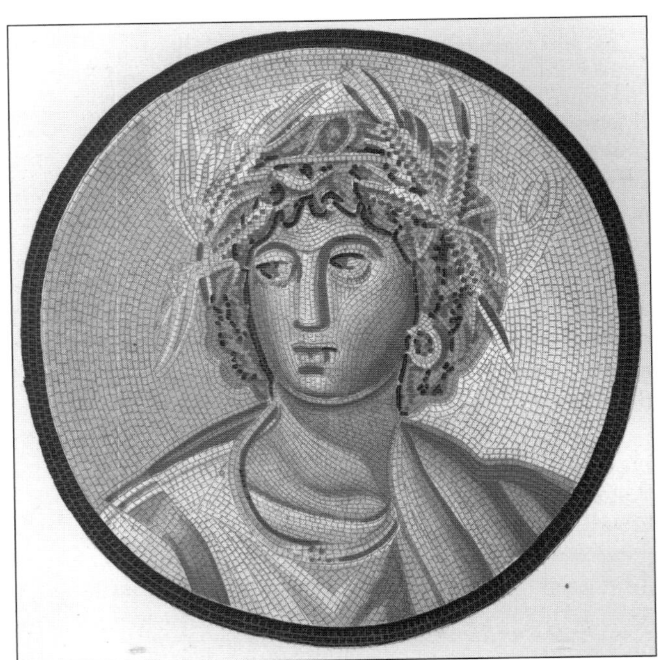

In a text of Diodorus Siculus, Davis found that worship of Ceres and Proserpina was introduced to Carthage according to a peace treaty imposed by Gelon (tyrant of Syracuse in 480 BC). In fact, although the Carthaginians suffered a famous defeat at the Battle of Himera in Sicily in that year, the introduction of the cult took place at Carthage only in 396 BC, perhaps in recompense for the desecration of Greek cults in Sicily by the Punic general Himilco.[35] Davis' claim that the Carthaginians did not give Ceres and Persephone their own temple, but associated them with the worship of Dido and Anna in one of the subsidiary chapels belonging to the Punic 'Temple of Astarte', seems to be based on his own theory that the Mosaic of the Months and Seasons belonged to such a subsidiary chapel, and showed these four, whom he considered to be goddesses of the Carthaginians, together.[36]

Davis believed that his mosaic fixed the site of the Punic chapel, and therefore of the 'Temple of Astarte,' for which he said that Dureau de la Malle had been unable to suggest a location. The latter had in fact said that the Temple of Astarte must have been near the Byrsa; the idea that was later widely accepted, that the temple lay on the hill of Juno, depends at least partly on his argumentation.[37] Dureau de la Malle was thinking of the Juno Coelestis or Caelestis of Roman Carthage, the equivalent to the Punic Astarte or Tanit. Davis himself had found no evidence of such a temple on the summit of the 'Hill of Juno,' but Beulé confidently considered the Hill of Juno to be its site after he found what he took to be a relief depicting the goddess on the north side of the Byrsa Hill. The relief does not prove his case, as it was actually a late Punic grave *stele* depicting a Carthaginian woman, not a goddess, as his drawing clearly shows.[38]

Although Davis conceded that the Punic temple complex had been entirely destroyed at the time of the Roman conquest, he thought that the text he ascribed to Prosper demonstrated that the Romans had later restored all the former aspects of worship. The literary evidence certainly indicates that the Temple of Juno Caelestis was still standing in AD 399, when it was rededicated as a Christian church; but the temple was razed on imperial orders in AD 421, after which the area became a cemetery.[39] Davis was oblivious to the extreme difficulty inherent in the idea that this particular mosaic floor, if indeed Punic, had survived these vicissitudes.[40] His archaeological justifications for a Punic date were as follows: the mosaic was of fine quality; it was found ten feet (3.0 m) below the surface (although earlier he had said that ruins pre-dating the last Punic War were at least twenty feet [6 m] down);[41] the mosaic was under the remains of two superimposed nondescript floors ('mortar mixed with small stones'), which his workmen broke up to reach the lower mosaic; the female figures were clothed in costumes which did not look Roman to his eyes;[42] and finally, the mosaic was laid over a mortar which was very thick, white and friable, unlike the mortars which he recognized as being Roman, which were thinner, very hard and made with lime, crushed brick and ash. This detail, which was clearly expressed by Davis, suggests a possible line of argument for dating the mosaic (see Appendix 3). Davis also described a thin layer of charcoal that overlay the mosaic, and he suggested that the building had been destroyed by fire.[43]

Davis' description of the excavation

Vaux expressed the disappointment occasioned at the British Museum by Davis' unscholarly account of his excavations. In a paper to the Royal Society, Vaux regretted that the reader of Davis' *Carthage and Her Remains* would not find there 'any connected narrative of the steps Mr. Davis followed in his excavations'.[44] Franks had also expressed a hope that Davis would present a full account of the circumstances of the excavation, but the latter himself had a very narrow view of his aims; success was the retrieval of fine art objects, and he was not interested in establishing the context of his finds in any detail. For the Mosaic of the Months and Seasons, on the other hand, Davis did discuss the excavation and the conservation of the mosaic in voluminous detail, although it has cost me a great deal of effort and time to make good sense of his account.

Davis described the field in which the mosaic was found as being in a highly disturbed state; the immediate area was a 'fearful scene of havoc and destruction'.[45] He described deep pits here, including one 300 ft across: an extent of over 90 m was of significant size in terms of the Roman city, since a city-block measured 140 m by 35 m. Davis wrote that the immediate area of disturbed ground over the mosaic was in a hollow which lay about six feet (1.8 m) below the surface of the surrounding fields.[46] The tremendously-disturbed six-feet deep hollow in the field directly over the mosaic certainly, I believe, represented the work of perhaps very recent stone robbers in removing the fallen superstructure of a massive stone building.

A relatively small area is sketched on the ground plan, which must cover only about twenty-five feet by twenty feet (7.6 m by 6.1 m), since Davis related points 'I' and 'D' on the plan to the surviving circular medallions of the mosaic, and the dimensions of the mosaic are known. I superimposed the ground plan on the mosaic at the same scale, clarifying what Davis found in his excavation (Fig. 7.9). Within the area of the ground plan there was a deep central robber trench ('C/B/C'), perpendicular to an imaginary line joining the two circular medallions. In a letter to Clarendon, Davis ascribed this trench to stone robbers ('rude Barbarians who dug through the mosaic in search of stone for building purposes'). On either side of the trench the ground plan showed high mounds of displaced soil, which were beginning to slump into the intervening trench. The damage to the fourth side, where the mosaic was completely lost, was ascribed by Davis to the Romans, 'who built new foundations through the Mosaic having evidently been ignorant of its existence'.[47] On his plan of the mosaic, he has marked 'pits' three times across this area. While it is possible to quibble with points of detail, it seems certain that one whole side of the mosaic was lost to a major building project in late antiquity. While the later building could have been constructed in the Vandal or Byzantine period, its monumentality and the fact that it was built on the same alignment as the Mosaic of the Months and Seasons suggest that it can be dated within the late period of the city's prosperity, and was

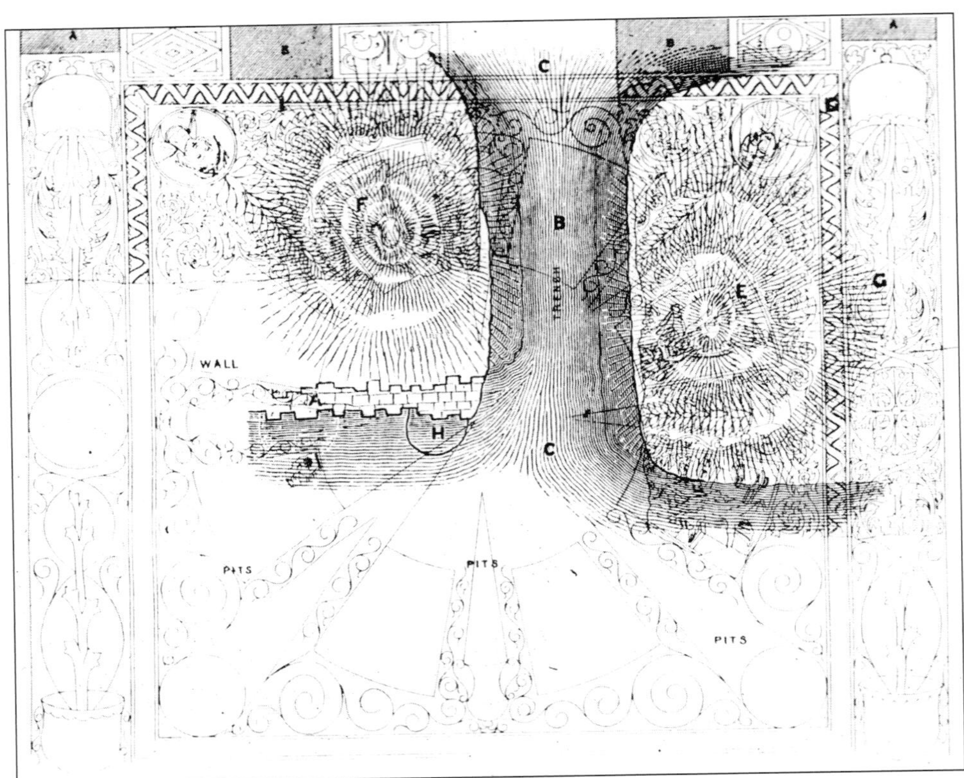

Fig. 7.9 Davis' drawing of the Mosaic of the Months and Seasons superimposed on his ground plan (compare Figs 7.2 and 7.3)

therefore built no later than the mid-sixth century. The standing walls of this great building were then robbed out before Davis' day. The wall at the foot of which the fragment of November was found was removed by him, but his ground plan shows that it was built with much smaller stones, which the stone-robbers had ignored; this wall was clearly later than and unrelated to the massive building which destroyed much of the mosaic. In contrast, the trench 'C/B/C' represented a perpendicular line of wall, probably belonging to the same massive late building, which had been removed in the very recent past, as the thrown-up heaps of soil on either side still attested to the work. This ancient building was certainly constructed with no respect for the existence of the earlier mosaic.

Regularly at Carthage stone walls, whether Punic or Roman, were built in a construction technique designated *opus Africanum* ('African work'), in which vertical columns of large rectangular cut-stone blocks alternated with an infill of smaller stones. The diligence of the stone robbers in displacing so much soil to retrieve the walls here suggest that these were fine ashlar walls preserved to a good height (although not necessarily above the surface of the ground), possibly from an important Vandal or Byzantine structure.

The neat and regular lines of the area missing between the two preserved pieces of the mosaic indicate that the stone-robbers were after a wall which, although later, was on the same orthogonal alignment as the walls of the room and building in which the mosaic lay (Fig. 7.2). Davis gave no trustworthy indication of the orientation of the mosaic *in situ* (one might argue that the threshold was on the north side, as it seems to be at the top of Ferriere's drawing), but the fact that the finished borders of the mosaic and the walls which cut through it later are on the same alignment means that the room and its house were aligned with the regular street-grid.

Davis' plan shows that the cut through the mosaic for the later stone wall (along the line 'C/B/C') varied from four and a half to five feet (1.4 m to 1.5 m) across. This relatively narrow cut, which was made at the time the wall was built, suggests that the latter probably did not have a wide foundation trench. The later robber-trench, as is typical for robber-trenches at Carthage at foundation level, was probably only as wide as the blocks retrieved.

The room implied by the mosaic is a strict rectangle, and belonged to a luxury house or a public building planned on orthogonal lines. Davis did not publish any evidence for the nature of the building; he did not describe the thickness, materials or construction style of the walls, for example, although the preservation of the edges of the mosaic makes it certain that he came up against the line of those walls. The survival of later floors, or possibly of layers of destruction debris, above this mosaic make it unlikely, although not impossible, that the walls of the earlier building to which our mosaic belonged were completely robbed out in antiquity.

Davis' discussion and plan clarify the state of the ground, but they are not very helpful in ascertaining the stratigraphic depth of the mosaic, despite Davis' statement that the mosaic was found ten feet (3.0 m) below the surface. Davis had earlier stated that Punic finds come from a depth of twenty feet (6.0 m), and this is not an unreasonable generality; but in his discussion of the Mosaic of the Months and Seasons he said that Roman pavements occurred at a depth of between two and five feet (0.6 m to 1.5 m), but Punic ones occurred at a depth of ten feet or more. I suspect that he modified his earlier opinion to agree with the facts of this excavation, and with his argument that this mosaic was Punic.

In his book he stated that there were two nondescript levels of pavement, respectively at one and two feet (0.3 m and 0.6 m) from the surface of the mosaic, made up of 'mortar mixed with small stones'.[48] In his earlier letter to Clarendon, on the other hand, he had said that his workmen had broken through 'no less than three distinct floors, before it was brought to light'.[49] The idea that there were three floors above the mosaic was followed by Franks, who relied on information in the letters, and subsequently repeated by Gauckler; the latter, however, who was an experienced archaeologist, was not convinced that Davis saw floors at all, and suggested that these may have been destruction layers ('three layers of superimposed rubble').[50]

Establishing the depth of the Mosaic of the Months and Seasons from Davis' evidence is impossible: while there is no reason to reject his claim that the mosaic was ten feet (3 m) below the surface, it is difficult to understand how this relates to the fact that the floor was found under a mound fourteen feet (4.3 m) high. Furthermore, we cannot know the real depth of the larger hollow in which the mosaic and its building lay. On the other hand, because Davis'ground plan shows two slumping peaks of soil thrown up on either side of trench 'C/B/C' (within a very restricted area), it is likely that each of these mounds was about four feet (1.2 m) high, and the fourteen-foot (4.3 m) depth which Davis described is the whole depth his workmen had to dig through to reach the mosaic (see Fig. 7.2).

Confusingly, three successive layers of *mosaic* pavement were discussed by Mr George Leighton Ditson, an American journalist for the *New York Tribune*.[51] Ditson had raved over the Mosaic of the Months and Seasons, defending a Punic date, and Davis quoted Ditson at length, possibly with a copy of the latter's newspaper article in hand. Ditson was a travel writer who had trained as a medical doctor but never practised. He wrote several books, and his observations on Davis' mosaics re-appeared in his book *The Crescent and the French Crusades* (1859), which was later reissued under the more transparent title *Adventures and Observations on the North Coast of Africa*.[52] Ditson visited Carthage in March and April of 1857 and, if he saw the mosaic before it was lifted, as he implies, probably arrived no later than mid-February. It seems, however, that Davis was taken with Ditson's account because the latter agreed with Davis that the mosaic was Punic. Ditson, however, thoroughly confused matters when he described three superimposed mosaic floors, the lowest one five feet (1.5 m) below the surface, while to the north and right there was a second, evidently visible in the cut and about three inches (7 cm) above. Three or four feet (*c.* 1 m) above that floor there was a third mosaic on the eastern side, at the same elevation as a figure of Victory, about which Ditson was also enthusiastic.[53] This does not agree at all with Davis' account of the nondescript floor levels noted above the Mosaic of the Months and Seasons.

Careful reading of this passage and of Davis' note indicates that Ditson was not describing mosaic floors above the Mosaic of the Months and Seasons, however, but at another site, the site of the Mosaic of Victory with Inscription (Site 13: Fig. 8.3), which can be certainly identified from Davis' description of it much later in the text. Davis discovered the Mosaic of Victory at Falbe's site 90, where Falbe himself had found mosaics on the sea-shore in 1824 and again in 1838. Davis was already digging this site in the spring of 1857, when Ditson was visiting Carthage, since these mosaics were among those shipped on HMS *Curaçoa* at the time of its second call at Carthage. As mentioned above (pp. 93–4), the *Curaçoa* arrived in London in August, and the finds, including the Mosaic of Victory with Inscription and three geometric mosaics stratigraphically below it, were catalogued in December of the same year. Ditson's observations are, therefore, not relevant to the floors and depth of soil over the Mosaic of the Months and Seasons; however, an understanding of the two sites he confused illuminates the later confusion of Wilmanns and Mommsen over the description and site of the Mosaic of the Months and Seasons.[54]

The real site of the mosaic according to Davis' text and map

The Mosaic of the Months and Seasons is itself well documented, as are the immediate circumstances of its excavation. Nevertheless, with no more than Davis' written description, it would be almost impossible to determine exactly where the mosaic was found. This is largely because Davis used his own idiosyncratic place-names for all the landmarks of ancient Carthage, while the archaeologists who followed him at Carthage over the next century did the same, creating an almost impenetrable confusion. It requires detailed, first-hand knowledge of the ancient city and its topography to make any sense of Davis' account and to locate the find-spot of the mosaic with confidence.

As noted above (p. 96), Davis identified the site of the Mosaic of the Months and Seasons with the 'Temple of Astarte'; his illustration of one of the circular corner busts of the mosaic was also labelled 'Head of Ceres from the Temple of Astarte' (Fig. 7.8 and Colour Plate 1).[55] Davis said that he found the mosaic in a spot he had previously investigated, which he knew as the 'Temple of Coelestis' or the 'Temple of Astarte.' Davis also called the site the 'Temple of Juno'.[56] This is all highly misleading. The site of the Mosaic of the Months and Seasons was certainly not on the Hill of Juno, as his designation may seem to imply. Davis' 'Temple of Astarte' (where he found the mosaic) lies in fact well over 100 m north-west of the summit of the Hill of Juno. The truth is that he only designated the site of the mosaic as the location of the 'Temple of Astarte' after he interpreted his find as a pavement in a temple belonging to the great precinct of the goddess.

Davis adopted from Dureau de la Malle the idea that the site of the temple could and should be identified, but he was not convinced by the somewhat open arguments of the French scholar, and felt perfectly justified in publishing his own ideas. He described the location of the two houses which he was excavating in October 1857, both of them in fact situated on what is now known as the Odeon Hill, as being on the 'Byrsa' and not far from the area where the 'first large mosaic' was excavated.[57] While scholars have ordinarily followed Dureau de la Malle in identifying the Saint Louis Hill, which was the highest hill (60.5 m above sea-level) in the geographical centre of Carthage, as the Punic Byrsa, Davis by contrast as we have seen (pp. 57–8) placed the Byrsa on Bordj-Djedid, a cliff above the shore on the north-eastern side of the city. Further-more, he did not limit his unconventional conception of the Byrsa to the modest height we call Bordj-Djedid today, but included the whole eastern and northern area of its continuation, the Odeon Hill, right up to the line of the Theodosian Wall on the northern side of the late Roman city. In other words, Davis described the site of the Mosaic of the Months and Seasons as either Bordj-Djedid or the Byrsa, whereas modern nomenclature would place Bordj-Djedid and the Byrsa Hill a kilometer apart. In actual fact, and in modern terms, the site of the Mosaic of the Months and Seasons is on the south-western slope of the Odeon Hill.

Correlations with the street-grid of Roman Carthage and modern maps that incorporate it allow the placement of Davis' site of the 'Temple of Astarte' in relation to the street-grid (Fig. 4.12). Davis discovered the Mosaic of the Months and Seasons in the northern half of the city, between the Hill of Juno and the Odeon Hill. The site is marked on both his sketch-maps, where the location of the site has only a relative value, as well as on his published map. He marked the site on his first sketch-map with the notation that meant 'no ruins, finds.' On it the site lay north-east (the sketch-map direction is not accurate) of his unproductive site on the Hill of Juno. On the second sketch-map, the site is shown on the south-western side of the summit of the Odeon Hill, just west of his 'Temple of Saturn.' The 'Temple of Saturn,' now generally known as the Circular Monument, is marked as Davis' site 16 on the published map, and is a reliable orientation point because it still exists on the ground. On this published map, which is topographically accurate, the site of the mosaic is labelled 'T[emple of] Astarte' with a point; the point is located on the south-western slope of the Odeon Hill. It lies at the south end of the block between *decumani* 3 and 4 north and between *cardines* 1 and 2 west. The elevation in this area is between forty and forty-five meters above sea-level.[58] There is no equivalent site on the plan of Falbe, which agrees with Davis' statement that the area had no ruins.

The point on Davis' published map lies on the short side of one Roman city-block west and immediately north of the *triclinium* (dining-room) containing the 'Mosaic of the Seasons' in the House of the Horses ('Maison des Chevaux'),[59] what is probably a large Roman house, that was not to be excavated until 1960 (Fig. 7.10). The House of the Horses has one of the most impressive programmes of mosaics, dated to the first quarter of the fourth century AD, yet to be found at Carthage. Because Davis' points are placed thirty to forty meters west of their real position in this area, as is shown by the accurate and indicated positions of the Circular Monument, the original site of the Mosaic of the Months and Seasons is probably one short block east of its position on Davis' map, that is, in the south end of the block between *decumani* 3 and 4 north and between the *cardo maximus* and *cardo* 1 west. This would place it immediately contiguous to the *triclinium* of the Mosaic of the Seasons in the House of the Horses; if this is indeed the correct location, as I believe, then the mosaic probably belongs to that great residential complex.

All of Davis' indicators locate the site of his 'Temple of Astarte' and Mosaic of the Months and Seasons on

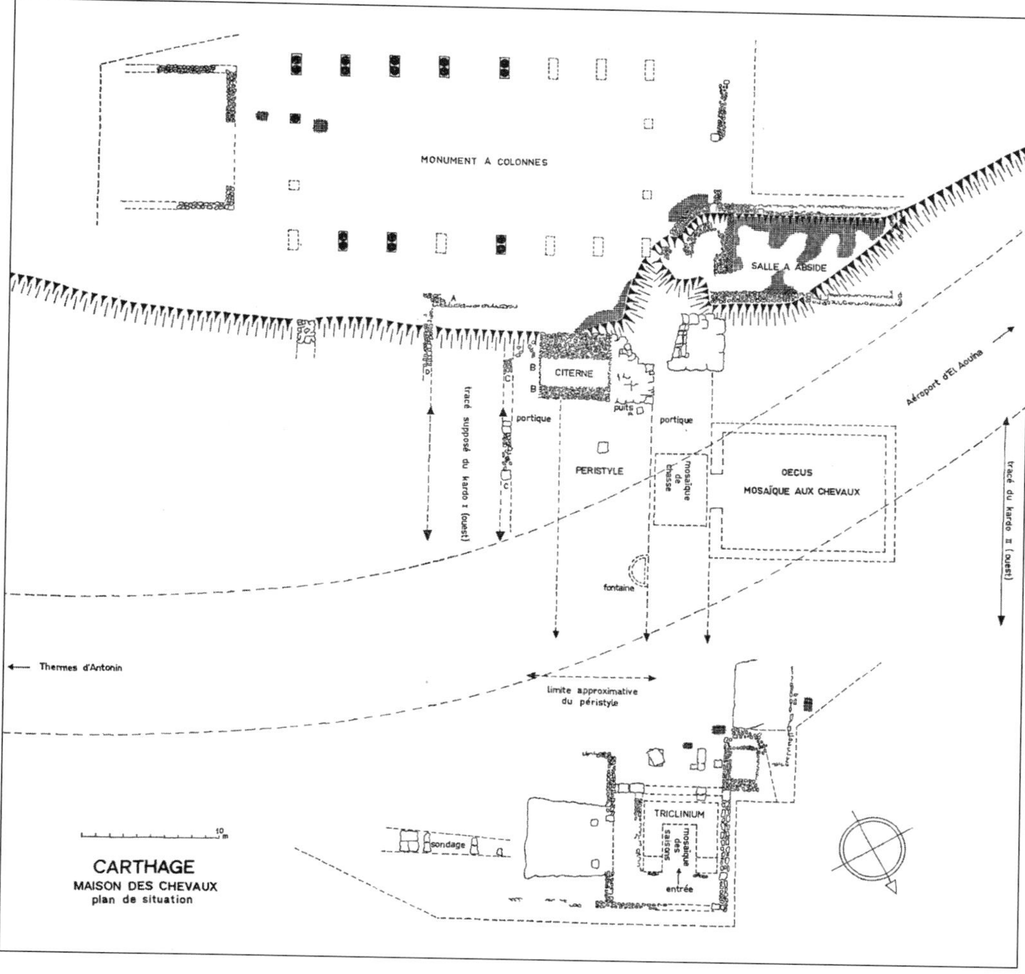

Fig. 7.10 Plan of the House of the Horses and the columnar hall. The latter and the adjacent apsed room (top right) were excavated in 1920–22, the rest in 1960 in advance of the building of a new road (the course of which is indicated by the dotted lines). The room containing the mosaic of the horses (Fig. 7.11) lay directly, as can be seen here, in the line of this new highway.

the south-western slope of the Odeon Hill. The site is immediately adjacent to the north side of the 'House of the Seasons.' The House of the Seasons, although it lay on the north side of the theoretical line of *decumanus* 3 north, was amalgamated with the 'House of the Horses' in such fashion that the line of *decumanus* 3 was absorbed. These houses are the sites of the Mosaic of the Horses, a Mosaic of Children Hunting, and a Mosaic of the Seasons. The Mosaic of the Horses, which survives nearly complete, is one of the most interesting and impressive mosaics ever excavated at Carthage (Fig. 7.11). The complex was also integrated with the great columned and vaulted halls immediately to the south (Figs 12.2–3), which had been identified by Delattre and later by Lézine as the 'Baths of Gargilius,' the site of an important church council in AD 411.[60] These halls are still referred to as the 'Baths of Gargilius' at Carthage today, although there is no evidence for this identification, and earlier scholars from the time of Dureau de la Malle onward had applied the same designation, probably also incorrectly, to the great baths at Falbe no. 54.

The whole complex of the 'House of the Horses' was identified by Picard as the headquarters of the racing faction of the 'Blues'.[61] While there are good reasons to consider the structures in the area as a unified complex, Picard's identification is not satisfactory. Salomonson more conservatively suggested that the complex was the home of an important magistrate of Roman Carthage.[62] I believe that the size of the complex, which incorporated domestic quarters as well as public halls, its location on the *cardo maximus* not far from the Forum on the Byrsa hill, and the elegance and 'political correctness' of its mosaic programme suggest that this complex was none other than the palace of the proconsul, the governor of the province of Africa.

The location of the palace of the proconsul at Carthage has not been convincingly identified. A Vandal or Byzantine edifice on the south corner of the artificial plateau of the Byrsa was not the Roman proconsul's palace, despite its location in the administrative heart of the Roman city.[63] The heavy foundations of this rectangular edifice lie over and across a major temple on the plan of the monumental structures of

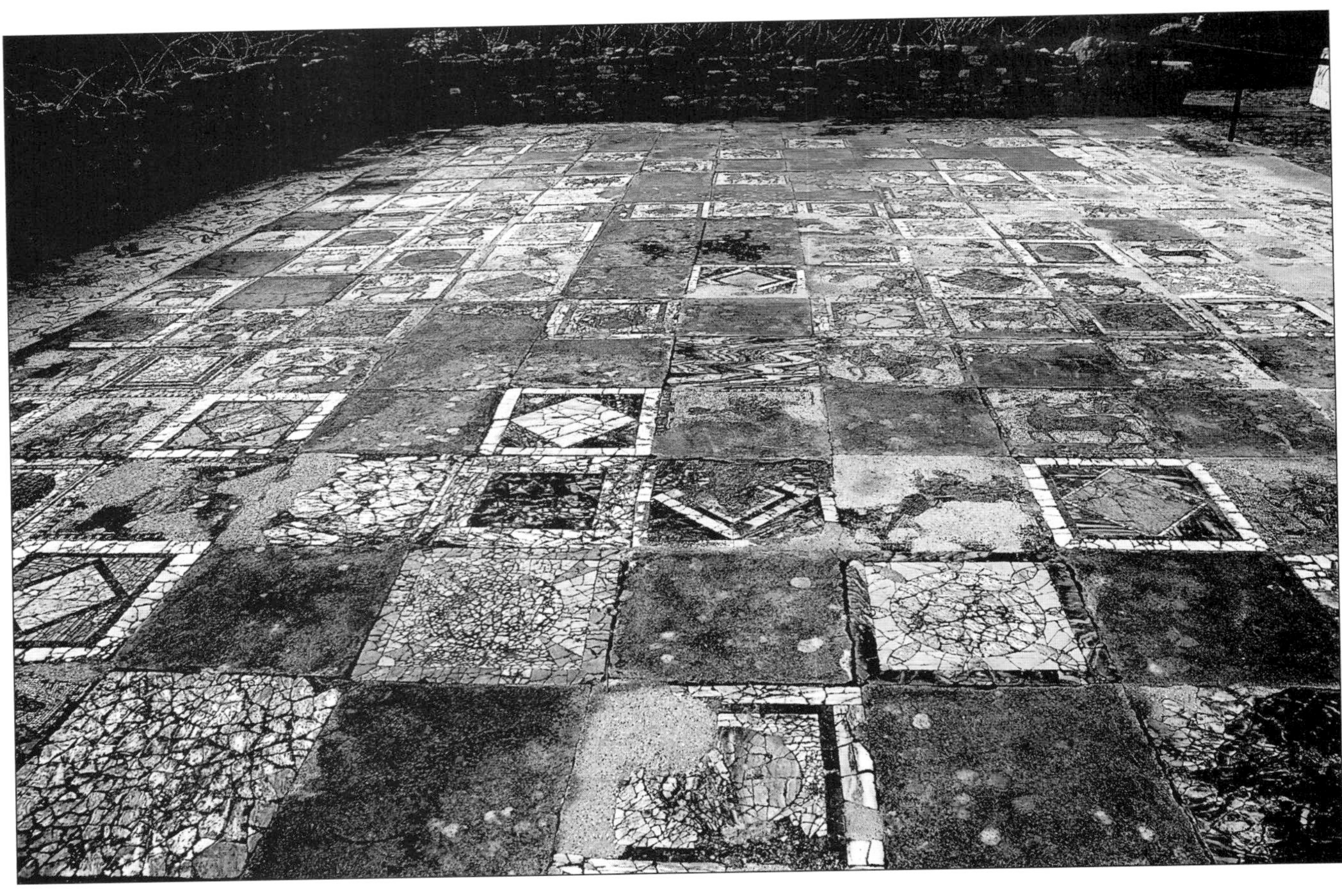

Fig. 7.11 The mosaic of the horses from the House of the Horses, first quarter of the fourth century AD, as relaid after its excavation in 1960 in the House of the Aviary, in the 'Archaeological Park of the Roman villas'

the second century AD. This so-called 'proconsular palace', therefore, disregards the monumental plan and must post-date the second-century structures, which survived at least to the beginning of the Vandal period.[64]

Lifting the Mosaic of the Months and Seasons

The 'Mosaic of the Months and Seasons' was Davis' most impressive find and the one that motivated him to devise a system for lifting mosaics with friable mortar in large intact sections. He was justly proud of having invented a method to raise this mosaic, since essentially the same method of lifting is still in use today. Once he had perfected his method, he was happy to apply it to any likely mosaic which he found. His ingenuity shows that Davis had real genius as a practical man.

He said that his first effort to remove a section of the Mosaic of the Months and Seasons by a coating of gypsum laid on above had proved unsuccessful. At some point, he had watched Touzon break up the fragment of November, as it was originally found, in an attempt to lift it. Davis also recounted the scene when a Maltese "expert," whose competence Davis had already had occasion to distrust, undermined a section of the symmetrical border next to the figure of March in order to lift it, only to have it collapse into rubble.[65] Horrified by the disaster which the destruction of the mosaic would mean to him personally, Davis wrote, 'The wind was howling its shrill notes among the solitary ruins, and the shades of evening were fast thickening around us. Everything in our immediate vicinity had the appearance as if some unheard-of crime had either been committed, or was on the very point of being perpetrated'. Galvanized by this failure, Davis then spent another sleepless night, in the course of which he came up with the long and tedious process of lifting the mosaic in pieces and crating them for shipping.

Once he had the process clearly in mind, he had to acquire supplies to carry it out, but this was not a great problem, as most of his requirements except for wood were easily available, and cheap. The accounts which he presented to Consul Wood for the month from

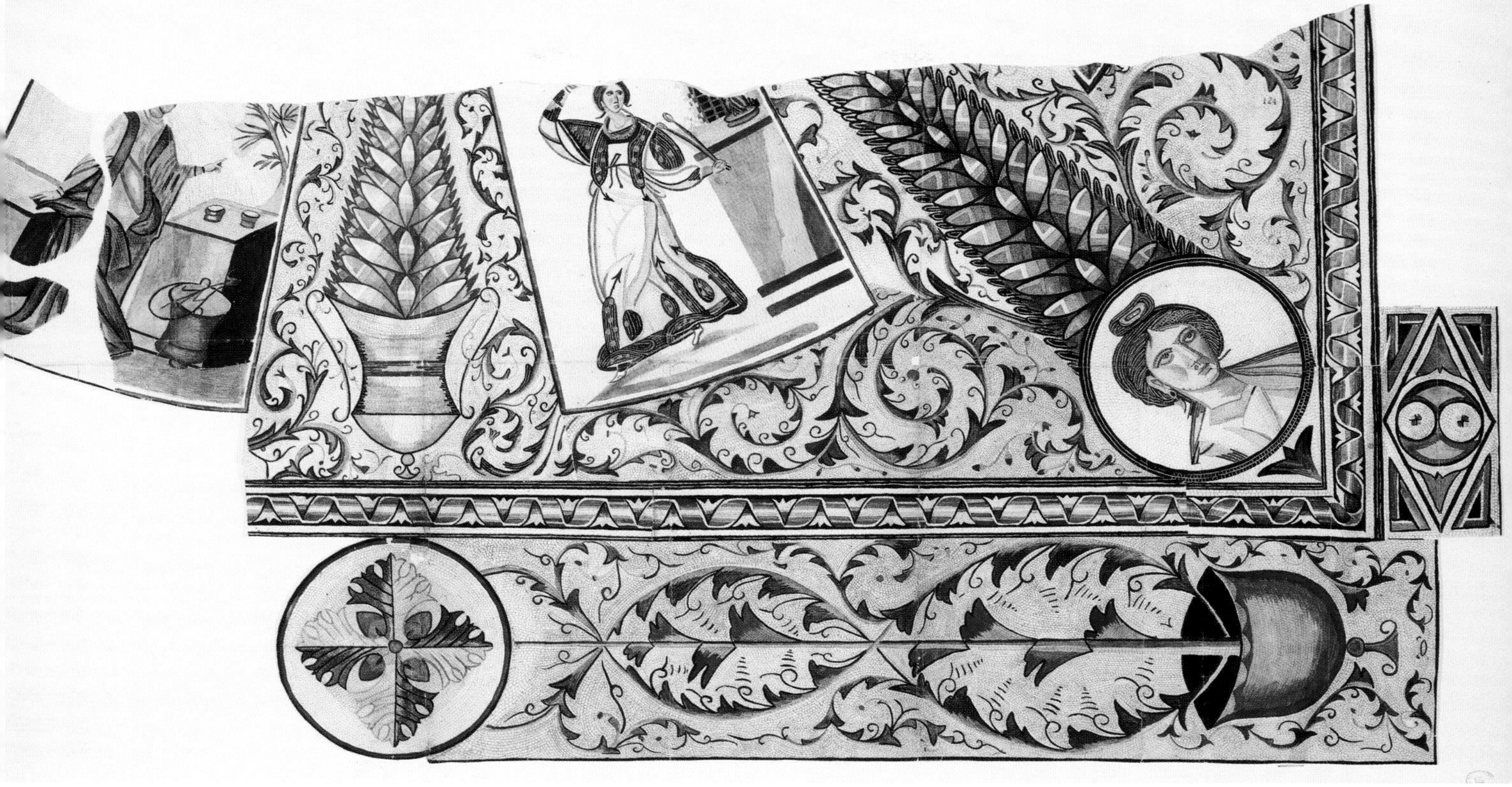

Plate 1 Carthage, Mosaic of the Months and Seasons, detail showing the Months of March (left) and April, and the personification of Spring (in the corner roundel); watercolour (1857) by an unknown artist, made while the mosaic was still in situ

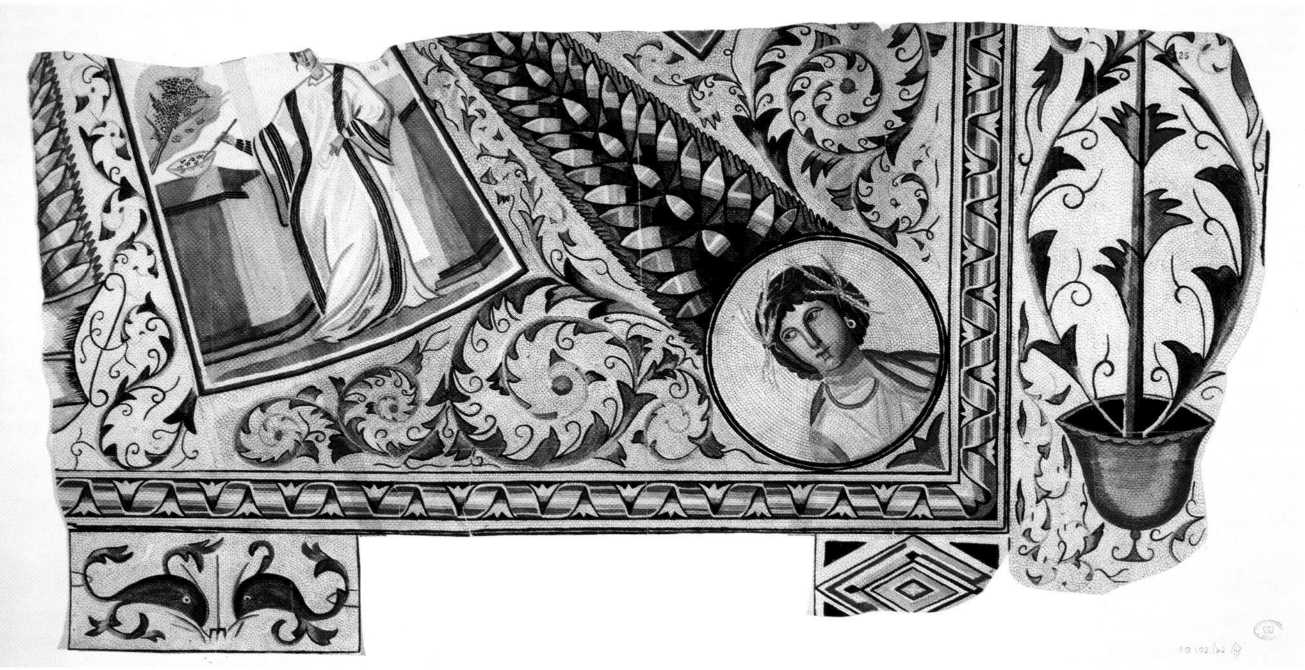

Plate 2 Carthage, another detail of the same mosaic, showing the Month of July and the personification of Summer, as depicted in another watercolour by the same artist as for Plate 1; the mosaic itself belongs to the last quarter of the fourth century AD.

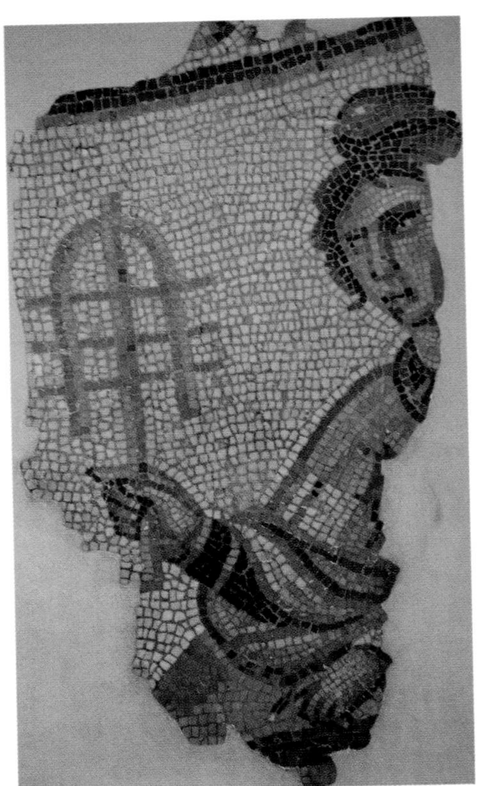

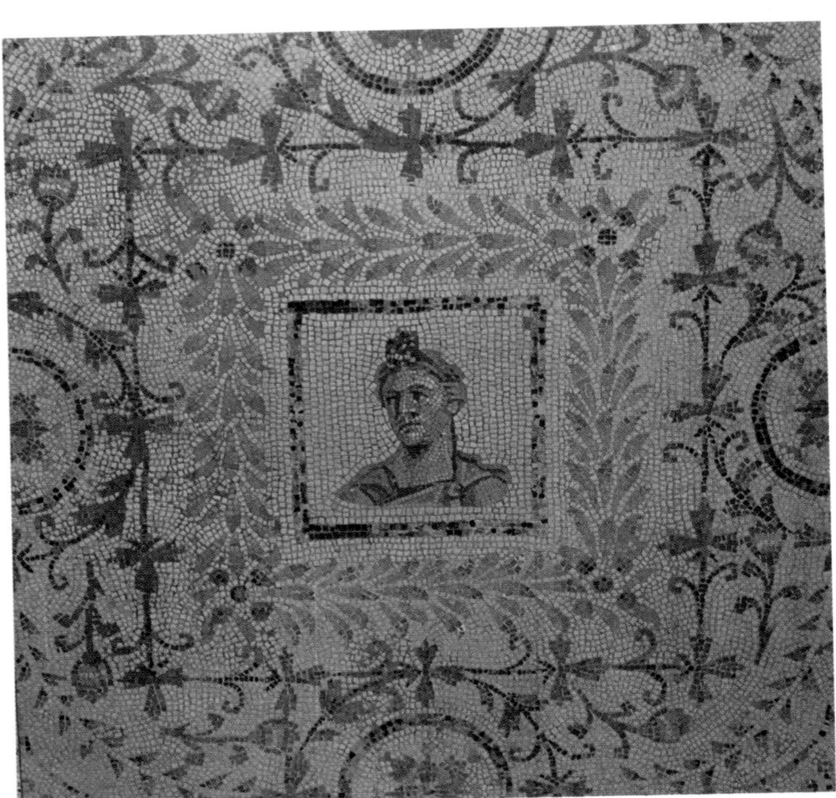

Plate 3 (above left) *Carthage, Mosaic of the Months and Seasons, fragmentary figure holding a* sistrum, *representing the Month of November (height of fragment: 0.71 m)*

Plate 4 (above right) *Gammarth, detail of the Mosaic of the Muses, showing the bust of a muse, surrounded by a laurel-wreath frame which in turn is set within a vine-trellis framework ('floral style'); probably mid-second century AD*

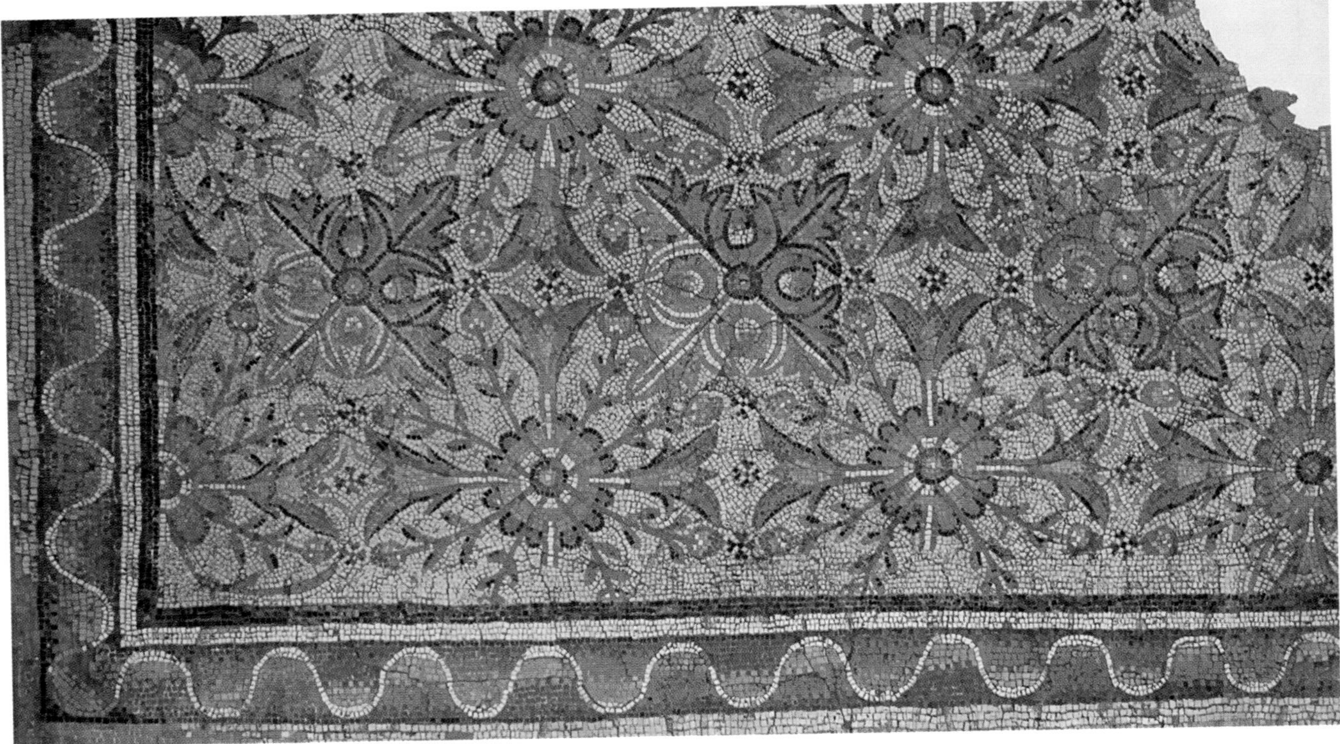

Plate 5 *Carthage, detail of the Mosaic of Rosettes and Lotus Buds, in a cruciform arrangement with eight small additional flowers; centralized compositions of four close-set acanthus leaves between. Mid- to late fourth century AD (or later)?*

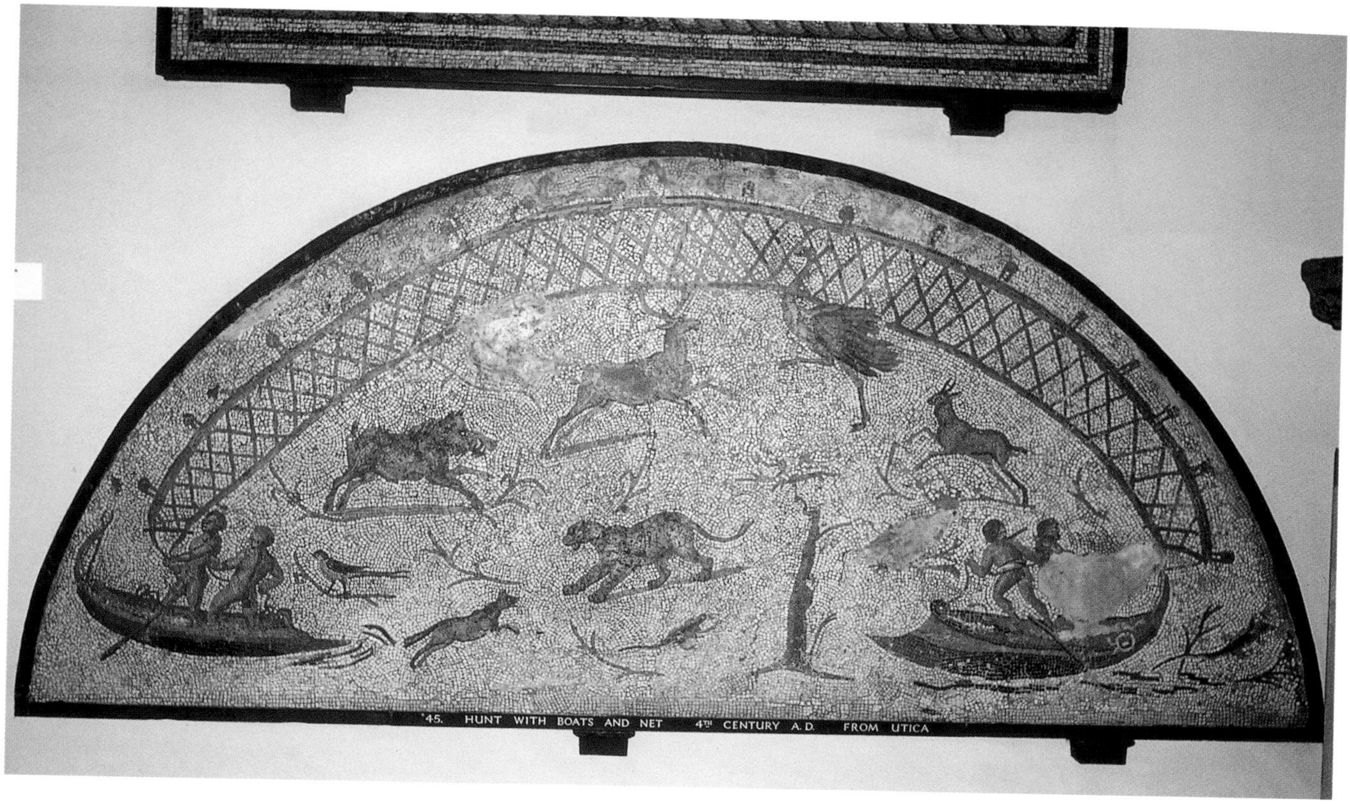

'45. HUNT WITH BOATS AND NET 4TH CENTURY A.D. FROM UTICA

Plate 6 Utica, Mosaic of the Fisher-Hunters (diameter 3.35 m): men in boats holding a net attempt to capture a variety of animals – a boar, a deer, an ostrich, a gazelle and a leopard. There is also a dog in attendance, and a bird, lizards, branches and a tree stump fill the spaces in the rest of the field. Probably end of the second century or beginning of the third century AD.

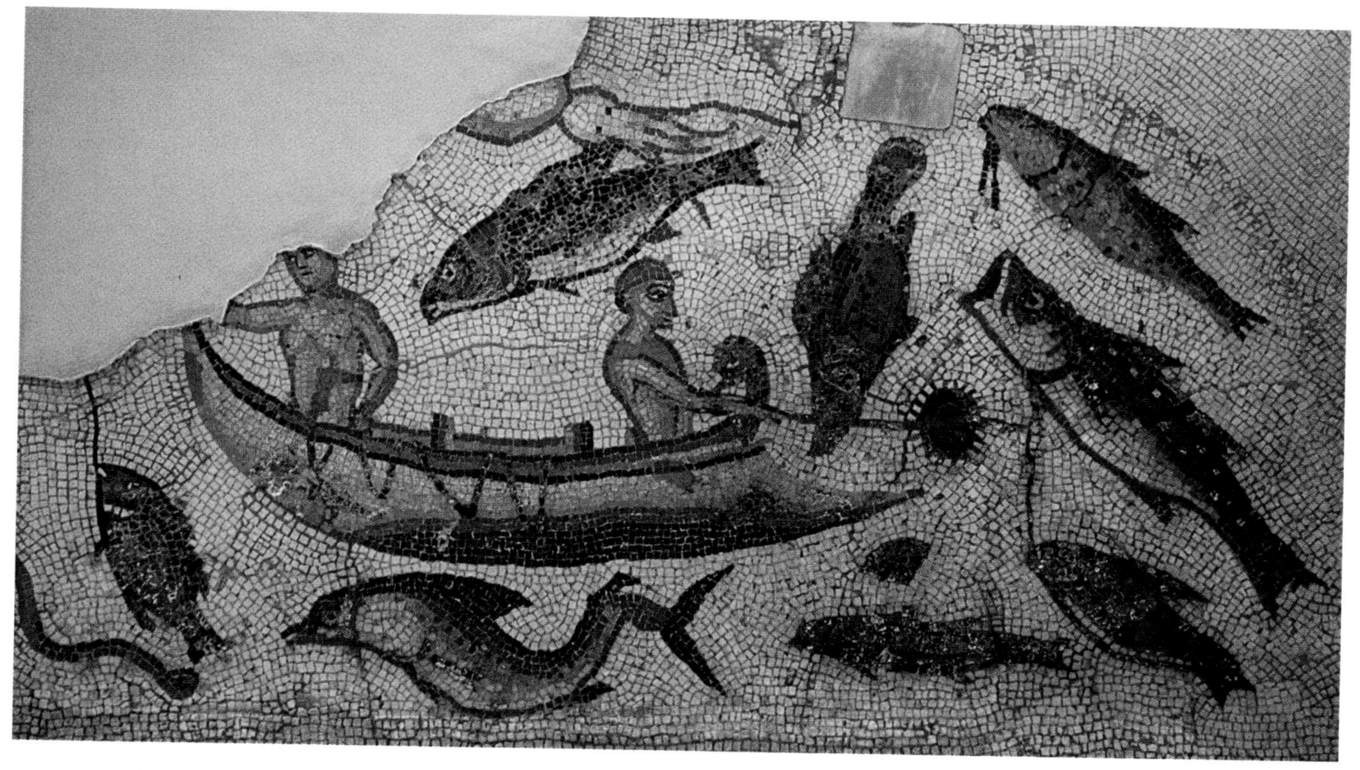

Plate 7 Utica, Mosaic of Two Fishermen in a Boat. The panel measures 1.38 m by 0.76 m; second half of the fourth century AD (?)

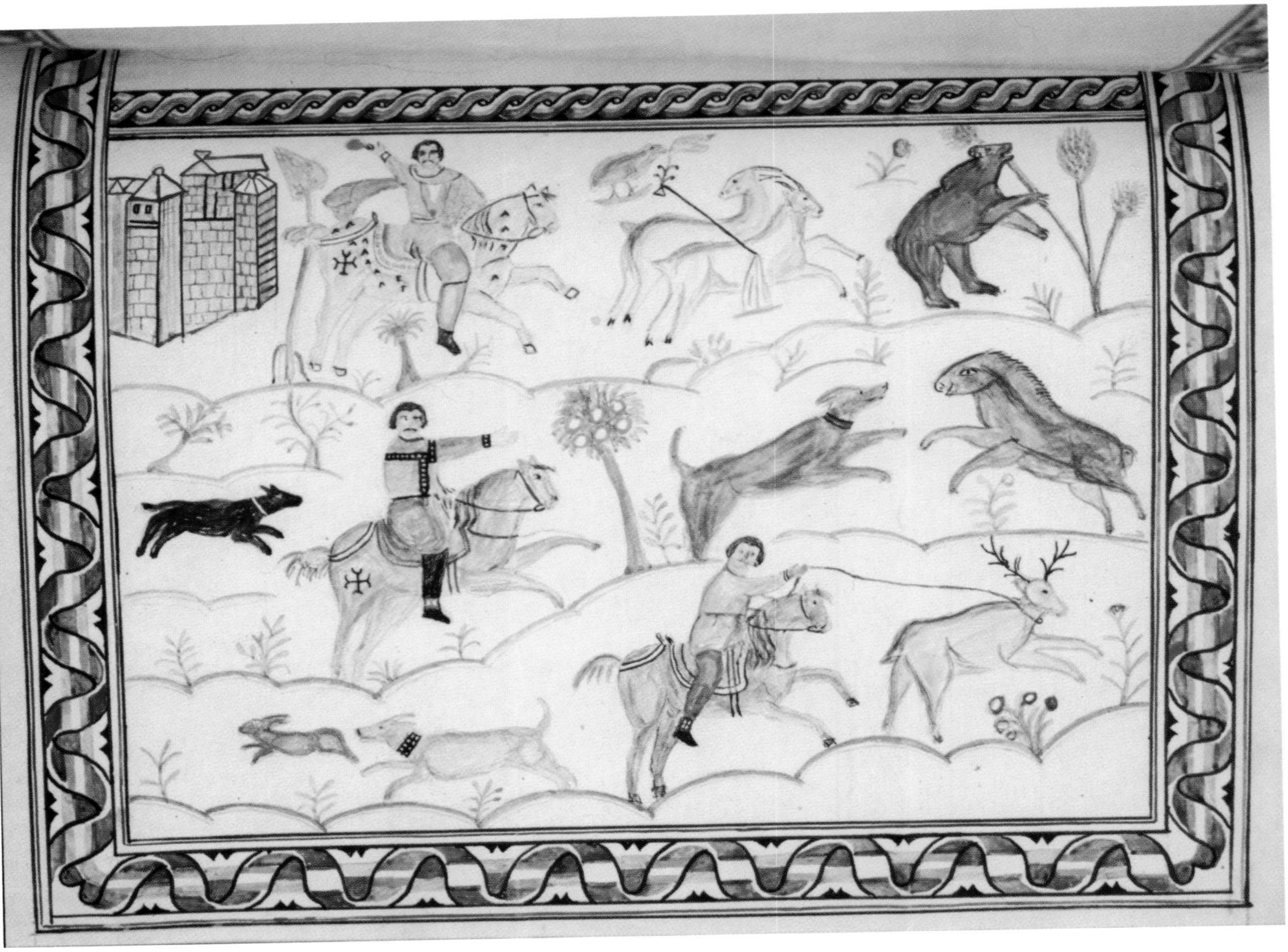

Plate 8 Carthage, Vandal Hunting Mosaic, Davis' coloured-pencil drawing (hitherto unpublished) of the floor while it was still in situ*; 11 by 14 inches (28 cm x 36 cm). The pavement was subsequently broken up into sections for transporting to London.*

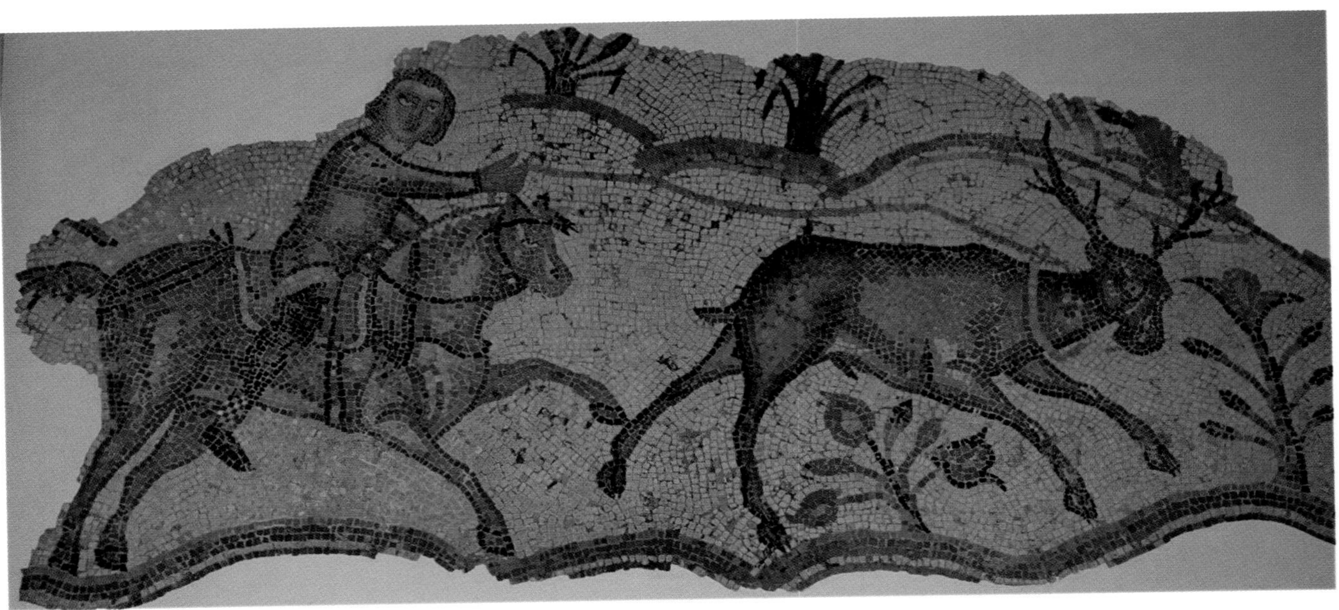

Plate 9 Carthage, Vandal Hunting mosaic, detail of a horseman lassooing a stag, belonging to the bottom right-hand part of the floor (see Plate 8); second half of the fifth century AD (?)

January 14th to February 14th, 1857, included the following list of supplies:[66]

4 pieces of canvas for mosaic
10 lbs. of glue ('common carpenters' glue')[67]
lime
coals for drying mosaic
2 flat irons for drying mosaic
2 watchmen for 29 days during which mosaic was down
2 temporary stoves for fieldwork
gluepot and brushes
2 jars
3 buckets
1 tub for preparing cement
2 knives and 3 long chisels
boards for boxes

In a letter to Clarendon, Davis described the process he had devised:[68]

> I glued common canvas upon a small piece of mosaic and when quite dry I severed it with very great care from its ancient cement by means of knives and chisels and placed it with the reverse side upwards in a case previously prepared for it. I now filled the case with fresh cement and screwed the top on it. In this state I left it for about ten hours. The case was then turned so that what was before the bottom now became the top. The lid was unscrewed[,] the canvas cautiously removed by means of hot water and the marble cleaned of the remains of glue which adhered to it. The experiment having worked so well I set to work the following day with greater assurance and succeeded after twenty-nine days of arduous labour in removing the whole mosaic upon canvass [*sic*]. In the course of these operations I became so confident of my method that I have taken up, and that most successfully, one piece nearly twelve feet in length by three in breadth.

The method even had the advantage of smoothing unevenness in the original floor; Davis noted that the cheek of his 'Ceres' ('Summer') was smoothed by the process. In fact, Davis' method of lifting mosaics bypassed the extensive work of conservation that would have faced the staff when the British Museum received mosaics lifted by Newton's conventional method.

Because Davis could not entrust this job to his workmen, he was forced to do it almost entirely by himself while his workmen sat by and told stories. He said that it took him twenty days (but elsewhere he said twenty-nine days) to lift the Mosaic of the Months and Seasons; he certainly had his equipment by the middle of February, so he should have finished this task by the middle or end of March. Davis elsewhere said that he had spent 'upwards of three months in encasing it', and that the whole process took to the end of March.[69] There is some discrepancy here with the report of the British Consul, Richard Wood, who had been asked by the Foreign Office to inspect the mosaic; Wood wrote on March 3rd that he had visited Davis' house but found the mosaic already packed into wooden boxes.[70] I suspect that Wood was not interested in continuing to the site to see what was going on there, although the distance was scarcely another kilometer from Davis' dig-house at Douar ech-Chott. While Davis was at work on lifting and packing the mosaic, he says that he was not able to undertake further excavation. In actual fact, however, the site of the Mosaic of Victory with Inscription was also being dug in the spring of 1857.

Davis made no systematic effort to catalogue the mosaic, but sent Clarendon a list of the pieces he was shipping. The mosaic arrived at the Museum in nineteen pieces, of which Davis' list appears below,[71] while a sketch of the surviving pieces which he enclosed with his reports clarifies the present identification of the fragments [in brackets]:

No. 1. Priestess sacrificing under sacred tree [not marked on plan, but certainly July];
No. 2. Priestess dancing before Idol [April];
No. 3. Flower pot [cantharus at mid-point of side];
No. 4. Large ornamental side piece [area of acanthus scroll under April];
No. 5. [Ditto] [area of acanthus scroll under July];
No. 6. Ceres [Summer];
No. 7. Dido [Spring];
No. 8. Broken tree [shorter surviving segment of border];
No. 9. Complete tree [longer surviving segment of border];
No. 10. Priestess before altar and tree with bird on it [March];
No. 11. Small side piece near Dido [area of acanthus scroll to right of Spring];
No. 12. Part of priestess with a sistrum in her hand [November];
No. 13. Small side piece near Ceres [area of acanthus scroll to right of Ceres];
No. 14. Fish [threshold with two dolphins facing on either side of trident];
No. 15. Circle joining top of tree [rosette in centre of side border];
No. 16. Piece of ornamental border [geometric lozenge from left side of threshold];
No. 17. [Ditto];
No. 18. Fragment of a vase [not marked on sketch];
No. 19. Fragment of border [second geometric lozenge from right side of threshold]

Subsequent accounts of the Mosaic

Davis published his *Carthage and Her Remains* in 1861, and Augustus Franks, a curator at the Museum (Fig. 7.12), had by that time already published a full scholarly account of the Mosaic of the Months and Seasons, as well as a brief description of some of the other

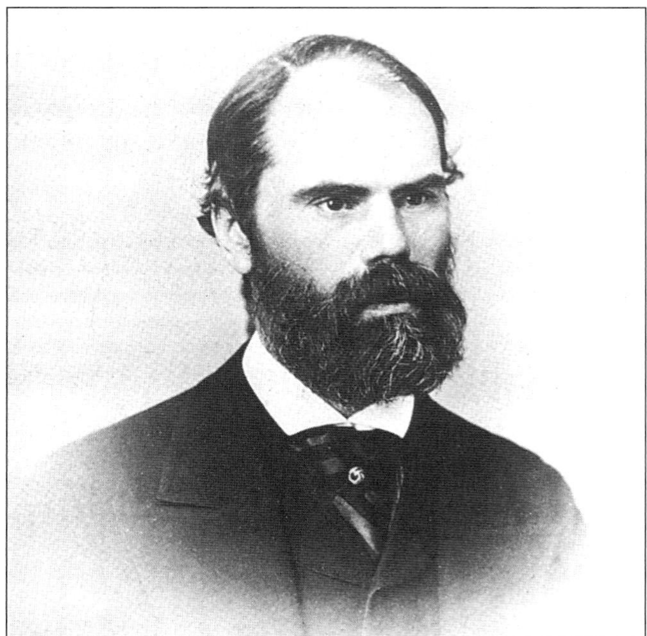

mosaics which had reached London from Davis on HMS *Curaçoa* and HMS *Supply* in time to be included in his report.[72] Franks' relatively lengthy treatment of the Mosaic of the Months and Seasons indicated that he found it by far the most interesting and important artefact among the objects shipped by Davis from Carthage. Franks published an outline drawing of his new reconstruction of the Mosaic of the Months and Seasons, which placed the twelve Months in the reconstructed design of the whole pavement (Fig. 7.13). Franks also published seven colour plates that fairly accurately (but not sympathetically) reproduced details of the mosaic down to the *tesserae*; scholars thus had much of what they needed in order to study the mosaic further.

Franks' immediate recognition of the significance of the iconography of the Mosaic of the Months and Seasons confirms his reputation as one of the most knowledgeable scholars of archaeology in his day.[73] A Cambridge man, he had been appointed Director of the Department of British and Medieval Antiquities in

Fig. 7.12 (above) *Sir Augustus Wollaston Franks (1826–1897), polymathic scholar, British Museum Keeper, avid collector, and generous benefactor to the Museum, in the only surviving photograph of him, taken c. 1870*

Fig. 7.13 (below) *Franks' reconstruction of the Mosaic of the Months and Seasons (compare Fig. 7.3)*

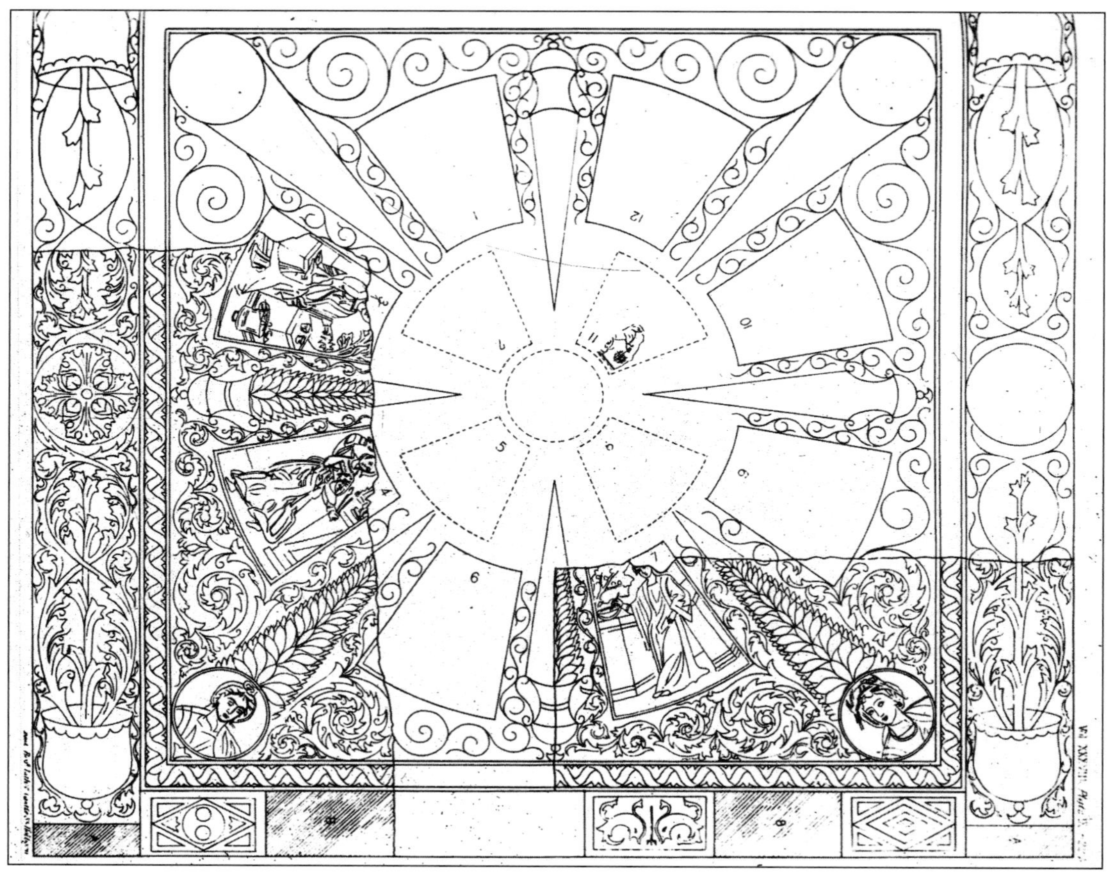

1851, when he was only twenty-six.[74] Franks was a life-long collector of museum-quality objects, most of which he left to the Museum in his will. He was a highly intelligent and discriminating scholar, and more of an archaeologist than a collector in these early years of his career.[75]

Davis read Franks' paper before finishing *Carthage and Her Remains* and therefore knew that the latter identified the mosaic as Roman, the full-length figures as Months, and the corner medallions as Seasons.[76] Franks also stated that the iconography of the figures was closely related to those on the equivalent months from the Codex-Calendar of AD 354, an important late Roman manuscript.[77] He therefore made the indispensable observation that fixed the cultural significance of the Mosaic of the Months and Seasons, and accomplished this scholarly feat within a year and a half of the arrival of the mosaic at the Museum, since he presented his paper in March 1859. Franks not only recognized the mosaic as Roman, but his observations correctly suggested a date for it in the late Roman period. He based his argument on the eighteenth-century publication by Montfaucon of a description of the Codex Vindobonensis, a manuscript copy of the Codex-Calendar dating to the sixteenth century. Franks also mentioned the relationship of the mosaic to the tetrastichs (verses in four lines), ascribed to Ausonius by Montfaucon, which accompanied the illustrations of the Months in the Codex-Calendar.[78] The first exacting iconographical study of the Codex-Calendar of 354 and its relationship to the known series of Roman mosaics of the Months was published by Strzygowski in 1888,[79] nearly thirty years after Franks' article appeared; but the illustrated manuscripts of the Codex-Calendar had earlier interested the great German scholar Theodor Mommsen, who wrote long discussions of them in 1850, 1863 and 1892.[80]

When Franks perceived the relationship of the Mosaic of the Months and Seasons to the illustrations of the Codex-Calendar, he was immediately able to identify the individual Months of March, April, July and November correctly (although they were not labelled as such on the mosaic), because they copy both the body positions and the essential attributes of the illustrations of those Months and their associated poetry in the Codex-Calendar. In the simplest terms, in the illustrations of the Codex-Calendar, March points to a swallow (Fig. 7.14), April dances with castanets, July eats mulberries and November holds a *sistrum*. Further parallels from other attributes and from the poetry associated with the images of the Months in the Codex-Calendar gave Franks far

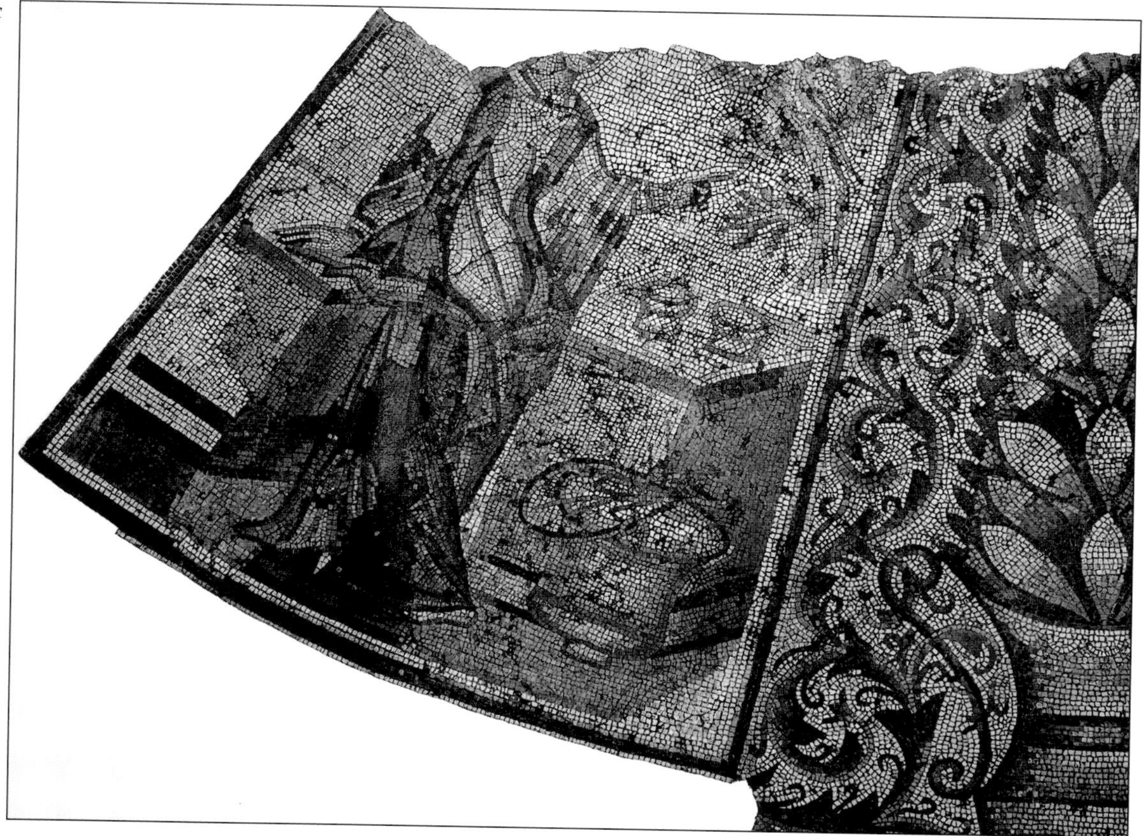

Fig. 7.14 Mosaic of the Months and Seasons, the panel showing March. She is shown between two square bases and partially leans on the left one, supporting herself there with her right hand. With her left she points towards a swallow in the tree on the right. Two small cups are on the right-hand base, and a large bucket with a loop handle stands on the ground in front of it.

more evidence than he required simply to clinch this identification.

The parallels with the Codex-Calendar suggest but do not demand a mid-fourth-century chronologyfor the mosaic. Gauckler dated it to the Antonine period,[81] and Hinks implicitly dated it to the third century by the order in which he placed it in his catalogue.[82] Dunbabin placed it in the second half of the fourth century,[83] however, and subsequently grouped it with the products of a mosaic workshop operating at Carthage around AD 400, judging by the similarity of border and decorative motifs.[84]

Although Davis was not at all convinced by Franks' interpretation, and was unable to see any similarity between the graceful and evidently feminine figures of his mosaic and the often ungainly men of the sixteenth century Vindobonensis illustrations that were reproduced in Montfaucon, he was somewhat mollified that Franks had used Davis' reports to the Foreign Office.[85] Davis noted that the find had also got into the newspapers, but the reports published there he thought very inaccurate.[86]

The plan of the Mosaic according to Franks

Franks must have had a copy of the reconstruction drawing, for to it he owed the information that two corners of the mosaic and the intervening space had been lost to three deep pits; that most of the centre was lost to a pit dug by Arabs in search of construction materials; and that a wall had destroyed part of the mosaic.[87] Only two large roughly rectangular outer fragments of the whole mosaic survive. Nevertheless, the remaining pieces are sufficient to show that the overall plan of the Mosaic of the Months and Seasons is a circle laid within a square. The fragments at their greatest extent reach less than half the radius of the circle. The eight figures which evidently filled trapezoidal framed sections of a wide circular outer band are a little over four feet (1.2 m) in height; that is, about three-quarters life-size.

Franks estimated that the mosaic came from a large floor, approximately twenty-eight feet (about 8.5m) square. He elsewhere described the mosaic as being twenty-three feet square (7 m), with the circular medallions in the corners being 2 feet 9 inches (0.84 m) across.[88] The mosaic, therefore, covered the floor of a very large room, suitable for formal public receptions. Such a room is larger than the ordinary requirements of a luxurious private house, but rooms of this size are certainly not unusual. At least two rooms excavated by Davis were larger; one, in a house to the east of the theatre on the Odeon Hill, measured thirty-five feet by thirty feet (10.7 m by 9.1 m), while a room with a hunting mosaic in a building of the Vandal era, to the north of the Hill of Juno, measured twenty-eight by forty feet (8.5 m by 12.2 m). A reception in a bare room of this size (8.7 m by 7.4 m, or about 64 m^2) would feel crowded with more than fifty people, but would be somewhat sparsely occupied with less than thirty. It would provide spacious and elegant accommodation for dinner in the fashion of the fourth century, on *stibadia* (curved couches), for twelve to twenty-four people, allowing plenty of room for entertainers and the circulation of servants.

Franks already knew in 1860 that the mosaic represented the Months; this meant that Davis' reconstruction, with eight symmetrically disposed sections of a circular band, could not be correct. In order to find space for twelve Months, Franks had to reorganize the plan of the mosaic, truncating the outer eight sections and supplying an inner circular band with four sections (Fig. 7.13). Beginning in the left-hand corner with Winter (not preserved), Franks placed January (not preserved) to the left in the lower band, February (not preserved) on the inner band, and March on the lower band to the right, followed by April. May (not preserved) would have been on the inner band, above the corner medallion of Spring (Fig. 7.15). June (not preserved) would have been to the right, followed by July, August (not preserved) on the inner band, Summer in the corner medallion and September (not preserved) to the right. The remaining months and medallions (October to December and Autumn), as well as the central motif, are lost, except for a fragment of a woman holding a *sistrum*, who is clearly November, which Franks placed on the next truncated section of the inner band. Franks' modified reconstruction is completely convincing; the only objection to his reconstruction is that the framed areas for February, May, August and November in the inner circle are accorded less space, and could not have been full-length figures at the same scale.

As noted above (p. 99), Davis' plan of the ground immediately over the mosaic can be correlated with the mosaic which he found below. I therefore placed an overlay of Davis' ground plan of the area over the mosaic, enlarged to the same scale, over his drawing of the mosaic, in order to check whether Franks' reconstruction worked with Davis' ground plan (Fig. 7.2). Interestingly, one can see that the placement of the pit 'H,' the site of the fragment of November, was corrected on Davis' ground plan from a point which would require agreement with his suggested reconstruction, to one which more nearly agreed with Franks placement. This suggests that Davis reconsidered the location of the pit, perhaps after reading Franks' argument. Davis, who saw the mosaic *in situ*, had allowed his artist to place November in the outer circle, but the

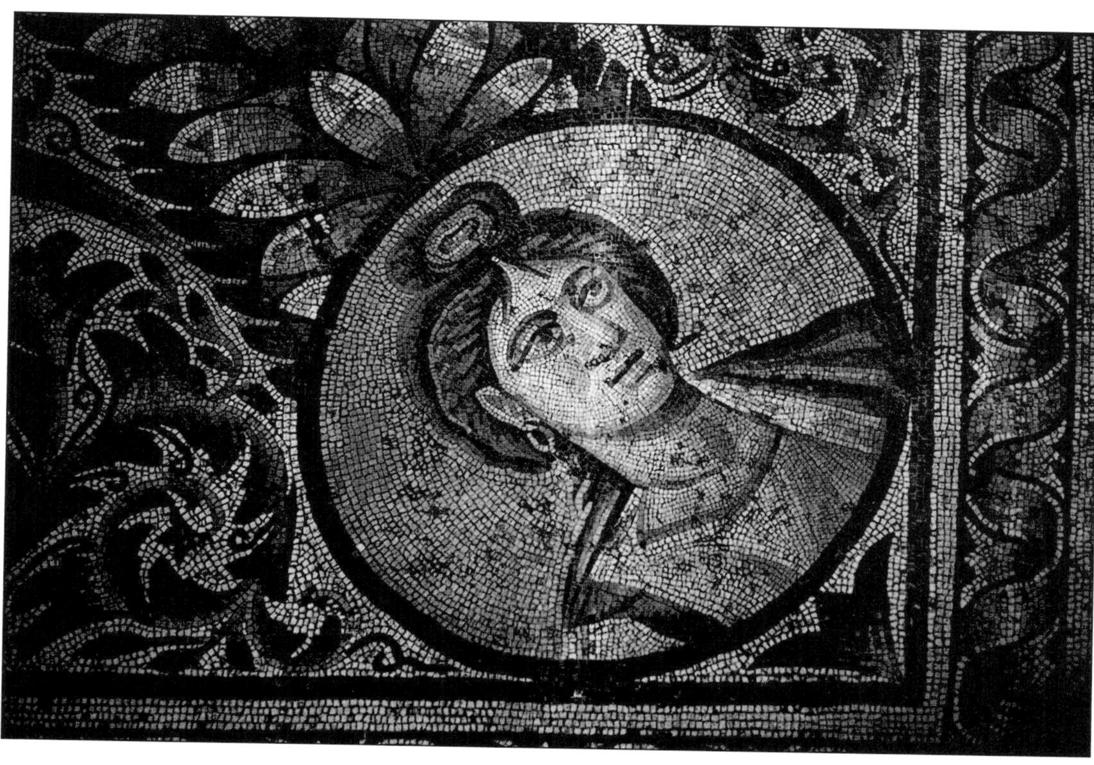

Fig. 7.15 Mosaic of the Months and Seasons, detail of the bust of Spring (diameter of roundel: 0.74 m)

section of the mosaic with November was just on the other side of a wall from the two large fragments, which may have confused Davis' perception of its location. Neither Davis' nor Franks' version of the mosaic correlates perfectly with the former's letters on the ground plan. Certainly, however, Franks' reconstruction is supported by Davis' ground plan and by the very fact of its emendation.

Confusion of the site by later scholars

The location of the site of the Mosaic of the Months and Seasons was confused before Davis even published his book, when Franks described it as being near Falbe no. 86.[89] The latter site, which Falbe described as 'ruins indicating the continuation of a street',[90] is on the alignment of *decumanus* 4 north; it is at least ninety meters north of the place Davis indicated. Since Davis' book had not yet been published, Franks must have correlated the site marked on the sketch-map with Falbe's plan, without stating that this was simply his best approximation on the basis of the evidence available.

Because Davis' Mosaic of the Months and Seasons had an image of Isis worship (the *sistrum*), Wilmanns and Mommsen in 1881 were to confuse the site with the so-called 'Temple of Sarapis,' where Sainte-Marie was to excavate in 1874.[91] They described the Mosaic of the Months and Seasons as follows: *Carthagine reperto in opero musivo Mensium Isidis aliisque imaginibus ornato, nunc Londinii in museo Britannico adservato,* that is, 'Found in Carthage, mosaic with images of the Months, of Isis and with other images, now preserved in the British Museum in London'; so far, so good. Then they added: *fortasse ad idem Serapidis templum pertinet, ad quod tituli sopra positi nn. 1002–1007*: 'perhaps it belongs to the same temple of Serapis to which belong the inscriptions nos 1002–1007, above'. As we shall see, this is incorrect.

Making matters worse, Wilmanns and Mommsen also conflated the inscription from the Mosaic of Victory with the images of the Mosaic of the Months and Seasons. In additional notes, furthermore, they ascribed one of their errors, that of linking the Mosaic of the Months and Seasons to the inscription on the Mosaic of Victory, to Beulé, saying that he described such a mosaic as having the names of the Months.[92] This is also incorrect, because the mosaic which Beulé described with the Latin names of the Months was a completely different pavement, which was also described by Davis (see above, Chapter 6). This chaotic confusion is all the more damaging because of the revered reputation of Mommsen and of that of the corpus of Latin inscriptions.

Additional notes in the next fascicle of the corpus did not correct the confusion about the site of the Mosaic of the Months and Seasons which Wilmanns and Mommsen had inadvertently sowed in their original entry, no doubt because Mommsen still thought their site attribution had merit. Sainte-Marie's 'Temple of Sarapis' is designated by the label 'Serapeum' on the 1896 Bordy map, on which it lay along *decumanus* 3 north and *cardo* 10 east. It is placed more accurately on Rives' 1995 map of Carthage, at the north end of the block between *decumani* 2 and 3 north and between *cardines* 10 and 11 east.[93] There is in fact no connection between the Mosaic of the Months and Seasons and the Serapeum, and the sites are approximately 400 m or about ten city-blocks apart.

The site of the Mosaic of the Months and Seasons has never been identified correctly since the original confusion. Hinks followed Gauckler, who said it was found at the foot of the Odeon Hill, *and* near Falbe no. 86 *and* near the presumed site of the Serapeum;[94] these are three different and widely separate sites. Gauckler ordered the Mosaic of the Months and Seasons with other mosaics from 'Dermech,' which is the area around the Antonine Baths, and very far from its real location. This explains why the site of the Mosaic of the Months and Seasons was given as 'Dermech, Antonine Baths, Douïmès' by Dunbabin in 1978;[95] this would place it in the general area of the Serapeum. When the mosaic is placed in its correct location, as part of the grandest residential complex in fourth-century Carthage, its true significance is clarified.

The Mosaic of the Months and Seasons was the first, the most finely made, and also the most iconograpically interesting of all Davis' mosaic finds, and it motivated him to invent a method to lift it successfully. His method allowed the intact preservation of the location of each mosaic *tessera* in the ancient design. This was a tremendous scientific advance over previous methodology, in which ancient mosaics were ordinarily broken up badly during the lifting process, and were then reconstituted by skilled mosaicists, who followed more or less faithfully the original intent of the design. The days when such destructiveness could be justified were over, once Davis had invented a reliable method of lifting mosaics intact. Furthermore, the experience of finding and lifting this mosaic showed him how to proceed at Carthage, and from this point onwards he looked specifically for sites which would yield fresh mosaic finds.

8

Excavations on other sites in the Spring of 1857

The chronology of work in the Spring of 1857

Davis ended the account of his lifting of the Mosaic of the Months and Seasons (Site 8) by evoking a scene of himself doing all the work while his workmen told stories.[1] When he next took up the account of his excavations, he was beginning to work at the 'Temple of Saturn' (Site 23) in fine November weather (the year was 1857, although Davis did not note it).[2] But while he thus implied that he did little digging between the find of the mosaic in January and its loading aboard the *Curaçoa* in late May 1857, much evidence shows that he did. The numbers on the first sketch-map, Ditson's quoted remarks about the Mosaic of Victory with Inscription, the receipt for thirteen cases of antiquities and two statues loaded on board the *Curaçoa* during its second stop in Carthage in July 1857,[3] and the British Museum accession records of the six mosaics which arrived in late August 1857,[4] all show that Davis certainly excavated at five more places before the second departure of the *Curaçoa*. Two additional sites fit best in this period. Two of these seven produced mosaics, while another yielded quantities of Punic *stelae*.

Davis said that finds from the first thirteen sketch-map sites were shipped on the *Curaçoa*. The central *emblema* (a figural area that could be made separately for portability) of the Mosaic with Baskets of Fish and Fruit was loaded on the *Curaçoa* together with the nineteen pieces of the Mosaic of the Months and Seasons, but the border of the former was only loaded when the ship returned for a second time in July 1857. The Mosaic of Victory with Inscription and three geometric mosaics from deeper on the same site were all loaded on the *Curaçoa* in July as well. These six were the only mosaics shipped on the *Curaçoa*. In addition, a case of Punic *stelae* from sketch-map site 13 was included in the first loading. Since the sketch-map sites were numbered in the order in which they were dug, his sites 9 and 10, which produced almost no finds, were also dug in the period between the discovery of the Mosaic of the Months and Seasons and the second loading of the *Curaçoa*. Davis' excavations at the great enclosure on the summit of Bordj-Djedid (Site 11) and at the Antonine Baths (Site 12) also belong at this time. Although there are no sketch-map numbers for these sites, their respective numbers on Davis' published map (8 and 5) are low, indicating that they were dug relatively early. The order in which they are discussed in Davis' book suggests that they were dug before sketch-map sites 11 (Falbe no. 90, the site of the Mosaic of Victory), 12 (the 'Punic mine') and 14 (the 'Carthaginian House'), and therefore also before the end of May 1857.

Davis' ninth site: the north side of the Circular Harbour

Davis recorded the first of these sites (Site 9) on the first sketch-map with the notation indicating 'ruins where nothing was found'. It lay immediately to the north of the Circular Harbour, in the south-eastern quarter of the Roman city-grid. Davis' first sketch-map indicates a rectangular enclosure running generally north–south at this point. On the second sketch-map, the site is marked north of the 'Cothon.' The equivalent site on the published map lay on the slope of the depression rising away from the north side of the Circular Harbour. Falbe marked three unnumbered small ruins in this immediate area on his plan. The site is in the block just north of the theoretical line of *decumanus* 4 south and between *cardines* 13 and 14 east; it must lie at an elevation less than five meters above sea-level.[5] At either this site or, more probably, the next, in a Roman ruin near the 'Cothon,' Davis found 'exquisite pieces of statuary embedded in cement'.[6] He has otherwise nothing to say about this excavation.

The same area, immediately to the north of the Circular Harbour, but in the southern quarter of the block between *cardines* 14 and 15 east, was excavated in the 1970s by the British UNESCO team at Carthage. Henry Hurst and his colleagues found a series of rooms built in *pisé* (unfired mud-brick) until the late Roman era, with consistent evidence of craft activities, and a particularly wide range of evidence related to cloth-making. The rooms faced on to a flagged area rather than a defined *decumanus* at the curving edge of the harbour.[7] The area was most unpromising for an excavator like Davis, who was hoping for finds of museum quality, and it is not surprising that he abandoned this site in short order.

Davis' tenth site: the 'Temple of Apollo' north of the Circular Harbour

Davis dug another site north of the Circular Harbour and also marked it with the notation 'ruins, nothing found' (Site 10). It lies in the south-eastern quarter of the city-grid, where the elevation is very low. This is the most problematic of all his sites in terms of its location and function. On the first sketch-map Davis indicated a large, almost square double enclosure here. On the second sketch-map, the point lies north of the Circular Harbour and west of the south end of a curved 'Line of small chambers' along the sea-front. The equivalent site on his published map is marked inside a large rectangular outline which Davis marked as the 'Temple of Apollo.' He indicated this with the same type of double outline as the Antonine Baths, suggesting that it was also an area of impressive ruins.

Davis noted that the ruins here were very disturbed; he believed that they had been excavated or robbed out previously. His only find was a small marble head of Apollo.[8] Both Falbe and Dureau de la Malle had cited ancient sources which placed the Temple of Apollo in the Punic 'Forum,' which (again according to the sources) lay between the circular harbour and the Byrsa. Davis evidently felt that his own site was a likely location for the 'Temple of Apollo', and he may have seen the small head of Apollo as confirmation of this idea. The site correlates somewhat imperfectly with Falbe no. 55, a huge irregular trapezoidal enclosure filling a space of about 80 m by 100 m – one of several sites identified by Falbe as 'temples and large buildings'.[9] Falbe no. 55 can be located exactly, between *decumani* 2 and 3 south and between *cardines* 11 and 13 east. Falbe himself did not call his site no. 55 the 'Temple of Apollo'; rather, as noted above (p. 74), he placed the latter at no. 54, at the south-western base of the Byrsa Hill, nearly 500 m north-west of Falbe no. 55. Beulé, who was to visit Davis' sites in 1859, idiosyncratically called this excavation both Falbe no. 55 and the 'Temple of Baal'; perhaps he was influenced by something which Davis had said, as the latter later wrote that he regarded the Apollo of Punic Carthage as equivalent to Baal.[10] Beulé said that all that remained on the site were the ruins of Roman concrete walls and other Roman debris.[11]

The location of the large structure which Davis indicated north of the Circular Harbour is eighty meters (two short city-blocks) too far west to agree with the placement of Falbe no. 55. Most of Davis' sites need to be corrected by one block to the east to bring them into agreement with their probable true locations, but here the error would be twice that, and Davis' building is also placed about fifty meters too far south to agree exactly with Falbe no. 55. Nevertheless, the enclosure drawn on Davis' published map cannot be meant to be anything else because of its size.

As mentioned above (p. 59), Falbe no. 55 formed the turning point of a line of ruins more than a kilometer long that ran across the falling elevation of the city from the eastern (or Bordj-Djedid) cisterns, and then continued west for most of another kilometer. The location, great size and irregular plan of Falbe no. 55 are possible clues to its function. Although it seems to be within the area which ancient sources identified as the Punic forum, like all the remains on Falbe's plan it is not Punic, but overlies earlier Roman remains; because of its irregular outline, it is most likely a structure of Vandal or Byzantine date. Although he did not link his observation to Falbe no. 55, Beulé wrote that Justinian built a fortress-monastery very close to the port, and that the Arabs called the area Abou-Soleiman, after Solomon, the Byzantine governor of Carthage;[12] Beulé did not link his observation to Falbe no. 55, and it has been suggested that since Solomon's fort was situated on high ground, the most likely location for it was Koudiat el-Hobsia, the artificial hill to the west of the Punic harbours.[13] Nevertheless, Falbe no. 55 may have formed part of the Byzantine fortification system.

Davis may have been echoing Falbe's map when he drew his large double enclosure on the first sketch-map, or he may have found traces of architectural remains in agreement with Falbe's conclusions. Beulé's observations suggest that the remains of Falbe no. 55, which were certainly impressive in Falbe's day, were hardly visible by Davis' time. The area was known to have received the most concentrated attention from stone-robbers. In 1876 Sainte-Marie was to describe the area of the Punic forum as wide and all at one level. He also said that Beulé did not try to dig in the area of the Punic 'Forum' between the ports and the Byrsa Hill, because when Beulé was at Carthage, the area was covered by fields awaiting the harvest.[14] By 1897, the Bordy map shows the whole area as a field 7.67 m above sea level, with no distinguishing characteristics; Bordy mapped Roman remains, but he evidently saw none here.

The point on Davis' published map is just south of *decumanus* 3 south, in the three blocks between *cardines* 8 and 11 east. In terms of the modern suburb of Carthage, his point falls just east of the mid-point of the 'Michigan sector' and just south of the Palaeochristian Museum erected by the Michigan team.[15] Excavation in the area just across Avenue Bourguiba from the Michigan site, in the long block to the north of Falbe no. 55, has revealed an enormous *triclinium* and well-preserved mosaics in an elaborate fourth-century Roman building.[16] A large 'House with Hunting Mosaics' lay a block or so southwest of Davis' site,[17] at the north end of the block between *decumani* 3 and 4 south and *cardines* 7 and 8 east.[18] The excavations of the 'House of the Greek Charioteers,' by the American UNESCO team, are about one long Roman block north of Davis' excavations. The late-fourth- or early-fifth-century house, which produced a number of mosaics, lies south of *decumanus* 2 south and on the west side of *cardo* 9 east. The excavators noted that the whole site was extremely mutilated, partly by the builders of the late Roman house, who cleared to the level of first-century floors before they began construction.[19] An early Christian basilica and ecclesiastical complex lie nearby to the north-east, between *cardines* 9 and 10 east. Although even the original basilica of the late fourth or early fifth century was built as a Christian church,[20] it seems likely that the city-blocks near Davis' site formed a pleasant residential area in the late Roman period.

Falbe drew a straight north–south line of small chambers parallel to the merchant harbour and about 750 m long. The line turns thirty degrees north-north-east halfway along the Circular Harbour to continue along the alignment of the Roman street-grid for another kilometer, ending at *decumanus* 2 north. The small chambers are largely submerged on Falbe's plan and lie along the shore between *cardines* 18 and 19 east on the Roman street-grid. The northern section of the line partly agrees with the relative placement of Davis' curved 'Line of Small Chambers' on his second sketch-map. Beulé was to describe the line of chambers as possible store-rooms of Roman construction, where deep excavation might reveal Punic remains. Beulé was thinking of the Punic city wall, and his idea that the Punic sea-wall lay along this same line has been proved correct.[21] During the UNESCO excavations, Rakob was to show the Punic wall continuing along the sea-front from the harbours and northward across the entire seaward face of the city (Fig. 8.1). Where evidence survives, the Punic wall lies straight as a die along the line of the later Roman sea-front street, *cardo* 18 east.[22] The fact that Davis drew the line of chambers as curved on his second sketch-map suggests that he had not observed the line carefully himself, and probably did not even realize that Falbe's chambers were partially submerged.

Davis' eleventh site: the large enclosure on the summit of Bordj-Djedid

Davis next returned to Bordj-Djedid, this time to a major complex of ruins on the summit, immediately north-west of the Turkish fort (Site 11). The site is an immense rectangular enclosure lying at about thirty meters above sea-level, with a steep drop to the sea.[23] As mentioned above (p. 57), Davis identified the place as the 'Temple of Aesculapius'. Ancient sources placed this on the Byrsa, which other scholars equated with the Saint Louis Hill; Davis, as we have seen (p. 58), located the temple on Bordj-Djedid, which he therefore considered to be the Punic Byrsa.[24] His point on his published map and the outlined enclosure fall on the summit of Bordj-Djedid in a northern extension of the north-eastern quarter of the city-grid, between *decumani* 6 and 7 north and between *cardines* 18 and 19 east.

Here Davis took on an extremely complex site of great archaeological and historical interest. Partly because it is a multi-period site, its history has never been clarified by its excavators, and the site is now inaccessible within the grounds of the Presidential

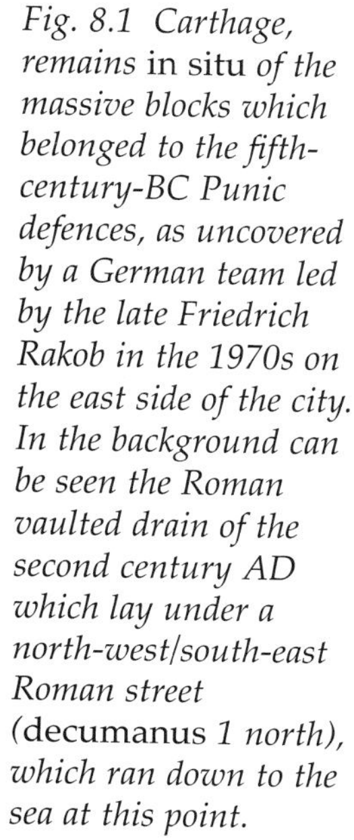
Fig. 8.1 Carthage, remains in situ *of the massive blocks which belonged to the fifth-century-BC Punic defences, as uncovered by a German team led by the late Friedrich Rakob in the 1970s on the east side of the city. In the background can be seen the Roman vaulted drain of the second century AD which lay under a north-west/south-east Roman street* (decumanus *1 north), which ran down to the sea at this point.*

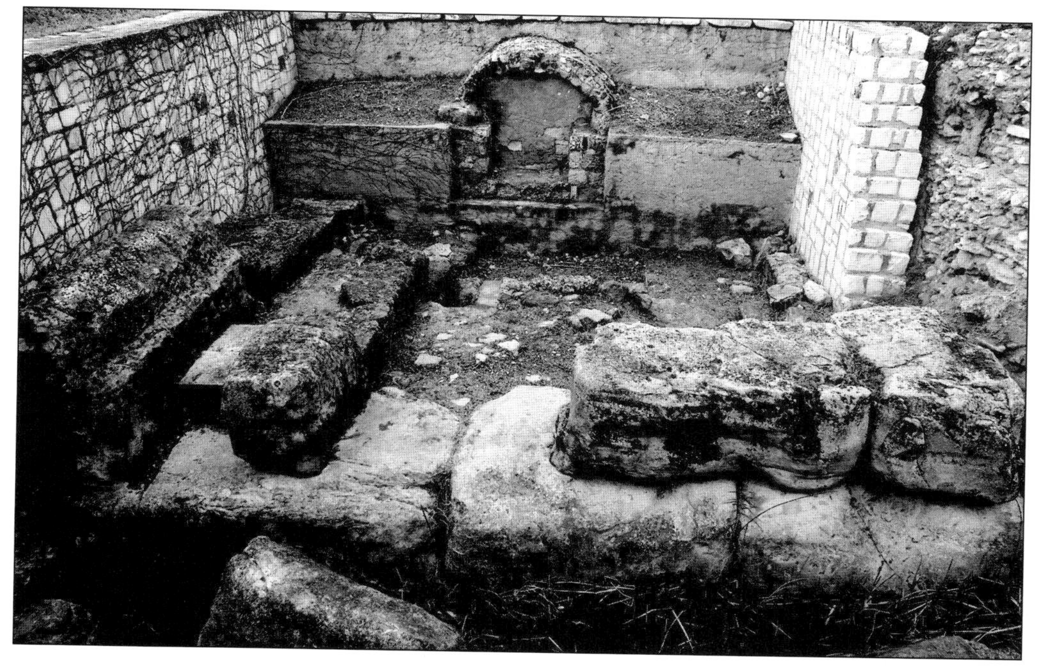

Palace. Davis described an enormous enclosure with an outer wall six feet (1.8 m) thick, enclosing a rectangular area of 613 ft by 340 ft (approximately 188 m by 104 m), and surrounding a 'temple' measuring 186 ft by 79 ft (approximately 57 m by 24 m). He dug a transverse trench, evidently inside the temple area, but he did not mention finds from here. He also noted huge rainwater cisterns within the larger enclosure.[25] Davis understandably did not continue his investigation of the site to beneath the Turkish fort, which lay immediately to the south-east over part of the outer rectangle, and which he outlined but did not label on his published map. His site is indicated on the latter by a point in the middle of a square enclosure just at the northern end of his label 'District of Aesculapius'. Davis believed that this ran along the 'Via Salutaria' ('Health Street') to the 'Temple of Aesculapius'; idiosyncratically (and mistakenly), he placed all three on his published map.

Beulé was to visit the site with Davis in 1859. He thought the summit of Bordj-Djedid was artificial and that the larger rectangle which Davis described was a retaining wall. Beulé also noted that Davis had found no architectural remains of a temple on this site.[26] Since Beulé not only believed that the Temple of Aesculapius was on the Byrsa Hill, but also was convinced that the marble architectural fragments from a temple in Corinthian style that he had found on the Byrsa were the remains of the Roman temple of Aesculapius, he had personally argued with Davis that the summit of Bordj-Djedid was too near the sea to be the acropolis of an ancient city, and could not therefore possibly be the site of the temple of Aesculapius. Ancient literary sources stated that the latter was approached by 60 steps, but Beulé pointed out that more than 120 steps would have been required for the grand staircase that led from the beach to the summit of Bordj-Djedid. Beulé therefore preferred the interpretation that, since there was ancient paving on the summit, the area was the 'Platea Nova', described by Victor of Vita in the Vandal period, and that the inner rectangle enclosed a garden.[27]

The closest point on the plan of Falbe is no. 34, but Falbe's description of it is not at all helpful.[28] His map indicates a rectangular enclosure on the summit of Bordj-Djedid. Whether he intended to indicate also a larger outer enclosure is not clear. On the other hand, his enclosure measures approximately seventy by twenty meters, is oriented to the street-grid, and is practically identical to the outline, location and size of an inner enclosure which was to be drawn and published by Lézine in 1961.[29] Delattre also described similar ruins on the summit of Bordj-Djedid. In 1897, Bordy showed a partial outline of the inner enclosure; on his map it is just a few degrees off the alignment of the Roman street-grid, which Bordy indicated here and there by heavy discontinuous lines. This alignment shows that the huge structure is in fact Roman.

According to the ancient sources, a Punic temple to Demeter and Persephone existed at Carthage from the early fourth century BC.[30] Grenville Temple was evidently the first to suggest that the summit of Bordj-Djedid, where he also noted 'the supports of a long and wide flight of stairs leading down to the sea', was the site of the Temple of Ceres (Ceres being the Roman equivalent of Demeter).[31] The area with the great double enclosure was to be marked 'Sanctuary of Ceres' and 'Punic necropolis' on the Bordy map (1897), reflecting the views of Delattre and Gauckler.[32] While excavating the Punic necropolis 'near Sainte-Monique,' which is actually in this same area, Delattre found a Punic inscription dedicating a shrine to Astarte and Tanit, numerous lamps of Hellenistic Greek form with the mark of Tanit, a Latin inscription of priests and priestesses of Ceres, a monumental marble head of Ceres, parts of a Roman statue of Aesculapius, a smaller statue of Ceres or Pomona, and Roman marble architectural debris, including an elegant Corinthian capital, all of which indicated to him that the temple must have been near the necropolis in both Punic and Roman times. Although the Punic temple of Demeter may have shared the summit with the Punic necropolis, it must in that case have been relatively limited in area.[33] While martialling the evidence that the massive rectangular structure was the Roman temple of Ceres, Delattre noted that Davis had sent to the British Museum an inscription of a Roman lady with the title 'Cerealis,' indicating a priestess of Ceres. Although Davis certainly excavated in the same area, the exact provenance of this inscription is unknown.[34] While he did not use them to argue Davis' point, Delattre's finds supported Davis' hypothesis that the Temple of Aesculapius was on the summit of Bordj-Djedid, and destroyed Beulé's objection that this site had no finds indicating a Roman temple. Nevertheless, modern scholars continue to consider the higher summit in the centre of the city the most likely site of the Punic Byrsa and the Punic temple of Eshmoun/Aesculapius, the site which is believed to have been completely destroyed by the extensive Roman rehandling of the Byrsa hill.

If the great Roman structure at Bordj-Djedid is indeed a temple, the Roman temple was built directly over the Punic necropolis. Delattre was to find many Punic shaft graves, mainly of the fourth/second centuries BC, in excavations within this quadrangle, and many of the finds described above were found in these shafts. The variable depth of the shafts also suggested to him that the summit of this hill had been levelled by the Romans,[35] no doubt to provide a level foundation for the massive structure. Punic shaft graves were also found here by Merlin and Drappier between 1906 and 1908; a detailed plan of their site, which they called Ard el-Kheraib ('Field of Ruins')[36] related both the great inner and outer walls to the shaft graves of the Punic necropolis.[37] The site names which French archaeologists chose for this necropolis are deliberately misleading; they were meant to draw the attention of tourists and locals away from the summit of Bordj-Djedid, which had become the site of a French military installation. In fact, the summit of this hill is one continuous Punic necropolis.[38]

Davis himself sent eight Punic tomb-markers, which he otherwise never mentioned, to the British Museum; they have now been published by Carole Mendleson.[39] The accession numbers show that seven of the eight were shipped on the *Curaçoa* in 1857, which indicates that Davis found these seven at one of his first fifteen sites. These uninscribed tomb monuments have a full-length figure in relief standing in a rectangular niche; the figure wears a long garment and holds its right hand raised, palm outward. Beulé found several examples of the same type on the north side of the Byrsa Hill, but the most numerous examples of this type of *stele* come from the excavations of Merlin and Drappier at 'Ard el-Kheraib' and the excavations of Delattre at 'Sainte-Monique'.[40] They were originally placed above ground to mark late Punic shaft graves.[41] Davis' eleventh site, the large enclosure on Bordj-Djedid, is by far the most likely source of the Punic tomb markers he found.

The huge double rectangular enclosure on the summit of Bord-Djedid was not a figment of Davis' imagination, as it was drawn and described (as noted above) in very similar terms by the architect Lézine a century later (Fig. 8.2). According to him, the area is the site of a large 'temple,' Lézine's point (13), marked with a rectangular enclosure on his plan of the north-eastern quadrant of the city. His 'temple' lies across *decumanus* 6 north and fills much of the area bounded by *cardines* 16 to 20.[42] Davis' published map placed the 'temple' about fifty meters north of its location according to Lézine, but within the same *decumani*. The measurements of the outer enclosure on the latter's map are in excess of 150 m by about 110 m, comparable to the dimensions reported by Davis. For comparison, the great Roman walled enclosure that created the foundation for the Roman forum on the Byrsa hill was four times as large, measuring approximately 223 m by 336 m.[43] The evidence from excavation is not adequate to identify the function of the enclosure, but if it surrounded a temple, the temple was an important one.

The theory that this structure is indeed a Roman temple has its dissenters. Gauckler argued that the site was a Roman military camp, and in this he was followed by Cagnat, who believed that the site was the *castrum* of the first urban cohort, the military unit assigned to Roman Carthage. Delattre also noted that fragments of an inscription listing soldiers were regularly recovered from this area.[44] The fact that Bordj-Djedid ('New Fort') was the site of a Turkish fort under the Regency of Tunis, and that a new fort was built at the same location by the French in 1898 under the Protectorate[45] shows that it was a natural defensive point, and it is possible that the Roman camp was indeed situated somewhere on this summit. Nevertheless, as Duval has rightly pointed out, the huge architectural ensemble described by Davis, Lézine and others bears absolutely no resemblance to a Roman *castrum*.[46]

A spring of fresh water was later to be excavated (in 1920) at the foot of Bordj-Djedid by Louis Carton, a medical man who excavated many sites in Tunisia. The stone construction of the captation chamber recalled Early Punic tombs to Carton, and pre-dated the Roman construction of a gallery with monumental entrance and a later reservoir, all of which lay closer to the sea. Carton called the site the 'fountain of a thousand amphoras'.[47] The face of the same cliff had been excavated by Delattre in 1906; although the latter did not find the spring, he found the cliff stabilized by a retaining wall backed by several thousand Roman amphoras, most of them imported from the north-eastern coast of Spain. The amphora types give the retaining wall a *terminus post quem* of the mid-first century AD.[48] As Carton pointed out, the date of the amphoras suggests that the Roman architectural enhancement of the spring pre-dated the construction of the Zaghouan aqueduct, for which a Hadrianic date is commonly accepted.[49]

The same summit was probably used by the army of Saint Louis (King Louis IX of France) when he came to Carthage in AD 1270. Beulé said that Saint Louis was never on the Byrsa Hill and cited Grenville Temple's statement that Bordj-Djedid used to be known as Fort Saint-Louis.[50] In fact, the French Crusaders camped first at a freshwater spring, which they found an unusual amenity at Carthage; in fact it is so unusual that it must be the same site as Carton's fountain. They then slaughtered a Saracen garrison who held a large defensive tower on a hill; many of the enemy were found hiding in the caverns with which the place abounded. The tower was considered the strong point of the whole surrounding region. The Crusaders cleared out the tower to make a hospital for the wounded and a refuge for the women, while the

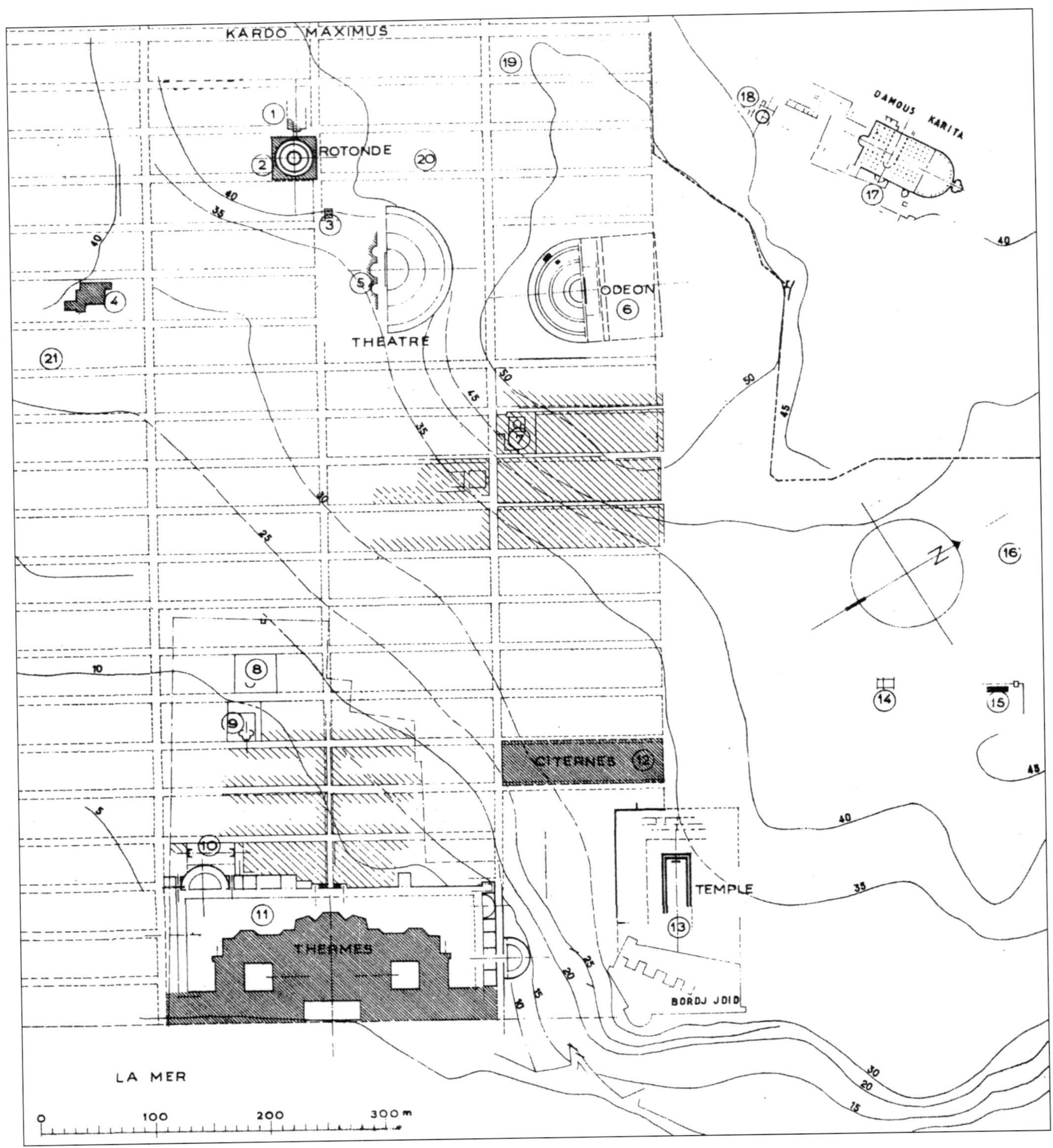

Fig. 8.2 Plan of the north-eastern quarter of Roman Carthage, as interpreted by Alexandre Lézine (1961)

main body of the army camped in the valley below.[51] Bordj-Djedid is obviously much more suitable than the Byrsa as a strong-point for the region, especially in an era when danger was from the sea.

The confusion of excavators who tried to identify the structures on the summit and slope of Bordj-Djedid was compounded by their search for a simple answer. It is certain that the area was a Punic necropolis from the early fourth century BC, but the Roman site is suited equally for either a military installation or a temple. It is certain that the huge double enclosure is a Roman structure, because of its alignment with the Roman street-grid. Beulé's judgment that the summit of Bordj-Djedid was artificial, and Delattre's evidence that the summit of the hill had been cut down harmonizes better with plans for the construction of a great temple rather than a fort, especially considering that the Roman military presence at Carthage, the capital of a peaceful province, was minor. If the great rectangular enclosures were built as the foundation of a Roman temple, it is a problem that the architectural remains of such a temple were almost entirely missing on the ground, although Delattre found significant architectural evidence for one in the Punic tomb shafts, which had clearly been opened in Roman times and again after the end of the Roman era. There is no evidence for the date of the monumental stairway, but it seems a natural complement to a great Roman temple, and a very unlikely approach to a Roman garrison fort. It is equally unlikely that the Vandal kings would have produced something so grandiose and impractical of access as an open plaza on the summit, although they might have incorporated a pre-existing monumental stairway into a new architectural ensemble. Perhaps the Vandals destroyed a great Roman temple and removed as much of the evidence as possible before building their new plaza. Perhaps the troops of Saint Louis did assault the summit of Bordj-Djedid and used the standing remains as a refuge. The incredible variety of evidence for the history and archaeology of this site provides some justification for Davis' stubborn belief that the Temple of Aesculapius stood here.

Davis' twelfth site: excavations at the Antonine Baths

Davis then returned to the area of the Antonine Baths (Site 12), again probably before the departure of the *Curaçoa*. He was back in the north-eastern quarter of the city street-grid, within a block or two of the sea. Davis dug several trenches here and marked two points in this area on the published map. One lies in the immediate centre of the outline of the main building of the Antonine Baths, while the other falls immediately to the west of the hemicycle/*caldarium* (the hot room of a Roman bath complex), just east of *cardo* 18 east and just north of the line of *decumanus* 4 north, although that Roman street was here interrupted by the western enclosure wall of the baths.

The Antonine Baths can of course be located exactly, but the complex is very large (see Figs 3.4–5 and Fig. 5.5).[52] Davis' two points here make sense and seem likely to be accurate within thirty meters or less, especially since he had the seashore as an immediate reference point. Comparison with Lézine's plan suggests Davis was digging just inside the western enclosure wall of the complex.[53] This would have been close to the line of the 'Esplanade' (*cardo* 18 east), the street that runs along the landward side of the bath-building. Roman houses, in particular the House of Black and White Mosaics, were be excavated a century later on the west side of this street.[54]

Davis did not know the massive complex of ruins on the sea-shore as the Antonine Baths. Although Falbe recognized his site no. 67 as 'the most impressive building of a bath',[55] Davis was not convinced by this identification. The latter's first sketch-map indicated the ruins by three enclosures, of which the one on the south-west corresponds to the south-west latrine, which has been discussed above (Site 4). His second sketch-map designated the main baths by a jumble of irregular circles, and Davis idiosyncratically labelled the area the 'Forum.' Since the ancient sources said that the Punic Forum lay between the harbours and the Byrsa, and since Davis had decided that the summit of Bordj-Djedid was the Punic Byrsa, the Antonine Baths became a possible site of the Punic forum.

His best find, and the only one which he mentioned in his text, was a grey granite column five feet (1.5 m) in diameter and ten feet (3.0 m) long, which was removed in order to be used in the construction of Mohammed Bey's new palace at the Bardo.[56] Beulé may have been unknowingly referring to Davis' find when he described a huge granite column brought to the Bardo by turning it into a wheel pulled by horses.[57] The find of the column confirms that Davis was digging inside the baths themselves.

Davis' thirteenth site: the Vandal Mosaic of Victory at Falbe no. 90

Unlike the four previous sites, Davis' next site (Site 13) proved very productive. This was where Davis discovered the Vandal Mosaic of Victory with Inscription (Fig. 8.3), as well as three geometric mosaics at lower levels. The site, Falbe no. 90, was on the sea-shore at the foot of a steep and somewhat inaccessible ravine, just to the north of the expanded city grid. Davis' first sketch-map indicated that the site had no ruins, but did produce finds. The second sketch-map marked the site on the north side of an inlet. It lies about half-way between the Turkish fort on Bordj-Djedid and the marked 'Ruins of Sea Gate,' which are *c.* 800 m farther north. The equivalent on the published map is marked on the sea-shore, at the foot of steeply-rising ground. It does not lie to the north of Falbe no. 72, as Hinks thought, following Franks.[58] Falbe no. 72 was the site described by Falbe as 'remains of a gate of the city'[59]

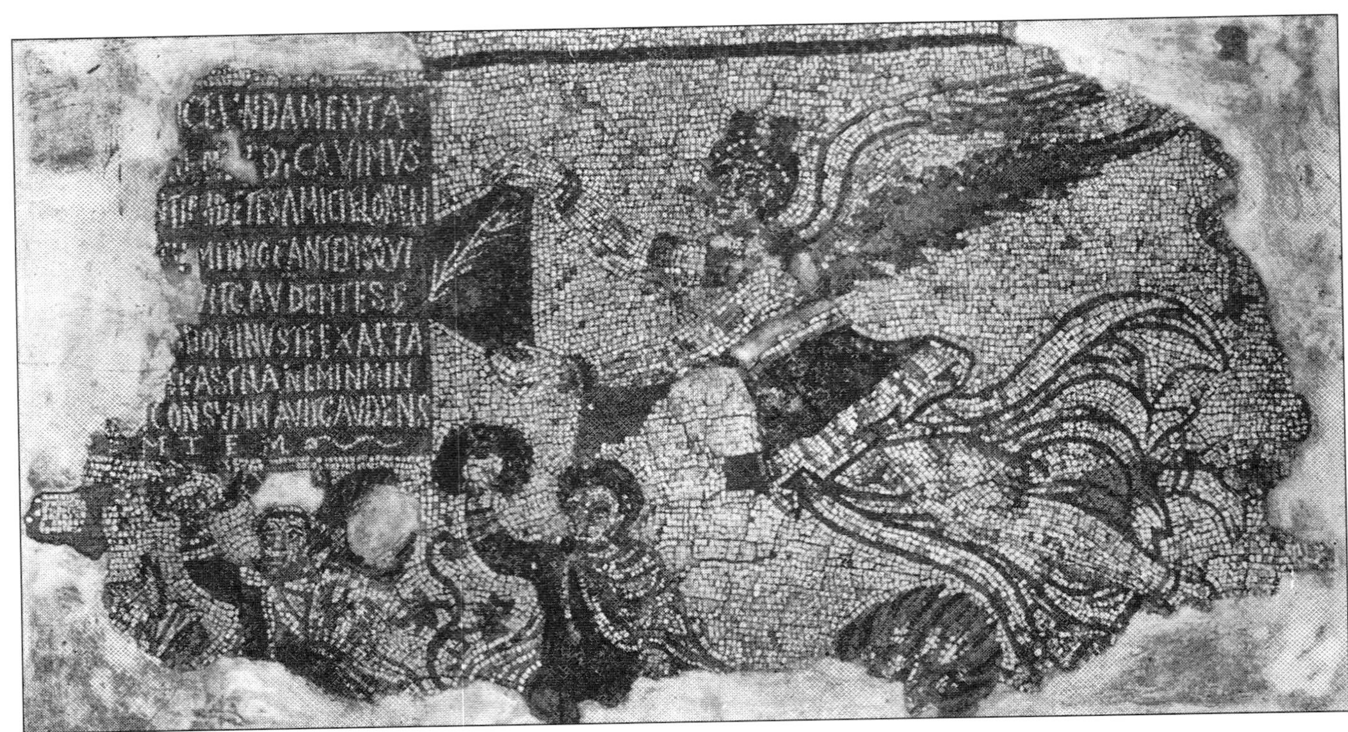

Fig. 8.3 The Mosaic of Victory with Inscription. It shows a winged Victory holding up a tabula ansata *(in red) bearing an inscription executed in white* tesserae; *there is a palm branch (symbol of Victory) in the handle* (ansa) *of the inscribed panel, and parts of two young men below holding wreaths and fans. This fragment measures 2.17 m by 1.20 m. Second half of the fifth century AD (?).*

and is also so marked on Davis' published map. The latter reached the place where the Mosaic of Victory was found from the summer residence of his friend the 'Lord Keeper of the Seal,' whose house was marked as site 11 on his published map. Davis said, 'From here a path leads down to an unfinished bathing establishment near a ravine to the right'. According to Davis, the path therefore led down on the left or north side of the ravine, and the site with the Mosaic of Victory was adjacent to an unfinished modern bathing house at the foot of the cliff. A person walking continued in the same direction, that is, along the sea and to the north, to reach the so-called 'Sea Gate'.[60]

Falbe had also marked his site no. 90 on the north side of the mouth of a narrow ravine, and described the spot as a 'ruin where I discovered a mosaic floor'.[61] While Davis' first sketch-map indicated that the site had no ruins, Falbe had reported ruins at site no. 90, and in another part of his book, Davis himself said there were numerous ancient ruins in the vicinity.[62] He also said that the site was chosen at random, and that, like the Mosaic with Baskets of Fish and Fruit (see below, p. 123), the Mosaic of Victory was found in an unmotivated test-trench.[63] The description and maps of the site of the Mosaic of Victory show that it was in the same restricted area as Falbe no. 90, however, and Davis' claim that the site was chosen at random is therefore unlikely to be strictly accurate. Falbe had excavated mosaics at site no. 90 in 1824 and 1838. Davis certainly knew about the find of a mosaic in 1824, since he had the plan of Falbe and its companion text, and he should have known of the further discoveries in 1838, since he had a copy of the report which Temple and Falbe prepared for their excavation society.

Davis' site lies on the sea-shore just beyond the north-eastern section of the expanded city street-grid and the line of the Theodosian Wall. It is situated to the north of the line of *decumanus* 8 north and east of *cardo* 21 east. The city street-grid was not laid out at the foot of the ravine, however, since the Danish excavators at Falbe no. 90 in the UNESCO campaign of the 1970s indicated that the extensive buildings which they found, crowded against the cliff wall, did not follow the alignment of the street-grid.[64]

The mosaics were first mentioned in a letter from Davis to the Foreign Office, dated May 28th, 1857.[65] George Leighton Ditson, the American travel writer mentioned above (p. 101), described the stratigraphy of these mosaics in a report for the *New York Tribune* as follows:[66]

> . . . three mosaic floors have been discovered, just so nearly one above the other as to allow a portion of each to be uncovered without removing either [*sic*] of them. I have seen them twice, and can therefore substantiate the fact. The lowest one was found in cutting away a hillside at the depth of about five feet; on its right, as you stand facing the north, and about three inches above it, there is another flooring of mosaic; three or four feet above the latter, and on its eastern side, there is still another; and at about the same elevation on the other hand is *the* [Ditson's or Davis' emphasis] 'Figure of Victory'.

Since Ditson described the site while it was still being excavated, he was visiting Davis' excavations in the spring of 1857.

Davis himself said, '. . . I discovered an edifice, scarcely anything of which but the pavements have remained and these mark distinctly the Punic and Roman periods of Carthage'. He described the uppermost mosaic he found at Falbe no. 90 as 'a fragment of mosaic representing a flying figure, of rather rough composition, bearing in her hands a portion of Latin inscription'.[67] A partially-preserved mosaic, seven feet by four feet (2.1 m by 1.2 m), depicted a winged and flying Victory holding the points of the right side of a *tabula ansata* (a characteristic Roman tablet with flared 'handles' on either side, widely copied in Roman inscriptions), on which a nine-line inscription, broken off on the left side, memorialized the construction of a building.[68] A palm branch decorated the right-hand side of the inscription. The Latin text was in white letters on a red ground;[69] below, the upper bodies of two youths face left holding wreaths and square fans with long handles (*flabella*); these fans do not seem to appear in art before the fourth century. The boys are dressed in grey tunics and white cloaks with conspicuous flying ties. The dress of the Victory is in red outline only, which also suggests a late date.[70] The placing of the three figures indicates that approximately half the width of the mosaic and the right-hand half of the inscription survive. The original width of the panel would therefore have been about fourteen feet (4.3 m). A plain horizontal line defines a border just above the inscription, but no other area of border is preserved. The fragment which Davis found was probably set within the design of a much larger mosaic floor.

Franks published a reading of the inscription as did Davis; the two are the same, except that the former understood a leaf-shaped sentence division where the latter read 'V.' Franks also supplemented the inscription to interpret the building as a 'basilica'. The inscription was subsequently published in the corpus of Latin inscriptions, where Wilmanns and Mommsen completed line 3 as *florem* and quoted an attempt by the Italian scholar, de Rossi, to complete the lines (see below).[71] Franks dated the style of the mosaic and inscription to the fourth century.[72]

[. . .]nc fundamenta
[. . .]tem dedicavimus
tibidete ❧ amici floren
deum invocantem ❧ qui
[. . .]vit gaudentes ❧
dominus te exalta
❧ fastilanem in min
consummavit gaudens
[. . .]emtem ❧

He suggested restoring the first lines as *basilicam hanc fundamenta tenus labentem dedicavimus* ('we have restored [actually, 'dedicated'] this basilica, which had collapsed to its foundations. . .'), but could not get further. Wilmanns or Mommsen noted that the meter of the lines was the *septenarius*, which limits the metrical possibilities for completion of the lines. None of the scholars who considered the inscription had any suggestion as to how deal with line 9. De Rossi was quoted in the corpus of Latin inscriptions, where Wilmanns and Mommsen obviously preferred his completion of the inscription to Franks' suggestions, as follows:

. . . nc fundamenta
[iecimus, . . fron]tem dedicavimus
. . . ti. Bidete, amici, florem
[Wandalorum?] deum invocantem, qui
[. . . exaudi]vit gaudentes
. . . Dominus te exalta
[vit per] Fastilanem immin
[entem operi]. . . [ ] consummavit gaudens
. . . emtem.

Bidete is late Latin for *videte*. A very rough translation of this inscription, as supplemented by de Rossi, would be '. . .we set down the foundations, we dedicated the façade. . . See, friends, the flower [of the Vandals?] calling on God, who heard [the people] rejoicing. . .God has exalted you, Fastila, as you encourage the work. . . [Someone] finished [the work] rejoicing . . . '. De Rossi interpreted 'Fastila' as a Vandal name, perhaps a female person, as the 'flower' [of the Vandals?], and he also suggested that the subject of *consummavit* ('he/she finished') in line 8 should be the name of a Vandal king. The inscription commemorated the construction of an important public building that is probably of the early Vandal period, dating to the second half of the fifth century.

Judging by the location of the site on Davis' published map, this building was located within fifty meters from the sea and on steeply rising ground. Ditson's description indicates that the Mosaic of Victory was found with earlier mosaics lying at a lower level and partly to the east (even closer to the sea) and north, rather than in a sequence directly beneath the Mosaic of Victory. Could the Mosaic of Victory have been the porch or entrance hall of a building that rose behind it and away from the sea? A grand Roman building, especially one on the sea front, would probably have been supported on vaults, which Davis reported as typical even for the private sea-front villas which he investigated further north at Gammarth;[73] but Davis clearly found that this Vandal mosaic had been laid at ground level, with underlying soil layers.

In comparing the upper mosaic with the lower ones, Ditson said that the topmost mosaic (the Mosaic of Victory with Inscription) was embedded in cement about an inch thick which was excessively hard and had to be taken up with the figures.[74] The extreme hardness of the cement was considered by Davis as a sign that the mosaic was Roman rather than Punic; in terms of our present understanding of the dating of these mosaics, it may be characteristic of the late Roman period, in contrast with that used for early Roman mosaics (see Appendix 3).

Three geometric mosaics from below the Mosaic of Victory

Davis found the fragmentary Mosaic of Victory four feet (1.2 m) below the surface, and another mosaic was found at about the same level, according to Ditson. Franks wrote that a second geometric mosaic was found three feet (0.9 m) farther down, and a third, with an elongated geometric design, was found six inches (15 cm) lower than that.[75] All four mosaics were among those sent to the British Museum on HMS *Curaçoa*, which left Carthage in July. Their accession numbers beginning '1857.12-18' (December 18th, 1857) prove they were a part of this shipment. Three geometric mosaics were dispatched: a black-and-white Mosaic of Back-to-Back Peltas, and two other more sophisticated geometric mosaics. In his 'Statement', Davis described these three as, first, decorating an entrance passage, while 'the remaining two are quarters of apartments, and which is all that has remained of the same [lower] structure'.[76] Davis may have meant that the lowest mosaics, which are similar in size, and both with borders on two adjacent sides, each made up about a quarter of the floor of its original room. He had earlier stated that scarcely anything but the pavements remained of the building in which these mosaics were located. His description implies that the lower mosaics were contemporary despite the fact that one is on a slightly higher level, and also that the building in which they were placed had been razed before the construction of the Vandal edifice with the Mosaic of Victory.

With regard to the two lowest pavements below the Mosaic of Victory, Franks described the upper one as having a [geometric] pattern only, the other, six inches lower, as an elegant geometrical design.[77] Davis quoted this description from Franks, but substituted the word 'elongated' for Franks' 'elegant'.[78] Franks did not explain his basis for deciding that one was upper, the other lower. Davis said that the third and lowest pavement had 'geometrical designs tastefully distributed'; he also noted that the lowest mosaic had a bedding of soft mortar.[79] To Davis, soft mortar indicated a mosaic of Punic date. Ditson, however, described the lower two pavements as obtained without the mortar, since after they have had cotton cloth glued down on the surfaces, the mortar was 'easily cut away by any sharp instrument',[80] implying that both had soft mortar. Davis removed 'such of these antiquities as were least injured', which suggests that all were fragmentary.[81] In his inventory of Tunisian mosaics, Gauckler later listed two geometric mosaics from this site, the first found four feet (this is not perfectly true to his sources) under the Mosaic of Victory, and the second six inches farther down, but Gauckler was incorrect in describing them as left in place and subsequently destroyed.[82]

The 'entrance passage' described by Davis must be the black-and-white geometric Mosaic of Back-to-Back Peltas, which is complete on three sides, as it is a relatively small mosaic suitable for a threshold (Fig. 8.4).[83] Ditson's stratigraphic description puts this pavement at about the same level as the Mosaic of Victory, but to the east and beyond the other two mosaics. The pattern is large, bold and simple for the size of the mosaic. Hinks dated it to the second century, listing related examples which suggest that it is approximately contemporary with the two lower mosaics from the same site, but it could equally well date a century or more later.

The remaining two mosaics are contemporary in style. The first of these is a geometric floor, the Mosaic of Hexagons Framing Hexafoils (Fig. 8.5), with a rigidly symmetrical repeating pattern on a white ground, based on six-pointed florets (hexafoils) on a black hexagonal ground inside hexagonal frames; the latter are arranged around squares and interspersed with four-pointed stars to create an overall pattern of interlocking circles. The mosaic is in black and white with accents in buff, red and some pink. The fragment which Davis sent to Britain is a corner with a triple border on two sides, the inner border a strong black

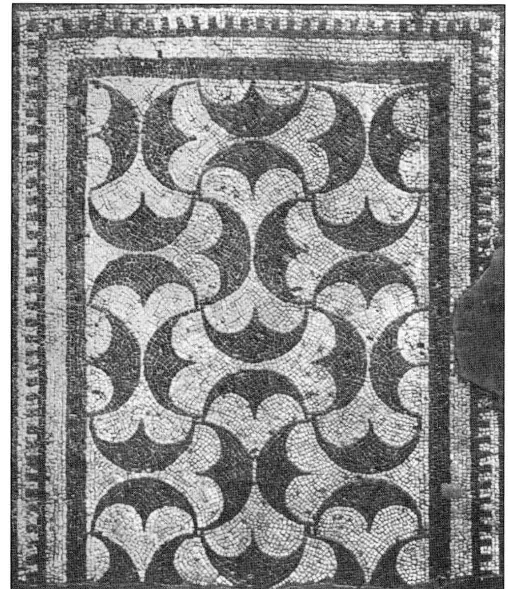

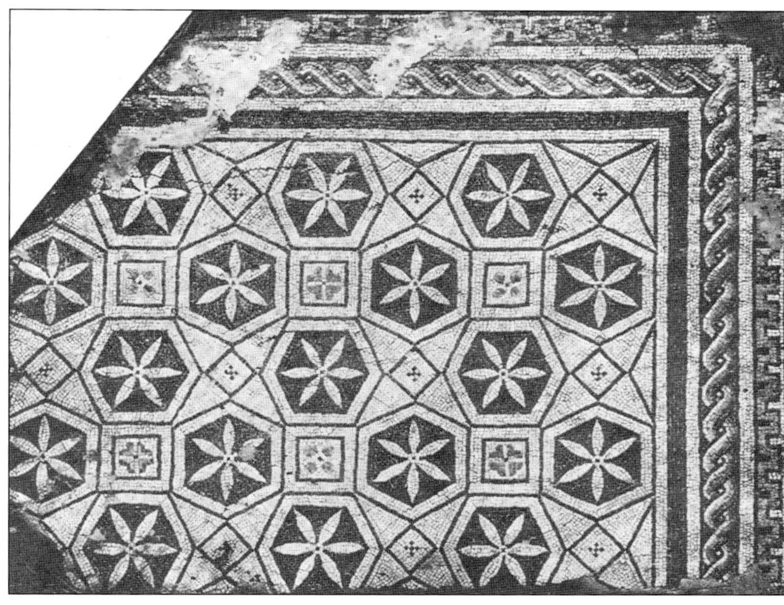

Fig. 8.4 (above left) *The Mosaic of Back-to-Back Peltas, with its 'running-pelta' pattern; the portion here, raised by Davis in 1857, measures 1.56 m by 1.37 m. It comes from the same site as Fig. 8.3 but at a slightly lower level; second half of the second century AD (?)*

Fig. 8.5 (above right) *The Mosaic of Hexagons Framing Hexafoils, the corner of a pavement from three feet lower than the pavement shown in Fig. 8.4; second half of the second century AD (?). The portion preserved measures 2.12 m by 1.65 m.*

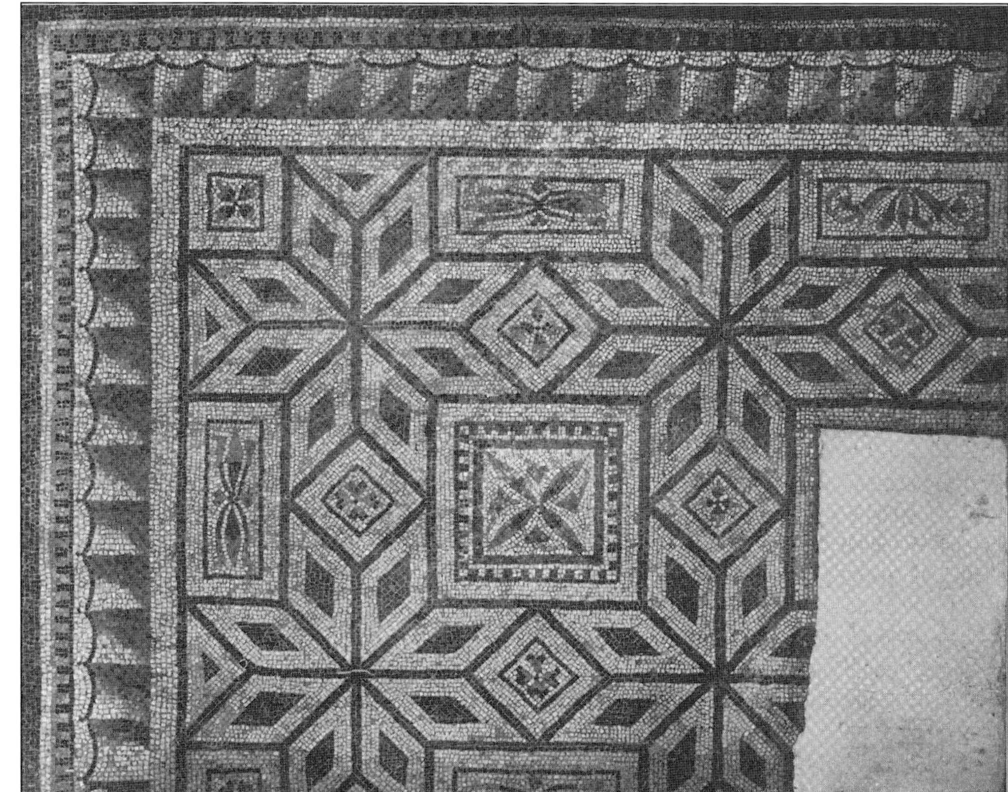

Fig. 8.6 The Mosaic of the Eight-Pointed Stars, in a pattern which encloses both squares and smaller squares set diagonally; the latter each contains a four-leafed floret, the larger square a four-petalled rosette with an accompanying hedera *(ivy-leaf) between each pair of petals. The border is made up of a continuous awning pattern and an outer row of dentils. Second half of the second century AD (?).*

line, the next a simple guilloche, and the outer border a simple meander consisting of an 'embattled' filet. Hinks ascribed the mosaic (his no. 8) to the second century.[84] The strong repeated pattern is pleasing but hardly 'elegant'.

The other was the Mosaic of Eight-Pointed Stars (Fig. 8.6), a polychrome geometric mosaic with an elegant shaded awning border, and octagonal stars that surround squares and rectangles framing delicate motifs, in the style of a floral carpet. Davis again sent a corner fragment of this floor. Hinks' measurements imply that the area of the mosaic shown in his photograph measures 2.18 m by 1.84 m, but the mosaic may continue somewhat beyond the photograph in two directions.[85] It seems likely to me that this mosaic (Hinks no. 9) would have been seen by Franks as more elegant than Hinks no. 8, discussed above. Although the sizes of the two fragments are similar, the orientation of the long and short sides is different. Since Hinks organized the catalogue of mosaics chronologically, his numbering of these two (Hinks nos 8 and 9) shows that he regarded them as approximately contemporary. These two mosaics very probably belonged to a private Roman sea-side house.

More archaeological evidence for Falbe no. 90

Although Davis was digging in the immediate area of Falbe no. 90, he was probably not working in the same building as that excavated by Falbe and Temple in 1838. Falbe had described this building as 'near the seashore where the piers come to an end',[86] and the space in the area is so restricted that Davis' site cannot be far away. Nevertheless, the mosaics retrieved by Davis are very different from the Marine Mosaic excavated by Falbe and Temple, and there is no evidence to associate Davis' mosaics with Falbe's plan of the suite of rectangular rooms which he and Grenville Temple excavated. Falbe provided a scale but not a north point or any other orientation for this plan. The layout of the rooms suggests that they form part of a small Roman bath-house (see Fig. 3.7). Falbe's notes on the Mosaic of a Nereid on a Hippocamp (Fig. 6.2) said that it formed part of a very damaged mosaic in room no. 1; the room number is not indicated on his sketch-plan of the house, but he probably meant one of the two large central rooms. The building was the same one that he had excavated fourteen years earlier at Falbe no. 90,[87] and the second large square room may have been the site of the mosaic lost in 1824.

Falbe had found the 1824 mosaic about eight to ten feet (2.4 m to 3.0 m) below the surface. Davis' Mosaic of Victory with Inscription was found at a depth of four feet (1.2 m), while one of the geometric mosaics, as already noted above (p. 120), was another three feet (0.9 m) farther down and the lowest of the geometric mosaics was six inches (15 cm) below that. The depth of the lowest mosaic is somewhat comparable to the depth of soil Falbe described over the mosaic destroyed in 1824. On the other hand, Ditson described the lowest mosaic in Davis' sequence as only about five feet (c. 1.5 m) below the surface. Davis' mosaics were found while digging away a slope, however, which makes the reported depths here somewhat meaningless, as downwash from the cliff immediately behind the excavations would have continually accumulated.

The area around Falbe site no. 90 was explored again in 1975 and 1977 by the Danish UNESCO team. The team was aware of the mosaics which Falbe had excavated at his site no. 90 in 1824 and 1838, but not of Davis' finds from the same area in 1857.[88] Although the Danish archaeological preserve, a triangle, is nearly 200 m long on the sea side, they chose to dig very close to the shore in the northern half of the defined area, where the ground rises steeply from the shore.[89] The long building on the west side of their site was built up against the slope in the first century, and perhaps already in the reign of Augustus, and seemed to serve originally as a pleasant villa facing east to the sea. Vaulted rooms were added at ground level in the second century, and there would have been new usable space above. Doorways between these rooms were later filled in, and the spaces were probably used as shops. In the late fourth or early fifth century, a Roman villa measuring 15.7 m by 24.5 m was built on the south-eastern area of the site, on a different alignment and even closer to the sea. All the buildings in the complex excavated by the Danes were in use together for a short period of time before the Vandal conquest in AD 439. Their excavated area was not inhabited during the Vandal period, but mass burials of early Vandal date were laid in and under the floors of three of the earlier vaulted rooms, probably around the middle of the fifth century, judging by the associated coins and pottery.[90]

Although the Danes did not find preserved mosaics, they did discover a surviving piece of mosaic border with a polychrome guilloche and a possible dentil pattern in a large room where the rest of the mosaic had been broken up or robbed out. Material found underneath this floor could be dated no later than the second half of the second century, and it was originally suggested by the excavators that this might be the room where Falbe's 'Mosaic of Oceanus and Nereids' was found.[91] Certainly a Roman mosaic floor was removed from this room at some time in the past, but Falbe described a wide border of fish for his Marine Mosaic.

Davis sent four mosaics from Falbe no. 90 to the British Museum (Hinks nos 8, 9, 11 and 59). None of these have a simple guilloche border: the Mosaic of Hexagons Framing Hexafoils is bordered by a single twisted guilloche, the Mosaic of Back-to-Back Peltas has dentils between simple lines, while the Mosaic of the Eight-Pointed Stars has a shaded awning border and the Mosaic of Victory has a simple black line around an area equivalent to a large *emblema*.[92] The guilloche border from the Danish site is similar to the guilloche that forms the border of Davis' Mosaic with Baskets of Fish and Fruit (Fig. 8.7)[93] and to the outer border of the geometric mosaic that Davis was to excavate at Utica (Fig. 11.10),[94] which may support the Danish evidence that their robbed-out mosaic is of second-century date.

Although the Danes used a north point, their plans do not show the relation of their excavations to the surrounding elevation or to the sea.[95] As they originally thought that they might be digging the same rooms dug by Falbe, their eastern suite of rooms must be very close to the sea, and they indicate that the western line of rooms was built up against the hillside. Subsequently the Danish excavators decided that their site had a very different history from Falbe's site. Although they found no extant remains of it, the Danish excavators believe that the site excavated by Falbe and Temple probably lay to the south of their own work, in an area where the archaeological evidence has now been completely destroyed.[96]

This example indicates that where three sites have been dug in clear relationship to a well-defined Falbe point, there may still be no overlap in the excavations. This is especially interesting since the width of available space before the steep rise of the hill is very limited. Nevertheless, the results from each excavation appear to be quite different. Falbe and Temple's excavation at Falbe no. 90 may have been no larger than the 19-meter-square room-complex drawn by Falbe; this is something more than half the width of the narrow side of a city-block at Carthage. Davis' trench could have been as small as four or five meters per side, since the Mosaic of Victory with Inscription was a fragment only 2.17 m by 1.20 m in size,[97] and the corner of the lowest geometric mosaic was about 2.2 m by 1.8 m. The Danish excavations of the 1970s were also narrow, although the area excavated was quite long: their site is approximately twenty-five meters wide by seventy meters long (north–south),[98] a little less than half a Roman city-block at Carthage. I think it likely that the sites excavated by Falbe and Davis were both south of the Danish site, closer to the foot of the ravine, and that the former was closer to the sea than the latter.

All three sites, nevertheless, show some similarity. All reported Roman mosaic floors that probably belonged to the middle or the second half of the second century AD. Rectangular rooms, a feature elsewhere of early rather than late Roman buildings, were described by both Falbe and the later Danish excavators. Davis found a (possibly early) Vandal building dedication, while the Danes found a well-preserved early Vandal mass-burial. It is possible to meld all this information for an understanding of the area that is not likely to be far wrong. The narrow and somewhat inaccessible beach area was the site of at least one Roman residence and a small Roman bath-house from the first to early third century, with some evolution into shops towards the end of this period. A new and larger integrated residential development was constructed in the late fourth or early fifth century, but these buildings were abandoned immediately after the Vandal conquest. The area then saw new construction with a more religious or official function, although it is impossible to say whether the Vandal mass burials came before or after the Vandal structure with the mosaic inscription.

Davis' fourteenth site: the early Roman Mosaic with Baskets of Fish and Fruit

While he was still digging at the sea-shore site with the Mosaic of Victory (Falbe 90), word was brought to Davis by his workmen that another mosaic had been found at an unmotivated test trench at the edge of a bean-field (Site 14). The site was most probably at a moderate elevation on the slope of the Hill of Juno and would have had a sea view. Here an elegant mosaic border had been discovered at a depth of about six feet (1.8 m).[99] Davis barely mentioned the mosaic in his book, but he said a little more in letters to the Foreign Office, written in May and July 1857. After getting permission from the landowner, on condition that the beans would be paid for, he cleared the room and took up two pieces of mosaic. The first, the *emblema* of the Mosaic with Baskets of Fish and Fruit (Fig. 8.7), was loaded on to the *Curaçoa* before its first departure.[100] Davis described the site of the find as being not far from the trench with Punic votive tablets.[101] In a letter of July 14th, he described additional cases sent on the *Curaçoa*, for which he received a receipt from Captain Forbes; this shows that the border (Fig. 8.8) had to wait for the second load. Davis noted that the latter came from the same room as the Mosaic with Baskets of Fish and Fruit, and that together the two pieces made up a third of the floor.[102]

The map evidence for the site of the Mosaic with Baskets of Fish and Fruit is both confused and confusing, as Davis used his site numbers inconsistently. On

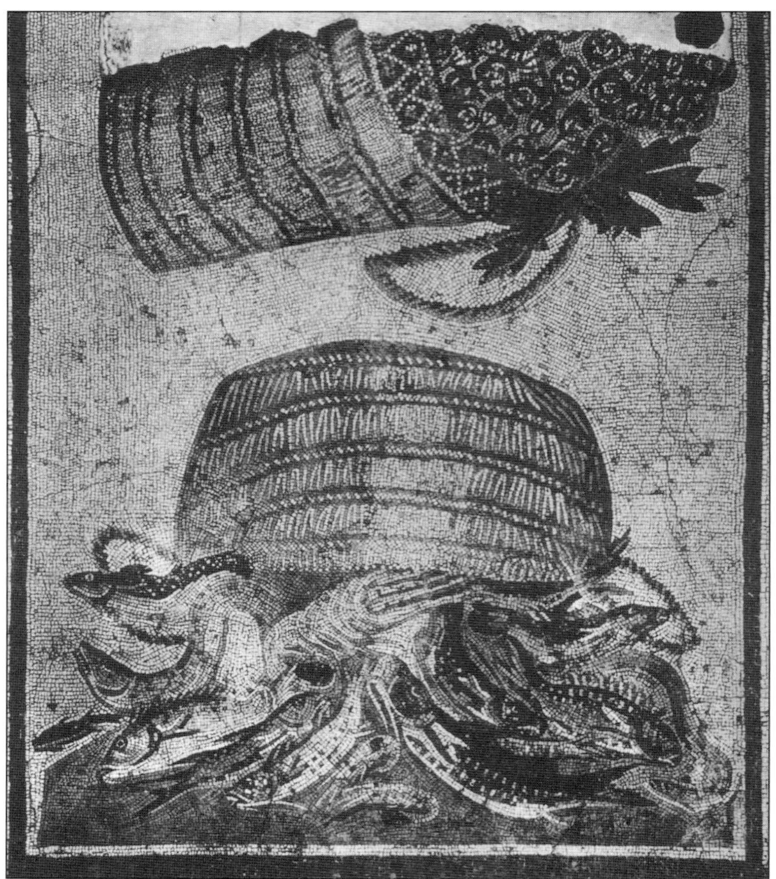

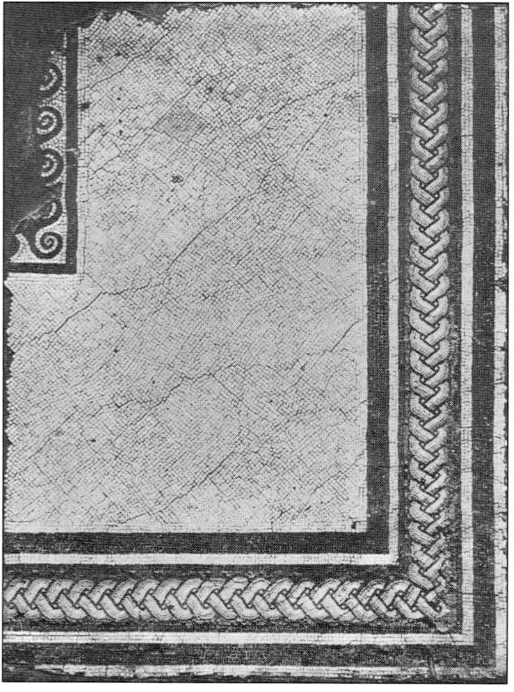

Fig. 8.7 (above left) *The* emblema *of the Mosaic with Baskets of Fish and Fruit (late first or early second century AD?). The motif of fish escaping from a basket is known elsewhere in north Africa, for example on mosaics at Hadrumetum (Sousse) and at Uzitta.*

Fig. 8.8 (above right) *A corner of the floor which contained the Mosaic with Baskets of Fish and Fruit at its centre, showing both the wave-pattern border which enclosed the latter and the three-strand guilloche border of the whole floor (late first or early second century AD?).*

his first sketch-map, which he enclosed with his letter of May 28th, 1857, site 12 was placed in fairly close proximity to, and north of, his 'Punic mine' (site 13, Fig. 4.13). The sketch-map indicates that the site had finds, but no ruins. On the second sketch-map, Davis reversed the location of these numbers, but in his 'Statement', which relates to the second sketch-map, site 12 was described as the site of the Punic mine. The relative placing of these two sites, one of which should be the site of the Mosaic with Baskets of Fish and Fruit, is therefore not necessarily different, but because Davis did not mention site 13 in the 'Statement', its identity is uncertain. On the other hand, both pieces of the Mosaic with Baskets of Fish and Fruit had gone to England on the *Curaçoa* in the summer of 1857 and the mosaic and its site were not relevant to the purpose of the 'Statement', which listed the cases on board HMS *Supply* in 1858. Davis changed the numbers for his sites again for the published map. Site 23 on the published map is certainly the 'Punic mine',[103] but he did not label and never discussed site 22, fifty meters to the north, and in the relative position of the Mosaic with Baskets of Fish and Fruit on the first sketch-map. Nevertheless, this number probably was meant to indicate the site. On the other hand (to confuse matters further), Davis' published map also places the Hill of Juno two blocks too far to the west, which contributes to the difficulty in locating both sites. The published map places site 23 (the 'Punic mine') on the north-east slope of the Byrsa hill, one third of the way between *decumani* 1 and 2 north and on *cardo* 3 east. For various reasons (see below, p. 127), I believe this should be corrected to *cardo* 5 east. The corresponding location of the discovery of the Mosaic with Baskets of Fish and

Fruit is therefore on the south-east slope of the Hill of Juno, on the line of *decumanus* 2 north and *cardo* 6 east.

On Davis' second sketch-map (Fig. 4.14), he also showed both sites lying immediately on the east side of a path running along the eastern base of the Byrsa and the Hill of Juno; this road ran from Douar ech-Chott to Sidi bou-Said. A similar path was also shown some forty years later on Bordy's 1897 map, running not far above the twenty-meter contour line. The relevant section of the Bordy path ran between cardines 6 and 7 east and between *decumani* 1 and 3 north. It seems certain that both the Mosaic with Baskets of Fish and Fruit and the site of the Punic *stelae* lay on the eastern side of such a road or path in 1857, but Davis specifically said that he had to divert this path as the site of the 'Punic mine' grew.

The overlay of the street-grid with Davis' published map, on the other hand (Fig. 4.12), shows the 'Punic mine' at *cardo* 3 east and the site of the mosaic at *cardo* 4 east. If these sites are corrected by one block to *cardo* 4 east and *cardo* 5 east, the two are both at the same elevation on the slope, but the elevation is forty-five meters above sea-level – one which could hardly be seen as near the foot of these two hills. It is very likely that the location of sites 23 and 22 on the published map is simply incorrect, and that they have been dragged too far west by the incorrect siting of the Hill of Juno. Moving the location of the sites one more short block east (a correction of two short-sided blocks in total, or about seventy-seven meters including the intervening street), to *cardo* 5 east and *cardo* 6 east, drops their elevation to about thirty meters above sea level, which agrees better with the second sketch-map, but is still a block too far west and ten meters too high to agree with Bordy's path in 1897. I think this is not too serious a problem, as the line of the road may have changed again with more frequent carriage traffic.

This correction would place the site of the Mosaic with Baskets of Fish and Fruit as lying beneath what is now the modern inner ring road (Rue Junon) running around the slope of the hill of Juno. This was an area of luxury housing with potential sea views in Roman times, just as it is today. The 'House of the Bird-Chariots' that was be excavated by Hanoune and published in 1969 is less than half a Roman city-block away to the south, and the 'House with the Mosaic of Dominus Julius' is one or two short blocks to the west. The House of the Bird-Chariots is sited between *decumani* 1 and 2 north and between *cardines* 5 and 7 east, lying across the line of *cardo* 6 east, at the base of the hill of Juno.[104] According to the excavators, the house with the Mosaic of Dominus Julius was situated 200 m north of the Chapel of Saint Louis (now demolished).[105] Therefore it lay on the line of *cardo* 3 east, half-way between *decumani* 1 and 2 north, on the north side of the modern outer ring road running around the hill of Juno.

The Mosaic with Baskets of Fish and Fruit was formed by a central rectangular pseudo-*emblema* on which two baskets are preserved, one of fish and one of fruit, surrounded by a plain white ground with a guilloche border. The photograph in Hinks' book (Fig. 8.7) suggests that about half the *emblema* is lost, including half the basket of fruit, which was evidently in the centre.[106] The wide inner border around the *emblema* is a framed band of running waves in black on white, and the outer border is a three-strand guilloche. Davis rightly described the mosaic as having very vivid colours.[107] The *emblema* incorporated some glass *tesserae* and its plain white ground would have made a cool and elegant impression, according to Franks.[108] The *emblema* is of fine quality and the white *tesserae* of the ground are placed diagonally, which gives the piece a particular elegance. This is stylistically the earliest mosaic discovered by Davis at Carthage, and may date as early as the late first century AD.[109]

The restored panel is on display in the Roman Empire Gallery (Room 70) in the British Museum. Despite Davis' description of 'a wooden hod filled with fruit',[110] both containers are clearly baskets with twisted rope handles, very similar to the alfa or esparto grass baskets produced in Tunisia today. The dimensions of the fragment with the *emblema* are 1.79 m by 1.30 m; the background with borders is 1.61 m by 1.32 m.[111] If the basket of fruit is at the centre of the *emblema*, I calculate the original size of the mosaic floor at approximately 3.4 m by 5.4 m, based on the dimensions of the surviving fragments. These dimensions for the room would agree roughly with Davis' observation that the preserved mosaic is equivalent to one-third of the original floor.[112] The room was a pleasant size and, especially given its location on the slopes of the Hill of Juno, it was probably a reception room in an elegant early Roman house.

Davis had spread himself too thin in the spring and early summer of 1857. After digging four sites with almost no finds (Sites 9–12), he was not prepared to record adequately the important mosaic finds that were revealed at the sea-side site, Falbe no. 90, and noted even less at the site of the early Roman Mosaic of Baskets of Fish and Fruit. At the same time another excavation was producing numerous finds of Punic *stelae*. For the third time, Davis was dealing with productive sites that were not marked on the plan of Falbe, and these experiences would lead him to rely more heavily on his own judgment in the future.

9

Punic votive stelae

Davis' fifteenth site: Punic *stelae* from the 'Punic Mine'

Davis' 'Punic mine' (Site 15) produced an impressively large group of nearly one hundred Punic votive *stelae*. Although he was able to read the inscriptions, aided by the similarity of the language to Hebrew,[1] and although he recognized that the inscriptions belonged to Punic rather than to Roman Carthage because of the form of the Punic letters,[2] his interpretations of them were otherwise fanciful.[3] Davis knew all the ancient sources on Carthaginian child sacrifice, which he discussed in detail as a 'cruel and inhuman rite',[4] but because the *tophet* (the precinct for the burial of sacrificial victims) was not to be discovered until 1922, Davis had no archaeological evidence to associate the votive *stelae* which he found with the cremated remains of the victims.[5]

According to Davis, the site of the 'Punic mine' was an unmotivated test trench, like that which had resulted in the find of the Mosaic with Baskets of Fish and Fruit. Only an insignificant fragment of ruin was noted by a scout at the site. Davis stated that it lay immediately alongside the south-eastern side of the road from Douar ech-Chott to Sidi bou-Said; the 'Punic mine' was so close to the road that Davis eventually had to lay down a lower, alternative road.[6] The site was described by Vaux as being at the western or upper end of the hollow running east–west down to the sea between the Byrsa and the Hill of Juno,[7] but Vaux's description may be based on Davis' published map.

The site is in the north-eastern quarter of the city grid; the footpath described by Davis lies on the north-eastern side of the Byrsa Hill, just above the twenty-meter elevation line (or possibly as high as the twenty-five-meter line), judging by the location of a path which fits Davis' description on Bordy's 1897 map. The hollow between the two hills is marked by contour lines on the Bordy map, and curves west as far as *cardo* 3 east. If we follow the street-grid correlations exactly, Davis' site is at *cardo* 3 east and between *decumani* 1 and 2 north. As its location is closely related to that of the Mosaic with Baskets of Fish and Fruit, the arguments above for the wherabouts of that site, further east and at a lower level, are equally relevant. In short, I place the 'Punic mine' at *cardo* 5 east.

The first Punic votive tablets from here were loaded on the *Curaçoa* at the end of May 1857.[8] The site was dug repeatedly and never completely abandoned during the course of Davis' excavations; for example, we know that he was digging here again in December 1857. The productive area excavated eventually measured about 200 feet (*c.* 77 m) per side; that is, it involved the area defined by the short sides of two city-blocks, suggesting that the structure which Davis said he was demolishing to recover the inscriptions was very large. On the other hand a great web of trenches in an adjoining field (Davis did not specify in which direction) did not yield any Punic *stelae*; he described his trenches there as looking like a spider's web, with an aggregate eventually of 300 feet (91.4 m) in length. The trenches varied from six to fifteen feet (1.82 m to 4.6 m) in length and were usually four feet (1.2 m) wide.[9]

Davis said that the Punic inscriptions had to be broken out of massive Roman, or more likely early Christian, walls. He dated the structure by the *spolia* (re-used architectural debris), including the *stelae*, which were incorporated in its walls. His excavations created havoc because his men had to destroy the walls in order to retrieve the *stelae*. Davis wrote: 'As we were determined to secure every trophy, we were absolutely compelled to demolish the walls in which they were embedded. This process of destruction, under other circumstances perfectly inexcusable, prevented us from ascertaining the real nature of the building itself'. As on his other sites, Davis was followed by stone-robbers, who removed the remainder of the walls when he moved on, an arrangement which he perceived as mutually agreeable.[10] The result is that he could say nothing whatever about the plan of the structure which he had destroyed.

Davis' men had found four or five Punic tablets immediately when they first assayed the site, and these should be among the ones which were packed in case 22 of Davis' first load on the *Curaçoa*. He explained that the votive *stelae* all bore the name of Baal Hammon, sometimes accompanied by a second deity, and then the name of the devotee (Figs 9.1–3).[11] Franks also commented extensively on the *stelae* in his paper on Davis' finds.[12] Some have simple line-drawn motifs, which are both Punic and Greek in inspiration, and Vaux, who first catalogued and published them in 1863, noted that some of the Greek motifs have parallels in the third and second century BC.[13]

Punic inscriptions, particularly votive *stelae*, had been found before, but the finds were isolated and

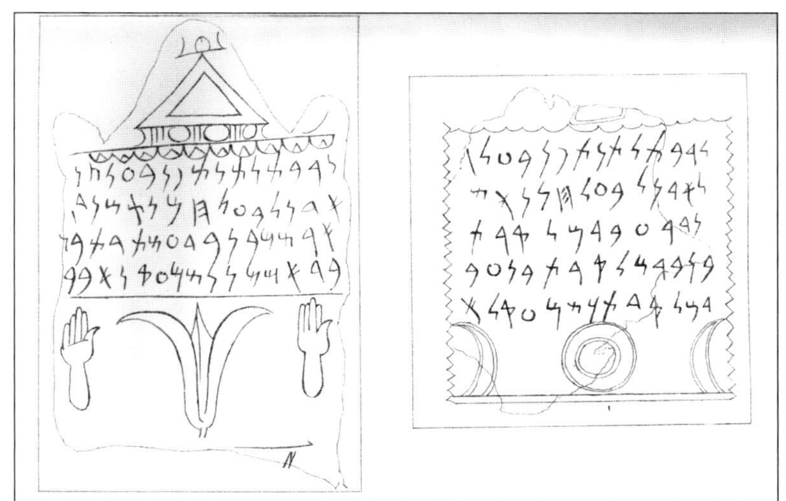

Fig. 9.1 Drawing of two of the Punic stelae *found by Davis, the only ones illustrated by him in* Carthage and Her Remains

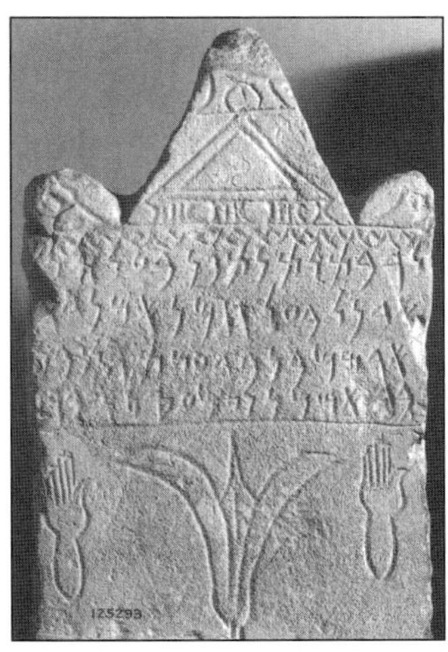

Fig. 9.2 (below left) The first of the stelae *shown in Fig. 9.1 as it is today. There is a 'symbol of Tanit' above, and a hand on either side of a lotus flower below; the Punic inscription reads 'To the lady to Tanit face of Baal, and to the lord to Baal Hammon, which vowed Arisham son of Bod'ashtart son of Bodeshmum, for he heard his voice and blessed him'. Height: 25 cm; width: 14 cm.*

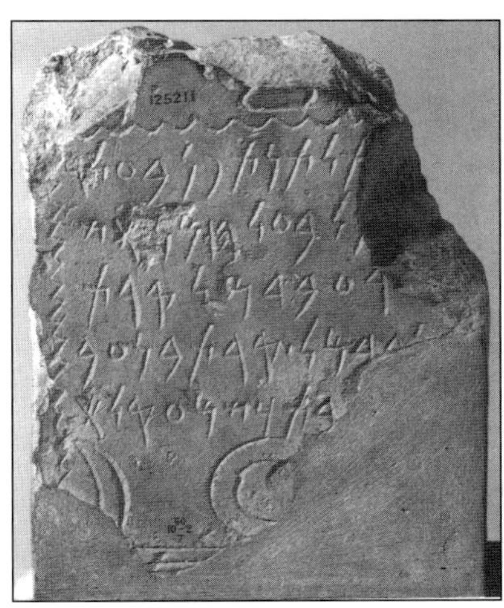

Fig. 9.3 (below right) The second of the stelae *in Fig. 9.1 as it is today. There is part of a large 'Tanit symbol' below, but the stone is badly damaged. The text reads '[To the la]dy to Tanit face of Baal, and [to the lord] to Baal Hammon, which [vow]ed 'Abdmelqart [son of] Bodmelqart [son of] 'Abdmelqart, for he heard his voice'. Surviving height: 17 cm; width: 13.7 cm.*

widely scattered. Humbert had been the first to discover Punic inscriptions in excavation at Carthage, in the area between the amphitheatre and the La Malga cisterns, and to publish his examples.[14] Falbe published a brief description of two Punic votive *stelae* and a Punic tomb-marker with his map of Carthage in 1833.[15] Although many of the Punic and neo-Punic *stelae* published as high-quality lithographs by Abbé Bourgade were not from Carthage, he said that two of his *stelae* (Carthage A and B) were found on the island of the circular harbour; another of Bourgade's inscriptions was on a Punic tomb-marker from Carthage.[16] Davis found several Punic inscriptions at the Roman house to the east of the theatre (Site 21).[17] Farthest away from the area of concentrated finds, Davis found three Punic *stelae* at the 'Carthaginian house' (Site 16),[18] which was in fact a late Roman house on the north side of the Roman city. In his review of previous finds of Punic votive *stelae*, Sainte-Marie was to note that those in the collection of the son of the Khaznadar were found particularly at the Bordj-Djedid cisterns (the 'great cisterns by the sea') and near the military port (the Circular Harbour).[19] A number of Punic *stelae* were to be found in the excavation of the house of Sidi Ismaïl,[20] which was on the sea-front and immediately south of the *decumanus maximus*. Shelby Brown later noted other scattered finds of Punic *stelae* at Carthage between 1845 and 1921. The list of early finds that she used, which is not comprehensive, was compiled in the course of research on Punic *stelae* discovered at the Punic ports.[21]

In his 1860 publication of Davis' finds, Franks reported that previously only seventeen Punic votive *stelae* had been published. Franks was following a source that attributed all the Punic *stelae* found by that time to a single site, Falbe no. 58,[22] which Guérin had identified as the 'Temple of Saturn.' Falbe no. 58 is along the line of *decumanus* 1 north, which is the line along which the greatest concentration of Punic votive *stelae* outside the *tophet* was subsequently found, and

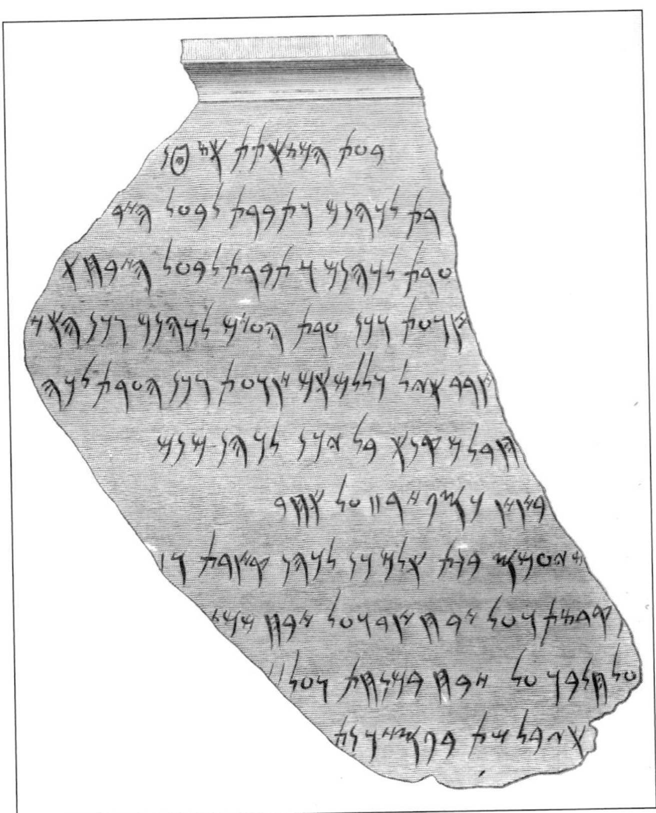

Fig. 9.4 The so-called 'Tariff Inscription' found by Davis, as illustrated by him in Carthage and Her Remains. *This fragmentary plaque was probably affixed to a temple or a sanctuary wall; it lists payments for sacrifices and stipulates which parts are to go to the priests and which to the offerand; 28 cm by 22 cm.*

between *cardines* 7 and 8 east, at an elevation of between twenty and twenty-five meters. Falbe only identified the site as among a number of 'temples or large buildings'.[23] There is no direct evidence for its original function, but like other large and irregular ruins on the plan of Falbe, it is likely to be of Vandal or Byzantine date. Nearly 150 years after Davis' excavations at Carthage, the site of Falbe no. 58 is still a very large and deep unmarked excavation.[24] This is not however Davis' 'Punic mine', which lay about 70 meters west of Falbe no. 58.

Davis eventually excavated most of the ninety publishable Punic votive inscriptions from this site. Vaux's publication included lithographs of each of Davis' *stelae* and provided a Hebrew transcription as well as a Latin translation. Davis himself published translations of eight examples, accompanied by a copious and erratic discussion.[25] The translations which he published were his own, although he may also have seen translations of the Punic into Hebrew and Latin provided to him by Vaux.[26] Davis also discussed one inscription of a different character, an important Punic inscription that described arrangements for payments to priests who organized sacrifices (Fig. 9.4).[27] He did not find this inscription in the trench he called the 'Punic mine', however, but at the Circular Monument, Davis' Site 23, which he called the 'Temple of Baal' or of Saturn.[28]

Sainte-Marie digs for Punic *stelae* in 1874 and 1875

Later nineteenth-century excavations tried to replicate Davis' finds of Punic *stelae* at Carthage. An account of these excavations and the location of their trenches may dispel some potential confusion about Davis' trench. Of crucial importance is the fact that Sainte-Marie excavated Punic *stelae* from a total of five trenches, but Sainte-Marie's site A, the trench which produced more than 2,000 examples, was located at an identifiable location quite a long way from Davis' trench. Delattre would (mistakenly) write that Sainte-Marie had found them at the site they called 'Feddan-el-Behim'; he added that he himself had since found 200 more, and Reinach and Babelon were exploring the site again at the time of his writing.[29] All three intended to dig in the same trench where Sainte-Marie had discovered the great mass of his finds of Punic *stelae* (his 'Site A'), and they believed, wrongly, that this trench was the site of Davis' excavations as well. In fact, the various nineteenth-century excavations conducted by Davis, Sainte-Marie, Delattre, and Reinach and Babelon, where Punic *stelae* were found, included at least five trenches dug by Sainte-Marie, but the other archaeologists did not excavate in the area which Sainte-Marie found to be the most productive. All five trenches lay on an east–west line with a length of more than 400 meters, parallel to and between *decumani* 1 and 2 north and running from *cardo* 5 to *cardo* 17 east. Davis' site was at the far western end of a long area in which concentrations of Punic *stelae* would eventually be excavated.

In 1874, fifteen years after Davis closed his excavations, a new appointee to the French consulate at Tunis, the aristocratic, classically-educated and academically-minded Evariste Pricot de Sainte-Marie, decided that since the Punic *stelae* were of such interest to scholars he would spend his evidently ample free time excavating for them. Sainte-Marie took his self-imposed task seriously and must have begun compiling his bibliography of previous research on Carthage at about the same time. He published the first version of this still useful work in 1875 and a revised version in 1878. He also published a brief summary of his knowledge of the site of Carthage in 1876.[30]

Through the great scholar Ernest Renan, Sainte-Marie was awarded a grant from the French Academy of Inscriptions, with the proviso that he only dig at sites which were known to have produced Punic *stelae* in the past. If the location of Davis' 'Punic mine' was known, it would have been an important potential site for Sainte-Marie, and Davis' name was mentioned among others in the instructions he received.[31] Sainte-Marie excavated in the area which he considered the Punic 'Forum', and found a total of more than 2,000 Punic *stelae* in a single trench.[32] By the 1880s, the editors of the newly organized corpus of Semitic inscriptions were busy with nearly 4,000 examples of Punic votive *stelae* from Carthage. By the 1890s at least one scholar was blasé enough to say that the inscriptions were repetitive, boring, and of no great significance.[33]

Although Sainte-Marie had sent squeezes of all these to the French national library, most of the *stelae* themselves were lost in the explosion of the French naval vessel, the *Magenta*, in the harbour of Toulon; a great number were recovered by divers by 1876. Despite Renan's explicit instructions, Sainte-Marie also excavated at a nearby site he called the 'Serapeum,' where he found six Roman inscriptions, which he sent to the Museum of Algiers. These inscriptions had been dedicated by Roman priests of Serapis. His 'Serapeum' lies in the north-eastern quarter of Carthage, at the northern end of the block between *decumani* 2 and 3 north and between *cardines* 10 and 11 east.[34]

Sainte-Marie drew maps that are our best evidence for establishing exactly where he excavated. A careful study of both these and his written account shows that Sainte-Marie excavated at five sites that produced Punic *stelae*, but only one, his 'Site A', the first he dug, produced great quantities. Sainte-Marie's map and the account of his excavations suggest that the site where Davis found Punic *stelae* was equivalent to Sainte-Marie's 'Site E', one of the less productive sites which Sainte-Marie dug. Davis' 'Punic mine' is ten short blocks (about 400 m) west of the area which Sainte-Marie first marked as producing Punic *stelae*.

Renan's brief instructed Sainte-Marie to produce a map and mark his sites on it, and Sainte-Marie did publish such a map in his *Mission à Carthage*. He claimed it was accurate, and it is useful, although it is very simple and at a very small scale (Fig. 9.5).[35] Sainte-Marie was led to his first site, 'Site A', by Arab informants. In the event, Site A produced nearly all of the more than 2,000 Punic *stelae* which Sainte-Marie found; no more than a hundred in total came from the other sites he dug.[36] Lines on the map in *Mission à Carthage* orientate the viewer. Sainte-Marie shows a straight line drawn from the centre of the Byrsa Hill, running east to the sea; this would approximate to the line of the *decumanus maximus*. He idiosyncratically labelled this line as the 'Via Salutaris;' he was thinking, with Dureau de la Malle, that the street would have led to the sixty steps up to the Temple of Aesculapius on the Byrsa Hill. All five of his sites that produced Punic *stelae* lay north of this line. On the same map, a less straight east–west modern path is marked more or less parallel to his 'Via Salutaris,' but about 190 meters to the north. Sainte-Marie labelled this path the 'Via Caelestis;' he was thinking that it ran to the Temple of Astarte on the summit of the 'Hill of Juno.' Sainte-Marie's 'Via Caelestis' lies about one-third of the way between *decumani* 1 and 2 north. All five of his trenches lay south of this line.

Sainte-Marie's map shows that Site A was also on another modern path running south from the west side of the Bordj-Djedid cisterns to the west side of the circular harbour. Between *decumani* 1 and 2 north, such a line falls between *cardines* 13 and 14 east. Sainte-Marie's Site A falls on the south-west corner where these two lines cross, between *cardines* 13 and 14 east and just north of *decumanus* 1 north. I know of no modern excavation in that exact area.[37] The German excavation plan shows that Sainte-Marie's Site A falls within the Punic orthogonal street-grid; it also indicates a major Punic street along the same line as the Roman *decumanus* 1 north. The Punic street ran east–west from the great Punic gate onto the sea and straight across the city.[38] Sainte-Marie said that his Site A lay about 200 meters south of the Roman 'Serapeum' (his Site H), and this agrees with the distance and the direction between the equivalent sites on the city grid.

Sainte-Marie began digging at Site A on August 25th, 1874, and within three days he had recovered twenty votive *stelae* from a tiny trench 1.1 m by 3.0 m in size, although he was only one meter down at this point, and had not yet found walls. He was digging again between October 19th and 31st, by which latter date he had extracted a total of 110 *stelae* from this trench. On October 20th, he first met a wall (1 m thick and 'Roman'), at two meters down. The wall was made with *spolia* from a monumental Roman building, as it included cut stone, columns, and capitals as well as the *stelae*; in short, it was constructed in very similar fashion to the walls which Davis had described (probably a wall of Byzantine type with ashlar face and rubble interior). By November 4th, Sainte-Marie had a total of 230 *stelae* from Site A. The trench was now twenty-four meters long and four and a half meters deep, but still only one meter wide. Back on site between November 15th and 21st, he went down to a depth of seven meters at Site A. The work of breaking

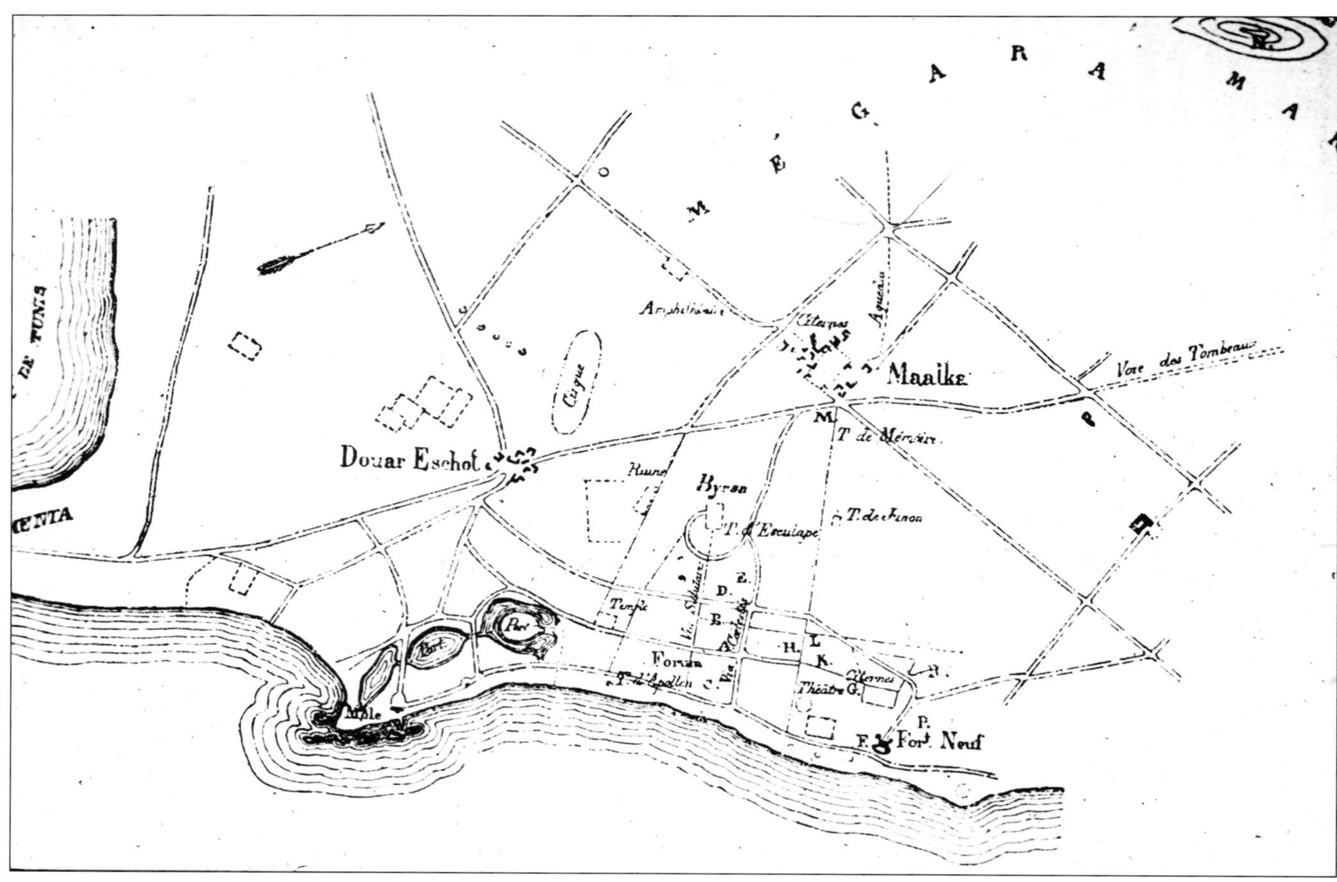

Fig. 9.5 Plan of Carthage, showing the excavation sites dug by Évariste Charles Pricot de Sainte-Marie (1884), as indicated by capital letters

up the walls was very difficult, but his men persevered, and the total was now almost 550 *stelae* from Site A alone. By November 26th, he had reached nine meters, but by this time, not surprisingly, collapses of the sides of the trench were making the work too difficult (one might indeed suspect that the work was also very dangerous for his workmen, who went on strike for better pay at the end of January). Although Sainte-Marie did not continue his detailed description, it seems clear that, having done one length of the wall, he continued to follow it around the three 'rooms' on his plan (Fig. 9.6), and as far down as it went, to end with a total of more than 2,000 *stelae* from the site.

Davis explicitly said that the *stelae* at his own site were broken out of walls by his workmen and that he destroyed the walls without recording them. Sainte-Marie not only said that the *stelae* he found at Site A were broken out of walls, but by contrast he also gave a plan of those walls, which his trenches evidently followed exactly. The *stelae* came from the walls of a suite of three contiguous 'rooms', each four meters square. Each was a very regular 1.05 m thick, and there was a semicircular shaft against the outer wall between the second and third rooms. There is a slot in the wall of the first room that seems too narrow to be a doorway. The structure he shows, with dimensions slightly over 17.0 m by 12.5 m, is not complete, and it is impossible to identify the building type. Sainte-Marie's description suggests that these walls were more than seven meters high, as he had not reached the foundation at nine meters depth. The proportions suggest that the 'rooms', with no doors or windows, were not designed for ordinary human occupation.

Site A and its mysterious structure fall at the ten-meter contour line on Andrew Wilson's map of Carthage (Fig. 4.1). The site is on the line of ruins that Falbe drew from the south-west corner of the Bordj-Djedid cisterns and southwards along *cardo* 13 east for a total of more than a kilometer. I have suggested above (p. 59) that this was most likely a Byzantine internal defensive wall. The line of ruins along *cardo* 13 east continued south past a large ruin on its west side (Falbe no. 56, which lies between the *decumanus maximus* and *decumanus* 1 south) to another

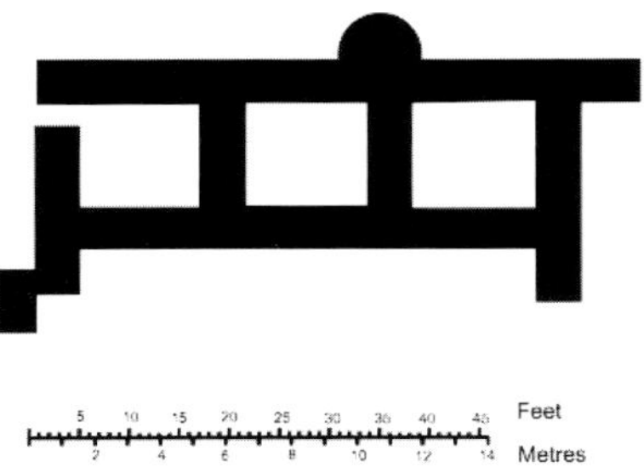

Fig. 9.6 Plan of the building demolished in order to excavate Punic stelae, *at Sainte-Marie's 'Site A'*

large ruin on its west side (Falbe no. 55, between *decumani* 2 and 3 south). It therefore seems possible that Punic *stelae* and Roman *spolia* were incorporated into a Byzantine defensive structure. Since Byzantine defensive walls were typically made up of squared stone, it may be that Davis' and Sainte-Marie's finds came originally from the mortared fill between two ashlar walls.

Falbe no. 56 is the site of a deep trench dug by Friedrich Rakob. The upper levels of the trench revealed the apse of an immensely large basilica of late Roman, Vandal or Byzantine date, while much deeper in the trench Rakob found evidence of an important Punic sanctuary.[39] In terms of the Roman street-grid, Rakob's site is immediately south of the *decumanus maximus* and between *cardines* 11 and 13 east.[40] Sainte-Marie's Site A is slightly more than one long Roman city-block north.

Sainte-Marie's efforts at four succeeding sites (his sites B, C, D and E), all between his 'Via Salutaris' and 'Via Caelestis,' produced hardly any Punic *stelae* by comparison with his Site A. Of the places he dug in this area, Site E correlates most closely with the location of Davis' 'Punic mine'. Sainte-Marie chose Site E, which was relatively high up the slope between the Byrsa and the Hill of Juno, because he was told that Punic *stelae* had been found there in the past. Sainte-Marie's Site E is on the line of *decumanus* 1 north, and approximately between *cardines* 5 and 6 east. Twenty-six Punic inscriptions were discovered here. He also found all sorts of mutilated Roman debris, including inscriptions. Davis' description of the 'Punic Mine' corresponds perfectly with Sainte-Marie's description of Site E. The fact that Sainte-Marie found *stelae* here at a rate not much different than that suggested by Davis' exploits implies that he was in the same type of context as that explored by Davis, if not in exactly the same trench. This tends to confirm my hypothesis that the correct location of Davis' 'Punic mine' is between *decumani* 1 and 2 north and along *cardo* 5 east.

Reinach and Babelon excavate for Punic *stelae* in 1884

In 1884, ten years after Sainte-Marie's excavations, Reinach and Babelon excavated in the 'Forum.' They considered the [Punic] 'Forum' to be the whole area from the ports to the Antonine Baths. They wrongly believed that they were re-excavating Sainte-Marie's Site A when they excavated a site called 'Feddan-el-Behim'. Delattre must have shown them it. He had arrived in Carthage in November 1875, when Sainte-Marie had just completed his excavations. Sainte-Marie left his trenches open; Delattre had also excavated in one of them in 1883 and found several hundred Punic *stelae*.[41] As Delattre was both knowledgeable and a trustworthy informant, it is certain that the trench dug by Reinach and Babelon had been begun by Sainte-Marie and re-excavated by Delattre, but these men evidently did not realize that it was only one of several trenches which Sainte-Marie had dug.

Reinach and Babelon drew detailed plans and elevations of their trench. It was marked as site XXXV (35) on the map of Carthage in the *Atlas archéologique*, which Reinach and Babelon were involved in producing in 1893. This map shows 'Feddan-el-Behim' between the *decumanus maximus* and *decumanus* 1 north and between *cardines* 10 and 11 east. In the original report of the excavation, Reinach and Babelon said that the site lay between Falbe nos 56 and 58.[42] A point half-way between these two ruins falls just north of the *decumanus maximus* and between *cardines* 9 and 10 east. The site is therefore close to *cardo* 10 east and three to four short Roman blocks (150 m) from Sainte-Marie's Site A. It is close or identical to Sainte-Marie's Site B, which, together with his Site C (which lay between the *decumanus maximus* and *decumanus* 1 north, and within two or three blocks from the sea), produced a total of only fifty *stelae*.[43]

Babelon later wrote that their excavation measured fifty-six by thirteen meters and was six to nine meters deep,[44] an enormously large trench. The published plan and sections suggest that the greatest depth excavated was 8.4 meters, although a significant extent at either end of the trench, with almost no structural finds, is no more than three meters deep.[45] They dug for most of April 1884, and employed eighty-five workmen. The *stelae* were found in infill and destruction of every sort, not shallower than four meters below the surface.[46] They found walls, cisterns, shafts and conduits in the central section, but no coherent structural plan. At fifty-six meters in length, Reinach and Babelon's east–west trench should have crossed a *cardo*. An elevation drawing of it shows a typical second-century Roman street-drain near the eastern end. Correlation with Bordy's map shows that this belonged to *cardo* 11 east. The street was only about 1.5 meters below the modern surface, suggesting that, since the first 1.5 m produced nothing structural, any building remains above Roman ground-level had previously been removed.

Reinach and Babelon recovered 330 epigraphic Punic *stelae* from this site, as well as 253 *stelae* without inscriptions,[47] plus pagan and Christian lamps and Latin inscriptions. Lamps from their sites included a small number of Punic examples with a range of dates. Punic inscriptions were concentrated within a limited area fifteen meters west of the drain of *cardo* 11, around a well-shaft which they thought was the one described by Sainte-Marie.[48]

Because Reinach and Babelon thought that their trench was Sainte-Marie's Site A, they believed that the latter had deliberately falsified the circumstances of his finds. They found no *stelae* in its walls. Babelon said that the *stelae* in their trenches were found lying all over the place in infill and destruction contexts, at no less than four meters deep. Since the *stelae* were designed to stand up, with their unfinished lower parts in earth, they were all discovered in secondary contexts.[49] Again, attacking Sainte-Marie, they said that they did not find any traces of mortar on the *stelae* which Sainte-Marie had sent to Paris.[50] They believed that his workmen actually dug the 'tunnels' (*mines*) which they found on their site, and that therefore he could not have drawn a plan of his walls. Furthermore, his plan did not agree with anything in their trench.[51]

Reinach and Babelon in my view showered Sainte-Marie with undeserved opprobrium. Sainte-Marie gave a dated day-by-day account of going down from one meter to nine meters in his trench at Site A, so the claim that he sent his workmen to tunnel for finds is unfounded, if not downright libellous. There are tunnels dug by human effort deep in the area of the 'Forum,' since Rakob also reported them.[52] Beulé found that an apse on the Byrsa had been undermined by one such tunnel; he said that they were made by Arabs, who, with the industry of moles, dug them looking for objects to sell; he had even found a rusted tool to support this hypothesis.[53] It is not likely that they originate with the French archaeologists of the nineteenth century, who described their open trenches; Beulé was unusual in using tunnels and even dynamite at times. Reinach and Babelon did not find the walls which Sainte-Marie described for two good reasons: first, Sainte-Marie had removed them completely, by inordinate labour on the part of his men; and second, Reinach and Babelon were digging in a different area, probably Sainte-Marie's Site B and not his Site A.

The combined excavation evidence shows that the Punic votive *stelae* were used in large numbers, along with Roman debris, for building material at Davis' 'Punic mine' and Sainte-Marie's Site A, while scattered finds appeared in a long area along *decumanus* 1 north and from *cardines* 5 east (Davis' 'Punic mine' and Sainte-Marie's 'Site E') as far as *cardines* 16 or 17 east (Sainte-Marie's 'Site C'). Ever since Delattre told Audollent that the Punic *stelae* were found half-way between the hill of Saint Louis and the house of Ahmed Zarouk, it has been accepted that they came from near the intersection of *cardo* 10 east and *decumanus* 1 north. In 1959 Hours-Miédan wrote that Sainte-Marie's Punic *stelae* had been discovered under the track of the 'TGM,' the light rapid transit train ('Tunis/Goulette/Marsa') laid down in 1907.[54] This is the general area of Reinach and Babelon's trench 35, and close to Sainte-Marie's Site B, but it is not close to the latter's Site A, the source of more than 2,000 Punic *stelae*, nor to Davis' 'Punic mine'. The three find-spots were in fact widely separated, related only by their proximity to the line of *decumanus* 1 north. This last road was on the same line as an important Punic street that debouched at the city's sea-gate. The point with by far the greatest concentration of Punic *stelae* was Sainte-Marie's Site A, just north of *decumanus* 1 north and between *cardines* 13 and 14 east. The Punic street formed part of an orthogonal grid dating to between perhaps the fifth century BC and the destruction of Punic Carthage in 146 BC, while the *stelae* excavated by the nineteenth-century excavators belong mainly to between the fourth and the second centuries BC. There is good reason to believe, however, as we have seen above, that the *stelae* originally stood in the *tophet* (the sanctuary where infants and young children sacrificed to Baal were buried), and were later moved to the area along *decumanus* 1 north when they were reused in the Roman period.

Davis' Punic *stelae* from Carthage

The Punic material which Davis excavated is today in the British Museum, and Carole Mendleson has recently published a catalogue of all the Punic *stelae* that the Museum possesses. Her monograph shows that Davis sent to London a total of eighty-eight inscribed Punic votive *stelae* (now 86 because of joins), a further ten uninscribed examples, and two other inscriptions. In addition to the ninety Punic inscriptions published by Vaux in 1863, ten uninscribed Punic *stelae* excavated or found by Davis have now been published by Mendleson.[55] Despite the fact that the *stelae* excavated by Davis have been published not only by Vaux but also by Euting in 1883 (the latter only as lithographs with no commentary) and in the corpus of Semitic inscriptions (1881 onwards), Mendleson's catalogue is important because it is systematic, and includes photographs, accurate translations and the original accession numbers. Although she is correct in saying that the British Museum has only a small collection of Punic votive *stelae* by comparison with the thousands held in individual museums elsewhere, the British Museum does have some of the earliest such finds, thanks to Davis' excavations.

The original catalogue numbers dating from 1857, 1859 and 1860 are written on the objects, guaranteeing the identification of the items sent by Davis. The numbers show that for each shipment the three main classifications of *stelae* in Mendleson's monograph (Punic tomb-markers, Punic votive *stelae*, and neo-Punic votive and tomb *stelae*) were recognized before their catalogue numbers were assigned. Davis grouped the finds in his packing, which would have facilitated the orderliness of the cataloguing. Since Davis explicitly stated that he excavated Punic votive *stelae* from the 'Punic mine' throughout the entire time that he excavated at Carthage, it is not surprising to find examples of them in each shipment. The inscribed slabs were also catalogued first in each shipment, indicating that the Museum staff saw them as of great significance. Vaux himself may have assigned the museum accession numbers. He recognized all the inscribed Punic *stelae*, including one that was originally catalogued apart from this group (57.12-18.51). One of the relevant catalogue-numbers (59.4-2.4) is now missing, and Vaux may have removed the object from the group. In another case two pieces of an uninscribed *stele* join.[56]

Davis sent thirty-eight inscribed and nine uninscribed Punic limestone votive *stelae* to the Museum in 1857. Of the inscribed *stelae* one is a variant, a red-brown limestone column.[57] Two years later, Davis sent thirty-four Punic *stelae* and a plinth in marble, which was possibly a statue base, with a dedicatory inscription.[58] In 1860 Davis sent seventeen Punic *stelae*, and an inscription which lists prices to be paid to priests for sacrifices.[59] As mentioned above (p. 128), the Punic 'tariff' inscription (Fig. 9.4) was not found in the 'Punic mine' but near the Circular Monument.

The Punic votive *stelae* in the British Museum collection are likely all to have come from the later levels of the Carthage *tophet*, and so belong to the period from as early as the fourth century to 146 BC (Fig. 9.7).[60] At the *tophet* they were markers which stood above small buried jars that held the cremated bones of babies, young children, or substituted sacrificial animals. There has been much exploration of the *tophet* since its first excavation in 1922, but the material in the latest defined stratigraphic group, 'Tanit III,' has always been extremely disturbed and minimally published. Poinssot and Lantier described the *stelae* of this period as smaller, with acroteria, and not as well worked.[61] On Cintas's excavation, the 'Tanit III' context seemed to have been damaged by

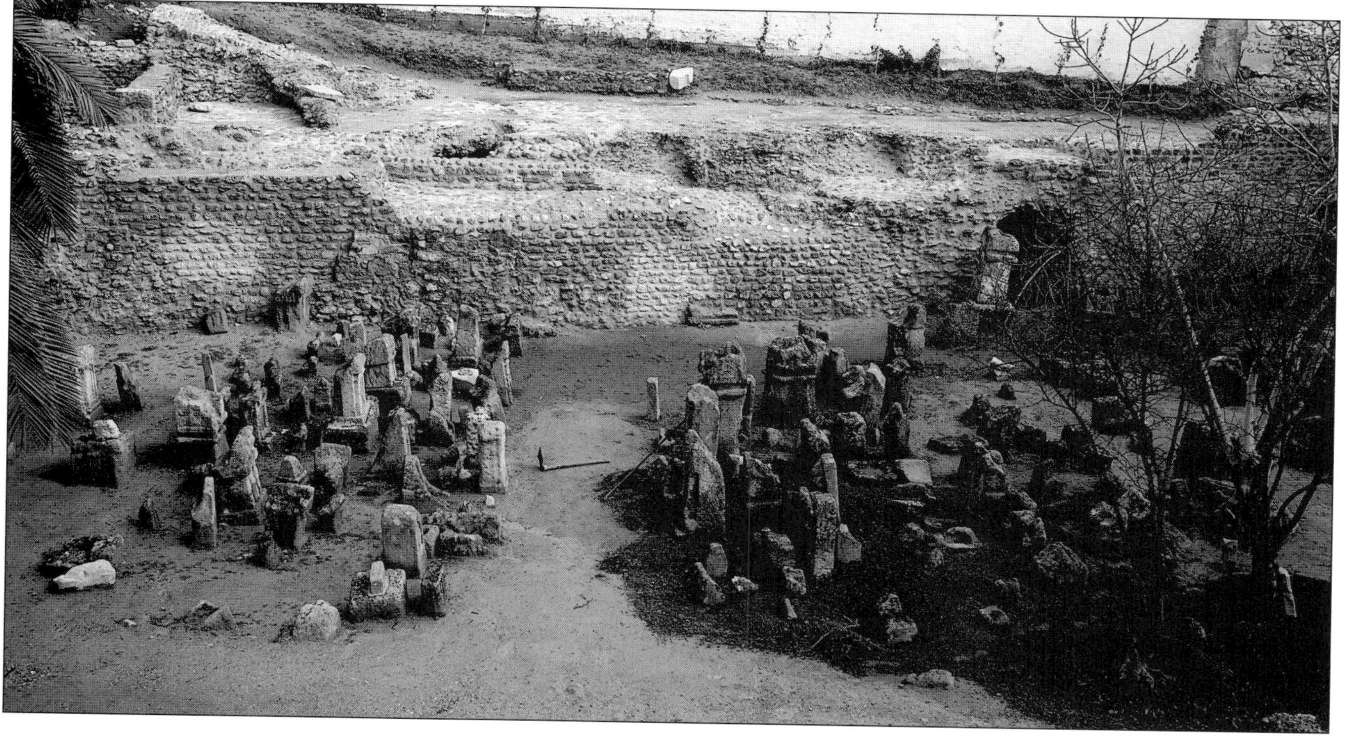

Fig. 9.7 The tophet *at Carthage as it appears today (foreground), with later, Roman vaulted structures beyond*

the Romans. The votive slabs in this context were described as gabled *stelae* with acroteria, or else 'obelisks' (probably simple gabled *stelae*) without acroteria, which is closer to the variety demonstrated by Davis' examples; but Cintas dated the whole context broadly, to 400/146 BC.[62]

Examples sent by Davis of rather short *stelae* with acroteria match the typology of the very latest votive *stelae*, from 'Tanit III', dated by Shelby Brown to 225/146 BC, while taller ones, whether with a simple gable or a gable and acroteria, are ascribed to the later part of Tanit II (*c*. 500/225).[63] Not all of Davis' Punic votive *stelae* are complete, but of the forty-eight that are well enough preserved to make the distinction, twenty-six have a simple pointed gable and twenty-two have a gable and *acroteria*.[64] It is likely, therefore, that Davis' *stelae* are not all of the latest period, and Mendleson's dating of *c*. 400 BC to 146 BC is a good approximation for the group as a whole.

The site of the *tophet* is two long Roman city-blocks south of the Roman city street-grid, and lies just to the west of the Punic and Roman merchant harbour. If the line of *cardo* 15 east were extended to the south, it would run through the *tophet*. Davis never dug in or near the *tophet*, and his finds of these *stelae* at Carthage were concentrated more than a kilometer further north. After the discovery of the *tophet* in the 1920s, Lapeyre was to suggest that the *stelae* excavated by nineteenth-century archaeologists elsewhere may have belonged to a Punic *favissa*, a deliberately and formally constructed pit to hold *stelae* cleared from the *tophet* to make space for new burials.[65] Hours-Miédan later suggested that there might have been a second and later *tophet* north of the Byrsa,[66] but this seems unlikely. It is possible that the people of Punic Carthage created a *favissa* for *stelae* in the northern half of the city, although none of the excavated Punic *stelae* came from a context that fits this description. Because they may originate from contexts of two different periods in the *tophet*, I think it is most likely that the Romans removed thousands of *stelae* from it to a dump in the northern half of the city as part of a massive operation intended to desecrate the Punic religious sanctuary where a rite was practiced (child sacrifice) which they abhorred. The fact that both Davis and Sainte-Marie report finding the *stelae* built into later (possibly much later) structures is compatible with either of these scenarios.

Individual Punic votive *stelae* may seem unimportant because museums today contain more than 10,000 of them, with an estimated 7,000 examples in the museums of Carthage and the Bardo alone.[67] By the general laws of archaeology, this cannot possibly approach the total number that once existed. The *stelae* in their great numbers illustrate the widely-shared intention of the individual citizens of Punic Carthage to propitiate their gods personally by the sacrifice of their children, and to memorialize their act in concrete form. Scholars have complained that the wording of the vow on these *stelae* was formulaic and the iconography generally rigid and simplistic.[68] On the other hand, the votives from the *tophet* are not anonymous, but proud declarations of a personal vow. Typically, the inscription follows a formula, as in the following example, where the inscription is complete: 'To the lady, to Tanit, the face of Baal, and to the lord, to Baal Hammon, [the vow] which vowed Kabdot, daughter of 'Azor, son of Abdo'.[69] The dedicant shows conscious pride in family, as the *stele* names the person who made the vow as well as his or her father, and the father's father. Although most dedications were erected by men, women carried out this duty where appropriate, and twelve of Davis' *stelae* are complete enough to show that a woman was the dedicant, as opposed to sixty-three which were dedicated by men.

Although Davis never stopped digging at the site of the 'Punic mine' until he was forced to give up excavation by the Foreign Office, he seemed to be much more excited by finds of mosaics. From the departure of the *Curaçoa* in the summer of 1857, he began to dig at two sites of Roman houses that he had chosen for reasons of his own, abandoning for the moment his earlier tactic of digging at Falbe's sites.

The Neo-Punic *stelae* purchased by Davis for the British Museum

In the meantime Davis was not exclusively interested in Carthage and kept his eyes open for other opportunities to enrich the British Museum. On June 29th, 1857 Davis wrote to Clarendon describing antiquities he had acquired from the collection of a German archaeologist named Honegger, who had died in London in 1849. According to Davis, Honegger had left no papers, 'unless Mr Vaux has them' – a reference to William Vaux, curator at the British Museum. Davis' account makes it clear that the neo-Punic *stelae* which he acquired from Honegger's collection were not excavated at Carthage; in this letter he stated specficially that the *stelae* in question were from Zama, El Kef (Sicca Veneria) and Baja (Vacca), all sites in the interior of Tunisia.[70]

The letter to Clarendon was written between the first and second departures of the *Curaçoa*. The antiquities in the second load included eight cases of bas-reliefs, among which Davis specifically mentioned Punic and Numidian inscriptions.[71] The original accession numbers show that he sent the greatest number of neo-Punic *stelae* to London in 1857, but thereafter, in the two later shipments, the numbers decreased markedly; twenty-nine *stelae* were shipped immediately (there would have been some time pressure in loading them on the *Curaçoa*), followed by thirteen more in 1859 and six in 1860.[72] Significantly, Davis kept back two *stelae* with Latin inscriptions until the last shipment.[73]

In *Carthage and Her Remains*, Davis wrote further about Honegger's collection of 'Punic, Numidian and Libyan inscriptions'. Davis piqued the curiosity of his readers by saying that the antiquities had been 'a cause of strife and litigation for some years past'. One of the parties to the quarrel was certainly Mr Honegger, who excavated other ancient sites, including the Antonine Baths at Carthage, for Sir Thomas Reade, the British consul at Tunis. Reade had paid the expenses of Honegger's excavations at Maktar, and therefore considered the finds excavated there to be his own property.[74] Both men had died in 1849, and the litigation must have been between their estates. Davis said that he had acquired the antiquities through Her Majesty's vice-consul at Sousse, a Mr Crow. Davis continues:

> We are unable to classify these antiquities for want of more minute details, and these we shall, in all probability, never obtain. Their interest is, however, great, as coming from Carthaginian Africa, of which there is no doubt whatever; and their value does not only consist in the inscriptions, but in the bas-reliefs which accompany them. These are symbolical, and relate to Punic theology, as intermingled with astronomy and astrology, and present a vast scope for conjecture and speculation.

Davis argued that the crude drawings of the bas-reliefs were examples of religious art and therefore were not to be judged in terms of technical sophistication.[75] He clearly thought that all were Punic rather than Roman, which implies that he was not thinking clearly about the fact that some of them have Latin inscriptions. At least ten of these *stelae* had been published by Abbé Bourgade in his *Toison d'or* in 1852. In that book Bourgade said that some of his inscriptions came from the collection of the late 'Honnegger', whose name he evidently mis-spelled. Bourgade also complained that, despite consulting the French Academy of Inscriptions, he could find no scholar in the 1840s able to enlighten him on the meaning of these *stelae*.[76] Carole Mendleson has catalogued the entire collection of sixty-one neo-Punic *stelae* in the British Museum (now sixty due to the discovery of a join), and her catalogue documents the fact that scholars have commented on them repeatedly. Although questions remain about their exact provenance, they are important as documents of the persistence of Punic religious beliefs in Tunisia into Roman times.

The neo-Punic *stelae* which Davis purchased are distinguished by typology from the similar examples, inscriptions and tomb monuments that he excavated at Carthage, none of which were published by Vaux. The *stelae* sent by Davis can be identified with certainty from their original accession numbers.[77] Forty-eight of the sixty-one examples in the Museum were acquired by Davis. Less than half of Davis' finds have inscriptions. The *stelae* not acquired by Davis can also be traced back to the excavations of Honegger, because they were acquired from Reade's collection by others. Of the two that were not Honegger's finds, one was excavated by Sir Grenville Temple at Maghrawa near Maktar in 1833/4.[78] This *stele*, with its dedicatory inscription by the ancient citizens of Maktar, is unique; it has similarities to a group which Honegger described (see below), but not to any other *stele* in the collection of the Museum. The other example not first acquired by Honegger was originally published in 1837, and belongs to one of the two main groups represented in Davis' acquisitions.[79]

The majority of the neo-Punic *stelae* in the British Museum collection fall into a few typological groups: most are votives, but a few are tomb markers. The votive *stelae* acquired by Davis fall into two main groups. The first has large and simple designs in raised relief, typically with a dedication to Baal in a rectangular frame (Fig. 9.8). Roman names appear in neo-Punic transcription on three examples, and in Latin letters on one example.[80] The second group, sometimes classified as 'La Ghorfa' *stelae*,[81] has crowded figural scenes in relief with frequent iconographic references to sacrifice (Figs 9.9–10). A frontal figure typically stands in a niche with rounded top, and the niche is often framed by a Greco-Roman *aedicula* (gabled shrine). These *stelae* are not ordinarily inscribed, but two have brief Latin inscriptions.[82] This second type made up half of Davis' acquisitions. Jennifer Moore studied forty-three examples of the 'La Ghorfa' group in museum collections, including the twenty-four examples in the British Museum.[83] Comparative material suggests that the so-called 'La Ghorfa' *stelae* originate from the region around Maktar.[84] They date mainly to the late first and second centuries AD, and combine elements from indigenous, Punic and Roman culture. It is clear that they are votives, but votives dedicated to gods who are not clearly identifiable.[85] The original accession numbers prove that all the *stelae* of the 'La Ghorfa' type now in the Museum were sent by Davis, of which Mendleson's identified nineteen examples, and Moore now twenty-four.[86]

When Davis wrote to Clarendon saying that Vaux might have papers referring to these *stelae*, he may have been aware of the existence of a letter from

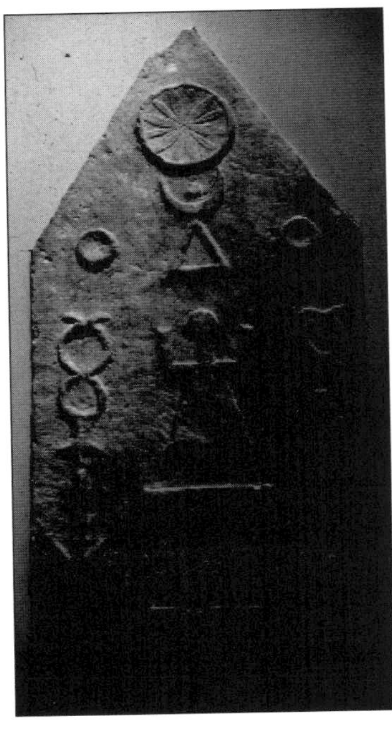

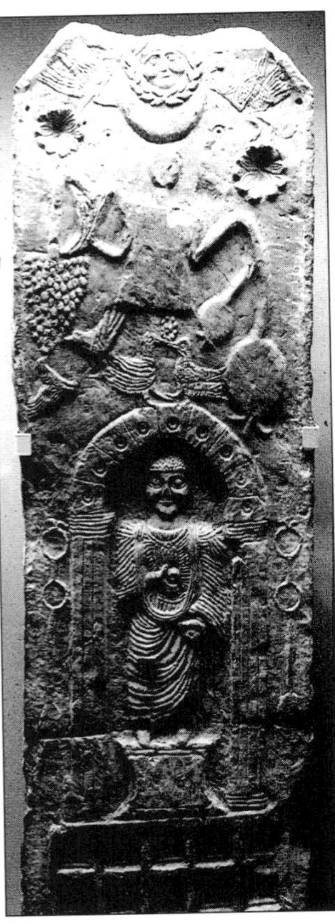

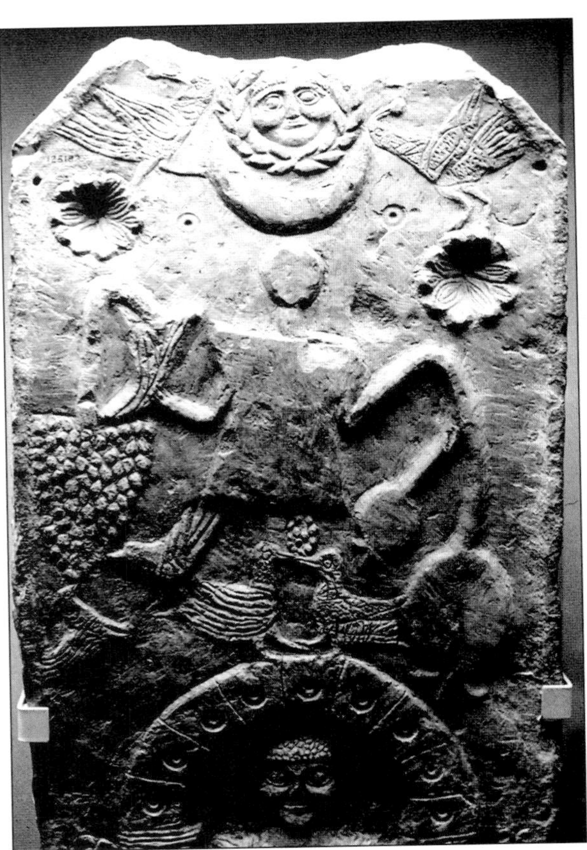

Fig. 9.8 (left) *A* stele *of Numidian type, probably from western Tunisia or eastern Algeria, of which the lower part is lost. Under a rosette disc at the top is a Tophet symbol incorporating a sun disc and a crescent moon; below is a more conventional Tanit symbol with hands upraised. It is flanked by a* caduceus *on either side, the shaft of each of which takes the form of an anchor. The inscribed panel in neo-Punic reads: 'To the lord to Baal a vow which vowed Gaius Julius Arish, son of Adinibaal, son of Addirbaal, for he heard his voice and he blessed him'. Width: 39 cm; first century BC (?).*

Fig. 9.9 (centre) Stele *of 'La Ghorfa' type, probably from Maghrawa in the region of Maktar in central Tunisia. A one-line neo-Punic inscription at the bottom contains the standard formula 'vow which vowed for he heard his voice (and) blessed him', but does not name the dedicant. Height: 130 cm; width: 40 cm.*

Fig. 9.10 (right) *Detail of Fig. 9.9. At the top is a traditional sun disc and a crescent moon below it, but here the sun has a face and a wreath around; the moon is flanked by birds. Below is an anthropomorphized Tanit symbol holding a giant pomegranate and a (drinking) horn containing a bunch of grapes; two birds nibble at the latter. Two more birds stand atop the arched structure below (an* aedicula*) containing a male figure, the dedicator.*

Honegger written in 1848 to the then keeper Edward Hawkins (and now in the archives of the British Museum) that offered twenty-seven inscriptions from Maktar for sale. The site lies eighty-one miles south-west of Carthage, and at least one inscription mentioned the *hamactharim* ('the people of Maktar').[87] Because Honegger's inflated description of the twenty-seven *stelae* he wished to sell in 1848, which he described as having 'Libo-Phoenician' inscriptions, does not match any group now in the British Museum, Mendleson concluded that none of the present collection came from Maktar. She preferred to accept the three provenances given by Davis, but in my opinion these are very insecurely based, and Davis gave no argument to support them. A Frenchman named Jomard published a letter in 1843 in which he said that Honegger had excavated a site near Maktar where forty bas-reliefs were found, some with Punic inscriptions.[88] Jomard's letter said that as of 1843 the finds had been removed to Tunis, and were to be sent to London. This did not happen quite as planned. The next notice of the vicissitudes suffered by Honegger's *stelae* is the letter to the British Museum from him in 1848, offering for sale to the trustees twenty-seven *stelae* (not forty) excavated by him near Maktar; but the Museum did not acquire them at this time.[89] Moore argued that the count of forty *stelae* found by Honegger near Maktar agrees well with the total number of examples of the 'La Ghorfa' group in museums today.

As mentioned above (p. 135), two of the 'La Ghorfa' *stelae* which Davis sent to the Museum have brief Latin inscriptions, and Latin inscriptions occur on examples in other collections as well. The Latin may be behind Davis' claim that the *stelae* could indicate to the uninformed that 'both Punic and Roman Carthage were alike rude, uncouth, and unpolished'.[90] The Latin inscription on the 'La Ghorfa' *stele* held back by Davis until 1860 reads *R·V·S·L·H* (Fig. 9.11).[91] Although he certainly recognized this as Latin, it may be that he did not know how to read it. Parallel examples show that Wilmanns was correct in interpreting the first letter as the abbreviation for a name (Wilmanns suggested 'Rogatus'), followed by the abbreviation, common on early Roman votive dedications at Carthage, of *V·S·L·A*, i.e. *votum solvit libens animo* ('he/she freely fulfilled this vow'), taking the 'H' as a engraver's error.[92] Another which Davis sent to the British Museum has a Latin inscription *L. Iuli / Urba(ni)*, 'of Lucius Julius Urbanus' (Fig. 9.12; for the design, compare a *stele* now in Tunis, of which a detail is Fig. 9.13). It was written retrograde, with some of its letters reversed. Not surprisingly, it was misunderstood as Punic by Abbé Bourgade, and Davis probably did not recognize it as Latin either. Bourgade described this, the last *stele* in his *Toison d'or*, as a Numidian inscription and bas-relief.[93] I have mentioned above that the Latin inscription of Lucius Julius Urbanus on this neo-Punic *stele* was republished in the corpus of Latin inscriptions.[94] To complicate the history of the *stele* further, Bourgade wrote that he had acquired it from among the antiquities of Mohammed, son of Mustapha Khaznadar. The son of the Khaznadar owned other examples of 'La Ghorfa' *stelae* which he also had probably acquired from Honegger. Wilmanns described this same *stele* as perhaps found at Hadrumetum, the Roman equivalent of modern Sousse.[95] This provenance is not correct, although the *stele* had spent time at Sousse while it was subject to litigation.

Davis may have known of another Latin inscription on a neo-Punic *stele* in Cubisol's collection;[96] but there is no evidence to show whether he knew of four more neo-Punic *stelae* of 'La Ghorfa' type with Latin inscriptions owned by Mohammed, the son of Mustapha Khaznadar. These all include some version of the formula *V·S·L·A*.[97] A total of seventeen 'La Ghorfa' *stelae* were at one time in the collection of Mohammed, housed at the family palace at Manouba. These *stelae* may also have originally been excavated by Honegger, and purchased from him by the son of the Khaznadar, who was an enthusiast for archaeological artifacts, but who did not excavate himself. The Khaznadar's son sent three *stelae* of the 'La Ghorfa' type to the Vienna exhibition in 1873 and they remain there to this day. The Khaznadar's successor as Prime Minister, Khereddine, sent two more to the Louvre, while the twelve 'La Ghorfa' *stelae* now in the Bardo Museum in Tunis must be the remnant of this collection.[98]

As we have seen (p. 135), another group of neo-Punic *stelae* has large and simple relief decoration and inscriptions. Davis' acquisitions include one *stele* of this type which Mendleson considered early, datable to the second or more probably the first century BC (Fig. 9.8).[99] Davis also acquired twelve examples of her relatively later group of fifteen inscribed *stelae* of this type.[100] The remaining three *stelae* in this group, and another that is certainly related, were acquired for the Museum from the former Reade collection by the Baronet Sir Thomas Phillipps.[101] All the examples of Mendleson's relatively later group come from the collection of Reade or Honegger, suggesting a common provenance, but there is no convincing evidence as to where they were originally found.

Eight of the neo-Punic *stelae* sent by Davis are not easily grouped. Five are tombstones of the Roman period, of which Bourgade published three in 1852. Of the five, three have Roman names in neo-Punic. One has the stereotyped Roman burial inscription of a woman named Maximilla, completely in Latin;[102] this was one of the inscriptions which Davis held back until 1860. Mendleson suggested a date in the first century AD for a tombstone that is typologically very similar.[103] The provenance of these neo-Punic funerary *stelae* is not known, but there is no evidence to link them with Carthage. Of the final three *stelae* acquired by Davis, two are atypical fragments with clear references to Greco-Roman mythology.[104] The last, while possibly related to the 'La Ghorfa' group, is unusually simple.[105]

As mentioned above (p. 30), Davis was acquainted with Abbé Bourgade when the Abbé was still resident in Tunis and wrote that he repeatedly, but unsuccessfully, offered to buy Bourgade's collection for the British Museum.[106] Davis evidently did not recognize that ten (eleven before the discovery of a join) of the neo-Punic *stelae* which he sent to the British Museum had been published by Bourgade in 1852, and again in 1856. The latter evidently acquired *stelae* from Honegger, with the idea of publishing them,

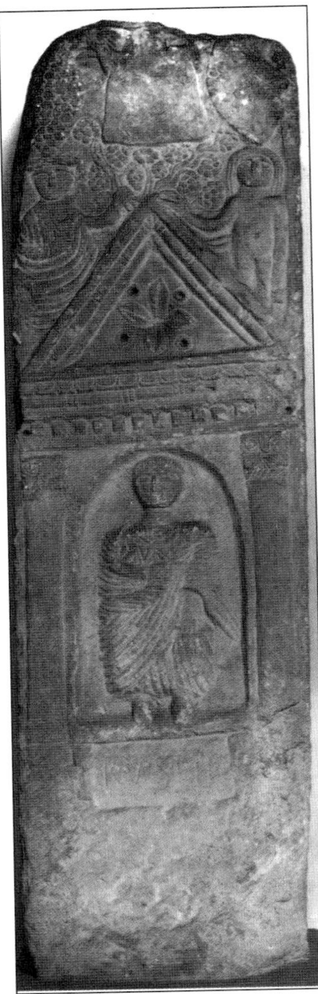

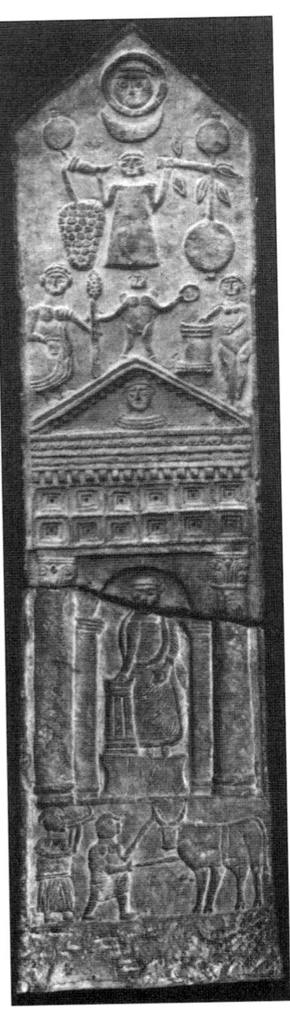

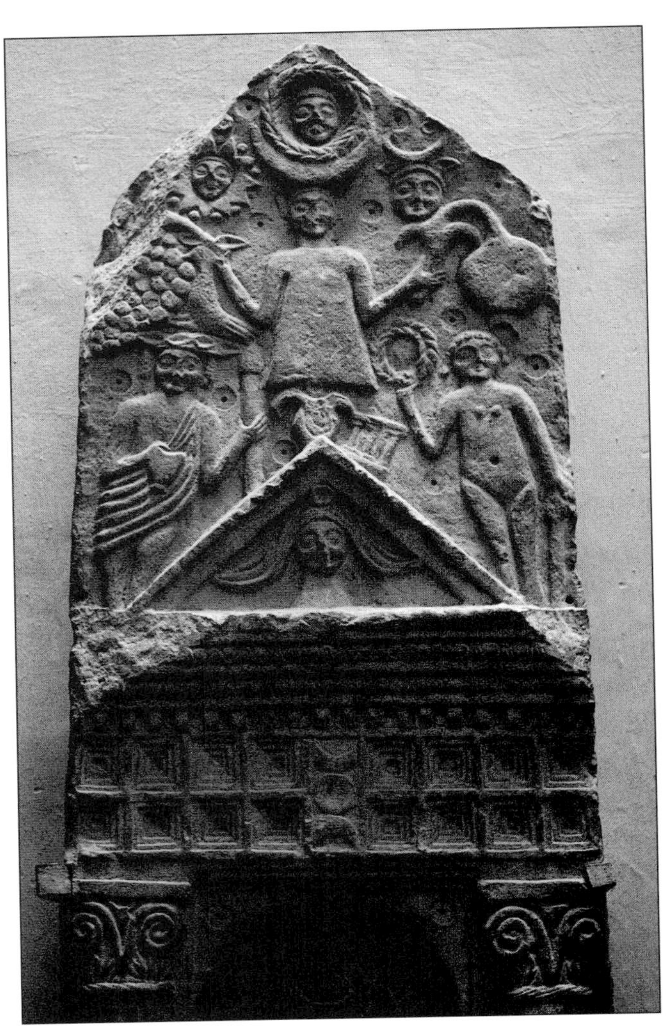

Fig. 9.11 (left) Stele *of 'La Ghorfa' type, damaged at the top, showing a Tanit figure, Dionysus (Liber in North Africa), and Venus; draped man standing in an irregularly-drawn* aedicula *below; the inscribed panel beneath reads* R S V L H, R(ogatus?) solvit votum libens (animo? *– if the H is a stone-cutter's error for an A), 'R(ogatus?) freely paid his vow'. Height: 123 cm; width: 34 cm.*

Fig. 9.12 (centre) Stele *depicting a man standing in an* aedicula, *making an offering at an altar. The pedestal on which he stands is inscribed in retrograde* L. Iuli(us) Urb(anus), *presumably the dedicator. The scene below, with a man playing double Phrygian pipes and another leading a bull to sacrifice, is unparalleled on 'Ghorfa'-type* stelae. *For the upper part of this* stele, *see the caption below to Fig. 9.13. Height: 170 cm; width: 45 cm.*

Fig. 9.13 (right) *Detail of a* stele *in the Musée du Bardo, Tunis, also in the 'La Ghorfa' series, with the same type of design as Fig. 9.12. In both there is a crescent moon surmounted by a sun disc, and below an anthropomorphized 'Tanit' figure, holding a (drinking) horn and outsize grapes (in her right hand) and one (or two, as on Fig. 9.12) pomegranates (in her left); below again stands a wreathed Dionysus/Liber, on the left, holding* thyrsus, *and a nude Venus on the right. Here on the Bardo* stele *Venus brandishes a wreath aloft, while on Fig. 9.12 she is sacrificing at an altar; the latter* stele *depicts also Eros with wings and wreath standing between Dionysus and Venus, not present on the Bardo* stele. *As often, in the* aedicula *below, there is a bust in the pediment and the horizontal ceiling coffering is also shown, but vertically as though serving as an architrave.*

which were later returned to Honegger's estate because of litigation. Even more of Bourgade's collection might be included in Davis' acquisition, because the second edition of Bourgade's *Toison d'or*, which I was unable to compare with Mendleson's account, included additional examples. According to Sainte-Marie, writing in 1884, Bourgade's collection of thirty to forty *stelae*, mostly neo-Punic, was supposedly sold to a Greek, but most were subsequently acquired by the British Museum;[107] Sainte-Marie's opinion seems to contain some grain of truth.

The *stele* of Julius Urbanus has the most complicated history: it was excavated by Honegger, perhaps in 1843 if it was part of Honegger's finds near Maktar, bought by the son of the Khaznadar, borrowed or bought from him by Bourgade in time for publication in 1852, perhaps mistakenly returned to Honegger's estate while its ownership was being contested, and finally bought by Davis in 1857 and sent to the British Museum. To complicate the story further, a few months before Davis acquired the neo-Punic *stelae* at Sousse, Lady Reade offered artefacts from her husband's collection to the British Museum.[108] It may be that the latter included the neo-Punic *stelae* acquired by Davis from her husband's estate soon afterwards.

Two more *stelae* which had been published by Bourgade and are now in the British Museum came by way of a donation of four *stelae* from Sir Thomas Phillipps, who acquired them from the Reade collection and presented them in 1858.[109] They are examples of Mendleson's group with simple designs in high relief. Even earlier, another nine *stelae* which had once been part of the Reade collection were offered for sale in a catalogue of Winstanley and Sons in 1850 and were acquired by the Museum at that time. Judging by their iconography, they are votives. They date to between the second and the late third or early fourth centuries AD,[110] and are later than anything which Davis acquired. Despite the implicit claim in the title of the sales catalogue, these anepigraphic *stelae* are certainly not from Carthage. Mendleson noted a similarity between three of these and a *stele* from El-Lehs.[111] This is probably the village of 'Lheys', mentioned by Sir Grenville Temple in 1835 as lying at a distance of an hour and a half from Maghrawa (the time required to make the journey on horseback). He noted similar bas-reliefs there to the one that he acquired at Maghrawa, differing in that the bas-reliefs from 'Lheys' were found in association with Roman inscriptions and sculpture.[112] It is likely that Temple mentioned this site as well as that at Maghrawa to his friend Sir Thomas Reade, and that Reade later sent Honegger there to investigate.

Fifty-eight of the sixty neo-Punic inscriptions now in the British Museum can therefore be traced back to excavations of Honegger and of his patron Sir Thomas Reade in the interior of Tunisia at some time before 1849, but a convincing history of their discovery is still lacking. The history of these neo-Punic *stelae* suggests the degree of complication and potential confusion involved in an inadequately-recorded excavation and the subsequent sale of antiquarian objects.

Although Davis had been hired by the Foreign Office to carry on excavations at Carthage, his acquisition of the neo-Punic *stelae*, finds which Davis knew were not from Carthage but from the Tunisian hinterland, demonstrates that acquiring finds for the British Museum was his overriding priority, and this explains why he immediately went beyond the site of Carthage when the opportunity arose.

10

Excavation at Carthage in the second half of 1857

Loading antiquities on the *Curaçoa* in the summer of 1857

By May 28th, 1857, Davis was digging at a new site on the north side of the Odeon Hill, which he called the 'Carthaginian House' (Site 16). He optimistically imagined that the job could be done in one or two weeks with a full complement of men. Meanwhile, however, HMS *Curaçoa* had arrived at La Goulette,[1] and Davis was then involved with the final packing and dispatch of the Mosaic of the Months and Seasons. The *Curaçoa* was homeward bound, but in no great hurry, as subsequent events showed, and was therefore available to transport the archaeological artefacts bound for the British Museum. The ship's carpenter, Mr Pollard, and his assistants helped with packing and loading, which occupied four days, and Davis received a receipt for twenty-six cases of antiquities from Lieutenant Durban, the ship's commander, on May 25th.[2] Packing completely depleted Davis' supply of wood, a rare commodity in Tunisia, and he asked for 300 to 400 boards in his letter to the Foreign Office.[3] The letter also mentioned that the officers attended a Bairam levée, a reception given by the Bey. Davis gave a special entertainment for the men of the *Curaçoa* before they left. The party was held on a newly-excavated mosaic floor, the Mosaic Imitating Green Marble, in the 'Carthaginian House'.[4]

The first twenty-six cases of finds included nineteen for the Mosaic of the Months and Seasons, and one for the figural *emblema* of the Mosaic with Baskets of Fish and Fruit. The six remaining cases included marble heads ('of Juno, Neptune, etc.') and other sculptural fragments; Punic votive tablets; torsos and other fragments of sculpture; fragments of stone balls found near the Circular Harbour which Davis described as 'believed to have been projected by Roman catapults', and lamps and other pieces of terracotta, including an early Roman amphora.[5]

Davis seems to have sent the greatest number of small finds in this first load, and they were later registered at the Museum. In his 1860 article, Franks wrote that the antiquities from Davis at Carthage were mostly Roman and 'neither very numerous nor of great importance'. He noted the amphora, several other pottery vases, and about forty-five lamps, of which some were early Roman, but the greater number were late Roman. Among these Franks noted one with a menorah, four with Christian monograms and another with a figure of a youth carrying a hare. Other finds included a brick tile stamped BARBARVS, bone spoons and pins, marble weights, and fragments of glass and bronze.[6] The range of finds described by Franks confirms what the mosaic finds suggest; Davis excavated almost entirely in contexts of the early Roman to late Byzantine eras.

The amphora is identifiable among those in the British Museum. It is an example of a very common Roman wine vessel from the west coast of Italy; the particular form dates *c.* 40/30 BC.[7] This amphora was probably retrieved from the assemblage known as the 'First Amphora Wall,' on the south-west side of the Byrsa hill at Carthage. Several thousand amphorae had been used to moderate drainage behind the high Roman terrace wall that surrounded the widened summit of the Byrsa; the assemblage has a *terminus post quem* of *c.* 15 BC.[8] The site was briefly excavated by Davis but not until December 1857 (Site 25), so he most probably purchased this amphora from the guardian of the chapel of Saint Louis. Beulé chanced upon the same amphora wall in 1859, and Delattre was to excavate it fully in 1883.[9]

The *Curaçoa* left La Goulette in order to continue its Mediterranean tour, but was soon to return. In mid-June 1857, the British Mediterranean squadron of four ships of the line and two frigates, one of them the *Curaçoa*, anchored off La Goulette under Admiral Lord Lyons, the commander of the Mediterranean fleet. Although he had certainly not finished with the 'Carthaginian House', Davis had just begun to work on another house on the south-east side of the Odeon Hill. Lord Lyons and Davis first met at this time.[10]

Lord Lyons had not brought the fleet to La Goulette on an innocent friendly visit. It was the role of both the British and French fleets at this time to put pressure on the Bey to guarantee the rights of Europeans and Jews, whom the European consuls had determined to protect.[11] A scandal had erupted when a drunken Jew, Samuel Batto Sfez, was accused of cursing Islam; despite the best efforts of the French and British consuls to prevent this outcome, the man was beheaded on June 24th, 1857.[12] Davis ignored the political implications of the presence of the fleet, but he tremendously enjoyed his opportunity to guide Lord Lyons over the site of Carthage. Davis was very favourably impressed by Lyons. The latter had been created vice-admiral in 1855, after a long and distinguished naval career, when he was already sixty-five, and was raised to the peerage in June 1856 with the title of Baron. Lyons was also known for his energy and good French. On his arrival at Tunis, the Admiral met with the Bey.[13] Davis reported that the Admiral was an able diplomat whose personal manner had made a positive impression on the Bey. Lyons became in turn an enthusiastic supporter of Davis, but he returned to England in 1858 and, unfortunately for Davis, died late in the same year.[14]

The squadron stayed for only a few days, leaving for Cagliari in Sardinia, with Davis, who had some business there, hitching a ride on board the *Curaçoa*.[15] He hired a photographer in Cagliari and probably visited his friend Canon Giovanni Spano. Spano was canon of the Cathedral of Cagliari, Principal of the University and editor of the *Bullettino archeologico Sardo*. He treated Davis as an intellectual equal, and was enthusiastically supportive of the latter's work at Carthage from its beginning. Spano showed Davis the *Lapide di Nora*, an early Punic inscription, as well as his collection of Punic antiquities, particularly from Pula and Tharros, a collection that Spano subsequently presented to the Museum of Cagliari.[16]

While in Sardinia, Davis visited the Punic site of Nora. He must have regaled the officers of the British fleet with his adventures, because he then led the Admiral and some of the captains on a visit to the site. Davis had intended to return to Carthage on a commercial vessel, but as it was delayed, he left Cagliari on board the *Curaçoa* once more, on Friday, June 19th. The *Curaçoa* was headed for Malta, but went by way of Carthage to drop Davis off. Admiral Lord Lyons told Davis to get the rest of the packing done, and he would have the boat stop again briefly on its way to London and board anything else that was ready to go.[17] The *Curaçoa* does not seem to have picked up antiquities at this time, but returned to Carthage as planned (in early July) for a second load. The latter consisted of thirteen cases of antiquities and two statues without their heads. Five more cases of mosaics were also loaded. They included the border fragment from the Mosaic with Baskets of Fish and Fruit, and the four mosaics from Falbe no. 90 (Site 13).[18] Davis said that finds from his first thirteen excavations, or sketch-map sites, went with the *Curaçoa*.[19] Although he had been working at the 'Carthaginian House' on the north wall of the city, which was the site of the Mosaic Imitating Green Marble, nothing from this excavation was sent with the *Curaçoa*. The ship left Carthage for England on July 10th.[20]

All six of the mosaics sent on the *Curaçoa* arrived in London in late August 1857,[21] and the lot was accessioned before the end of the year, as is implicitly shown by the catalogue number, beginning '57.12-18,' i.e. December 18th, 1857. The museum was overwhelmed with the accessioning of new finds at the time, including sculptures from Assyria, and sculptures, architectural remains and other finds from Newton's major excavations at the Mausoleum at Halicarnassos on the west coast of Turkey. The mosaics from Carthage were consigned to a newly-cleared basement and, with those that arrived later, were still largely not on display in 1870.[22]

Repercussions of the diplomatic incident in the summer of 1857

Admiral Lyons and his fleet arrived at La Goulette at least once again, the visit this time occasioned by the beheading of the Jew who had blasphemed against Islam. A draft of a letter in Italian from Consul Wood to the Bey, dated July 24th, 1857, protested about the atrocity.[23] Wood reported to the Admiralty that the French fleet was in the Bay of Tunis at the beginning of September as France's protest against the incident.[24] By late September, the Bey was promising reforms, including a constitution, with the result that instructions to Lord Lyons at that time to proceed with the fleet to the Bay of Tunis were countermanded.[25] A subsequent visit by the British fleet may have occurred in November of 1857, as Davis noted such a visit not long after he received permission from the Foreign Office to be taken by admiralty ships to Cap Bon, and letters in the Foreign Office files show that he received this permission in late October.[26] Davis noted that Lyons brought two English ladies with him, one his niece, Miss Pearson. The ladies wished to see the palace of the Bey, and Davis recounted that therefore two other English ladies, 'who possessed some knowlege of Arabic', accompanied the visitors to the harem of the palace at La Marsa. It seems certain that Davis is here discreetly referring to his wife and Miss Rosenberg, her young companion.

According to Davis, the Admiral and his party had a separate formal audience with the Bey at the palace. Since Mohammed Bey had enacted a charter granting equal rights to all people under his jurisdiction on September 20th, 1857, the intention of the visit was undoubtedly pacific and congratulatory.[27] Before the end of the audience, all four ladies were ushered in to the gentlemen's presence, where chairs were provided for them and the Bey carried on a polite conversation with the whole party. Davis described this as the first occasion on which Christian ladies were publicly received at the Bey's court, and explained it as a groundbreaking diplomatic move to establish that the Bey was not the monster that international opinion was making him out to be.[28]

Davis' sixteenth site: the Late Roman 'Carthaginian House'

In the late spring of 1857, having gained some experience of Carthage, Davis began to dig at a site he had chosen for clearly formulated reasons of his own (Site 16).[29] His headman, Ali Karema, was not pleased at the choice of site, but Davis had great hopes for it. He marked out three oblique trenches four feet wide and twenty-five feet long, placing them twenty-five feet apart. Perceiving the line of the wall on the north side of the city, he chose to dig just to the south of a great walled enclosure, which was outlined but not numbered on the plan of Falbe. Davis shows a similar but not identical enclosure on his own plan. Nevertheless, he said that at the point where he chose to dig there were no vestiges above ground.[30] He implicitly believed that he was digging on the site of the Punic city wall, and at the time of his letters to the Foreign Office, he indicates that he was expecting to find Punic housing. As he actually found a house here, the site was indicated on the sketch-map as a 'Carthaginian House'. It lay on the north side of the city, near the declivity that was to be determined by excavation in the 1970s as formed by the Theodosian Wall of AD 425. The Roman city of Carthage had not been surrounded by walls until this time.

Davis perceived that his site lay on the city walls because of the ruins of several 'forts' flanking a line of 'wide and deep trenches' (this is his attempt to describe the conformation of the land determined by the line of the wall); he chose to dig at a site on the right (east) side of the road which led to one of these forts.[31] His description and the location of the relevant point on the published map suggests that he was digging in the Roman city-block between *decumani* 5 and 6 north and approximately on the line of *cardo* 2 east, about eighty meters east of the point where the line of the *cardo maximus* north crosses the line of the Theodosian Wall. The site is also about eighty meters east of Bab el-Rih (the 'Gate of the Wind') (Site 7). The area between the *cardo maximus* and *cardo* 2 east at this point is now covered by a large modern mosque. The portion of Theodosian Wall and Roman houses that were occupied at least until the wall's construction in AD 425 were excavated along the line of *decumanus* 6 north extending from slightly west of *cardo* 2 east to just east of *cardo* 3 east by the second Canadian team under the late Colin Wells during the UNESCO 'Save Carthage' project in the 1970s and 1980s. Late Roman houses, shops and bath-houses solidly occupied the area here and also further to the east in a zone that lay inside the wall from the time of its construction.[32]

In the summer Davis' men left him to attend to the barley harvest.[33] He was still full of energy as he neared the end of his first full year of excavation, and he resented the men's unwillingness to work in July and August.[34] After the second departure of the *Curaçoa*, on July 10th, 1857, it was still harvest-time; Davis, far too optimistically, reported the harvest as 'nearly over' on July 14th.[35] Almost certainly work did not resume on the site before September. At the beginning of October, Davis reported that his excavations were going well. He wrote that '. . . two houses of which there was no vestige above ground have nearly been cleared'.[36] He was planning to remove and case the antiquities which he had found at the two houses, of which the 'Carthaginian House' was one.

To confuse posterity, Davis said that he was digging on the 'Byrsa,' or at the same point where the 'large mosaic' had been discovered. His published map shows the 'Byrsa' on relatively low ground south of the long summit of Bordj-Djedid and the Odeon. He meant that he was working on the Odeon Hill, for which he had no specific name, the same hill on which the 'large mosaic' had been found. The latter was either the Mosaic of the Months and Seasons, or the large geometric mosaic from the Roman house east of the theatre (Site 21; see below, p. 146), which measured thirty-five by thirty feet (11.0 m by 9.1 m). Franks interpreted Davis' statement to mean that two houses were uncovered at one site, but Davis meant merely that he had excavated two houses with mosaics on what we now know as the Odeon Hill.

The two houses excavated at this time were widely separated; they are more than 300 m apart. Davis enclosed a drawing of the floor-plan of a 'Carthaginian House' (Fig. 10.1) with his description of the cases shipped on the *Supply*.[37] In addition, he marked the position of the 'Carthaginian House' on his second sketch-map. The house which he excavated east of the theatre (Site 21) was described as a suite of eight rooms; the same might be said for the plan of the 'Carthaginian House', but Davis indicated that the major mosaic from the house east of the theatre came from a large room, thirty-five by thirty feet in size, whereas the ground plan of the 'Carthaginian House' which he enclosed with his letter to the Foreign Office shows that it contains no room as large as this.

Davis wrote of the 'Carthaginian House' as follows: 'The accompanying ground plan gives some idea of the building, although there were other chambers, which evidently belonged to it, traces of which we discovered, but were unable to satisfy ourselves as to their connexions, in consequence of having been obliged to restore the land to the owner for agricultural purposes'. Davis marked one of the small rooms on this plan 'Bath Room', and continued, 'On the walls were faint remains of fresco paintings, and in one of

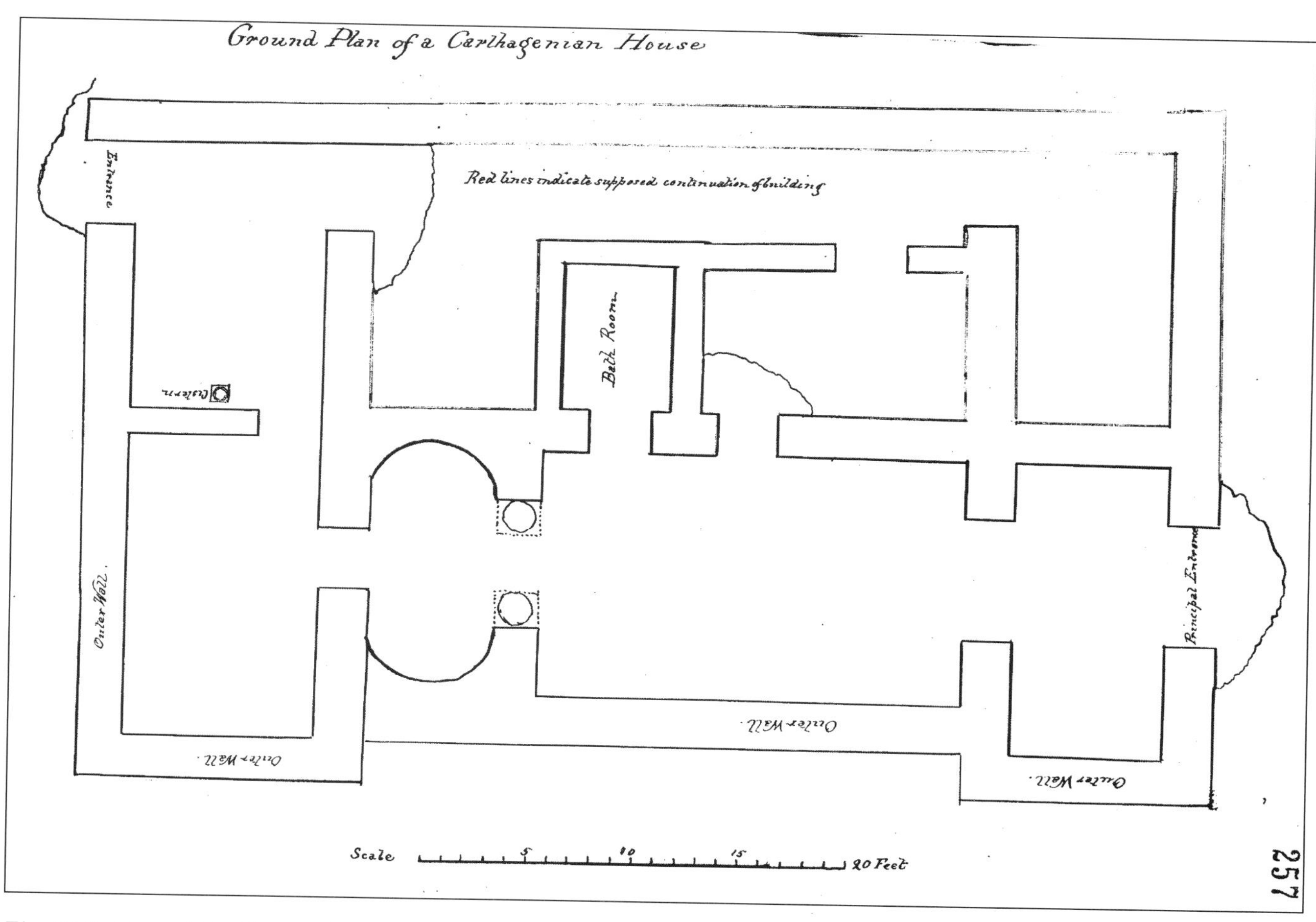

Fig. 10.1 Plan of the 'Carthaginian House', as it appears in Davis' hitherto unpublished original drawing

the chambers, or rather alcoves, we found the lower portion, about a foot in depth, lined with thin slabs of white marble'.[38] The architecture of the 'Carthaginian House', as well as the mosaics which Davis found, imply a fourth-century date, a chronology in harmony with the late Roman decoration of houses in this neighborhood known from later excavation.

As mentioned above (p. 140), Davis gave a party for the officers of the *Curaçoa* on this site, and a drawing illustrating the excavated rooms and mosaic floors still *in situ* was published in Davis' text;[39] a very similar one had appeared earlier in the *Illustrated London News*, in the issue for May 29th (Fig. 10.2). The site was, therefore, at least partly dug by the date of the first departure of the *Curaçoa* on May 25th, as the party dinner was held just before that date. Davis walked his readers from the hill of Bordj-Djedid to this site, to explain its location and the circumstances of his dinner party, and the line of the walk can be retraced.[40]

The drawing of the site showed a mosaic made up of rectangular areas laid to suggest mirroring slabs of green marble. Davis described the pavement, in 'beautiful shades of green marble, representing slabs of *verde antico*', but also as 'an excellent imitation' of a *cipollino*. Davis confused two different types of marble here; the type of marble represented on Davis' pavement was in fact an imitation of *cipollino*, which has green streaks on a white ground. The drawing shows a border that may have been formed by rectangular *opus sectile* (cut marble pavement or revetment), as Gauckler thought, and two geometric threshold mosaics with patterns of oblique diamonds, the first on a smaller scale than the second. A drawing of the excavation of this mosaic, by Arthur Hall, was, as we have seen (Fig. 10.2), published in the *Illustrated London News*.[41] The drawing in Davis' text is very similar, and both were made from the same vantage point. The drawings, however, pose a problem for the location of the 'Carthaginian House'. If the perspective is correct as drawn, the horizontal lines of the mosaic floor converge in front of and below the Chapel of Saint Louis, at a point between *cardines* 5 and 6 east. According to the laws of perspective, the room with the mosaic should be placed along a line between

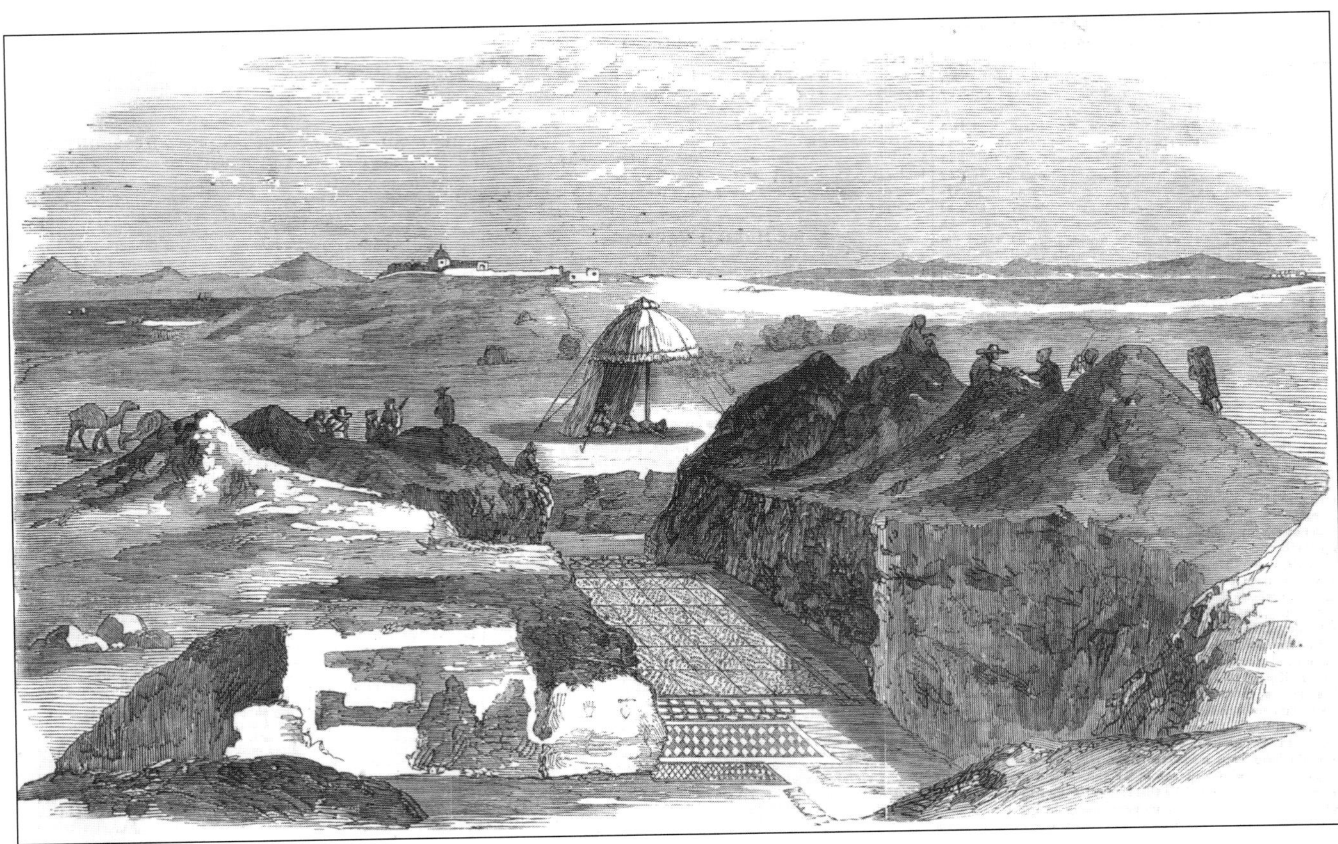

Fig. 10.2 The excavation of the 'Carthaginian House' in progress, as shown in an engraving in The Illustrated London News *on May 29th 1858. The accompanying article notes that 'the colours and design of the mosaic are as perfect as the day the pavement was first put down', and comments on the plaster in the foreground, where 'the well-known charm against the "evil eye" and a heart scratched on the plaster look as if done but yesterday'. A hand and a* hedera *(ivy leaf) – rather than a 'heart' – are just visible in the original engraving.*

these streets. The house lay not far from the northern edge of the Roman city and the fortifications which Davis described, but a house along this line and with this view would lie on the site of the Odeon. The huge structure of the Odeon precludes a house on its site from its construction at the beginning of the third century AD to the end of Byzantine Carthage, even though the Odeon was massively damaged at the beginning of the Vandal era, after which it went out of use. But the small scale of the rooms in the 'Carthaginian House' makes it unlikely that they can be interpreted as rooms in a public building. I therefore think that the perspective of the drawings is not correct, and that the 'Carthaginian House' must have lain near *cardo* 2 east and *decumanus* 6 north, as I have argued above (p. 142).

Hall explained the symbols on a wall that appears to stand on the line of the threshold as follows: 'To the left in the foreground the plaster of the wall is partly broken away, but enough remains to show that a portion of it was covered with fresco. The well-known charm against the 'evil eye,' [the drawing shows a raised hand] and a heart scratched on the plaster, look as if done but yesterday'. What these symbols mean is uncertain, but they clearly were meant to meet the eye of someone entering this room.

The Mosaic Imitating Green Marble was found twelve feet (3.7 m) down[42] in a large building (in his 'Statement', Davis specified ten feet [3 m] down). The floor of the room was cleared, probably as quickly as possible, with the intended dinner party in mind. At the time of the drawing published in Davis, the mosaic may have been only half-cleared. If the depth of soil is twelve feet (3.7 m), the cleared portion in this drawing is perhaps twelve by twenty feet (3.7 m by 6.1 m). In line with this, the largest room in the 'Carthaginian House' measured twelve by twenty feet, according to the scale given on the ground-plan. Three Punic *stelae*, or 'Phoenician inscriptions', 'and some mosaics' were also found at this site.

The Mosaic Imitating Green Marble itself was not lifted, as it does not appear in the accession lists of the

British Museum. William Gregory, the Irish MP, visited Davis in early November 1857. The latter took Gregory to visit his excavations, who wrote that Davis 'had just laid open a series of chambers paved with the most beautiful mosaic'. Gregory noted that the rooms, especially the bedrooms, were small. He also told a shocking story which explains the loss of the Mosaic Imitating Green Marble. He said that officers of Lord Lyons's fleet had tried to take souvenirs from the site and had broken up the mosaics with pickaxes. Davis had come along in time to save the floors from total destruction, but they were badly damaged, perhaps too heavily to make retrieval possible.[43] A small piece of a mosaic also closely imitating green marble is on display in the National Museum of Carthage,[44] which may possibly have been recovered later from the same site; on the other hand, mosaics with this general pattern are not uncommon.

As we have seen, Davis mentioned additional mosaics from the excavation of the 'Carthaginian House'. In his 'Statement' of December 1858, he correlated the numbers marked on the cases sent on the *Supply* with the sketch-map site-numbers. As the case numbers were recorded on the accession lists, these numbers show that three geometric mosaics came from that site.[45] Hinks later suggested a range of dates from the third to the fifth century AD for these mosaics. These suggestions are not particularly coherent; the floors all belong to a single structure and most likely all date to the fourth or early fifth century.

The Mosaic of Cubes in Perspective (Fig. 10.3) was surely the larger threshold panel illustrated in the room with the Mosaic Imitating Green Marble. This floor has juxtaposed cubes with white tops, and alternating red and grey-green sides. A black-and-white toothed border is preserved on three sides, and a zigzag polychrome pattern on one side in white, red, black, green and orange is framed by a shallow curving line, and laid against a plain white ground. The pavement from border to border is evidently more than a meter wide, but the length cannot be determined from Hinks's photograph, because the longer direction of the mosaic is cut off. Furthermore, the different cataloguers disagreed widely on the dimensions of this mosaic, which I have not seen.[46] Hinks dated it to the third century from comparanda scattered across the Roman empire. Another mosaic from the same site, the Mosaic of Latticework, is a small square polychrome geometric floor with an all-over pattern in white, red and greys, with a plain black-and-white line border on all four sides. The mosaic is just over a meter square. According to Hinks, the latticework motif is paralleled elsewhere in mosaics, and also appears in stone relief decoration. Only the order of Hinks' numbering implies a third- or fourth-century date for this mosaic.

The third geometric mosaic lifted from the 'Carthaginian House' is a small threshold mosaic, the Mosaic of Intersecting Green and Red Circles (Fig. 10.4). The pavement is framed by plain, straight black-and-white lines on the short side and two long sides, and has green and red interlaced circles on a white ground; each circle frames a simple cross. The mosaic has no glass *tesserae*, but nevertheless has pleasing colour intensity. Hinks dated this mosaic to the fourth or early fifth century; the circles have interior dentils, and this motif provided the basis for his argument. A more elegant version of the same design was to be

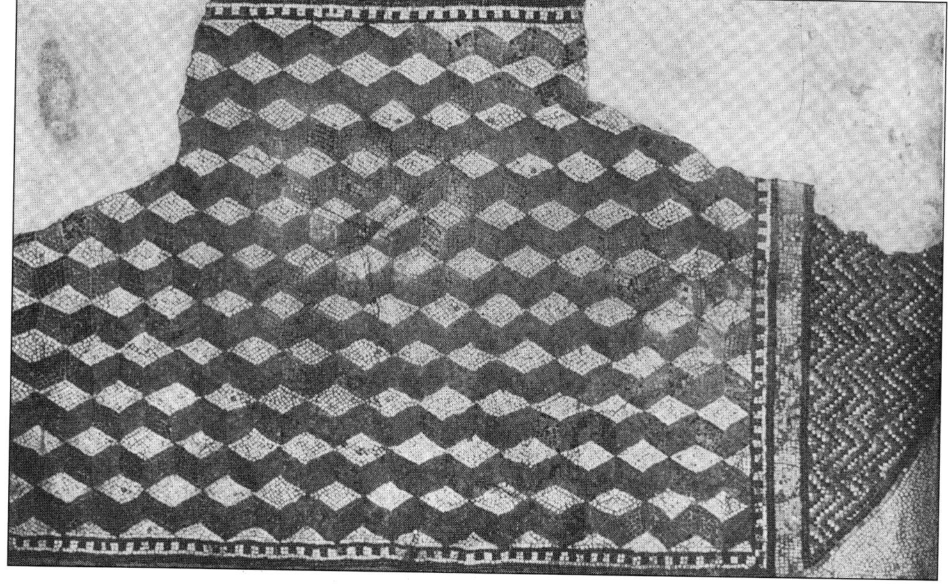

Fig. 10.3 The Mosaic of Cubes in Perspective, from the 'Carthaginian House', detail; it can be seen in situ *in the foreground of Fig. 10.2 (the second panel from the front). The main field shows white, red and grey-green cubes in perspective; there is an enclosing dentil border. There is a more intricate zig-zag panel at one end, but overall the mosaic is poorly executed. Later fourth or early fifth century AD (?).*

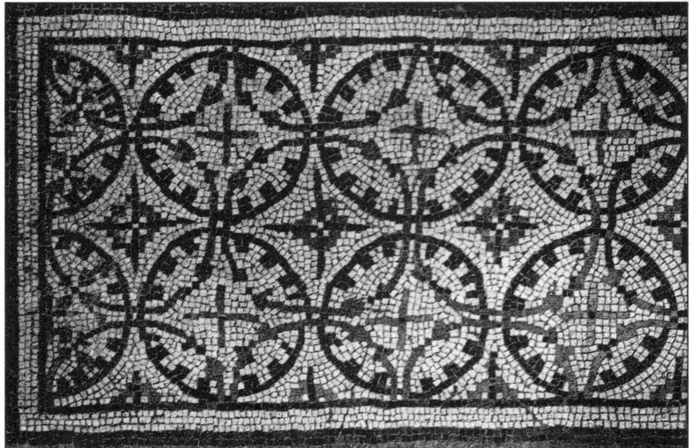

Fig. 10.4 The Mosaic of Intersecting Green and Red Circles, from the 'Carthaginian House', detail; its original position was at the opposite end of the main part of the pavement (in the background of Fig. 10.2) from where Fig. 10.3 came. Also very poorly drawn and executed, the intersecting circles (a red band with inner dentils; perfunctory green vine tendrils) define concave squares containing simple crosses. Later fourth or early fifth century AD (?).

excavated but not lifted by Sainte-Marie in 1874; his mosaic came from the slope between the Turkish fort and the Antonine Baths, an area of Roman housing where Davis had also excavated (Site 5).[47] Lézine published a mosaic of similar pattern which he associated with renovations to the Antonine Baths in AD 389.[48]

It was also in the autumn of 1857 that Davis dug at four sites (Sites 17–20) where he said he found nothing. These are not identified on any of Davis' maps. Although the actual sites may be marked on the published map as points, with or without numbers, there is no evidence for which ones they might be. An unnumbered site with a prostrate column (Site 24), which Davis described at length and which appears on his published map as a point without a number, may be one of these four 'unproductive' sites.

Davis' twenty-first site: the Roman House east of the theatre

Davis continued with a site on the south-east summit of the Odeon Hill, which he had chosen for its panoramic view (Site 21). This site is indicated on the second sketch-map with a point, but no descriptive label. There are two possibly relevant points on the published map. There is no equivalent site on the plan of Falbe, but Falbe did indicate, with crude horizontal lines, the steep slope that formed the hollow of the *cavea* (raked seating area) of the then unrecognized Roman theatre. The choice of this site was due to Davis' independent judgment, as he noted that this was a likely location for luxury housing because of its high situation and wide sea-view; there were no visible ruins above ground.[49]

Here Davis in fact chose to dig one of the best sites for Roman housing at Carthage. The general area is the same as the furthest western extent of Gauckler's later excavation of a district of luxury Roman houses that is now part of a protected archaeological park on the Odeon Hill (Fig. 10.5). Gauckler's 'Villa de la Volière' (House of the Aviary), which he excavated in 1903 (Fig. 10.6), is a now partially restored house that takes up an

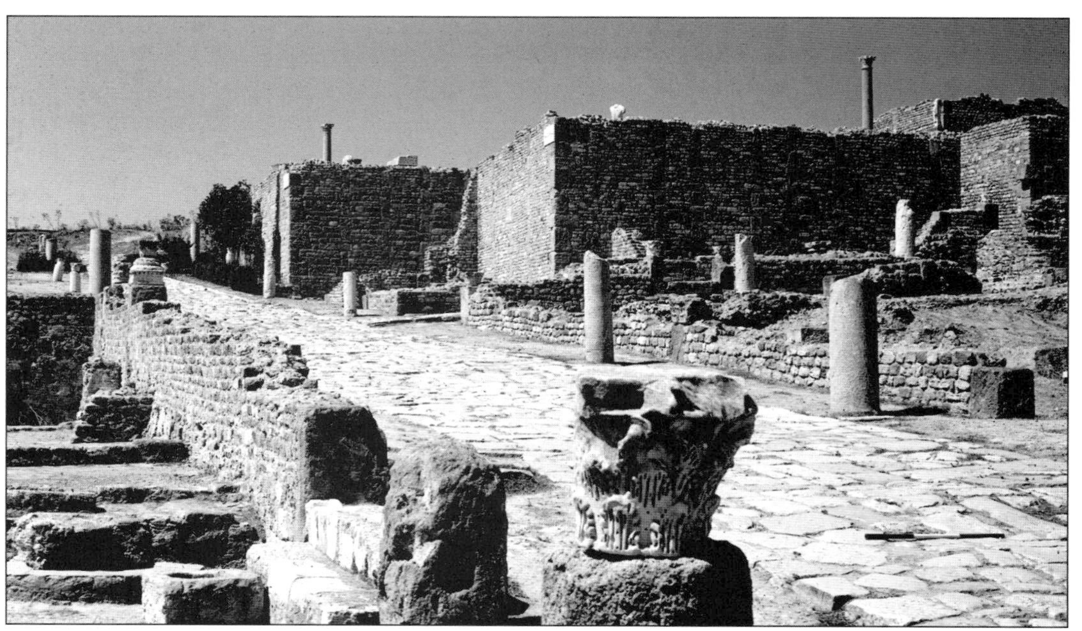

Fig. 10.5 View of part of the 'Archaeological Park of the Roman villas' (from the south), as it appeared in the summer of 1973 when excavation was in full swing. Davis excavated to the left (south) of the structures visible here. The paved street is decumanus *5 north.*

entire Roman city block (Fig. 10.7).[50] It lies slightly higher than Davis' site, on the north side of *decumanus* 5. This housing area rises up the eastern slope of the Odeon Hill to end at *cardo* 7 east; the eastern enclosure wall of the Odeon is on the west side of this same *cardo*. Davis found his greatest concentration of mosaics here in one block, between *decumani* 4 and 5 north and on either the west or the east side of *cardo* 8.

The site of the house east of the theatre is in the north-eastern quarter of the city-grid. The two points on Davis' published map fall on and just north of *decumanus* 4 north and between *cardines* 5 and 6 east, or right on the line of the eastern *cavea* and enclosure wall of the theatre. But Davis' excavation at these points was near the summit of the Odeon Hill, and he uncovered luxury Roman houses, so the location of the points cannot be correct. To have the view Davis described, while being in the area he indicated, the site should be at the top of the south-east side of the theatre incline, on the rising slope of the Odeon Hill. Indeed it must lie on the south side of *decumanus* 5 north in order to agree with Davis' description of its fine view. The real location of these two points must be almost two short blocks (about fifty meters) to the north-east of his points on the published map, and therefore between *cardines* 7 and 8 east. The site would then overlie the west end of the area of Roman luxury housing still extant on the Odeon Hill and be at an elevation of forty to forty-five meters, while the nearby summit of the hill is about fifty meters above sea-level.[51] The fact that the Davis' locations do not agree perfectly with his description can be explained by the lack of fixed points in the immediate area, since the sites of the theatre and odeon were not recognized at the time.

Davis chose to describe the location of the house in as obscure a way as possible, and without his map it would be impossible to locate it. He said the site was 'on an elevation which faces the modern fort built on the site of what I believe to have been the temple of Aesculapius, and overlooks the range of cisterns, which were supplied by rainwater, from which it is a little more than a couple of hundred paces'.[52] The site is in fact more than a quarter of a mile (more than 400 meters) from the eastern cisterns to which he refers, and the Turkish fort is beyond the cisterns. Davis here simply wanted to take advantage of an opportunity to refer to his idiosyncratic identification of the site of the 'Temple of Aesculapius.' He meant that the site of these houses was on an elevation (the Odeon Hill), which hill faced the fort on the Bordj-Djedid hill,

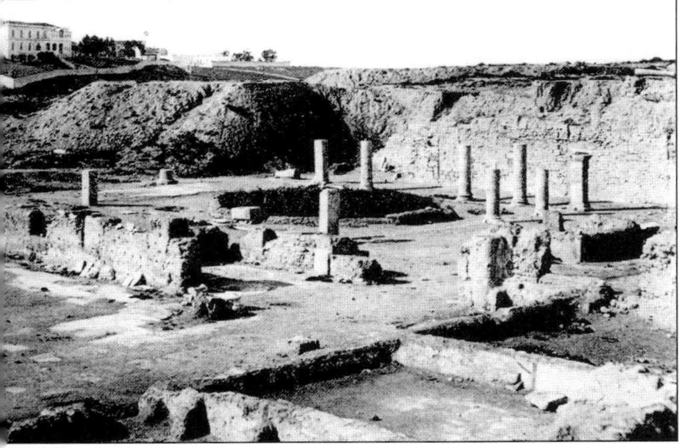

Fig. 10.6 (above) *Paul Gauckler's excavation of the House of the Aviary in progress in 1903, looking north-westwards up the hill*

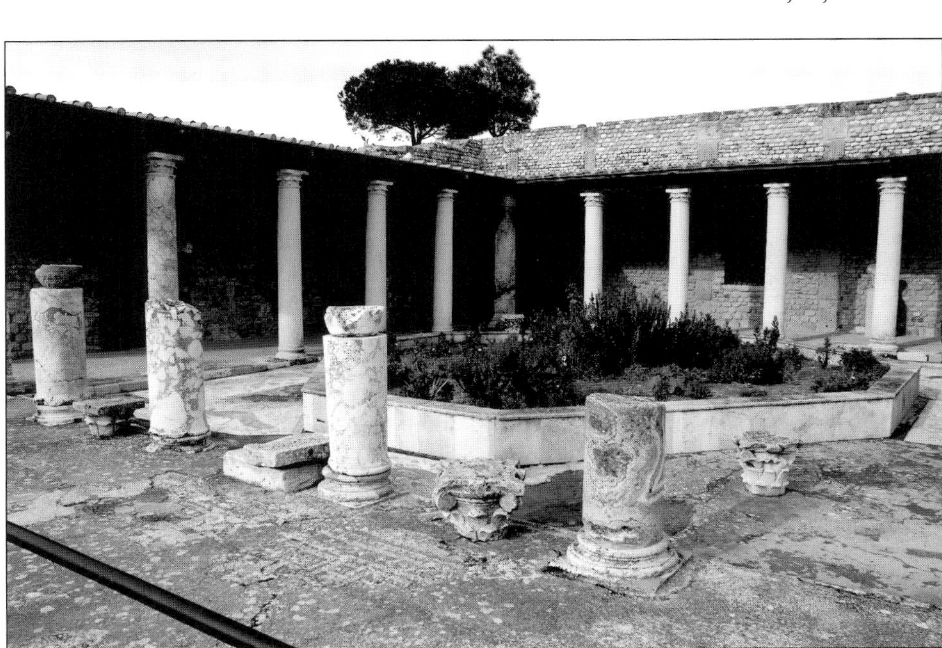

Fig. 10.7 (right) *The House of the Aviary as it looks today, from the same orientation as Fig. 10.6 (but closer to the peristyle), showing how much of the house was reconstructed in the twentieth century*

where Davis located the 'Temple of Aesculapius,' which overlooked the range of cisterns.

His excavation of this house began in the spring and early summer of 1857, as early work on the site was contemporary with the excavation of the Mosaic of Victory, but at that time Davis may have thought he had exhausted the latter site.[53] One of the mosaics from the house was discovered by the date of the second departure of the *Curaçoa* in July 1857, but Davis shipped finds only from the first thirteen sketch-map sites on that occasion. Excavation was continuing at the beginning of October 1857.[54] William Gregory also visited this site with Davis; he said that the latter had exposed a very large chamber with a Roman pavement of coarser materials than the ones in the 'Carthaginian House'; Gregory imagined that this new pavement, the Mosaic of Interlaced Squares Forming Starred Octagons, would make a fine floor for a large room in the British Museum.[55]

Although there were no ancient remains above the ground, and the land produced a regular crop, making excavation arrangements more difficult, Davis laid out two long trenches oriented north-east/south-west, and about thirty yards (27 m) apart. He concentrated his men here for a time, and they eventually cleared three of eight chambers.[56] Coming down at a depth of three feet (elsewhere described as four or five feet) upon three (four according to Davis' later 'Statement' to the Foreign Office) neatly-built and mortared stone tombs with a common floor, he was with difficulty able to convince his men that these were not Muslim tombs. Davis was certain that they were neither Muslim nor Christian because of their orientation. Once convinced, his men, 'with a fanatical zeal', demolished the tombs in less than an hour. Davis was unconcerned at the loss of evidence of tombs which he thought were Roman, with no architectural pretensions.[57] Since the three geometric mosaics subsequently discovered at a depth of nine feet (2.7 m) below the tombs were Roman mosaics of the second or third century, it seems possible that these neatly constructed tombs, placed on a site with a wide view of the sea, if indeed not Muslim, may have been crusader burials.

The men first proceeded six feet (1.8 m) farther down, at which depth they met two strata of reddish clay, which the headman at first thought was 'natural'; they then encountered building debris two feet (0.6 m) below that, then a little more than a foot (0.3 m) of fine sand, and finally a mosaic, a total of nine feet (2.7 m) below the graves and thirteen feet (4.0 m) below the surface. This is the only occasion when Davis attempted to interpret the stratigraphy: 'the fragments of ruin were undoubtedly portions of the fallen roof, and the deposit of sand the remains of decomposed cement, while the layers of reddish earth appear only to have been washed into the ruin by very heavy rains . . .'.[58]

Davis eventually found eight chambers on the site, and said that the house was more extensive than the

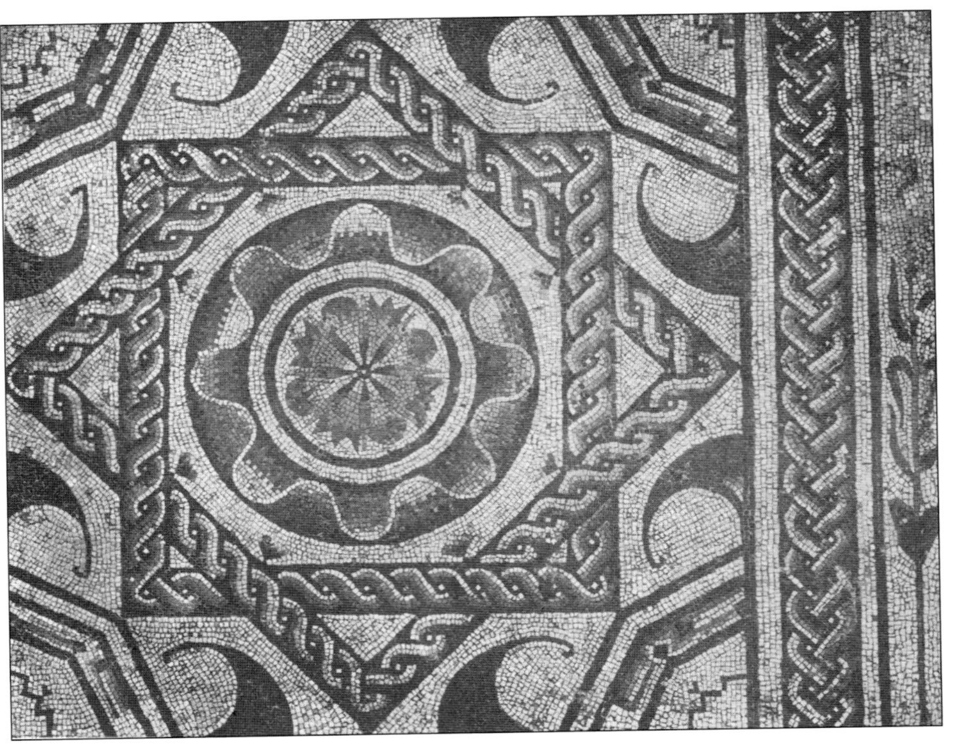

Fig. 10. 8 Portion of a geometric pavement found '200 m north of the Bordj Djedid cisterns' – the Mosaic of Interlaced Squares in simple guilloche, forming eight-pointed stars and enclosing irregular octagons; within the latter, undulating rainbow-pattern circles enclosing rosettes. Part of the three-strand guilloche inner border of the mosaic, and an outer border of millet stalks, are also visible (see also Fig. 10.9). This fragment measures 2.06 m in by 1.68 m; probably third century AD.

1859

Date.	No.	Description.
4-2	72	Mosaic pavement quadrangular portion coarse work, ornaments in black with red grey + yellow details. H. 4ft 10" × 4ft. 9½".
	73	——— another panel of same pattern with border to one side only. Central ornament of square panel different. 4ft 8" × 4ft 9".
	74	——— quadrangular piece with interlaced squares in the middle of them a circle with chevron border, enclosing four leaved flower. Border round two sides of compartment of interlaced pattern. W. 6ft 8". [upper part covered with cement].
	75	——— another piece of same pavement. identical in pattern. border round two sides (much broken) 6ft 7 × 6f
	76	——— no border; same border to central ornament, but different centre [imperfect in parts] 5ft 4" × 5ft 8".
	77	——— circular pattern, border on one side only; central ornament different having a nebulé border + eight petalled flower, on one side a bull-rush. 6ft 9" × 5ft 6"
	78	——— border on one side only, same border to central ornament but different centre [which is much injured] 6ft 4 × 5ft 5
	79	——— no border same border to central ornament but different centre 5ft. 6" × 5ft.
	80	——— frgt. border on one side, same border to central ornament which is destroyed. 5ft. × 2ft 8".

Fig. 10.9 Part of a page from the British Museum Registry, showing entries for the 2nd April 1859. Nos 72–73 together with the (uppermost) illustration provide our only knowledge of the Mosaic of Squares and Peltas, a pavement not included in Hinks' catalogue of 1933. The illustrated fragment shows a central square (with right-angled z-pattern border) containing a rosette, the whole framed by pairs of opposed peltae *attached to poised squares; there are further squares at the corners. Probably third century AD. Entry 74 illustrates and describes another fragment of the pavement to which Fig. 10.8 belongs, as do also nos 75–80. Fig. 10.8 is here entry 77 (the millet stalk of which is here called a 'bullrush').*

line of rooms he was able to investigate. He described these eight rooms as running on a north-east/south-west line, which suggests they lay along the alignment of the Roman *cardines*. The rooms were all at the same level, and since the hill was steep, it is likely that the site had been levelled for the house. Little of the stone and mortar walls had survived.[59] The materials of the walls, both stone and cement, seemed to Davis to be of Punic date, which may suggest that the mortar was soft, and therefore possibly belonging to the early Roman or mid-Roman periods. Alternatively, he could have been referring to construction of the walls in *opus Africanum*, a method of construction (as we have seen: p. 100) common at Carthage in both the Punic and Roman eras, in which stone pilasters of large squared blocks alternate with smaller stone infill. In his later 'Statement', Davis said there was evidence of fire in a layer over all these rooms.[60]

The first mosaic from this house was found in a very large room, measuring thirty-five by thirty feet

(10.65 m by 9.15 m); the whole was cleared and the polychrome pavement was much admired. This is the Mosaic of Interlaced Squares (Hinks 25: Fig. 10.8). According to Franks' description, this large floor had an effective design, a 'geometric mosaic of large circular medallions inscribed in octagonal stars formed by two interlaced squares'. Franks noted, on the other hand, that the mosaic was Roman and not early, with coarse execution and poor colour and materials. He suggested as a parallel a pavement at Cirencester,[61] indicating that the design belonged to a widespread western Mediterranean tradition. Hinks' order implies that the mosaic was datable, according to him, to the third century. None of the descriptions before Hinks mention it, but the floor depicted a large millet stalk against a white background in a border along one side.[62] The millet plant is a symbol of a prominent amphitheatre faction, or else a simple fetish, whch is often worked into the mosaics of Africa Proconsularis and Byzacena.[63] 'The objects we recovered . . . consist chiefly in a variety of elegant [mosaic] designs', according to Davis. Four geometric mosaics, of which two are certainly from this site, and two more which probably are, were sent to London on HMS *Supply* in October 1858. Ten large square pieces of the largest mosaic were received in London; Davis explained in his 'Statement' that the floor was shipped in ten cases, nos 4–12 and 14.[64]

Another mosaic, the Mosaic of Squares and Peltas, which was among the finds excavated by Davis and accessioned in 1859, is problematic. Its find-spot is in doubt because of confusion in its labelling. It arrived in two large pieces, one of which was sketched in the accession list (Fig. 10.9). It correlates with two case-numbers mentioned by Davis in his 'Statement': case 25, which Davis attributed to the 'Carthaginian House' near the north gate of the city, and case 13, which he assigned to the house east of the theatre. Both fragments are approximately one and a half meters square; one is a corner with a border on two sides, and the other has a border on one side only. The mosaic is black on white with red, grey and yellow details, according to notes in the accession list. The style of the mosaic, a complicated geometric design that includes peltas and poised squares arranged around large squares, is not very different in effect from the very large mosaic from the house east of the theatre. The pieces lifted are also comparable in size. Despite the fact that this mosaic is clearly described in the accession list, it was not catalogued in Newton's *Guide* of 1876, and therefore Gauckler did not know of it when he came to assemble his catalogue. The fact that Hinks did not include it in his work is harder to explain; perhaps he simply did not find this mosaic in the storerooms. Since the pavements at the 'Carthaginian House' seem to have been of late Roman date, and this mosaic ought to belong to the second or the third centuries, it most probably comes from a room in the house east of the theatre. There, however, Davis said that eight rooms were defined, but only three emptied; we are not specifically told that any floor from here was raised.

The Mosaic of Hexagonal Laurel Wreaths (Hinks 21: Fig. 10.10), which has an all-over pattern of which variants are common at Carthage, also came from the house east of the theatre. Davis sent three large fragments of this mosaic to the Museum. One is a corner with a wide cable border on two sides. In the 'Statement', Davis said that this pavement ('the fragments contained in cases marked 27, 28 and 29') was found twenty feet (6.1 m) away from the largest room

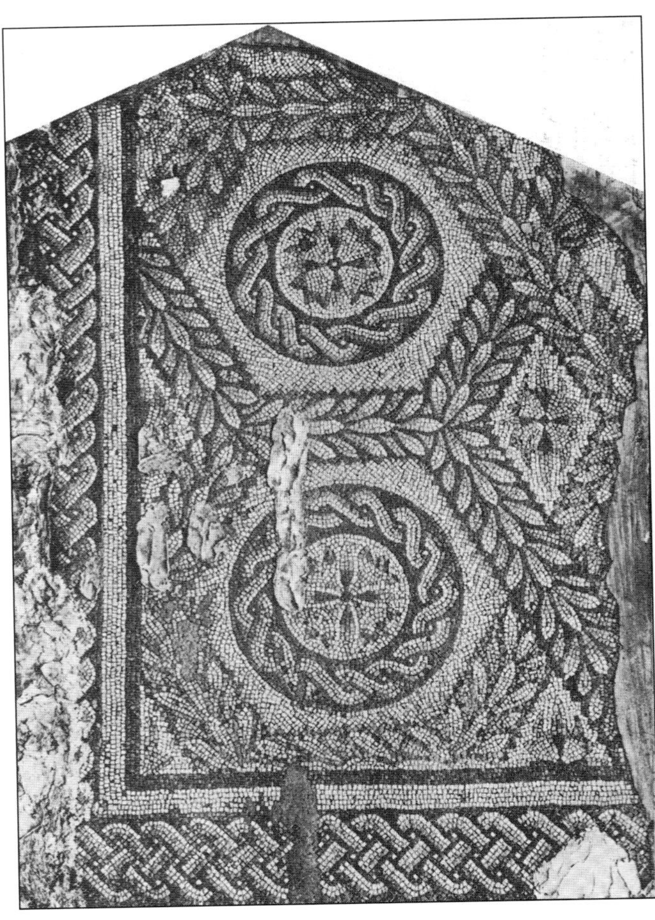

Fig. 10.10 Mosaic of Hexagonal Laurel Wreaths, consisting of adjacent hexagons and lozenges formed by interlaced laurel-wreath borders; in each hexagon is a simple guilloche circle enclosing a four-petalled floral design. Probably second half of the third century or first half of the fourth century AD.

in a line of eight rooms, and to the south-west. This seems to be opposite to the direction which Davis actually meant, given his further comments on the site (see below). Franks used the word 'adjoining' to describe the location of the room,[65] but this does not seem to be correct either. Since the alignment of the house with eight rooms was north-east/south-west, and the distance described is only between six and seven meters, the floor may have come from a non-contiguous room near the line of eight rooms. Hinks did not date this mosaic, but the order he put it in his catalogue implies that he thought it belonged to the second or third century AD. In my opinion, the mosaic pattern is typical of the second half of the third century or the first half of the fourth century.[66]

Davis found a solidly-constructed well in the immediate area of this mosaic, which, when cleared out, reached a depth of 150 ft (45 m). It was evidently of a much later date than the house with the mosaics, since the mouth of the well was nine feet (2.7 m) above the level of the Mosaic of Hexagonal Laurel Wreaths. Davis argued at length, but very unconvincingly, that the existence of this well proved that the floor was Punic. In fact, the mouth of the well was evidently at the same level as the tombs nine feet above the floors of the house, and therefore the well may have been contemporary with the burials, which I have already suggested above (p. 148) may have been Muslim or even crusader tombs. Confusingly, because it is unlikely that there were two such deep wells investigated by Davis in this area, a point marked 'well 150' appears on the second sketch-map, but it is quite far to the north of the Mosaic of Hexagonal Laurel Wreaths and not to the south-west.

A black-and-white geometric mosaic was found on the same level as the pavements described above, in the last room (the north-easternmost) of the range of eight rooms. Davis also described this room as being next to the room in which the Mosaic of Hexagonal Laurel Wreaths was found, which means that both these mosaics must come from north-east of the largest mosaic. The black-and-white geometric mosaic came from a small room only eight feet (2.4 m) square. Davis said three graves, neatly laid into the wall, lay on the floor of the room,[67] but elsewhere he said only that there were human bones on the black-and-white mosaic floor, and that two graves were found on the floor of a similar-sized room nearby.[68] Although he did not describe these graves, they are clearly not the same as the built tombs found three (or four) feet below the original surface of the excavation. At some point in the Vandal period or later, when burials within the boundaries of the city became accepted practice, it was common for burials to be placed in shafts dug down to the level of a mosaic floor, which formed an attractive and level resting-place for the corpse.

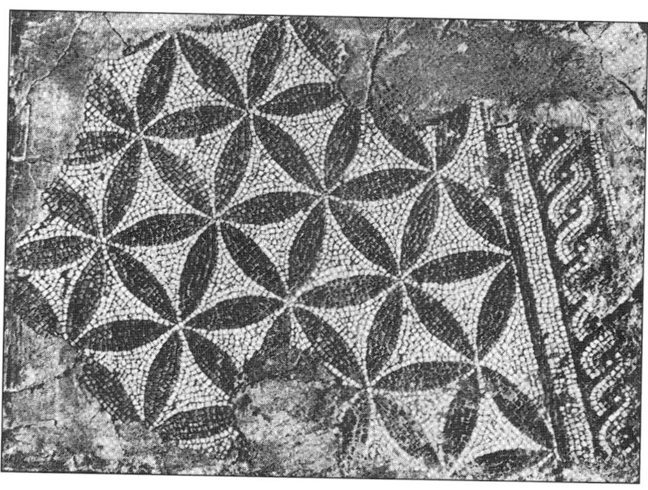

Fig. 10.11 Fragment of the Mosaic of Intersecting Circles Forming Hexafoils (here in black), leaving concave triangles (in white) between; simple guilloche border. Probably second century AD; maximum surviving width: 97 cm. An identical mosaic, found at Utica in 1881, is now in the Musée du Louvre in Paris.

The small black-and-white mosaic was lifted and packed in case no. 38.[69] While many of the case-numbers are marked in the accession list for Davis' finds registered in 1859, case no. 38 was not. Only two black-and-white mosaics in the group shipped on the *Supply* in 1858 are missing their case numbers. The other is a Mosaic of Ivy Leaves, which if from this context probably would have received some comment. The order implicit in Hinks' 'no. 10' suggests that the other black-and-white geometric mosaic dates to the second half of the second century AD. It is therefore fairly certain that the fragment of black-and-white Mosaic of Intersecting Circles Forming Hexafoils (Fig. 10.11), which has a red and buff simple guilloche border, comes from the smallest room at the north-eastern end of the line of eight rooms.

Gauckler's excavations of houses east of the Theatre and Odeon

Gauckler was to undertake extensive excavation in exactly the same area east of the theatre and Odeon forty years later, uncovering several Roman city-blocks of luxury housing. In his inventory of Tunisian mosaics, Gauckler referred to a house excavated by Davis[70] and suggested that it might be in the same area as his own mosaics nos 639 and following, which come from this area of luxury housing. Gauckler could not tell from his reading of Davis and Franks, both of whose published accounts were (as we have seen) very

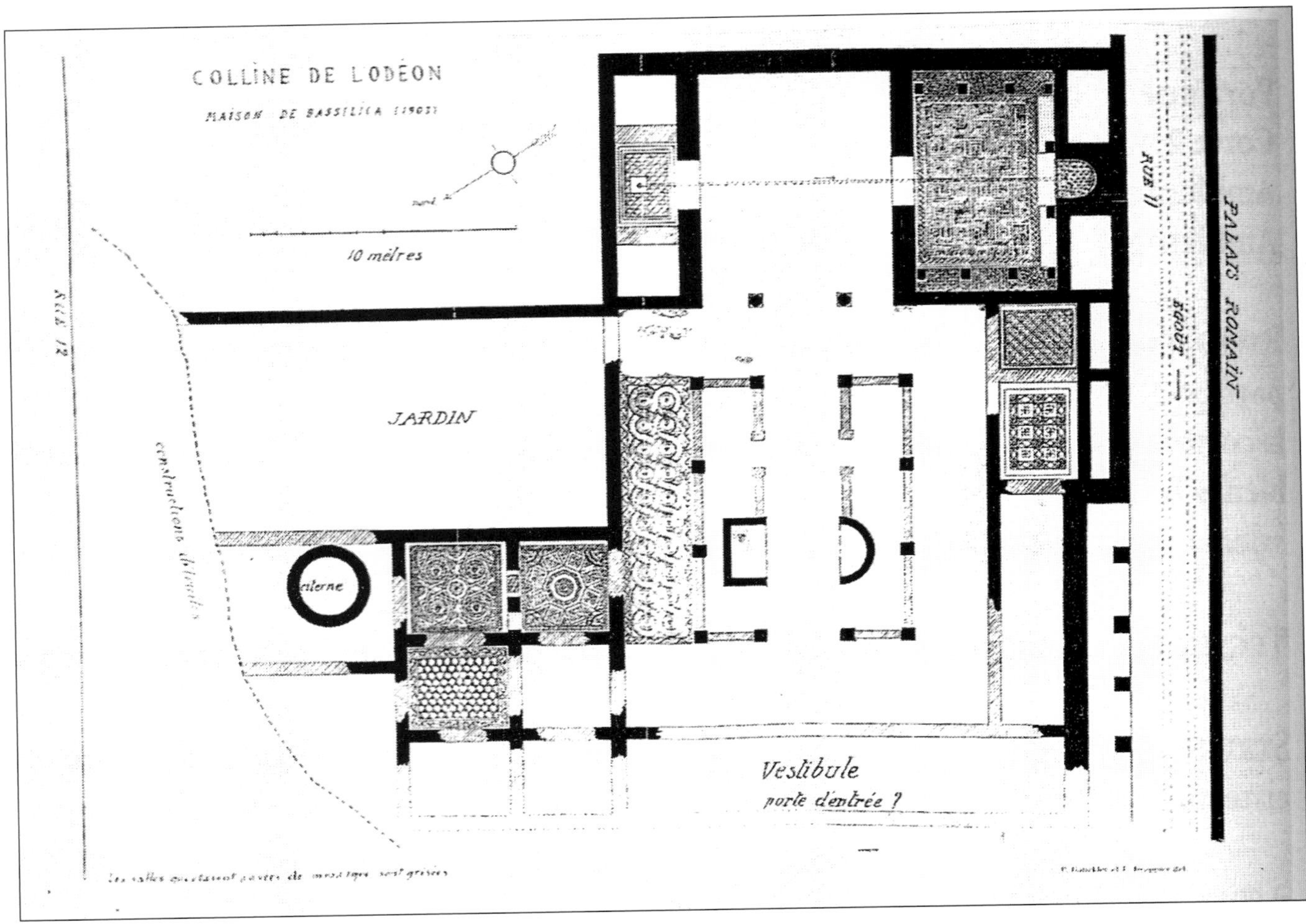

Fig. 10.12 Plan of the 'House of the Bassilica', as excavated by Paul Gauckler in 1903, which produced mosaic floors of broadly fourth-century date. One carried an inscription mis-spelling the word 'basilica' – hence the house's name.

unclear, that the mosaics to which he appended this note belonged to Davis' 'Carthaginian House' from a different area of Carthage. The latter lies on the north-western edge of the Odeon Hill, whereas Gauckler was referring to six houses which he had dug on the upper south-eastern slope of the Odeon Hill, between *decumani* 4 and 6 north and *cardines* 7 and 11 east.[71]

Probably Gauckler did not check his own inventory numbers when he wrote this note, for no. 639 is the last mosaic which he listed from the house he called the Maison de Bassilica (the 'House of the Bassilica;' the term is mis-spelled on the mosaic to which the name refers: Fig. 10.12). The 'House of the Bassilica' lies immediately east of the Odeon and on the north side of *decumanus* 5 north, just below the top of the slope of the hill, at an elevation of forty-five meters. Gauckler's statement is interesting, because there are close similarities on the one hand between the mosaics which Davis described from the house or houses he dug on the upper south-eastern slope of the Odeon Hill, and mosaics on the other hand which Gauckler dug in the exact same area. In my opinion, Davis' house with a view, placed east of the theatre on the Odeon Hill, was most likely Gauckler's 'house south of the House of the Bassilica', which lay between *decumani* 4 and 5 north and *cardines* 8 and 9 east,[72] or, less likely, Gauckler's house between *decumani* 4 and 5 north and *cardines* 7 and 8 east, which lies immediately east of the upper *cavea* of the theatre.

Although the house closest to the theatre minimizes Davis' error in placing the point on his published map, there are no close mosaic parallels from this house. Gauckler excavated it in 1903, and described it as very ruined, with only the inner walls remaining, yet he also noted a peristyle, drains, cisterns, a fountain, and particularly the mosaics of an *oecus* (a reception hall which typically is open on one side) and its two wings, which opened through three doorways onto the peristyle. The main floor of the *oecus* was laid out in twelve medallions with Bacchic themes in *opus vermiculatum* (very fine mosaic work, often with irregularly-shaped tiny *tesserae*). A Mosaic of the Seasons, of which only Winter survived, ornamented the threshold. A semi-circular fountain basin in the court opposite the *oecus* was ornamented with a mosaic of fish. The floor in the wing to the right of the *oecus* imitated *opus sectile*, while the wing to the left had a floor in which medallions alternated with rosettes composed of four flaring peltas. The mosaics in this house are quite elegant, but they are not particularly close parallels for Davis' pavements from the house east of the theatre.[73]

Alternatively and preferably, Davis' site is the house which is the immediate neighbour to the south in relation to Gauckler's 'Maison de Bassilica'; that would place it in the next block to the east of the house immediately east of the theatre. My interpretation that Davis and Gauckler both dug in the exact same area is strongly supported by the latter's description of the mosaics which he found in his excavations of this house in 1897. The upper half of the block to the south of the 'House of the Bassilica' rises very steeply, from thirty-five to forty-five meters (Fig. 10.13). The extensive mansion in this block had superimposed mosaics from three different eras. In one area of the house, Gauckler reported a 'Byzantine' geometric design of squares and lozenges as being the latest mosaic floor. The next lower level was an 'Antonine' mosaic with a geometric pattern formed of octagons made of two interlaced squares, bordered by bands with oblique markings. The design of this mosaic is clearly related to Davis' Mosaic of Interlaced Squares. In another area of the same extensive house, the latest mosaic was another 'Byzantine' pavement, with squares filled with *xenia* (representations of food and drink), a 'barbarous' mosaic which Gauckler dated to the fifth or sixth century.[74] Below this, he excavated a floor with circular medallions of laurel wreaths surrounding birds.[75] On the same level in the same house, he found another mosaic made up of large laurel garlands delineating squares, each containing a mask.[76] The mosaics with laurel wreath surrounds are similar in style to Davis' Mosaic of Hexagonal Laurel Wreaths. The earliest layer of pavement in this area of Gauckler's house, a plain white mosaic with a toothed border, was below both of these.[77]

The fact that Gauckler discovered a mosaic with octagons formed of two interlaced squares in one 'Antonine' floor in this house, as well as pavements with circular medallions of laurel wreaths containing birds as well as large squared laurel garlands containing masks, matches closely the general style of the mosaics of second- or third-century date excavated by Davis; it makes the location of Davis' house nearly certain. The 'house to the south of the House of the Bassilica' uncovered by Gauckler was certainly decorated in the same style and at the same time as the rooms (very probably in the very same house) excavated by Davis. Mosaics reported by Gauckler from the House of the Bassilica in the block to the north are also comparable. For example, one mosaic design in that house also included two interlaced squares forming eight-pointed stars.[78] Ennabli and Ben Osman suggest-

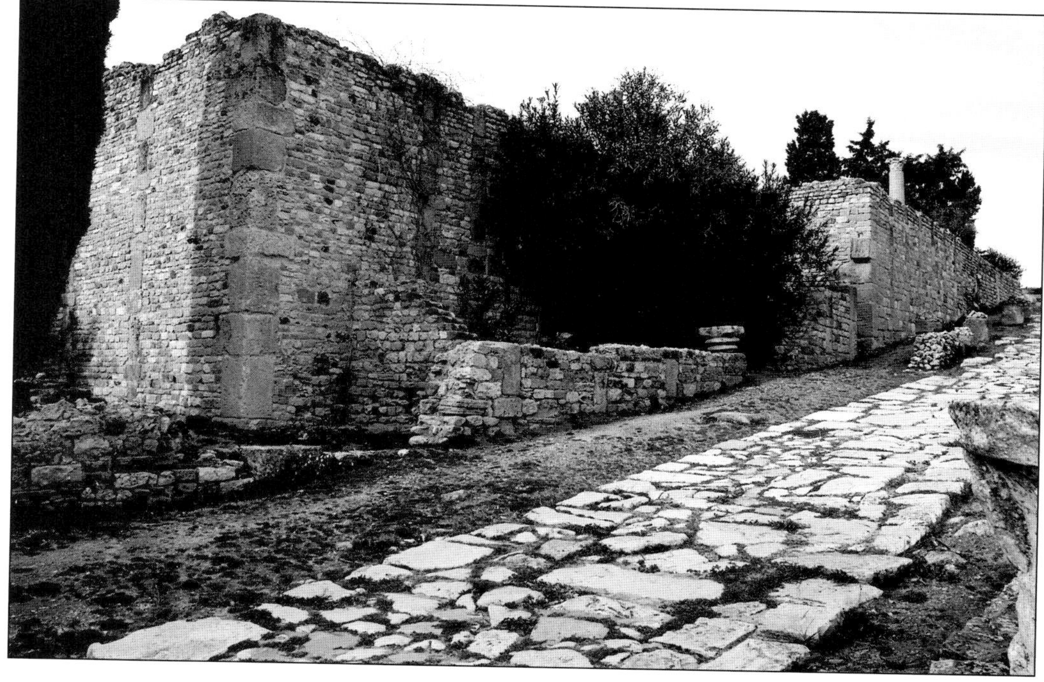

Fig. 10.13 The south-east retaining wall of the House of the Aviary, showing the steeply rising and terraced ground on which the houses of this area were built; cardo 9 *east is in the foreground.*

ed that the lay-out of the luxury houses in this 'development' went back to the occupation at the time of the Augustan *colonia*, i.e. perhaps as early as 29 BC. The styles of the mosaics suggest that renovation was general in the second and third centuries AD, the probable date of the three mosaics recovered from here by Davis. As Gauckler noted, where there were later floors, they were of late Roman or Byzantine date.[79]

Davis' twenty-second site: the nearby House with the Mosaic of Two Gazelles

Davis next dug at a site (Site 22) slightly north of the house with the line of eight rooms. He regarded this as the same as the house east of the theatre.[80] This was, however, a dwelling with much later mosaics than those in the house just described. He noted the secondary site as lying 'behind' the house east of the theatre, and about forty yards (36.6 m) away.[81] In his 'Statement', he said that Site 22 was 'a little above and close to the last-mentioned chamber', that is, close to the small room eight feet square. If he meant 'behind' from the view-point of the Hill of Saint Louis, a common reference point for early archaeologists at Carthage, then the secondary site was forty yards to the north and at an elevation about four to six meters higher than the house which Davis originally dug. The site, therefore, almost certainly correlates with the unnumbered point just to the north on Davis' published map. It is another forty meters or so north along the line of *cardo* 8 east, the most probable location for the house east of the theatre. Correcting Davis' position on the published map to agree with my argument for the placement of Site 21, the real location of Davis' secondary house site (Site 22) lay immediately on the south side of *decumanus* 5 north and probably between *cardines* 8 and 9 east. I think that both of Davis' sites lay south of *decumanus* 5 north, since the House of the Aviary lies on the north side of this street, and was shored up by a high retaining wall along the *decumanus* (Fig. 10.13). Lézine shows the block with Davis' probable sites rising steeply from thirty to forty-five meters above sea level.[82] A rectangular 'Villa' is delineated in the north end of this block on Bordy's 1897 map, above the thirty-six-meter contour line. While Davis regarded this site as essentially the same as that of the eight-room house with the fine view, the sharply-rising elevation and contrasting style of the mosaics calls this judgment into question. Franks, however, following Davis, considered the mosaics from this house also to come from what he called site no. 5,[83] while Gauckler ascribed the mosaics which Davis and Franks described to the 'same excavation, same house'.[84]

Davis referred to the location of Site 22 by describing himself riding towards 'the hill facing the site of the Temple of Aesculapius, on which stands the modern little Moorish fort called Burj-Jedeed', where, he said, his men had excavated a mosaic of two gazelles drinking at a fountain.[85] This is confusing. Davis, who had no name for it, was in fact riding on the Odeon Hill towards Bordj-Djedid; the heights of the two hills are separated by a saddle depression. Bordj-Djedid is the site of the Turkish fort where, as we have seen (pp. 57–8), Davis also believed that the Temple of Aesculapius was situated.

The Mosaic of Two Gazelles at a Fountain (Hinks 48: Fig. 10.14) lay under only about two feet (0.6 m) of soil. It looks like an *emblema*, as it is a rather small rectangular mosaic, measuring just 1.2 m by 0.7 m, neatly framed by a double line of dark *tesserae* on all four

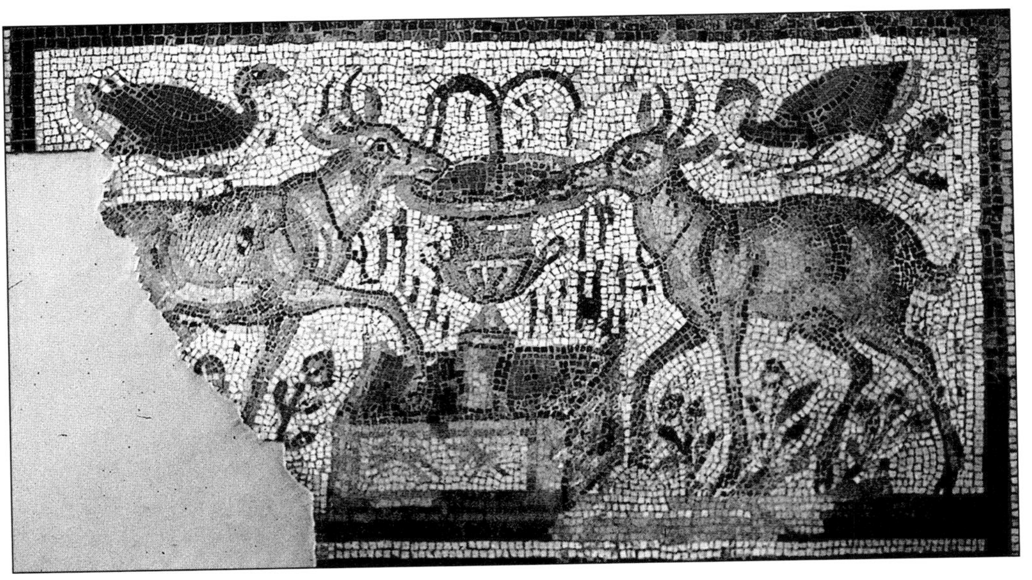

Fig. 10.14 Carthage, Mosaic of Two Gazelles at a Fountain. Each has an amulet round its neck. Jets of water cascade down from the fountain into a basin below; plants with red flowers fill spaces below the gazelles, a pair of birds above. Close parallels for such an arrangement are attested in early Christian church mosaics in Tunisia. Width: 1.19 m; height: 0.685 m; sixth century AD (?).

sides;[86] but Davis said that it was found in 'an entrance passage',[87] and there is no reason to doubt this. It is not earlier than the fifth century or more likely belongs to the sixth century; its theme has clear Christian significance. The subject matter of the Mosaic of Two Gazelles suggests that the site, if a house rather than a chapel, had an owner with Christian affiliations. Davis shipped two mosaics from this site, the Mosaic of Rosettes and Lotus Buds in cases 1, 2 and 3, and the Mosaic of Two Gazelles in case 31.[88] The museum accession-list also records these case numbers, and since the accession-lists date before the arrival of Davis' 'Statement', they prove the correlation of these two mosaics with this site.

According to Franks, the geometric mosaics associated with the Mosaic of Two Gazelles have cruciform patterns and are inferior in design to that of other mosaics from the general area.[89] However, Davis only described one geometric mosaic as coming from the same area, although it arrived in three cases and three large pieces, one over ten feet (3 m) long. The Mosaic of Rosettes and Lotus Buds (Hinks 20), a polychrome mosaic with large and dense floral motifs (Colour Plate 5), was dated to the second or third century by Hinks. In fact the style and the shaded wave border suggest a date not earlier than the fourth century. The late mosaics from this site corroborate Gauckler's comments that houses in this area have three layers of mosaics, of which the latest is 'Byzantine'.

Davis' twenty-third site: the late Roman 'Circular Monument'

Perhaps because of the frustration of digging four unproductive sites in a row (Sites 17–20), Davis once again tried a site marked on the plan of Falbe, Falbe no. 70. This site (Site 23), known today as the Circular Monument, had impressive standing remains of concrete pilasters and arches, of which Davis published a plan and an engraving (Figs 10.15–16).[90] He was aware that Falbe and Temple had excavated here to a depth of twenty feet (6.0 m) in 1838; they had somewhat thoughtlessly identified the remains as belonging to a 'house'.[91] Davis himself identified the site as the 'Temple of Saturn' or Baal Hammon, expending considerable argument upon its symbolic interpretation. The order of the sketch-map site-numbers suggests that Davis excavated at the Circular Monument in the autumn of 1857: he explicitly says that he was digging at this site in November. He sank a shaft in the centre of the structure at least fifteen feet (4.6 m) deeper than the previous excavators. Here, beneath a collapsed vault, he found evidence of burnt earth mixed with bones, and then the natural rock. The burnt earth and bones convinced him that he had found the site of the child sacrifices to Moloch, another name for Baal.

The fact that Davis dug this site is crucial to an evaluation of the accuracy of his published map, because the exact site of the Circular Monument is certain. It lies at the north end of the block between *decumani* 3 and 4 north and between *cardines* 2 and 3 east. On his second sketch-map, Davis marked the site with circles indicating a ruin, and labelled it the 'Temple [of] Saturn'. The equivalent site on the published map is labelled '[Temple of] Baal.' This site is no. 70 on the plan of Falbe, marked as a circle within a square in exactly the correct location (Fig. 3.2). Falbe had originally described no. 70, together with another unrelated site, as 'Temples'.[92]

The site lies in the north-eastern quarter of the city-grid, just above the 40-m elevation line according to the Bordy map of 1897. Correlations between Davis' map and the street-grid put the Circular Monument on the line of *cardo* 1 east in the northern half of the block, between *decumani* 3 and 4 north (Fig. 4.12). The 'Circular Monument' in fact fills the northern third of the block between *decumani* 3 and 4 north and between *cardines* 2 and 3 east.[93] The real position of the Circular Monument is thirty-five meters east of its position as marked on Davis' map.

Somewhere near here, 'in the vicinity of the Temple of Saturn', Davis also found a fragment of the 'Carthage Tariff' or 'Price List,' an important and beautifully-cut Punic inscription that described payments to priests for sacrifice (Fig. 9.4).[94] The association of this inscription with the Circular Monument undoubtedly confirmed his opinion that the Circular Monument was the 'Temple of Saturn.' The Punic inscription was later greatly to interest scholars because of its unusual content. Delattre found another piece of the same inscription in 1883, and sent it to the editors of the corpus of Semitic inscriptions. Philippe Berger, one of the editors, went from Paris to the British Museum to compare the new find with the two pieces already there, and argued that all three fragments belonged to one inscription.[95] Two other inscriptions with the same content existed in other collections.[96] Later still, Saumagne was to find at Carthage a yet further piece of the Punic price list.[97]

Davis opened other trenches in the outer galleries of the Circular Monument, and retrieved a fragment of mosaic with geometric designs from a pavement at a depth of twenty-five feet (7.6 m) in the first circular gallery,[98] although it is not clear whether he was reckoning from the centre or the outer casement of the structure. As noted above, Davis said that he went down fifteen feet deeper than the previous excavators, who had excavated to a depth of twenty feet, to a total

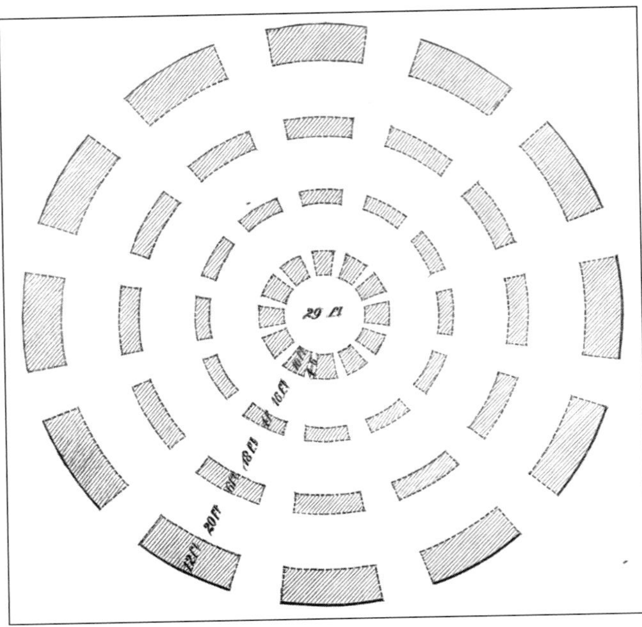

Fig. 10.15 (above) *Plan of what Davis interpreted as the 'Temple of Saturn', and Fig. 10.16* (below) *Davis' illustration of the 'Temple of Saturn', both as recorded by him in* Carthage and Her Remains *(see also Figs 10.17 and 10.18)*

of thirty-five feet (10.7 m), but this may only apply to the central area, where he reached bedrock. He found the mosaic pavement in the first circular gallery, in the remains of what he considered 'a more ancient building'. He also reported finding a fluted column three and a half feet (1.1 m) in diameter, standing complete to a height of five feet (1.5 m) above the pavement, and embedded in a later (concrete) pilaster. He took this to mean that the entire structure of the Circular Monument was originally built with similar fluted columns. In fact the combination of Roman floor and such an impressive column might suggest that the earlier structure which Davis had uncovered was a Roman basilica or public portico rather than a house, although it is not clear from his description whether the footing of the column was originally set on the mosaic pavement. After digging to this depth, he abandoned the site, as it needed too much labour to continue, and, as he said, he was not interested in describing architectural remains for their own sake.[99]

The date of the mosaic which Davis excavated precedes the construction of the Circular Monument, which is not Punic, as Davis thought. Although Pierre Senay, the most recent excavator of the site (Fig. 10.17), has argued that the monument is the *Aedes Memoriae* ('Temple of Memory') attested in ancient sources, I

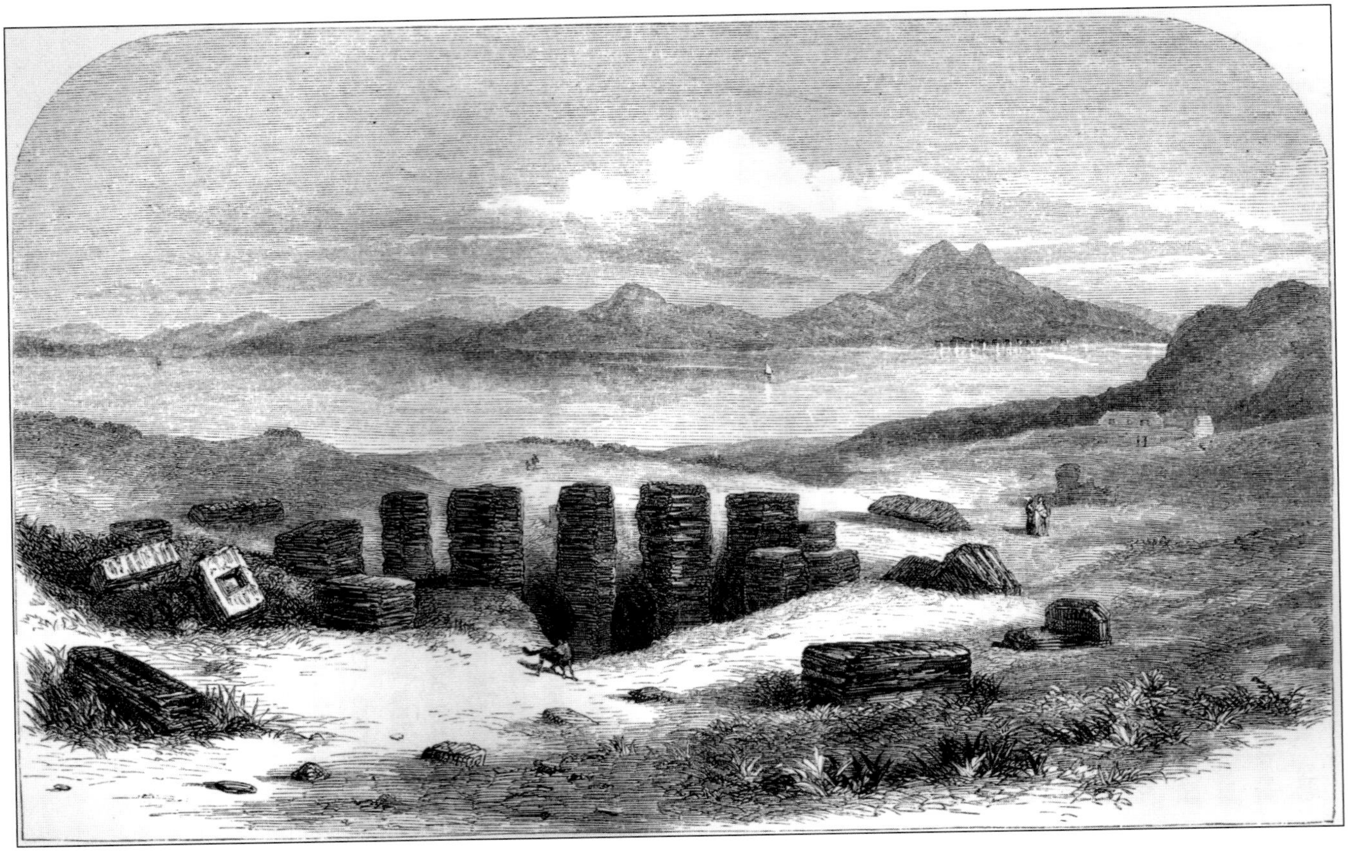

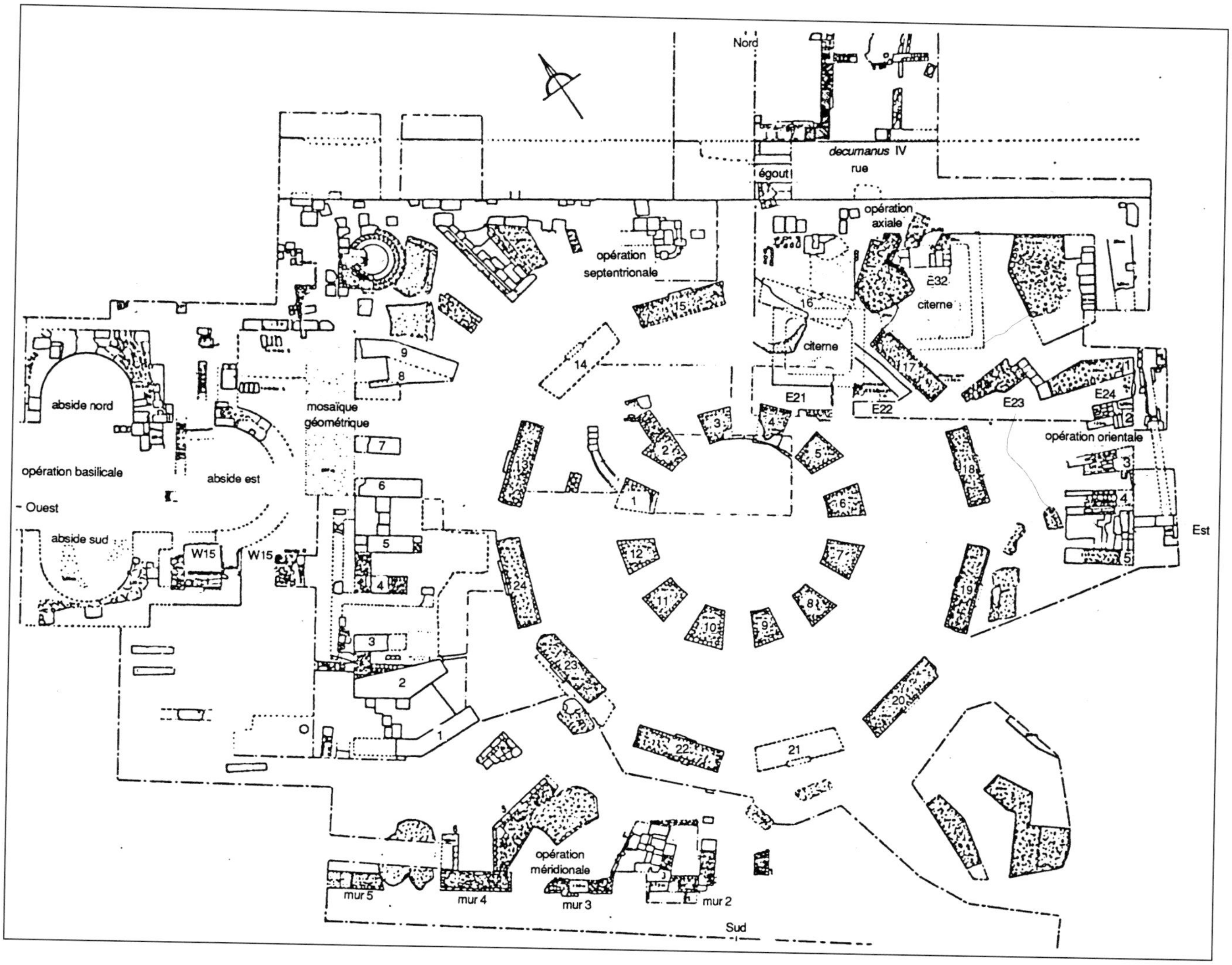

Fig. 10.17 (above) *Plan of the same building as that shown in Fig. 10.15 (now called the 'Circular Monument'), after renewed excavation since 1976 by Pierre Senay; second half of the fourth century AD.*

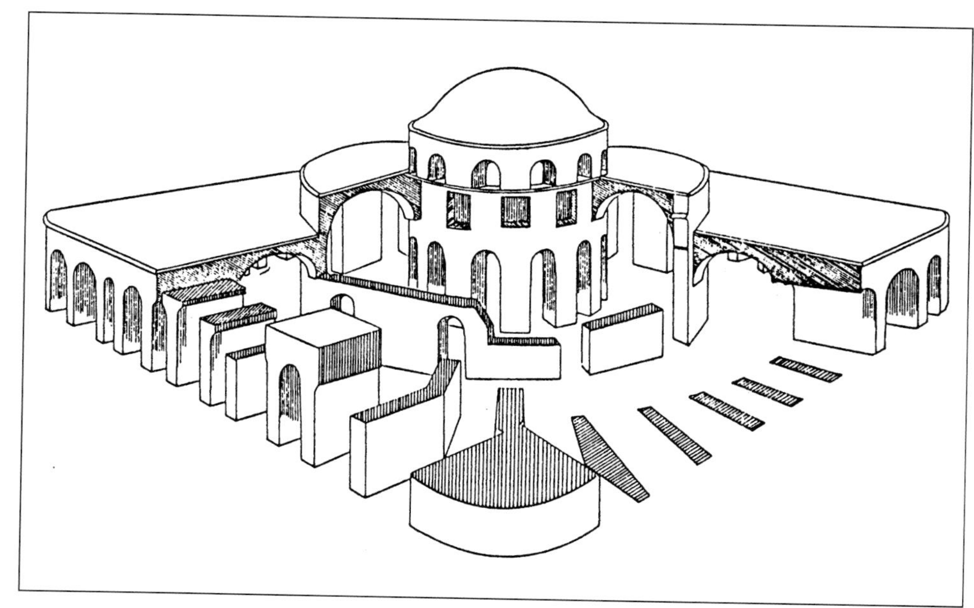

Fig. 10.18 (right) *Pierre Senay's interpretation of the 'Circular Monument' as the* Aedes Memoriae, *a building at Carthage mentioned by Hydatius and Victor of Vita*

prefer the argument of Hallier and of Liliane Ennabli that the Circular Monument is an unidentified *memoria* (a monument honouring a Christian saint), dating to the second half of the fourth century (Fig. 10.18).[100] Davis described the mosaic which he retrieved from this building only as 'a design', the word which he usually used to denote a geometric mosaic.[101] Beulé wrote that this floor was very simple and of Roman date.[102] If a pavement was indeed 'recovered' from the Circular Monument, as Davis said, and sent to the British Museum, it would naturally have gone with the third packing round, on the *Supply*. Beulé, who came to Carthage in spring 1859, could only have actually seen this mosaic among Davis' finds if it was not sent with the *Supply* in October 1858.

The Circular Monument and its related buildings cover an area of housing dating to the second and third centuries AD,[103] and the mosaic which Davis found might therefore belong to a floor of this date. There is no candidate among the collection of mosaics which certainly arrived on the *Supply* and have accession numbers in the British Museum, but it is just possible that the pavement in question is a fragment of mosaic with no accession number, namely the Mosaic of Squares and Oblong Hexagons Forming Irregular Octagons (Hinks 40: Fig. 10.19). This simple geometric mosaic with a pattern commonly found at Carthage appears to have come from Davis' excavations in the area of the Circular Monument, although there is not enough evidence to consider its provenance as absolutely certain. The floor has an outline pattern of interlaced octagons comprised of squares and lozenges on a white background. The small fragment, which is among Davis' mosaics currently on display in the British Museum, has been ascribed to 'Carthage' since 1876. Hinks also ascribed it to Davis' excavations.[104]

In 1976 Senay's team was also to uncover a fragment of a simple geometric mosaic floor, oriented on the same alignment as the street-grid, just below the level of the foundations of the outer arches of the Circular Monument but towards the building's interior.[105] The mosaic fragment is illustrated in the first publication of Senay's excavations at Carthage. This pavement could also be described as lying at the base of the first gallery. It is a black-and-white mosaic of simple small black flowers composed of four tassels, on a white background divided into squares and rectangles. The mosaic has a surviving piece of straight-line border. The preserved fragment measures about 1.40 m by 1.0 m, and the squares with black flowers are 0.40 m across.[106] Finds reported from under the mosaic included six pieces of African Red Slip pottery, two coins, a fragment of violet glass and a piece of lamp,

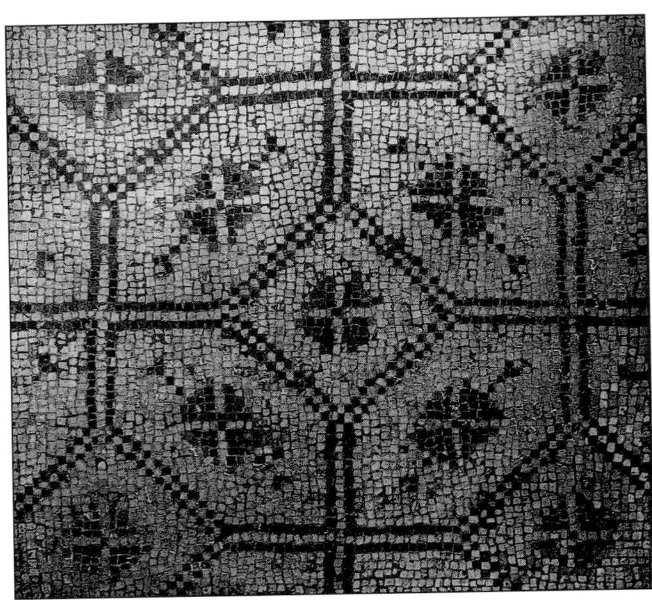

Fig. 10.19 Carthage, fragment of the Mosaic of Squares and Oblong Hexagons Forming Irregular Octagons. There are elongated rosettes in the oblongs and squares; on the complete pavement the octagons would be seen to intersect with other octagons on their longer sides. 94.5 cm by 89 cm; third century AD (?).

not further described; these finds, considered with the context, as well as the design of the mosaic itself, suggest that the mosaic may date to the second or early third century. Because modern infill was removed to reach this mosaic, Senay's team identifed it as a mosaic uncovered by Lézine. Senay may not have been aware that Davis had also excavated to this level. There is nothing, however, exactly similar to the mosaic excavated and illustrated by Senay in the collection of mosaics which Davis sent to the British Museum.

The design of the Mosaic with Squares and Oblong Hexagons (Hinks 40) also appears in a house with three geometric mosaics excavated by Senay's team just to the west of the Circular Monument in the block between the *cardo maximus* and *cardo* 1 east.[107] A Roman house with geometric mosaic floors and wall frescoes was excavated at the lower levels of his excavations in the area of the presumed Christian basilica associated with the Circular Monument. Three contiguous geometric mosaics, part of the flooring of a Roman house, one on either side of a mosaic-paved hall at the base of stairs, are shown on a plan of the site (Fig. 10.20). Isabelle Chabot has described one of the mosaics in detail; she also described the wall paintings associated with the floor. In my opinion this mosaic belongs to a house of the third century AD.[108]

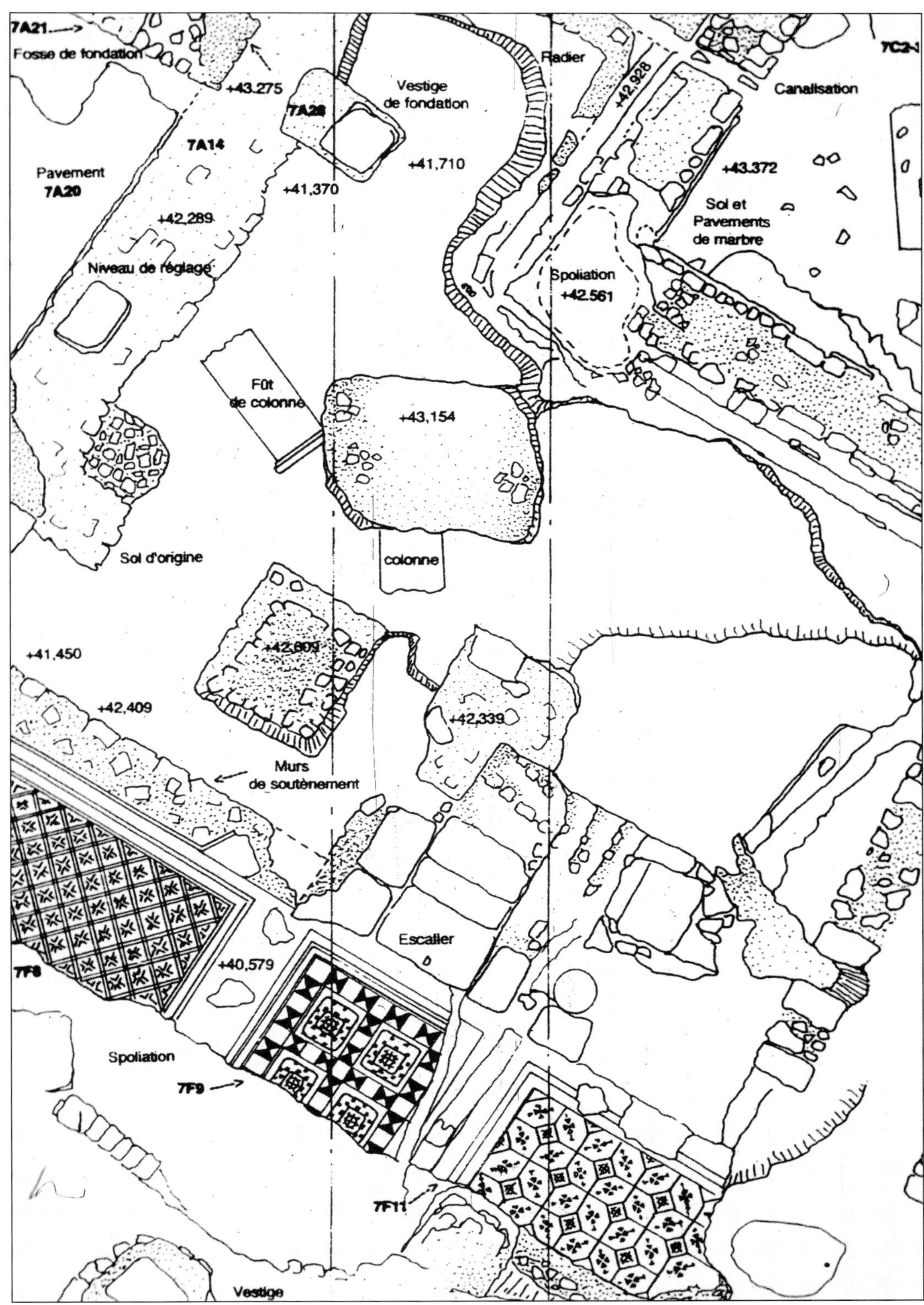

Fig. 10.20 Plan of Pierre Senay's excavation between the cardo maximus *and* cardo 1 *east*

The third of these pavements, on the north side of the hall at the base of stairs, is identical in its design and in the dimensions of its motifs to the mosaic which in my opinion was recovered by Davis from beneath the foundations of the Circular Monument (Hinks 40), although the colours may be different. The mosaic discovered in Senay's Roman house lies in the surviving corner of a room and has a simple line border on two sides. The dimensions of the fragment are about 2.5 m by 1.15 m. The original size and function of the room cannot be determined, although the house as preserved suggests that it belonged to a fairly elegant establishment. General stylistic considerations indicate that the fragment of mosaic in the British Museum (Hinks 40), the three fragments in the house published by Chabot, and the mosaic fragment discovered by Senay beneath the foundations of the Circular Monument are all contemporary. Davis' statement that he retrieved a mosaic pavement from the Circular Monument makes it very likely that Hinks 40 is the fragment in question. On the other hand, this simple pattern is common at Carthage; for example, a mosaic displayed on the floor of the Bardo museum, with a basically identical pattern, comes from the House of the Peacock in the Archaeological Park associated with the Antonine Baths.[109]

Davis' twenty-fourth site: the collapse of a prostrate column

Later in the autumn of 1857, Davis dug at a site between the 'Temple of Astarte' and the 'Temple of Baal' (Site 25) – that is, between the site of the Mosaic of the Months and Seasons and the Circular Monument. No such site is indicated on the second sketch-map, but an unlabelled and un-numbered point is indicated on Davis' published map between the 'Temple of Astarte' and the 'Temple of Baal.' It lies about forty meters to the south-west of the Circular Monument. No equivalent site is indicated on the plan of Falbe, and in fact Davis described this spot as an unmotivated test trench, chosen 'for a mere temporary research'.[110]

Correlations between Davis' published map and the street-grid put the site in the northern half of the street-grid, close to the *cardo maximus*. The point falls towards the south end of the block between *decumani* 3 and 4 north, and lies on or just east of the *cardo maximus*. A beautiful prostrate column, fourteen feet (4.3 m) long, but still well-secured by soil at its base, with a Corinthian capital nearby, was found lying transverse in this trench. While unsupervised, Davis' workmen had undermined the column and were evidently working below it when a great collapse of soil, which half-buried and stunned a workman who did not make his escape quickly enough, led to the abandonment of the trench.[111]

Interestingly, a monolithic column, 0.8 meters in diameter, broken in two pieces, was found in the excavations of Pierre Senay within the northern half of the block between *decumani* 3 and 4 north and between the *cardo maximus* and *cardo* 1 east. The two pieces, which are clearly marked on Senay's plan (Fig. 10.20),[112] are

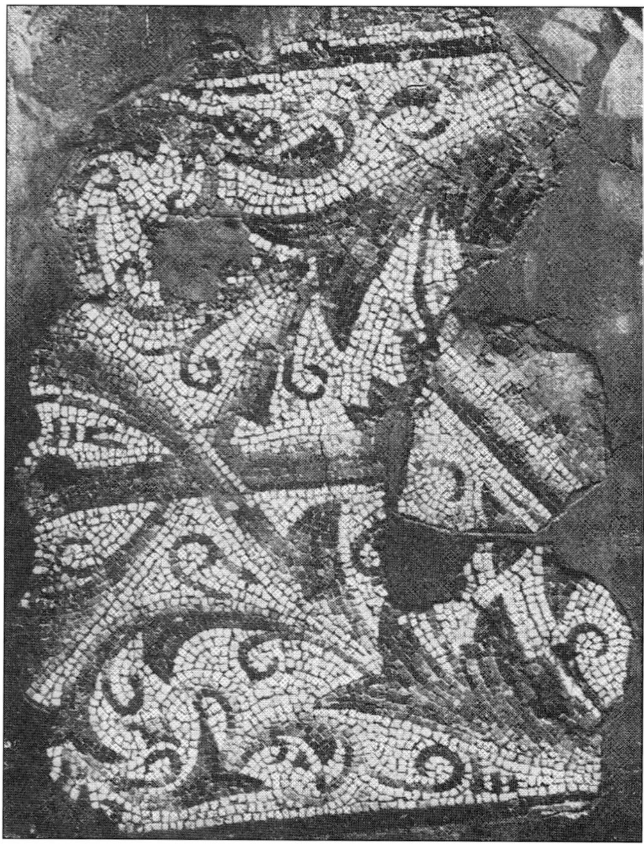

Fig. 10.21 Carthage, two pieces of the fragmentary Mosaic of Acanthus Tendrils, probably early fourth century AD; maximum surviving height 0.89 m.

not more than four meters west of the Roman house with the mosaic published by Chabot. The area may be the site of a Christian basilica of the fourth century which originally lay to the west of the Circular Monument. There are other less impressive remains of monolithic columns on the site; the interest of this particular column is that it lies at a level about a meter and a half lower than one would expect for the remains of the late Roman basilica, a fact which Davis' story would explain. I believe that this is the site described by Davis, which can therefore be located exactly: it is about thirty meters north-east of its location on his published map.

Davis said that a fragment of a Mosaic of Acanthus Tendrils (Hinks 30: Fig. 10.21), which was packed in case 43, among the materials sent home on the *Supply*, belonged to the mosaic sent on the *Curaçoa*. The acanthus fragment was the first mosaic to be given an accession number in April 1859, and the person who wrote the notes suggested that the scroll was similar to fragments of the Mosaic of the Months and Seasons. Also noted was an extra fragment, depicting fruit and two leaves, 'from one of the panels with figures', also enclosed within case 43. The piece of the Mosaic of Acanthus Tendrils was not actually part of the Mosaic of the Months and Seasons, as Davis and the anonymous cataloguer thought, because the style of the two is not the same. The freedom of the drawing of the acanthus suggests that the former dates to the early fourth century. Hinks dated both to the late third century, but the Mosaic of the Months and Seasons is now dated, as we have seen (p. 108), to the late fourth century. Davis' comment nevertheless suggests that the mosaic was excavated in the immediate area of the Mosaic of the Months and Seasons.

Davis' twenty-fifth site: debris on the south-west slope of the Hill of Saint Louis

In December Davis also dug on the south-western slope of the hill of Saint Louis, or the Byrsa (Site 25). The year was still 1857, as is revealed by an incident during the excavation in which he jumped into the trench and attacked a workman who had accused him of cursing Islam (cf. p. 72). The political incident that made this accusation dangerous had taken place 'only a few months before', in July of 1857.[113]

The top of the Hill of Saint Louis is indicated by a square double enclosure on Davis' first sketch-map, but it was not numbered as a site. On the second sketch-map the summit was marked as Saint Louis, but no excavation is marked on the slope of the hill. Davis had asked the French consul, Léon Roches, for permission to dig on the Byrsa Hill, although he did not explain his motivation for excavating there. After waiting in vain for a response, he dug on areas of the hill which were not claimed by the French,[114] who in fact claimed only the summit and not the slopes.[115] The site is in the centre of the ancient Roman city, just within the southern half of the street-grid. The area marked by Davis is between *decumani* 1 and 2 south and immediately along the line of the *cardo maximus*. *Decumanus* 1 south lay at the foot of the terrace wall which enclosed the artificial summit of the Roman forum, and this east–west street sloped downhill from fifty meters above sea-level at the *cardo maximus* to thirty meters above sea-level where it crossed *cardo* 4 east, losing 20 m of altitude in about 170 m, almost a twelve per cent grade.[116] When Davis dug here, a slope made up of material washed down from above must have obscured the vaulted enclosure wall. He dug Roman triple vaults that sound very similar to the vaults that were to be excavated by Beulé in the spring of 1859; the vaulted chambers which Davis found measured ten feet by twenty-two feet (3 m by 6.7 m) with communicating doors, and were fourteen feet (4.3 m) high at the beginning of the vault.[117] They are similar in size to the vaults at the first site which Davis excavated, east of the circus (pp. 73–4).

In 1893 Delattre was to publish an accurate map of his own excavations on the south-western side of the Hill of Saint Louis, and along *decumanus* 1 south.[118] The UNESCO excavations of the French team have shown that the discontinuous paved area (IV) which Delattre marked to the west of a line of vaults is *decumanus* 1 south, and the heavy rectangular structure to the north is part of the foundation for a temple now known to lie on the east side of the *cardo maximus* and the north side of *decumanus* 1 south.[119] Davis knew nothing of this, but he was digging along the line of *decumanus* 1 south.

Two of Davis' finds should come from the south-west side of the Hill of Saint Louis. The first is the amphora mentioned above (p. 140) which probably belonged to the 'First Amphora Wall.' The amphorae lay on the north side of *decumanus* 1 south immediately behind the vaulted chambers which buttressed the terrace wall.[120] Davis sent the amphora home on the *Curaçoa* long before he actually started excavation in this area, so he probably bought it, as we have seen (p. 48), from the guardian of the Chapel of Saint Louis. The same could be the case for the second find, a small marble slab with low relief imitating a wooden lattice. Beulé was later to find similar marble fragments at the foot of the same terrace wall.[121]

Davis said that he found nothing worthwhile on the south-western slope of Saint Louis, although there were traces of ruins above ground here. His finds were all Roman and Byzantine. He found Christian tombs, broken columns and composite capitals, but everything was so broken up it could not even be drawn.[122] When Beulé excavated in this area in the spring of 1859, he too said that the devastation here was terrible.[123] Perhaps this is why Beulé did not hesitate to use dynamite to reveal the vaulted wall along the north side of *decumanus* 1 south. He, too, did not recognize the Roman street-grid, and thought the vaulted wall was Punic.

Davis' twenty-sixth and twenty-seventh sites: Roman tombs

Davis also dug Roman tombs along the line of the road leading from La Malga to Sidi bou-Said (Sites 26 and 27). Since he said that his men were digging at the house east of the theatre at the same time as they dug here, the tombs were probably dug between October and December 1857.[124] This ancient road lined with tombs lies on the east side of the La Malga cisterns. The road that runs from here to Sidi bou-Said is a primary demarcation line of the ancient rural grid. Together with other indicators, it is clearly marked on

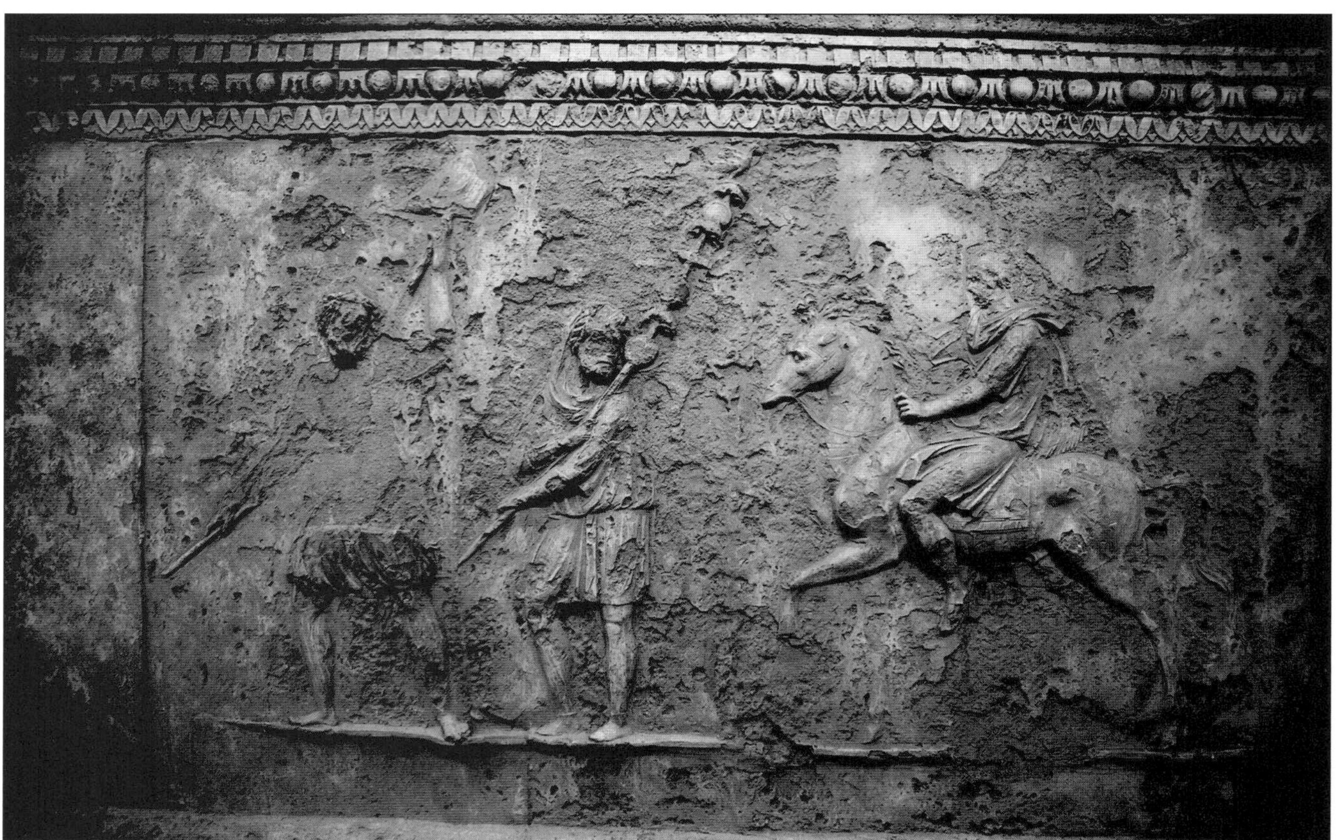

Fig. 10.22 Decoration on a Roman tomb at Carthage in white stucco, of the type found also in a funerary context by Davis. This example, of the middle of the second century AD, shows a man on horseback (the provincial governor?) preceded by a military vexillarius *and a* signifer *(standard-bearer) (Tunis, Musée du Bardo).*

the plan of Falbe. This road and some other evidence for the rural grid also appear on Davis' map. The road lies oblique to and across the street-grid of the Roman city, and defined the north-western boundary of the developed ancient built-up area, on a line from the *decumanus maximus* to *decumanus* 6 north.

Davis dug at two sites along the east side of this road, and to the north of the city street-grid. On his published map the sites are marked by points about 100 and 200 m beyond the declivity caused by the Theodosian wall. The area lies between thirty-five and forty meters above sea-level, in gently rolling terrain. Falbe no. 80, where ruins are indicated on both sides of the road, is equivalent to Davis' Site 26. Falbe considered his nos 80 to 83 to be part of 'ruins which indicate immense structures, and which form the boundary of Vandal Carthage'.[125] Falbe's points lie outside the line of the Theodosian Wall, which was built in AD 425 to protect the city from the Vandals. Falbe nos 80 to 82 lie along the line of the road from La Malga to Sidi bou-Said, while no. 83 is a large rectangular enclosure on a perpendicular line of the rural grid, to the north-east of the city. On Davis' published map, Falbe no. 83 had bcome the site of the summer villa of the Lord Keeper of the Seal, from which Davis' photographer friends took their panoramic view of the site of Carthage. In 1897 Bordy was to mark 'Roman tombs' on the west side of the road that goes from La Malga to Sidi bou-Said, not far from Davis' two sites. The latter did not explain why he selected these sites, although he seemed aware that the road was ancient. He explored an area of some 300 to 400 yards (between about 275 m and 365 m), which he described as 'an ancient "Père la Chaise", only a few feet underground, for we meet here with the last dwelling places of the rich and poor promiscuously'.[126] He was not greatly impressed with his finds, however, and soon abandoned the site, with the comment that the burials would not repay the expense of further excavation.

What Davis did discover here was an excellently-preserved Roman funerary *cippus*, a rectangular tomb with something of the appearance of an altar, at one of these two sites, about two feet (0.6 m) under the surface:

> This tomb was built of stone and mortar, and cemented over so beautifully that, when new, it must have had the appearance of a pure white marble sarcophagus. On the side, at a raised part, there were the remains of a bas-relief male figure in stucco, not at all badly executed, and at the head a marble slab was inserted, bearing this inscription:
>
> . . . . . .NIBVSSACR
> DAPHNISCANDIDAPIA
> VIXITANNISXXXVII S . .
> NIC . . . IS CONIVBIRNA
> . . . LDPIISSIMA . . FECIT

Wilmanns gave a corrected reading in the corpus of Latin inscriptions, noting that Davis had copied it badly:[127]

dis m]ANIBVS · SACR
DAPHNIS · CANDIDA · PIA
VIXIT · ANNIS · XXXV · H · S · E
NICETES · CONTVUBERNA
LI · PIISSIMAE · FECIT

The inscription reads: 'Sacred to the spirits of the dead. Here lies Daphnis Candida, who lived virtuously for thirty-five years. Nicetes made this for his most faithful mate'.

Davis' description of the tomb makes it clear that he and his men completely dismantled it:[128]

> In the centre, at the top of a square turret, or higher part of the sepulchre, we found an earthen pipe, which seems to have acted as a chimney, and to the left end, and below an arched part, we found a triangular opening, which was closed up by a brick slab two feet square. In removing this we found the whole of the interior of the tomb filled with charred wood and human bones, among which we also discovered an earthen lamp and a few coins.

He interpreted what he found to mean that the cremated corpse was actually burned inside the tomb; but, although the bones of the dead woman are no doubt interred in the *cippus*, Davis' views do not square with the reality of the temperature of the fire required to consume a corpse, and the vulnerability of stucco to combustion.

Such a tomb has many parallels, mostly of the first and second centuries AD, that were to be described later by Delattre as coming from two cemeteries, including the cemetery of the *officiales* (slave and freedman administrators seconded to Carthage from the imperial family), which was found on the west side of the amphitheatre,[129] and in the early Roman cemetery to the south-west of the circus which Naomi Norman was to excavate at Yasmina in the 1990s.[130] Figured stuccoes from tombs in the cemetery of the *officiales*, now on display in the Bardo (Fig. 10.22), and from Yasmina, allow us to imagine the stereotyped male figure, perhaps carrying a torch, on the side of the tomb.

By December 1857, only a little over a year since he had begun his project, Davis had opened twenty-six excavation sites and found a total of nineteen mosaics, of which he had retrieved seventeen. At this point he evidently felt that he had exhausted the possibilities of the site of Carthage, for he was soon to move north, first to Gammarth, which was within the area seen by scholars as part of the suburbs of Punic and Roman Carthage, and then to Utica. The next year would reveal both the benefits and the costs of his new policy.

11

Davis moves outside Roman Carthage

A threat to the continuation of Davis' excavations

During the three years which Davis dug at Carthage, he had official permission to excavate from the Bey, and was generously funded, as we have seen (p. 37), by the British Foreign Office. The situation with the Foreign Office, however, was not as straightforward as it appeared to Davis. He was evidently unaware that he had a problem with the Foreign Office and with Panizzi at the British Museum as early as January 1858. Davis dedicated *Carthage and Her Remains* to the Earl of Clarendon, and mentioned that his original proposal went to him,[1] whom he found to be the ideal interested patron. Much of the practical liaison with Davis was in the hands of Edmund Hammond, however, a career diplomat who probably did not act independently when he wrote to both Richard Wood and Antonio Panizzi in January 1858, after fifteen months of Davis' excavation, asking if the latter should be allowed to continue. Panizzi advised the Foreign Office that Davis should be stopped. Wood, on the other hand, thought that Davis should be allowed to continue through the spring of 1858, and until his latest finds could be evaluated.[2] It was therefore Wood's recommendation which gained Davis another year of work in peace. In February 1858 Clarendon even authorized Davis to hire Dr Heap as an assistant supervisor;[3] the latter was actually to begin work in April.[4]

Panizzi's lack of enthusiasm for Davis' finds was partly due to the fact that the British Museum had no space for the great influx of bulky antiquities which Newton and Davis were dispatching. The problem was first noted at meetings of the Trustees in the summer of 1857, and repeatedly thereafter.[5] It did not help that Davis did not write directly to Panizzi, so that the latter received any reports second-hand and through the kindness of the Foreign Office. In January 1858 an annoyed Panizzi told Hammond that he had never had a direct communication from Davis, and no news at all since October 31st, 1857, when a letter to Clarendon of October 8th, 1857, had been copied to him by the Foreign Office. He went on to say that 'if [recent?] excavations of which I know nothing give no good ground for hoping that more successful discoveries will be made than has hitherto been the case, then it is hardly worthwhile to continue the [diggings?]'.[6] Panizzi was not particularly impressed by the Roman mosaics which Davis sent in quantity; he later said, in a private opinion to Edmund Hammond, 'We never got anything of old Carthage and nonetheless enough from the more recent of that city'.[7]

Davis' letter of April 1858 was his earliest letter addressed to the Earl of Malmesbury,[8] who, in what was to be a brief change of government, had succeeded the Earl of Clarendon as Foreign Secretary by this date. Davis would have been informed of this change by Consul Wood. The new Foreign Secretary was on close personal terms with Napoleon III, and would perhaps have been easily influenced to see the French point of view on matters to do with Tunisia. In fact, he seems to have taken no interest in Davis, and neglected to pass the latter's letters along to Antonio Panizzi at the British Museum until November 1858, with the result that Panizzi heard nothing of Davis and his excavations for most of the year. Davis evidently did not write directly to Panizzi until January 1859; the confidential but formal tone of the two letters which he sent then is quite winning, and suggests that Davis would have done far better to have corresponded with Panizzi on a regular basis.[9] By this time, however, Panizzi had been advocating the closing down of Davis' excavations for a year.

Malmesbury was hardly supportive of Davis, but he nevertheless did not immediately consider bringing Davis' work to an end, despite the accusation against Malmesbury which Davis later addressed to the subsequent Foreign Secretary, Lord John Russell. The appointment of Malmesbury was unfortunate for Davis, however, since he cut the lines of communication between Davis and the Museum. This was especially bad for Davis because letters and reports from C. T. Newton, by contrast, were constantly being reviewed in meetings of the Trustees in 1858.[10]

Davis' twenty-eighth and twenty-ninth Sites: Roman villas on the sea at Gammarth

Unaware of all this, Davis removed his researches three or four miles (about 5 to 6 km) north to Gammarth. As we have seen, he actually moved his household as well, perhaps by the late fall of 1857. His one-year lease on a house at Douar ech-Chott would have run out by December, but he kept this house on as a working headquarters for Dr Heap.

Late in 1857, Davis first excavated at a villa by the sea near Gammarth (Site 28). The site is marked on the seashore on his published map. It is more than half a mile north of 'Cape Camart' as the crow flies. No equivalent site is marked on the second sketch-map, which shows only the second Roman villa Davis excavated at Gammarth (Site 29), another half mile to the north-west. Davis identified this area, three to four miles north of the ancient Roman city street-grid, as the 'Megara' of Punic Carthage, an area of estates that he thought were still within the northern suburbs of the Punic city, and inside the area where land and sea defences joined.[11] He was influenced in this by Falbe, who said, however, that there were only a few ruins of houses along the shore north-east of Cape Gammarth, with some small [supporting] vaults.[12] The plan of Falbe shows the shore along the coast as precipitously steep all along this area. Davis began to excavate here in the rainy season, between November and December 1857, as he dug in the catacombs of Gammarth immediately subsequently, in January 1858.

Davis found the remains of several sea-side villas on the sea front, 'built either upon arches [vaults] or on pilasters through which the sea could beat freely'.[13] A pavement with a similar design and execution to that of the mosaics at the second site was discovered at the more southerly villa, but was evidently not successfully lifted. Davis cited Justin to support his view that the more southerly villa belonged to Hannibal Barca, who had owned a sea-side villa in a sheltered bay.[14] Fortified with this opinion, Davis must have been greatly disappointed if the mosaic which he found here could not be retrieved. Forty years later Audollent was annoyed by Davis' claim and wrote that the latter's pavements from the area of Gammarth not only were not shown to be Punic, but also were not certainly from villas owned by individuals.[15] Perhaps Audollent did not believe that villas were likely in an area so far to the north of Carthage proper, but Davis' mosaic finds certainly indicate the presence of elegant Roman second-century sea-side villas at these two sites.

Davis was much more successful at the second of the two villas (Site 29), which was located on the shore four miles north of the city street-grid. This villa was the site of the Mosaic of the Muses, the first Mosaic of Nereids and Tritons, and the elegant Mosaic of the Circular Awnings. In a letter to the Foreign Office of January 23rd, 1858, Davis reported finding chaste and elegant mosaic designs 'within the last few days'. These should be the mosaics from the sea-side villas at Gammarth. All three mosaics which Davis sent to the British Museum from this site (Hinks 18A–B and 19) are fine examples of the floral carpet style, a fashion which began in north Africa under Hadrian and blossomed in the Antonine period in the mid-second century AD, continuing into the third century.[16]

Sophia Cracroft reported a visit on Saturday, May 15th, 1858, together with Lady Franklin, to the mosaics at one of these sites during her stay with the Davis family. Miss Cracroft reported:[17]

> We had to wade over a sea of sand hills – the sea before us is that intense blue wh[ich] I have hitherto seen only in a picture, wh[ich] must be seen to be believed in! We found the mosaics close to the shore, imbedded in a bank overhanging – singularly perfect and of beautiful regular patterns, the prevailing colours dark red, black, dark green, dark blue and relieved by white. They were on a flat surface, evidently the floor of a house.

Although Miss Cracroft's account does not allow a definitive identification of the mosaics which she saw, it is clear that as late as May some lovely polychrome mosaics of regular pattern had not as yet been lifted from this site.

In his statement of December 21st, 1858, Davis described the more northerly of the two villa sites at Gammarth as 'close to the beach and ten feet (3 m) above the level of the sea, abruptly cut down. Above we had only deep sands and hence nothing to guide us. From the sea we had faint marks of ancient remains, and these indications led us to determine upon digging here . . .'.[18] An almost superhuman effort was required to remove these floors successfully. Davis wrote:[19]

> It required the greatest possible care to clear the sand from this pavement and when cleared the minutest attention was necessary in cleaning it for removal. The sand which covered it having been saturated by the heavy rains, and the sea having lashed its waves over it for centuries, loosened it almost completely from its cement. With the most perfect ease might the whole have been swept together into a heap of marbles, and thus forever destroyed its form. However, by dint of great exertion and attention, I succeeded in removing it and in embedding it in its present cement. We were obliged to build a temporary wall on the side of the sea to secure standing room for the men, to enable us to reverse it successfully.

Davis gave no information about the depth of the mosaic, which was under deep and shifting sand. The fact that the floor was completely loosened from its bedding would have suggested the use of soft mortar and so an 'early' date to Davis.

Davis recorded the numbers of these five cases,[20] but they were not recorded on the Museum accession lists. Two mosaics certainly come from one particular house on the sea-shore at Gammarth, however, since Davis clearly described the find and lifting of the first mosaic, and the second has the same border and stylistic date.[21] They are the Mosaic of the Muses (Fig. 11.1

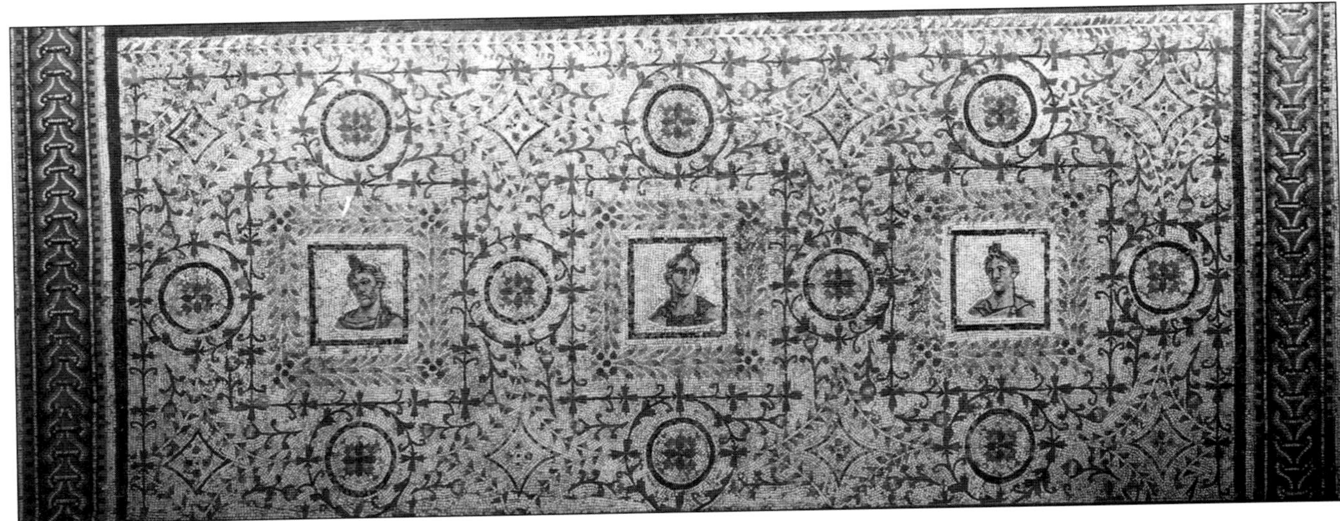

Fig. 11.1 Gammarth, sea-side villa, Mosaic of the Muses; this was part of a larger pavement which would have contained nine busts in all. There are no attributes enabling more specific identification of each muse. Each bust is surrounded by a laurel-wreath frame which is set within a formal framework of vine tendrils, typical of the so-called 'floral style' at Carthage in the mid- and later second century AD. See Colour Plate 4 for a detail. Probably c. *AD 150; length of preserved fragment: 4.13 m; height: 1.51 m.*

and Colour Plate 4) and the associated Mosaic of Nereids and Tritons (I). The first fragment of mosaic showed three framed female busts on a floral carpet background, the border a double cable. Three busts were taken up in one large piece, measuring about sixteen by five feet (4.9 m by 1.5 m). Two additional fragments of the same mosaic, with more busts, were also sent by Davis. Franks judged this mosaic among the finest found at Carthage, although he did not believe it was 'early' and noted its many glass *tesserae*. Gauckler thought the busts were possibly Seasons and the work very fine. Hinks dated this mosaic to the second or third century by the small size of its *tesserae* and its naturalistic drawing; a date in the mid-second century seems most likely. Dunbabin was the first to note that the female busts represent Muses.[22]

There is no evidence for the excavation of the Mosaic with Nereids and Tritons (Fig. 11.2) as distinct

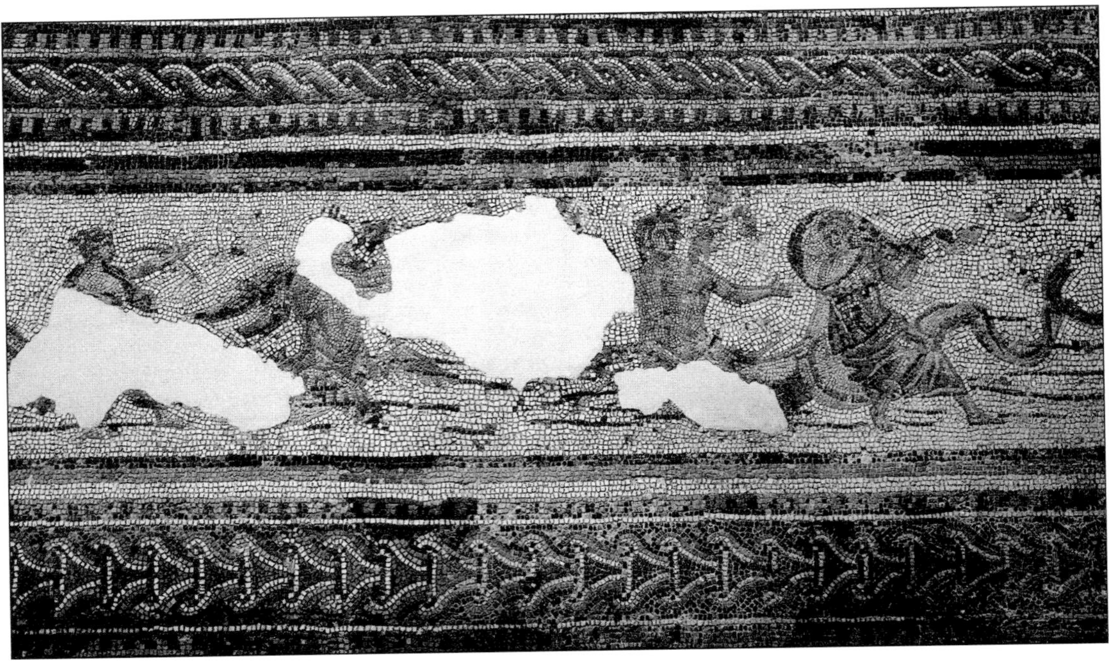

Fig. 11.2 Gammarth, Mosaic of Nereids and Tritons, detail from a long border with the same theme throughout. It comes from the same site as Fig. 11.1, and was also laid around the middle of the second century AD. Height of the figured panel: 0.43 m.

from that of the Mosaic of the Muses. Hinks realised that the panel with Nereids and Tritons and the Mosaic of the Muses were both part of the floor of one room, as they share the same tightly braided double guilloche border (with straight 'tongues' in the middle). The wide strip of mosaic has a dentil border at the top and bottom, and there are two symmetrical groups of Nereids on Tritons with dolphins on either side. Only earth colours of marble or stone were used, including dull green. Gauckler described this as a threshold mosaic, broken off at the left.

Because Davis used the term 'design' to describe geometric floors, the most likely candidate for another mosaic from this site among the pavements sent on the *Supply*, and accessioned with them, is the Mosaic of Circular Awning Patterns (Fig. 11.3), an elegant polychrome floral carpet mosaic, with a design arranged in squares around circular 'awning' patterns that give the effect of a parasol. This pavement has a complicated and well-designed border on two contiguous sides. The border is made up of a simple guilloche flanked immediately on either side by rows of dentils and straight lines. It is a mid-second-century mosaic, and correlates well with the style of the other two mosaics from the site. It immediately follows the Mosaic of the Muses and the Mosaic of Nereids and Tritons in the accession list at the British Museum. Since there were five cases shipped from this site, and the first two mosaics were packed in four of them, the order of the accession numbers supports the argument that this mosaic is the third example from the more northerly sea-side villa at Gammarth.

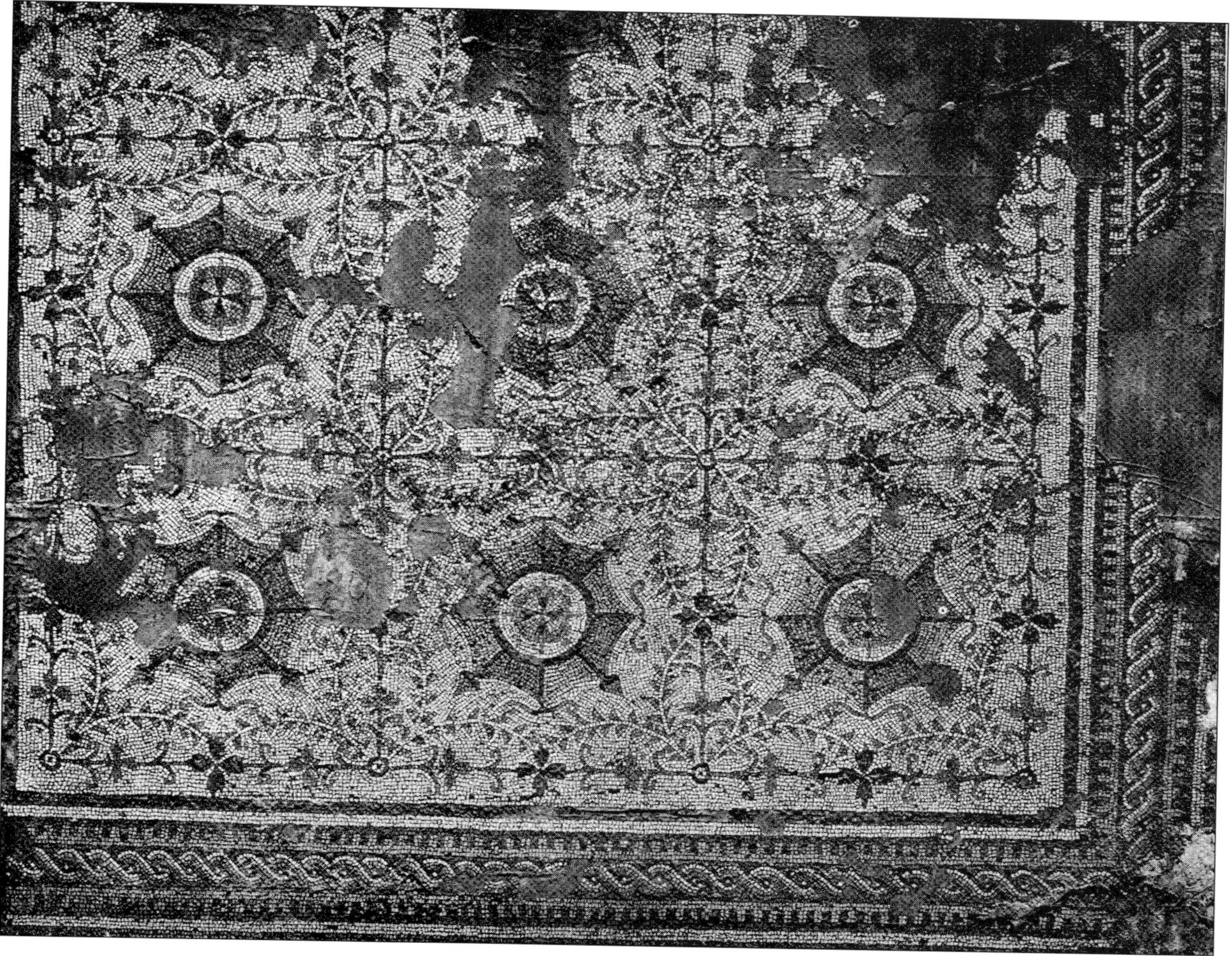

Fig. 11.3 Gammarth, Mosaic of Circular Awning Patterns, each set at the centre of a square vine-trellis grid; between circle and square grid is a less prominent concave octagon pattern, made up of simple stems with pairs of shoots springing from either side. This portion measures 2.05 m by 2.49 m; mid-second century AD.

Davis' thirtieth site: the catacombs dug into the Hill of Gammarth

Davis had begun to dig at Gammarth in the autumn of 1857, but he had moved his excavations to the catacombs west of Cape Gammarth (Site 30) by January 1858. He marked and numbered the site on the second sketch-map with the labels 'Ancient Catacombs' and 'Camart.' By contrast, the published map has numerous scattered points in the area of 'Jebel Khawi' and the 'Catacomb Hill,' but none are numbered, so Davis' excavations in this area can only be generally located.

While digging at the Roman sea-side villas to the north of Gammarth, Davis rode by the village of Gammarth and over the hill of Djebel Khaoui ('Empty Mountain') nearly every day. In doing so he noticed square apertures in the ground, but did not investigate them until he saw a hyena entering one.[23] He was not the first to explore these burials, since Falbe had mentioned tombs at Gammarth at Falbe nos 92 and 93, and said that the walls in the interior of these tombs had square compartments for the bodies, similar to tombs around Antioch.[24] Here Davis found various adjoining underground rock-cut rectangular chambers, dug into the limestone of the hills, with long perpendicular niches where the bodies of the dead were once placed. He described this area as 'the burial ground of the Carthaginians' in his letter to the Foreign Office.[25] Consul Wood reported Davis' work at Gammarth in the same letter of February 1858 in which he suggested that Davis' excavations should continue at least until his finds could be evaluated.[26] In one chamber, Davis found a wall-painting of a seven-branched candlestick (the Jewish *menorah*), a blocked niche and behind it a skeleton, which immediately disintegrated.[27] The catacombs provided a difficult challenge, as his men were very nervous of them, there were few finds, and it was difficult to make sense of the area; this prompted Davis to remark that excavation there was 'a cure for nervous impatience'.[28] He nevertheless continued to work at the catacombs until the arrival of HMS *Harpy* in May 1858.[29] In the autumn of 1859 Beulé was also to excavate at these tombs and publish a plan of one of them (Fig. 13.5).

Delattre later wrote that Sainte-Marie had also explored the tombs of Gammarth (this would have been in 1874 or 1875) and, despite his view that he had found absolutely nothing of value, Sainte-Marie had copied six inscriptions from there.[30] In 1887 and 1888 the catacombs were again explored by a group of black Sudanese boys who had been rescued from slave traders in 1876, and whose education at Carthage was arranged by Archbishop Lavigerie of Algiers. As teenagers they were enthusiastic about archaeology, and Delattre encouraged them to explore the tombs at Gammarth in their long vacation. The Sudanese boys left a record of their excavations that Delattre organized and published later. The evidence suggested that the tombs were Jewish burials of Roman date.[31]

Davis' thirty-first site: a Byzantine mausoleum on the Hill of Gammarth

Davis discovered the mausoleum with the Mosaic of Vases Linked by Intersecting Semicircles (Hinks 49) on the hill of Gammarth (Site 31) in the first week of April 1858 (Figs 11.4–5). It would have been Davis' most recent mosaic find at the time of the Sunday dinner which he hosted in May and which was attended by Flaubert and Lady Franklin (pp. 32–4). In Davis' 'Statement', he wrote: 'On the brow of the hill, toward the north, I observed some masonry above ground which I cleared and found there the mosaic packed in cases 15, 16 and 17. It appears to have been the mausoleum of some opulent Roman'. He described the pavement as 'a rather superior mosaic with various birds and animals'.[32] In his text he noted that he had found 'some portions of a pavement', with no further description, along with a mutilated statue of a woman.[33] According to Franks, the most remarkable of Davis' sculptural finds was a statue of a lady in grey Parian marble, found near La Marsa;[34] Gammarth is only slightly north of La Marsa, and it is likely that Franks meant the same Roman statue of a draped female that Beulé noted from Davis' mausoleum site. Davis said that the mosaic was lifted and sent to the museum in three cases. Although the case-numbers were not noted in the British Museum accession catalogue of 1859, the three mentioned by Davis correlate with the fact that the mosaic was catalogued in three large pieces.

Davis' second sketch-map (Fig. 4.15), which is topographically quite inaccurate for the area to the north of Carthage, shows the site in immediate juxtaposition to the catacombs of Gammarth, well inland, and to the west rather than to the north of the Jewish tombs. The combined evidence of Davis' letters and sketch-map suggests that the site of the Mosaic of Vases Linked by Intersecting Semicircles was indeed in the immediate area of the tombs at Gammarth, but do not allow it to be located exactly. Beulé, who was to excavate among the tombs at Gammarth in the autumn of 1859, described Davis' site as a series of mausolea on a vast esplanade supported by terrace walls. The esplanade was on the northern slope of Djebel Khaoui and overlooked the shallow salt lake (the Sebkha de la Soukra) to the north.[35]

Franks must have read Davis' letter, as he associated this mosaic with Gammarth and with the tombs which Davis described there. Franks noted similar

Fig. 11.4 (below) *Gammarth, part of the Mosaic of Vases Linked by Intersecting Semicircles. Between the right-hand pair of chalices a fountain flows in four separate streams from a shell, labelled* FONTES, *with two animals (a stag and a deer) drinking from it; there is a bird between the vases on the left. Underneath the semicircles are a flower, a peacock, a gazelle (?) and a pheasant; ivy leaves are set above the chalice handles. Width: 2.72 m; sixth century AD.*

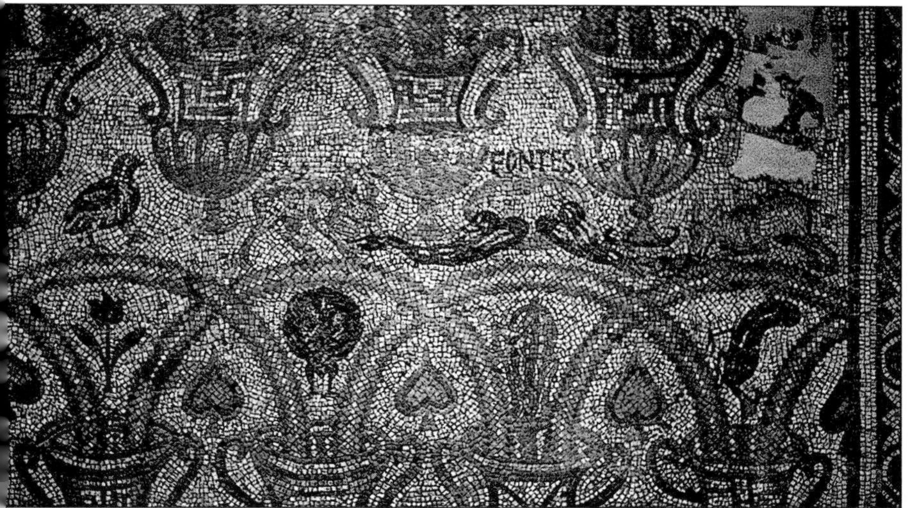

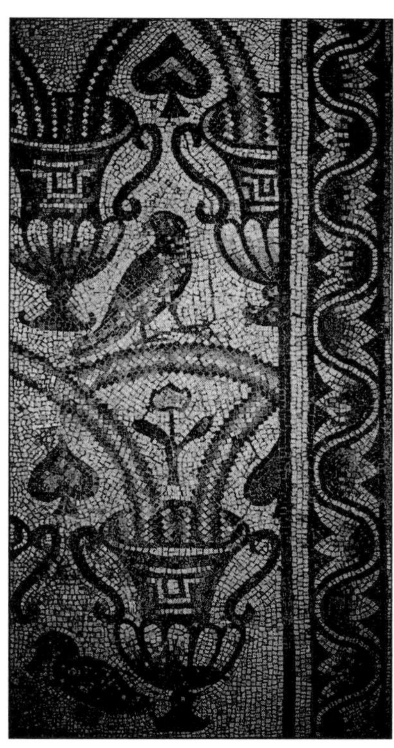

Fig. 11.5 (above right) *Gammarth, Mosaic of Vases Linked by Intersecting Semicircles, another detail, with birds, ivy leaves and a flower between the chalices with their S-shaped handles; the border itself is of trifid calices, alternately inverted, separated by an undulating line.*

decoration in Roman mausolea on the via Appia near Rome. Gauckler later described a pavement with a related design from his excavation at the 'House of the Bassilica' on the Odeon Hill (Fig. 10.12). He described a room with a fountain in the centre and, around the basin, a rectangular mosaic with interlaced arcs, each one sheltering a heart-shaped leaf;[36] this corresponds exactly to a narrow band of the design that appears twice on Davis' mosaic. Gauckler's mosaic had a border of simple lines; Davis' mosaic by contrast has a border of an undulating line separating opposed flowers. The same design of intersecting semicircles and vases also occurred in the curved apses of the baptistery of the Byzantine basilica next to the House of the Greek Charioteers; the relevant phase of that complex dates to the mid-sixth century AD.[37]

Franks was the first to describe this mosaic, which showed volute craters joined by arches that rise from the vases, with birds perched above the arches. He noted that the mosaic was not early and showed coarse workmanship; it used bright colours and some glass *tesserae*. Gauckler quoted the size of this fragment from Newton's *Synopsis* of 1876 as 4 ft 7 in by 9 ft (1.4 m by 2.7 m). There are actually three large fragments of this mosaic, all displayed in the north-west stairwell of the British Museum (two are illustrated in Figs 11.4–5). The display label dates the mosaic to the late fourth or early fifth century, but this is too early. Mosaics with Christian themes are not common at Carthage before the church buildings associated with the Byzantine reconquest in the second half of the sixth century AD. The design is not rare and belongs to a group of mosaics which Dunbabin has ascribed to a Byzantine workshop at Carthage operating in the Justinianic era.[38]

A mosaic without provenance

There is no evidence for the specific site of the Mosaic of Ivy Leaves (Hinks 12), a fairly large threshold mosaic with a border on all four sides, which has a slightly irregular scatter of fifty-two black ivy leaves in four rows over a white background (Fig. 11.6). The mosaic was certainly found by Davis at Carthage, because it was shipped on the *Supply* and its accession number belongs to Davis' finds, but no case-number was noted in the accession list. The Mosaic of Ivy Leaves was catalogued immediately after the Mosaic of Two Gazelles from the secondary house to the east of the theatre on the Odeon Hill, but the pavement does not have any obvious connections with that site. The evidence provides nothing in the way of further clues, since Davis excavated seventeen sites (Sites 16–32) between the

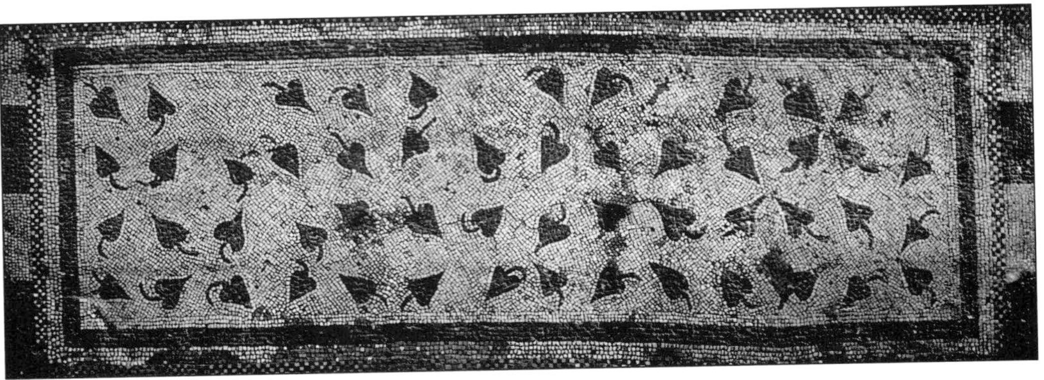

Fig. 11.6 Carthage (?), Mosaic of Ivy Leaves, with black hederae *scattered in four neat rows but in varied orientations on a white ground. Length: 2.85 m; probably second century AD.*

loading of the *Curaçoa* and that of the *Supply*. Davis either tells us enough about these seventeen sites to lessen the likelihood that the mosaic was found there, or tells us so little that a hypothesis for its location cannot be justified.

Hinks's catalogue order implicitly dates the mosaic to the second or even the third century. The style of the Mosaic with Ivy Leaves is dissimilar from the floors from Gammarth or Utica. The mosaic is also so distinctive that it seems surprising that, if it had come from these sites, Davis did not mention it. Perhaps it was excavated by Dr Heap, which might explain Davis' indifference. Alternatively, it may have been among the finds which Davis mentioned from near the house of the Bey at La Marsa, which were shipped on the *Supply* in cases 48 and 49, but which Davis did not describe further.[39]

Interlude at Utica, June 1858

Davis devoted a whole chapter of *Carthage and Her Remains* to his excavations at Utica,[40] and he also mentioned his work there briefly in his 'Statement' of the contents of the cases sent on the *Supply* in October 1858. In his book, Davis included Utica in the list of sites which he had wished to investigate, but it is clear from the correspondence between Davis and the Foreign Office that Utica was not a part of his original plan. The project developed from his request 'to investigate the opposite shores of the Bay of Carthage'. He had written to Clarendon in October 1857 to ask if he could be ferried to Cap Bon by a ship of the fleet.[41] He had originally focused on Nisua (also called Sidi Daoud) and Cerebis, or modern Korbous.[42] The first site was mentioned by Sir Grenville Temple as 'Misoua or Nisoua near the marabou of Sidi-Daood' in his description of his travels in Tunisia. Davis had a copy of Temple's account of this voyage, which was published in 1835. The latter, who captained his own boat, and therefore had more freedom to explore than Davis did, described the site of Nisoua as having mosaic floors noted in the eighteenth century by Shaw.[43] Temple himself had set Arab workmen to dig on the site, and recovered lamps, vases, and funerary inscriptions; he was particularly delighted by a terracotta of a lady in her bath being scraped down by a female assistant. Temple was following in the footsteps of Sir Thomas Reade, who had collected many finds at the same site the previous year.[44] It therefore seems that Davis' main interest was in exploring an archaeological site that would be more productive than Carthage.

The two sites are marked on an authoritative map of eastern Africa Proconsularis published in 1881.[45] 'Missua' ('Sidi Daud') is on the north-western side of the Cap Bon peninsula, more than 30 miles (48 km) from Carthage by sea, while 'Curubis' is on the lower eastern shore of Cap Bon, two-thirds of the way from Kelibia to Nabeul, and not less than 110 miles (177 km) from Carthage by sea. By contrast Utica is in the opposite direction along the coast, about 20 miles (32 km) north-west of Carthage (Fig. 11.7). The Admiralty approved the plan to visit Cap Bon as of November 21st, 1857,[46] but evidently the lack of an available ship delayed putting the plan into action. Subsequently Davis was promised the co-operation of the crew of the *Harpy* by Admiral Lord Lyons.[47] In the event, Davis dropped his plans to excavate at the sites on Cap Bon and concentrated on Utica.

HMS *Harpy* arrived at La Goulette at exactly the time which Lyons had specified, in mid-May 1858, at which time Lady Franklin and her niece noted its presence in port.[48] In the meantime, British Consul Wood had made arrangements for Davis and his colleagues to be received hospitably by the local authorities at the various sites, including Utica, which Davis wanted to investigate.[49] The ship's brief was to give every assistance to Davis, a command that gave him a good deal of freedom of action. On May 14th, 1858, Davis reported to the Foreign Office that the *Harpy* had arrived, and that he had used the opportunity to explore three sites, one of which was Utica.[50] On May 19th, Mr and Mrs Davis sailed to Utica on the *Harpy*, while a note in Sophia Cracroft's journal suggests that she and Lady

Franklin made their way by land to neighboring Porto Farina the following day.[51] By June 1858, Davis had abandoned his excavations at Gammarth in order to dig at Utica.[52]

The captain of the *Harpy*, Lieutenant Edwin Porcher (Fig. 1.2), was one of the group that welcomed Lady Franklin and her niece to Tunis, and he was also present at the Sunday dinner at the home of the Davises at which Lady Franklin and Flaubert were among the guests (p. 35). My impression is that the plan to dig at Utica was formulated with Porcher's encouragement.[53] Porcher may have had a personal interest in Utica, an interest that could easily have developed out of a conventional classical education.

It may be partly due to the influence of Davis and his experiences at Utica that Porcher and another officer, R. M. Smith of the Royal Engineers, not long thereafter excavated five temples at Cyrene, recovering statues and architectural remains which they sent to the British Museum. The excavation at Cyrene was published with dispatch, and fifty-four drawings and plans from this volume were signed by Porcher, who was an accomplished artist.[54] In the 1860s Porcher produced attractive watercolours of the scenes which he met on a tour of duty in British Columbia.[55] In *Carthage and Her Remains* Davis published two elegant nature scenes from Utica, as well as a map of the site and a plan of the room with three mosaics. The original copy of the map was signed and dated by Porcher, and the drawings and plan are probably by him as well.

Work begins at Utica

The 'halifa' or lieutenant governor of the area around Utica was friendly and cooperated with Davis' expedi-

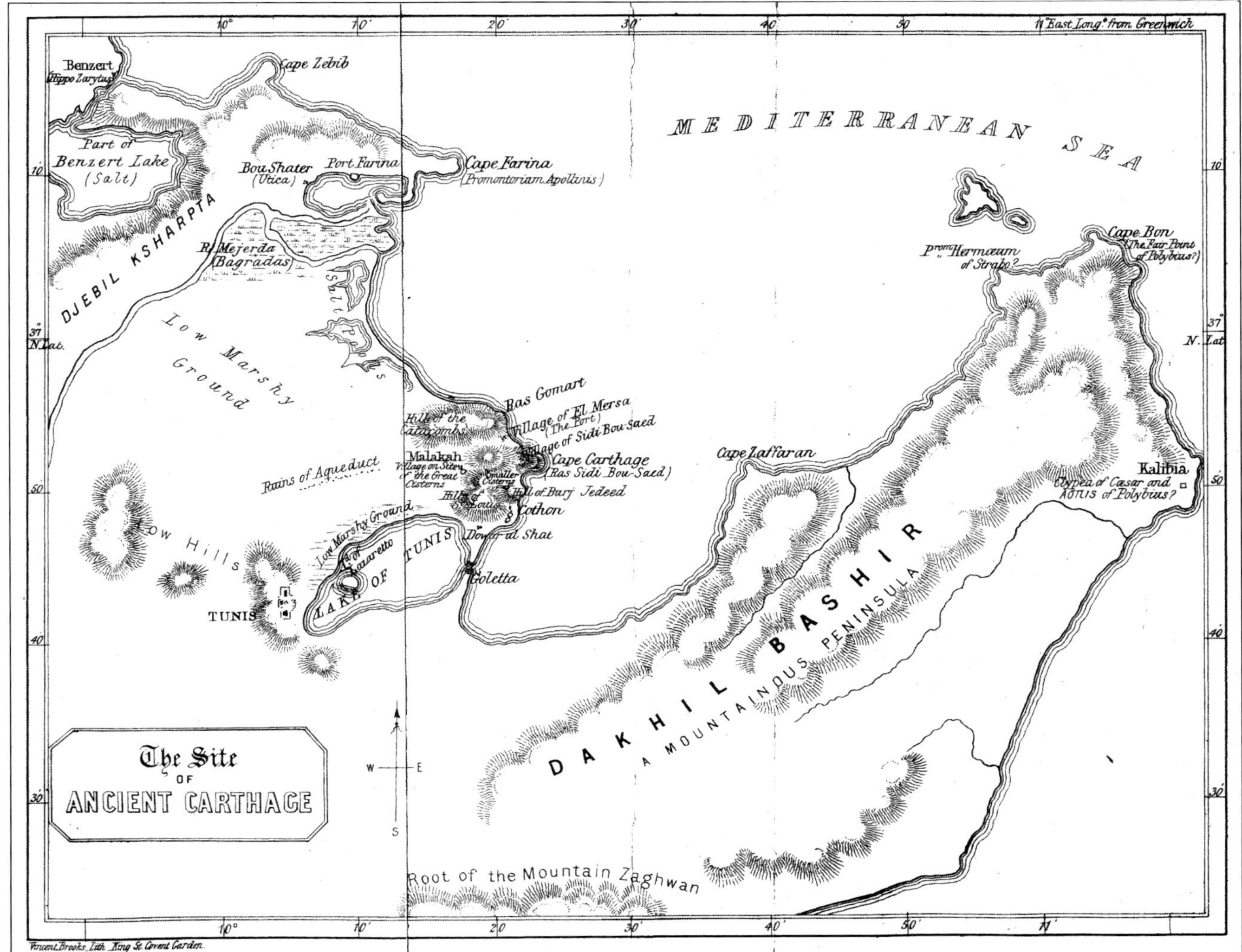

Fig. 11.7 Map of Northern Tunisia published by Joseph Williams Blakesley (1859). Utica (Bou Shater) is marked at top left.

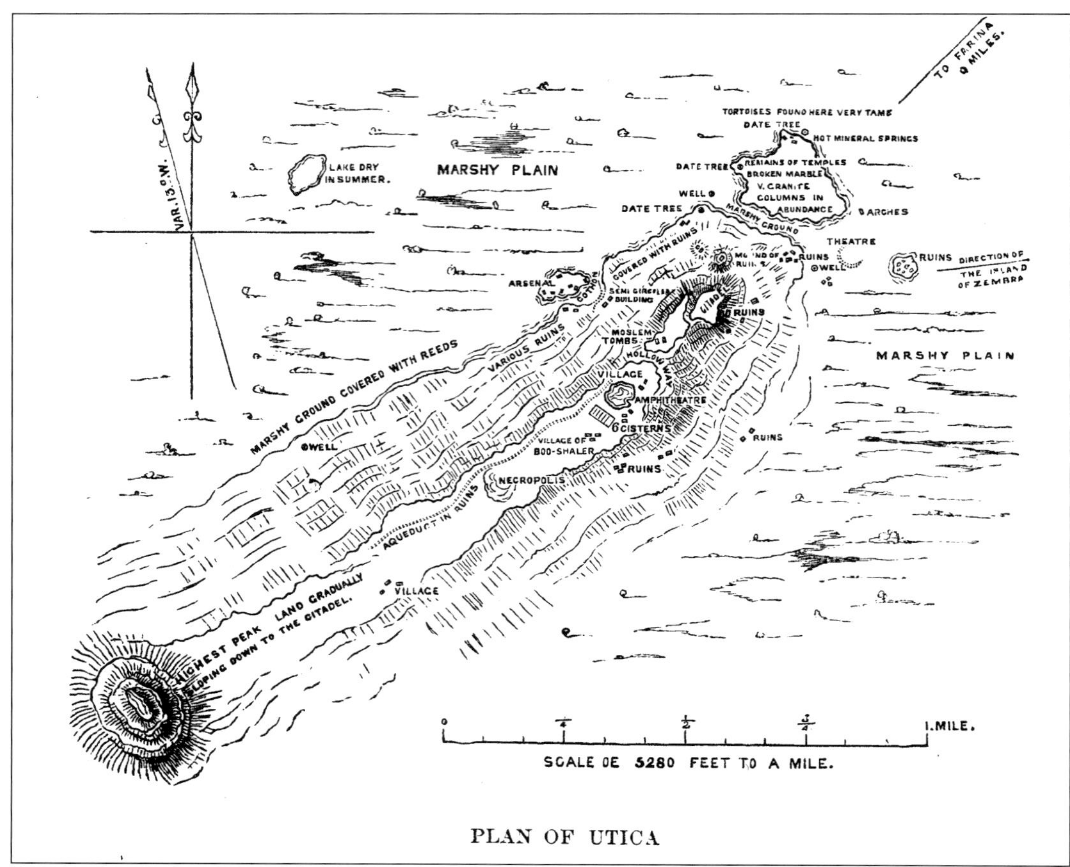

Fig. 11.8 Utica, map of the site by Lieutenant Edwin Augustus Porcher (see Fig. 1.2); the modern village is here labelled as 'Boo Shaler' (cf. Fig. 11.7)

tion; however, Count Raffo, who owned fisheries nearby, was minded to oppose it. Davis said that by the time they had pitched their tents at the site they were joined by Lady Franklin;[56] this was a little disingenuous, as he does not mention that she had been staying at his home and had certainly not happened on this isolated site by chance. On June 26th, 1858, Davis reported that he had been digging at Utica for the last twenty-one days, aided by Lieutenant Porcher and fifteen men from the crew of the *Harpy*. The boat could not be anchored nearby, and it seems that a good portion of the crew stayed with it in the nearby harbour of Porto Farina. Those who lived in tents on the site were harassed by insects, and Davis himself suffered intensely.[57] The sailors who participated in the excavation astonished the local Arabs by their strength and competence with spades and wheelbarrows. Davis conceded, however, that the British marines ate and drank not only much more, but a significantly more sustaining diet than his Arab workmen.[58]

Porcher's map of the site of Utica (Fig. 11.8) was enclosed in this letter.[59] The map, which was also published in *Carthage and Her Remains*, shows the site as a long promontory jutting in a north-easterly direction through a marshy surround. Utica had been an important port in ancient times, but was already seven or eight miles (between 11 km and 13 km) from the sea by Davis' day.[60] This silting up was comparatively recent, as Davis knew. Only twenty-five years earlier, Falbe had described the site as four miles (4.7 km) from the sea.[61] The latter knew Utica intimately and had drawn a plan of the site that he was unfortunately forced to suppress, because he could not get diplomatic permission to publish it.[62]

It is not certain that Davis worked with a map at Utica other than the plan of the site drawn by Porcher. Daux was to publish a view of Utica 'as it looked in 46 BC' in the 1860s, at which time he was exploring the site on a commission from the emperor Napoleon III; but that came too late for Davis' expedition.[63] Although Daux's plans and drawings of Utica are generally attacked as fantasist, Tissot was strongly influenced by them and would later publish his own versions of Daux's plan.[64] Since Daux's plan was made only five or six years after Davis' expedition to Utica, it is illuminating to compare his restoration of the city with Porcher's plan, and also with another drawn by the French architect Lézine in the 1960s after modern excavation.[65] Interestingly, these comparisons are very favorable to the acumen of Daux. While Daux labelled the sites he drew over-imaginatively, and freely restored the site to what he believed was its ancient condition, his plan is still recognizably of the site of Utica,[66] with the same cape, 'Citadel,' military port, theatre, amphitheatre and cisterns which Davis and Porcher saw. Furthermore, Daux recognized a great deal of evidence for an orthogonal street-grid on the slopes to the north-east of the citadel and on the headland which Davis referred to as the 'cape', a topographically natural designation, as Porcher's map of the promontory in its marshy surround shows.[67] Daux mistakenly understood the 'cape' to be separated by an artificial harbour from the second rise of the promontory on which the Citadel stood.

In his own description of Utica, Davis mentioned the amphitheatre, the well-preserved cisterns and the aqueduct. The Arabs told him that there was an ancient necropolis west of the cisterns where they often found pottery and lamps. According to Count Hérisson, the later owner of the site of Utica, Davis also excavated at the necropolis,[68] but Davis explicitly denied knowing anything of the necropolis from his own excavation.[69] Porcher marked and labelled all these sites on his map. The map is clear and well-labelled, but Davis did not refer to the places noted by Porcher in exactly the same way. On the long north side of the promontory, for example, there were remains of a harbour which Davis designated the 'Cothon', with an island in the centre 'upon which are the ruins of what may have been the admiral's palace'.[70] It is interesting that Daux, whose work did not appear until 1869, also labelled his plans and elevations of this site the 'Admiral's Palace.'[71] This is the hill labelled 'Arsenal' by Porcher. Here the remains of a very large building with a symmetrical ground-plan were identified by Lézine in the 1960s as a great Roman bath-building. Porcher's map marked the much larger 'island' (the 'cape') at the north end of the promontory as 'Remains of temples, V. [?] granite columns in abundance'. Lézine identifed a forum and columned street in this area, all on a regular grid-plan (Fig. 11.9).[72] The plan of Daux foreshadows the results of later excavation clearly enough to argue that the remains of many of these buildings were still visible in his day, and therefore also to Davis and Porcher.

Neither Davis nor Porcher divined that much of Roman Utica was laid out on a regular street-grid. Like Carthage, Utica was a Roman *colonia*, and a good part of the city, particularly the lower ground on the north and east side of the long promontory (the side away from the sea in ancient times), was divided up on a street-grid, eventually developed with Roman buildings and houses. The blocks of the Roman city of Utica were rectangular, like those at Carthage, but not as long; following Lézine's plan of the site, I estimate their dimensions at 41 m by 89 m.

Davis mentioned excavating at only two sites at Utica. He found mosaics at both, firmly stating that they came from two different sites, which he said were marked as 'A' and 'B' on Porcher's map. Unfortunately, neither the published version of the map nor the original in the Foreign Office files has these two sites marked. The only clues as to their location are what Davis wrote when he described the sites of his excavations. Davis stated that he immediately went to work with the fifteen marines from the *Harpy* on excavations

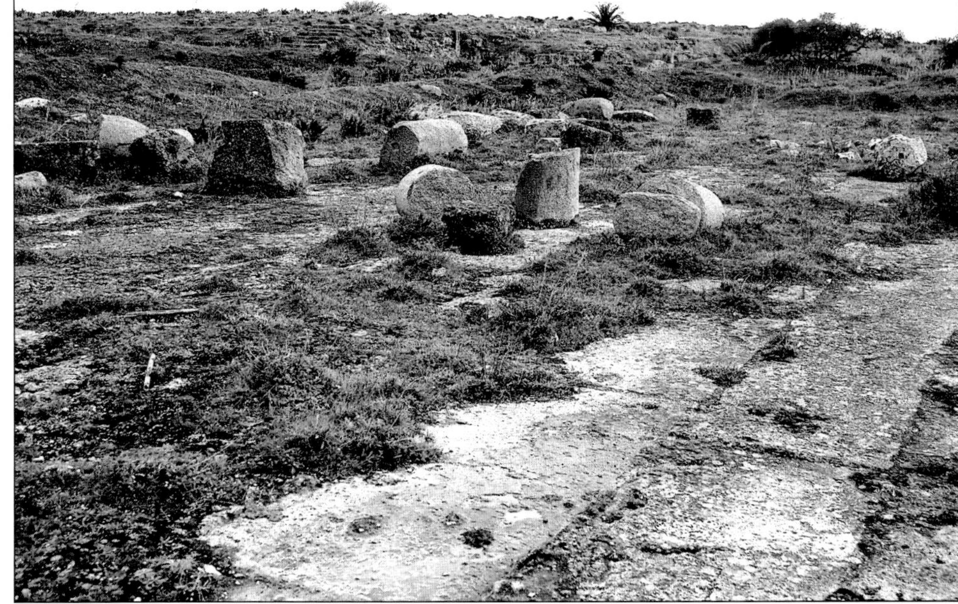

Fig. 11.9 Utica, building once paved in marble (the impressions remain) and furnished with granite columns (fragments of fallen shafts are visible), as it appeared in 2009, looking north-east. It lies between the 'temple désaffecté' and the 'House of the Large Oecus'. Although this area has been cleared since Davis' day (by Lézine), the generally desolate appearance of the site is not far different from how it looked in the middle of the nineteenth century. Renewed excavation here in 2010 tentatively suggested that this may be part of Utica's basilica.

near the cape, an area which he found very disturbed. He thought that this might have been the area excavated by Count Camillo Borgia, who had dug at Utica forty years earlier.[73] Davis found scattered but impressive Roman marble building-debris, including columns, capitals and cornices of every description. He thought that the cape 'must have been the quarter inhabited by her wealthy citizens', and that 'here, in all probability, stood the proconsular palace'.[74] This description fits very well with Daux's plan, which shows large orthogonal public buildings and temples on the cape, and with Lézine's later identification of the area as a forum and columned street.

The Mosaic of Two Fishermen in a Boat

The Mosaic of Two Fishermen in a Boat (Hinks 44: Colour Plate 7) was discovered first, after only a few days' work. This must have made a gratifying change from the frustrations of digging at Carthage. Davis also mentioned the finding of two (or three) marble heads, which eventually made their way to the British Museum.[75] One of these was stolen from the excavation site, but it was later returned after Davis had made sufficient fuss with the local authorities. He believed that its disappearance was engineered by a European, and he seemed to have someone specific in mind. Count Raffo is the natural suspect, but as Davis neglected to say any word of appreciation for the kindness of Baron Bogo, who owned the site of Utica and the land around it at the time, and whom he mentioned in this very context,[76] it is possible that he felt that the owner of the land had ulterior motives in supporting the excavation, and was perhaps not above arranging a theft.

Correlations with Davis' description of the packaging of the finds which were shipped on the *Supply* make it clear that both the Mosaic of Two Fishermen in a Boat and the marble heads came from one site, which Davis called 'Site B'. Count Hérisson later said that Davis worked at Utica with fifty seamen from the *Harpy* and found several heads in white marble on the 'Island', 'below the temple, of which one still sees the vestiges'.[77] The Count was not the most trustworthy informant. He lived and worked at Utica twenty years after Davis' excavations, and the latter's statement that he worked with fifteen seamen from the *Harpy* is certainly more accurate. Furthermore, the Count's later description of his own excavations at Utica caused a scandal which was reported in all the French newspapers, since a number of his 'finds' were not from Utica at all. They were acquired from earlier excavations at Carthage and had already been published.[78] Nevertheless, the Count's claim agrees with the evidence I have gathered, which locates 'site B' in the area near the forum, and probably in the blocks of Roman houses at a lower elevation.

The Mosaic of Two Fishermen in a Boat would be more suitable as a pavement for a house than a public building; this small mosaic is charming rather than impressive. On the other hand, even the blocks of housing in this area were clearly dedicated to luxury homes of people of high status. In keeping with this are the marble busts from the site, which included a fine head of the emperor Titus (AD 79–80), as well as a very lovely head of a Roman lady that dates to about AD 100.[79]

The House of the Fisher-Hunters

'Site A' is the only other site which Davis mentioned as having been selected for excavation; it was 'at the foot of the hill on which the citadel, the Byrsa of Utica, stood'. Porcher's map shows the 'Citadel' at the north end of the peninsula at the highest point on the second rise of the promontory, and inland from the area which Davis described as the cape. Since the latter said that the view from the hill included Carthage, the site must have been on the east side of the hill. Davis said the place 'faced the plain' and also was 'at a short distance from our tents',[80] neither of which piece of information is helpful, since plains surround the promontory. Since however early explorers saw the western and northern sides of the ancient promontory as the site of the harbours and the sea, Davis' excavations should certainly be placed on the east side of the promontory. Porcher's map shows ruins on the eastern plain immediately below the 'Citadel,' near a 'well' and a 'theatre'. Lézine's plan shows that the theatre was beyond the Roman street-grid, and it seems most likely that Davis' 'site A' was about half-way between the ten- and twenty-meter contour lines on Lézine's plan, and within the street-grid of the Roman city. If we take Porcher's indication of the direction to the island of Zembra, which lies directly east (Fig. 11.8), as equivalent to the line on which the site fell, 'site A' might fall half-way between the Citadel and the 'House of the Cascade,' which are about 250 m apart.[81]

At this site the marines came upon a geometric mosaic floor (Hinks 6: Figs 11.10–11) in a rectangular room measuring twenty-seven feet by twenty-four feet (8.2 m by 7.3 m), and as the floor was damaged, they selected panels for removal. Davis said that the remains of the wall that defined this room were very low. He had his men dig a second trench beyond the wall, where they discovered a raised semicircular mosaic which Davis very naturally thought belonged to the same room. The Mosaic of Fisher-Hunters (Hinks 45) depicts men in two boats pulling a net to draw in various wild animals on a flooded plain

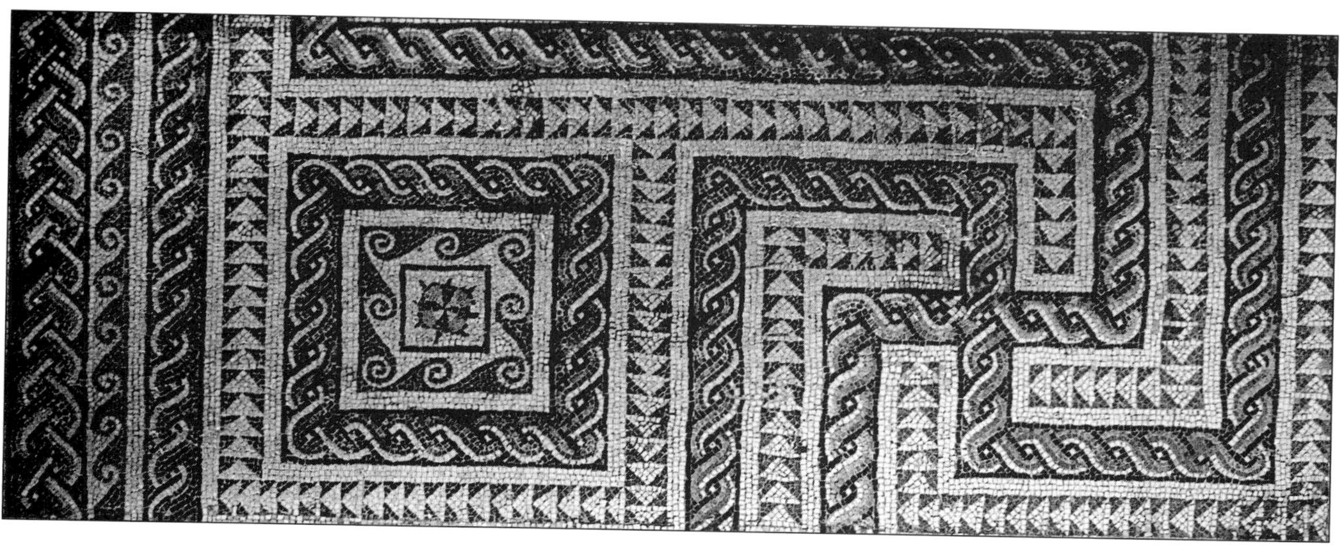

Fig. 11.10 (above) *Utica, Site 'A', a portion (2.14 m by 0.85 m) of geometric mosaic floor which came from the main rectangular room off which opened the apse containing the mosaic shown in Colour Plate 6; probably end of the second century or early third century AD. The composition is made up of spaced swastika meanders in simple guilloche, with square panels between, also framed in guilloche.*

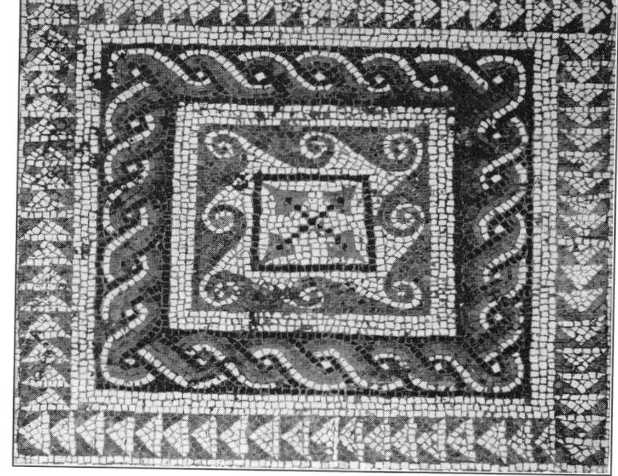

Fig. 11.11 (right) *Utica, Site 'A', a further square panel from the same floor as that illustrated in Fig. 11.10, with a different design in the central square panel (here crossed* hederae)

(Colour Plate 6). Davis wrote, in his account of his excavations: 'It is extraordinary that we should have found at Utica two mosaics, and upon each a water-scene.'[82] His statement implied that the two figural mosaics from Utica that are clearly identifiable from his text are the only significant mosaics which he sent to London from Utica.

A plan of the complex of rooms at 'site A', no doubt drawn by Porcher, was published in *Carthage and Her Remains* (Fig. 11.12).[83] The plan gives the impression of an articulated audience hall ending in an apse. This is a misinterpretation, however, as Lézine's plan of Insula 2 and the adjoining *insula* to the north make clear.[84] Both these city blocks are occupied by Roman housing, of which the most impressive house is the 'House of the Cascade' in Insula 2. Within these two blocks there are four examples of a repeated architectural ensemble, in exactly the same relationship and on a similar scale as the 'room' in Davis' complex. Two of the examples occur on two sides of one peristyle in a house in the block immediately to the north of Insula 2. The raised semicircular alcove flanked by columns is not an apse at the end of an audience hall; instead, Davis' large rectangular room is an *oecus*, or rectangular reception hall, which would have opened onto a roofed and columned peristyle. If the treatment of the entrance was symmetrical, as is ordinarily the case, Davis' hall had three contiguous entrances. They were separated from each other by massive piers, one of which appeared in Porcher's measured drawing. The piers in any case preclude the possibility that the whole ensemble is one room. These piers would have partially blocked the light coming into the *oecus*, which might have been desirable; a similar arrangement exists in the house to the west of the House of the Cascade in Insula 2, where the *oecus* entrances open to the north. The central threshold between the pilasters was paved by the Mosaic of Six Birds (Hinks 43: Fig. 11.13), and opened onto the hallway of a peristyle. On the other side of the hallway, within the open air of the

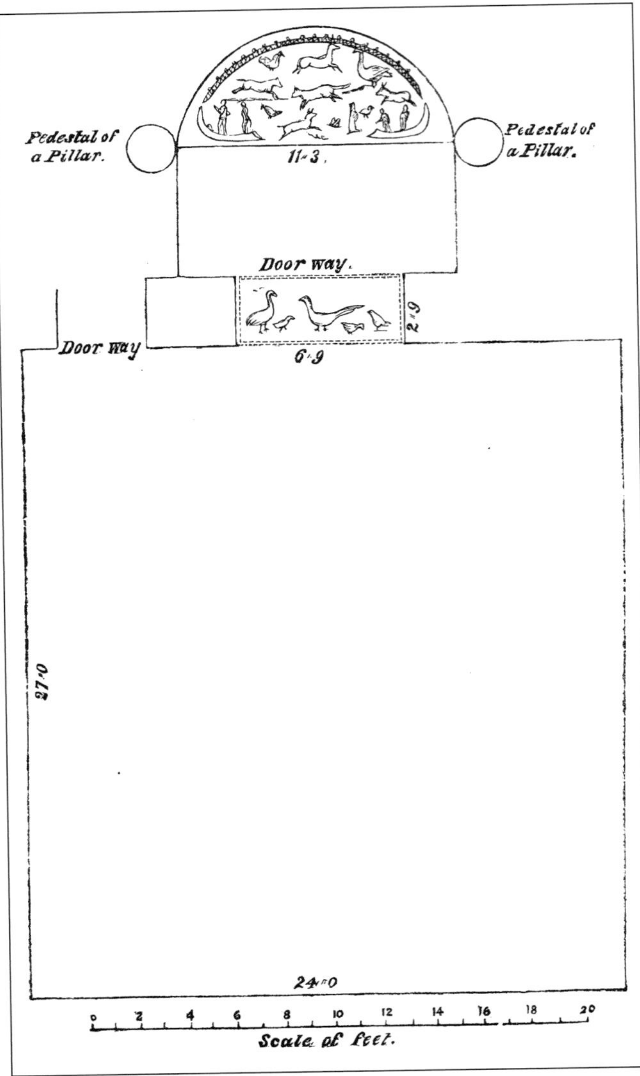

peristyle, but facing towards the central entrance to the *oecus* and aligned with it, was the raised semicircular alcove, which is ordinarily the basin of a fountain, although Rebuffat has pointed out that this type of apsidal structure was not always a fountain basin and may at times have had a purely decorative purpose.[85] The examples illustrated by Lézine show that this detail of domestic architecture is particularly typical of Utica, and it is in fact common in elegant North African domestic architecture.[86] There is an example of the same ensemble at Carthage in the Roman house excavated by Gauckler that was closest to the east side of the theatre (p. 152).[87]

Hinks did not know the plan published by Davis which implied that these three pieces of mosaic belonged to the same room. He separated them as nos. 6, 44 and 45, dating the geometric floor (his 6: Fig. 11.10), to the first or second century, but the threshold Mosaic of Six Birds (44), and the apsidal figural Mosaic of Fisher-Hunters (45), to the fourth century.[88] The correct interpretation of the layout drawn by Porcher and published by Davis explains some disquieting points about the plan and the ensemble of mosaics. An apsed room is typical of houses of late Roman date, but the geometric floor in the large rectangular

Fig. 11.12 (left) *Utica, Site 'A', Porcher's plan of the excavated rooms*

Fig. 11.13 (below) *Utica, Site 'A', mosaic of Six Birds, a threshold panel (2.06 m by 0.75 m) which lay between the hall containing the geometric mosaic shown in Fig. 11.10, and the apse featuring the hunting mosaic shown in Colour Plate 6 (see Fig. 11.12); probably end of the second century or early third century AD.*

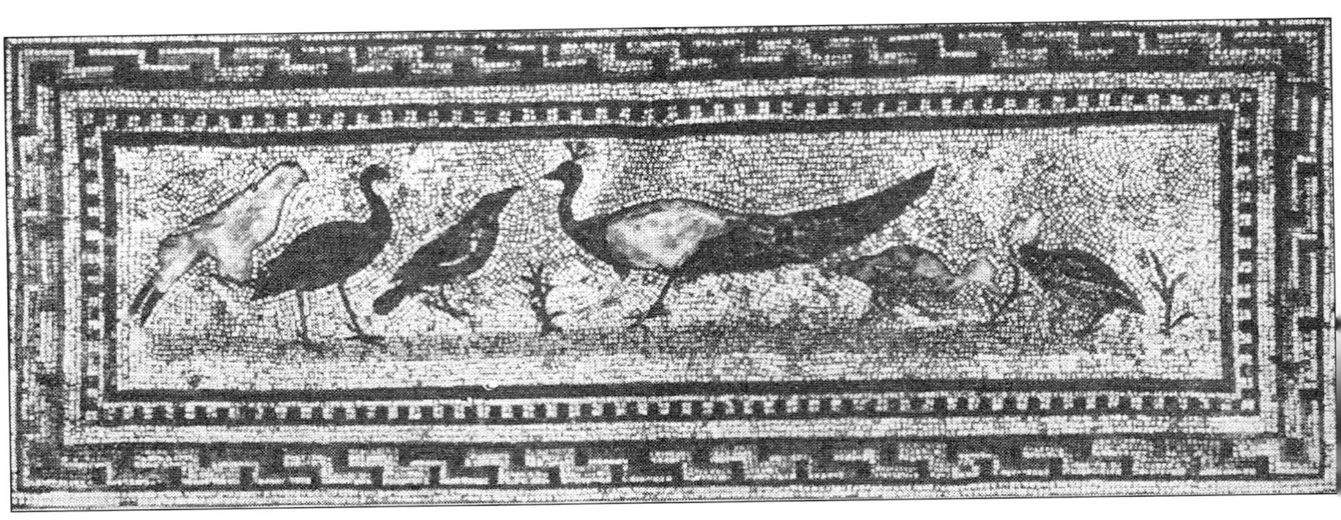

room at 'site A' has many early comparanda;[89] the correct interpretation of the layout suggests a Roman house belonging to either the second or the third century AD.

Porcher's plan implied walls running across the peristyle hall to close the 'apsed room,' but his walls have no thickness, and the columns on either side of the semi-circular mosaic are tangent to its outer edges. The location of the columns makes perfect sense if they and the raised semicircular area belong to a peristyle. The columns are slender, only about a foot in diameter; they are similar to the diameter of the columns in the peristyle of the 'House of the Cascade.' The likely explanation for Porcher's error in representing the hall as a closed room is that the two trenches which Davis described were never joined, so that Porcher simply extrapolated walls to conform to Davis' judgment that the mosaics all belonged to one room. If the intervening area was not excavated, this explains why the plan does not show any detail of the pavement between the Mosaic of Fisher-Hunters and the threshold Mosaic of Six Birds.

The theme of the Mosaic of Fisher-Hunters (Colour Plate 6) is a flood, as was noted by Alexander and her team of mosaic specialists, following Franks.[90] It is a natural theme for a mosaic-lined basin in a peristyle, the central space of which was open to the air and weather; the basin might also have been fed by running water. It is not as natural for a raised apse at the back of a closed room, which might more probably have been used to feature a statue or, in later Roman times, as a kind of frame for the owner of the house when giving an audience. Another problem with the mosaics that were taken up from this complex is the fact that the styles of the various pavements conflict. Even if they are in fact all of the same date, the geometric pattern of the floor in the *oecus* is strong and colourful, especially when compared to the threshold Mosaic of Six Birds, while the scene of the Mosaic of Fisher-Hunters is in a third, different style. These problems with the ensemble are largely mitigated when the complex is seen in its correct architectural context.

Scholars and the mosaics of Utica

A comment by a historian of the British Museum who was a contemporary of Davis that the mosaics which the latter recovered from Utica were more interesting than those from Carthage seems gratuitous,[91] but the fact that four of the mosaics from Utica are on display in the Museum today may reflect that early opinion. Most recently published by Alexander and her colleagues in a volume of the *Corpus des Mosaïques de Tunisie*, the mosaics themselves are there described in great detail, but the authors did not provide a trustworthy description of their find-spots. The site of the rooms with three mosaics was ascribed to the 'House of the Fisher-Hunters.' Naming the house implies that the location of the mosaics could be recognized in the plan of a specific Roman house at Utica, but the evidence does not support this. The sub-title of Alexander's volume refers to *Mosaics without a precise location*. Again, the Corpus states that the house was located near the large cisterns, but no clear argument supported this claim.[92] On Porcher's map, major cisterns are marked to the west of the amphitheatre, well away from the northern end of the promontory. There is no evidence in *Carthage and Her Remains* or in Davis' papers that he dug in this area, and in fact, Davis specifically noted the area west of the cisterns as a necropolis where he had not dug.[93] In the Corpus, the general area of the site of the house is marked at 32.5 m above sea level, but Davis described it as lying 'at the foot of the hill on which the citadel . . . stood'.[94] Furthermore, the Corpus described the Mosaic with Two Fishermen as being from the same area as that from the House of the Fisher-Hunters; but Davis clearly wrote in his 'Statement' that the mosaics came from two different sites.

The fountain basin Mosaic of Fisher-Hunters, the threshold Mosaic of Six Birds, and five panels of the geometric mosaic (the floors from 'site A'), were lifted and are now in the British Museum. Alexander thought that mosaics from Utica in general belong to the second or third century.[95] They dated all the pieces of mosaic from Davis' 'site A' to the first half of the third century. No doubt they were influenced by Davis' published plan of the 'room' containing the ensemble of mosaics, which they republished.[96]

A fisherman mosaic from an apse in the 'Villa of Scorpianus' at Carthage[97] is similar to the Mosaic of Fisher/Hunters in subject and style. The 'Villa of Scorpianus' also has a fine floral carpet mosaic, which Salies described as an example of the full Antonine style of the mid-second century.[98] This so-called villa is a bath-house rather than a private villa; Roman bricks, one dating to AD 126, have been found in the construction of the building, and suggest a date in the mid-second century.[99] It therefore seems possible that the ensemble from the 'House of Fishers/Hunters' at Utica could be significantly earlier than the date suggested by Alexander's team. They dated the Mosaic of Two Fishermen in a Boat to the second half of the fourth century,[100] although they did not realize that it came from Davis' 'site B', which is some distance away from his 'site A'. In addition, the authors of the mosaic corpus catalogued a small square section of a Mosaic of Rosette in Square Frame, which is also from Utica and from 'site A' according to the number (case 40) of the case in which it was shipped;[101] this fragment was not included in Hinks' catalogue.

Davis' work at Utica comes to an end

The excavation at Utica was brief, unexpectedly so, as the *Harpy* was called away to Malta after only twenty (or twenty-one) days of excavation,[102] and Davis was left to regret that a dig of a few months was not possible. The accession numbers show that the mosaics from Utica were returned to London on the *Supply* in October 1858, and therefore that they were lifted as soon as possible after they were found, for once the *Harpy* had departed there would have been no further opportunity to retrieve them.

Davis' excavations at Utica were relatively successful, for a significant number of discoveries were made in a short period of time. As his finds also provided indirect evidence for the Roman houses of Utica, his excavations could have been quite informative for the time if they had been more carefully documented. As it was, lifting the mosaics that were found must have absorbed most of the team's energies in the three short weeks when they were at work on the site. Although it seems that Davis was both stimulated and thoroughly delighted by his expedition to Utica, it is likely that the severe and debilitating illness which he suffered in the autumn of 1858 was contracted during his work there.

12

Davis' late mosaic finds

Davis falls ill in the autumn of 1858

In early October 1858 Davis complained to Malmesbury that the cases of finds were exposed to the weather and needed rescue.[1] HMS *Supply*, a steamship that had done yeoman service with Newton's excavations, and was already heavily loaded with antiquities from Halicarnassos and Cnidos,[2] arrived at Carthage in mid-October. There the ship took on fifty-one cases of finds from Davis' excavations. This was evidently done without his supervision, as he had fallen seriously ill, and the evidence suggests that he was completely incapacitated from October to December 1858.

The *Supply* left Carthage on October 18th, 1858.[3] It arrived safely at Woolwich nearly six weeks later, on November 30th, 1858[4] and at London the next day,[5] after 'a very rough, and indeed, a very boisterous passage'.[6] Meanwhile, on November 6th, 1858, Davis wrote to the Foreign Office saying he could not yet make up the list of contents because of illness, but hoped to do it in a few days.[7] In fact, he was only well enough to write his ten-page 'Statement explanatory of the contents of fifty-one cases of antiquities embarked on board the H.M.S. Supply' on December 21st. Once the statement was written, there were more delays before it was sent off, enclosed in a letter to the Foreign Office in mid-January 1859.[8] The finds actually arrived in London six weeks before Davis was able to despatch his description. His statement was then copied to Panizzi by the Foreign Office on February 3rd, 1859.

Although there is no direct evidence for the cause of his illness, it is very likely that Davis contracted malaria during his expedition to Utica. He had expatiated at length on the terrible insects at the site, which he recommended for scientific study, although he said nothing specifically about mosquitoes. In Daux's popular account of his own work at Utica for Napoleon III, he would say that the marshy site of Utica had a reputation for fatal miasmas and fevers, and that the yellowed skin of the natives he met there was not reassuring. Daux refused to be driven from the field in the face of these warnings, and either escaped the fever or had not yet experienced it when he wrote this account.[9] Forty years before, when Count Camillo Borgia had excavated at Utica, one of his colleagues contracted fever there and died of it, and this was the probable cause of Borgia's own death, although Beulé blamed it on the ports of Carthage.[10]

After Davis' recovery he was kept occupied by the visit of Prince Alfred in the first two weeks of January 1859, which further delayed the despatch of the 'Statement'. In his letter of this date Davis put a good face on the situation, writing 'since the departure of the *Supply* we have opened two new excavations'. Davis may have been depending on Dr Heap to manage the excavations for him, but it is just as likely that the two new excavations to which he referred had only been opened in the last few weeks of 1858.

Davis' thirty-second site: unrecorded excavations at La Marsa

Finds from one more excavation site, for which almost no information was recorded, went with the *Supply*. In his 'Statement' Davis said that the materials shipped on the *Supply* in Cases 48 and 49 were found at La Marsa near the Bey's palace.[11] There is no mention of this site elsewhere in Davis' book or letters, which may suggest that he himself did not excavate it. Could the Bey have decided to try his hand at excavation? Or were these perhaps chance finds? In his 'Statement' Davis noted the finds from La Marsa immediately after those from Utica, and since the cases came on the *Supply* they must have been packed before October 1858. La Marsa was inside the suburbs of Roman Carthage, as a number of later finds have shown: for example, a stucco tomb with a Roman lady in three scenes was discovered March 15, 1883, and Charles Tissot had earlier acquired a fine marble statue of Venus which was recovered from a well at La Marsa.[12]

The visit of Prince Alfred

At about the same time that Davis' recovery from his illness was complete, and when he had evidently returned to excavation with full vigour, Prince Alfred's ship, HMS *Euryalus*, appeared before Carthage.[13] This must have been a very exciting event for Davis as the date, January 2nd, 1859, is the only complete date which he supplied in *Carthage and Her Remains*. In January of 1859, Prince Alfred, Queen Victoria's fourth child and second son, was fourteen years old and had been a midshipman in the Royal Navy for only a few months.[14] Alfred was an attractive, intelligent and healthy teenager, whose love of ships and the sea was marked from babyhood. HMS *Euryalus*, his first posting, was a large steam frigate armed with fifty guns. The *Euryalus* cruised the Mediterranean for over a year and the visit to Carthage was intended as an educational experience for the prince in a year in which he also visited Gibraltar, Morocco, Malta, Egypt, Palestine and Syria. His travels were followed avidly at home. Alfred lived a double life during this time, in training as a naval officer on board, but receiving full military honours at every port.[15]

The prince told Consul Wood that a visit to Carthage was an important purpose of his journey and he stayed in the area of Tunis until January 15th. When Prince Alfred spent a long day touring the site of Carthage with Davis a few days after his arrival, Davis' workmen had just cleared the three sirens in the Mosaic of the Sirens (Hinks 46), which Davis described as being in the area of the 'Temple of Astarte.' As we have seen, however (p. 58), he defined the area of the 'Temple of Astarte' extremely loosely. One side of the Vandal Hunting Mosaic (Hinks 57) had also been cleared and was seen by the prince. On the following day, Davis accompanied the prince and his suite to Oudna.[16] After the Prince's visit, Davis settled back into his regular archaeological occupations, and half the mosaic chamber at the 'Temple of Astarte' was cleared, revealing more of the Vandal Hunting Mosaic.

In Davis' letter to the Foreign Office of January 15th, 1859, he reported continued success and a new find of 'an edifice of some importance, and in all probability a temple [Davis' usual but mistaken interpretation]. We have already discovered several figures in mosaic, one of which will throw some light on the architecture of the Carthaginians and the other on their dress and habits'. This was the find of the Vandal Hunting Mosaic, which Davis noted was first discovered just before the visit of Prince Alfred.

The Foreign Office attempts to close Davis' excavations

In January 1859, Davis wrote directly to Panizzi for the first time, complaining that Malmesbury was ignoring his letters.[17] Thus alerted, Panizzi borrowed Davis' letters of that year from the Foreign Office and placed them before the Trustees. Quite by chance, Davis had written to Panizzi for the first time immediately after the latter had again advised Hammond that Davis' work should be brought to an end. At this moment Davis was probably suffering from too high an estimate of his own importance, having spent the first two weeks of January introducing young Prince Alfred to the attractions of archaeology.

Panizzi's complaint was that Davis had produced no Punic material but more than enough Roman finds, and he was concerned also about the expense incurred by the government.[18] This time the Foreign Office acted immediately, sending a letter to Consul Wood on January 22nd, 1859, asking him to give Davis his notice, which Wood did around the end of January.[19] The directions to Davis to quit, delivered in a way that was insulting and unappreciative, crossed with his own letters reporting on the important work accomplished with the shipping of fifty-one cases of finds on the *Supply*. For Davis, Wood's news must have been a serious shock.

On February 12th, 1859, Consul Wood reported back to the Foreign Office that he had followed his instructions, but had found that Davis was not completely cooperative. Although Davis sent home most of his workmen, he thought that the commencement of the excavations of the French archaeologist, Charles Beulé, at the very same moment as he had received Wood's directive, made this an ill-starred time for him to quit.[20] Edmund Hammond at the Foreign Office realized that the method used to bring Davis' excavations to an end was not appropriate, and he wrote a more polite and appreciative letter to Davis for Malmesbury's signature.[21]

Although Davis blamed his summary cashiering on Malmesbury, and said so when he later wrote to Lord John Russell, the next Foreign Secretary, the decision against him had really been made by Hammond and Panizzi. As mentioned above (p. 162), Hammond solicited a letter from Panizzi for his opinion of Davis' work already in January 1858, at which time Panizzi replied that 'it is hardly worthwhile to continue'.[22] Hammond then went to Wood, who said that Davis had collected forty cases of objects, and while it was Wood's opinion that much of the material other than the mosaics and Punic inscriptions might not be very important, he suggested that the finds should be evaluated by experts, and that he should be allowed to excavate until the spring of 1858 in order to give him a fair trial.[23] Davis was then allowed to continue, almost certainly without any word of these exchanges reaching his own ears.

Hammond was again soliciting Panizzi's opinion a year later, in January 1859, and Panizzi said, 'The excavations at Carthage ought to be put an end to . . . We never got anything of old Carthage and nonetheless enough from the more recent [finds?] of that city'.[24] Despite the fact that the cases from the *Supply* had not been opened at this point, it is clear that Panizzi felt that Davis had done enough in principle, especially considering the costs, and would have been unmoved by the new finds.

There was probably no special animus against Davis and his finds in this decision. Lack of space was a great problem for the Museum, with the overwhelming number of finds coming in from C. T. Newton at Halicarnassos and Cnidos,[25] as well as the smaller number of cases from Davis. In fact, Newton received instructions from Malmesbury to bring his own excavations to a close very shortly after Davis did.[26] Newton was still packing up finds in May 1859, while awaiting the arrival of the *Supply*, but declared himself quite relieved to return to England 'after three years of rough life on the coast of Asia Minor'. On the other hand, Newton was looking forward to a new diplomatic post, the consulship at Rome.[27]

Franks therefore believed that Davis' excavations ended in 1858 and that the materials which arrived on the *Supply*, which he included in his article published in 1860, completed the collection excavated by Davis.[28] The Mosaic of the Sirens, the Vandal Hunting Mosaic and the second Mosaic of Nereids and Tritons (Hinks nos 17A–B) were not treated in Franks' 1860 article, as the latter had evidently not heard of them. He may have been aware that Davis had been ordered to bring his excavations to a close by Malmesbury before February 12th, 1859, the date of a meeting of the Trustees at which a letter was read which had been written by Davis to Panizzi complaining of the fact. In this letter Davis had in fact said that, while he had dismissed the majority of his workmen, he intended to continue limited excavation.[29]

Davis therefore ignored Malmesbury's letter and continued his third year with more digging at Carthage in the general area of the 'Temple of Astarte'. The Vandal Hunting Mosaic, excavated from January 1859 onwards, and the second Mosaic of Nereids and Tritons, excavated subsequently, did not arrive at the Museum until 1860, and were not given accession numbers until October 2nd, 1860. Since the Mosaic of the Sirens was being dug at the same time as the Vandal Hunting Mosaic, it should have reached the Museum in the same lot, but it was evidently not given an accession number either then or afterwards. Eighty years later, when Hinks catalogued the mosaics from Carthage, he was not aware that the Mosaic of the Sirens was certainly from Carthage and among Davis' finds there.[30] The result of all this was that the last year of Davis' excavations was by far the most poorly documented, despite the importance of the finds.

Davis' thirty-third site: the Roman Mosaic of the Sirens

Davis' workmen came upon the Mosaic of the Sirens (Hinks 46: Fig. 12.1) just at the time of the visit of Prince Alfred, who saw part of it being unearthed in early January 1859. The scene shows three Sirens sur-

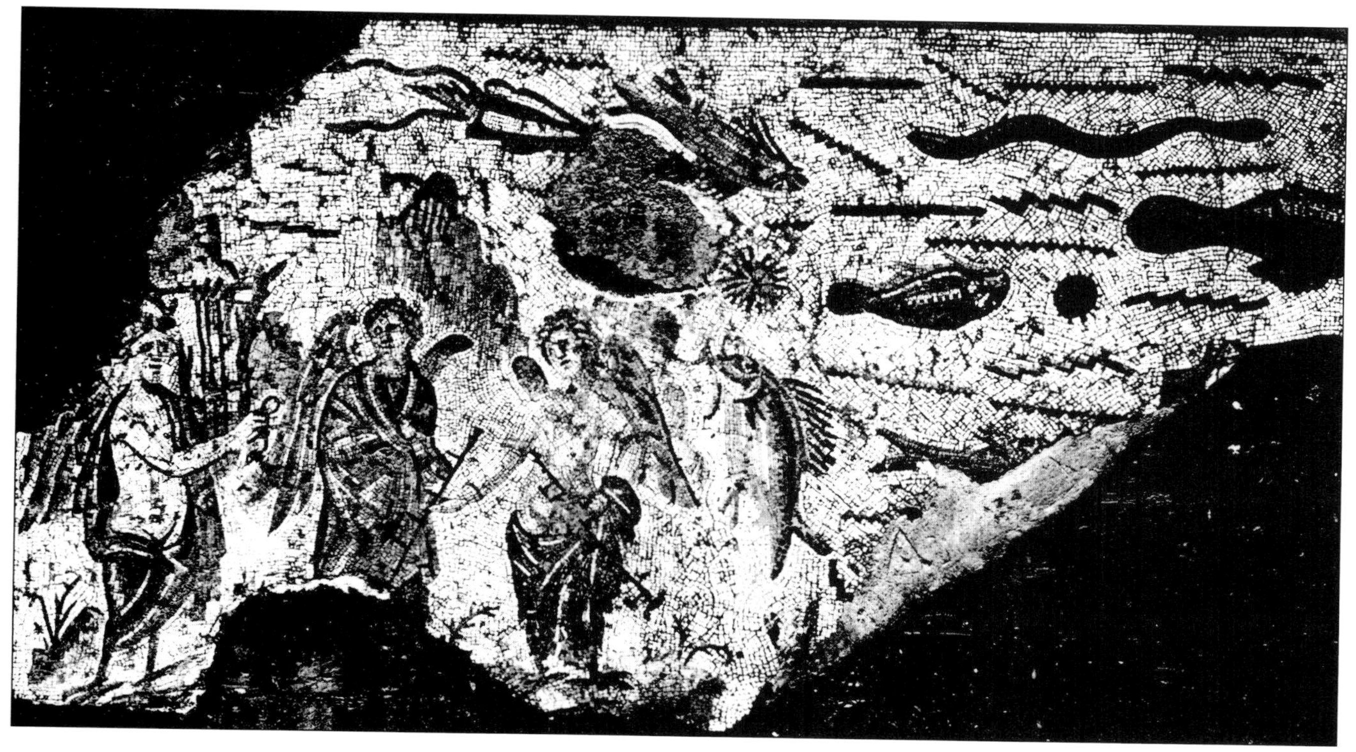

Fig. 12.1 Carthage, Mosaic of the Sirens; two of the three are naked to the waist, the central one is clothed. The siren on the left carries a lyre, that on the right two pipes. They stand against a mountainous backdrop; the fish around are grossly out of proportion with the sirens. Date uncertain (c. AD 300?). Height of fragment: 1.38 m; length: 2.44 m.

rounded by fish; some of the fish are dead, but one is listening intently. The Sirens were winged females with clawed birds' feet, to the horror of Davis' headman, Ali Karema.[31] In his later catalogue, Hinks counted nine marine animals, without noting that most were on their backs. The mosaic uses a very wide range of colours, and its style suggests a date in the later third or early fourth century AD.

The find of the Mosaic of the Sirens post-dated the despatch of the second sketch-map, and the site is not labelled on Davis' published map. He did not discuss either his motivation for excavation at the site, nor its stratigraphy; but it seems clear that he had returned to the extensive area he thought of as the 'Temple of Astarte.' A point is marked on the published map (Fig. 4.4) on the north-western side of the summit of the hill of Juno which corresponds with Davis' description of the location of the site of the Mosaic of the Sirens. Davis sets the site in context by relating it to the Mosaic of the Months and Seasons and the Vandal Hunting Mosaic. He notes that the Vandal Hunting Mosaic was found about 200 yards (*c.* 180 m) from the Mosaic of the Months and Seasons ('our first discovery'), and the Mosaic of the Sirens was a 'very little higher up, and in the direction of the hill of St. Louis'.[32] The Mosaic of the Months and Seasons was discovered at site 7 on Davis' published map, the 'T[emple of] Astarte,' which lies 40 m above sea level, while the location of the Vandal Hunting Mosaic, at the unnumbered point labelled 'T[emple of] Diana,' is *c.* 170 m to the north-west (about 200 yards) at approximately 45 m above sea level. The un-numbered point on the north-western side of the Hill of Juno, towards the hill of Saint Louis, should therefore be the site of the Mosaic of the Sirens. It is also at about 40 m above sea level on Davis' published map, so not actually at a higher elevation, but a hollow between the two points might have misled Davis. The points marking the 'Temple of Diana' and the 'Temple of Astarte' are both about 200 yards from the likely site of the Mosaic of the Sirens and form an approximation of an isosceles triangle.

The site of the Mosaic of the Sirens falls between *cardines* 4 and 5 west and on the line of *decumanus* 2 north. Davis' published map, however, puts the western edge of the summit of the Hill of Juno two blocks (75 m) to the west of where it really lies. I believe he meant this point to fall on the north-western slope of the Hill of Juno. In that case, the Mosaic of the Sirens would be almost contiguous on the west to the site which today is called the 'Baths of Gargilius'. The columns of this monument were re-erected *c.* 1930 (Fig. 12.2). A great complex here includes the columned hall and the adjacent vaulted hall to the south (Fig. 12.3), which together lie five meters above the immediately adjacent House of the Horses (see Fig. 7.10). The halls at a higher level share both a party wall and a late Roman cistern with this house, which has spectacular mosaics.[33] As noted above (p. 103), Picard thought the entire complex was the headquarters of the racing faction of the Blues, but in my opinion this complex was in fact the palace of the proconsul of Africa.

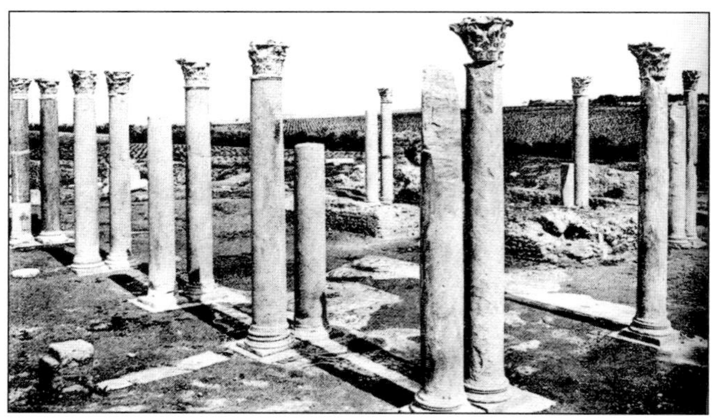

Fig. 12.2 (above) *Carthage, 'Monument of the Columns', immediately after their re-erection c. 1930. Some portions of mosaic pavement are also exposed. In the background is an extensive vineyard belonging to the White Fathers.*

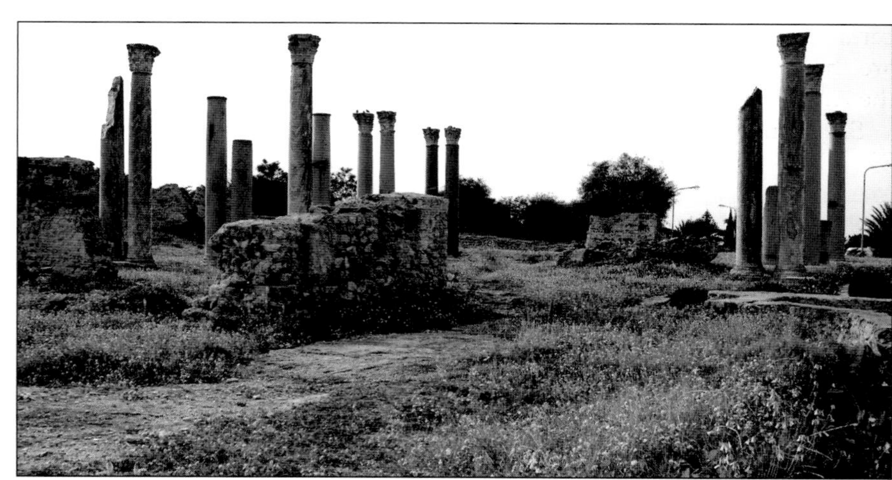

Fig. 12.3 (right) *The 'Monument of the Columns', as it is today; for a plan of this monument, see Fig. 7.10.*

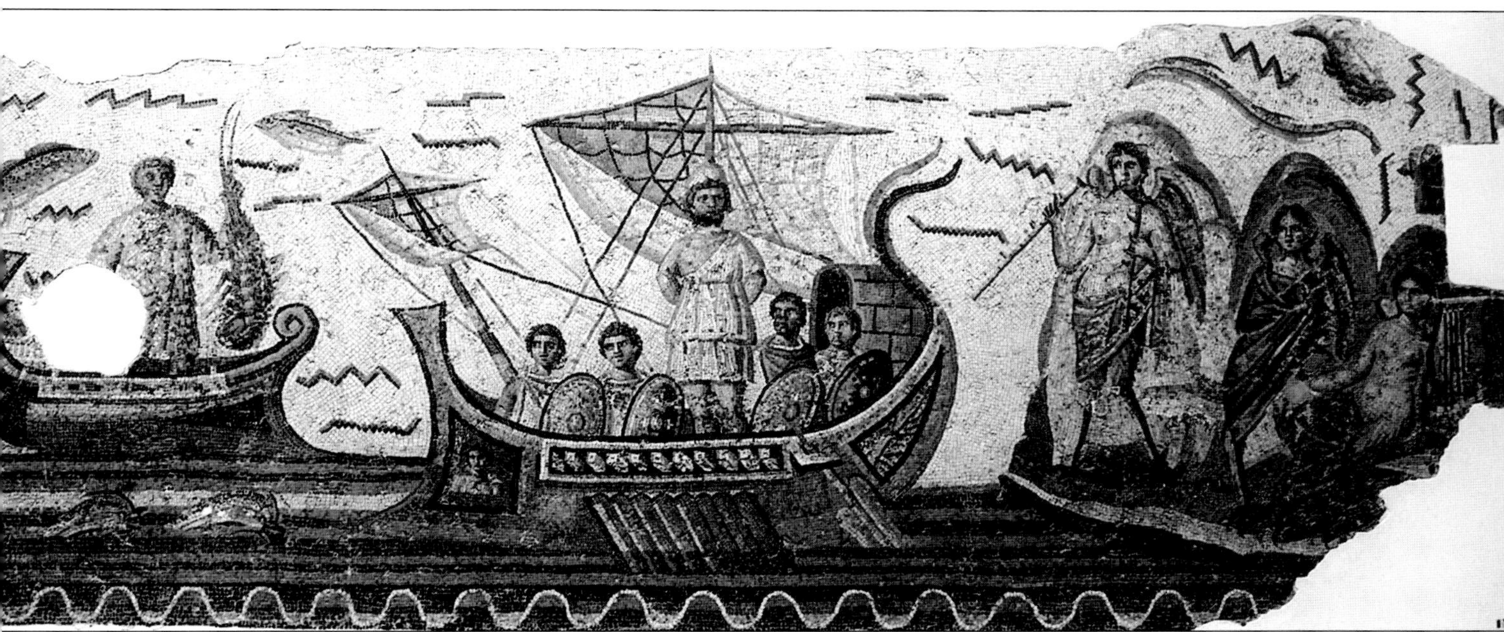

Fig. 12.4 Dougga, mosaic panel showing Ulysses and the Sirens, from the House of Dionysus and Ulysses, middle of the third century AD. Ulysses, bound fast to the mast, is allured by the sirens' song; his crew, with wax in their ears, look steadfastly in the opposite direction. As on Fig. 12.3, the sirens have wings and bird's feet (Tunis, Musée du Bardo).

The closest equivalent site to that of the Mosaic of the Sirens on the plan of Falbe is the latter's no. 79; this lies along the northern wall of a large rectangular enclosure which Falbe marked on the north-west corner of the summit of the Hill of Juno. Arguing from what we know about the terracing of the Byrsa Hill, Falbe's plan indicates that this area of the summit of the Hill of Juno was also supported on vaulted arcades and shored up by terrace walls. The western side of Falbe no. 79 and the western side of the summit of the Byrsa hill lie along *cardo* 2 west. *Cardo* 2 west also runs along the western side of the columned hall; it seems certain, therefore, that the walls marked at Falbe no. 79 are the same as the western and northern outlines of the columnar hall.[34]

Sir Grenville Temple excavated briefly at Falbe no. 79 in 1838, but evidently the site, which Dureau de la Malle had identified as the 'Temple of Saturn,' was not productive.[35] Nevertheless, it seems that Davis had chosen to dig here. If so, this was the first time he had followed Falbe and been rewarded by a significant mosaic find. The site of the Mosaic of the Sirens should lie immediately west of the great complex which I think of as the site of the palace of the proconsul. It is not far from the centre of the city, but in the north-western quarter, an area about which relatively little is known from excavation.

The subject of the mosaic would have been appropriate for a private luxury house. The same subject appears on a mosaic from the House of Dionysus and Ulysses at Dougga, now in the Bardo Museum in Tunis (Fig. 12.4). Although the drawing and workmanship of the Dougga mosaic is of somewhat finer quality, the similarities between the two representations of the Sirens are very close. There the mosaic appeared as a part of the decoration around a pool in a courtyard of a luxury house, and the scene was balanced by a scene of Dionysus' victory over the Tyrrhenian pirates. The different subjects of the mosaic floor at Dougga are most obviously connected by their marine theme, and two other rooms of the same house also have Dionysiac subjects. Picard's suggestion that the floor was an analogy of the struggles of the soul, and Poinssot's idea that the repeated Dionysiac themes suggest that the house was used by a Dionysiac fraternity, were both rejected by Dunbabin, who saw the choice of mosaic themes as dependent on nothing more complicated than the decorative preferences of the owner. I think it is more likely that the themes ordinarily did have some intellectual significance for the patron who commissioned the mosaic. Dunbabin dated the House of Dionysus and Ulysses at Dougga to the middle of the third century.[36] She dated the Mosaic of the Sirens, listed among mosaics of undetermined provenance at Carthage, to the late third or early fourth century.[37]

Davis' thirty-fourth site: the Vandal Hunting Mosaic

The Vandal Hunting Mosaic (Hinks 57 and 58) had just been discovered when Prince Alfred arrived, and was not completely cleared until a month after his departure. This site also lay in the north-western quarter of the Roman city. It is Davis' 'Temple of Diana,' marked with a point and labelled as such on his published map: as he describes, this is about 200 yards from the Mosaic of the Months and Seasons, and was found within a large precinct which was understood by Davis, although not clearly delimited, to be the 'Temple of Astarte.' There is no direct evidence to explain why Davis selected this site. The point lies in the middle of the block defined by *decumani* 3 and 4 north, on *cardo* 6 west. In relation to the *cardo maximus* north, it is in the opposite direction from Bordj Djedid. Almost nothing is known about this area of the north-western quarter of the city from published excavation.

According to Davis, the mosaic was found 'in the ruins of an edifice of great solidity',[38] on the slope of a hill, covered by between 8 and 20 ft (*c.* 2.5 m to 6.0 m) of soil.[39] Scenes with a walled structure, part of a horse and rider, and some fish and birds, had been uncovered at the time of the visit of Prince Alfred, but only the section of the mosaic covered by the least depth of soil had been exposed. By the day after Prince Alfred's departure, the complete width of the mosaic and approximately half of the room had been cleared. A panel with a hunting scene was now evident. The description of a building on the scene suggests that the lower left side of the mosaic was uncovered first. The complete chamber measured 40 by 28 ft (12.2 m by 8.5 m),[40] and the mosaic is therefore comparable in size to the Mosaic of the Horses, which is the largest mosaic known from a house at Carthage.

A drawing in coloured pencils of the complete mosaic *in situ* was included in a letter from Davis to Panizzi, dated February 12th, 1859 (Colour Plate 8). The drawing was placed before a meeting of the Trustees together with Davis' letter, and is now preserved in the archives of the British Museum. The letter was written less than a week after Davis had received his notice from Malmesbury to cease excavation.[41] Davis had written to ask Panizzi for guidance on how to divide up the mosaic in order to lift it, since it was far too large to be lifted in one piece, and the all-over placement of the figures did not allow it to be divided easily into rectangular sections.

Hinks clearly did not know of the existence of this drawing, which I discovered in the Museum Archives in October 2001. The drawing, which measures approximately 11 by 14 inches (28 cm x 36 cm), is somewhat primitive in style but essentially accurate. It was done in colour pencils, perhaps by Davis himself or one of his older children, and shows that the mosaic was complete when found. The rectangular mosaic

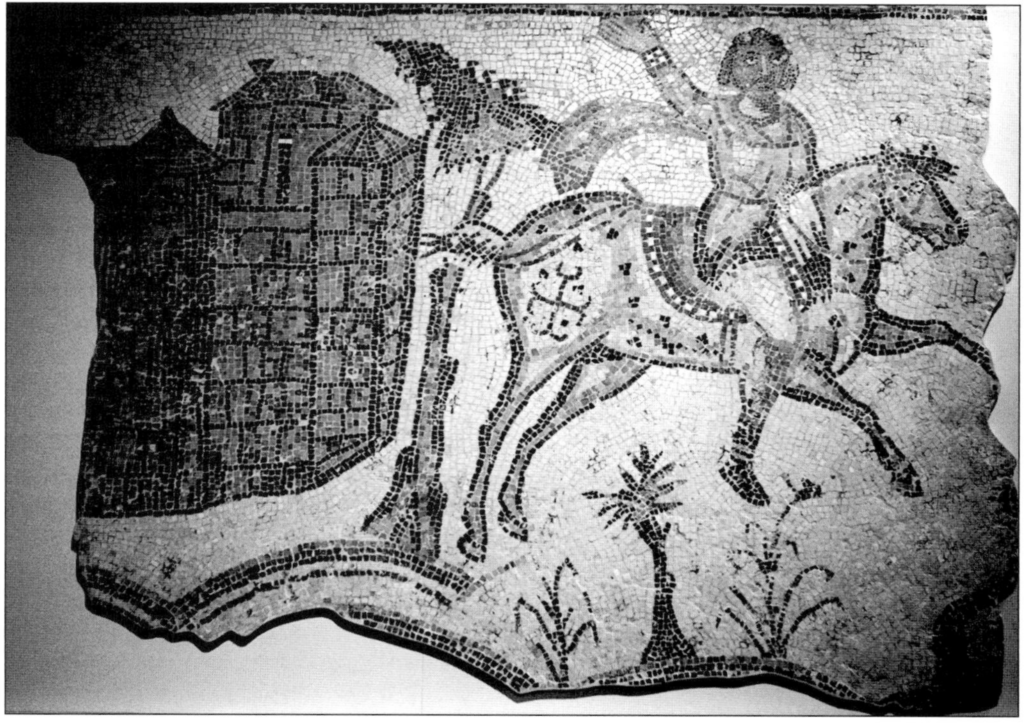

Fig. 12.5 Carthage, detail of the Vandal Hunting Mosaic: the dominus *on horseback leaves the city. This part comes from the upper left of the composition (see Colour Plate 8). The cross on the hind quarters of the horse is a branded stable-mark, commonly found on North African mosaics. Probably second half of the fifth century AD; height of this fragment: 1.69 m; length: 2.45 m.*

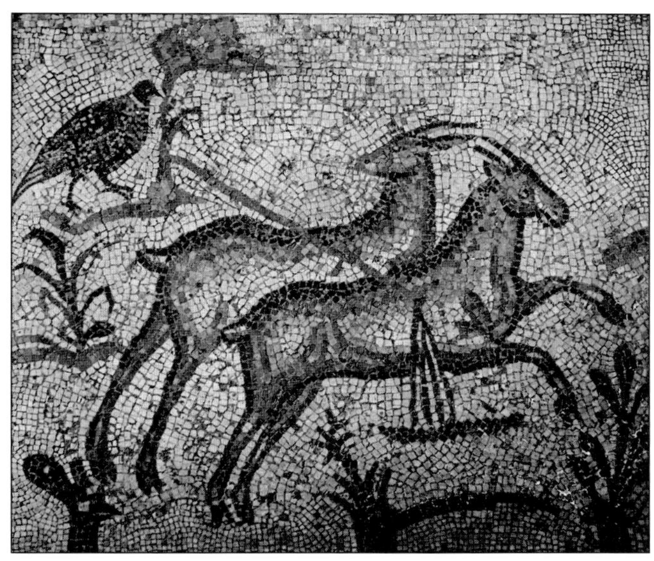

Fig. 12.6 (left) *Another detail of the Vandal Hunting Mosaic (from centre, top, of the composition), showing a partridge (?) and two gazelles, one wounded by a hunting spear; height: 1.27 m; length: 1.43 m.*

Fig. 12.7 (below) *The Vandal Hunting Mosaic, detail showing a huntsman and hunting dog (from the mid-left part of the floor); height: 1.29 m; length: 2.66 m.*

Fig. 12.8 (bottom) *Vandal Hunting Mosaic, detail, a hunting dog and a boar confront one another (from the mid-right part of the floor); height 1.26 m; length 2.58 m.*

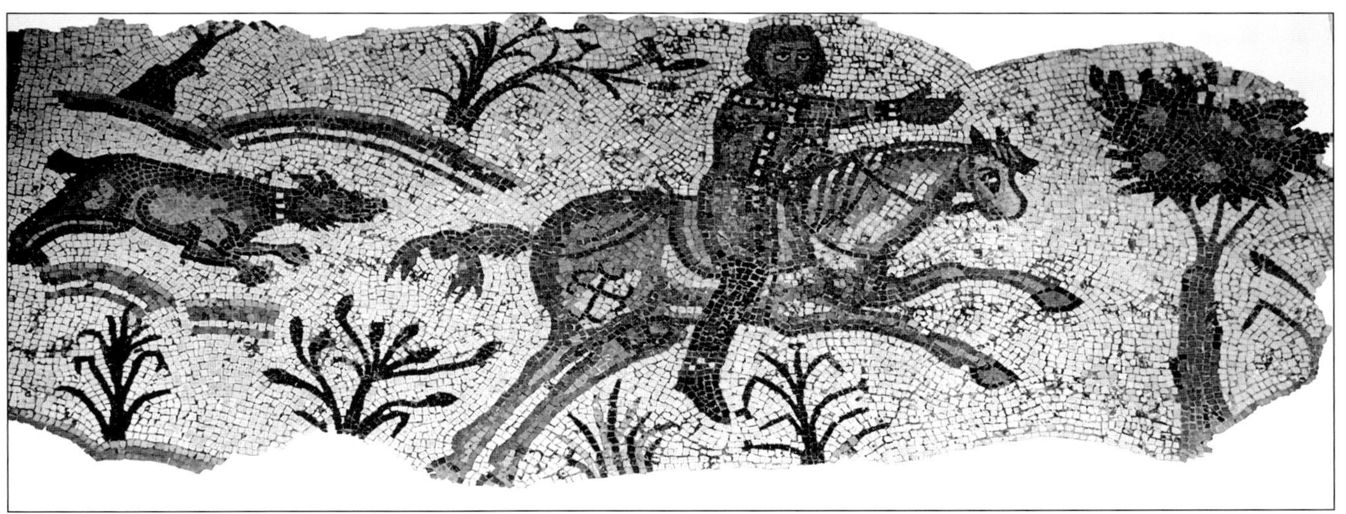

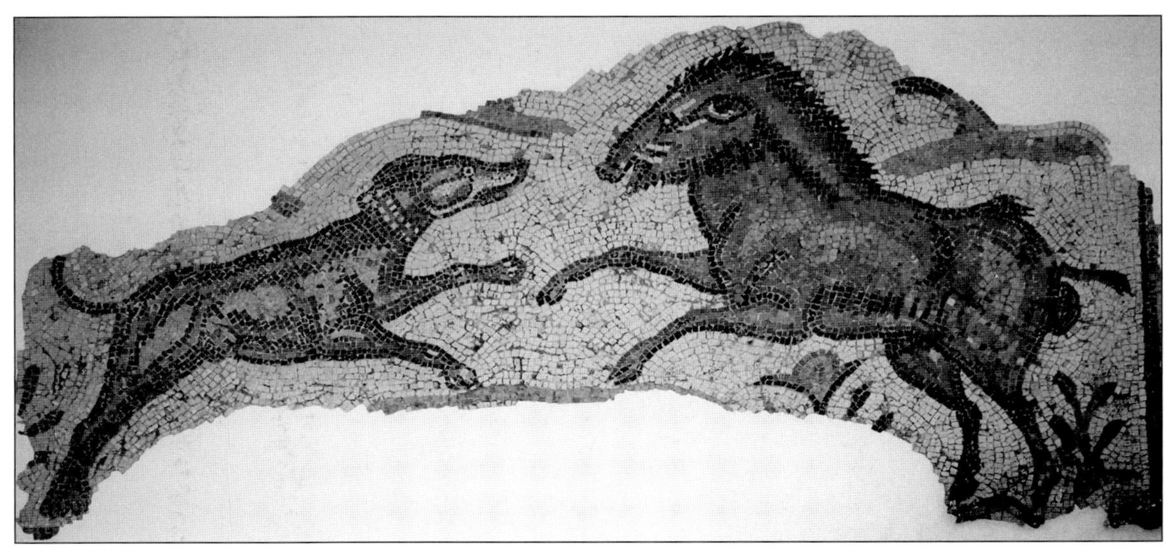

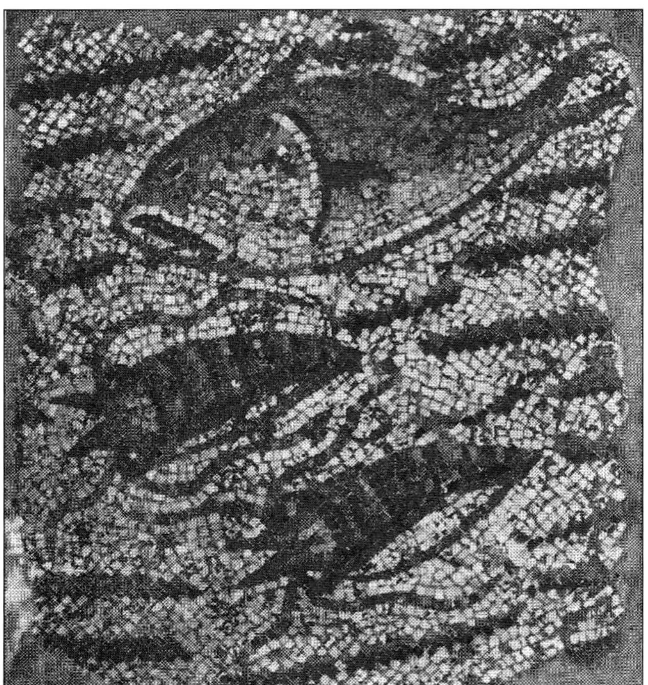

Fig. 12.9 Carthage, one of two fragments of a mosaic with fish and birds lifted from another part of the same floor as the Vandal Hunting Mosaic. Probably second half of the fifth century AD (?). Height of this fragment: 1.06 m.

was surrounded by an elegant ribbon and lotus border. About two-thirds of the area of the floor was devoted to an open field filled with fish and birds (Hinks' description of the fish and birds as appearing in medallions is incorrect). The lower one-third was divided from the rest. Inside this third the hunting motifs were disposed in an informal and rhythmic layout on irregular ground lines, not in strict zones, but in a one-directional arrangement. This panel, 28 ft (8.5 m) wide, represented a hunting scene, with three horsemen in Germanic costume and animals being hunted. The building to the left was a gate to Davis' eye, the costumes 'certainly not Roman'.[42]

Seven fragments of the Vandal Hunting Mosaic (Hinks 57) were lifted in large pieces with irregular edges (Figs 12.5–8 and Colour Plate 9). In addition, two fragments of the area of the mosaic with fish and birds were catalogued separately by Hinks (Hinks 58: one is Fig. 12.9). The latter suggested a date for the mosaic in the late fifth or early sixth century, during the Vandal era at Carthage.[43] The mosaic is probably not later than the second half of the fifth century; the ribbon and lotus border and the layout of the design suggest that, while the style of the figures looks Vandal, it should be dated earlier rather than later in the Vandal period, probably AD 450/475.

The Foreign Office brings Davis' excavations to a close

As mentioned above (p. 180), when Wood informed the Foreign Office that Davis was balking, a more polite and appreciative notice to quit was drafted for Malmesbury's signature.[44] It did not have the desired effect, as Davis simply continued to excavate. He was most unwilling to quit at this point, partly because he had recently uncovered two important figured mosaics, the Mosaic of the Sirens and the Vandal Hunting Mosaic, which it would take significant time to lift and package for shipment. An underlying issue, however, was that the work of Davis and Charles-Ernest Beulé,[45] both important archaeological pioneers at Carthage, overlapped in time, as Beulé arrived in January 1859, just as Davis received instructions to bring his excavations to an end.

Davis responded to this sudden and stressful turn of events by writing an obviously resentful letter to Panizzi, saying that he had no intention of closing his excavations. He was particularly incensed that Malmesbury had ignored his letters and his services to the nation, and that this was his first communication to Davis. In Davis' letter to Panizzi, dated February 12th, 1859, Davis reported that he had received Malmesbury's first directive on the very day that 'M. Brule [*sic*], professor of archaeology at Paris, commenced his excavations. He [Beulé] brought me a letter of introduction from Wm. Vaux, and promised in no way to interfere with my labours. Had he however been aware of the peculiar state of my affairs he would undoubtedly have taken possession of the field'.[46]

A political and administrative decision that Davis' project had outlived its usefulness had already been taken both in the Foreign Office and at the British Museum; but Davis completely disagreed. He refused to quit; as he wrote to Panizzi, the work was too important for him to stop at this point. In the same letter, he wrote: 'My mind is made up for the present not to abandon Carthage. I say this not in a spirit of opposition, but as a duty I feel incumbent on me'.

In early 1859 Malmesbury was replaced as Foreign Secretary by Lord John Russell, who already had a long career as a statesman.[47] Russell had been an active Trustee of the Museum in the past year, attending nearly every one of their meetings. This fact suggests that he might have been favorably disposed towards Davis if the latter had managed his relations with the Museum better. In July 1859 Davis wrote a letter to Russell, praising Clarendon's support for his project, and explaining that he would like to continue excavation at Carthage for a few more months; he also wrote that he would then like to be considered for the job of Vice-consul at Benghazi, where he could spend much of his energy on archaeology. Russell consulted Hammond, who pointed out with some indignation that Davis had been told to quit at Carthage twice, but was still at work there.[48] Hammond's comments make it clear that he personally did not approve of the expenditure of excavation. Russell therefore wrote to Davis, again instructing him to close his operations. A letter to him dated September 12th, 1859, told him that he had been instructed to close his operations by Malmesbury in February 1859, and that he was now to do so at once.[49] Davis subsequently presented bills for his salary to October 14th, 1859 and for expenses of £100 over this year. Consul Wood paid these bills, and was evidently able to justify the costs in the face of questions from the Foreign Office.[50] Davis left another twenty boxes of finds with Wood at this time.[51] It was therefore in October 1859 that Davis' work at Carthage was brought to an end with his own acquiescence,[52] although the Foreign Office had been trying to dislodge him since January.

In his book, Davis' story was that he was sent notice by the Foreign Office to close his excavations while still excavating the Vandal Hunting Mosaic, and that he at once 'took the requisite steps to bring the excavations to a close'.[53] These steps included the packing of the two mosaics excavated in the meantime, which might well have taken several months, judging by the time it took to lift the Mosaic of the Months and Seasons. Nevertheless Davis felt continued excavation was justified and even necessitated by the presence of Beulé. Davis himself stated that the second Mosaic of Nereids and Tritons (Figs 13.3–4) was excavated even after he had received his notice to quit. Although he was working with a much-reduced complement of workmen, there is no way of ascertaining that he did not also excavate unsuccessfully at the same time at other sites. In the light of his earlier mosaic finds, it seems most unlikely that he should have dug at only three sites, each of which just happened to have produced a figured mosaic.

13

Davis in competition with Beulé

Beulé enters the field

It was not pleasing to the French that a British archaeologist should control excavation at Carthage, but I have found no evidence that Charles Beulé's sudden appearance on the scene was politically engineered. Nevertheless, the latter had a passion for his country and certainly came to Carthage as a kind of knight-errant and champion of France. Beulé praised his friend Léon Roches' sponsorship of the rebuilding of the Carthage aqueduct, at a cost to the Tunisians of 7,000,000 francs (a cost that was ruinous for the Tunisian economy), saying that France was 'not like another country I could name' in its support of 'wise reforms, a regular administration, tolerance and the spread of the virtues of civilization'.[1] Beulé was a self-consciously professional archaeologist and scholar, who had had great success in his excavation of the 'Beulé Gate' at the entrance to the Acropolis in Athens, work which he had begun in 1852.[2] Beulé eventually published a lively description of this excavation, which was achieved with the regular application of explosives; characteristically, he ascribed the whole glory of his achievement to France.[3]

Beulé was young in the eyes of his academic contemporaries (born in 1826, he was probably still thirty-two when he first met Davis at Carthage), and both impetuous and intense. Like Davis, Beulé was inspired by the recent finds at Nineveh and Babylon.[4] Furthermore, it is likely that he wanted to use archaeology to confirm the advances made at Carthage a quarter of a century previously by Falbe and Dureau de la Malle. Given his conviction that the Phoenician and Punic city could be uncovered, he boldly set out to test his ideas on the spot. He had evidently read second-hand reports of Davis' work at Carthage, and he was challenged by the latter's intimations that the remains of Punic Carthage were not to be found;[5] and he was positively galvanized by Davis' claim that the Byrsa of Punic Carthage was to be identified with Bordj-Djedid. Beulé must have been strongly motivated to discredit Davis, since he did not hesitate to enter the field while the latter was still excavating at Carthage. Although it never occurred to Beulé that he might learn from Davis, he was evidently influenced by him, since about half of Beulé's work focused on two sites where Davis had preceded him: the south-western side of the Hill of Saint Louis and the tombs at Gammarth. In both cases, Beulé's motivation was at least partly to demonstrate, in contrast to Davis' work, the proper way to proceed.

Davis, having just received a directive to close his excavations, was doubly upset by the unexpected arrival of the French archaeologist. The relationship between the two men was described in the most positive terms by an eye-witness, an anonymous enthusiast for archaeology at Carthage, who wrote, 'Till recently Mr. Davis stood alone in the field; but during the last few weeks M. Beulé, professor of archaeology of Paris, has been most actively and judiciously occupied . . . This effort of the learned professor must not be regarded as an opposition movement. On the contrary, the greatest possible harmony exi[s]ts between him and the English excavator. They are often seen on the ruins together, and cordially aid each other in fixing the topography of the mysterious city of Dido'.[6]

Beulé and Davis soon had an opportunity to argue their views on which hill was to be identified as the ancient Byrsa. One can imagine them walking over the slopes of Bordj-Djedid together, for Beulé stated his opinions on Bordj-Djedid in the context of his altercation with Davis. According to Beulé relations between the two men were cordial, despite the fact that he did not hide from Davis his disagreement with the latter's view that Bordj-Djedid was the acropolis of the Punic city. The ancients, he told Davis, would never have put an acropolis by the sea-shore, and the great stairway up Bordj-Djedid was too high to fit the description of the sixty steps that led to the Byrsa. He did agree that the summit of Bordj-Djedid was artificial; on the other hand, he pointed out that Davis' excavation within the great rectangular enclosures had not revealed any architectural remains of a temple.[7] These open discussions did not change the fact that each took an intensely competitive attitude to the other. Neither was minded to be of much help to the other and each saw much to criticize. Davis and Beulé each had reason to regard the other man as an obstruction. The summit of the Hill of Saint Louis had been deeded to France by a treaty of 1830, and the French consul, Léon Roches, had barred Davis from excavating in this area by ignoring his requests for permission.[8] The latter must have been annoyed by Beulé's excavations in the spring of 1859 on the summit and especially on the south-western slope, where Davis himself had already excavated in December 1857 (his Site 25).

Beulé published a brief note in the spring of 1859 on Davis' finds of Roman and Byzantine mosaics and inscriptions in a prestigious French academic journal, which was also quoted by the French newspaper *Le Moniteur* for May 14th, 1859. Davis had evidently told Beulé that he could not expect success in his goal of finding the remnants of Punic Carthage.[9] In return, Beulé was unkind enough to suggest that the value of Davis' mosaic finds was limited.[10] For the *Moniteur* article, Beulé coolly wrote, as quoted by Davis, 'It is true that the British Museum owes a certain number of Roman and Byzantine mosaics, of *stelae* and of inscriptions, to the zeal of Mr N. Davis'.[11] Davis, who believed that his mosaics were Punic, fumed that Beulé had never seen them. While all of the former's finds before January of 1859 had already been shipped to London, this implies that Davis did not invite Beulé to inspect the Mosaic of the Sirens or the Vandal Hunting Mosaic, both of which he was still clearing and lifting when Beulé arrived on the scene.

Beulé's note would also allow for an interpretation that the *stelae* and inscriptions that Davis found were likewise all Roman or Byzantine, and that was in fact Beulé's opinion, as he wrote: 'All the Punic inscriptions that one finds among the ruins of Carthage are later than the Roman conquest'.[12] When arguing against Beulé's implicit suggestion that his Punic *stelae* were Roman, Davis lost his head to the point of declaring that he had not found any Latin inscriptions. This was not true, since, in the corpus of Latin inscriptions, Wilmanns and Mommsen listed nine inscriptions on stone which had been sent to the British Museum by Davis.[13]

Beulé said that his relations with Davis were courteous,[14] while Davis declared, 'Personally, he knows full well, we can have no ill feelings towards him'.[15] In fact, the two regarded each other with scorn, and both allowed ironic comments on the other's work to slip into print. As already noted, Beulé had expressed the opinion, which might well have been shared by some contemporary academics, that Davis' mosaics were nothing of special interest.[16] Davis did not restrain himself from sardonic comments on Beulé, such as: 'Punic remains were the special object of his search, and what else but Punic relics can he be expected to find?'.[17] More aggressively, he referred to Beulé's interpretation of the Saint Louis Hill as the Punic Byrsa, surrounded by a Punic defensive wall, as 'a mere concatenation of misrepresentations'.[18]

Davis and Beulé were completely incompatible in their personal styles. Reinach later described the latter as a charming man, with the taste of an artist and the concerns of an academic,[19] while Davis, lacking the advantages of wealth and family, presented himself as a practical man and an adventurer. Beulé was a highly qualified academic and prolific scholar, who had already achieved public acclaim in France. Although fourteen years younger than Davis, he had been appointed professor of archaeology at the Bibliothèque Nationale in Paris, among the first to hold such a position. Furthermore, because Greece had had laws protecting its archaeological patrimony since 1827, and exporting archaeological finds from Greece therefore was strictly forbidden, archaeologists at Athens could pride themselves that their work was scientific research rather than plunder.[20] In 1865, the vapid Armand de Flaux wrote that while Davis was looking for works of art at Carthage, Beulé was 'a higher type'.[21] It seems likely that Beulé made Davis aware both of the great renown and the supposed faultless professionalism of his rival, as well as of the differences in their goals.

Davis found it nearly incomprehensible, and a bitter pill to swallow, that Beulé was elected to the French Academy of Inscriptions in 1860, only a year after his exploits at Carthage. The Academy wished to confer upon Beulé an honour equal to 'his efforts and sacrifices', and he was elected from among six candidates by an absolute majority.[22] From Davis' point of view, Beulé received this signal honour on the basis of his incorrect identification of the retaining wall on the south-western side of the Hill of Saint Louis as the great Punic defensive wall of Carthage, thus creating, as Davis said, a 'stupendous pedestal for his fame'. Beulé's glory was certainly achieved partly at Davis' expense, as the latter suspected when he wrote that Beulé's 'aim evidently [was] to depreciate the researches of others'.[23] Beulé's rise in the academic world of France was meteoric: he became Perpetual Secretary of the French Academy of Fine Arts in 1862. Davis probably never knew that his rival's subsequent political career was not distinguished, and that Beulé became a frustrated and embittered man.[24]

Beulé's excavations at Carthage

Beulé personally funded the expenses of his excavations at Carthage, which suggests that he was a man of considerable wealth: he and his wife (who drew antiquities for him) stayed in the French consulate at La Marsa, a former summer palace of the Bey. This was at the invitation of Consul Roches, whom Beulé described as a warm and supportive friend. Roches' enthusiasm for Beulé and his work was easily stimulated because, as Beulé noted, Roches did not want France to come second to Britain. He probably helped Beulé acquire workmen and provided further by paying the expenses for ten of the men out of his own pocket.[25] Beulé made slightly acidic comments on his Arab workmen, noting that they moved with 'Biblical dignity', and used baskets that 'would not hold twenty oranges'.[26]

He began excavating in early February of 1859. During his first short period of work at Carthage, he occupied himself on the summit of the Byrsa or Hill of Saint Louis. Beulé was used to the strictures of excavation in Greece, where the exportation of antiquities was already illegal. He left at least some of his finds in the enclosure around the Chapel of Saint Louis, intending to found a little site museum.[27] The guardian sold these objects, however, so that there was nothing left by the time of the arrival of the White Fathers in 1875.[28]

Beulé accomplished a prodigious amount of work in about seventy days of excavation,[29] compressed into two seasons, in the spring and fall of 1859. Davis was still at work in Carthage throughout Beulé's first campaign, but he had wrapped up his excavations when the latter carried on his second campaign. In his first campaign Beulé surveyed the summit of the Hill of Saint Louis (the Byrsa) and excavated two important series of apses along the eastern and south-western limits of the rectangular plateau. He had no clear plans to return to Carthage until he learned in the fall of 1859 that Davis had closed his excavations, but once the field was clear he returned to Tunisia immediately. In his second campaign he explored the tombs of Gammarth, where Davis had worked in the spring of 1858, and excavated at least one of them thoroughly by November.[30] Finally, he turned to the military and merchant harbours of Carthage, and opened three hundred little trenches in order to map the outline of the ports, before packing up his expedition for good in December.[31] Beulé repeatedly insisted that his focus was architecture as opposed to Davis' interest in objects;[32] one could describe his methods less favorably as 'wall-chasing.'

Having accomplished what he could personally afford, Beulé published his excavations at Carthage promptly. In fact his report on his excavations on the Byrsa must have been completed in the spring of 1859, perhaps even before he left Carthage for the first time, and the report on the ports and Gammarth were evidently completed immediately after he finished those excavations, since they were originally published in serial form in the *Journal des Savants* from August 1859 to September 1860. Davis seems to have read these reports as they appeared, as he reacts to them in his own book. Beulé never edited or re-evaluated his first impressions; four letters from his excavations at Carthage published in 1873 were also written in 1859. His account stuck much closer to matters of interest to scholars than Davis' volume did; nevertheless Beulé's account was also disorganized, and his interpretations were often wrong.

Beulé's preconceptions

Beulé saw that although Roman Carthage had been destroyed, a recognizable plan still existed. Punic Carthage, on the other hand, lay at a level so low that it had not yet been reached by any earlier excavator, including Davis.[33] Beulé believed that one of the greatest cities of the ancient world could not have been destroyed without trace. Since to his mind the circuit of the Punic city was 20 kilometers,[34] and since the Punic city covered 18 million square meters, it could not have been 'removed'.[35] Beulé estimated the Punic city at more than four times the size of the Roman city, as defined by the street-grid. He included the area north to La Marsa and Gammarth, where he believed the wealthy of the Punic city resided.[36]

Like Davis, Beulé was minimally interested in the finds of Roman Carthage, and stated that one little fragment from Punic Carthage would have far more value for science than poor-quality Roman mosaics, or objects from Roman cemeteries. Beulé belittled the great difficulty which Davis had had in discovering anything of archaeological interest at Carthage. He did not hesitate to cast scorn on the latter's finds of Roman mosaics, and boasted that he himself could have found hundreds of meters of them with shallow trenches placed anywhere.[37] He ignored the fact that, until Davis started to discover and lift such pavements, no one knew that mosaic floors were characteristic of Roman Carthage. Like other nineteenth-century scholars discussing Carthage, including Davis, Beulé devoted page after page to a rehearsal of the ancient sources, particularly Appian.[38] This obsessive reference to the texts suggests that for him the purpose of excavation was to illustrate and confirm the accounts of ancient historians. On the other hand, when a text disagreed with his considered views, he did not hesitate to discard it; he gave no weight to Orosius' claim that the Punic fortifications had been reduced to dust, for example.[39] Beulé praised Dureau de la Malle, who had never visited Carthage, but who knew his ancient sources 'so completely one cannot criticize'.[40] Careful consideration of the evidence of the ancient sources was not an error in principle, but like most other scholars of his day (with the exception of Dureau de la Malle), Beulé did not differentiate clearly between evidence which applied to Punic (as opposed to Roman) Carthage, and regarded all ancient sources as being of potentially equal value.

Beulé contrasted his own disinterested goals with Davis' search for objects.[41] Beulé believed that his own methods, which emphasized the importance of architecture, were more scientific. In fact, he was cavalier in his rejection of artefacts in and of themselves, noting very few of them, although occasionally he recorded his observations or interpretations. Most of the finds that interested him were sculptural or architectural; a number were drawn by his wife and reproduced on six plates. His remarks on the Punic temples of Carthage are confused enough to confirm his complete lack of interest in them.[42] He justified his attitude by arguing that they had all been rebuilt in Roman times. The great Punic walls and ports had been recorded in impressive detail by Appian, and Beulé may have hoped to confirm these accounts, but the necropolis at Gammarth, which had been previously explored only by Davis, was not described by any ancient author. Here Beulé's interest seems to have been aroused both by the latter's work and by recent publications of comparable tomb complexes in the Levant.

Some of Beulé's ideas about Carthage changed as he wrote and excavated. He originally believed that the Temple of Juno Caelestis, which was two miles in circumference according to the ancient sources, must have been outside the Punic city, since temples of Hera were placed well outside Greek cities. He later changed his mind and followed Dureau de la Malle in considering the hill to the north of the Byrsa the Hill of Juno, when he found 'a relief of Juno Caelestis' while tunnelling into the north side of the Byrsa Hill. This was actually an uninscribed late Punic grave *stele* showing a woman with lifted hand.[43]

Beulé's observations on the Byrsa Hill

Beulé described his completed excavations on the Hill of Saint Louis in a letter written on March 19th.[44] Roches had been happy to make the site available, within certain limits, to Beulé, at a time when the latter believed that it would be ungentlemanly for him to dig elsewhere at Carthage.[45] The forced choice of site was no problem, because Beulé also believed, against Davis, that the Hill of Saint Louis was the ancient Byrsa, the acropolis of the Punic city. Beulé also believed, with Falbe and against Davis, that the great Punic fortifications described by Appian not only ran across the isthmus, but also encircled the Byrsa. On the other hand, he rejected Barth's observation, with which Davis agreed, that the topography of the hill was man-made, created by artificial terracing. Beulé's own incorrect interpretation was that the Byrsa had been created by nature for its role as an acropolis, although the summit was cut down. To his mind, confirmation came from his discovery of 'bedrock' at a depth of between 2.5 and 3.5 m in his trenches 'A,' 'B' and 'C' near the middle of the plateau. Beulé described this 'bedrock' as pale yellowish clayey sandstone; he said it was friable when dry, compact when wet, and easily cut, but a solid base for a foundation.[46] He also argued, against Dureau de la Malle, that the Byrsa was only an acropolis, not a whole quarter of the ancient city, since according to the ancient sources the circuit of the Byrsa was two miles (2,600 m) around the crest of the hill.[47] These sources posed a problem, because Beulé's own measurements of the Byrsa showed a circuit of only 1,400 m at the crest. He therefore decided that the walls were not at the crest but about half-way down the slope of the hill. Davis derided Beulé's judgment that the Hill of Saint Louis was the Byrsa, and asked rhetorically how there could have been room for the more than 50,000 refugees inside the circuit of the walls during the Third Punic War.[48] Beulé in fact had calculated that if the walls were located as he proposed, the space allowed for each of the 50,000 was eight square meters, but he left any structures out of these calculations.

Davis was so unimpressed by the remains on the summit of the Hill of Saint Louis that he said that it was impossible for a rational man to imagine it covered by temples and palaces;[49] his comment suggested that familiarity breeds contempt. Although the ruins were neither impressive nor obviously co-ordinated, Beulé's survey of the surface recorded useful information. At first he found only scattered walls, underground cisterns of widely varying types and masses of Roman concrete, sometimes from collapsed vaulting. Beulé's sketch-map was meant to be as detailed as possible, although the plan was not accurate or drawn to scale. He did not mention the circumstances under which his plan was drawn, and hardly refers to it in his text, but it does provide independent evidence for his finds and his preconceptions (Fig. 13.1).[50]

Subsequent excavation has confirmed the existence of the apses which Beulé described and drew from his excavations, lending credibility to his representation of other finds on the summit. We know exactly where he was digging in his two most important excavations. These were 'G,' Punic fortifications on the south-western side of the Byrsa to Beulé, but actually the vaulted apses of the Roman retaining wall along the north side of *decumanus* 1 south which supported the huge terracing project of the early Augustan era, and 'I,' larger apses on the east side of the summit, the palace of the proconsul to Beulé, but actually the vaulted platform along the west side of *cardo* 4 east which supported Carthage's Roman judicial basilica of the mid-second century AD.

Beulé believed that the Temple of Aesculapius was on the Byrsa hill, following Appian, who said it was on the side of the plateau facing the forum and the sea,

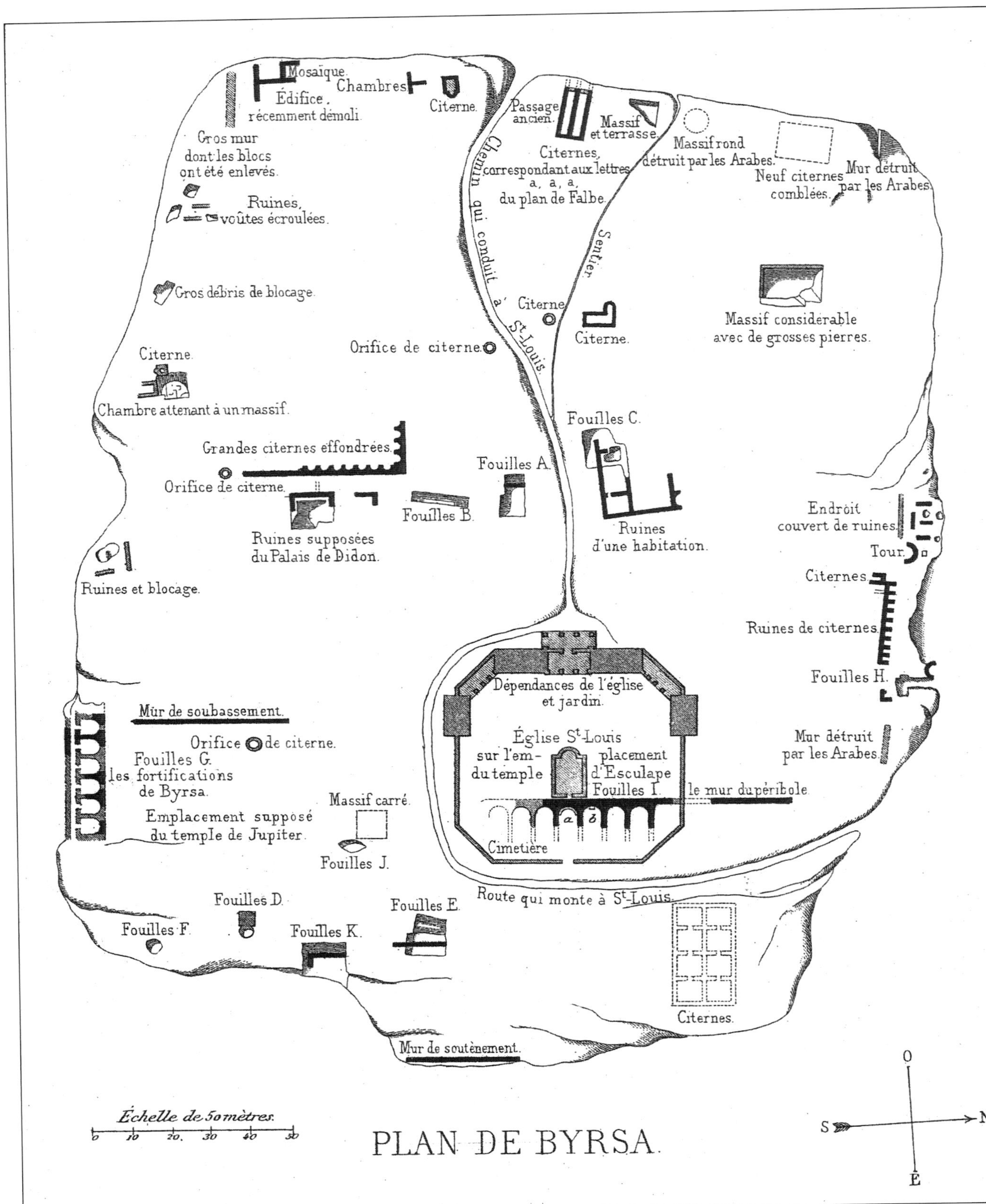

Fig. 13.1 Map published in 1861 by Charles Ernest Beulé (1826–1874) of remains that he recorded on the Byrsa hill

and was approached by a stairway of sixty steps.[51] Beulé therefore thought that the site of the temple was on the east or seaward side of the hill on the site of the Chapel of Saint Louis, and that remains of the temple must have been visible at the time the chapel was built. He ignored the fact that the French traveller Chateaubriand (who devoted just one paragraph to the ancient site),[52] had found only fragments of marble on the surface of the Byrsa when he visited it briefly in 1807. Furthermore, the chapel was not built until 1842, and any significant remains on its site would have appeared on Falbe's plan, which was drawn ten years before. On the other hand, the last bey of Algeria had got the materials for his palace at Constantine from the Hill of Saint Louis at Carthage, and the architect of the chapel, a Frenchman named Jourdain, had excavated columns of Numidian marble there which were still on the site.[53] Beulé had also been told that the chapel was not on a solid foundation, but built partly over an ancient cistern (in fact it was built over a vaulted platform supporting a Roman basilica).[54] While he felt hampered and frustrated by the presence of the Chapel of Saint Louis and its subsidiaries, they in fact covered less than ten per cent of the summit. By 1884 a third of the summit had been built over by the White Fathers, and the opportunity which Beulé had to survey the site no longer existed.

In his efforts to understand the Byrsa Hill, Beulé certainly consulted Falbe's map. Falbe indicated the Hill of Saint Louis as a regular and enormous rectangle, with steep slopes on four sides. Falbe had left the summit, which he designated site no. 52, almost completely blank, but he described no. 52 in his text as the 'Byrsa or Acropolis'.[55] Beulé said that Falbe meant the letters 'a, a, a' on the west and north sides of the summit to designate the vaults for the triple wall surrounding the Byrsa;[56] Beulé rather thought that the letters actually marked two Roman cisterns on the west side of the summit, contiguous and parallel, lined with water-resistant mortar, of which the fronts had been demolished and the interiors used as homes by Arab families. He thought that the cisterns lay to the north of the escape passage for the 50,000 people mentioned by Appian, and therefore marked an 'ancient passage' next to them on his plan. Not having found a great deal of help in Falbe's plan, Beulé dismissed Falbe as no archaeologist.[57]

Beulé found that the slope on the west side of the summit had been recently disturbed by Arabs looking for construction materials. His map described the house in the south-west corner, where the Mosaic of the Months with Latin Inscriptions had been discovered, as an 'edifice recently demolished', and labelled three other sites as destroyed by Arabs.[58] On the northern edge of the summit Falbe had marked conspicuous and massive walls. Beulé noted nothing similar on his plan except a line of wall 25 m long which he labelled as 'cisterns' and 'ruins of cisterns'. He also noted two 40-m stretches of wall running across the summit, both marked on the same north–south alignment. The first he labelled as belonging to great 'collapsed cisterns' on the south centre of the summit, and the other 70 yds to the east as a 'retaining wall'. All of this was more or less disappointing, but Beulé's careful observations make it clear that already in his day there were no standing Roman public monuments, much less Punic ones, on the summit of the Byrsa Hill.

Beulé's excavations on the Byrsa Hill

Beulé's first excavations were at the centre of the summit, at sites he marked 'A,' 'B' and 'C.' At 'B' he discovered an Arab cemetery, which he thought might date to the twelfth century; one grave used an elegant late Punic *stele* as its cover. He documented the remains of two houses on the summit; one was the site where the Mosaic of the Months had been excavated. His trench 'C' revealed the ruins of another large house, about 20 m square. His plan of the summit shows the house as off the Roman alignment, and he himself identified it as Vandal or Byzantine; an older house lay directly below.[59] These sites and the Arab silo (an excavated granary) which he found at trench 'D' show that there was some casual Byzantine and Arab occupation on the summit, but that even this could only be revealed by excavation.

Beulé next planned to dig along the south-western slope to find the line of the Punic defensive wall he thought Appian had described. His next trenches, 'J,' 'D' and 'F,' near the south corner of the summit, were meant to discover the depth to bedrock, on which he was certain that the great defensive walls must have been founded. It was only a little over 1 m to bedrock at 'J,' and 3.40 m at 'D,' an Arab silo filled with debris. In this trench he found a small bas-relief, about 1 ft square, depicting a shrine which he interpreted as the Temple of Jupiter.[60] He considered this one of his most significant finds, which indicates how unrewarding his discoveries generally were.[61] At 'E,' further along the eastern side of the hill, he dug down the face of a heavy wall, rebuilt in Roman times, to a depth of 7.55 m at which bedrock was reached. Lastly, he dug the circular pit 'F,' at the extreme south corner of the summit, which was filled with debris of every sort, including 'Greek vases from Sicily' (more likely black gloss Hellenistic 'Campana' wares) and mosaic; here his men reached bedrock at 19 m,[62] a feat which must have posed extreme dangers for them. The spectacular depth of fill did not sway Beulé's conviction that the

Byrsa Hill was an entirely natural acropolis, but he did have some qualms about the difficulty of digging through such a depth of fill, and about the extreme destruction which he and earlier excavators (a reference to Davis) had found.[63]

When Beulé dug trench 'K,' probably his last excavation on the Hill of Saint Louis, he found a stretch of Roman *opus reticulatum* wall 10 m long with large foundation blocks of El Haouaria sandstone: the blocks had been taken from more ancient buildings, but rebuilt and mortared. When he removed one of the large stone blocks, newly-broken amphorae cascaded down. Although he recognized that the amphorae were Roman by their Latin inscriptions, the amphorae made Beulé think that the apses had been storerooms in Punic times. The size of the containers, their double-rolled handles, and the name and monogram of 'Mescellius'[64] (actually Maesius Celsus) on one of them all serve to identify them as Italian wine amphorae. The specific type is from Northern Campania and dates, along with the rest of the 'First Amphora Wall', to some time around 15 BC.[65] This was the east face of the same terracing wall which Beulé had found on the south-western slope of the hill and considered Punic, but he did not recognize the structural relationship between the two walls.

His first major excavation site was at trench 'G' on the south side of the Hill of Saint Louis. Although Beulé did not mention the fact, Davis had already dug extensively in the same area. Beulé said that he found the 'Theodosian wall' first; as he could not budge the core, he attacked it with dynamite.[66] He then pushed further toward the interior of the hill and found what he believed to be the Punic defensive walls. Five more meters down he reached the base of the foundation and bedrock, at 56 ft below the modern surface. The bedrock was covered with more than a meter of black ash, with large pieces of carbonized wood and fire-damaged metal debris as well as much fine thin glass. He also found many unused small terracotta projectiles. In this area, three kinds of pottery were common: a yellowish ceramic fabric with red paint, Hellenistic black-glazed wares, and a bright orange fabric which he thought was locally made.[67] To Beulé this material was all Punic, and some of it certainly was, but the glass he described was blown glass and therefore of Roman date; a nearly complete pot in the local orange fabric sounds like an early thin-walled mug in 'African Red Slip,' a Roman pottery fabric.[68]

These walls Beulé believed to be the Punic fortifications of the Byrsa and already built in the sixth century BC; he argued that the stones were not ashlar blocks, but cut and fitted on site like archaic construction techniques of the sixth century BC.[69] Beulé found contiguous apses of cut and fitted stone with a hallway and wall in front of them, 10 m thick from one side to the other, as Appian had said. He therefore felt that he had confirmed Orosius's description of walls in cut stone, and Appian's description of hollow and covered walls. The walls he found provided tremendous terracing force, as Beulé recognized. He also observed that some parts showed Roman rebuilding right down to the foundation – for example, an area 8 m high in *opus reticulatum*, which he recognized as a Roman construction method. Since the walls generally only stood 5 m high, he could not demonstrate that there were three storeys as the ancient sources describe, but he thought the burnt wood came from the floors.[70] Given his own experience of the site, Davis was outraged by Beulé's claim to have found Punic walls, and on this question Davis was correct; the walls are Roman terracing walls which supported an immense artificial plateau, as the French excavations of the 1970s demonstrated.

Beulé's second major excavation site was in the area immediately east of the Chapel of Saint Louis, where he expected to find the Roman temple of Aesculapius surrounded by public buildings. Here he excavated a series of large contiguous apses (Fig. 13.2), the back wall of which, he thought, formed the *peribolos* (enclosure wall) of the Temple of Aesculapius. He found four apses, postulated a total of seven and carefully excavated two. The interior of the central apse had been covered in *opus sectile* made of a variety of marbles, and the floor was also of destroyed *opus sectile*. The second apse was less elegant, with stucco decoration, but had a great statue base or *tribunal* at the back. A process of elimination of possibilities in the ancient sources led Beulé to the conclusion that these apses belonged to the palace of the proconsul.[71] He recognized that the white marble architectural debris of columns, Corinthian capitals and cornices which he found on surface layers down-slope from these apses belonged to a Roman public building, although he was too quick to assign them to the temple of Aesculapius.[72]

His excavation at sites 'G' and 'I' on the Hill of Saint Louis was first given some of its true significance when Charles Saumagne used Beulé's vaulted walls as part of a demonstration of the layout of the street-grid of Roman Carthage.[73] Beulé's excavations of the apse-reinforced walls along the south-western side of the Byrsa summit and of the vaults along the east side have also been re-evaluated in the course of the French UNESCO excavations of the 1970s. As explained above (p. 161) in discussion of Davis' Site 25, the apsed walls running east–west at excavation 'G' were part of Roman retaining walls along *decumanus* 1 south that

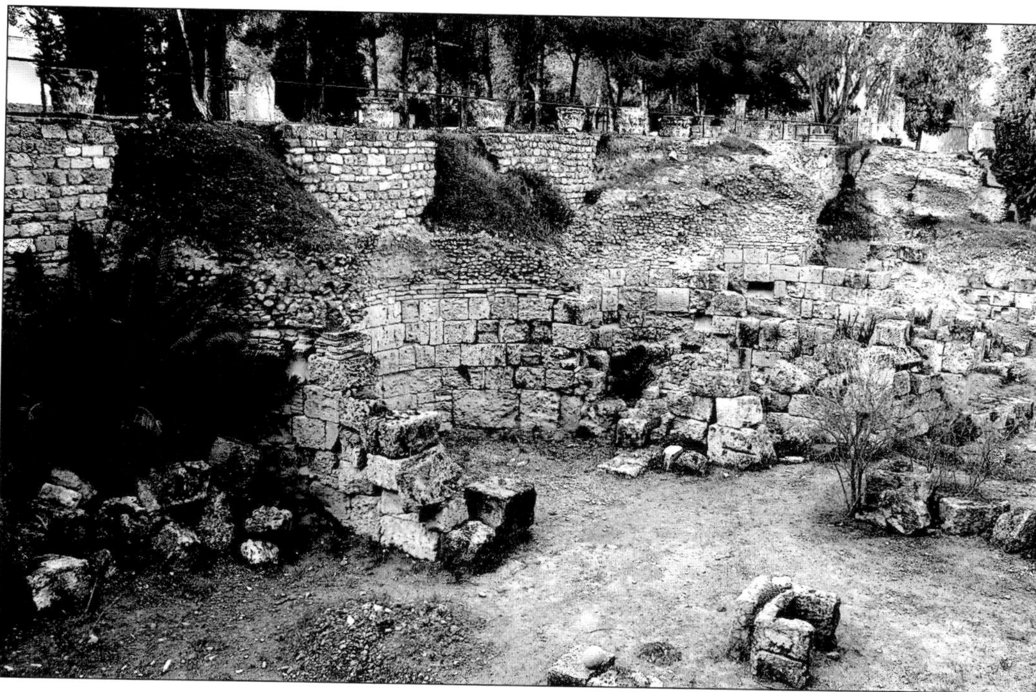

Fig. 13.2 Apsed retaining structure for the Roman basilica, built on the north-east side of the Byrsa hill. It was uncovered by Beulé in 1859, and interpreted by him as part of the Roman governor's palace.

supported a massive artificial terrace. This terracing was built immediately after 15 BC and entirely buried an area of late Punic housing (Fig. 3.9).[74] Beulé had found the continuation of the same terrace enclosure on the eastern side of the Byrsa when he dug his trench 'K' and released the fall of early Roman amphoras. Thousands of early Roman amphoras had been laid in rows behind the terrace wall to moderate drainage. Delattre excavated a significant extent of the 'First Amphora Wall' in 1893 and published the epigraphy on the amphoras in 1894. The larger vaulted apses on the east side of the summit, which Beulé was the first to investigate, were, as noted above (p. 193), the eastern-facing vaults of a huge Roman concrete platform, supporting a judicial basilica belonging to the middle of the second century AD.[75]

Davis' thirty-fifth and last site: the second Mosaic of Nereids and Tritons

Although Davis' excavations were closed by October 1859, he kept some workmen on until then, partly to mislead Beulé and the French about the status of his project. Perhaps in the spring or summer of that year, Davis again set his men to digging at the village of Douar ech-Chott. The site was within the village itself, as the latter's buildings are outlined on both the plan of Falbe and on Davis' published map: Davis' thirty-fifth and last excavation at Carthage, site 20 on his published map, falls among them. The site is very close to the house which Davis had originally hired. He was no longer living in the house, but Dr Heap had made it his headquarters, and Davis used it as a workshed and storeroom. He may have set his workmen to excavate close by in order to keep an eye on them while he occupied himself with packing.

He described this site as 'in the field adjoining the cemetery at Dowar Eshutt', adding that this was the very same field in which he had first broken ground at Carthage. On the published map, points 1 and 20 are about 200 m apart, with point 20 to the south-west, and Davis is either being very approximate or describing a very large field. The Muslim cemetery at Douar ech-Chott was outlined on the Bordy map in 1897; it was undoubtedly in exactly the same location in Davis' day. It was on the north side of the village, just east of the road from La Goulette to La Marsa. The site also lies about 70 m south-east of the circus. Davis identified the site as the 'Temple of Neptune' on his map, but almost certainly the name reflects nothing more than the subject matter of the mosaic which was found there.

The site is in the south-eastern quarter of the city, between *decumani* 5 and 6 south and on the line of *cardo* 1 east. Davis described the site as being a very few hundred feet from the military harbour in the direction of Douar ech-Chott,[76] but it actually lay about 400 m from the harbour. It is also so close to the Circus that this seems a very disingenuous way to describe the site; given the subject matter of the mosaic, Davis may have been indicating its proximity to the sea, but again, in terms of the topography of Carthage, the sea is not near.

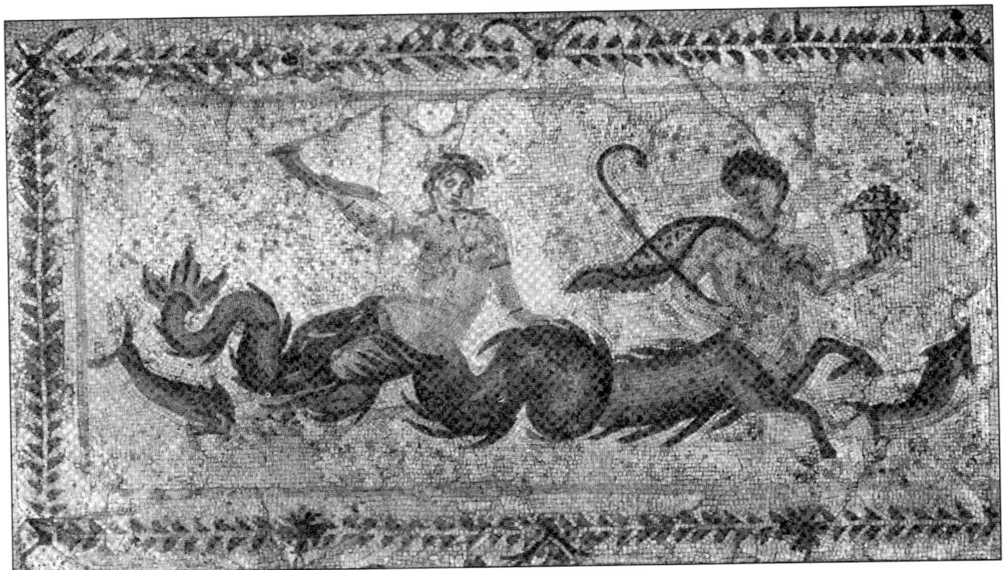

Fig. 13.3 Carthage, second Mosaic of Nereids and Tritons (see Fig. 11.2 for the other mosaic with the same theme found by Davis): the nereid (left) holds a drinking horn, the triton a shepherd's crook (pedum) *and a basket. Two small dolphins are in attendance. Part of a long frieze (height of field: 1.04 m). The border consists of simple stems with pairs of shoots springing from either side, similar to those in Figs 11.1 and 11.3. Mid-second century AD.*

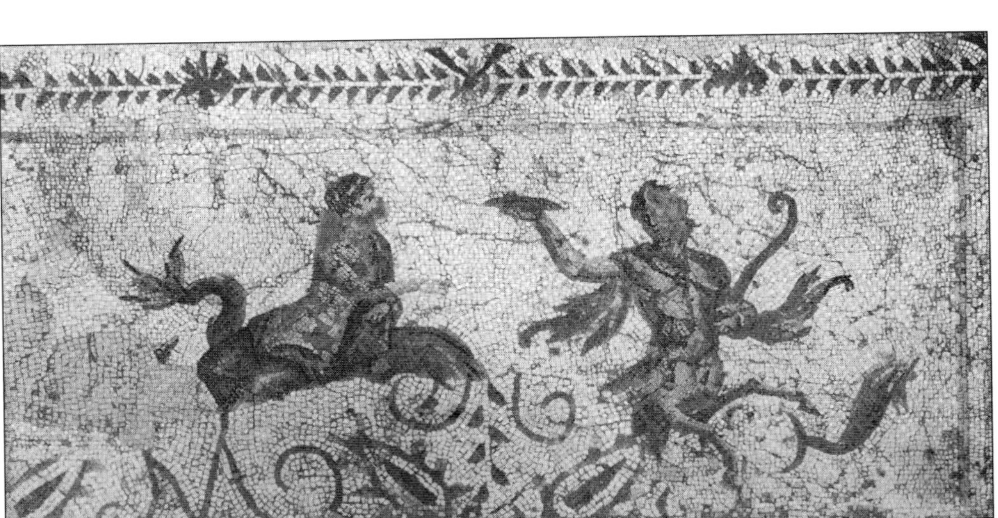

Fig. 13.4 Another detail from the same Mosaic of Nereids and Tritons as that shown in Fig. 13.3. The triton holds a curved stick (or a ship's aplustre?) and an offering dish (patera). *The lower bodies of both the nereid and the triton are incomplete; the lower part of the mosaic had been repaired in antiquity ignoring the original design.*

The excavation at Site 35 was not casual, as Davis said that he dug 18 ft (5.5 m) down to reveal a mosaic pavement with intermittently inlaid panels.[77] This was the second Mosaic of Nereids and Tritons.[78] It is possible that this mosaic was found after Davis' letter to Lord Russell in July 1859, as he did not mention it then. Davis himself was not impressed with the quality of the pavement, but it attracted a continuous stream of the local Tunisian nobility; the readers of Davis' book were invited to see it at the British Museum, or to wait for his planned work *Carthaginian Remains Illustrated*.[79] The mosaic consisted of two sections (Figs 13.3–4) from a long frieze of marine deities of Nereids and Tritons, which were evidently repeated at intervals of 10 ft (3 m). One of the fragments has poor-quality ancient repair, such that the Triton's body is mostly missing (Fig. 13.4). According to Davis the panels were in a direct line with a pedestal 4.5 ft (1.4 m) high, but this statement does not make any obvious sense. A length of pavement 25 ft (7.6 m) long was uncovered, and rough tessellation continued for 35 ft (10.7 m) more. The friezes formed the '*emblema*' of the pavement; each frieze has a delicate foliate-pattern border on each long side. Hinks gave the dimensions of the width of the field between the borders as just over a meter (1.04 m to be precise). The design is very similar to the first Mosaic of Nereids and Tritons from the seaside villa excavated by Davis at Gammarth and certainly is closely contemporary.

Davis' second mosaic of Nereids and Tritons was evidently found next to the large *turris aquaria* (water tower) which is outlined on the map of the water supply of Roman Carthage published by Andrew Wilson (Fig. 4.1);[80] this large building, which occupied more than half of a city block, lay immediately to the south of the mosaic. It seems possible that this Mosaic of Nereids and Tritons paved a forecourt for the water tower; in that case it might have defined a public court and shrine leading to fountains or pools which could easily have been designed in association with the water tower. If this mosaic is related to the construction of a water tower, it would also relate to the construction of the aqueduct, suggesting a date around the mid-second century, a date which is generally confirmed by the style of the mosaic.

Davis' second (or third) notice from the Foreign Office came from Lord John Russell and was written on September 12th, 1859. The death of Davis' patron, Mohammed Bey, followed shortly thereafter, perhaps even before Russell's letter reached Davis, as the new Bey, Mohammed-es-Sadok, succeeded on September 23rd, 1859. Since Davis had relied on the support of Mohammed Bey, his death was a significant event which may have convinced Davis that his project had reached an end. The second Mosaic of Nereids and Tritons was the last of the twenty-six mosaics which Davis sent to the British Museum from Carthage, and all of his subsequent efforts focused on packing and arranging for the finds to be sent to Britain.

Beulé's excavations at the necropolis of Gammarth

Beulé had finished his first season of excavation under pressure, as he had to hurry back to Paris in the spring of 1859 to teach his course on archaeology.[81] He returned to Carthage in October, immediately after learning that Davis had closed his excavations. He came back bored with the Byrsa, or perhaps stung that the government had not granted his request through the Academy for 6,000 francs to continue excavation there.[82] To Beulé's displeasure, the walls he had exposed on the south side of the Byrsa had been dismantled in the short intervening months that he had been away.[83] He was looking for fresh questions, and decided to investigate the necropolis of Gammarth and the ports of Carthage.

Already on November 13th, Beulé sent a description of his completed excavations among the tombs at Gammarth to a colleague.[84] Gammarth, four miles north of the Roman city, was the site of an ancient necropolis which Davis had explored in the spring of 1858 (Davis' Site 30) and which he thought covered more than a square mile.[85] Beulé believed that these were Punic tombs, because the site would have been within the line of Punic walls which ancient sources said ran across the isthmus. Great numbers of chamber tombs were tunnelled into the limestone under the hill of Djebel Khaoui, the 'empty mountain,' on the more gently sloping north side, away from the city. Beulé's exaggerated claim that there were thousands of tombs and millions of burials on the site were to be revised by Delattre to an estimate of between 200 and 250 tombs and perhaps 3,400 burial spaces.[86] At first Beulé explored the tombs alone, as his men refused to enter them. His account of slipping into a partly dirt-filled tomb, and sliding through the empty niches that had been prepared for the corpse into the next chamber, exactly paralleled Davis' account, except for the fact that Davis allowed an Italian ('Giovanni') who had some mining experience to do the exploring, noting that he was equipped with candles and matches.[87]

Beulé then began his excavations by clearing the topsoil from an undisturbed space of 15 by 20 m to reach the surface of the harder rock that overlay the tombs. A cut in this led his men to the entrance of a tomb, which he emptied of soil when he found the ceiling and plaster intact. The tombs varied little in type and Beulé thought they were aligned, with possible traces of streets and drainage above. Steps led down a narrow passage to the rectangular and symmetrical tomb chamber, with long narrow niches cut perpendicular to the walls for inhumation burials (Fig.13.5). Beulé found no trace of Christian symbolism in the tombs, although he noted that they were used into Byzantine times since he found a coin of Heraclius (AD 610–41) at the feet of a skeleton in a tomb he unsealed.[88] The almost complete lack of finds in the tombs, particularly lamps, had already been noted by Davis[89] and Beulé only found skeletons behind those niches which still had intact plaster flat with the wall. Although he had been asked to recover a skull for the Jardin des Plantes in Paris, this was impossible because the bones were soft as paste when found, and turned to powder when they had dried out.

Beulé improved on Davis' popularizing account by publishing the plan of a superior intact tomb, and noting scholarly parallels to Jewish tombs in the Holy Land: among them was the family tomb popularly identified as that of Joseph of Arimathea at the Church of the Holy Sepulchre in Jerusalem.[90] Beulé believed that these tombs had served the Punic city for seven centuries, and for seven more after the arrival of the Romans.[91] He was certainly wrong in this, since shaft tombs, first published by Delattre in 1885, demonstrate that the Phoenician and Punic Carthaginians buried their dead within the city. Nevertheless Beulé's plan confirms that the tombs of Gammarth have clear Palestinian models, and that the necropolis flourished from Roman to Byzantine times. The cemetery of Gammarth raises important questions about the numbers and status of Jews in the Roman city.

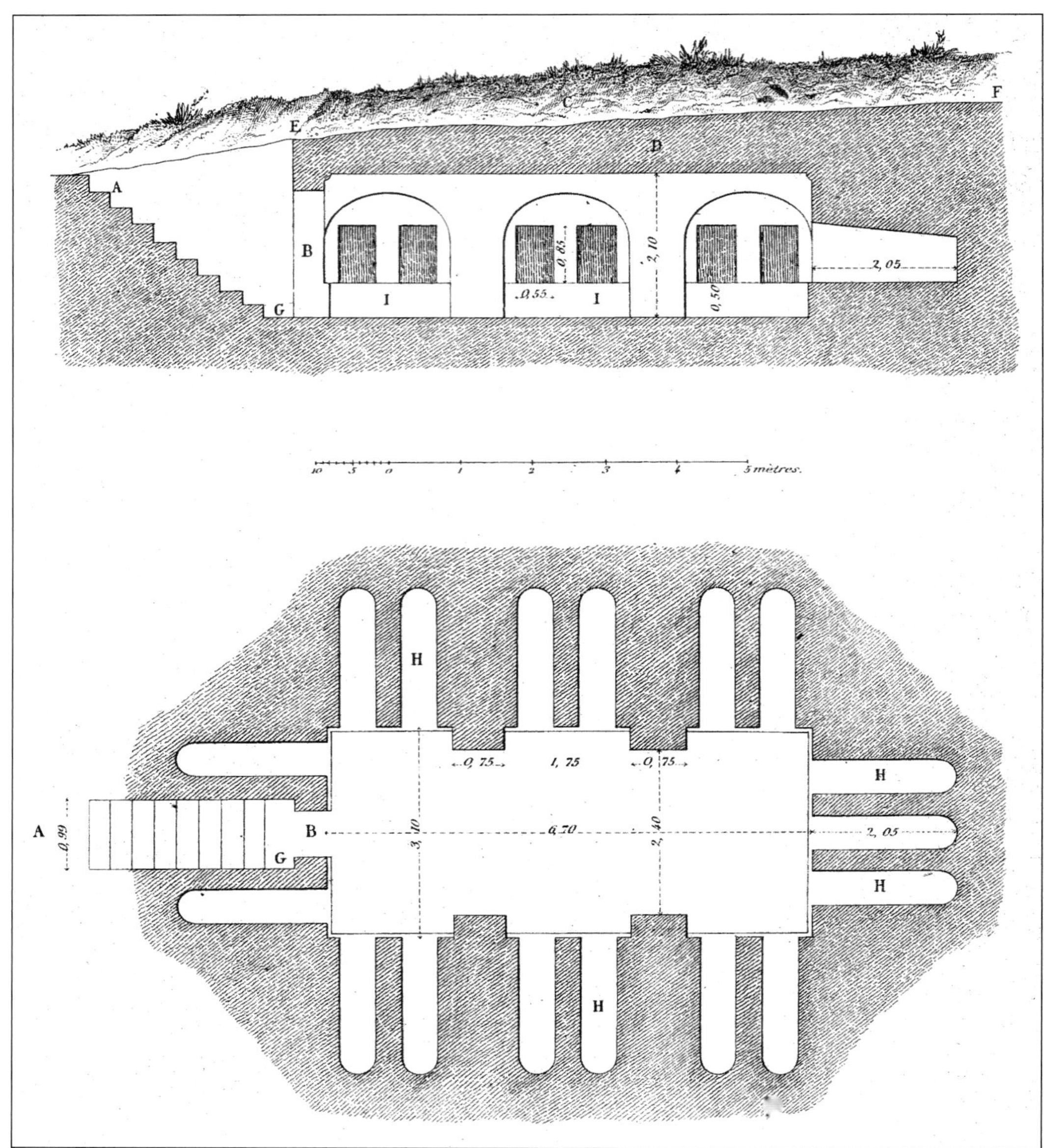

Fig. 13.5 Gammarth, section and plan of a Jewish family tomb, excavated by Beulé

Beulé's excavation of the ports of Carthage

Beulé wrote to an unnamed correspondent about his completed excavations at the ancient ports of Carthage on December 15th, 1859. These excavations resulted in a simple plan that outlined the walls defining the circular or military harbour with its central island (Fig. 13.6), and a larger almost rectangular merchant harbour to the south.[92] Beulé came to Carthage already certain that the ports had been dug out by human labour, because of the definition of '*cothon*' in an ancient source (a word of Semitic root used by Latin sources to refer to an artificial harbour),[93] and he recognized that the nearby hill known as Koudiat el-Hobsia (no. 74 on the plan of Falbe) was formed by the excavated soil from it.[94]

In order to excavate at the ports, Beulé needed the permission of the powerful Mameluke ministers of the Bey, the Khaznadar and Khereddine, Minister of the Marine, who both had summer villas on the site. Beulé commented that the Prime Minister, Mustapha Khaznadar, 'showed his Greek blood' by offering Beulé access to his gardens; the Khaznadar was urbane enough to assure him that any damage from his excavations would be a valued souvenir.[95] Permission to dig was one obstacle; fear of contagion from the fetid and sloppy black mud was another. Beulé believed that Camillo Borgia had died of a fever contracted while exploring the ports, and Beulé's Arab labourers worked enveloped in their white wool cloaks, which they believed protected them from fever. Finally, as

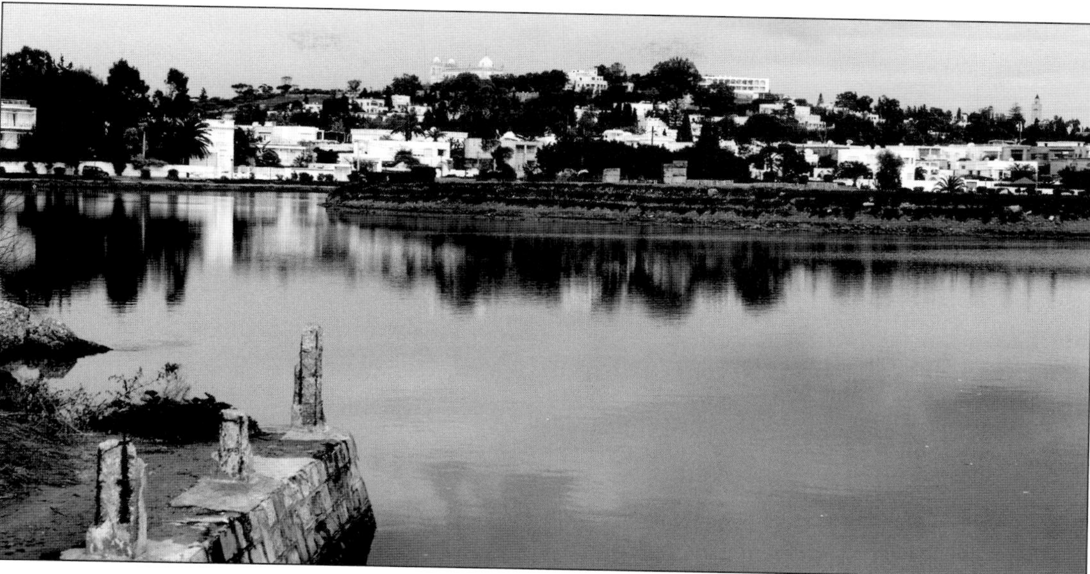

Fig. 13.6 The circular harbour as it appears today, from the south, with the island at centre, and the Byrsa hill crowned by the large French church (1884) on the sky-line

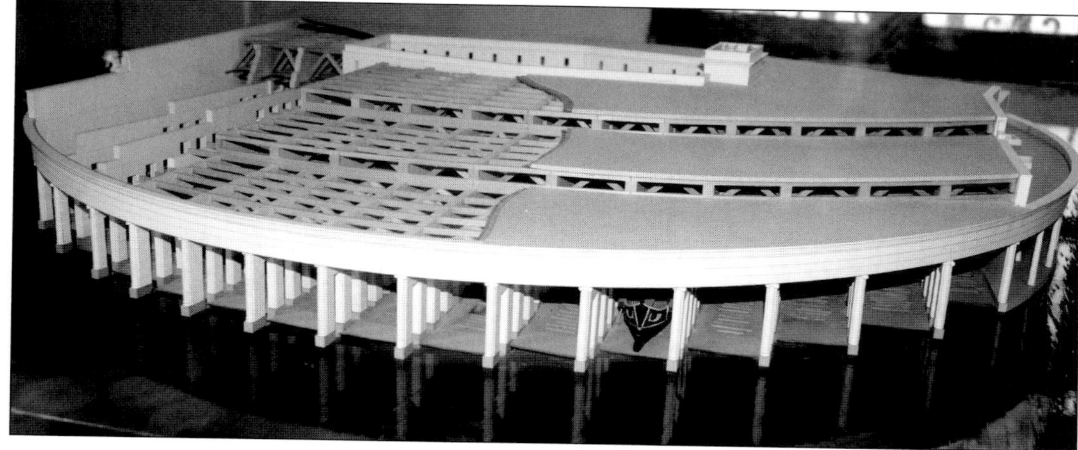

Fig. 13.7 Model of the Punic shipsheds on the circular island (shown with Ionic columns supporting the roof), based on the evidence of the 1970s excavations (Carthage, Antiquarium of the Harbours)

Davis had predicted, much of the work was done below the water table, which Beulé found only two or three meters down. As Beulé said, the goal of his research was to follow the walls;[96] once the water had settled in each small trench, he was able to draw the defining wall.[97]

Beulé first worked on the island of the circular harbour, excavating the tops of walls to determine its measurements. The walls he found were Roman, but he said they followed the plan Appian had described. After tracing the quay that crossed the harbour from the island northward, Beulé also correctly recorded the width of the Punic shipsheds on the outer side of the harbour. He openly stated that he here destroyed Roman architecture without scruple in order to find precious Punic remains.[98] On the island itself his finds included large blocks of Punic stone. He also described singular heavy cornices, covered in thick stucco and painted red and yellow, which, despite his interest in architecture, he hesitated to identify as Punic.[99] He was looking for the Ionic columns described by Appian, and although he found no trace of the capitals, he did find two fragments of engaged fluted Greek columns, 47 cm in diameter, that were covered with fine white stucco surfaces.[100] These he considered adequate proof of Appian's description; the whole military harbour was clearly inspired by Greek models. More than a century later, Hurst's team excavated a fragment of volute from an Ionic capital and other architectural debris that tend to confirm Beulé's conception of the Punic ports (Fig. 13.7).[101]

Beulé and his men also worked their way around the plan of the merchant harbour (Fig. 13.8), sinking fifty small, discontinuous trenches to follow the walls; this land belonged to the village of Douar ech-Chott, but the villagers were more than cooperative. In contrast, the south-east corner of the merchant harbour, where Beulé expected to find the entrance to the whole harbour complex, lay within a gun battery manned by military guards. Beulé knew he had no chance of obtaining a permit to dig there, so he simply deployed sixty workmen, who were told not to answer questions. The guardsmen sent an officer to La Goulette for instructions; the officer took his time, and when he returned with a military escort, it was already evening and the work had been completed.[102] The results of this effort suggested to Beulé that the narrow entrance to the port along the southern edge was 126 m long and only 6 m wide.[103]

The result of Beulé's few weeks of work was a clear plan of the two ports. Subsequent work has shown that he was generally correct in his mapping of the island of the Circular Harbour, with its surrounding ring of water, although he did not draw the outer ring of shipsheds because he did not have evidence for their length. Beulé also did not guess that the Circular Harbour as described by Appian was first built only in the first half of the second century BC, shortly before the Third Punic War.[104] By contrast, his plan of the merchant harbour has been completely superseded (Fig. 13.9). A method that could quickly produce enough evidence to define a circle was not adequate to draw a rectangle of unknown size. The port as he drew it was at least two and a half times larger in area than

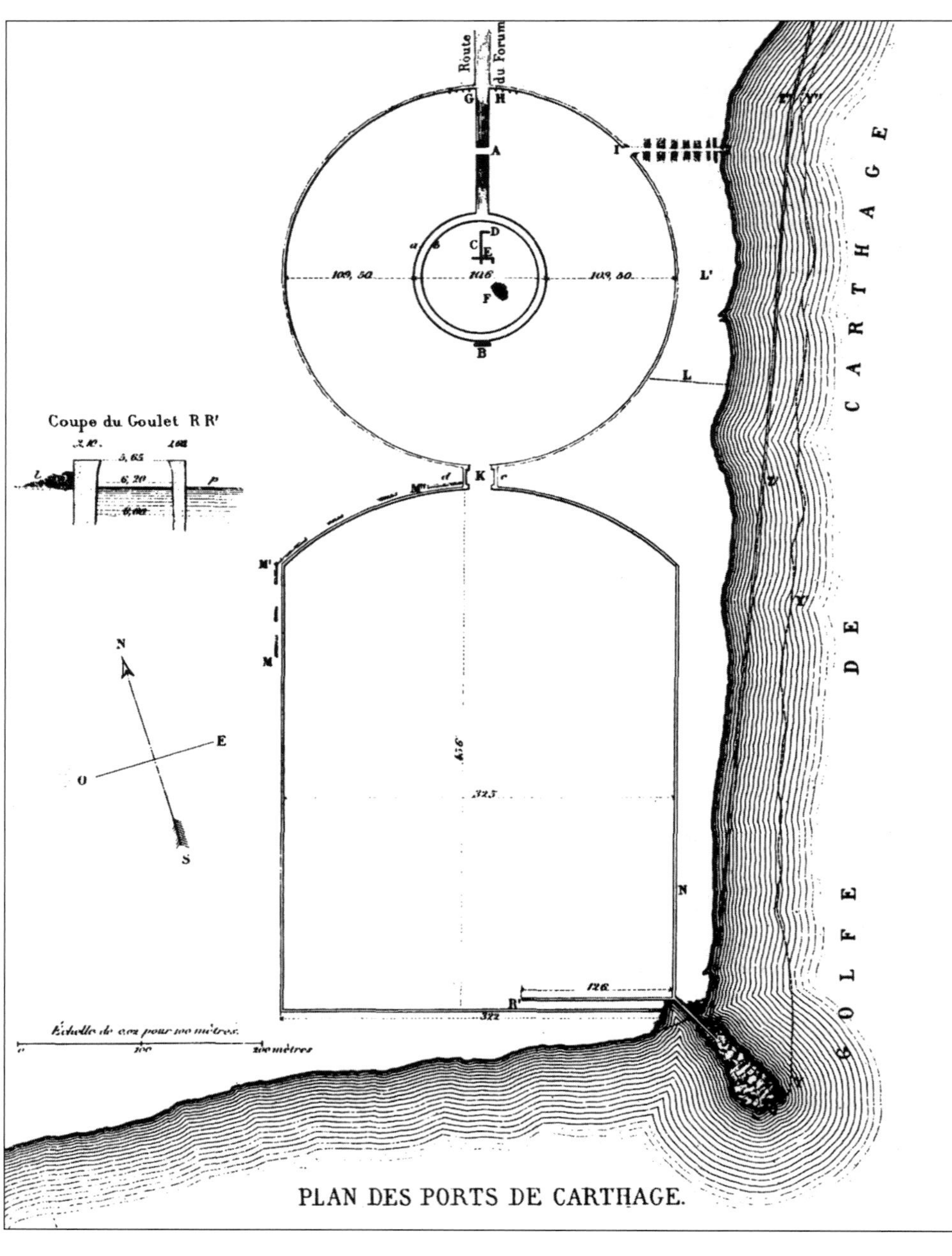

Fig. 13.8 Beulé's plan of the Punic harbours (1861). He was the first to detect remains of the Punic shipsheds on the north side of the harbour, at points marked G and H at the top of this plan.

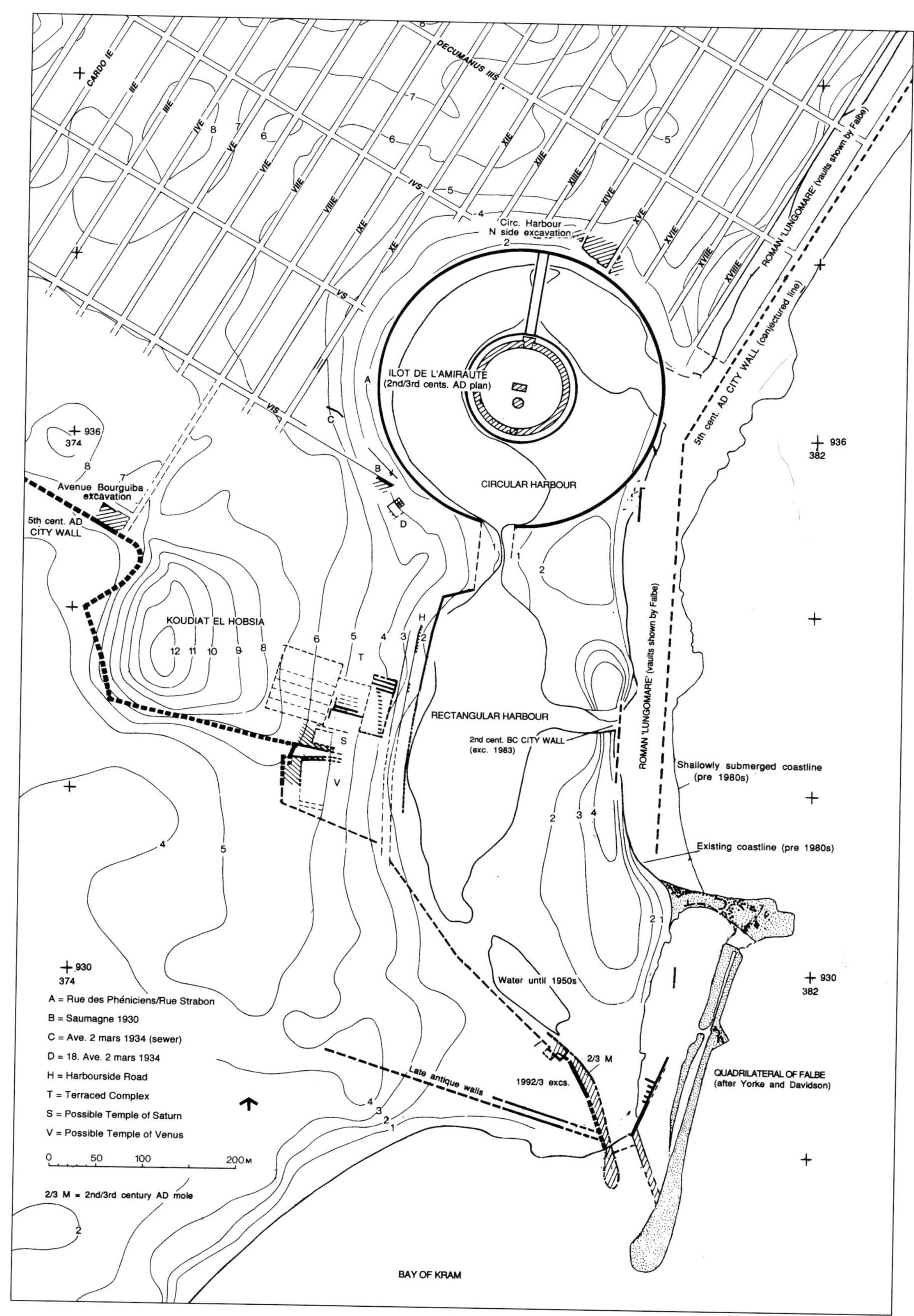

Fig. 13.9 Plan (1994) of the area of the harbours during the Roman period, on the basis of the most recent research

the outline accepted today,[105] and Beulé also rotated the north–south axis of the ports 20°, so that the axis of the complex lies on a north-north-east alignment.

In the 1970s a team led by Larry Stager was to excavate at the *tophet* and on the west side of the merchant harbour as part of the UNESCO campaigns. Because the commercial harbour was flanked by the *tophet*, it could never have been as wide as Beulé thought. Furthermore Stager's excavation showed that a canal about 50 m wide running north–south preceded both harbours, and the quay of the commercial harbour was first built only in the third century BC. A section of the quay wall on the north-west side of the commercial harbour was built of seven courses of ashlar blocks in El Haouaria sandstone, but only the lowest three courses belong to the Punic harbour, which was only two and a half meters deep. In the second or third century AD, the shape of the harbour was changed to a long hexagon, as the blocks form a corner with an angle of 120°. Beulé could perhaps have mapped the quay wall which Stager found with the underwater method that the former described, but Stager's wall indicates that the commercial harbour was less than 150 m in width, whereas Beulé's plan indicates a width of 325 m.[106] Furthermore, the double line of wall which Beulé thought formed the southern limit and entrance to the harbour was re-excavated by Henry Hurst's team in the early 1990s. These walls are in concrete, almost certainly a different material to that used for the walls which Beulé's men were following elsewhere around the commercial harbour. According to Hurst, the concrete walls post-date the fifth-century-AD Theodosian Wall, and may even belong to after the Justinianic conquest in the sixth century. They lie between 60 and 70 m south of the Roman mole which was built in the second or third century AD ('2/3 M' on Fig. 13.9), and were built close to the water, on land which had only silted up over the preceding few hundred years. The entrance to the Punic commercial harbour was probably even further north at the end of the Punic period.[107] Although Beulé looked for the merchant harbour in the right general area, he clearly oversimplified the problem and mis-used the evidence that he found, partly because he did not imagine how complicated the geological and archaeological history of the area was.

Beulé also described a submerged line that he drew parallel to and east of the ports as the 'Theodosian Wall',[108] but there is no surviving evidence that the Theodosian Wall, which was built *c.* AD 425 to defend against landward attack by the Vandals, ever ran along the seafront. A more or less comparable line on the plan of Falbe was the southern continuation of the 'line of small chambers' which Beulé himself had earlier described as Roman storerooms, perhaps built above the line of Punic sea-wall. Evidence from east of the merchant harbour for the Punic city wall of the third/second century BC, including robber trenches and stuccoed architrave blocks,[109] does lie on this same line. Beulé's confusion about the identification of this wall is inexplicable.

The excavation of the harbours was the last of Beulé's exploits at Carthage. His account of his work ends abruptly, without any summing up. It seems that he came to Carthage with certain preconceptions, and, as he said, worked only 'until the diverse elements necessary to the solution of the problem could be discovered'.[110] The scholarly acclaim with which he was received on his return may have confirmed his belief that he had sufficiently dealt with Carthage, since he showed no further interest in the site.

Davis leaves Carthage

After bringing his excavations to a close in October 1859, Davis may have left Tunis, if only temporarily. He must have set seriously to work on his account of his excavations, as his book was ready for publication less than a year later. Davis nevertheless found time for a tour with American consul Nicholson around southern Tunisia in April of 1860, a trip that he described in the last chapters of *Carthage and Her Remains*. Davis had left Tunisia again by June 15th, 1860, when Wood wrote to Hammond reporting that Davis had left twenty cases of antiquities with him. The peripatetic Davis at that time set off for Cagliari in Sardinia, where he hoped to visit the Neolithic remains. In the event, he had to give up this plan because it was malaria season in Sardinia.[111]

HMS *Supply* was reported to be in transit for England from Malta with antiquities from Carthage sent by Consul Wood, according to a letter of Wood dated July 15th, 1860;[112] the ship arrived at London in August 1860.[113] The accession numbers of two mosaics, including seven fragments from the Vandal Hunting Mosaic, and one fragment from the second Mosaic of Nereids and Tritons, show that they were first catalogued in the Museum on October 2nd, 1860.[114] As noted above, the Mosaic of the Sirens may also have been included in this shipment, but it never received an accession number.

It is also possible that the Mosaic of the Sirens was shipped with the twenty further packages of antiquities from Carthage which were sent by Wood on HMS *Kertch*, as Wood reported in a letter of August 21st, 1860. Besides these cases, the shipment also included a bas-relief with four figures and a horse, and eight other smaller marbles. These packages had been left at Douar ech-Chott by Davis, who left a receipt for them as well as a receipt for the tools which he had left behind, as well as three cases of antiquities which he did not think worth sending (pieces of bas-reliefs and 38 Punic epigraphic fragments, as well as 26 scraps of Greek and Latin inscriptions).[115]

On August 30th, 1860, Davis wrote to the Foreign Office from a new address in England to announce the imminent publication of *Carthage and Her Remains*, asking if the office would care to buy copies.[116] The book was published with Richard Bentley in London in 1861. Davis set off in the spring of the same year with Henry Ferriere and American consul Nicholson for a more ambitious tour of Tunisia, collecting the material for his next book. Davis said this tour was undertaken one year later than the journey which he had described at the end of *Carthage and Her Remains*; it was contemporary with work by a French company to repair the ancient aqueduct bringing water from Zaghouan to Tunis.[117] His boasting of his control of an unmanageable stallion indicated that Davis had completely recovered his health and native buoyancy at this time.[118] The little group traveled in April and May, according to Davis' detailed table of each day's weather conditions, but, as usual for him, the year was omitted.[119] He delivered the manuscript of *Ruined Cities* to the publishing house of John Murray in 1862. In November of 1862, the unreliable Flaux reported that Davis was at Pisa writing a history of the Barbary pirates, a project that Davis had mentioned in *Carthage and Her Remains*.[120] From this point I have found nothing further about Davis' career or his whereabouts until the last year of his life. He revisited Tunis two decades later, in 1881, after the takeover by the French. The trip overtaxed him (he was seventy years old) and he may have contracted pneumonia; he died in Florence, where his daughter Margaret Piccioli had made her home with her family, in the January of 1882.[121]

14

The contribution of the pioneer archaeologists at Carthage

Davis and Beulé in the opinion of contemporary and later scholars

From the moment the competition between Davis and Beulé arose, the latter was able to establish himself as the 'better man' in an academic sense. The sophisticated Franks, described by one biographer as a European at heart,[1] was inclined to favour Beulé and his methods over those of Davis. Franks, for example, in his 1860 article on Davis' finds, included a long postscript on the results of Beulé's excavations at Carthage. He accepted Beulé's opinions that the vaults which the latter had uncovered on the south-western slope of the Saint Louis Hill were part of the Punic triple wall around the Byrsa, and that the vaults excavated on the eastern face of the hill belonged to the Roman palace of the proconsul, or perhaps to the library of Carthage. Franks concluded his paper on Davis' finds by expressing gratitude to Beulé for his disinterested investigations into the topography of Carthage, as the latter was 'not looking to be rewarded by the discovery of ancient works of art'.[2] Thus even a curator of the British Museum was prepared to disparage on principle the kind of work which Davis had done, even though it had supported Franks' own professional career.

The French academic establishment did not hesitate to harm Davis' reputation while championing that of Beulé. In 1886 Salomon Reinach described Davis' character as 'malicious'; Reinach was referring to Davis' relations with, and comments on, Beulé.[3] The French archaeological establishment had not forgiven Davis for the jaundiced view which he took of Beulé and his efforts. The idea that Davis was hostile and unfair to Beulé became accepted among academics; for example, in 1888 Strzygowski took Davis' negative comments on the figures in the Mosaic of the Months, excavated at the south corner of the Saint Louis hill, as an aspersion cast at Beulé.[4] This was certainly not the case, because Davis knew that that mosaic had in fact been discovered by the guardian of the Chapel of Saint Louis, and had no connection at all with Beulé.

French prejudice against Davis has not moderated over the years. In the 1950s Dupuy, when noting Davis' work, said that 'his activity was far from being as disinterested as that of M[onsieur] Beulé, who was a real archaeologist'. In the same context, Dupuy gave a polite nod of recognition to Alphonse Rousseau, Léon Roches and Abbé Bourgade, who all had the distinction of being French.[5] Rousseau was a desultory if enthusiastic amateur of archaeology, with nothing remarkable to offer in terms of scholarly method, while Abbé Bourgade, although a serious scholar of the Punic texts which he collected, was an antiquarian and not an archaeologist. Consul Roches, although he sent artifacts to Berbrugger at the Museum of Algiers,[6] was not particularly distinguished, even as an antiquarian.

The competition between Beulé and Davis was exacerbated by the long-established rivalry between France and Britain in Tunisia. The arrival of the former at Carthage marked the beginning of more than a century of French ascendancy in Tunisia and in Tunisian archaeology. The immediate result, however, of Beulé's demonstration that Davis' methods could be improved on, and that he was the man to do it, was to bring academic archaeology at Carthage to an abrupt halt. Beulé had dared to confront Davis, but, with Davis removed, Beulé's exalted status made the questioning of his results unwelcome. No French academic was in a position either to challenge his results or to improve on them.

Armand de Flaux excavated for a month at Carthage in 1862, but declared the field exhausted; he tried to save face in his report to his patron, Count Walewski, by criticizing both Davis and Beulé, but his criticisms are ludicrously feeble.[7] In 1862, Gouvet, a French engineer commissioned by the Bey to restore the Bordj-Djedid cisterns, dug a trench as much as 100 m long and 10 m deep in the Roman block south of the cisterns. This was an amateurish archaeological effort with exciting results, as Gouvet's excavation went through early Christian and Roman layers to Punic levels, but his excavation was never published.[8] The enterprising Auguste Daux, with a commission from the emperor Napoleon III in the 1860s, was to claim that he himself had excavated and mapped the triple wall around the entire extent of Punic Carthage. Daux's unsupported claims did not challenge Beulé, however, but indirectly supported his views. Tissot incorporated Daux's description of the Punic walls into the map of Carthage which he published in 1884. Tissot then encouraged Reinach and Babelon to excavate at Carthage, where common sense forced them to expose Daux's evidence for these walls as completely unreliable.[9] Subsequent maps omit them.

Flaux, Gouvet and Daux did not publish their work, and their efforts are largely forgotten.

The situation changed when Sainte-Marie took up excavation at Carthage in 1874; significantly, that was the year of Beulé's death. Young Father Alfred-Louis Delattre, who was posted to a mission on the site of the Chapel of Saint Louis in 1875, soon followed Sainte-Marie's example. In 1878 Sainte-Marie, surveying the past from the French point of view, declared that Falbe, Dureau de la Malle and Beulé were the three greatest contributors to an understanding of the topography of Carthage.[10] This Francophile ranking has never been seriously challenged, although Falbe was a great topographer but certainly not a great archaeologist, and Dureau de la Malle was not an archaeologist at all. Although political history may suggest that the story of the earliest archaeologists at Carthage is about the triumph of France, this is a serious misinterpretation of the evidence. From an archaeological viewpoint the first pioneers at Carthage were men of varying backgrounds who had the earliest opportunities to create and apply scientific methodology to the physical remains of the ancient city. Whether they were French or not is of peripheral significance.

Humbert, Falbe, Temple and Reade

The very earliest archaeologist to have worked at Carthage was the Dutch engineer Jean Emile Humbert. Humbert sent the Rijksmuseum in Leiden a collection of pottery and small finds. It seems likely from the fact that Humbert dug along the western road which bounded the ancient city that he intended to investigate tombs, believing that he would be most successful in collecting finds for the Rijksmuseum by following this method. If this was in fact the case, he had some awareness of the topography of the Roman city and the function of this area. Humbert may not have consciously formulated his hypothesis, but he had his reasons for his individual approach. His pottery finds were later catalogued by Holwerda along with other pottery in the museum's collection.[11] The catalogue in turn provided examples of complete forms of pottery from Carthage which John Hayes was later to use in his seminal work on the chronology of the Roman pottery of Tunisia.[12] Tunisia was a major exporter of pottery from the second to at least the sixth century AD, and archaeologists today depend heavily on identification of these wares and forms to date sites belonging to the time of the Roman Empire. The simple fact that Humbert sent his Carthage finds to a museum allowed them to be used to advance knowledge of Roman material culture more than a century later.

Falbe is a giant in the story of the early archaeology at Carthage, although his greatest contribution was as a topographer. His map of the topography of the ancient city (Fig. 3.2) was a crucial advance, because it allowed excavation to be based on hypotheses, not necessarily consciously formulated, about the function of different areas. Falbe's map convinced Dureau de la Malle that the site of the Roman city was identifiable, and that the Punic city lay beneath it. Falbe, however, was more distinguished as an antiquarian than as an archaeologist. In his own day, he was probably best known as a numismatist. Numismatists today go to the publication of the Royal Collection of Coins and Medals in the Danish National Museum for the Punic coins of Carthage; a collection based on donations by Falbe.[13] He was a discerning collector who published original and early observations on these coins.[14]

Falbe brought Grenville Temple and the funds of the Society for the Exploration of Carthage to excavate at four particular sites which he had mapped and which he seems to have thought would produce mosaics or other significant finds. His map showed that remains of architectural interest survived in each of these places, but there is no evidence that Falbe formulated an argument that these sites would be productive of finds for collectors, and in two cases they evidently were not. As an archaeological team, Falbe and Temple never published their results at Carthage, but, once again, many of their scattered finds have ended up in museums where they have been made available to scholars.

Thomas Reade's archaeological interest in Carthage was evidently limited to the site of the Antonine Baths, and only politeness would allow anyone to consider his plundering of the site's architectural remains as archaeology. Nevertheless, although he never published any account of the excavations he sponsored, occasional finds from his excavations have also reached museums.

The contrast between Davis and Beulé

Davis and Beulé made more solid contributions to archaeology, but are distinguished from each other by starkly contrasting methodologies. Davis saw the whole site of Carthage as an untapped opportunity to find cultural treasure for the British Museum, and took the advice of curators at the British Museum to supply himself with maps, including the plan of Falbe. Davis saw his function as an archaeologist in terms of the physical process of unearthing finds and despatching them to the British Museum. He left the publication and analysis of his finds to the curators of the Museum, whom he imagined were better suited than himself to that role. Digging at Falbe's sites did not produce finds for Davis, and he was more successful after he formulated his own hypothesis that the topographical locations which seemed to him to be suitable for luxury housing would have been equally suitable for that purpose in ancient times. Sites that fit this description brought him mosaics and other finds. Whether Davis' finds have fared better for being removed from their archaeological context is an ethical concern. The Punic *stelae* were published immediately by Vaux, and have now been re-published by Carole Mendleson with more documentation explaining their significance.[15] We know much more about these individual artefacts than we would otherwise have gleaned, simply because Davis retrieved them from Carthage. The mosaics are a more debatable case. Certainly those which reached the British Museum have been carefully preserved, and that of course is crucial. Those on display have undoubtedly had a large audience, and a majority of that audience may identify through them with Roman culture more generally; but that is not to say that the mosaics themselves have necessarily been better understood. They have been relatively neglected by scholars, a situation that this book is intended to remedy.

Beulé burst on to the scene with the conscious intention of discrediting Davis' efforts and his finds, and with the less clearly formulated intention of proving that Appian's description of Punic Carthage could be demonstrated by fieldwork on the ground. In his knowledge of and dependence on ancient texts, Beulé had something in common with Schliemann at Troy and Mycenae. Beulé attacked the south-west side of the Byrsa Hill in order to prove that the Byrsa identified by Falbe would be surrounded by the Punic defences which Appian had described. On his return to Carthage he first excavated and mapped tombs at Gammarth, but here he seems to have been drawn away from his original goals because of the interest which Davis' work in the tombs had aroused in him. Beulé hypothesized that these were the tombs of the earliest Carthaginians; but he was unable to demonstrate this, and his results showed only that they had Semitic cultural parallels and were in use until the Arab conquest. With scant time and perhaps scant money left, he then set out to demonstrate by excavation that Appian's description of the ports could be justified. His excavations at Carthage were of short duration. Furthermore, despite his superior academic and social status, as well as the support of the French consul, his private funds did not allow him to dig on Davis' gargantuan scale. His results at the ports were seriously compromised by the shortage of both time and money.

Davis dug to produce Punic finds to enrich the British Museum, while Beulé dug to record Punic architecture. Both wanted Punic finds and disdained Roman material remains, a prejudice that was to some extent shared by their contemporaries. Although Davis did not abandon Roman and later small finds such as lamps and pottery, he would have considered his excavations a total failure if this had been the extent of his finds. Davis advanced understanding of Punic culture by excavating re-used Punic *stelae* that were immediately properly published by Vaux. He contributed to Roman archaeology by discovering and lifting many Roman mosaics. Beulé's major contribution to an understanding of Punic culture was his plan of the Circular Harbour and the evidence which he found for the Punic shipsheds there. The apsed vaults which he recorded on the Byrsa (Fig. 13.2) and his plan of a Jewish tomb at Gammarth were somewhat accidental contributions. He has been considered a giant of early archaeology at Carthage, and certainly the fact that he dug to test hypotheses represented a great contribution to archaeology as a discipline; but the fact that he largely abandoned his finds was clearly a major flaw in his methodology. Furthermore, archaeologists have had to re-excavate his sites in order to understand what he found. On the other hand, at least in the cases of his excavations at the harbours and on the Byrsa Hill, he did at least leave plans which have allowed these sites to be identified with comparative ease.

Advances in method before archaeological theory

In the first fifty years of excavation at Carthage archaeologists were struggling to learn how to carry out archaeology at the same time as they were gradually accumulating knowledge about the ancient city. Carthage was a difficult location at which to learn. Firstly, the surfaces of the site were extremely disturbed. Second, because of the reality of deep stratigraphic layering, finds generally revealed the culture of Byzantine, Vandal and Roman Carthage, which were discovered by and large not far below the surface, with only the occasional glimpse of Punic culture, the remains of which lay buried at a greater depth. The early archaeologists deliberately excavated ancient remains, rather than simply collecting antiquities, but their concept of context was no more specific than 'Carthage.' They did not understand the crucial significance of the link between artefact and specific context, and in the course of this first half-century of excavation they did not learn to understand it.

In terms of the history of archaeology of Carthage, this was the period in which choosing a specific excavation site on the basis of a hypothesis was born. Planning projects in order to test a hypothesis is a more intellectually respectable procedure than digging somewhere in the blind hope of finding something.

Working from a hypothesis was a position which had been gained through experience and criticism of past procedure, in which blind digging not only took place, but also was seen as an essential first step. It is possible to surmise that Humbert used this methodology in digging tombs on the western periphery of the ancient city; Davis certainly used it while looking for Punic housing, and Beulé used it too, although without articulating it, when he tried to establish that Appian's descriptions of the Byrsa and the ports were reliable.

Realities limiting Davis' achievement

Although Davis' great energy, ambition and resourcefulness demand respect, his personal will was only one of a number of crucial factors which determined the success or failure of his excavations. His work took place in a limited window of time and at a fortunate, if all too brief, intersection of national and international political interests, the availability of funding, and archaeological reality, the last of which determined what he would find. There is no doubt that his efforts would have been without result if any of these factors had not been favorable. With so many of the variables in his favour, it was archaeological reality which gave Davis his greatest difficulties, as the site of Carthage refused to give up its Punic treasures.

The problem was that Punic treasures, where they existed, were concentrated in shaft graves of which even the tops were often situated deeper in the ground than Davis ever dug. These Punic tombs and cemeteries did not lie outside the Roman city of Carthage; in fact, like Davis' own sites, they were concentrated in the hills on the north side of the city.[16] There were archaic Punic tombs and cemeteries on the south-west side of the Byrsa Hill, where Davis dug; rich tombs mainly of the fifth century BC (Douïmès), close to his site of the Mosaic with Baskets of Fish and Fruit; more tombs lay on lower ground near the Antonine Baths (Dermech); and slightly later shaft graves were found in the immediate area of Davis' excavations on the summit of Bordj-Djedid (Sainte-Monique).[17] Apart from Gouvet, Delattre (Fig. 14.1) was the earliest excavator to discover Punic tombs at Carthage. He first found archaic Punic tombs in deep trenches on the summit of the Hill of Juno in 1880, and published a first paper on a Punic tomb in 1885. This tomb was from exactly the area where Davis and Beulé had excavated, on the south-west side of the Saint Louis Hill.[18]

The great originality of Davis' contribution to archaeology at Carthage was that he revealed a Roman Carthage studded with mosaic floors. He was empowered by his mistaken belief that many of these mosaics were Punic, although his critics were aware from the first that they were of Roman date. Beulé was marked-

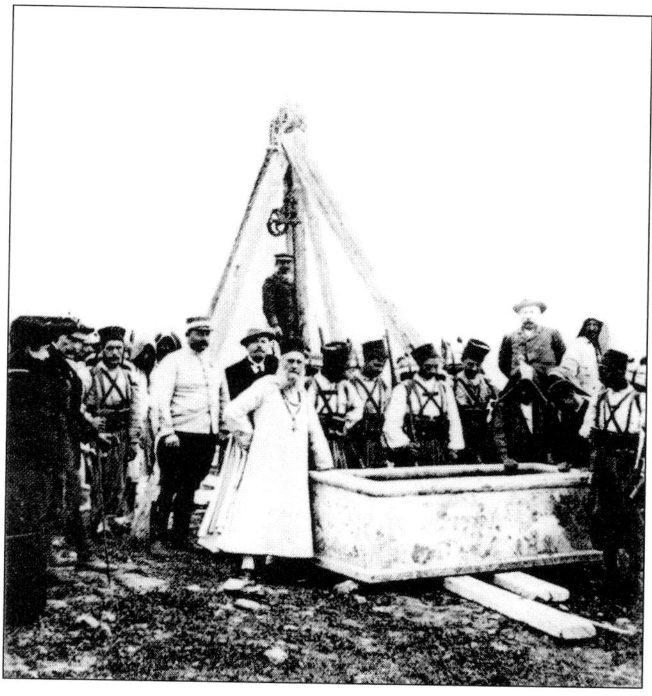

Fig. 14.1 Carthage, necropolis of 'Les Rabs' on the Sainte Monique Hill, c. 1902: Père Alfred Louis Delattre (1850–1932) at the raising of a Punic sarcophagus from a deep shaft tomb, accompanied by an officer and soldiers of the Fourth Zouave Regiment who had assisted in the operation

ly unfair to Davis when he said that he himself could have found hundreds of meters of them, since mosaics were ubiquitous and one only needed shallow trenches to find them. Beulé's claim that all the ground of Roman Carthage is covered with mosaics is not strictly true; furthermore, Davis often had to dig very deep trenches before he found mosaics. His scholarly contemporaries tended to be blasé about the significance of his mosaic finds, not wishing to give too much credit to a man who was not an academic and who considered his finds Punic when they were clearly Roman. Davis himself said that mosaics and inscriptions 'proclaim their own origin',[19] and, in fact, classically-trained scholars such as Franks, von Maltzan and Beulé had no difficulty recognizing Davis' mosaics as of Roman rather than Punic date. Nevertheless, the widespread use of polychrome figural and geometric mosaics was an aspect of the lifestyle of Roman Carthage which had hardly been imagined before Davis' excavations.

By sending the mosaics which he found back to England, Davis made them available for detailed study. Although scholars of the nineteenth century still attributed infinitely more value to inscriptions and knew relatively little about mosaics (on which publication was limited), they found them worthy objects of scholarly interest. Despite Beulé's opinion, not all the mosaics which Davis recovered were coarsely made and of little interest to science.[20] Although he had more to say about figural mosaics in his book, the collection in the Museum shows that Davis returned both figural and geometric mosaics from Carthage with equal zeal. Figural mosaics were naturally of far more interest to the early scholars than the geometric ones. More impressive to academics in his day, however, given the then general enthusiasm for inscriptions, were the ninety inscribed Punic votive *stelae* which Davis sent to the Museum. Six more *stelae* excavated by him went to the museum of Cagliari in Sardinia; it is likely that he made a gift of these to his esteemed friend, Canon Spano.[21] The Trustees of the British Museum approved the publication of the ninety *stelae* which they received, although the number of copies of this expensive volume of lithographs seems to have been limited.[22]

The size of the challenge

Like other archaeologists, whether early or not, Davis is liable to criticism for indiscriminate digging and for the fact that he destroyed many sites during his excavations at Carthage. The indiscriminate nature of his work was partly an unavoidable consequence of his being a very early archaeologist at Carthage, with little to guide him in his choice of excavation sites. It is true, however, that he pockmarked the site of Carthage with trenches. Some statistics may put Davis' destructiveness in perspective. As mentioned above, the street-grid of Roman Carthage covered an area approximately 5,790 feet by 5,528 feet square (1.471 km by 1.404 km). This does not sound like a very large surface area for the urban centre of one of the most important cities of the ancient world; however when it is considered as an archaeological site, such a surface area is intimidatingly large, at approximately thirty-two million square feet (slightly over two million square meters). It must have been particularly intimidating for Davis, who did not know where to look for the Punic remains which he hoped to find. Furthermore, I estimate that the site of Carthage has an approximate average deposition layer of 25 ft (7.6 m) from the surface down to natural, so that the entire city could in theory be excavated by the removal of 800 million cubic feet (about 15 million m^3) of soil and archaeological remains. In fact, Davis' trenches were relatively small, often covering no more than 400 sq ft (37 sq m) of surface area, with the removal of no more than 4,000 cubic feet (282 m^3) of soil, accomplished by pick and shovel. If this is multiplied by the 25 sites which Davis dug inside the city street-grid, one can estimate that he dug approximately 100,000 cubic feet (approximately 7,000 m^3) of soil. This was a little over 1/10,000th of the soil available for excavation in the urban centre of Carthage. No matter how intense Davis' efforts, they were puny by comparison with the sheer magnitude of the ancient site available for excavation.

In its upper layers, however, a notable percentage of this soil had already been disturbed. Especially when Davis chose to dig at ruins which were marked on the plan of Falbe, and therefore visible above the ground, he was doomed to deal with the dug-over remains left by the stone robbers who had often preceded him. Everyone who has excavated at Carthage knows that the site has been a stone quarry for centuries, and has had the experience of identifying a wall, not by its remains, but by a robber trench marking its former line. In a few cases, particularly at Falbe no. 54 and perhaps at Falbe no. 90, Davis also dug into soil disturbed by earlier archaeologists. In short, he, like Humbert, Reade, Falbe and Temple before him, and like Reinach, Babelon and Sainte-Marie after him, had many things going against him when he came to dig at Carthage. It was only with the excavations of Delattre, who had the advantage of living on the site and the option of choosing to excavate promising sites at the moment of their discovery, that the process of archaeological excavation at Carthage became less haphazard and more reflective of reasoned judgment of a particular site's potential.[23]

Beulé's place in the history of the archaeology of Carthage

Beulé came to Carthage as the model of a scholar and an experienced archaeologist, with the implicit intention of undermining Davis' credibility. Beulé strongly believed and easily convinced his contemporaries that the archaeologist's proper subject was architecture, and that the mere collection of artefacts for display was an improper goal. His convictions put Davis in the wrong, but it is also easy to see Beulé as narrow and rash. Like Davis, he believed that some cultures were more significant than others; and, at Carthage, Punic culture was infinitely to be preferred over Roman. Furthermore, while Beulé occasionally mentioned and described specific artefacts, he did not link them to stratigraphy, or see the value of dating them accurately, or collect them for future analysis. These were faults of his training, but it was undoubtedly a fault of his personality that Beulé's hypotheses quickly became incontrovertible preconceptions.

What, then, was Beulé's contribution? He took on three very large projects in his limited time at Carthage. Taking into consideration that he expended about twice as many man-hours at Carthage as Humbert, or as Grenville Temple and Falbe, and about one-sixth of the man-hours expended by Davis, he accomplished a prodigious amount of work. Although he did not understand their significance, he was the first to find two important series of apsed vaults on the Byrsa, describe them clearly and place them on a plan. He was the first to map a tomb at Gammarth, and his detailed plan agrees well with plans which Delattre published later; he also made the association between these tombs and Jewish tombs in the Levant. Most significantly, he was the first to excavate to recover the plan of the Punic ports, taking Dureau de la Malle at face value (who had said 'Falbe's plan leaves no doubt'), and showing that Appian's description of the Punic harbours could be confirmed on the ground. Although even a hundred years later there were scholars who missed this point, Beulé's excavations at the ports proved that, at least by the time of the Third Punic War, the Punic city of Carthage certainly occupied much the same site as the Roman city,[24] which itself could be recognized by the Roman monuments identifiable on the plan of Falbe.

Beulé's acquaintance with Carthage was nevertheless superficial and bookish; he came to the site to demonstrate what he already knew, and wrote for scholars who shared his knowledge and preconceptions. Yet as an archaeologist Beulé used scientific methods capable of providing objective and incontrovertible results. It is therefore all the more disconcerting to see that although he made brilliant observations on the Circular Harbour, his exploration of the merchant harbour was a rushed and botched job. One can see in his accounts of his excavations that Beulé had an agile mind, was quick to provide interpretations of his results which corroborated his hypotheses, and evidently had never encountered the experience of finding archaeological evidence which completely overturned them. But only in the case of the Circular Harbour have both his excavations and his interpretations stood the test of time. His poor results in the commercial harbour proved that, as Davis guessed, he did not have the time or resources to excavate it properly, and science would have been better served if his outline of it had never been published. His excavation and plan of a tomb at Gammarth provided useful data, and he was on the right track with scholarly parallels, but he was wrong in interpreting these 'Semitic' tombs as Punic rather than Jewish.

Because of Beulé's confident assertions that he had found a Punic wall around the Byrsa, the Saint Louis Hill was subsequently accepted as the Punic Byrsa by the majority of scholars. Although he may well have been correct in his identification of the Byrsa, his excavations did not prove his hypothesis. More than half a century later, his plans of the apsed vaults on the Byrsa helped Saumagne demonstrate something completely different: that the pattern of the Roman street-grid proved that the Byrsa was the centre of the Roman city. In short, Beulé was brilliant but unreliable. He fired the imaginations of the many later scholars who were to follow him to the ports of Carthage, and it was also his work which inspired the French to come back to the Byrsa in the UNESCO campaign, partly to shed further light on his excavation results, and partly to find evidence there for the Punic Byrsa in which Beulé had so ardently believed.

Davis' place in the history of the archaeology of Carthage

The acquisition of a large and significant collection of Roman mosaics and Punic *stelae* from Carthage by the British Museum, a feat that was unlikely in every way, was owed to a number of circumstances working in concert. The first of these was the initiative of Davis himself, the right man at the right time, particularly because of his practical genius at lifting pavements intact when mosaics became his major category of finds (Fig. 14.2). Second was the amenability of the Foreign Office to a project which was not purely politically motivated and which was unquestionably expensive.[25]

Davis' excavations were remarkable for the number of areas which he opened and for the quantity of soil displaced. His was no minor effort, and it is not surprising that he scorned Beulé, who, as Davis pointed out, spent a total of seventy days in excavation at Carthage. Davis' own difficulties at Carthage demonstrated that a person not interested in architectural remains could only pursue a satisfactory archaeological career with difficulty. The treasures of the Punic era were not easily to be found; and while he had chanced upon a notable deposit of re-used Punic votive inscriptions, he seemed somewhat bored by them and did not adequately record the circumstances of their excavation. Davis discovered many important mosaics, but he provided almost no direct evidence for the housing or architecture of Roman Carthage, hampered as he was by his conviction that the finer mosaics were from Punic temples. His methods and intemperate zeal may provoke derision, but his goals were not far out of line with those of other archaeologists of the day, and his work represented a tremendous advance over pure looting. His goal of collecting museum-quality antiquities led to his development of a fine method of lifting mosaics. In a number of ways, Davis' work was path-breaking, and set standards of professionalism for archaeologists of the future. He had written per-

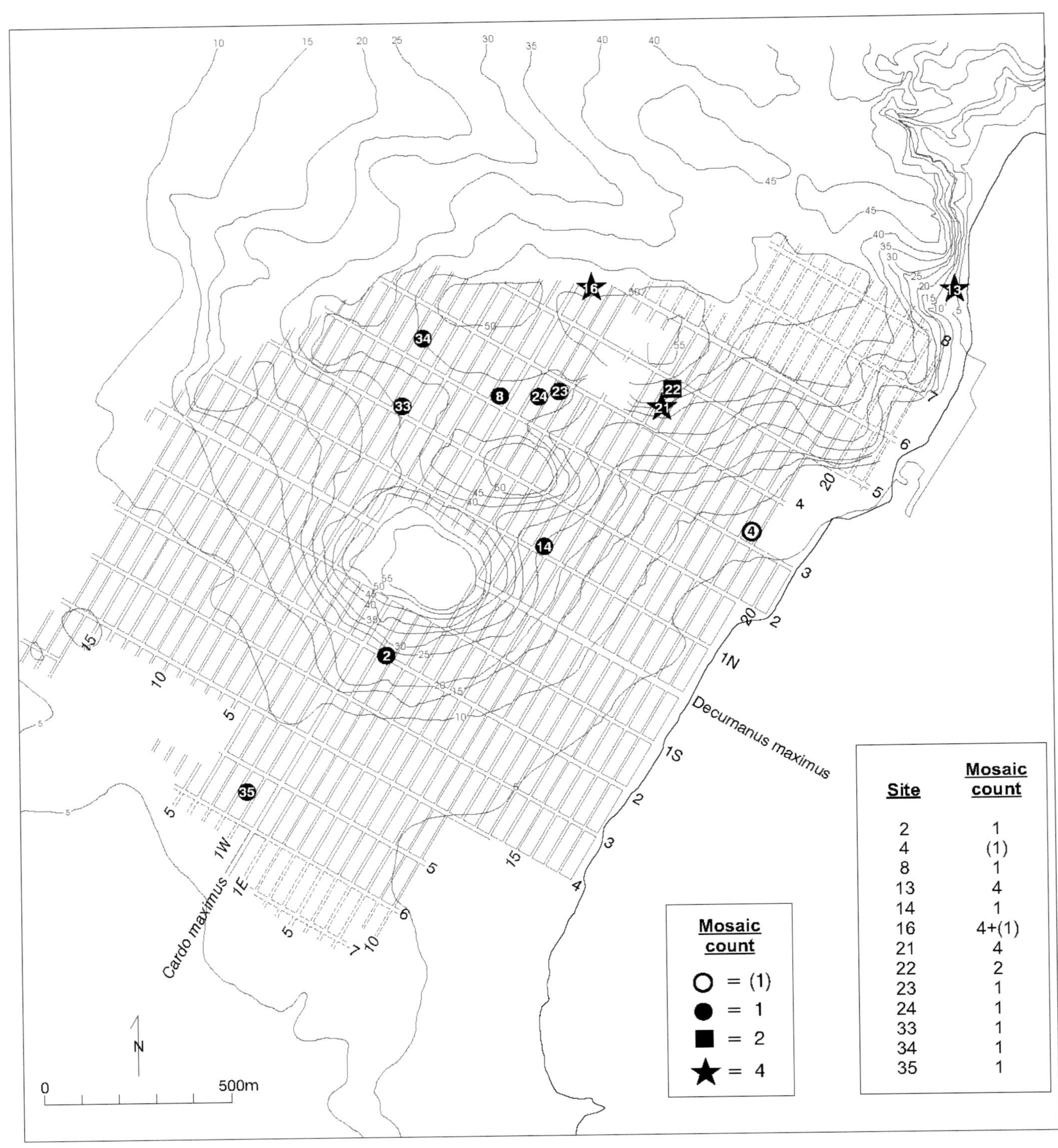

mission from the Bey and the approval of the British Museum; he had adequate funding from the British government, sufficient for him to carry out his intentions and to pay his men fairly; he excavated finds from contexts which were recorded, if minimally, and preserved them for an interested public, which included scholars as well as the 'holiday-going public' whom Blakesley deplored. He had a good working knowledge of Arabic and other useful languages, and the administrative and inter-personal skills to manage

Fig. 14.2 (opposite) *Map of Carthage showing the likely locations of Davis' trenches in which mosaic pavements were uncovered. The site numbers are the author's, as used throughout this book and as indicated in parentheses in the caption to Fig. 4.4, as follows:*
2 *Bath-house (Falbe no. 54);*
4 *Latrine of the Antonine Baths;*
8 *Mosaic of the Months and Seasons;*
13 *Mosaic of Victory (Falbe no. 90);*
14 *Mosaic of Baskets of Fish and Fruit;*
16 *'Carthaginian House';*
21 *House East of the Theatre;*
22 *Mosaic of Two Gazelles;*
23 *'Circular Monument' (Falbe no. 70);*
24 *Prostrate Column;*
33 *Mosaic of the Sirens;*
34 *Vandal Hunting Mosaic;*
35 *Second Mosaic of Nereids and Tritons.*
Four more mosaics were excavated at sites 29 and 31 near Gammarth, north of Carthage itself. In all twenty-four mosaics were found within the area of this map, of which twenty-two were excavated and sent to the British Museum. The mosaic at Site 4 (Fig. 5.7) and one of the five mosaics (the main one) at Site 16 (Fig. 10.2) were not retrieved: they are indicated here in the key by numbers in parentheses.

a gargantuan excavation and large teams of workmen. He acquired and read the scholarly works available, which were mostly in French, staked out measured rectangular trenches, placed his sites on an accurate map, sent along information on the contexts which he excavated for the Foreign Office, arranged for photographers and draftsmen, presented his work to reporters for the public press, safely delivered the booty to the British Museum, and published an account of his work promptly. He had the support and probably the advice of scholars at the British Museum, whom he counted on to produce scholarly publications of his finds, and his reports to the British Foreign Office were useful to Franks when he wrote up Davis' finds.

A major flaw in Davis' methods was his lack of properly detailed excavation journals, particularly when combined with his obliviousness to dates. Although it has proved possible to determine the provenance of the mosaics by using every scrap of evidence which Davis recorded, the small finds which he sent to the British Museum seem not to have been even listed by Davis, much less catalogued by him. He further undermined the usefulness of his work by not explicitly correllating his excavations with Falbe's site numbers and Dureau de la Malle's comments, especially since he was heavily dependent on both these authors. Also reprehensible was his total lack of interest in architectural evidence and his almost complete failure to record it, since he did not see it as part of his brief; even worse was the fact that he ignored architectural evidence in the course of destroying it.

In an important survey of archaeological developments in North Africa between 1834 and 1892 from a French point of view, Charles Diehl said that the heroic age of archaeology in North Africa ended with the establishment of the French protectorate in Tunisia in 1881.[26] He was thinking of the French line of archaeological work beginning around 1830 with the conquest of Algiers. Diehl was not aware of Humbert's work at Carthage, and probably would in any case have excluded the latter from his survey because he was not French. In Tunisia he would have included Falbe (always tacitly claimed by the French) and Dureau de la Malle, as well as Beulé, Guérin and Sainte-Marie. Diehl would certainly not have included Nathan Davis among his heroes, but I see Davis as a kind of Odysseus among the early archaeologists, too universal in his abilities to observe any ordinary limits, and too limited in his judgment to escape censure for his actions. He was largely unconscious of the fact that his work built directly on that of Falbe and Dureau de la Malle. In fact, if Davis had made his dependence on their work explicit by locating his sites in relation to the numbers on Falbe's plan, and explaining his procedures as tests of the hypotheses of Dureau de la Malle, he might have joined the direct line of great early contributors to the exploration of Carthage. Instead he only complained about the inadequacy of his predecessors, who, on the other hand, were deeply respected by the French academic establishment.

Furthermore, his bombastic and disorganized writing style made it extremely difficult for scholars, and especially for the French scholars who subsequently dominated the field of archaeology in North Africa, to use his work. It is because Davis stood apart from the academic world, and particularly from the French academic world, that Diehl would certainly not have included him among his heroes. Nevertheless, I believe that Davis rightly deserves to be ranked with these early giants of archaeology at Carthage, and that his serious academic flaws were more than offset by his vigorous practical virtues, qualities which are also crucial to the successful conduct of archaeological projects in the field.

Appendix 1: Some observations on Davis' mosaic finds

How do Davis' mosaics compare with others found at Carthage since? Only a subjective answer is possible. Gauckler listed approximately 300 mosaics from Carthage in his catalogue of 1910 (nos 588–902), and about 300 mosaics have been discovered since that time. These counts are very approximate and include mosaics of all periods, mosaics that were merely noted and not lifted, fragments of pavements, and mosaics that were destroyed. Only about fifty of the floors catalogued by Gauckler in 1910 survive;[1] Davis lifted half of them. Since the latter described or lifted a total of twenty-eight mosaics at Carthage, he discovered less than five percent of a possible total of 600 mosaics from the city, but of those perhaps no more than one hundred and fifty are in museums, on display *in situ*, or adequately published today.

It is more helpful to compare Davis' count with the figural mosaics that have been discovered at Carthage. About twenty figural mosaics are listed by Gauckler, of which Davis excavated seven. Not more than twenty figural mosaics have been discovered at Carthage since the publication of Gauckler's catalogue. This means that in three seasons Davis excavated about a sixth of all the figural mosaics found at Carthage in the last century and a half, an amazing rate, almost ten times as high as the rate of discovery of figural mosaics in the period since his excavations. Furthermore, Davis' Mosaic of the Months and Seasons is arguably the highest-quality pavement of its period and the most iconographically interesting figural mosaic from the city. Gauckler, who was trying to be brief, gave it two pages of description, more than he gave to any other mosaic at Carthage.[2]

The mosaics sent from Carthage by Davis as of the end of 1858 were first published in 1860 in a scholarly account by Augustus Franks, a curator at the British Museum. Franks' article is particularly important, because he was the first to see the connection between Davis' Mosaic of the Months and Seasons and the Codex-Calendar of 354,[3] a manuscript calendar that clarifies the meaning of the mosaic and provides clues to its date. Davis continued to dig throughout much of 1859, and at least three other important figural mosaics, which were not known to Franks when he wrote his article, were received by the museum early in 1860. All these mosaics are still in the collection of the Museum, where those on display were first published by C. T. Newton in 1876.[4]

Paul Gauckler, who directed the Antiquities Service in Tunisia in the late nineteenth and early twentieth century, lifted many mosaics at Carthage, particularly in an area of Roman houses on the Odeon Hill. Gauckler was unusually broadminded among French scholars of his day, in that he did not regard the mosaics which Davis had excavated as lost. His catalogue of the Roman mosaics of Tunisia included these pavements and Gauckler used an admirable variety of published sources to trace them. On the other hand, Gauckler's numbering was arbitrary, as he sometimes included several mosaics in one entry or entered a mosaic more than once by following several sources. While Gauckler's disinterested desire to document Davis' mosaics is praiseworthy, and he did indeed list the majority of the mosaics that the latter excavated, my research shows that he introduced or perpetuated a number of serious errors in the provenances for these mosaics (see Appendix 2 for the details). This is unfortunate, because mosaic specialists have generally followed Gauckler's attributions of Davis' mosaics to broad areas of Carthage.

There is a notable discontinuity between the way the mosaics from Carthage in the British Museum have been studied, as opposed to the pavements that have remained *in situ* or have been removed to the Bardo Museum at Tunis. From the mid-twentieth century, mosaic discoveries at Carthage have been interpreted in terms of their themes, and evaluated in the light of their provenance in the city and the type of building in which they occur,[5] while it has been taken too much for granted that similar questions cannot be posed or answered for Davis' mosaics. Hinks' catalogue of the mosaics in the British Museum is now nearly eighty years old; he described Davis' mosaics, found comparanda where possible, and suggested dates, but his concern with their provenance and excavation was minimal, and on these questions, he understandably followed Gauckler.[6]

In the years since Hinks' catalogue, Davis' mosaics have been relatively neglected by scholars, although his figural pavements figured in Dunbabin's study of the mosaics of Roman North Africa,[7] and the Mosaic of the Months and Seasons was also discussed by Parrish.[8] Both Dunbabin and Parrish accepted Gauckler's provenances without further discussion. Davis' mosaics have not been included, on the other hand, in the stunningly-illustrated publication of

Tunisian mosaics by Blanchard-Lemée and her colleagues, nor in other, equally spectacular, compendia.[9]

In his catalogue of mosaics at the British Museum, Hinks listed twenty-eight mosaics from Carthage excavated by Davis.[10] According to my count, fifteen of the latter's excavation sites produced mosaics out of a total of thirty-five known places that Davis dug in the ancient city; in all Davis sent twenty-six mosaics to the British Museum from Carthage. Among Carthaginian mosaics I include four floors from the suburb of Gammarth, a few miles to the north of the city. Two additional pavments from the city proper were excavated and described by Davis but not lifted. In addition he sent five pavements (four from one house) from two separate Roman houses at Utica. The counts for Carthage are somewhat arbitrary, as I reckon as two separate mosaics floors which come from the same room but which have very different themes; on the other hand, I group fragments which clearly belong to one and the same unified design as belonging to a single floor. Fifteen of Davis' mosaics are currently on display in the British Museum, thirteen in the north-west stairwell, and another two in the Roman Empire Gallery (Room 70).

From the vantage point of what we know today, one of the most striking aspects of Davis' mosaic finds is that their find-spots formed a particular pattern. Of the four important figural mosaics that he found within or immediately outside the city grid – that is, the Mosaic of the Months and Seasons, the Mosaic of Victory with Inscription, the Mosaic of the Sirens, and the Vandal Hunting Mosaic – all are from the northern half of the city, three of them in the area which we now see as the most desirable residential district enjoying the highest elevation in the city. Besides the four figural mosaics, there are also two more figural mosaics, the Mosaic with Baskets of Fish and Fruit, and the Mosaic of Two Gazelles at a Fountain, from the northern half of the city. This was, as Davis correctly divined, the area most likely to be devoted to luxury housing.

In fact, of twenty mosaics certainly retrieved by Davis within or adjacent to the Roman city street-grid, seventeen are from the northern half of the city (twelve of them from the Odeon Hill) and thirteen are certainly from the north-eastern quarter. In contrast, the mosaic with the long *emblemata* of Nereids and Tritons was an isolated find in the low-lying southern half of the city. This Mosaic of Nereids and Tritons undoubtedly comes from a public monument. The small Mosaic of Birds in Square Frames comes from near the *cardo maximus* and *decumanus* 1 east, south of the centre of the city and just beyond the circuit of the Byrsa Hill. The site was almost certainly a large public bathhouse; neither of these two sites were Roman houses.

When Davis' geometric and all-over carpet-pattern mosaics known to be from specific sites are added to the total, the pattern becomes one of a few concentrations of mosaics. This is particularly clear in the north-eastern quadrant of the city, the area of luxury housing. The 'Carthaginian house', just inside the Theodosian wall on the northern side of the city, produced four mosaics that were returned to the British Museum, and also the Mosaic Imitating Green Marble which was evidently lost to vandalism. The house to the east of the theatre produced four geometric or patterned mosaics, while its subsidiary site, forty meters farther north up the hill and probably in the same city block, produced the Mosaic of Rosettes and Lotus Buds as well as the Mosaic of Two Gazelles. Similarly, a site on the seashore, Falbe no. 90, produced three more geometric mosaics beneath the Mosaic of Victory with Inscription. By contrast, the Mosaic with Baskets of Fish and Fruit was the one mosaic lifted from its particular site and sent to Britain. Davis said that further excavation at this site was abandoned, because a bean crop had been disturbed in its excavation. The site seems to have been an early Roman house, and more extensive excavation here would probably also have recovered additional floors.

Fifteen mosaics sent to the British Museum, therefore, came from the north-eastern quadrant of the city. In addition to these, two more almost certainly came from the northern half of the city – the geometric Mosaic of Squares and Oblong Hexagons Forming Irregular Octagons, which I have identified as probably coming from below the Circular Monument, and the fragmentary Mosaic of Acanthus Tendrils, which Davis described as coming from the same site as the Mosaic of the Months and Seasons. The provenance of the Mosaic of Ivy Leaves is entirely uncertain. It was shipped to the Museum on HMS *Supply* with material excavated at Carthage between the spring of 1857 and the spring of 1858, as well as with material from Utica. It seems to have come from Carthage rather than Utica, as Davis did not mention it in connection with the excavations at the latter. It would therefore have most likely been found during the period in which Davis was excavating the houses on the Odeon Hill, but there is no real evidence for a provenance in the north-eastern quadrant of the city.

The north-eastern quadrant was also the site of the Mosaic of Monochrome Scales from the south-west latrine of the Antonine Baths, a floor that Davis excavated but understandably (in view of its size and the simplicity of its design) did not try to lift. While the majority of the mosaics from the north-eastern quadrant of the city are certainly from residential contexts, the Antonine bath-building was a public monument; it is also situated on the seashore. A lower elevation clearly correlates with public monuments that were dependent on water supply, such as baths and the circus of Carthage; the latter had pools and even fountains down the length of its central *euripus*.

Three of the mosaics dispatched to the British Museum from the north-western quadrant of the city were figural, which makes this area, still relatively poorly understood today, the most prolific in terms of Davis' finds of figural mosaics. The excavation of the House of the Horses, with the spectacular Mosaic of the Horses (Fig. 7.11), and Mosaic of Children Hunting, confirms that this was another area of the city with impressive residences and/or public buildings.

Three of the figural mosaics excavated by Davis, the Mosaic of the Sirens, the Vandal Hunting Mosaic and the second Mosaic of Nereids and Tritons, also came from his last year of excavation (i.e. October 1858 to October 1859), when he returned to the central area of the city. As we have seen, he received his first notice to close his excavations in January 1859. The fact that these mosaics were each lifted alone from their contexts suggests that Davis had by then modified his practice, deciding to spend his now limited resources in lifting only the figural floors, since he had learned that they were of far more interest to scholars than simple geometric mosaics, and as a result brought him more credit for his expenditure of effort.

Davis gave some information on the stratigraphical depth of the pavement for ten of his mosaic excavations (the number includes both figural and geometric floors): the soil cover varied from two to twenty-five feet or more (0.6 m to 7.6 m). Operating free of the stringent archaeological methodology of the present, Davis dug through ungratifying soil layers as quickly as he liked. It seems that under these conditions, Davis unearthed Roman mosaics which date across the whole period of the Roman occupation of Carthage.

All of the floors discovered by him at Carthage are Roman rather than Punic; the earliest dates to the later first century AD while the latest are Byzantine (post-AD 534 at Carthage). The nine figural mosaics are evenly divided between the early Empire and the late Roman/Vandal/Byzantine periods. Hinks made an explicit effort to date most of the floors, both figural and geometric, indicated implicitly by the order in which he placed them in his catalogue. His chronology holds quite well for the earlier mosaics, but less well for the later floors. I see a strong tendency for the pavements to cluster in the second and early third centuries, and then again in the fourth to sixth centuries. Hinks dated the Mosaic of the Months and Seasons (Hinks no. 29) and the Mosaic of Acanthus Scrolls (Hinks no. 30) to the third century, while in fact they are now known to belong to the fourth century. Hinks' dating seems to be also wrong for the Mosaic of Rosettes and Lotus Buds (his no. 20), which he dated to the second or third century but which I believe dates to the fourth century or later. In addition Hinks dated the Mosaic of Birds in Square Frames (his no. 42) to the fourth century, but it probably dates to *c.* AD 500. I agree with his generally Vandal dates for the Mosaic of Victory with Inscription (no. 59) and the Vandal Hunting Mosaic (nos 57 and 58). On the other hand, the Mosaic of Two Gazelles at a Fountain (Hinks no. 48) is certainly not earlier than the fifth century, and the Mosaic of Vases Linked by Intersecting Semicircles (no. 59) is certainly Byzantine (post-AD 534); both were ascribed by Hinks to the 'fourth or fifth century'.

Several interesting observations can be made on the subject matter of the figural mosaics at Carthage from Davis' collection. In general, it is limited and disappointing, particularly for the early Empire. For example, the Mosaic with Baskets of Fish and Fruit, which is lively, colourful and well executed, probably dates to the end of the first century. It is a charming but somewhat anonymous floor, hardly indicating the individual interests of its patron. On the other hand, the locally-made baskets and local species of fish suggest that the mosaic is a true product of Carthage.

More seriously disappointing is the 'tired' quality of the mythological scenes in the mid-second century mosaics, two of which feature Nereids and Tritons. One of the very few floors excavated previously at Carthage included an important and very large marine mosaic which featured a head of Oceanus with a subordinate scene of a Nereid on a hippocamp, but there is nevertheless a striking lack of originality in subject matter in the economically-thriving second/third-century city. Janine Lancha's study of mosaics with intellectual reference, in particular to the Muses, found almost nothing of relevance at Carthage.[11] Davis' Mosaic of the Muses is the only mosaic with this theme known at Carthage even today; it uses the busts of the Muses as small medallions in a floral carpet, a design which exploits their decorative potential and minimizes their symbolic meaning. The Mosaic of the Sirens, which dates to the late third or early fourth century, is the only figural mosaic derived from mythology that has some liveliness. Here too the floor is not unique, as the Mosaic of Odysseus and the Sirens from Dougga (Fig. 12.4) developed the same theme in a very similar way, but the subject matter of the mosaic at least does suggest some intellectual interest on the part of the patron who commissioned it.

From the late Roman to the Byzantine period, Davis unearthed four figural mosaics, the Mosaic of the Months and the Seasons, the Mosaic of Victory with

Inscription, the Vandal Hunting Mosaic and the Mosaic of Two Gazelles at a Fountain. These are very disparate in quality. The first, the Mosaic of the Months and Seasons, from the later fourth century, turned to an intellectual concept for its theme, which is unusual at Carthage. It is stimulating and original in its design and subject matter, as well as being very fine in its execution. The second is an example of a Christian building-dedication, from perhaps the second half of the fifth century, which however uses iconography that would be entirely acceptable in a pagan building. The third, though most likely a Vandal mosaic from the middle of the fifth century, is an example of a genre that was fairly common at Carthage, that is, illustrations of the lifestyle of the wealthy in general, and of hunting in particular. The fourth mosaic, which is likely from its subject matter to be Byzantine (mid-sixth century?), although a fifth-century date is not impossible, illustrates a Christian theme, the water of life, expressed in a symbolic nature-scene. Insofar as Davis' finds of figural mosaics foreshadowed the discovery of future figured pavements at Carthage, they had already demonstrated that finds of the later Roman period were likely to be far more interesting than those of the early Empire. On the other hand, the fact that only two mosaics have very clear Christian iconography would also later be confirmed as characteristic of Carthage, where the appearance of Christian iconography is certainly rare before the full Byzantine era.

Appendix 2: Gauckler's errors on the provenances of Davis' mosaics

Modern mosaic analysts tend to trust the inventory of Tunisian mosaics, compiled by Paul Gauckler.[1] He was the first authoritative scholar to treat Davis' mosaics systematically after Franks. As director of the Antiquities Service for Tunisia in the late nineteenth and early twentieth century, Gauckler was intimately involved in the excavation and lifting of many mosaics, particularly in order to create the early collection in the Bardo Museum in Tunis. Although his mosaic catalogue was actually published some years after he left Tunisia, he was the person best placed to make such a list.

My research has shown, however, that Gauckler is not completely trustworthy on the mosaics which Davis excavated at Carthage, and that he is particularly unreliable on questions of provenance. This is not because Gauckler was an intrinsically unreliable scholar. He was trying to create a systematic catalogue of all the Roman mosaics from Tunisia, a gargantuan task that made it impossible for him to approach the sources for Davis' pavements analytically. In his attempt to document them, Gauckler conscientiously followed published sources, which were mostly in English, but he was confused by the fact that these different sources had different purposes.

In *Carthage and Her Remains*, Davis described his exploits, but did not provide a catalogue of artefacts. Any description of specific mosaics was incidental to Davis' purposes. Franks, on the other hand, wanted to establish the importance of the Museum collection, and worked from excellent sources, including the mosaics themselves, the accession lists of 1857 and 1859 (which he may have compiled himself), and from Davis' letters and drawings; but Franks did not intend to publish a systematic catalogue.[2] Gauckler also did not realize that Franks' publication did not include all the mosaics that had arrived at the museum in 1859, and he omitted three that were to arrive later.

Newton's *Synopsis* of 1876, which Gauckler did use, was an excellent source as a published catalogue,[3] but the author only treated mosaics on display. Furthermore, Newton was primarily interested in an accurate description of the artefacts themselves, was only minimally interested in the contexts of the mosaics, and had evidently not consulted either Davis' accounts or the Museum's records in any great detail. Gauckler also used Morgan[4] and Audollent,[5] but apart from illustrations, Morgan added almost nothing of value, and Audollent's interest was in summing up Roman mosaic finds at Carthage, among which he considered Davis' finds to be of relatively little interest.

Gauckler listed twenty-nine inventory numbers as coming from Davis' excavations, but he reached this total in a very haphazard way. Six mosaics are listed more than once, because in following several sources, he did not note that they referred to the same mosaic. Two of these pavements are listed more than once because he gave separate numbers to different pieces of the same mosaic. He also listed some floors twice because he did not understand Davis' admittedly obscure descriptions. In the final analysis, he counted four mosaics twice, one mosaic three times, and one mosaic four times. In a different type of confusion, four mosaics are grouped as two, and two pieces of one mosaic (the Mosaic of Wreathed Rosettes) are counted as two separate mosaics without clear supporting evidence.

When these anomalies are eliminated, Gauckler attested twenty-two of Davis' twenty-eight mosaics from Carthage, and twenty of the twenty-six mosaics which were lifted and are now in the British Museum. Six of Davis' mosaics from Carthage slipped through Gauckler's net; they were noted in the museum's accession list but were not published until Hinks' catalogue (the Mosaic of Squares and Peltas did not appear in Hinks).[6] Of these, the Mosaic of the Sirens and the Mosaic of Circular Awnings are the most important. In terms of the sources which Gauckler had to work with, his cataloguing of Davis' mosaics was not bad.

Gauckler is unreliable, however, as a guide to the provenance of Davis' mosaics. Of the twenty-six mosaics Davis sent to the Museum from Carthage, Gauckler gave the correct provenance for only four. Of the remaining sixteen mosaics he knew, he gave an incorrect provenance for thirteen, and considered the other three to be of undetermined location. In fact, only two mosaics certainly excavated by Davis are of unknown location, and I have proposed a probable provenance for one of these.

Gauckler, who had worked at Carthage for fifteen years and knew the Roman city very well, was best placed to understand Davis' topographical references, read his map, and interpret him correctly, but he did not notice that Davis used the term Bordj-Djedid to refer to most of the northern part of the city. Eight of Gauckler's incorrect identifications of provenance stem from this confusion. Davis included with the hill which Gauckler knew as Bordj-Djedid the whole extent of what is today referred to as the Odeon Hill. Davis knew of no Odeon Hill, since it was Gauckler who first discovered and excavated both the odeon and the theatre. The points on Davis' map make it clear to anyone who knows Carthage that some of his most important sites were on the Odeon Hill. Gauckler may have missed what should have been obvious to him, simply because he took for granted that no accurate provenance could be determined for Davis' mosaics from Carthage.

Appendix 3: The mortar of Davis' mosaics

Davis explicitly stated the idea, and reiterated it several times as he introduced new examples of mosaics which illustrated it, that some of his mosaics, in particular the ones which he considered Punic, were laid in soft friable mortar, while others which he considered Roman were laid in very hard and tough mortar. The Mosaic of the Months and Seasons, which is now dated to the second half of the fourth century AD, was the latest in date of Davis' mosaic finds for which he explicitly mentioned that the mortar in which the floor was laid was soft. He said that the Mosaic of the Months and Seasons was laid over a mortar which was thick (in terms of feet and inches) and friable, unlike the mortars that he recognized as being 'Roman' [*sic*], which were thinner, very hard and made with lime, crushed brick and ash. The Mosaic of the Months, which was excavated by the guardian of Saint Louis, was another example of a floor that Davis regarded as 'Roman' because of its mortar,[1] which was therefore relatively thin but very hard. As usual, however, Davis was not perfectly clear. He wrote:[2]

> The bed upon which Punic mosaics were placed we found to be much thicker than that of the Roman, but its adhesive power had entirely perished. The stones peeled off with perfect ease, whilst the cement which joins the marbles is much stronger *than* [*sic*, emphasis mine; see below] those which are undoubtedly of the Roman period. The latter we were obliged to remove with the cement in which it was imbedded, varying in thickness from two inches to one foot, and is generally composed of lime, pounded bricks, and a sprinkling of ashes, whereas the only apparent ingredient in the Punic is lime. The cement in the remains of walls we found in connexion with the Roman mosaics was as firm as the stone itself, whereas in those of the Punic era the stones could be severed from it with the most perfect ease.

Davis' statement is problematic, because he said that the cement of the mosaics which he considered Punic was soft, yet the cement between the actual *tesserae* was very hard. Ditson repeated this idea, evidently quoting directly from Davis. If Davis meant to say this, he was implying that the chemical composition of the mortar between the *tesserae* was different from the mortar in the bedding immediately below. This is possible but not very likely. Furthermore, the so-called 'Punic' mosaics would have been rigid on the canvas to which they had been glued while they were being turned onto the bed of the wooden boxes in the process of lifting that Davis devised. Davis' use of the phrase 'peeled off' does not suggest that the *tesserae* and their mortar were rigid. If the mosaic was rigid when lifted, the cheek of 'Ceres' could not have been smoothed by the lifting process.[3] Furthermore, Davis' description of the lifting of the mosaics from the seaside villas at Gammarth makes it clear that the floors there were threatened with complete disintegration, although their constant wetting with sea-water made them a special case.

The Mosaic of the Muses was no longer held together either by its mortar bed or by the mortar between the *tesserae*. In describing the process of lifting this mosaic, Davis wrote, 'The mosaic itself was quite loosened from the bed of cement on which it lay, so that it required the greatest attention to remove it without damaging it'.[4] Furthermore, Davis stated that the whole pavment could easily have been 'swept together into a heap of marbles', destroying the design.[5] I believe that he intended to say that the mortar that joined the marble *tesserae* was stronger *in* the 'Roman' mosaics.

According to Ditson, the Mosaic of Victory with Inscription, which is now dated to the Vandal era, had mortar very different from that of the geometric mosaics several feet below. He reckoned that the Mosaic of Victory was embedded in cement about an inch thick, that it was excessively hard, and that it had to be taken up with the figured surface. In contrast, Davis noted that the lowest mosaic in this sequence, the Mosaic of Interlaced Squares, had a bedding of soft mortar, and Davis therefore considered it to be Punic. Ditson more specifically described the lower two mosaics in this sequence, both the Mosaic of Hexagons Framing Hexafoils, and the Mosaic of Interlaced Squares, as being obtained by the Museum without the mortar, since after they had had cotton cloth glued down on the surfaces, the mortar was 'easily cut away by any sharp instrument'.[6] His statement implies that both of the two lower mosaics, which date to the second century, had soft and friable mortar, at least in their bedding.

Davis described the floor of the south-west latrine at the Antonine Baths as 'of extraordinary solidity',[7] a description implying a very tough mortar. The most recent study of mosaics from the Antonine Baths suggested that this floor dated to the original Antonine construction of the building in the mid-second century,[8] which undermines Davis' general argument. On the other hand, this building was undoubtedly constructed on the order of the emperor and built to last for centuries. In contrast, the Mosaic of the Muses, which was lifted with great difficulty by Davis because it was directly on the sea front and kept wet by the sea, was embedded in a mortar that was completely friable. The Mosaic of the Muses also dates to the middle of the second century, but was part of the decoration of a private house.

Completely contradicting Davis' observations, Gauckler a half century later stated that there were no correlations between the date of a mosaic and its type of mortar. Gauckler was making observations on the dating evidence for Roman pavements at Carthage based on his finds of sequences of mosaics in the area of luxury Roman housing on the Odeon Hill. He said that the construction of mosaics could not be used to date them; neither materials, type of *tesserae*, nor the quality of the mortar, had any chronological significance. Gaukler was strongly of the opinion that mosaics could only be dated by style and accessory decorative motifs, but he specifically stated that there is no sign of different composition of the mortar or cement at different periods.[9]

It certainly seems to be the case that not all mosaic floors used the harder mortar once it was introduced. For example, the team that recorded the mosaics from the Archaeological Park associated with the Antonine Baths sunk a trial trench under a small square of mosaic on the mid-line of the Christian basilica known as Dermech I, and found a broken and mutilated statue of Venus. They found no ash in the nucleus of the mosaic, only sand and mortar in equal amounts – a mortar Davis would have regarded as Punic. They dated the mosaic to the first half or the middle of the sixth century AD.[10]

The use of ash, which produces a harder and more chemically stable mortar, is associated with the Theodosian Wall of AD 425. Williams carried out tests showing that the Theodosian Wall was constructed with such a mortar, but Williams was not convinced that the motivation for creating it was necessarily to produce a stronger mortar. He suggested that ash was mixed in to the mortar of the defences simply because the job was rushed and the method of lime-burning was careless.[11]

Certainly the date of any change in the general use of mortar mixed with ash has not been established. For example, in 1965 Picard said, in a somewhat circular argument, that the mortar in fourth-century mosaic floors used ash.[12] In 1976, Senay noted that no study of mortars at Carthage had been made, and he therefore questioned the arguments of Lézine and Picard, who thought that the construction of the Circular Monument was Constantinian because its mortar contained ash.[13] Henry Hurst recently described the yellow *opus caementicium* (construction cement) that distinguishes the major monuments of the later second and third century AD at Carthage from late antique structures of the sixth century AD, the latter being constructed in grey charcoal-flecked cement; but Hurst's observations here left the date of such a change wide open.[14]

The Swedish UNESCO team excavated a small Roman public bath-house on the northern slope of the Byrsa hill. The bath-house has two phases, and in her summary of the dating evidence Hansen has stated that the later complex used grey mortar, clearly distinguishable from the mortar of the earlier Roman building. She pointed out that a mosaic with acanthus scrolls from the second phase of the later complex has comparanda suggesting a date at the end of the fourth century AD, and that this date agrees with the chronology which has been suggested earlier for the use of grey mortar.[15] Here she cited an earlier suggestion by Hurst and Roskams that grey mortar was used at Carthage only after the earthquake that occurred in AD 365.[16]

Gros also referred to the major earthquake of July 21st, 365, which caused widespread and severe damage in the eastern Mediterranean, relating it to the fact that the Antonine Baths needed and received restoration work in 389.[17] Liliane Ennabli has also argued that the north side of the Circular Monument had to be rebuilt because of earthquake damage in the late fourth century.[18] There has in fact been a lively debate over whether this earthquake could have affected Carthage, since the main areas of attested damage are in the eastern Mediterranean. Lepelley denied that it had any impact at Carthage, although there is apparently evidence for it at Sfax and Sbeitla in southern Tunisia.[19] During his tour of Algeria and Tunisia in 1859, Blakesley observed an inscription that recorded the effects of an earthquake (*'terrae motibus'*) at Guelma (Calama) in Algeria, an inland city well to the west of Carthage. The inscription dated the earthquake to the reign of Valens and Valentinian, and therefore most likely this refers to the earthquake of 365.[20]

I believe that the earthquake of 365 did at least some damage at Carthage.[21] For example, in Naomi Norman's excavation of a Roman cemetery at Yasmina, a monument made of ashlar blocks collapsed to one side in a destruction pattern typical of earthquake damage and hardly attributable to any other cause. This damage was first attributed to the earthquake of AD 365, but as material under the fallen blocks was found to date to the fifth or sixth centuries

AD, that chronology cannot be right.[22] Nevertheless, it seems clear that earthquake damage could and did affect Carthage.

There is also a pattern of late Roman cistern-building at Carthage, which perhaps implies a break in the service of the aqueduct; very slight earthquake damage can cause a complete breakdown of the water supply. A cistern which lies along the north side of *decumanus* 6 north, on the sector of Theodosian wall excavated by a Canadian team, was constructed over a major pottery deposit in a building which was filled in as early as AD 200 and certainly no later than AD 350. The cistern walls were cut down to the base at the time of the construction of the Theodosian Wall in AD 425, as the latter runs across the cistern's south-eastern corner.[23] This cistern therefore predates the Theodosian Wall of 425 and might well postdate the earthquake of 365. The cistern in the peristyle of the House of the Horses, which compromises the plan of the reception area and the elegant mosaic decoration of the early fourth century,[24] may also be a response to earthquake damage to the aqueduct in 365. One further argument supports the likelihood that earthquake damage to the aqueduct was experienced at Carthage in AD 365: there is an attested famine at Carthage in AD 366/7, when the proconsul, Julius Festus Hymettius, was remembered for his controversial aid to the people of Carthage.[25]

A possible general change in the composition of construction mortar in the late fourth century is clearly a real issue which has not been adequately resolved and which I cannot attempt to resolve here because of the complexities of the question. I believe that Davis, who was the first to lift mosaics at Carthage and who was forced to concern himself with the toughness of the mortar he found, observed a real, if undeniably not an absolute, correlation between mortar composition and chronology. The fact that Davis specifically described the mortar of the Mosaic of the Months and Seasons as soft suggests that this pavement is among the last in date before the beginning of a general change in the composition of mortar. It would therefore be most useful if a new review of the evidence is conducted on whether and when such a change took place; it would, for example, be important for the dating of the Mosaic of the Months and Seasons if a chronology pre-dating AD 365 could be confirmed on the evidence of its mortar bedding.

Notes

Note to reader

A much-cited book in the *Notes* here is Davis 1861, Nathan Davis' own account of his excavations. Two editions were issued by the publisher Richard Bentley, with the same date and the same illustrations, but one is more generously laid out, with a total of 631 as compared to 504 pages. The version with longer pagination is later, since it includes a corrected figure title and an added note. Page numbers of the edition with shorter pagination are given first in the notes, with the later and longer edition's page number(s) placed in brackets after it.

Notes to Chapter One

1. Falbe 1833; Gran-Aymerich 2001, 244–5. I have seen Falbe's rare text at the New York Public Library and at the Bibliothèque Nationale de France; the British Library and the Bibliothèque Nationale de France have the separate large folio of plans.
2. Dureau de la Malle 1835.
3. Davis 1861.
4. Franks 1860, 222–3.
5. Newton 1850.
6. Beulé 1861; Beulé 1873. Gran-Aymerich 2001, 71.
7. Gran-Aymerich 1998, 47.
8. Newton 1865, vol. 1, 28; Gran-Aymerich 2001, 485–6. On such rules of procedure as there were in Tunisia at this time, Halbertsma 2003, 83.
9. Gran-Aymerich 1998, 146.
10. Dunant 1858, 235. Dunant later founded the International Red Cross, for which he received the Nobel Prize in 1901.
11. Beulé 1861, 57.
12. Adkins 2003; Gran-Aymerich 2001, 397–9.
13. MacPherson 1857, especially 46, 53 and 128–9.
14. Wroth in Lee 1909; Cooper 1872, 287; *Athenaeum*, January 14th, 1882, no. 2829, 65; Boase 1965; Kirk 1902.
15. Davis 1854.
16. Davis 1862.
17. Dumas, in Murch 1959, *passim*.
18. Davis 1861, 341–2 (427).
19. Davis 1861, 416 (517).
20. Endelman 1979, 109.
21. Letter of Panizzi to Clarendon, July 28th, 1856: FO 102/62, 5–8.
22. Endelman 1979, 218.
23. Davis 1854, vol. 2, 113.
24. Edwards 1870, 666, note.
25. Davis 1861, fig. on 343 (facing 428).
26. Brown 1974, 388.
27. Holloway, with Bright-Holloway, January 6th, 2003 [website]. Nathan Davis died in Florence of lung congestion on January 6th, 1882: W. Wroth in Lee 1909. He was buried in the Modern Protestant Cemetery according to its records, but my informant, Assunta d'Aloi, was not able to find his grave. His age at death is incorrectly given as 62 (he was 70). His personal names are confused with those of his son Alfred George Davis, who is also buried in this cemetery: Holloway, personal communication, September 6th, 2004.
28. Endelman 1979, 25, 45–6, and 170–6.
29. Manly 2004, 21 and note 2.
30. Endelman 1979, 229–30, 241 and 260.
31. Endelman 1979, 261.
32. Letter from Davis to Wood, March 22, 1857: FO 335/108/7.
33. Davis 1861, 437–63 (544–75): chapter 25.
34. Mommsen 1881, xxx and xxiv.
35. Davis 1861, 39 (32).
36. Perry 1869, 541. Davis' employment as a Protestant missionary: Gidney 1908, 194–5.
37. Endelman 1979, 229–30, 257–60, and 273.
38. Gidney 1908; Endelman 1979, 71–7; Soumille and Peyras 1993, 62.
39. Vernau 1981.
40. Sebag 1958. Sebag published an excerpt from Davis' *Tunis* (1841), and quipped that he hoped his readers would not think the French translation an 'unmerited honour' for Davis: Sebag 1958, 161.
41. Davis 1841, 40–7.
42. Davis 1844, dedication.
43. A daughter, Margaret Davis, was born at Tunis on October 23rd, 1846, according to the inscription on her grave in the Modern Protestant Cemetery in Florence: Julia Bolton Holloway and Assunta D'Aloi, personal communication, September 4th, 2004.
44. Davis 1844, 200.
45. Davis 1861, 50 (43–4).
46. Grandchamp 1944, chart between 132 and 133.
47. Brown 1974, 127–34.
48. Davis 1854, vol. 1, xii, 8 and 30.
49. Davis 1854, vol. 2, 76.
50. Davis 1852: issue 7, November 1852, 196–8.
51. Davis and Davidson, n.d. [1854].
52. Gregory 1859, vol. 2, 372; Cooper 1872, 440–1.
53. The 'Certificate of Candidate for Election' for N. Davis was signed May 16th, 1855, and again on his election, June 11th, 1855.
54. Burkhardt and Smith 1989, 510–11, with notes.
55. Four letters of Mrs C. Davis in the Archives of the RGS.
56. Dunant 1858, 23.
57. Tissot 1884–1888, vol. 1, 657; Gran-Aymerich 2001, 663–5.

58. Sainte-Marie 1878a, 132–5.
59. Audollent 1901, 13–17, and 15, note 3.
60. Flaux 1865.
61. Sainte-Marie 1878a, 133, no. 95.
62. Reinach 1886, 87.
63. Sainte-Marie 1884.
64. Von Maltzan 1870, 269–315, especially 296 and 304.
65. Edwards 1870, 666, note.
66. Davis 1861, ix–xi (vii–x), and 116 (130).
67. Davis 1861, 346–9 (431–4); Tacitus, *Annals* XVI.1.2.
68. Hinks 1933.
69. Franks 1860, 202–36; Vaux 1863a.

Notes to Chapter Two

1. Rousseau 1864, 397.
2. Sainte-Marie 1878b, 144; Rousseau 1864, 397.
3. Brown 1974; Perkins 1997, s.v. 'Ahmad Bey'.
4. Gandolphe 1951.
5. Davis 1841, 46.
6. Gregory 1859, vol. 2, 325; Davis 1861, 164–5 (197).
7. Gregory 1894, 173.
8. Davis 1861, 477 (594).
9. Gregory 1859, vol. 2, 186.
10. Perkins 1986, 61.
11. Grandchamp 1944, chart between 132 and 133.
12. Ganiage 1985, 171–2.
13. Perkins 1997, s. v. 'Mamluks'.
14. Gregory 1859, vol. 2, 198.
15. Davis 1862, 361.
16. Martel 1967, 79.
17. Faucon 1893, vol. 1, 195–6.
18. Davis 1861, 354–5 (441–2).
19. Dunant 1858, 230–1.
20. Guérin 1862, vol. 1, 70.
21. Davis 1861, 157 (186).
22. Gregory 1859, vol. 2, 386–8.
23. Davies 1858, 131–7; Anon. 1861, 198, with fig. on 195.
24. Gregory 1859, vol. 2, 190.
25. McGoogan 2005, 365–6.
26. Rawnsley 1923, 125, quoting a letter of Sophia Cracroft, May 26th, 1858 at Tunis = SPRI MS 248/247/52–68.
27. Delavoye 1999, 108.
28. Gregory 1859, vol. 2, 339.
29. Brown 1974, 228, fig. 7, for a portrait of Raffo; cf. 227, n. 46.
30. Kobelt 1885, 376.
31. Brown 1974, 348–9, n. 24.
32. Davis 1861, 157–8 (186–7).
33. Davis 1861, 51–2, 156–7, 252; (43–47), (185–7), (316–7); Brown 1974, 35, 96, 219, 328 and 347.
34. Letter of Davis to Clarendon, July 19th, 1856, FO 102/62, 1–4.
35. Davis 1861, 128 (148), note and 157 (185); Brown 1974, 96 and 219.
36. Dunant 1858, 76.
37. Perry 1869, 394.
38. Koestler [website], '4th generation, Capt. David Porter 1754–1808'. Captain Porter was the father of Margaret (Peggy) Porter, the wife of Dr Samuel Davies Heap (1781–1853); Cohen 1988, 9–40, with portraits of Dr Heap and his wife Margaret facing 10.
39. Perry 1869, 550–1, for the American consuls at Tunis between 1824 and 1867; Davis 1854, vol. 2, note on 317.
40. Dauber 1967a, 828–9.
41. Outrescaut 2000 [website], for the French consuls at Tunis in the nineteenth century; Revault 1984, 102.
42. Dupuy 1954, 26, n. 51.
43. Lambert 1912, s.v. 'Roches (Léon)'.
44. Danziger 1977, 158.
45. Davis 1862, 172.
46. Emerit 1947, 81–105.
47. Flaux 1865, 53–4.
48. Perkins 1997, s.v. 'Wood, Richard'; Marsden 1971, frontispiece, for a photograph of Wood; Estournelles de Constant 1891, 29, fig. 2, for a later photograph.
49. Ganiage 1971, 39, n. 2.
50. Journal of Sophia Cracroft for Tuesday, May 18th, 1858: SPRI, MS 248/232/2; BJ.
51. Gregory 1859, vol. 2, 196.
52. Chamam 2002, 75, n. 25.
53. Chamam 2002, 70.
54. Martel 1967, 80.
55. Letter of Malmesbury to Wood, March 10th, 1858, a directive to Wood in regard to his letter of November 28th, 1857, which informed the Foreign Office of the action against Davis [not in file]: FO 102/62, 194–7.
56. Draft of letter of Wood to Davis, March 18th, 1857; letter of Davis to Wood, March 22nd, 1857: FO 335/108/7.
57. Journal of Sophia Cracroft for Monday, May 17th, 1858: SPRI MS 248/232/2; BJ.
58. Guérin 1862, vol. 1, 17; Davis 1861, 65 (63), estimating the population at 200,000; Brown 1974, 375–8.
59. Bard 1854, 82.
60. Salinas 1990, 182–5.
61. Brown 1974, 35, n. 13.
62. Flaux 1865, 55.
63. Guérin 1862, vol. 1, 17.
64. McGoogan 2005, 365.
65. Davis 1862, 2.
66. Bard 1854, 86.
67. Bard 1854, 83.
68. Blakesley 1859, 378.
69. Davis 1861, 65 (63).
70. Davis 1841, 37.
71. Guérin 1862, vol. 1, 15 and 33; Perkins 1986, 75–6.
72. Dupuy 1954, 18–19, relying on Flaux 1865.
73. Dupuy 1954, 16 and 18.
74. Dunant 1858, 229–30.
75. Guérin 1862, vol. 1, 19; Sainte-Marie 1878b, 125; Lambert 1912, s.v. 'Sutter'.
76. Dupuy 1954, 17.
77. Dunant 1858, 227–35.
78. Arrouas 1932, s. v. 'Le comte Joseph, Marie, Jean-Baptiste Raffo'; Chamam 2002, 75.
79. Dunant 1858, 126; Delavoye 1999, 229–30.

80. Davis 1841, 46.
81. Flaux 1865, 52, 56 and 66.
82. Sainte-Marie 1878b, 126. From the Catholic point of view, their numbers were derisory; Sainte-Marie counted 50 Protestants in the whole country in 1878, compared to 16,287 Catholics.
83. Moorehead 1998, 12–13.
84. Davis 1861, note on 325 (408).
85. Letter of Wood to Clarendon, March 10th, 1857: FO 335/108/3.
86. Journal of Sophia Cracroft for Tuesday, May 18th, 1858: SPRI MS 248/232/2; BJ; Dauber 1967b, note (*) on 534.
87. Perry 1869, 550–1; Davis 1861 and 1862, passim.
88. Dauber 1967a, 829; Koestler [website]; Perry 1869, 552.
89. Dunant 1858, 229–30; Long 1970, 313–14.
90. Cohen 1988, 25, with portraits of the younger Heaps on the facing page.
91. Perry 1869, 551.
92. White 1959a and b.
93. Dunant 1858, 229–30.
94. Dauber 1967b, 533–4. After the war Heap hoped to be re-appointed Consul General at Constantinople, but fell ill and died of consumption in August of 1866.
95. Wilmanns and Mommsen 1881, part 1, 145; Sainte-Marie 1884, 7.
96. Gozlan 1982, 179–87, pls CVI–CXIII.
97. Lund 1986, 21, citing a letter of Falbe to the Danish crown prince, March 23rd, 1838.
98. Davis 1861, 50–2 (44–7).
99. Wilmanns and Mommsen 1881, *CIL* VIII.1021, cf. *additamenta*, 929; *CIL* VIII.1026, and 10536; Gran-Aymerich 2001, 66.
100. Sainte-Marie 1878a, s.v. 'Rousseau (Alphonse)', 172, no. 308.
101. Rousseau 1850, 260–1 and pl. 143.
102. Soumille 1992.
103. Bourgade 1852/1856. On the title page of the second edition (1856), Bourgade is styled 'chaplain of the Imperial Chapel of Saint Louis, founder and director of the Collège Saint-Louis at Tunis, apostolic missionary, honorable canon of Algiers, knight of the imperial order of the Legion of Honour, and officer of the order of Nichan-Iftikhar [an honour bestowed by the Bey of Tunis]'.
104. Mélia 1939, 163–7.
105. Gandolphe 1940, 522; portrait of Bourgade: facing 518.
106. Ashbee 1889, 13.
107. Bourgade 1856, 12; Mendleson 2003, 37–48.
108. Delattre 1883, 5.
109. Gandolphe 1951, 279 and 292.
110. Delavoye 1999, 44.
111. Davis 1861, 110–11 (124).
112. Bendana 2000, 512–26; Gran-Aymerich 2001, 663–5.
113. Guérin 1862, vol. 1, xiii–xiv; Sainte-Marie 1875b, 107, no. 218.
114. Tissot 1884, vol. 1, 659.
115. Davis 1861, 245 (307); Guérin, 1862, vol. 1, 277–8, nos 475–6; Sainte-Marie 1878a, 131–2, no. 90; Euting 1883, nos 120–9 (pls 70–5, Punic *stelae* previously published by Cubisol). For Charles Cubisol, Lambert 1912, s.v. 'Cubisol (Joseph)'.
116. *CIL* VIII.1010, 1016, 1024, 1028, 1034, 1045, 1056, 1093 and 1113.
117. Journal of Sophia Cracroft for Thursday, May 13th, 1858: SPRI MS 248/232/2; BJ.
118. Perry 1869, 151.
119. For Margherita Davis (1846–1916), her marriage to Cesare Piccioli (1840–1902), and their four children, Alberto (1873–1890), Beatrice (1873–1912), Arturo (1875–1940) and Franklin (d. 1947), see Holloway 2003 [website].
120. Journal of Sophia Cracroft for Sunday, May 16th, 1858: SPRI, MS 248/232/2; BJ.
121. Coda to letter of Sophia Cracroft, May 26th, 1858, from Malta; also journal entry of Sophia Cracroft for Sunday, May 16th, 1858: see note 120.
122. Davis 1862, 339.
123. Blakesley 1859, 381.
124. Dunant 1858, 181.
125. Anon. 1858d, 397–8. Bacon 1976 led me to stories about archaeological discoveries made during the nineteenth century that were published in *The Illustrated London News*. Bacon considered the archaeological news 'thin' for the years 1857 to 1861, recording only Newton's excavations at Halicarnassos and Cnidos, and incorrectly citing the excavations of the 'Revd. W. Davies' at Carthage (1976, 31).
126. Davis 1861, 352 (438).
127. Wall 2001; Troyat 1992.
128. Troyat 1992, 163; Wall 2001, 246–7.
129. Blakesley 1859, 376–7.
130. Spufford 1997, 115–29. Woodward 1951 (introduction) noted that Jane Franklin's papers are now at the Scott Polar Research Institute in Cambridge, England.
131. McGoogan 2005; Beattie and Geiger 1987, with nineteenth-century bibliography.
132. Holloway 2003 [website], for evidence that in 1859 Mrs Davis was to give birth to another child, Alfred George Davis (1859–1894), a British citizen born in Tunis. Despite the fact that Alfred George's father's name is recorded as 'Natale', this family affiliation seems certain.
133. This whole section is based on a letter of Sophia Cracroft, May 26th, 1858, quoted in Rawnsley 1923, 119–27 = SPRI MS 248/247/52–68; D.
134. Gregory 1859, vol. 2, 166 and 173.
135. Journal of Sophia Cracroft for Saturday, May 15th, 1858: SPRI MS 248/232/2; BJ.
136. Davis 1854, vol. 2, 43.
137. Delavoye 1999, 67.
138. Dupuy 1954, 26.
139. Letter of N. Davis to Norton Shaw, May 15th, 1858, in the Archives of the RGS.
140. Letter of Davis to Malmesbury, 10th April 1858: FO 102/62, 198. Flaubert did not arrive at Tunis until April 18th, 1858.

141. Delavoye 1999, 203, quoting a letter of Flaubert to Jean Clogenson, Paris, May 25th, 1857.
142. Delavoye 1999, 66.
143. Walford 1882, 152–3.
144. Perkins 1986, 63. Hamuda Bey was Bey of Tunis from 1782 to 1814.
145. Osler 1835, 207–29; Perkins 1997, s.v. 'Exmouth, first viscount (Edward Pellew)'.
146. Journal of Sophia Cracroft for Saturday, May 15th, 1858: SPRI MS 248/232/2; BJ.
147. Revault 1974, 142 and 150–1.
148. Davis 1861, 384 (482–3).
149. Noah 1819, 290–1.
150. Gregory 1859, vol. 2, 173.
151. Blakesley 1859, 407.
152. Rawnsley 1923, 126, quoting a letter of Sophia Cracroft, May 26th, 1858 = SPRI, MS 248/247/52–68; D.
153. Delavoye 1999, 110.
154. Journal of Sophia Cracroft, for Sunday, May 16th, 1858: SPRI MS 248/232/2; BJ.
155. Dupuy 1954, 20, note 34, quoting Flaubert's letter. Since the French word *ministre* can refer to a Protestant minister, his term *ministre anglais* should refer to Davis. The person in question was involved in archaeological excavations, and Flaubert had been invited to his house several times.
156. Flaux 1865, 60–1; Triulzi 1971b, 160–2.
157. Salinas 1990, 190–1.
158. Dupuy 1954, 20.
159. Delavoye 1999, 67, with n. 1 on 181, and 110–11; for the dates, 196–7, notes.
160. Journal of Sophia Cracroft for Sunday, May 16th, 1858: SPRI MS 248/232/2; BJ.

Notes to Chapter Three

1. Letter of Davis to Clarendon, July 19th, 1856: FO 102/62, 1–4.
2. Villiers 1938.
3. Letter of Panizzi to Clarendon, July 22nd, 1857: FO 102/62, 131.
4. Miller 1973, fig. facing 161; Miller 1967. Antonio Panizzi, later Sir Anthony Panizzi, KCB (1797–1879), was Keeper of Printed Books (1837–1856) and later Principal Librarian (1856–1866) at the British Museum.
5. Letter of Clarendon to Panizzi, July 21st, 1856: FO 102/62, 5, and letter of Panizzi to Clarendon, July 28th, 1856: FO 102/62, 6–8.
6. Miller 1973, 144.
7. Jenkins 1992, 168–95; Gran-Aymerich 1998, 178–9 and n. 164 on 178.
8. Newton 1865, vol. 2.
9. Unsigned letter of February 6th, 1857, from the Foreign Office to the Admiralty: FO 102/62, 54. Chandler's views: Triulzi 1971a, 667–8.
10. Davis 1861, xi (ix).
11. Unsigned note, written September 1st, 1859, on the back of a letter of Davis to Lord John Russell, dated July 30th, 1859: FO 102/62, 292–4.
12. Letter of Davis, August 4th, 1856, placed before the Trustees on August 9th, 1856: BM Archives, C9069–70.
13. Report of the meeting of the Trustees for October 11th, 1856: BM Archives, C9080–1.
14. Davis 1861, 57 (47–8).
15. Davis 1861, 52 (47); cf. Miller 1973, 294–5, n. 1. William Hokham Carpenter (1792–1866) was Keeper of Prints and Drawings from 1845 to 1866.
16. Davis 1861, xi (x).
17. Miller 1973, 192–3; Vaux 1863a.
18. Letter of Ferriere to Clarendon, August 4th, 1856, with note from Hammond: FO 102/62, 9–10; letter of Clarendon to Ferriere, August 7th, 1856: FO 102/62, 11.
19. Letter of Davis to Clarendon, August 19th, 1856: FO 102/62, 14.
20. Letter of Davis to Clarendon, August 19th, 1856, and letter of Clarendon (probably written by Hammond) to Davis, September 6th, 1856: FO 102/62, 14 and 17.
21. Letter of Davis, October 21st, 1856, at Tunis, to Clarendon: FO 102/62, 21–22.
22. Davis 1861, 53 (48).
23. The costs paid for Davis' expenses in 1857: January 26th, 1857, salary: £96 and 12 shillings; April 14th, 1857, expenses: £200; April 20th, 1857, salary: £94 and 10 shillings; July 14th, 1857, quarterly salary [amount missing]; August 26th, 1857, expenses: £200; November 5th, 1857, salary: £96 and 12 shillings; December 11th, 1857, expenses: £200. Source: letters of Wood to the Foreign Office: FO 335/108/3.
24. Davis 1861, 54 (48–9). The receipt of Davis for tools and twenty cases of artefacts left in the care of the British consul in Tunis, May 14th, 1860, was enclosed in a letter of Wood to the Foreign Office, June 15th, 1860: FO 102/62, 304.
25. Letter of Davis to Clarendon, October 21st, 1856: FO 102/62, 21; Davis' first report of expenses, January 26th, 1857: FO 102/62, 47.
26. Davis, 1861, 54–5 (49–50).
27. Letter of Davis to Clarendon, October 21st, 1856: FO 102/62, 21; Davis 1861, 56 (51).
28. Davis 1861, 158 (187).
29. Davis 1861, 355 (443).
30. Davis 1861, 58 (54).
31. Davis 1861, 63 (60).
32. Receipt for one year's rent from Anna Stellina, December 1st (?), 1856: FO 102/62, 49; Davis 1861, 58–9 (55); Davis 1862, 3.
33. Davis 1861, 57 (52) with fig. on 59 (facing 56); 'Moalka' facing 363 (facing 457).
34. Davis 1861, 58 (54–5).
35. Davis 1861, 145 (171).
36. Letter of Panizzi to Hammond, January 21st, 1857: FO 102/62, 41–2.
37. Letter of Hammond to Davis, January 22nd, 1857: FO 102/62, 43.
38. Letter of Davis to Panizzi, January 15th, 1859, read to the Trustees on February 12th, 1859: BM Archives, C9521.

39. Letter of Davis to Malmesbury, January 15th, 1859: FO 102/62, 244.
40. Dunant 1858, 229–30.
41. Letter of Sophia Cracroft, September 15th, 1858, quoted by Rawnsley 1923, 137.
42. Gallagher 1983, 5–7. In Davis' day, Tunisia suffered epidemic cholera in 1849–50 and again briefly in 1856.
43. Letter from the Foreign Office to Panizzi, February 8th, 1858: FO 102/62, 188; letter of Davis to Malmesbury, April 10th, 1858: FO 102/62, 198.
44. Davis 1861, 384 (483).
45. Letter of Davis to Malmesbury, January 15th, 1859: FO 102/62, 244.
46. Davis 1861, 117 (130) and 164 (197).
47. Davis 1861 55 (61); Sainte-Marie 1875b, 82, no. 60 for Dedreux.
48. Dureau de la Malle 1835.
49. Dusgate 1834; cited by Sainte-Marie 1878a, 138, no. 112.
50. Temple 1835, first quoted by Davis 1861, 42 (35–6).
51. Sainte-Marie 1875b.
52. Ashbee 1889, 2.
53. Sainte-Marie 1878a.
54. Sainte-Marie 1875b, 83–4, no. 69; Sainte-Marie 1878a, 123, no. 46.
55. Falbe 1833; Revault 1974, Plate G, facing p. 54. A copy of the plan of Falbe with clearly inscribed numbers (a few incorrect), and a list of his sites, was published in *CEDAC Carthage 2*, June 1979, centrefold, 22–3.
56. Hérisson 1881, 276.
57. Sainte-Marie 1875a, map at the back of the volume.
58. Sainte-Marie 1884, 209 and 217–18; Lancel 1992, 440, fig. 248, reproduced Sainte-Marie's version.
59. Tissot 1884, vol. 1, 565–613 and map facing 564.
60. Daux 1869; Kolendo 1988, 252–3, nn. 5, 6 and 8. Amos Perry, the American consul at Tunis from 1862 to 1867, gave his name as Auguste Daux, saying that he had been a personal acquaintance for more than five years: Perry 1869, v.
61. Napoléon III 1865–1866. The final volume, which might have included Daux's maps of North Africa, never appeared.
62. Reinach 1886, 85, n. 1.
63. Cf. Hurst et al. 1994, 51–2.
64. Noah 1819, 275–80.
65. Debergh 2002.
66. Davis 1861, 107–15 (119–28).
67. Dureau de la Malle 1835, 18–20.
68. Audollent 1901, 15.
69. Debergh 2000; Mommsen, 1881.
70. Debergh 2000, 468, n. 53.
71. Noah 1819, 263–4.
72. Halbertsma 1995, frontispiece.
73. Halbertsma 2003, 71–111; Debergh 2002, 471–2.
74. Davis 1861, 107 (119).
75. Halbertsma 1995, 26–7 and 205; Humbert 1821.
76. Debergh 2000, 460.
77. Debergh 2000, map, pl. 8.
78. Debergh 2000, 472–4.
79. Davis' published site 12 is just beyond the intersection of the lines of *decumanus* 6 north and *cardo* 4 west; neither street extended to this point.
80. Holwerda 1936, especially 38–63, nos 474–937.
81. Hayes 1972.
82. *CIL* VIII.1098 and 1101; *CIL* VIII.1075 and 1118.
83. 'Inventaire des matériaux relatifs à la régence de Tunis provenant de M. le Lieutenant Colonel Humbert', at the Museum of Leiden, unpublished notes [not seen by me].
84. Janssen 1843.
85. Halbertsma 1995; 2003.
86. Falbe et al. 1860–1874 (reprinted 1984). Ashbee listed a numismatic work by Falbe dated to 1837: Ashbee 1889, 27.
87. Neira Jiménez 2000, 804, n. 19; Hurst et al. 1994, 250; Jenkins 1969.
88. Lund 1986, 8–24. Destruction of mosaic in 1824: Falbe 1833, 43; Halbertsma 2003, 84.
89. Temple 1835.
89. Guérin 1862, xii, citing Temple 1835.
90. Kobelt 1885, 449.
91. Letter of S. D. Heap to his father, with enclosures, February 15th, 1827, quoted in Cohen 1988, 13–22, especially 17–18.
92. Dumas, quoted in Murch 1959, 131.
93. Revault 1974, 55–72. The British consuls Reade and Wood used 'El-Abdalliya' as a summer residence.
94. Temple 1835, vol. 1, 89–90, 98 and 116–17.
95. Temple 1835, vol. 1, 5.
96. Temple 1835, vol. 1, 85–7.
97. Temple 1835, vol. 2, 69.
98. Temple 1835, vol. 1, 108; quoted by Audollent 1901, 824.
99. [Falbe and Temple] 1838.
100. Audollent 1901, 10, n. 3, citing [Falbe and Temple] 1838, vi.
101. Gandolphe 1952, 152–6, reproduced the articles of the Society *verbatim*.
102. Lund 1986, 13–21.
103. Falbe 1833, 43.
104. Lund 1986, 13 and 22, n. 6.
105. Letter of Falbe to the Danish Crown Prince, March 23rd, 1838, cited by Lund 1986, 21.
106. Davis 1844, 140 and note.
107. Beulé 1861, 27; Guérin 1862, vol. 1, 62.
108. Dupuy 1954, 28 with n. 52.
109. Delattre 1884–1885, 107.
110. Letters of Florence Ogg, Director of Exhibits, Collections and Historic House, Suffolk County Vanderbilt Mansion, Planetarium, Museum, August 6th and 21st, 2002. I thank Betty Leventhal for bringing these columns to my attention.
111. Audollent 1901, 242.
112. Gauckler 1910, 235, no. 699, citing Kennedy 1846, vol. 2, 35; Lézine 1968, 42, figs 35–8 and 62–5; Ben Abed-Ben Khader et al. 1999 for the mosaics.
113. Sainte-Marie 1875b, 101, no. 177; Sainte-Marie 1878a, 169, no. 292.

114. *CIL* VIII.1052.
115. Audollent 1901, 11–12; [Falbe and Temple] 1838, cited by Sainte-Marie 1875b, 85, no. 78, and 106, no. 209.
116. Temple 1835, vol. 2, 26.
117. Davis 1861, 261 (330).
118. Audollent 1901, 12, quoting [Falbe and Temple] 1838, xi–xii.
119. Audollent 1901, 12, note 2, citing [Falbe and Temple] 1838, Pl. IV, figs 1 and 7.
120. Temple 1835, vol. 1, 104–5.
121. Cf. Lund 1986, 14, fig. 3, and 16, fig. 4.
122. Falbe 1833, folio volume of maps and figs, pl. IV, no. 2.
123. Wilson 1998, 82, fig. 11, citing Babelon et al. 1893. On Carthage's water supply, see also Casagrande 2008, 65–85 (72–74 on Bordj-Djedid).
124. Sainte-Marie 1878b, fig. facing 10.
125. Davis 1861, 313 (393).
126. Anon. 1857, 448, illustrated with two figures, 'Remains of Carthage: the cisterns' and 'Remains of Carthage: the aqueduct'.
127. Lund 1986, 17, citing a letter of Falbe, March 23rd, 1838, to the Danish Crown Prince.
128. Falbe 1833, 10.
129. Lund 1986, 18, fig. 5.
130. Falbe 1833, 37, translation by Lund 1986, 19 and 23, n. 18.
131. Storz 1991. The building lies in the northern extension of the street grid, in the block between *cardines* 13 and 14 east and *decumani* 6 and 7 north.
132. Storz 1991, 44–5 and fig. 3.
133. Storz 1991, 49–57, with fig. 6 on 49 and fig. 12 on 54.
134. [Falbe and Temple] 1838, cited by Davis 1861, 228, note (285, note).
135. Davis 1861, 46 (38).
136. Lund 1986, 19, citing a letter of Falbe, March 23rd, 1838, to the Danish Crown Prince.
137. Lund 1986, 21, citing a letter of Falbe, May 19th, 1838, to the Danish Crown Prince.
138. Halbertsma 2003, 84.
139. Gauckler 1910, 236, no. 704.
140. Picard 1983, 12–13.
141. Wilmanns and Mommsen 1881, 'Tituli parisini': *CIL* VIII.1165–1169a.
142. Audollent 1901, 7.
143. Audollent 1901, 11.
144. Franks 1860, 207, citing Judas 1847, pl. 9.
145. In terms of the Roman street-grid, Falbe no. 58 lay on the line of *decumanus* 1 north and between *cardines* 7 and 8 east.
146. Sainte-Marie 1876, 17.
147. Davis 1861, 110 (124); Beulé 1873, vol. 2, 4; cf. Sainte-Marie 1878b, 148 and Franks 1860, 222. Cf. now also Giroire and Roger 2007, 53–4. A plaster cast of the bust is displayed in the National Museum of Carthage.
148. Gros et al. 1985, 147, note 47.
149. Gros 1995, 48, fig. 2.
150. Audollent 1901, 281.
151. Beulé 1861, 18; Gandolphe 1952, 157–8.
152. Davis 1861, 303 (383).
153. Lancel 1979; Lancel et al. 1982; Lancel 1983.

Notes to Chapter Four

1. Delattre 1906, 70–1.
2. Lavigerie, letter of 1875, 1884, vol. 2, 365–6.
3. Temple, cited in Davis 1861, 42 (36).
4. Delattre 1906, 7–8.
5. Gandolphe 1951.
6. Audollent 1901, 262.
7. Wells 1996, 157–8.
8. Davis 1861, 309 (388).
9. Gregory 1859, 162.
10. Chabrely 1885, 34.
11. Lancel 1979, fig. 95, facing 78.
12. Barth 1849, 93.
13. Guérin 1862, vol. 1, 46; Beulé 1861, 30.
14. Delattre 1883–1884; reprint, 20.
15. Colin Wells, director of excavations at the Odeon, personal communication.
16. Lancel 1979, fig. 613, facing 382.
17. Falbe 1833, 2–4.
18. Morsy 1984, 169–74.
19. Falbe 1833, 3–4.
20. Hurst 1994, 42–3 with fig. 4.1 on 41.
21. Sainte-Marie 1875b, 86; 1878a, 142–3, and s.v. 'Caillat (Philippe),' 126.
22. Falbe 1833, 4.
23. Falbe 1833, 5 and 39.
24. Bordy [1897].
25. Falbe 1833, 8–11.
26. Beulé 1861, 21.
27. Falbe 1833, 46–7.
28. Falbe 1833, 17–20.
29. Appian, Books VIII and IX; Strabo XVII.3.14–15.
30. Falbe 1833, 28 and 39–40.
31. Falbe 1833, 31–5.
32. Beulé 1861, 19; cf. Chalon et al. 1995.
33. Falbe 1833, 37–8.
34. Falbe 1833, 45–6.
35. Davis 1861, 295–9 (372–7).
36. Falbe 1833, 27–31.
37. Lund 1986, 19 with fig. 5 on 18.
38. Falbe 1833, 38.
39. Hallier 1995, 203, fig. 2; 205, fig. 3.
40. Dureau de la Malle 1835.
41. Davis 1861, 311 (392); Beulé 1861, 25.
42. Audollent 1901, 9.
43. Falbe 1833, 13.
44. Sainte-Marie 1876, 28–9; Sainte-Marie 1878b, 14.
45. Sainte-Marie 1878b, 31–2 and fig. facing 32.
46. Davis 1861, 56 (52).
47. Davis 1861, 109–10 (122).
48. Davis 1861, 116–17 (130–1).
49. Beulé 1861, 90.
50. Davis 1862, 347.
51. Beulé 1861, 92–3, citing Festus and Servius.
52. Beulé 1873, vol. 2, 46.

53. Guérin 1862, vol. 1, 69.
54. Beulé 1873, vol. 2, 46.
55. Audollent 1901, 201, n. 1; Sainte-Marie 1878b, 7.
56. Davis 1861, 117 (130–1).
57. Clover 1978, 9, citing the *Chronica Gallica*.
58. Davis 1861, 102–04 (115–18).
59. Davis 1861, 138 (162) note, and cf. 290–304 (369–84).
60. Davis 1861, 302 (381–2).
61. Guérin 1862, vol. 1, 64.
62. Delattre 1883, 6.
63. Davis 1861, 340 (424), note*.
64. Ennabli 1992.
65. Golvin 1999.
66. Norman 1988, 31.
67. Falbe 1833, 41.
68. Colin Wells, personal communication, May 2006.
69. Pringle 1981, 119.
70. Pringle 1981, 146–7.
71. Pringle 1981, 139.
72. Letter of Falbe to the Danish Crown Prince, March 23rd, 1838, cited by Lund 1986, 23–4, n. 22.
73. Delattre 1886, 80–91; Vernaz 1887, 11–27, 151–70, with pl. 13.
74. Davis 1861, 340 (424).
75. Chatelain 1937, 232; Février 1989, vol. 1, 59.
76. Lézine 1961, map facing 40; Gauckler 1910, 208–21. Lézine marked the area of Roman housing excavated by Gauckler on the slope of the Odeon Hill as lying between *decumani* 4 and 6 north and between *cardines* 7 and 11 east; Gauckler himself called *decumanus* 5 north his 'rue III' and *decumanus* 6 north his 'rue IV,' while the *cardines* 7 to 11 east correspond to Gauckler's 'rues 12–8' (retrograde count).
77. Gauckler 1903, 11–13; cited by Picard 1951.
78. Haverfield 1913, 114, fig. 24.
79. Saumagne 1924; Saumagne 1931, 145–57.
80. Davin 1930.
81. Hurst 1994, 117; cf. 4, fig 1.1.
82. Humphrey 1978b, 516–17.
83. Wightman 1980, 29–46.
84. Wells et al. 1998.
85. Falbe 1833, 54–7.
86. Saumagne 1924, 133, fig. 1.
87. Trousset 1997, 95–109.
88. Vernaz 1887, 159.
89. Rakob 1984, plan 7 = Rakob 1986, 20, map.
90. U. S. Naval Observatory website, consulted November 20th and 21st, 2003. The latitude and longitude of Carthage is 36 degrees N 51′ and 10 degrees E 21′. The table for June 21st, 1890 (the summer solstice) shows the mid-point of the rising sun on the horizon at 60 degrees east of north at 05:05, and the mid-point of the setting sun at 300 degrees east of north (west-north-west) at 19:35. These degrees and hours vary slightly over time.
91. Lézine 1961, 37.
92. Trousset 1994, 70–81.
93. Delattre 1906, 71. The French 'cathedral' of Carthage is now deconsecrated and was never properly a cathedral of the Catholic Church; Delattre called his church the 'primatiale.'
94. Trousset 1997, 99, citing Hyginus.
95. Audollent 1901, 16, n. 1.
96. Hurst 1999, 8, fig. 1.
97. Davis 1861, 315 (394).
98. Davis 1861, lower figure on 148 (facing 177).
99. Senay 2000.
100. Hallier 1995; Ennabli 1997, 98–102.
101. Falbe 1833, 10.
102. Lund 1986, 19–21 with fig. 6 on 20.

Notes to Chapter Five

1. Davis 1861, 101–02 (114).
2. Davis 1861, 327 (409).
3. Davis 1861, 325 (407).
4. Letter from the Foreign Office to Davis, February 23rd, 1857: FO 102/62, 66–8, with a list of Davis's expenses and the names of his workmen.
5. Letter of Wood to Clarendon, December 20th, 1856: FO 102/62, 29.
6. Davis 1861, 148, fig., upper (between 176–7). The figure is incorrectly entitled 'The northern portion of the regency of Tunis' in the earlier edition, with the corrected title of 'Ground Plan of the First Discovery' in the later edition.
7. Davis 1861, 40 (32), 52 (47), 437 (544).
8. Davis 1861, 302 (facing 385); 308 (facing 388), and 331 (facing 414).
9. Davis 1861, ix (ix); note on 448 in the edition with longer pagination only; 436 (543).
10. Letter of Davis at Tunis to Clarendon, December 2nd, 1856: FO 102/62, 27.
11. Dondin-Payre 2000, 2119–46.
12. Morgan 1886, 246.
13. Gran-Aymerich 1998, 183 and 232.
14. Letter of Davis, June 29th, 1857, to Clarendon: FO 102/62, 120.
15. Davis 1861, 145 (171).
16. Davis 1861, 316 (395).
17. I thank Ron Ross for pointing this out.
18. Davis 1861, 357 (445).
19. Davis 1861, 435 (541–2).
20. Davis 1861, 62 (60).
21. Davis 1861, 175 (213).
22. Davis 1861, 115 (128).
23. Davis 1861, 60 (56).
24. Delattre 1883 [reprint], 6.
25. Beulé 1861, 7, 36, 39, 44, 58 with n. 3, 63, 100–01.
26. Davis 1861, 57 (53).
27. Davis 1861, 151–2 (177–8); 154 (182).
28. Davis 1861, 151 (177).
29. Davis 1861, 116–17 (130); Beulé 1873, vol. 2, 56.
30. Davis 1861, 101 (113).
31. Letter of Davis at Tunis to Clarendon, December 2nd, 1856: FO 102/62, 27–8.
32. Anon. 1858a, 480: sketch by Arthur Hall.
33. Davis 1861, 360–1 (449–51).

34. Ling 1967, 14; Perkins 1986, 73.
35. Khun de Prorok 1926, 105.
36. Davis 1861, 410 (511–12).
37. Davis 1861, 399–419 (499–519): 'Excavation at Utica'.
38. Davis 1861, 352 (438). Lord Lyons (1790–1858): *DNB* vol. 12, 1909.
39. Spufford 1997, 51–4.
40. Davis 1861, 167–71 (201–06).
41. Davis 1861, x (ix).
42. Davis 1861, 115 (127); fig. facing 112 (128).
43. Davis 1861, 330 (414); fig. on 43 (facing 35); fig. on 330 (414).
44. Anon. 1858a, 480.
45. Davies 1858.
46. Anon. 1858b, 545, sketch by Arthur Hall.
47. Anon. 1859c, 251; sketches by Arthur Hall on 252–3.
48. Davis 1861, 404 (506) (Lady Franklin), and 428–9, 432 (532–3, 536) (Prince Alfred).
49. Blakesley 1859, 373.
50. Blakesley 1859, 'Notice' [no page number].
51. Blakesley 1859, 397–9.
52. Beulé 1861, 28.
53. Davis 1861, 56–64 (51–62): 'The First Attempt'.
54. Norman 1988, 9, n. 8.
55. Saumagne 1928–1929, especially 635.
56. Davis 1861, 59–61 (55–7).
57. Anon. 1884, 112; Reinach and Babelon 1886.
58. Reinach and Babelon 1886, 18–19.
59. Davis 1861, 61–3 (58–60).
60. Falbe 1833, 27–30.
61. Lézine 1961, 45, n. 2, and Salomonson 1965, 10, n. 1, citing Augustine, *ad Donatistas post collationem*, xxv.43 and xxxv.58.
62. Rousseau 1850, 260–1 and pl. 143.
63. Gauckler 1910, 200.
64. Clover 1986, 3.
65. Gauckler 1910, 200–02, no. 598.
66. Clover 1986, 3–5.
67. Davis's 'Statement', December 21st, 1858: FO 102/62, 250.
68. Davis 1861, 312–1 (392–4), fig. on 313 (facing 393).
69. Ben Abed-Ben Khader et al. 1999 with Miller's plan 8, insula X.
70. Wilson 1998, 66, fig. 1.
71. Wilson 1998, 81–4 and passim; cf. also Casagrande 2008, 72–74.
72. Delavoye 1999, 82–3 and notes on 183.
73. Perry 1869, 437.
74. Ben Abed-Ben Khader et al. 1999, pl. 1. Miller's plan shows not the 'tranchée Vernaz' south of the Bordj-Djedid cisterns, but Gouvet's trench, in '*insula* X' (between *decumani* 4 and 5 north and *cardines* 15 and 16 east).
75. Vernaz 1887, 27.
76. Poinssot 1929, 5 and 36.
77. Wells et al. 1998, 15.
78. Daux 1869, 56–8.
79. Vernaz 1887, 11–27, 151–70 and pl. 13.
80. Falbe 1833, 37–8.
81. Falbe 1833, 10.
82. Temple 1835, vol. 1, 110.
83. Cagnat 1887, 171–9.
84. Sainte-Marie 1876, 30. Sainte-Marie described a site 500 meters south of the eastern cisterns; the distance to the latrine of the Antonine Baths is only about 300 meters, but there is no other likely possibility for the building he described, and his description of the marbles agrees with other observations of the latrine.
85. Davis 1861, 310 (389).
86. Ben Abed-Ben Khader et al. 1999, Miller's plan 8.
87. Davis 1861, 312 (392).
88. Davis 1861, 312 (392); Gauckler 1910, 235, no. 698, following Davis exactly.
89. Ben Abed-Ben Khader et al. 1999, 14 with pl. 22; Lézine 1968, 42. Lézine suggested that the mosaic belonged to the renovations of AD 389 because the *tesserae* were in Chemtou marble, but Chemtou marble was certainly in use much earlier.
90. Ben Abed-Ben Khader et al. 1999, Miller's plan 3.
91. Davis 1861, 312 (392).
92. Wilson 1998, 66, fig. 1; Lézine 1961, plan facing 40.
93. Lézine 1961, plan facing 40; Ben Abed-Ben Khader et al. 1999, Miller's plan 1.
94. Temple 1835, vol. 1, 107.
95. Davis 1861, 302 (facing 381).
96. Beulé 1861, 28.
97. Lézine 1961, plan facing 40.
98. Babelon 1896, 171, citing Beulé 1861, 29 and Delattre 1886, 86.
99. Delavoye 1999, 84.
100. Gauckler 1910, 250, no. 750.
101. Falbe 1833, 10.
102. Falbe 1833, 37–8.
103. Dureau de la Malle 1835, 174; Wilson 1998, 66, fig. 1.
104. Beulé 1861, 37 and 44.
105. Delattre 1884–1885.
106. Khun de Prorok 1923, 39 with fig.
107. Khun de Prorok 1926, 108–09; 131.
108. Wilson 1998, 66, fig. 1.
109. Babelon, Cagnat and Reinach 1893 [atlas], citing Tissot, 1884–1888, vol. 2, 805; Babelon 1896, 151; Lavigerie 1881, 49; Falbe 1833, 10.
110. Rakob 1984, translated 1986, 20 with fig.
111. Tissot 1884–1888, vol. 2, plate VII.

Notes to Chapter Six

1. Neira Jiménez 2000, 798–800.
2. Whitehouse 2001, 70–5.
3. Werner 1997.
4. Kenneth Uprichard, Head of Stone Conservation at the British Museum, noted that the mosaics from Halicarnassos still have considerable portions of Roman mortar on their backs, but had been heavily restored: personal communication, June 20th, 2002.
5. Hinks 1933, for Newton's mosaics.
6. Newton 1865, vol. 2, 81–2; Podany 2006.

7. Franks 1860, 222–3.
8. Rousseau 1850, 260–1, and pl. 143.
9. [Falbe and Temple] 1838, xi and colour pl. iv.
10. Neira Jiménez 2000, 804, note 19.
11. Lund 1986; Neira Jiménez 2000, 804, note 19.
12. Rousseau 1850, 260–1.
13. Parrish 1984, 128–31, cat. no. 16 and pls 25–26.
14. Baratte 1978, 76–8, cat. nos 38a–c (Ma 1788, 1789, 2999); Rousseau's drawing, fig. 69 on 76.
15. Franks 1860, 236.
16. Davis 1861, 166–7 (200).
17. Neira Jiménez 2000, 804, n. 19.
18. Parrish 1984, 128–31, especially 129, and pls 25–26, especially 26a.
19. Falbe 1833, 11 and. 43; Gauckler 1910, 235, no. 701.
20. Falbe 1833, 10 and 31.
21. Falbe 1833, 9 and 42.
22. A large public building is marked at this point on a modern map, entitled simply *Banlieue* (1996). The structure lies on the north side of the highway from Tunis airport to La Marsa, a road which still follows the rural grid.
23. Falbe 1833, map volume, plate IV, no. 1.
24. Falbe 1833, 4.
25. Falbe 1833, 43.
26. Lund 1986, 14–15 with n. 9, citing Falbe 1833, 46.
27. Franks 1860, 222, citing Falbe 1833, 43.
28. Halbertsma 2003, 84.
29. Davis 1861, 152 (178–9) with note.
30. Lund 1986, 15, citing a letter of March 23rd, 1838 from Falbe to the Danish Crown Prince.
31. Neira Jiménez 2000, 797, n. 6, citing the register of the Danish Royal Museum of Art for 1842.
32. Lund 1986, 17, with Falbe's plan, 10 with fig. 2 on 12.
33. [Falbe and Temple] 1838, xi with pl. iv.
34. Dunbabin 1978, 149–54.
35. Lund 1986, 15.
36. Falbe, quoted by Lund, 1986, 15.
37. Baratte 1978, 71, no. 35, cited by Lund 1986, 23, n. 13.
38. Neira Jiménez 2000, 804 and 811, pl. III.2; Lavagne 1983.
39. Lund 1986, 15.
40. [Falbe and Temple] 1838, 108 with pl. iv.1.
41. Lund 1986, 15.
42. Letter of Falbe, March 23rd, 1838, to the Danish Crown Prince: cited by Lund 1986, 15.
43. Lund 1986, 22, n. 10, citing museum inventory entry of 1842.
44. Neira Jiménez 2000, pl. II.2, 810 with fig. 2 on 809; cf. [Falbe and Temple] 1838, pl. iv.
45. Lund 1986, 15; Neira Jiménez 2000, 805.
46. Neira Jiménez 2000, 807, with pls I–II. The dimensions of the Nereid mosaic are not given, but I estimate that the piece is about 0.75 m by 1.50 m (the *tesserae* of the Louvre fragment are about 0.8 cm per side).
47. Lund 1986, 15.
48. Morgan 1886, 242 and 267 with colour plate.
49. Gauckler 1910, 236, no. 704.
50. Hinks 1933, 74–5, no. 15.
51. Anon. 1849, 16, with engraving of the Mosaic of Ocean. Its provenance was incorrectly listed as Athens.
52. Jenkins 1992, 57 and fig. 13 for Richard Westmacott (1775–1856).
53. Kenneth Uprichard, Head of Stone Conservation at the British Museum, said that in the modern process of restoration of this mosaic it was clear which parts were ancient and which belonged to the nineteenth-century restoration: personal communication, May 2003.
54. Hinks 1933, 74, no. 15, and pl. XXVIII, top.
55. Dunbabin 1978, 150.
56. Lund 1986, 17, citing Dunbabin 1978, 149–54.
57. Dunbabin 1978, 150 with n. 64.
58. Dunbabin 1978, 128; 153 (Themetra I a); 272, pl. 144 (in colour, Ben Abed-Ben Khader 2003, fig, 346).
59. Dunbabin 1978, 151–2 (Sétif 4), pl. 143.
60. Dunbabin 1978, 152.
61. Dunbabin 1978, 151 with n. 76.
62. Baratte 1978, 71, cat. no. 35 (Ma 1795), with fig. 62.
63. Lavagne 1983, 58.
64. Lavagne 1983, 59; comments by Darmon and Lavagne.
65. Rousseau 1850, 260–1 with pl. 143.
66. Dunbabin 1978, 59.
67. Parrish 1984, 130–1.
68. Clover 1986, 3–5; 4, n. 22, citing Luxorius, *Anthologia Latina* 301.
69. Rousseau 1850, 260.
70. Gauckler 1910, 201.
71. Wilmanns and Mommsen 1881: *CIL* VIII.10539.
72. Cf. Parrish 1984, 128–31, no. 16, and pls 25 a–c.
73. Beulé 1861, 37 with pl. 1.
74. Davis 1861, 166–7 (200–01).
75. Letter of Davis to Malmesbury, April 10th, 1858: FO 102/62, 200.
76. Korsunska 1933, 277–83; Parrish 1992, 483, no. 8, Hermitage 1069.
77. Gorbunova and Saverkina 1975, no. 114.
78. Davis 1861, 355 (443).
79. Parrish 1992, no. 16, 484.
80. Strzygowski 1888, 68–9 with fig.
81. Temple 1835, vol. 1, 109.
82. Gauckler 1910, 235, no. 699, citing Kennedy 1846, vol. 2, 37; Audollent 1901, 242 and notes.
83. Ben Abed-Ben Khader et al. 1999, 1–20 and corresponding nos and pls.
84. Gauckler 1910, 236–7, no. 705.
85. Audollent 1901, 12 and notes.
86. Neira Jiménez 2000, 808, n. 24.
87. Falbe 1833, 31.
88. Falbe 1833, 42.
89. Neira Jiménez 2000, 812, pl. IV; no scale.
90. Neira Jiménez 2000, 806 with n. 31.
91. Neira Jiménez 2000, 809, pl. I. A Roman lamp to one side of the mosaic provided the basis for my estimate of the mosaic's size.
92. Parlasca 1958, 183, n. 175; Neira Jiménez 2000, 809, pl. 1.
93. Storz 1991, 41–60, especially 54 with fig. 12.
94. Storz 1991, 53, with fig. 6 on 49.

95. Storz 1991, 49, fig. 6 and 54, fig. 12.
96. Storz 1991, 52–3.
97. M'Charek 1988, 746.
98. Gozlan 1983, 186 note.
99. Gozlan 1983, 179–87 and pls CVI–CXIII.
100. Sainte-Marie 1884, 27–31; fig. on 31.
101. For the site, Sainte-Marie 1875a.
102. Gauckler 1910, 202–03, no. 600, with bibliography.

Notes to Chapter Seven

1. Letter of Davis to the Foreign Office, January 13th, 1857: FO 102/62, 39–40.
2. Davis 1861, 101 (113).
3. Davis 1861, 145–58 (171–88): 'The First Discovery'; 159–85 (189–219): 'Its Antiquity'.
4. Letter of Davis to Clarendon, May 28th, 1857: FO 102/62; letter of Davis to Clarendon, June 29th, 1857: FO 102/62, 120, with two drawings. The originals are now in the map collection of the British National Archives: FO 102/62, MFQ 616 (3) and (4).
5. Letter of Davis to Clarendon, May 28th, 1857, Carthage: FO 102/62, 98; letter of Davis to Clarendon, July 14th, 1857, Carthage: FO 102/62, 123.
6. Jenkins 1992, 253.
7. The mosaic, in several pieces, is registered as MLA 1857.12–18.126–144. The designation 'MLA' indicates its present allocation to the Department of Medieval and Modern Europe in the British Museum, formerly the Department of Medieval and Later Antiquities.
8. Franks 1860, 202–36.
9. Davis 1861, 145–6 (171–3).
10. Marcel Gandolphe, 'Le R. Delattre', an undated article clipped from an unidentified Tunisian paper, in the Archives of the White Fathers (*Archivio Generale dei Missionari d'Africa*) in Rome, with material on Delattre in folder Y1, 'Anecdotes.'
11. Sainte-Marie 1884, 7.
12. Blakesley 1859, 396–7.
13. Flaux 1865, 268; the report to Count Walewski, 271–86.
14. Flaux 1865, 264–5.
15. Davis 1861, 146–9 (173–5).
16. Davis 1861, 149 (174).
17. Franks 1860, 224.
18. Davis 1861, plan, 148 (facing 177); description, 152 (178). The plan is correctly labelled 'Ground Plan of the First Discovery' in the edition with longer pagination and in the reprint of 1985.
19. Davis 1861, 150 (176). In his letter of January 13th, 1857, to Clarendon, Davis estimated the size of this piece at 18 ft by 7 ft (5.5 m by 2.1 m). Based on the diameter of the corner medallions, given by Franks as 2 ft 9 in (0.8 m), I estimate that the fragment is 17 ft 6 in by 9 ft 5 in (5.3 m by 2.9 m).
20. Davis 1861, 150 (176).
21. Davis 1861, 155 (184).
22. Davis 1861, drawing between 154–5 (between 184–5); between 182–3 in the reprint.
23. Sketch in the bound volume, *Papers Relating to Mr. Davis's Excavations at Carthage*, in the Department of Greek and Roman Antiquities at the British Museum.
24. Franks 1860, 227.
25. Receipt from Lieutenant Durbin at Tunis, May 25th, 1857: FO 102/62, 102.
26. Davis 1861, 176 (214).
27. Dureau de la Malle 1835.
28. Tissot 1884–1888, vol. 1, 653, n. 2, quoting *de prom. et praed.* III.38.5: *cuius platea lithostrata pavimento ac pretiosis columnis et moenibus decorata*; 'its open area decorated with stone-laid pavement and costly columns and walls'.
29. Davis 1861, 179 (218), suggested AD 425. The work quoted by Davis is now attributed to Quodvultdeus: Lancel 1988, 654–5; Hurst 1999, 90–1, provides a translation.
30. Wilson 1998, 66, fig. 1.
31. Davis 1861, 162 (193), citing Justin, *Epitome Pompei Trogi* 18.6.(8).
32. Davis 1861, 162 (193–4).
33. Ovid, *Fasti* III.523–710.
34. Beulé 1861, 8, citing Silius Italicus, *Punica* VIII. 25–231.
35. Lancel 1992, 114 (1995, 193), citing Diodorus Siculus XIV.77.5.
36. Davis 1861, 162–3 (194–5).
37. Dureau de la Malle 1835, 21.
38. Beulé 1861, 38 and pl. 3.
39. Cagnat 1894, 194–5, citing *Cod. Theod.* XI.1.34.
40. Davis 1861, 161–3 (194). Hurst 1999, especially 32, fig. 18, placed the sanctuary of Tanit or Astarte on the artificial hill Koudiat el-Hobsia near the *tophet*.
41. Davis 1861, 62 (60).
42. Davis 1861, 169–71 (203).
43. Davis, 1861, 175 (212–13).
44. Vaux 1863b, n. on 444.
45. Davis 1861, 146 (172).
46. Davis 1861, 150 (176).
47. Letter of Davis to Clarendon, January 13th, 1857: FO 102/62, 39.
48. Davis 1861, 175 (212) and 153 (180).
49. Letter of Davis to Clarendon, January 13th, 1857: FO 102/62, 39.
50. Gauckler 1910, 223.
51. George Leighton Ditson (1812–1895); *Who Was Who* 1967. I have not found Ditson's article in the *New York Tribune*, but his observations on North Africa were probably carried as a serial before their publication as a book in 1859.
52. Kirk 1902, vol. 1, s.v. 'Ditson, George Leighton.'
53. Davis 1861, 167–9 (201–6).
54. Wilmanns and Mommsen 1881, *CIL* VIII.1072, and *additamenta*, 929.
55. Davis 1861, 146–9 (191–3) and plate facing 160 (facing 193).
56. Letter of Davis to Clarendon, May 28th, 1857: FO 102/62, 101.
57. Letter of Davis to Clarendon, October 8th, 1857, forwarded to Panizzi by the Foreign Office; no copy in Foreign Office file = BM letter IX.

58. Wilson 1998, 66, fig. 1.
59. Salomonson 1965, 16, plan, fig. 2; Bullo and Ghedini 2003, 152–4.
60. Lézine 1961, 45–55.
61. Picard 1964, and 1965, 59–97. Picard's fascinating and informative book was written for a popular audience and he did not cite his sources.
62. Salomonson 1965, 89–91.
63. Lavan 1999, 159–60. The remains of this building are now encased in a concrete platform on the south corner of the Byrsa summit.
64. Deneauve 1990, 151–2, figs 9–10, with Robine's plan; Deneauve and Gros 1980, 326, with plan, fig. 11.
65. Davis 1861, 182–4 (222–4).
66. Davis' 'Carthaginian Excavation Expenditures, Monthly abstract of account from 14th Jan. to 14th Feb. 1857', enclosed with a letter of March 24th, 1857, from Wood to the Foreign Office: FO 102/62, 81–9.
67. Davis 1861, 183 (224).
68. Letter of Davis to Clarendon, March 25th, 1857; Davis 1861, 183–5 (224–5); Franks 1860, 223–4.
69. Davis 1861, 185 (225–6).
70. Letter of Wood to Clarendon, March 3rd, 1857: FO 335/105/3.
71. Receipt from Lieutenant Durbin at Tunis, May 25th, 1857: FO 102/62, 102.
72. Franks 1860, 202–36.
73. Wilson 1984, 17 and 41.
74. Miller 1973, 194.
75. Caygill and Cherry 1997.
76. Davis 1861, 165 (197–8).
77. Salzman 1990; Stern 1953. Both are indispensable on the subject matter of the Mosaic of the Months and Seasons.
78. Franks 1860, 228 and note; Montfaucon 1719 (translated by Humphreys in 1725). I have seen only the reprint for the supplement volumes: Supplement vol. I, 14–22 and figs.
79. Strzygowski 1888.
80. Salzman 1990, xix.
81. Gauckler 1910, 224, nos 666–8.
82. Hinks, 1933, 89–96, no. 29, figs 98–105 and pl. xxix.
83. Dunbabin 1978, 251, Carthage 16.
84. Dunbabin 1980, 85–127 and pls 6.1–7.
85. Davis 1861, 165–6 (198).
86. Davis 1861, 159 (190).
87. Franks 1860, 224.
88. Franks 1860, 224 and 227. Franks said that the lower sections of the circular band measured 4 ft (1.2 m) wide at their base and were 4 ft 4 in (1.3 m) high. Hinks 1933, 89, described the mosaic as a square approximately 8.4 m per side. Extrapolating from Franks' diameter of 2 ft 9 in (0.8 m) for the corner medallions, the complete floor measured 28 ft 9 in (8.8 m) by 24 ft 5 in (7.4 m).
89. Franks 1860, 224.
90. Falbe 1833, 10.
91. Wilmanns and Mommsen 1881: *CIL* VIII.1072.
92. Wilmanns and Mommsen 1881: *CIL* VIII. 929, *additamenta*.
93. Rives 1995, xiv (Map 1).
94. Gauckler 1910, 223.
95. Dunbabin 1978, 251, Carthage 16.

Notes to Chapter Eight

1. Davis 1861, 185 (226).
2. Davis 1861, 228 (285).
3. Receipt of Captain Arthur Forbes, July 10th, 1857: FO 102/62, 127–8.
4. Report of the meeting of the Trustees, October 10th, 1857: BM Archives C9272.
5. Wilson 1998, 66, fig. 1.
6. Davis 1861, 62 (59).
7. Hurst et al. 1994, 13 (fig. 1.7), 64–70 and 92–8.
8. Davis 1861, 421–3 (522–23).
9. Falbe 1833, 10.
10. Davis 1861, 421 (521–2).
11. Beulé 1861, 44 and 81.
12. Beulé 1861, 82, citing Procopius, *De aedificiis* VI.5 and *De Bello Vandalico* II.26; Beulé 1861, 95, quoting Barth 1849, vol. I, 92.
13. Pringle 1981, 172.
14. Sainte-Marie 1876, 13.
15. Eadie and Humphrey 1977, 3, fig. 1.
16. Brown, Humphrey and MacLennan 1976, 2; Eadie and Humphrey 1977, 6.
17. Mahjoubi 1967, 264. The site of the house was cut by the line of the 'TGM' tram line.
18. Eadie and Humphrey 1977, 7.
19. Brown, Humphrey and MacLennan 1976, 1–3; Bullo and Ghedini 2003, 166–7.
20. Ennabli 2000, 11.
21. Beulé 1861, 82.
22. Rakob 1986, 20, plan 7.
23. Wilson 1998, 66, fig. 1.
24. Davis 1861, 'Disputed topography', especially 293–303 (369–84).
25. Davis 1861, 301–2 (381–2).
26. Beulé 1861, 29.
27. Beulé 1861, 12 and 28–30, quoting Victor of Vita, *platea nova cum gradibus in media civitatis*: 'a new plaza with steps in the middle of the city'.
28. Falbe 1833, 9, 'Sidi Daoud II'.
29. Lézine 1961, plan facing 40.
30. Lancel 1992, 193, citing Diodorus Siculus XIV.77.5.
31. Temple 1835, vol. 1, 107.
32. Delattre 1899.
33. Delattre 1900.
34. *CIL* VIII.1041.
35. Delattre 1901, 435.
36. On the Bordy map of 1897 the term 'Ard el-Kheraib' referred to the area on the eastern side of the city from the Circular Harbour to *decumanus* 1 north; to Bordy, Gauckler and Delattre it was roughly equivalent to the Forum of Punic Carthage. Merlin and Drappier arbitrarily adopted the term for their excavations on the summit of Bordj-Djedid.
37. Duval, Lancel and Le Bohec 1984, 81, plan, fig. 11.

38. Vercoutter 1945, map facing 40; Benichou-Safar 1982, 56, fig. 30.
39. Mendleson 2003, 19–20 and pls on 65–6 (TM1–8).
40. Mendleson 2003, 19.
41. Benichou-Safar 1982, 71–8, with figs 39.1–3 on 73.
42. Lézine 1961, plan facing 40, point 13.
43. Deneauve 1983, 92 and 102, fig. 3.
44. Duval, Lancel and Le Bohec 1984.
45. Anon. 1898, 295.
46. N. Duval, in Duval, Lancel and Le Bohec 1984, 83 and n. 99.
47. Carton 1920, plan on 263.
48. Delattre 1906b; Freed 1996; 1998.
49. Carton 1920, 267.
50. Beulé 1861, 16–17, citing Temple 1835, vol. 1, 104.
51. Audollent 1901, Appendix II, 800–03; also 450–2 and 664–6.
52. Lézine 1968, 5–77.
53. Lézine 1961, plan facing 40.
54. Ben Abed-Ben Khader et al. 1999, Miller's plan 1; Bullo and Ghedini 2003, 150–1.
55. Falbe 1833, 10.
56. Davis 1861, 309 (388–9).
57. Beulé 1861, 19.
58. Franks 1860, 225.
59. Falbe 1833, 10.
60. Davis 1861, 330–3 (414).
61. Falbe 1833, 11.
62. Davis 1861, 333 (414).
63. Davis 1861, 329 (412).
64. Dietz 1985, especially 109; full bibliography and plan in Bullo and Ghedini 2003, 112–14.
65. Letter of Davis to Clarendon, May 28th, 1857: FO 102/62, 98–101.
66. Davis 1861, 168 (202).
67. Letter of Davis to Clarendon, May 28th, 1857: FO 102/62, 99–100.
68. Davis 1861, 330 (413–14).
69. Hinks 1933, 149, no. 59 with fig. 168. Compare the inscription on a mosaic dedication from the Basilica of Cresconius at Djemila: Dunbabin 1978, pl. LXXV, no. 194.
70. Dunbabin 1978, 151, n. 77.
71. Wilmanns and Mommsen 1881; *CIL* VIII.1072, and *additamenta*, 929.
72. Franks 1860, 224–5.
73. Davis 1861, 373 (467).
74. Davis 1861, 168 (202), quoting Ditson.
75. Franks 1860, 225, site no. 2, quoted by Davis 1861, 330 (413).
76. Letter of Davis to Clarendon, July 14th, 1857: FO 102/62, 123.
77. Franks 1860, 225.
78. Davis 1861, 330 (413).
79. Letter of Davis to Clarendon, July 14th, 1857: FO 102/62, 123.
80. Davis 1861, 168 (202–3), quoting Ditson.
81. Letter of Davis to Clarendon, May 28th, 1857: FO 102/62, 100.
82. Gauckler 1910, 254, no. 757.
83. Hinks 1933, 72, no. 11 and 73, fig. 79; dimensions 1.56 m by 1.37 m.
84. Hinks 1933, 60–70, no. 8, fig. 76.
85. Hinks 1933, 70-1, no. 9, fig. 77.
86. Falbe 1833, 43, cited by Lund, 1986, 13.
87. Lund 1986, 11, fig. 2, and 15.
88. Dietz and Trolle 1979, 10, 15 and especially 17.
89. Storz 1991, 42, fig. 1.
90. Poulsen 1986.
91. Dietz and Trolle 1979, 48 and 49, figs 29 and 30, mosaic C. T.
92. Hinks 1933, 149, no. 59, fig. 168.
93. Hinks 1933, 67, no. 4, fig. 73.
94. Hinks 1933, 68, no. 6, fig. 75.
95. Dietz 1986; Andersen's plans, especially 118, fig. 5.
96. Lund 1986, 10, stated that Falbe's villa was farther to the *north* (my italics) than the site excavated by the Danes in the 1970s, but on 17 he suggested that Falbe's villa was farther to the south and nearer the beach than the Danish excavations. The idea that Falbe's villa was farther to the south and closer to the sea seems to be the interpretation intended.
97. Hinks 1933, 149.
98. Dietz 1985, 115–18, Andersen's plans 1–5.
99. Davis 1861, 329 (412).
100. Itemized receipt from Lieutenant Durbin, May 25th, 1857: FO 102/62, 102.
101. Letter of Davis to Clarendon, May 28th, 1857: FO 102/62, 100.
102. Letter of Davis to Clarendon, July 14th, 1857: FO 102/62, 123; receipt from Captain Forbes, dated July 10th, 1857: FO 102/62, 127.
103. Davis 1861, 355 (442–4).
104. Hanoune 1969, 219–56 with fig. 17 on 220; cf. also Bullo and Ghedini 2003, 157.
105. Merlin 1921.
106. Hinks 1933, 67, no. 4, fig. 73 and pl. xxvi.
107. Davis 1861, 329 (412).
108. Franks 1860, 225.
109. Hinks 1933, 66, no. 4.
110. Davis 1861, 329 (412).
111. Hinks 1933, 66, no. 4.
112. Letter of Davis to Clarendon, July 14th, 1857: FO 102/62, 123.

Notes to Chapter Nine

1. Davis 1861, 241 (301).
2. Davis 1861, 239 (298).
3. Davis 1861, 196–227 (242–84): 'The Religion of the Carthaginians'.
4. Davis 1861, 228–44 (285–305): 'Saturn and His Victims'.
5. Stager 1992.
6. Davis 1861, 356 (443–5).
7. Vaux 1863a, [3].
8. Letter of Davis to Clarendon, May 28th, 1857: FO 102/62, 102.
9. Davis 1861, 355–9, 361–2 (442–5).

10. Davis 1861, 146 (173).
11. Davis 1861, 205–6 (256).
12. Franks 1860, 208–21.
13. Vaux 1863a, [3].
14. Humbert 1821; Halbertsma 1995, 26–7, 205.
15. Falbe 1833, map volume, pl. V, nos 3–4; Guérin 1862, vol. 1, xii; Benichou-Safar 1982, 221, no. 63, citing Falbe 1833, 110.
16. Bourgade 1856, 11; Euting 1883, pl. 8, no. 16 and pl. 9, no. 17; Benichou-Safar 1982, 223, no. 64 = Bourgade 1852, 18 and pl. = Euting 1883, pl. IX, no. 18.
17. Davis 1861, 346 (430).
18. Davis 1861, 323–4 (405).
19. Sainte-Marie 1884, 6.
20. Sainte-Marie 1875a, page not noted.
21. Brown 1991, 241, fig. 2; Wilson 1975.
22. Franks 1860, 208.
23. Falbe 1833, 10.
24. Falbe no. 58 is just north of *decumanus* 1 north and between *cardines* 7 and 8 east.
25. Davis 1861, 205–27 (256–72), with figure facing 206 (256).
26. Davis 1861, 240 (301) and 356–8 (446), with note *.
27. Davis 1861, 237–9 (296–8) and fig. on 223 (facing 281); Mendleson 2003, 30 and plate on 85 (Pu74).
28. Davis 1861, 237 (296); Beauregard and Senay 1976, 74, citing Toutain 1915.
29. Delattre 1884–85, 207; Reinach and Babelon 1886, 9.
30. Sainte-Marie 1876.
31. Sainte-Marie 1884, 3–4.
32. Sainte-Marie 1884, 9, map; Benichou-Safar 1989.
33. Berger 1900, 602.
34. *CIL* VIII.1002–7. The Bordy map indicates the position of the Serapeum; cf. Rives 1995, xiv, map 1.
35. Sainte-Marie 1884, 9, plan. I calculate that 1.0 cm on Sainte-Marie's plan equals approximately 275.6 m.
36. Sainte-Marie 1884, 31.
37. Hanoune 1969, 220, fig. 1 (map).
38. Rakob 1986, pl. 7.
39. Rakob 1991a; 1991b, plan (fig. 3) between 70 and 71.
40. Graham 1978, 10–11, map, where this site is not specifically marked or labelled.
41. Berger 1886; Babelon 1896, 132.
42. Reinach and Babelon 1886, 9.
43. Sainte-Marie 1884, 31.
44. Babelon 1896, 131–2.
45. Reinach and Babelon 1886, plan V between 34 and 35.
46. Babelon 1896, 69.
47. Reinach and Babelon 1886, 11.
48. Reinach and Babelon 1886, plan and sections between 34 and 35.
49. Babelon 1896, 69.
50. Reinach and Babelon 1886, 11–12.
51. Reinach and Babelon 1886, 37.
52. Rakob described these tunnels in a tour of his deep Punic trench, on the site of Falbe no. 56, which he led in the 1990s (the late Friedrich Rakob, personal communication).
53. Beulé 1861, 71.
54. Hours-Miédan 1959, 19.
55. Mendleson 2003, 19–20 and pls on 65–6 (TM 1–8).
56. Objects with British Museum catalogue numbers beginning with 57.12-18, 59.4-2 and 60.10-2 are from Davis's three shipments. Davis returned eight late Punic tomb markers, 100 Punic *stelae* and 50 neo-Punic *stelae* (among which there are two joins) to the British Museum, calculating from the concordances in Mendleson 2003, 55–8. Cf. Mendleson 2003, 21 and pl. on 68 (Pu5).
57. Mendleson 2003, 29–30 and pl. on 84 (Pu71).
58. Mendleson 2003, 30 and pl. on 85 (Pu72).
59. Mendleson 2003, 30 and pl. on 85 (Pu74).
60. Mendleson 2003, 7.
61. Brown 1991, 79, no. 3.
62. Brown 1991, 47.
63. Brown 1991, 51, with fig. 49 on 291. Brown dated 'Tanit III' to the later third and second centuries BC, and 'Tanit II' to *c.* 500–225 BC.
64. My own count, based on Mendleson 2003.
65. According to Brown 1991, 45, Lapeyre found many intentionally broken *stelae* neatly piled in a *favissa* (ritual burial trench) near the *tophet*, and suggested that Sainte-Marie had also discovered a *favissa*.
66. Brown 1991, 81, citing Hours-Miédan 1950, 16.
67. Brown 1991, 84.
68. Cf. Lancel 1992, 333–8, figs 206–11, for the range of Punic *stelae*.
69. Mendleson 2003, 33 and 91 (Pu97), from Davis' finds.
70. Letter of Davis to Clarendon, June 29th, 1857: FO 102/62, 120; Mendleson 2003, 61, Appendix 2.
71. Letter of Davis to Clarendon, July 14th, 1857: FO 102/62, 126.
72. Mendleson 2003. The original accession numbers are GR 57.12-18.38–67, excluding 51; GR 59.4-2.36–48, and GR 60.10-2.117–121 and 124.
73. Mendelson 2003, 47–8 and pl. on 111 (NPu58), an epitaph completely in Latin = *CIL* VIII.1052; and Mendelson 2003, 44 and pl. on 106 (NPu38), with inscription R· S· V· L· H· = *CIL* VIII.1011 = here Fig. 9.11.
74. M'Charek 1988, 736.
75. Davis 1861, 350–1 (435–7).
76. Bourgade 1856, 12.
77. Mendleson 2003, 37–48. Mendleson's catalogue provides the basis for my arguments in this section.
78. Mendleson 2003, 40 and pl. on 102 (NPu21).
79. Mendleson 2003, 37 and pl. on 97 (NPu1).
80. Mendleson 2003, 37–40 and pls on 97–101 (groups NPu1–2 and NPu3–17).
81. Mendleson 2003, 5 and n. 14. Mendelson indicates that the catalogue of the Musée Alaoui (now Musée du Bardo) stated that such *stelae* were found in excavations by the Khaznadar and his son at the village of La Ghorfa between 1860 and 1873. Bourgade had already published at least one *stele* in their collection in 1852, and the excavations as described are very unlikely.
82. Mendleson 2003, 41–5 and 102–05 (group NPu24–42).
83. Moore 2000, 238–55, Cat. 13–36, illustrated on 308–31 (figs 13–36); also 263–4 (concordances).

84. Moore 2000, 223–4, citing M'Charek 1988.
85. Moore 2000, 200–13.
86. Moore added NPu 19, 22, 23, 43 and 45 to Mendleson's group NPu 24–42. British Museum curator Jonathan Tubb subsequently discovered a join between Davis' NPu31 and 43, reducing the total count to 23: Mendleson 2003, 43 and 45 with pl. on 104 (= Fig. 9.12).
87. Mendleson 2003, 59–60, Appendix I: letter of J. B. Honegger at Holborn to Edward Hawkins at the British Museum, October 2nd, 1848.
88. Jomard 1843, quoted by M'Charek 1988, 735–6; both cited by Moore 2000, 217.
89. Moore 2000, 222.
90. Davis 1861, 351 (437).
91. Mendleson 2003, 44 and pl. on 106 (NPu38): Fig. 9.12.
92. *CIL* VIII.1011; Moore 2000, 252–3, Cat. 33, and 328, fig. 33. Wilmanns incorrectly described this *stele* as found at Carthage.
93. Bourgade 1856.
94. *CIL* VIII.1145.
95. Moore 2000, 244–5, Cat. 21, and 316, fig. 21 = *CIL* VIII.1145; Bourgade 1853, 23; Bourgade 1856, 47.
96. *CIL* VIII.1010: NIGER / V·S·L·A.
97. *CIL* VIII.1009 and 1142–44.
98. Moore 2000, 220.
99. Mendleson 2003, 37 and pls on 97 (NPu1 and 2).
100. Mendleson group NPu3–17. The original catalogue numbers indicate which *stelae* Davis acquired.
101. Mendleson 2003, 37–40 (NPu 3) and 16–17 (NPu 18) are certainly related.
102. Mendleson 2003, 47–8 and pls on 110–11 (NPu57–61), of which NPu58 is entirely in Latin.
103. NPu59 = Bourgade 1852, 18, no. 16; NPu58 = *CIL* VIII.1052.
104. Mendleson 2003, 40 and 46, with plates NPu 20 and 47.
105. Mendleson 2003, 45 and plate NPu44.
106. Davis 1861, 110–11 (124).
107. Sainte-Marie 1884, 7.
108. BM Archives C9191; a letter from Lady Reade offering artifacts to the Museum was discussed in the meeting of the Trustees, April 25th, 1857.
109. Mendleson 2003, 37, 40 and plates NPu3 and 18.
110. Mendleson 2003, NPu46, 48–50 and 52–56; Mendleson cited lots 38–45 from Anon. 1850.
111. Mendleson 2003, 47 and plates NPu53, 55 and 56.
112. Mendleson 2003, 62, Appendix 3, quoting a letter of Temple from 1835.

Notes to Chapter Ten

1. Letter of Davis to Clarendon, May 28th, 1857: FO 102/62, 98–101.
2. Receipt from Lieutenant Durbin, Tunis, May 25th, 1857: FO 102/62, 102.
3. Letter of Davis to Clarendon, May 28th, 1857: FO 102/62, 99.
4. Davis, 1861, 316–18 (396–7) with fig.
5. Receipt from Lieutenant Durbin, Tunis, May 25th, 1857: FO 102/62, 102.
6. Franks 1860, 232.
7. Joann Freed and Paul Roberts 1997–2000, unpublished catalogue of amphoras in the British Museum Department of Greek and Roman Antiquities, no. 61 = GR 1857.12-18.151, Dressel 1B Italian Tyrrhenian wine amphora, height 115 cm.
8. Delattre 1893 and 1894.
9. Freed 1996; Freed and Moore 1996.
10. Davis 1861, 324 (405–6).
11. Perkins 1986, 72–3.
12. Attal and Sitbon 1986, xix–xx.
13. Draft of letter of Wood to Clarendon, June 15th, 1857: FO 335/108/3.
14. Davis 1861, 352 (438); *DNB* 1909, s.v. 'Lyons, Edmund'.
15. Davis 1861, 324–6 (407).
16. Davis 1861, 34–5 (25) and note; 54–5 (49–50) and note.
17. Davis 1861, 324–5 (407).
18. Letter of Davis at Carthage to Clarendon, July 14th, 1857: FO 102/62, 123–4.
19. Davis' 'Statement' of December 21st, 1858: FO 102/62, 246.
20. Receipt of Captain Forbes, July 10th, 1857: FO 102/62, 127; letters of Davis, June 29th, 1857: FO 102/62, 120; and July 14th, 1857: FO 102/62, 123–4.
21. Meeting of the Trustees, October 10th, 1857: BM archives, C9272.
22. Edwards 1870, 668; Jenkins 1992, 184 with n. 116.
23. Draft of a letter of Wood to the Bey of Tunis, July 24th, 1857: FO 335/08/5.
24. Draft of a letter of Wood to the Admiralty, September 3rd, 1857: FO 335/08/5.
25. Letter of Clarendon to Wood, September 24th, 1857: FO 335/108/1.
26. Letter of Hammond to the Admiralty, October 28th, 1857: FO 102/62, 159–60.
27. Attal and Sitbon 1986, xx.
28. Davis 1861, 351–5 (437–42).
29. Letter of Davis to Clarendon, October 8th, 1857 (no copy in Foreign Office file, but = BM letter IX).
30. Davis' 'Statement' of December 21st, 1858: FO 102/62, back of 246.
31. Davis 1861, 316 (395–6).
32. Wells, Freed and Gallagher 1988; Wells, 1992; and in brief, Bullo and Ghedini 2003, 119–21.
33. Letter of Davis to Clarendon, May 28th, 1857: FO 102/62, 101.
34. Davis 1861, 245 (306).
35. Letter of Davis to Clarendon, July 14th, 1857: FO 102/62, 124.
36. Letter of Davis to Clarendon, October 8th, 1857 (no copy in Foreign office file, but = BM letter IX).
37. Floor plan of 'Carthaginian house', no copy in BM file, enclosed with Davis's 'Statement' of December 21st, 1858: FO 102/62, 257.
38. Davis' 'Statement' of December 21st, 1858: FO 102/62, 245–6.
39. Davis 1861, 317 (facing 396).
40. Davis 1861, 315–16 (394–5).

41. Anon. 1858b, 545.
42. Davis 1861, 316 (396).
43. Gregory 1859, vol. 2, 163–4.
44. Blanchard-Lemée et al. 1996, 271 and 294, fig. 212; Ling 1998, 82, fig. 57.
45. Hinks 1933, nos 13, 38 and 41 (GR 1859.4-2.69–71) correlate with cases 23, 24 and 26.
46. BM accession list, GR 1859.4-2.71; Anon. 1876; Hinks 1933, 74, no. 13, fig. 81.
47. Sainte-Marie 1884, 31, with fig. on 27.
48. Lézine 1968, 42 with fig. 38 on 65; cf. also for dating, 72.
49. Davis 1861, 327 (409).
50. Gauckler 1910, 214–19, nos 640–9; Bullo and Ghedini 2003, 125–7.
51. Lézine 1961, plan facing 40.
52. Davis' 'Statement' of December 21st, 1858: FO 102/62, 247–8.
53. Davis 1861, 324 (406).
54. Letter of Davis to Clarendon, October 8th, 1857 = BM letter IX (no copy in Foreign Office file).
55. Gregory 1859, vol. 2, 166.
56. Davis 1861, 336 (419); Franks 1860, 225–6, site no. 5.
57. Davis 1861, 328 (410).
58. Davis 1861, 334–5 (416–17).
59. Davis 1861, 346 (430).
60. Davis' 'Statement' of December 21st, 1858: FO 102/62, 249.
61. Franks 1860, 226.
62. Hinks 1933, 85, no. 25, with fig. 93; Ling 1998, cover of paperback edition.
63. Dunbabin 1978, 170–2.
64. The British Museum accession list correlates the ten pieces of mosaic, 1859.4-2.74–83, with their shipping cases and with Hinks 25 a–j.
65. Franks 1860, 226.
66. Hinks 1933, 81–2, no. 21 and fig. 89.
67. Davis 1861, 336 (420).
68. Davis 'Statement' of December 21st, 1858: FO 102/62, 245–6.
69. Davis 'Statement' of December 21st, 1858: FO 102/62, 249.
70. Gauckler 1910, 257, no. 768.
71. Lézine 1961, plan facing 40.
72. Gauckler 1910, 209–10, nos 621–5; Bullo and Ghedini 2003, 123–4 for the House of the Bassilica.
73. Gaucker 1910, 210–12, nos 626–30.
74. Gauckler 1910, 209, no. 621.
75. Gauckler 1910, 209, no. 622.
76. Gauckler 1910, 210, no. 623.
77. Gauckler 1910, 210, no. 624.
78. Gauckler 1910, 214, no. 638.
79. Ennabli and Ben Osman 1983a and b.
80. Davis' 'Statement' of December 21st, 1858: FO 102/62, 250.
81. Davis 1861, 346 (430).
82. Lézine 1961, plan facing 40.
83. Franks 1860, 226.
84. Gauckler 1910, 255, nos 760 and 762.
85. Davis 1861, 428 (531).
86. Hinks 1933, 122–3, no. 48 with fig. 139. The same theme (but more perfunctorily executed) occurs in the sixth-century church at Henchir Ounaïssia (El Ouara) in the region of Sbeitla: Ben Abed-Ben Khader 2003, fig. 395; Badisches Landesmuseum Karlsruhe 2009, 282, cat. 207. For other North African parallels, see H. Maguire in Stevens et al. 2005, 321–4. The motif is inspired by verse 1 of *Psalm* 42 : 'As the deer longs for the running brooks, so longs my soul for you, O God'.
87. Davis 1861, 346 (430).
88. Davis' 'Statement' of December 21st, 1858: FO 102/62, 250.
89. Franks 1860, 226.
90. Davis 1861, 229 (fig. facing 289).
91. [Falbe and Temple] 1838, cited by Davis 1861, 228 (285), note.
92. Falbe 1833, 10.
93. Lézine 1961, plan facing 40; Hallier 1995, fig. 2.
94. Davis 1861, 237 (296).
95. Mendleson 2003, 30 and pls on 85 (Pu73 and Pu74). The latter is Davis' Punic price list, reproduced in Davis' original drawing here as Fig. 9.4.
96. Anon. 1883, 154.
97. Berger 1910, 57; Toutain 1915.
98. Davis 1861, 232 (288).
99. Davis 1861, 228–32 (285–9).
100. Ennabli 1997, 102.
101. Davis 1861, 233 (289).
102. Beulé 1861, 44.
103. Ennabli 1997, 101.
104. Hinks 1933, 117–18, no. 40 with fig. 132.
105. Beauregard, Guimond and Senay 1976, 54–5, trench 1CC3b, Plan VIII, at back of volume.
106. Beauregard, Guimond and Senay 1976, 54; Beauregard and Senay 1978, 'mosaïque isotrope', Plan I in back pocket.
107. Senay 2000, plan, 119, fig. 1 (here Fig. 10.20); cf. also Bullo and Ghedini 2003, 122.
108. Chabot 2000; for mosaic 7F11, 136, figs 24 and 25; Senay 2000, 135, fig. 21 for the fallen column, and Plan II.
109. Balmelle et al. 1985, 260, pl. 169c; Ben Abed-Ben Khader et al. 1999, 142–3, no. 163, pl. LXIV; Bullo and Ghedini 2003, 136.
110. Davis 1861, 335 (417).
111. Davis 1861, 335–6 (417–18).
112. Senay 2000, Plan II, and fig. 1, 119 (= Fig. 10.20 here).
113. Davis 1861, 360–1 (449–51); Ling 1967, 14.
114. Davis 1861, 355 (443).
115. Beulé 1861, 20.
116. Wilson 1998, 66, fig. 1.
117. Davis 1861, 55 (59).
118. Delattre 1893, 95, pl. xi. The plan of Delattre's excavation is reproduced without explanation in the 1985 reprint of Davis' *Carthage and Her Remains*, between 388 and 389.
119. Deneauve and Gros 1980, with Robine's plan, 326, fig. 111.
120. Deneauve 1990, 151–2, with figs 9–10.

121. Franks 1860, 234; Beulé 1861, pl. II, figs 3–4.
122. Davis 1861, 355, 360–1 (442–3, 450–1).
123. Beulé 1861, 46.
124. Davis 1861, 334 (416–17).
125. Falbe 1833, 10.
126. Davis 1861, 333–4 (413–16).
127. *CIL* VIII.1044.
128. Davis 1861, 334 (416).
129. Cagnat and Schmidt 1891.
130. Norman 1994.

Notes to Chapter Eleven

1. Davis 1861, 53 (48); Jenkins 1992, 176 and n. 63, quoting a letter from Davis to Clarendon, dated August 4th, 1856. Jenkins found this letter, which I have not seen, among the papers of the Trustees, BM Archive.
2. Letter of Wood to Hammond, February 5th, 1858: FO 102/62, 186–7.
3. Letter probably of Hammond to Panizzi, February 8, 1858: FO 102/62, 188.
4. Letter of Davis to Malmesbury, April 10th, 1858: FO 102/62, 198.
5. Meetings of the Trustees, July 11th, 1857: BM Archives, C9239; January 22nd, 1858: C9322–3; June 12th, 1858: C9410; and December 11th, 1858: C9490.
6. Letter of Panizzi to Hammond, January 12th, 1858: FO 102/62, 179.
7. Letter of Panizzi to Hammond, January 15th, 1859: FO 102/62, 258.
8. Cooper 1872, 650, s.v. 'Malmesbury (Earl of), The Right Hon. James Howard Harris, G. C. B. (1807–1889)'.
9. Two letters of Davis to Panizzi, dated January 15th and February 12th, 1859, were presented to meetings of the Museum Trustees on February 12th and 26th, 1859: BM Archives, C9521 and C9533.
10. Gunning 2009, 174–5. Letter of Davis to Russell, July 30th, 1859: FO 102/62, 292.
11. Davis 1861, 372–3 (465).
12. Falbe 1833, 44.
13. Davis 1861, 373 (467).
14. Davis 1861, 374 (469), citing Justin, *Lib.*, 31.1.2 (Justin, *Epit. Trogi*, 31.2.3–5).
15. Audollent 1901, 160, n. 1.
16. Salies 1974, 41–3 and 138, no. K396.
17. Journal of Sophia Cracroft, Saturday, May 15th, 1858: SPRI MS 248/232/2; BJ.
18. Davis' 'Statement' of December 21st, 1858: FO 102/62.
19. Franks 1860, 226; his source is Davis' 'Statement'.
20. Davis' 'Statement' of December 21st, 1858: FO 102/62, 252.
21. Franks 1860, 227.
22. Dunbabin 1978, 252, Carthage 30b.
23. Davis 1861, 375 (470–1).
24. Falbe 1833, 43–4.
25. Letter of Davis to Clarendon, January 23rd, 1858: FO 102/62, 184.
26. Letter of Wood to Hammond, February 5th, 1858: FO 102/62, 186–7.
27. Davis 1861, 386 (486).
28. Davis 1861, 375–7 (470–4).
29. Davis 1861, 390 (489).
30. Delattre 1889, 14–15, citing Sainte-Marie 1884, 33.
31. Delattre 1894–1895.
32. Letter of Davis to Malmesbury, April 10th, 1858: FO 102/62, 198.
33. Davis 1861, 390 (488–9).
34. Franks 1860, 222.
35. Beulé 1861, 141.
36. Gauckler 1910, 213, no. 635.
37. Ennabli 2000, 44, plan 4; 68, fig. 105; and 69, fig. 108.
38. Dunbabin 1985, 14 and 28, fig. 4. The motif of the fountain with four individual water-sources is closely paralleled at Bir Ftouah in mosaic details found in 1897, now in the Louvre and the Bardo, and in the 1990s: H. Maguire in Stevens et al. 2005, 304, figs 6.1–2, and 320, fig. 6.15. For the Bardo example, Ben Abed-Ben Khader 2003, fig. 385. Cf. also note 86 of Ch. 10.
39. Davis' 'Statement' of December 21st, 1858: FO 102/62, 255.
40. Davis 1861, 399–41 (499–519): 'Excavation at Utica'.
41. Davis 1861, 352 (437–8); letter of the Foreign Office to the Admiralty, October 28th, 1857: FO 102/62, 159.
42. Davis 1861, 351 (437).
43. Shaw 1757, cited in Wilmanns and Mommsen 1881, xxv.
44. Temple 1835, vol. 2, 26.
45. Wilmanns and Mommsen 1881: *CIL* VIII, vol. I, pt. 2, pl. II, 'Provincia Africa.'
46. Letter from Admiralty to Clarendon, November 21st, 1857: FO 102/62, 166–7.
47. Davis 1861, 352 (438).
48. Letter of Sophia Cracroft, May 26th, 1858, quoted in Rawnsley 1923, 126.
49. Davis 1861, 399–404 (499).
50. Letter of Davis to Malmesbury, May 14th, 1858: FO 102/62, 202–3.
51. Journal of Sophia Cracroft, Wednesday, May 19th, 1858, with pencil note, Thursday, May 20th, 1858: SPRI MS 248/232/2; BJ.
52. Davis 1861, 390 (489).
53. For Porcher and his watercolours, Smith 2000.
54. Smith and Porcher 1864; also Thorn 2007.
55. Smith 2000.
56. Davis 1861, 404 (506).
57. Davis 1861, 412 (514–5).
58. Davis 1861, 409–10 (511).
59. Porcher's plan, dated June 1858, is in the Map Room of the British National Archives: FO 102/62 MFQ 616 pt. 2 (5).
60. Davis 1861, 402 (503); Wilmanns and Mommsen, 1881: *CIL* VIII, vol. 1, pt. 2, pl. II.
61. Falbe 1833, 14.
62. Falbe 1833, 1.
63. Daux 1869, 113–274 and pl. IX. For plans of Utica ascribed to Daux: Hérisson, 1881, map at end of volume. Alexander et al. 1976, Plan 1 and 1B, at the end of the volume, is Hérisson's map.

64. Tissot 1884–1888, vol. 2, plates II and VI. Hérisson acquired Daux's papers and shared them with Tissot: Tissot 1884, vol. 1, 577, note.
65. Lézine 1968, 82, fig. 1.
66. Kolendo 1998, 249–64.
67. Davis 1861, fig. facing 415 (516).
68. Hérisson 1881, 278.
69. Davis 1861, 407 (508).
70. Davis 1861, 404 (506–7).
71. Daux 1869, Pl. V, figs 1–3 and pl. VI, figs 1–2.
72. Lézine 1968, 82, fig. 1.
73. Davis 1861, 409 (510).
74. Davis 1861, 410 (512).
75. Davis' 'Statement' of December 21st, 1858: FO 102/62, 254.
76. Davis 1861, 410 (511–12).
77. Hérisson 1881, 278.
78. Berger et al. 1881, cited by Ashbee 1889, 84; Baratte 1971.
79. These two heads are displayed in the British Museum, Roman Empire Gallery (Room 70).
80. Davis 1861, 415 (516).
81. Lézine 1968, 87, fig. 4.
82. Davis 1861, 419 (518–19).
83. Davis 1861, facing 416 (518).
84. Lézine 1968, fold-out plan fig. 2, facing 82.
85. Rebuffat 1974, 446.
86. Rebuffat 1969; 1974.
87. Gauckler 1910, 210–12, nos 626–30.
88. Hinks 1933, 67–8, no. 6 with fig. 78 and 119–20, nos 44–5 with figs 135–7.
89. Hinks 1933, 67.
90. Alexander et al. 1976, 32.
91. Edwards 1870, 668.
92. Alexander et al. 1976, 29–33, nos 278A–B and 279, with a proposed location for the site on Plan 2C.
93. Davis 1861, 407 (508).
94. Davis 1861, 415 (516).
95. Alexander et al. 1976, viii.
96. Alexander et al. 1976, 29–33, nos 278–9.
97. Gauckler 1910, 274, no. 820.
98. Salies 1974, 42.
99. Rossiter 1998, 113–15.
100. Alexander et al. 1976, 33–4, no. 280.
101. Alexander et al. 1976, 34, no. 281: BM 1859.4-2.109.
102. Davis' 'Statement' of December 21st, 1858: FO 102/62, 253; letter of Davis to the Foreign Office, June 26th, 1858: FO 102/62, 207.

Notes to Chapter Twelve

1. Letter of Davis to Malmesbury, October 9th, 1858: FO 102/62, 210.
2. Davis 1861, 420 (520); Newton 1865, vol. 2, 67–8, 147.
3. Letter of Davis to Foreign Office, November 6th, 1858: FO 102/62, 212–13.
4. Letter from Admiralty to Hammond, November 30th, 1858: FO 102/62, 238; Jenkins 1992, 253 and 187, note 151.
5. Letters from Admiralty and commander of the *Supply* to the Foreign Office, both dated December 1st, 1858: BM Archives C9490.
6. Davis 1861, 420 (520).
7. Letter of Davis to Malmesbury, November 6th, 1858: FO 102/62, 212.
8. Letter of Davis to Malmesbury, January 1st, 1859: FO 102/62, 244–5.
9. Daux 1868, 261.
10. Debergh 2000, especially 472 and nn. 69–70 for Borgia; also Debergh 2002, 469–71 with notes; also Beulé 1861, 98.
11. Davis' 'Statement' of December 21st, 1858: FO 102/62, 254–5.
12. Delattre 1883–84, 'La Marsa', 293–8.
13. Davis 1861, 428 (532).
14. Prince Alfred, Duke of Edinburgh and Saxe-Coburg and Gotha (1844–1900); Van der Kiste and Jordaan 1984, especially 17–18 and 31–4.
15. Anon. 1859b, 98.
16. Davis 1861, 428–32 (532–6).
17. Copy of letter of Davis to Panizzi, January 15th, 1859, with report of the meeting of the Trustees, February 12th, 1859: BM Archives C9520–21.
18. Letter from Panizzi to Hammond, January 19th, 1859: FO 102/62, 258.
19. Letter from the Foreign Office to Wood, January 22nd, 1859: FO 102/62, 259; letter of Wood to Malmesbury, February 1st, 1859: FO 102/62, 281–2.
20. Letter of Davis to Wood, February 7th, 1859: FO 102/62, 283.
21. Letter of Malmesbury to Davis, February 28th, 1859: FO 102/62, 285.
22. Letter of Panizzi to Hammond, January 12th, 1858: FO 102/62, 179.
23. Letter of Wood to Hammond, February 5th, 1858: FO 102/62, 186.
24. Letter of Panizzi to Hammond, January 19th, 1859: FO 102/62, 258.
25. Anon. 1859a, 83 and fig. on 85.
26. Newton 1865, vol. 2, 256, letter dated March 15th, 1859.
27. Newton, 1865, vol. 2, 257, letter dated May 25th, 1859; also 264, letter dated June 18th, 1859.
28. Franks 1860, 206–7.
29. Copy of letter of Davis to Panizzi, February 12th, 1859, read to the meeting of the Trustees, February 26th, 1859: BM Archives C9533.
30. Hinks 1933, 120–1, no. 46 with pl. xxxi.
31. Davis 1861, 431 and 433 (534 and 538).
32. Davis 1861, 431 (532).
33. Salomonson 1965, 16, fig. 2.
34. Cf. Hanoune 1969, 220, fig. 1.
35. Lund 1986, 21, citing a letter of Falbe to the Danish Crown Prince, dated May 19th, 1838.
36. Dunbabin 1978, 42 (with n. 26), 147 and 183; also 257, Dougga 8a with pls 15–16.
37. Dunbabin 1978, 254, Carthage 48.
38. Davis 1861, 428 (531); Gunning 2009, 186–7.
39. Davis 1861, 431 (536).

40. Davis 1861, 434 (542).
41. Copy of letter of Davis to Panizzi, February 12th, 1859, read to the meeting of the Trustees, February 26th, 1859: BM Archives, C9533.
42. Davis 1861, 432 (541). For this portion of the mosaic in colour, see Badisches Landesmuseum Karlsruhe 2009, 237, Kat. 156.
43. Hinks 1933, 148.
44. Letter of Malmesbury to Davis, February 28th, 1859: FO 102/62, 285.
45. Beulé 1861; 1873.
46. Copy of letter of Davis to Panizzi, February 12th, 1859, reported by Panizzi in the meeting of the Trustees of February 26th, 1859; BM Archives C9533.
47. *DNB* 1897, s.v. 'Lord John Russell, first Earl Russell (1792–1878)'.
48. Letter of Davis to Russell, July 30th, 1859: FO 102/62, 292; with some notes of Hammond to Russell written on the back.
49. Letter from Foreign Office to Davis, September 12th, 1859, with a copy to acting British consul Werry at Tunis: FO 102/62, 297–8.
50. Letter from Foreign Office to Wood, June 11th, 1860: FO 102/62, 301–2.
51. Letters of Hammond to Wood, May 31st, 1860 and June 11th, 1860: FO 102/62, 300–1.
52. Audollent (1901, 13, n. 1) gave the date as October 22nd, 1859.
53. Davis 1861, 435 (541).

Notes to Chapter Thirteen

1. Beulé 1873, 27–8.
2. Beulé 1873, 6.
3. Beulé 1872 (reprint), 34–5 and 42.
4. Beulé 1861, 20 and 35.
5. Beulé 1873, 1–4.
6. Anon. 1859c, 251.
7. Beulé 1861, 27–9.
8. Davis 1861, 355 (443).
9. Beulé 1859, 33–4.
10. Beulé 1861, 35.
11. Davis 1861, 164 (196) and note; Beulé 1859, 34, n. 1.
12. Beulé 1873, 41.
13. *CIL* VIII.1011, 1041, 1044, 1045, 1069, 1073, 1083, 1104, 1105; also 1052 and 1145.
14. Beulé 1861, 28.
15. Davis 1861, 298 (377).
16. Beulé 1861, 35.
17. Davis 1861, 117 (130).
18. Davis 1861, 299 (377).
19. Reinach 1888 (reprint), 88.
20. Gran-Aymerich 1998, 201.
21. Flaux 1865, 278.
22. Davis 1861, 295 (372); cf. *CRAI* 1860, 14, report of session of February 3rd.
23. Davis 1861, 164 (196–7).
24. Prévost 1954, in Prévost and d'Amat 1948, s.v. '2. Beulé (Charles-Ernest)'.
25. Anon. 1859c, 251.
26. Beulé 1873, 4–5 and 48.
27. Beulé 1861, 57.
28. Lavigerie 1881 (reprint), 10.
29. Davis 1861, 160 (196).
30. Beulé 1873, 32–43.
31. Beulé 1873, 44–58.
32. Beulé 1861, 78.
33. Beulé 1861, 21 and 35.
34. Beulé 1873, 44.
35. Beulé 1861, 11.
36. Beulé 1861, 83.
37. Beulé 1861, 35.
38. Beulé 1861, 33 and 90.
39. Beulé 1861, 11, citing Orosius 4.23.
40. Beulé 1861, 25.
41. Beulé 1861, 78.
42. Beulé 1861, 43–4.
43. Beulé 1861, 26, 38, and pl. III at bottom.
44. Beulé 1873, 3 and 5.
45. Beulé 1861, 87.
46. Beulé 1861, 5.
47. Beulé 1861, 26 and 33.
48. Davis 1861, 295 (371).
49. Davis 1861, 300–01 (380).
50. Beulé 1861, 36 and pl. I.
51. Beulé 1861, 9.
52. Beulé 1861, 24.
53. Beulé 1861, 18.
54. Beulé 1861, 67.
55. Falbe 1833, 10.
56. Beulé 1861, 36, citing Falbe, 1833, 29.
57. Beulé 1861, 25, 36 and pl. I.
58. Beulé 1861, 37 and pl. I.
59. Beulé 1861, 41–2 and pl. III, upper right.
60. Beulé 1861, 76 and pl. II, fig. 6.
61. Davis 1861, 297 (375).
62. Beulé 1861, 39–42.
63. Beulé 1861, 46.
64. Beulé 1861, 39.
65. Freed 1996, 151 with n. 60.
66. Beulé 1861, 50.
67. Beulé 1861, 50–58.
68. Beulé 1861, 57.
69. Beulé 1861, 10 and pl. II, fig. 2.
70. Beulé 1861, 60–64.
71. Beulé 1861, 66–74.
72. Beulé 1861, 12, 29, 66, 70 and 75.
73. Saumagne 1924.
74. Lancel 1981, 184, fig. 14.
75. Gros et al. 1985.
76. Davis 1861, 116–17 (130).
77. Davis 1861, 435 (542–3).
78. Hinks 1933, 76, no. 17a–b, with figs 83–4.
79. Davis 1861, 434–6 (543) and 448, note * in the version of Davis' text with the longer pagination; there is no note on the corresponding page (359) of the edition published earlier the same year.
80. Wilson 1998, 66, fig. 1; Saumagne 1928–1929, 629–47;

Casagrande 2008, 76 (who describes it as 'una struttura estremamente bizzarra').
81. Beulé 1861, 72.
82. Beulé 1861, 87–9.
83. Beulé 1861, 97.
84. Beulé 1873, 32–43; Beulé 1861, 121–43.
85. Davis 1861, 390/489; Delattre 1889, 115.
86. Beulé 1861, 124; Delattre 1895 (reprint), 46–7. See now Stern 2011.
87. Davis 1861, 376–7 (471–4, 481).
88. Beulé 1873, 43.
89. Davis 1861, 386–9 (487–8).
90. Beulé 1861, 126; Vogüé 1860 (reprint 1973), 125 and pl. VI.1.C.
91. Beulé 1861, 140.
92. Beulé 1861, pl. IV.
93. Beulé 1861, 5, citing Servius *in Aen.* I.427, and 92–3.
94. Beulé 1861, 101.
95. Beulé 1873, 48.
96. Beulé 1873, 54.
97. Beulé 1861, 96–8.
98. Beulé 1861, 108; Hurst et al. 1994, 10–12.
99. Beulé 1861, 103 and 105, pl. V, figs 1–5.
100. Beulé 1861, 109 and pl. V, figs 8–9; Beulé 1873, 58.
101. Hurst et al. 1994, 291–2 and fig. 16.1.
102. Beulé 1873, 48–9.
103. Beulé 1873, 57 and pl. IV.
104. Hurst et al. 1994, 11, fig. 1.6 (Beulé's plan); 37, fig. 3.3 (Gibson's plan); dating on 48.
105. Hurst and Stager 1978, 341.
106. Stager 1992, 75–78 with fig. (77); Hurst et al. 1994, 42.
107. Hurst 1993, 15–16, fig. 2 and pl. 5; 1994, 55 (corrected plan).
108. Beulé 1861, 113.
109. Hurst et al. 1994, 48–51.
110. Beulé 1861, 15.
111. Davis 1861, 503 (630).
112. Letter of Wood to Hammond, July 15th, 1860: FO 102/62, 304.
113. Panizzi, report to the meeting of the Trustees, October 13th, 1860: BM Archives C9824.
114. GR (now MLA) 1860.10-2.129–134, plus 136a and b; GR 1960.10-2.135.
115. Letter of Wood to the Foreign Office, August 21st, 1860, with a receipt from Davis dated May 14th, 1860: BM Department of Greek and Roman Antiquities.
116. Letter of Davis to the Foreign Office, August 30th, 1860: FO 102/62, 306.
117. Davis 1862, 9–10.
118. Davis 1862, 26–7.
119. Davis 1862, Appendix II.
120. Flaux 1862, 278; Davis 1861, 158 (188), note.
121. *DNB* 1888, s.v. 'Davis, Nathan (1812–1882)'. For Margaret Piccioli, see Chapter 2, note 119.

Notes to Chapter 14

1. Wilson 1984, 41.
2. Franks 1860, 233–6.
3. Reinach 1888, 87.
4. Strzygowski 1888, 69–70.
5. Dupuy 1954, 23.
6. Anon. 1858c.
7. Flaux 1865, 261–83.
8. Vernaz 1887, 27.
9. Reinach and Babelon 1886, 34.
10. Sainte-Marie 1878a, 123, no. 46.
11. Holwerda 1936.
12. Hayes 1972.
13. Jenkins 1969.
14. Falbe, Lindberg and Müller 1843–60.
15. Mendleson 2003.
16. Lancel 1992, 26, fig. 25.
17. Benichou-Safar 1982, pl. 3.
18. Delattre 1885, 241–6 and pls XXIV–VI.
19. Davis 1861, 163 (196).
20. Beulé 1861, 35.
21. Davis 1861, 35 and note (25 and note on 26); also 54–5 and note (49–50 and note).
22. Davis 1861, 356–9 (444–8); Vaux 1863a. A copy now in Special Collections at the library of the University of Alberta once belonged to Franks.
23. Freed 2001.
24. Hurst and Stager 1978, 341.
25. Gunning 2009, 137–88.
26. Diehl 1892, 21.

Notes to Appendix One

1. Bairem-Ben Osman 1981, vol. 4, xiii.
2. Gauckler 1910, 223–5, no. 666.
3. Franks 1860, 228–30.
4. [Newton] 1876.
5. Cf. Picard 1965; Salomonson 1965.
6. Hinks 1933.
7. Dunbabin 1978.
8. Parrish 1984, 113–16, no. 10 with pls 17–18.
9. Blanchard-Lemée et al. 1996; Fantar et al. 1994, Yacoub 1995; Ben Abed-Ben Khader 2003; Ben Abed 2006.
10. Hinks 1933, Appendix I, 3.
11. Lancha 1997, 379.

Notes to Appendix Two

1. Gauckler 1910 and 1913.
2. Franks 1860.
3. [Newton] 1876, 66–87.
4. Morgan 1866.
5. Audollent 1901, 659–66.
6. Hinks 1933, 65–149 with pls xxvi–xxxii.

Notes to Appendix Three

1. Davis 1861, 355 (443).
2. Davis 1861, 175 (212).
3. Davis 1861, 185 (225).
4. Davis 1861, 375 (469).
5. Davis' 'Statement' to Malmesbury, December 21st,

1858: FO 102/62, 252.
6. Ditson, quoted in Davis 1861, 168 (202–03).
7. Davis 1861, 312 (392).
8. Ben Abed-Ben Khader et al. 1999, 20, no. 36.
9. Audollent 1901, 663–4; Gauckler 1896, 618.
10. Ben Abed-Ben Khader et al. 1999, xxi.
11. Williams 1984, 81.
12. Picard 1965, 22.
13. Beauregard, Guimond and Senay 1976, 82.
14. Hurst 1999, 18.
15. Hansen 2002, 117.
16. Hurst and Roskams 1984, 15.
17. Gros 1985, 113, citing Ammianus Marcellinus, *Histories* 26.10.15.
18. Ennabli 1997, 101.
19. Hallier 1995, 213, n. 37.
20. Blakesley 1859, 357–8.
21. Freed and Ros 1990, 19–22.
22. Norman 1994, 13.
23. My own observations, based on the analysis of the pottery from this unpublished context and observations of the site.
24. Salomonson 1965, 16, fig. 2.
25. Picard 1965, 57.

Bibliography

Abbreviations

BA/BCTH	*Bulletin archéologique du Comité des Travaux Historiques*
BAA	*Bulletin trimestriel des antiquités africaines* (1882–1885)
BEG	*Bulletin épigraphique de la Gaule* (1881–1886)
BM Archives	Central Archives of the British Museum
BSAF	*Bulletin de la Société Nationale des Antiquaires de France*
BSAS	*Bulletin de la Société Archéologique de Sousse*
CEDAC Carthage	*Centre d'Études et de Documentation Archéologique de la Conservation de Carthage*
CEA	*Cahiers des études anciennes* (Trois Rivières, Québec)
CIL	*Corpus inscriptionum latinarum*
CIS	*Corpus inscriptionum semiticarum*
CMT	*Corpus des Mosaïques de Tunisie*
CNRS	Centre Nationale de la Recherche Scientifique, Paris
CRAI	*Comptes rendus des séances de l'Académie des Inscriptions et Belles-Lettres*
DBF	*Dictionnaire de biographie française*
DNB	*Dictionary of National Biography*
EMC/CV	*Échos du monde classique/Classical Views*
FO	The British National Archives at Kew, formerly the Public Record Office, Foreign Office File
GR	British Museum Department of Greek and Roman Antiquities
ILN	*The Illustrated London News*
INAA	Institut National d'Archéologie et d'Art (Tunis)
JRA	*Journal of Roman Archaeology*
MDAI(R)	*Mitteilungen des deutschen archäologischen Instituts, Rome*
MEFRA	*Mélanges de l'École française de Rome. Antiquité.*
MLA	British Museum, Department of Medieval and Later Antiquities, now the Department of Medieval and Modern Europe
RGS	Royal Geographical Society
RSAC	*Recueil des notices et mémoires de la Société Archéologique du Département de Constantine* (Algeria)
SPRI	Scott Polar Research Institute, Cambridge, England
WA	British Museum, Department of Western Antiquities

Bibliography

This bibliography is divided into five sections:

I Archival documents
II Published maps
III Reference works
IV References to published sources cited in the notes and appendices
V Websites

I Archival documents

(a) Foreign Office files in the British National Archives (formerly the Public Record Office)

1. FO 102/62: Excavations on the site of ancient Carthage, 1856–1860

In this file letters from a variety of correspondents have been organized chronologically, bound and paginated 1–316. The items date from July 19th, 1856 to December 8th, 1860. This is the fundamental primary source for Davis' excavations. 52 letters from this file are cited above. Copies of ten of these letters and two enclosures exist in the Department of Greek and Roman Antiquities in the British Museum, which also has a total of four letters that do not appear in the Foreign Office file (see below).

FO 102/62, 1–4: Letter of Nathan Davis, July 19th, 1856, 14 Brunswick Square, London, to Clarendon at the Foreign Office

FO 102/62, 5: Letter of Clarendon at the Foreign Office to Panizzi, July 21st, 1856

FO 102/62, 6–8: Letter of Panizzi at the British Museum to Clarendon at the Foreign Office, July 28th, 1856

FO 102/62, 9–10: Note from Hammond attached to a letter of Lewis Ferriere; letter of Ferriere, in London, to Clarendon, August 4th, 1856

FO 102/62, 11: Letter of Clarendon to Lewis Ferriere, August 7th, 1856

FO 102/62, 14, Letter of Davis, 14 Brunswick Square, London, to Clarendon, August 19th, 1856

FO 102/62, 17: Letter of Clarendon, probably written by Hammond, to Davis, September 6th, 1856

FO 102/62, 21–2: Letter of Davis at Tunis to Clarendon. October 21st, 1856, BM letter I

FO 102/62, 27–8: Letter of Davis at Tunis to Clarendon, December 2nd, 1856, BM letter II

FO 102/62, 29: Letter of Wood to Clarendon, December 20th, 1856

FO 102/62, 39–40: Letter of Davis at Tunis to Clarendon at the Foreign Office, January 13th, 1857, BM letter III

FO 102/62, 41–2: Letter of Panizzi to Hammond at the Foreign Office, January 21st, 1857

FO 102/62, 43: Letter of Hammond to Davis in Tunis, January 22nd, 1857

FO 102/62, 47: Davis' first report of expenses, January 26th, 1857
FO 102/62, 49: Receipt for one year's rent from Anna Stellina, December 1st (?), 1856
FO 102/62, 54: Unsigned letter from the Foreign Office to the Admiralty, February 6th, 1857
FO 102/62, 66–8: Letter from the Foreign Office to Davis, February 23rd, 1857, approving his expenses, with a list of his expenses from January 14th to February 14th and names of fifteen to twenty workmen in January and fourteen workmen in February
FO 102/62, 81–9: 'Carthaginian Excavation Expenditures, Monthly abstract of account from 14th Jan. to 14th Feb. 1857', enclosed with a letter of Richard Wood at Tunis to the Foreign Office, March 24th, 1857
FO 102/62, 98–101: Letter of Davis at Carthage to Clarendon, May 28th, 1857, BM letter V
FO 102/62, 102: Itemized receipt from Lieutenant George Durbin at Tunis for twenty-six cases of antiquities, May 25th, 1857, BM enclosure VI with BM letter V
FO 102/62, 120: Letter of Davis to Clarendon, June 29th, 1857, BM letter VII
FO 102/62, 123–6: Letter of Davis to Clarendon, July 14th, 1857, BM letter VIII
FO 102/62, 127–8: Receipt of Captain Arthur Forbes, July 10th, 1857
FO 102/62, 131: Letter of Panizzi to Clarendon, July 22nd, 1857
FO 102/62, 159–60: Letter of Hammond to the Admiralty, October 28th, 1857
FO 102/62, 166–7: Letter of Admiralty to Clarendon, November 21st, 1857
FO 102/62, 179: Letter of Panizzi to Hammond, January 12th, 1858
FO 102/62, 184: Letter of Davis to Clarendon, January 23rd, 1858, BM letter X
FO 102/62, 186–7: Letter of Wood to Hammond, February 5th, 1858
FO 102/62, 188: Letter from the Foreign Office (probably from Hammond) to Panizzi, February 8th, 1858
FO 102/62, 194–7: Letter of Malmesbury to Wood, March 10th, 1858, as a directive to Wood in regard to his letter of November 28th, 1857, which informed the Foreign Office of the action against Davis [not in file]
FO 102/62, 198–200: Letter of Davis to Malmesbury, April 10th, 1858
FO 102/62, 202–3: Letter of Davis to Malmesbury, May 14th, 1858
FO 102/62, 207: Letter of Davis to Foreign Office, June 26th, 1858
FO 102/62, 210: Letter of Davis to Malmesbury, October 9th, 1858
FO 102/62, 212–13: Letter of Davis to the Foreign Office, November 6th, 1858
FO 102/62, 238: Letter of Admiralty to Hammond, November 30th, 1858
FO 102/62, 244: Letter of Davis at Carthage to Malmesbury, January 15th, 1859, BM letter XI
FO 102/62, 245–55: Davis' 'Statement', December 21st, 1858, enclosed with letter of January 15th, 1859, BM enclosure XII with BM letter XI
FO 102/62, 257: Floor plan of 'Carthaginian house', enclosed with 'Statement' of December 21st, 1858 [no copy in BM file]
FO 102/62, 258: Letter of Panizzi to Hammond, January 19th, 1859
FO 102/62, 259: Letter from the Foreign Office to Wood, January 22nd, 1859
FO 102/62, 283: Letter of Davis to Wood, February 7th, 1859
FO 102/62, 281–2: Letter of Wood to Malmesbury, February 12th, 1859
FO 102/62, 285: Letter of Malmesbury to Davis, February 28th, 1859
FO 102/62, 292–4: Unsigned note, written September 1st, 1859, probably from Hammond to Russell, on the back of a letter of Davis to Lord John Russell, dated July 30th, 1859
FO 102/62, 297–8: Letter from Foreign Office to Davis, with a copy to acting British consul Werry, September 12th, 1859
FO 102/62, 304: Letter of Davis at Tunis, May 14, 1860, enclosed in a letter of Wood at Tunis to the Foreign Office, June 15th, 1860
FO 102/62, 300: Letter of Hammond to Wood, May 31st, 1860
FO 102/62, 301–2: Letter of Hammond to Wood, June 11th, 1860
FO 102/62, 304: Letter of Wood to Hammond, July 15th, 1860
FO 102/62, 306: Letter of Davis, Bridge House, Twickenham, to the Foreign Office, dated August 30th, 1860

2. FO 335/108/1–7: Miscellaneous correspondence of Consul Richard Wood, 1857

These are unsorted bundles, from which the following letters have been cited:

FO 335/108/1: Letter of Clarendon to Wood, September 24th, 1857
FO 335/108/3: Receipts for Davis's expenses in 1857, dated from January 26th to December 11th, 1857
FO 335/108/3: Letter of Wood to Clarendon, March 3rd, 1857
FO 335/108/3: Letter of Wood to Clarendon, March 10th, 1857
FO 335/108/3: Draft of letter of Wood to Clarendon, June 15th, 1857
FO 335/108/5: Draft of letter of Wood to the Bey of Tunis, July 24th, 1857
FO 335/108/5: Draft of letter of Wood to the Admiralty, September 3rd, 1857
FO 335/108/7: Draft of letter of Wood to Davis, March 18th, 1857
FO 335/108/7: Letter of Davis to Wood, March 22nd, 1857

In addition, I have used:

FO 335/110/4: Letter of Davis, January 23rd, 1858
FO 335/110/10: 1856–1860: Unsorted bundle of letters and receipts from Davis [most not seen by me]

(b) Map room of the British National Archives

'Plan of the Peninsula of Carthage exhibiting the present excavations' (May 25, 1857), FO 102/62 (1) = MFQ 616 part 1 (1)

'Floor plan of large mosaic excavated at Carthage' (June 29, 1857), FO 102/62 (2) = MFQ 616 part 1 (2)

Untitled, two large detailed colour drawings of mosaic (Mosaic of the Months and Seasons) excavated at Carthage, FO 102/62 (3) (4) = MFQ 616 (3) (4)

'Plan of Utica', June 1858, by Lieut. E. A. Porcher, R. N., lat. 37 degrees 4' N. long. 10 degreees 0' E. (June 26th, 1858). FO 102/62 (5) = MFQ 616 pt. 2 (5)

'Plan of Carthage', originally enclosed with Davis' 'Statement' of December 21st, 1858, FO 102/62 (6) = MFQ 616 pt. 2 (6)

(c) British Museum, Department of Greek and Roman Antiquities

1. Papers relating to Mr Davis' excavations at Carthage
This bound volume contains copies of 10 letters and 2 enclosures from Davis to the Foreign Office that were numbered at the museum. Davis' letters of March 25th, 1857 and October 8th, 1857 (letters IV and IX) exist only in this collection, as they were never returned to the Foreign Office. I did not find the additional letters of May 14th and August 21st, 1860 in the Foreign Office file.

BM letter I: Letter of Davis, October 21st, 1856, Tunis, to Clarendon: FO 102/62, 21

BM letter II: Letter of Davis at Tunis to Clarendon, December 2nd, 1856: FO 102/62, 27

BM letter III: Letter of Davis to the Foreign Office, January 13th, 1857: FO 102/62, 39–40

BM letter IV: Letter of Davis to Clarendon, March 25th, 1857 [no copy in Foreign Office file]

BM letter V: Letter of Davis to Clarendon, May 28th, 1857: FO 102/62

BM enclosure VI with BM letter V: Letter of Davis to Clarendon, Carthage, May 28th, 1857: FO 102/62, 102

BM letter VII: Letter of Davis to Clarendon, June 29th, 1857: FO 102/62, 120

BM letter VIII: Letter of Davis to Clarendon, July 14th, 1857: FO 102/62, 126

BM letter IX: Letter of Davis to Clarendon, October 8th, 1857, forwarded to Panizzi by the Foreign Office [no copy in Foreign Office file]

BM letter X: Letter of Davis to Clarendon, January 23rd, 1858: FO 102/62, 184

BM letter XI: Letter of Davis to Malmesbury, Carthage, January 15th, 1859: FO 102/62, 244

BM enclosure XII with BM letter XI: Davis' 'Statement', December 21st, 1858: FO 102/62, 250

Letter of Wood to the Foreign Office, Tunis, August 21st, 1860, with a receipt from Davis for items left at 'Dowar el Shatt', dated May 14th, 1860; these two items survive with copies of Davis' letters in the Department of Greek and Roman Antiquities, but are missing from the Foreign Office file

2. Greek and Roman Department Register of Antiquities
This is the accession list kept year by year in the Department of Greek and Roman Antiquities; I have seen 1856 to 1861 inclusive.

3. 1876 Synopsis by C. T. Newton
This is a bound volume entitled *Interleaved Synopsis of the Contents of the British Museum*, in the library of the Department of Greek and Roman Antiquities (contains notes on the mosaic finds, their whereabouts and their publication)

4. Unpublished catalogue of amphorae
Written by Joann Freed and Paul Roberts, 1997–2000, deposited in the Department of Greek and Roman Antiquities, British Museum

(d) British Museum, Central Archives

Documents of Meetings of the Trustees, entries relevant to Davis' excavations at Carthage (C = Standing Committee: Minutes of Meetings), vols 27–29, July 1855–July 1862. I have cited four letters found among the Minutes of Meetings:

BM Archives, C9490: Letters from the Admiralty and the commander of the *Supply* to the Foreign Office, both dated December 1st, 1858

BM Archives, C9520–21: Copy of letter of Davis to Panizzi, January 15th, 1859, with report of the meeting of the Trustees, February 12th, 1859

BM Archives, C9533: Copy of letter of Davis to Panizzi, February 12th, 1859, read to the meeting of the Trustees, February 26th, 1859

(e) Manuscripts in the Scott Polar Research Institute, Cambridge

The Scott Polar Research Institute holds many papers of Jane, Lady Franklin (1791–1875) and of her niece, Sophia Cracroft (1816–1892), which are catalogued in Clive Holland (ed.), *Manuscripts in the Scott Polar Research Institute: A Catalogue*, Garland: New York 1982. Items prefixed MS 248 formed part of the Lefroy Bequest of 1941 (Holland 1982, vlii). The following entries are relevant to Nathan Davis (thanks to the kindness of archivist R. K. Headland, Meg Armstrong consulted these for me on September 23rd, 2003):

[Franklin, Jane] See Cracroft, Sophia. Letters (17) to her mother and sisters, 1858. [21st June 1858: account of Lady Franklin's presentation to the Queen of Greece]

MS 248/247/52–68; D. (Holland 1982, 269 and 172)

Cracroft, Sophia, 'Journal kept in the Near East and Greece', 13th April–17th July 1958, 3 vols in h o l o g r a p h: vol. 1, 13th April–12th May; vol. 2, 13th–20th May; vol. 3, 3rd June–17th July [The time frame covers the visit to Carthage]

MS 248/232/1–3: BJ (Holland 1982, 169–170)

(f) Manuscripts in the Archives of the Royal Geographical Society

The Royal Geographical Society has a few papers relating to Davis, written during the years that he was a Fellow of the RGS. I visited the RGS on July 28th, 2004. I thank Archivist Sarah Strong for kindly allowing me to see the following:

'Certificate of Candidate for Election' for N. Davis, proposed May 16th, 1855, elected June 11th, 1855, removed 1861

Four letters from Mrs C. Davis, incorrectly described in a note as wife of 'Rev. Nathaniel Davis', addressed to unnamed members of the Society or its Council, December 6th, 1855 (two letters), December 10th, 1855 and January 4th, 1856

Letter of Rev. N. Davis, from the Ruins of Carthage, Tunis, May 15th, 1858, to Dr Norton Shaw, editor of the *Journal of the Royal Geographical Society*

(g) Item from the Archives of the Missionaries of Africa (Archivio Generale dei Missionari d'Africa), Via Aurelia, Rome

Marcel Gandolphe [no date], 'Le R. Delattre', from an unidentified Tunisian newspaper, in folder Y1, 'Anecdotes', material on Alfred-Louis Delattre

II Published maps

BABELON, E., CAGNAT, R. and REINACH, S. (eds) 1893 *Description de l'Afrique du Nord, Atlas archéologique de la Tunisie. Edition spéciale des cartes topographiques publiée par le ministre de la guerre, accompagné d'un texte explicatif* (Paris: Ernest Leroux), 7 vols, with map of Carthage (1:50,000) inserted between 'El Ariana' and 'La Marsa' and with commentary on Carthage in vol. 3 (the map of Carthage and commentary are reprinted in Babelon 1896)

Banlieue nord de Tunis, La Marsa, Sidi Bou Said, Carthage, La Goulette, 1996, Plan de ville 1/10,000 (Tunis: Office de la Topographie et de la Cartographie)

BORDY, L'Ing. [1897] *Carte topographique et archéologique des environs de Carthage, avec le concours de MM. le R. P. Delattre, le général Dolot and P. Gauckler*, scale 1/5,000 (Paris: Service Géographique de l'Armée)

FALBE, C. T. (1791–1849) 1833 *Recherches sur l'emplacement de Carthage suivies de renseignements sur plusieurs inscriptions puniques inédites, de notices historiques, géographiques, etc., avec le plan topographique du terrain et des ruines de la ville dans leur état actuel et cinq autres planches* [map] (Paris: Imprimerie Royale)

GOLVIN, J.-C. 1999 *Restitution du site de Carthage à l'époque romaine*, Visualisation de Jean-Claude Golvin, Assistance scientifique de Abdelmajid Ennabli (Tunis: Édition de l'APPC)

GRAHAM, W. A. 1978 'Carthage. Plan archéologique d'étude', *CEDAC Carthage* 1, 10–11

III Reference works

ANON. 1857 *Men of the time: biographical sketches of eminent living characters; also, biographical sketches of celebrated women of the time* (London: Kent and Co.)

ANON. 1967 *Who was who in America? Historical volume, 1607–1896* (Chicago: Marquis Who's Who)

BOASE, F. 1965 [reprint] *Modern English biography, containing many thousand concise memoirs of persons who have died between the years 1851–1900*, 6 vols, 1892–1921: Vol. I, A–H (London: Frank Cass & Co Ltd)

COOPER, T. (ed.) 1872 *Men of the time: a dictionary of contemporaries containing biographical notices of eminent characters of both sexes* (London and New York: George Routledge and Sons)

KIRK, J. F. (ed.) 1902 *Supplement to Allibone's critical dictionary of English literature and British and American authors*, vol. 1 (London: J. B. Lippincott)

LEE, S. (ed.) 1897 *Dictionary of national biography*, vol. 49, Robinson–Russell (London: Smith, Elder and Co)

LEE, S. (ed.) 1909 *Dictionary of national biography*, vol. 12, Llwyd–Mason; vol. 14, Damon–D'Eyncourt, s.v. 'Davis, Nathan,' by W. Wroth [original entry 1888] (London: Smith, Elder and Co.)

PREVOST, M. and D'AMAT, R. (eds) 1948 *Dictionnaire de biographie française*, vol. 4, Aubernon–Baltard, s.v. 'Babelon, Ernest'; 1954, vol. 6, Bergeron–Bournon, s.v. '2. Beulé (Charles-Ernest)' by M. Prévost (Paris: Librairie Letouzey et Ané)

VERNAU, J. (ed.) 1981 *British Library general catalogue of printed books to 1975*, vol. 78 (1981), Davie–Decca (London, Munich, New York, Paris: K. G. Saur)

IV References to published sources cited in the notes and appendices

ADKINS, L. 2003 *Empires of the plain: Henry Rawlinson and the lost languages of Babylon* (New York: Thomas Dunne Books)

ALEXANDER, M. A., BESROUR, S, ENNAIFER, M. et al. 1976 *Corpus des Mosaïques de Tunisie. Vol. 1, fasc. 3. Utique. Les mosaïques sans localisation précise, et El Alia* (Tunis: Institut Nationale d'Archéologie et d'Art)

ANON. 1849 untitled note, *ILN* vol. 14, January 6th 1849, with engraving of the Mosaic of Ocean

ANON. 1850 *Curious Carthagenian Antiquities, marbles, valuable porphyry columns, fragments, terra cottas, &c. A catalogue of antiquities which will be sold by T. Winstanley and Sons on the 18th of February, 1850* (Liverpool: T. Winstanley and Sons) [*non vidi*]

ANON. 1857 'The site of Carthage (From the sketch-book of a recent tourist)', *ILN* vol. 31, October 31st 1857, 448 with figs, 'Remains of Carthage: the cisterns' and 'Remains of Carthage: the aqueduct'

ANON. 1858a 'Arabs excavating at the ruins of Carthage', *ILN* vol. 32, May 15th 1858, 480, fig. by Arthur Hall

ANON. 1858b 'The excavations at Carthage', *ILN* vol. 32, May 29th 1858, 545, with fig.

ANON. 1858c Untitled note, *Revue africaine* 2, 327 [on artefacts sent by Roches and Rousseau to Berbrugger at the Museum of Algiers]

ANON. 1858d 'An excursion from Tunis to Zowan', *ILN* vol. 33, October 30th 1858, 397–8

ANON. 1859a 'The arrival of the remains of the Tomb of Mausolus at the British Museum', *ILN* vol. 34, January 22nd 1859, 83

ANON. 1859b 'Prince Alfred at Tunis', *ILN* vol. 34, January 29th 1859, 98

ANON. 1859c 'The ruins of Carthage', *ILN* vol. 34, March 12th 1859, 251

ANON. 1861 'A recent wild-boar hunt in Algeria', *ILN* vol. 39, August 24th 1861, 198

ANON. 1882 'Fine-art gossip', *Athenaeum* no. 2829, January 14th 1882 [brief obituary of Nathan Davis]

ANON. 1883 untitled note in *CRAI* 1883, 154 [on Delattre's find of a fragment of the 'Punic price list']

ANON. 1884 untitled note in *BAA* 1884, 112 [on the excavations of Reinach and Babelon]

ANON. 1898 untitled note in *CRAI* 1898, 295 [on finds in the construction of the French battery on Bordj-Djedid]

ARROUAS, A. 1932 *Livre d'or, Régence de Tunis, figures d'hier et d'aujourd'hui* (Tunis: SAPI)

ASHBEE, H. 1889 *A bibliography of Tunisia from the earliest times to the end of 1888, in 2 parts, including Utica and Carthage, the Punic Wars, the Roman occupation, the Arab conquest, the expeditions of Louis IX and Charles V and the French Protectorate* (London: Dulau and Co.)

ATTAL, R. and SITBON, C. 1986 'From Carthage to Jerusalem, the Jewish community in Tunis', in *De Carthage à Jerusalem. La communauté juive de Tunis. Beth Hatefutsoth Musée de la Diaspora Juive Nahoum Goldmann, Tel Aviv, printemps 1986 / From Carthage to Jerusalem. The Jewish Community in Tunis. Beth Hatefutsoth, The Nathan Goldmann Museum of the Jewish Diaspora, Tel Aviv, Spring 1986* [exhibition catalogue], xvii–xxiv (Tel Aviv: Musée de la Diaspora Juive)

AUDOLLENT, A. 1901 *Carthage romaine, 146 avant Jésus-Christ–698 après Jesus-Christ* (Paris: Bibliothèque des Écoles françaises d'Athènes et de Rome 84)

BABELON, E. 1896 'Topographie de Carthage,' in *Carthage. Guides en Algérie et en Tunisie, à l'usage des touristes et des archéologues* (Paris: Leroux), 120–79

BACON, E. (ed.) 1976 *The great archaeologists: the modern world's discovery of ancient civilizations as originally reported in the pages of the* Illustrated London News *from 1842 to the present day* (London: Secker and Warburg)

BADISCHES LANDESMUSEUM KARLSRUHE (ed.) 2009 *Erben des imperiums in Nordafrika: das Königreich der Vandalen* (Mainz am Rhien: Verag Philipp von Zabern)

BAIREM-BEN OSMAN, W. 1981 *Catalogue des mosaïques de Carthage: Musée du Bardo, Musées des Thermes d'Antonin, quartier de Dermech, quartier de l'Odéon,* unpublished doctoral thesis, directed by M. Euzennat, submitted December 1980, Université d'Aix-en-Provence

BALMELLE, C. et al. 1985 *Le décor géometrique de la mosaïque romaine, vol. 1. Répertoire graphique et descriptif des compositions linéaires et isotropes* (Paris: Picard)

BARATTE, F. 1971 'Une curieuse expedition 'archéologique' en Tunisie. La 'mission' Hérisson', *Revue du Louvre* 21, 335–46

BARATTE, F. 1978 *Catalogue des mosaïques romaines et paléochrétiennes du musée du Louvre* (Paris: Éditions de la Réunion des musées nationaux)

BARD, J. 1854 *L'Algérie en 1854. Itinéraire général de Tunis à Tanger. Colonisation–paysages–monuments–culte–agriculture–statistique–hygiène–industrie–commerce–avenir* (Paris: L. Maison)

BARTH, H. 1849 *Wanderungen durch die Küstenländer des Mittelmeers in 1845–1847*, vol. 1, (Berlin: W. Hertz)

BEARD, M., 2000 *The invention of Jane Harrison* (Cambridge, Massachusetts, and London, England: Harvard University Press)

BEATTIE, O. and GEIGER, J. 1987 *Frozen in time: unlocking the secrets of the Franklin expedition* (Saskatoon: Western Producer Prairie Books)

BEAUREGARD, M., GUIMOND, L. and SENAY, P. 1976 'Fouilles du monument circulaire', *CEA* 6 = *Carthage* 1 (Montréal: Presses de l'Université de Québec), 21–68

BEAUREGARD, M. and SENAY, P. 1976 'Le monument circulaire', *CEA* 6 = *Carthage* 1, 71–85

BEAUREGARD, M. and SENAY, P. 1978 'Fouilles du monument circulaire', in P. Senay (ed.), *CEA* 9 = *Carthage* 2, 44–88

BEN ABDULLAH, Z. 1986 *Catalogue des inscriptions latines païennes du Musée du Bardo* [Collections de l'École française de Rome 92] (Rome: Ecole française de Rome)

BEN ABED-BEN KHADER, A. et al. 1999 *Corpus des Mosaïques de Tunisie. Vol. 4, fasc. 1. Karthago (Carthage). Les mosaïques du parc archéologique des Thermes d'Antonin* (Tunis: Institut Nationale du Patrimoine)

BEN ABED-BEN KHADER, A. (ed.) 2003 *Image in stone: Tunisia in mosaic* (Paris: Arts Latina and Tunis: Agence National du Patrimoine)

BEN ABED, A. 2006 *Stories in stone. Conserving mosaics of Roman North Africa* (Los Angeles: J. Paul Getty Museum/Getty Conservation Institute, and Tunis: Institut National du Patrimoine)

BENDANA, K., 2000 'Être archéologue à Tunis dans la deuxième moitié du XIXe siècle: l'exemple de Charles-Joseph Tissot (1828–1884)', in J. Alexandropoulos and P. Cabanel (eds), *La Tunisie mosaïque: diasporas, cosmopolitanisme, archéologies de l'identité* (Toulouse: Presses Universitaires de Mirail), 512–26

BENICHOU-SAFAR, H. 1982 *Les tombes puniques de Carthage. Topographie, structures, inscriptions et rites funéraires* (Paris: Éditions CNRS)

BENICHOU-SAFAR, H. 1989 'Les stèles dites "de Sainte-Marie" à Carthage', in H. Devijver and E. Lipinski (eds), *Punic Wars. Proceedings of the Conference held in Antwerp from the 23rd to the 26th of November 1988 = Studia Phoenicia* X (Leuven: Peeters), 353–64

BERGER, P. 1886 'Note sur trois cents nouveaux ex-votos de Carthage', *CRAI* 1886, 381–7

BERGER, P. 1900 'The excavations of Carthage', *Smithsonian Report for 1898* (Washington, DC: Smithsonian Institution), 601–14 [translated from *Revue des deux mondes* 153 (1899), 658–76]

BERGER, P. 1910 Untitled note in *CRAI* 1910, 57

BERGER, P. et al. 1881 'L'Exposition de la Cour Caulaincourt au Louvre', *Revue archéologique* 1881 [*non vidi*]

BEULÉ, C.-E. 1859 'Fouilles faites à Carthage. Découverte des murs puniques et d'importantes constructions plus modernes (1)', *CRAI* 1859, 33–7

BEULÉ, C.-E. 1861 *Fouilles à Carthage, aux frais et sur la direction de M. Beulé* (Paris: Imprimerie Impériale) [originally published as a serial in *Journal des Savants*, August 1859–September 1860]

BEULÉ, C.-E. 1872 'Journal de mes fouilles', *La Gazette des Beaux-Arts*, April and June 1872, 273–95 and 491–513 (reprint, Paris: Imprimerie de J. Claye)

BEULÉ, C.-E. 1873 'Lettres de Carthage', *Fouilles et découvertes résumées et discutées en vue de l'histoire de l'art, vol. 2, Afrique et Asie* (Paris: Didier et Cie), 3–58

BLAKESLEY, J. W. 1859 *Four months in Algeria, with a visit to Carthage* (Cambridge and London: Macmillan and Co.)

BLANCHARD-LEMÉE, M. et al. 1996 *Mosaics of Roman North Africa: floor mosaics from Tunisia* (London: British Museum Press) [translated from *Sols de l'Afrique romaine* (Paris: Imprimerie Nationale 1995)]

BOURGADE, F. 1852 *Toison d'or de la langue phénicienne* (Paris: Librairie de Benjamin Duprat) [second edition 1856 *non vidi*]

BROWN, L. C. 1974 *The Tunisia of Ahmad Bey, 1837–1855* (Princeton NJ: Princeton University Press)

BROWN, S. 1991 *Late Carthaginian child sacrifice and sacrificial monuments in their Mediterranean context* (Sheffield: Sheffield Academic Press)

BROWN, R., HUMPHREY. J. H. and MacLENNAN, J. 1976 'Preliminary field report', in Humphrey 1976, 1–19

BULLO, S. and GHEDINI, F. (eds) 2003 Amplissimae atque ornatissimae domus (*Aug.*, Civ. *II, 20, 26*). *L'edilizia residenziale nelle città della Tunisia romana. Schede* [Università degli Studi di Padova, Dipartimento di Scienze dell'Antichità: Antenor Quaderni 2.2] (Rome: Edizioni Quasar)

BURKHARDT, F. and SMITH, S. (eds) 1989 *The correspondence of Charles Darwin. Vol. 5, 1851–1855* (Cambridge: Cambridge University Press)

CAGNAT, R. 1887 'Sur l'inscription des thermes de Carthage', *Revue archéologique* 9, 171–9

CAGNAT, R. 1894 'Le capitole ou le temple de Junon Céleste à Carthage', *Revue archéologique* 24, 188–95

CAGNAT, R. and SCHMIDT, J. 1891 'Sepulcreta duo familiae domus Augustae Carthaginensis', *CIL* VIII, part 2, supplement vol. 1, 1301–2, nos 12590–13214

CARTON, L. 1920 'Découverte d'une fontaine antique à Carthage', *CRAI* 1920, 258–69

CASAGRANDE, M. 2008 *Gli impianti di adduzione idrica romani in Byzacena e in Zeugitana* [Studi di Storia Antica e di Archeologia 4] (Ortacesus: Nuove Grafiche Puddu)

CAYGILL, M. and CHERRY, J. (eds) 1997 *A. W. Franks, nineteenth-century collecting and the British Museum* (London: British Museum Press)

CHABOT, I. 2000 'La mosaïque et les fresques de la maison romaine', in P. Senay (ed.), *CEA* 36 = *Carthage* 11, 102–8

CHABRELY, F. 1885 *Une excursion à Carthage, avec une lettre de S. E. le cardinal Lavigerie* (Paris: Palmé)

CHALON, M. et al. 1985 'Memorabile factum. Une célébration de l'euergetisme des rois vandales dans l'Anthologie latine', *Antiquités africaines* 21, 207–62

CHAMAM, I. 2002 'An Ottoman Sir Wood, in Tunis: the man, diplomacy and politics', *Revue d'histoire maghrébine* 29, 69–78

CHATELAIN, Y. 1937 *La vie littéraire et intellectuelle en Tunisie de 1900 à 1937* (Paris)

CLOVER, F. M. 1978 'Carthage in the age of Augustine', in Humphrey 1978a, 1–14

CLOVER F. M. 1986 'Felix Carthago', *Dumbarton Oaks Papers* 40, 1–15

COHEN, E. G. 1988 *Family Facts and Fairy Tales*, 2nd edition (Pasadena, California: Hope Publishing House)

CUBISOL, C. 1867 *Notices abrégées sur la Régence de Tunis* (Paris: Challamel) [*non vidi*]

DANZIGER, R. 1977 *Abd al-Qadir and the Algerians. Resistance to the French and internal consolidation* (New York and London: Holmes and Meier)

DAUBER, L. G. 1967a 'Samuel Davies Heap – a footnote to American diplomatic history', *Military Medicine* 132 (10), 826–30

DAUBER, L. G. 1967b 'David Porter Heap – from Carthage to the Capitol City', *New England Journal of Medicine* 277, 533–4

DAUX, A. 1868 'Voyages et recherches en Tunisie', *Tour du Monde* 1868, 257–72

DAUX, A. 1869 *Recherches sur l'origine et l'emplacement des emporia phéniciens dans le Zeugis et le Byzacium (Afrique septentrionale), faites par ordre de l'Empereur* (Paris: Imprimerie impériale)

DAVIES, E. W. L. 1858 *Algiers in 1857. Its accessibility, climate and resources described with especial reference to English invalids. Also details of recreation obtainable in the neighbourhood, added for the use of travellers in general* (London: Longman, Brown, Green, Longmans & Roberts)

DAVIN, P. 1930 'Étude sur la cadastration de la Colonia Iulia Carthago', *Revue tunisienne* 1930, 73–85

DAVIS, N. 1841 *Tunis; or selections from a journal during a residence in that Regency* (Malta: G. Muir)

DAVIS, N. [1844] *The Carthaginian church; or a brief sketch of the history of the introduction, progress and extirpation of Christianity in North Africa* (Edinburgh: Paton and Ritchie)

DAVIS, N. 1844 *A voice from North Africa, or a narrative illustrative of the manners of the inhabitants of that part of the world, with an historical introduction and appendix* (Edinburgh: William Ritchie)

DAVIS, N. (ed.) 1852 *The Hebrew Christian Magazine*, nos 1–7, May–November, 1852 (London: Hebrew Christian Magazine)

DAVIS, N., and DAVIDSON, B. [1854] *Arabic reading lessons; consisting of extracts from the Koran, and other sources, grammatically analysed and translated; with the Elements of Arabic Grammar* (London: S. Bagster and Sons)

DAVIS, N. 1854 *Evenings in my tent, or wanderings in Balad Ejjareed, illustrating the moral, religious, social and political conditions of various African tribes of the African Sahara*, 2 vols (London: A. Hall, Virtue)

DAVIS, N. 1861 *Carthage and her remains, being an account of the excavations and researches on the site of the Phoenician metropolis of Africa* (London: Richard Bentley, two editions with different pagination; New York: Harper, with shorter pagination) [reprinted 1985 (London: Darf Publishers Limited, with the longer pagination)]

DAVIS, N. 1862 *Ruined cities within Numidian and Carthaginian territories* (London: John Murray) [reprinted in 2001 (London: Darf Publishers), and in 2003 (Chestnut Hill, Maryland: Elibron Classics)]

DEBERGH, J. 2000 'L'aurore de l'archéologie à Carthage au temps d'Hamouda Bey et de Mahmoud Bey (1782–1824): Frank, Humbert, Caronni, Gierlew, Borgia', in Khanoussi et al. 2000, 457–74

DEBERGH, J. 2002 ''Voici les ports.' 'Non.' Jean Emile Humbert et la localisation des installations portuaires de Carthage', *L'Africa romana* 14, 469–80

DELATTRE, A.-L. 1883 'Carthage', *Exposition internationale et coloniale d'Amsterdam. Section tunisienne. Objets archéologiques exposés par le R. P. Delattre* (Tunis: Imprimerie de B. Borrel)

DELATTRE, A.-L. 1883–1884 'Inscriptions de Carthage, 1875–1882', *BEG* 3, 25–8, 85–8, 182–5, 293–8

DELATTRE, A.-L. 1884–1885 'Inscriptions de Carthage, 1875–1883', *BEG* 4, 26–31, 105–10, 205–12 and 315–21

DELATTRE, A.-L. 1885 'Le tombeau punique de Byrsa et son mobilier funéraire', *BAA* 3, 241–6

DELATTRE, A.-L. 1886 'Inscriptions latines de Carthage, épigraphie païenne. Inscriptions provenant de la cité dite et des faubourgs (1884–1886) (suite). II. Colline de Junon', *BEG* 6, 80–91

DELATTRE, A.-L. 1889 'Epigraphie chrétienne de Carthage (1). VII. Gammarth (2)', *Cosmos*, no. 167, April 7 1889, 14–19

DELATTRE, A.-L. 1893 'Fouilles archéologiques dans le flanc sud-ouest de la colline de Saint-Louis en 1892', *BA/BCTH* 1893, 94–123

DELATTRE, A.-L. 1894 'Le mur à amphores de la colline Saint-Louis à Carthage', *BA/BCTH* 1894, 89–119

DELATTRE, A.-L. 1894 and 1895 'Gammart, ou la nécropole juive de Carthage', *Missions catholiques* December 1894, 589–91, 601–3, 613–16, 625–6 and 627; January 1895, 9–11 and 20–22 [reprinted in Lyon, 1895]

DELATTRE, A.-L.1899 'Sur l'emplacement du temple de Cérès à Carthage', *MSAF* 58, 1–20 (with an appendix by Antoine Héron de Villefosse: 21–6)

DELATTRE, A.-L. 1900 'La nécropole punique voisine de la colline de Sainte-Monique. Second mois des fouilles (février 1899 [*sic* for '1898'])', *Cosmos* 42, fasc. no. 788, March 3rd 1900, 273–6; and fasc. no. 789, March 10th, 304–8

DELATTRE, A.-L. 1901 'Carthage. La nécropole punique voisine de la colline de Sainte-Monique. Deuxième semestre des fouilles, 1898, juillet–décembre', *Cosmos* 45, fasc. 871, 435–40

DELATTRE, A.-L. 1906a *Un pèlerinage aux ruines de Carthage et au Musée Lavigerie, avec un plan de Carthage*, 2nd edition (Lyons: Imprimerie de J. Poncet)

DELATTRE, A.-L. 1906b 'Un second mur à amphores découvert à Carthage', *BSAS* 4, 33–48

DELAVOYE, C. M. (ed.) 1999 *Flaubert: carnet de voyage à Carthage, texte établi par Claire-Marie Delavoye* (Rouen: Publications de l'Université de Rouen)

DENEAUVE, J. and GROS, P. 1980 'Hypothèses sur le centre monumental de la Carthage romaine, d'après les recherches récentes sur la colline de Byrsa', *CRAI* 1980, 299–332

DENEAUVE, J. 1983 'Le tracé monumental de Byrsa à l'époque romaine. État actuel de recherches', *CEA* 16 = *Carthage* 6 [Actes du congrès (première partie)], 88–104

DENEAUVE, J. 1990 'Le centre monumental de Carthage. Un ensemble cultuel sur la colline de Byrsa', in *Carthage et son territoire dans l'antiquité*, vol. 1 [Actes du IVe colloque international réuni dans le cadre du 113e Congrès national des Sociétés savantes (Strasbourg, 5–9 avril 1988)] (Paris: Editions du Comité des Travaux Historiques et Scientifiques), 143–55

DIEHL, C. 1892 'Les découvertes de l'archéologie française en Algérie et en Tunisie', *Revue internationale de l'enseignement* 15th August 1892 (reprinted, Paris: A. Colin)

DIETZ, S. and TROLLE, S. 1979 *Premier rapport préliminaire sur les fouilles danoises à Carthage. Les campagnes de 1975 et 1977* [Working Papers 10] (Copenhagen: Nationalmuseet)

DIETZ, S. 1985 'Fouilles danoises à Carthage, 1975–1984', *CEA* 16 = *Carthage* 6 [Actes du congrès (première partie)], 107–13

DITSON, G. L. 1860 *Adventures and observations on the north coast of Africa; or the Crescent and the French Crusades* (New York: Derby & Jackson)

DONDIN-PAYRE, M. 2000 'Le premier reportage photographique archéologique en Afrique du Nord: les fouilles du Tombeau de la Chrétienne en 1855–1856', *Africa romana* 14, 2119–46

DUNANT, H. 1858 *Notice sur la Régence de Tunis* (Geneva:

Imprimerie de Dr Jules-Guillaume Fick; reprinted 1975)

DUNBABIN, K. M. D. 1978 *The mosaics of Roman North Africa. Studies in iconography and patronage* (Oxford: Clarendon Press)

DUNBABIN, K. M. D. 1980 'A mosaic workshop in Carthage around A.D. 400', in Pedley 1980, 85–127

DUNBABIN, K. M. D. 1985 'Mosaics of the Byzantine period in Carthage: problems and directions of research', *CEA* 17 = *Carthage* 7 [Actes du Congrès (deuxième partie)], 8–29

DUPUY, A. 1954 *En marge de Salammbô. Le voyage de Flaubert en Algérie-Tunisie (avril–juin 1858)* (Paris: Librairie Nicet)

DUREAU DE LA MALLE, A.-J.-C.-A. 1835 *Recherches sur la topographie de Carthage, avec des notes par Dusgate* (Paris: Firmin-Didot Frères)

DUSGATE, A. 1834 *Appendices au livre de Dureau de la Malle sur la topographie de Carthage* (Paris: Firmin-Didot)

DUVAL, N., LANCEL, S. and LE BOHEC, Y. 1984 'Études sur la garnison de Carthage. Deux documents nouveaux – les troupes de Proconsulaire – le camp de la cohorte urbaine' *BA/BCTH* n.s. 15–16, Fasc. B, 33–89

EADIE, J. W. and HUMPHREY, J. H. 1977 'The topography of the southeast quarter of later Roman Carthage', in Humphrey 1977, 1–19

EDWARDS, E. 1870 *Lives of the founders of the British Museum, with notices of its chief augmentors and benefactors, 1570–1870* (London: Trübner and Co.)

EMERIT, M. 1947 'La légende de Léon Roches', *Revue africaine* 91, 81–105

ENDELMAN, T. 1979 *The Jews of Georgian England, 1714–1830. Tradition and change in a liberal society* (Philadelphia: The Jewish Publication Society of America)

ENNABLI, A. and BEN OSMAN, W. 1983a 'La Maison de la Volière à Carthage: L'Architecture', in *Mosaïque. Recueil d'hommages à Henri Stern* (Paris: Éditions Recherches sur les Civilisations), 129–45

ENNABLI, A. and BEN OSMAN, W. 1983b 'Étude des pavements de la Villa de la Volière' *Mosaïque. Recueil d'hommages à Henri Stern* (Paris: Éditions Recherches sur les Civilisations), 147–56

ENNABLI, A. (ed.) 1992 *Pour sauver Carthage: Exploration et conservation de la cité punique, romaine et byzantine* (Paris: UNESCO and Tunis: INAA)

ENNABLI, L. 1997 *Carthage: une métropole chrétienne du IVe à la fin du VIIe siècle* [Études d'Antiquités Africaines] (Aix-en-Provence: Éditions CNRS)

ENNABLI, L. 2000 *La Basilique de Carthagenna et le locus des sept moines de Gafsa, Nouveaux édifices chrétiens de Carthage* (Aix-en-Provence: Éditions CNRS)

ESTOURNELLES DE CONSTANT, P.-H.-B. B., d' 1891 *La politique française en Tunisie: Le protectorat et ses origines (1854–1891) par P. H. X.* (Paris: E. Plon)

EUTING, J. 1883 *Sammlung der Carthagischen Inschriften* vol. 1 (Strasbourg: Karl J. Trübner)

FALBE, C. T. 1833 *Recherches sur l'emplacement de Carthage suivies de renseignements sur plusieurs inscriptions puniques inédites, de notices historiques, géographiques, etc., avec le plan topographique du terrain et des ruines de la ville dans leur état actuel et cinq autres planches* (Paris: Imprimerie Royale)

[FALBE, C. T. and TEMPLE, G.] 1838 *Excursion dans l'Afrique septentrionale par les délégués de la Société établie à Paris pour l'exploration de Carthage* (Paris: Gide et Arthus Bertrand)

FALBE, C. T., LINDBERG, J. C. and MÜLLER, L. 1860–74 *Numismatique de l'ancien Afrique, ouvrage préparé et commencé par C. T. Falbe et J. Chr. Lindberg, refait, achevé et publié par L. Müller*, 3 vols (Copenhagen: Imprimerie B. Luno; reprinted Bologna: Arnaldo Forni Editore, 1984)

FANTAR, M. H., PICARD, G.-C., BEN MANSOUR, M., JEDDI, N., SLIM, H., KHANOUSSI, M., YACOUB, M., FOUCHER, L., BÉJAOUI, F. and GHEDINI, F. 1994 *La mosaïque en Tunisie* (Paris: CNRS Editions, and Tunis: les Éditions de la Méditerranée)

FAUCON, N. 1893 *La Tunisie avant et depuis l'occupation française, histoire et colonisations*, 2 vols (Paris: A. Challamel)

FLAUX, A. de 1865 *La Régence de Tunis au dix-neuvième siècle* (Paris: Challamel Ainé)

FRANKS, A. W. 1860 'On recent excavations at Carthage and the antiquities discovered there by the Rev. Nathan Davis', *Archaeologia* 38, 202–36

FREED, J. and ROS, K. 1990 'Tunisian amphoras of the fourth century A.D. built into the Roman theater at Carthage', *CEDAC Carthage* 11, 19–22

FREED, J. and MOORE, J. 1996 'New observations on the earliest Roman amphoras from Carthage: Delattre's First Amphora Wall', *CEDAC Carthage* 15, 19–28

FREED, J. 1996 'Early Roman amphoras in the collection of the Museum of Carthage', *EMC/CV* 40, 119–55

FREED, J. 1998 'Stamped Tarraconensian Dressel 2–4 amphoras at Carthage', in *II Colloqui Internacional d'Arqueologia Roman (Badalona 6/9 de Maig de 1998). Actes. El vi a l'antiguitat: economia , producció i comerç al Mediterrani occidental* [Monografies Badalonines 14] (Badalona: Museu de Badalona), 350–6

FREED, J. 2001 'Bibliography of publications by Alfred-Louis Delattre (1850–1932)', *CEDAC Carthage* 20, 1–60

GALLAGHER, N. E. 1983 *Medicine and Power in Tunisia, 1780–1900* (Cambridge: Cambridge University Press)

GANDOLPHE, M. 1940 'Le centenaire de la chapelle de Saint Louis', *La Tunisie catholique*, September 1st, 1940, 518–26

GANDOLPHE, P. 1951 'Saint-Louis de Carthage (1830–1950)', *Cahiers de Byrsa* 1, 269–307

GANDOLPHE, P. 1952 'Origines et débuts du Musée Lavigerie', *Cahiers de Byrsa* 2, 151–78

GANIAGE, J. 1971 'France, England and the Tunisian affair', in P. Gifford and W. R. Louis (eds), *France and Britain in Africa, imperial rivalry and colonial rule* (New Haven and London: Yale University Press)

GANIAGE, J. 1985 'North Africa', in R. Oliver and G. N.

Sanderson (eds), *Cambridge History of Africa. Vol. 6, c. 1870 – c. 1905* (Cambridge), 159–207

GAUCKLER, P. 1896 'Extrait des procès-verbaux de la section archéologique du congrès de Carthage', *Revue tunisienne* 3, 610–22

GAUCKLER, P. *Compte rendu de la marche du service en 1896, 1897, 1898, 1899, 1900, 1901, 1902, 1903* Régence de Tunis, Direction des Antiquités et des Beaux-arts (Tunis: Imprimerie Rapide)

GAUCKLER, P. 1907 'Inscriptions diverses de Carthage (1901–1905)', *Nouvelles archives des missions scientifiques* 15, 423–43

GAUCKLER, P. 1910 and 1913 *Inventaire des mosaïques de la Gaule et de l'Afrique, vol. 2. Afrique proconsulaire (Tunisie)*, text (1910) and plates (1913) (Paris: Ernest Leroux)

GIDNEY, W. T. *The History of the London Society for Promoting Christianity amongst the Jews, from 1809 to 1908* (London: London Society for Promoting Christianity amongst the Jews)

GIROIRE, C. and ROGER, D. 2007 *Roman art from the Louvre* (New York: American Federation of Arts, and Manchester, Vermont: Hudson Hills Press)

GORBUNOVA, X. and SAVERKINA, I. 1975 *Greek and Roman Antiquities in the Hermitage*, translated by B. Bean and M. Orzhevskaya (Leningrad: Aurora Art Publishers)

GOZLAN, S. 1983 'Deux mosaïques de Carthage au Kunsthistorisches Museum de Vienne', in *Mosaïque. Recueil d'hommages à Henri Stern* (Paris: Éditions Recherches sur les Civilisations), 179–87

GRAN-AYMERICH, È. 1998 *Naissance de l'archéologie moderne, 1798–1945* (Paris: CNRS Éditions)

GRAN-AYMERICH, È. 2001 *Dictionnaire biographique d'archéologie, 1798–1945* (Paris: CNRS Éditions)

GRANDCHAMP, P. 1944 'Arbre généalogique de la famille Hassinite (1705–1944)' [fold-out chart], originally published in *Revue tunisienne* 38 (1936), 475 [republished in Martel and Sebag 1966, between 132 and 133]

GREGORY, W. H. 1859 *Egypt in 1855 and 1856; Tunis in 1857 and 1858*, especially Vol. 2, *Tunis in 1857 and 1858*, 151–400 (London: J. R. Smith, printed for private circulation)

GREGORY, A. (ed.) 1894 *William Henry Gregory, an autobiography, 1817–1892; with alternate title Sir William Gregory, formerly Member of Parliament and sometime Governor of Ceylon, an autobiography* (London: J. Murray)

GROS, P. et al. 1985 *Mission archéologique française à Carthage. Byrsa III. Rapport sur les campagnes de fouilles de 1977 à 1980: la basilique orientale et ses abords* [Collections École française de Rome 41] (Rome: École française de Rome)

GROS, P. 1995 'Le culte impérial dans le basilique judiciaire du forum de Carthage', *Karthago* 23, 45–56

GUERIN, V. 1862 *Voyage archéologique dans la Régence de Tunis*, 2 vols (Paris: Henri Plon)

GUNNING, L. P. 2009 *The British Consular Service in the Aegean and the collection of antiquities for the British Museum* (Farnham: Ashgate)

HALBERTSMA, R. B. 1995 *Le solitaire des ruines. De archeologische reizen van Jean Emile Humbert (1771–1839) in dienst van het Konikrijk der Nederlanden* [Collections of the National Museum of Antiquities at Leiden, IX] (Leiden: Rijksmuseum van Oudheden)

HALBERTSMA, R. B. 2003 *Scholars, Travellers and Trade: The Pioneer Years of the National Museum of Antiquities in Leiden, 1818–1840* (New York and London: Routledge)

HALLIER, G. 1995 'Le monument circulaire du plateau de l'Odéon à Carthage: précisions sur la conception et la géométrie d'un parti original', *Antiquités africaines* 31, 201–30

HANOUNE, R. 1969 'Trois pavements de la Maison de la Course de Chars à Carthage', *MEFRA* 81, 219–56

HANSEN, C. G. 2002 *Carthage: results of the Swedish Excavations, 1979–1983, Vol. 1. A Roman Bath in Carthage* (Stockholm: Paul Aströms Verlag)

HAVERFIELD, F. J. 1913 *Ancient Town Planning* (Oxford: Clarendon Press)

HAYES, J. W. 1972 *Late Roman Pottery* (London: The British School at Rome)

HERISSON, I. d'1881 *Relation d'une mission archéologique en Tunisie* (Paris: Société Anonyme de Publications Périodiques)

HINKS, R. P. 1933 *Catalogue of the Greek, Etruscan and Roman paintings and mosaics in the Brititsh Museum* (London: Trustees of the British Museum)

HOLWERDA, J. H. 1936 *Het Laat-grieksche en romeinsche Gebruiksaardewerk, uit het Middellandsche-Zee-Gebied in het Rijksmuseum van Oudheden te Leiden* ('S-Gravenhage: Algemeene Landsdrukkerij)

HOURS-MIEDAN, M. 1959 *Carthage* (Paris: Presses Universitaires de France)

HUMBERT, J.-E. 1821 *Notice sur quatre cippes sépulcraux et deux fragments; découverts, en 1817, sur le sol de l'ancienne Carthage* (The Hague: M. de Lyon) [*non vidi*]

HUMPHREY, J. H. (ed.) 1976 *Excavations at Carthage conducted by the University of Michigan*, vol. 1 (Tunis: American Schools of Oriental Research and INAA, Cérès Productions)

HUMPHREY, J. H. (ed.) 1977 *Excavations at Carthage conducted by the University of Michigan*, vol. 3 (Ann Arbor: Kelsey Museum and the University of Michigan)

HUMPHREY, J. H. (ed.) 1978a *Excavations at Carthage conducted by the University of Michigan*, vol. 4 (Ann Arbor: Kelsey Museum and the University of Michigan)

HUMPHREY, J. H. 1978b 'North African newsletter I', *American Journal of Archaeology* 82, 511–20

HUMPHREY, J. H. (ed.) 1998 *Carthage papers: the early colony's economy, water supply, a public bath, and the mobilization of state olive oil* [JRA Supplementary Series 28] (Portsmouth, Rhode Island)

HURST, H. 1975 'Excavations at Carthage 1974: first interim report', *Antiquaries Journal* 55, 11–40

HURST, H. R. 1993 'Excavations in the southern part of the Carthage harbours, 1992–1993', *CEDAC Carthage* 13, 10–19 (with corrected plan of the area around the harbours, 1994, *CEDAC Carthage* 14, 55)

HURST, H. R. et al. 1994 *Excavations at Carthage. The British Mission vol. 2, 1 The Circular Harbour, North Side. The Site and Finds Other Than Pottery* (INAA and British Academy Tunisia Committee, Oxford)

HURST, H. R. et al. 1999 *The sanctuary of Tanit at Carthage in the Roman period: a re-interpretation* [JRA Supplementary Series 30] (Portsmouth, Rhode Island)

HURST, H. R. and ROSKAMS, S. 1984 *Excavations at Carthage, the British mission. Vol. 1, 1. The Avenue du Président Habib Bourguiba, Salammbo: the site and finds other than pottery* (Sheffield: University of Sheffield)

HURST, H. R. and STAGER, L. E. 1978 'A metropolitan landscape: the late Punic port of Carthage', *World Archaeology* 9, 334–46

JANSSEN, L. J. F. 1843 *De grieksche, romeinsche en etrurische Monumenten van het Museum van Oudheden te Leyden* (Leiden: H. W. Hazenberg)

JENKINS, G. K. 1969 *Sylloge Nummorum Graecorum. Royal Collection of coins and medals in the Danish National Museum, Copenhagen* (Copenhagen: Munksgaard)

JENKINS, I. 1992 *Archaeologists and aesthetes in the sculpture galleries of the British Museum* (London: British Museum Press)

JOMARD, E. F. 1843 'Extrait d'une lettre de M. P. de Laporte à son père', *Bulletin de la Société de Géographie* 19, 128–9

JUDAS, A. C. 1847 *Étude démonstrative de la langue phénicienne et de la langue libyque* (Paris: F. Klincksieck) [*non vidi*]

KENNEDY, J. C. 1846 *Algeria and Tunis in 1845. An account of a journey made through the two regencies by Viscount Feilding and Captain Kennedy*, 2 vols (London: Henry Colburn)

KHANOUSSI, M., RUGGERI, P. and VISMARA, C. (eds) 2000 *L'Africa romana 13. Geografi, viaggiatori, militari nel Maghreb: alle origini dell'archeologia nel Nord Africa*, 2 vols (Rome: Carocci 2000)

KHUN DE PROROK, B. 1923 'The excavations of Carthage, 1921–1922', *Art and Archaeology* 15, 38–45

KHUN DE PROROK, B. 1926 *Digging for lost African gods: the record of five years' archaeological excavation in North Africa* (New York and London: P. Putnam's Sons)

KOBELT, W. 1885 *Reiseerinnerungen aus Algerien und Tunis* (Frankfurt am Main: Moritz Diesterweg)

KOLENDO, J. 1988 'Le cirque, l'amphithéâtre et le théâtre d'Utique d'après la description d'A. Daux', *Africa romana* 6, 249–64

KORSUNSKA, S. 1933 'Zu den römischen Monatsbildern', *MDAI(R)* 1948, 277–83

LAMBERT, P. 1912 *Choses et gens de Tunisie. Dictionnaire illustré de la Tunisie* (Tunis: C. Saliba Ainé)

LANCEL, S. (ed.) 1979 *Mission archéologique française à Carthage. Byrsa I. Rapports préliminaires des fouilles (1974–1976)* [Collections École française de Rome 41] (Rome: École française de Rome)

LANCEL, S. 1981 'Fouilles françaises à Carthage. La colline de Byrsa et l'occupation punique (VIIe siècle–146 av. J.-C.). Bilan de sept années de fouilles', *CRAI* 1981, 156–93

LANCEL, S. et al. 1982 *Mission archéologique française à Carthage. Byrsa II. Rapports préliminaires sur les fouilles 1977–1978: niveaux et vestiges puniques* [Collections École française de Rome 41] (Rome: École française de Rome)

LANCEL, S. 1983 *La colline de Byrsa à l'époque punique* (Paris: Éditions Recherches sur les Civilisations)

LANCEL S. 1988 'Victor de Vita et le Carthage vandale', *Africa romana* 6, 649–61

LANCEL, S. 1995 *Carthage: a history*, translated by Antonia Nevill (Oxford and Cambridge, Massachusetts: Blackwell)

LANCHA, J. 1997 *Mosaïque et culture dans l'occident romain (Ier–IVe s.)* (Rome: L'Erma di Bretschneider)

LAVAGNE, H. 1983 'Une mosaïque de Carthage à la Bibliothèque de Versailles et les débuts de l'exploration de la Tunisie', *BSAF* 1983, 58–9

LAVAN, L. 1999 'Late antique governors' palaces: a gazeteer', *Antiquité tardive* 7, 135–64

LAVIGERIE, C.-M. A. 1875 'Lettre aux missionaires d'Alger, récemment chargés de garder et desservir le tombeau de saint Louis, Roi de France, sur les ruines de Carthage', in *Oeuvres choisies de S. E. le Cardinal Lavigerie*, vol. 2 (Paris: Poussièlgue Frères)

LAVIGERIE, C.-M. A. 1881 *Lettre à M. le Secrétaire Perpetuel de l'Académie des Inscriptions et Belles-Lettres sur l'utilité d'une mission archéologique permanente à Carthage*, 17th April 1881 (Algiers: A. Jourdan)

LEGENDRE, M. 1957 'Note sur la cadastration romaine', *Cahiers de Tunisie* 5, 135–66

LÉZINE, A. 1961 *Architecture romaine d'Afrique: recherches et mises au point* (Tunis: Presses Universitaires de France)

LÉZINE, A. 1968 *Carthage-Utique. Études d'architecture et d'urbanisme* (Paris: Éditions CNRS)

LING, D. L. 1967 *Tunisia: from Protectorate to Republic* (Bloomington, Indiana: Indiana University Press)

LING, R. 1998 *Ancient mosaics* (London: British Museum Press, and Princeton, NJ: Princeton University Press)

LONG, D. F. 1970 *Nothing too daring. A biography of Commodore David Porter, 1780–1843* (Annapolis, Maryland: United States Naval Institute)

LUND, J. 1986 'The archaeological activities of Christian Tuxen Falbe in Carthage in 1838' *CEA* 18 = *Carthage* 8 [Actes du Congrès (troisième partie)], 8–24

MACPHERSON, D. 1857 *Antiquities of Kertch, and researches in the Cimmerian Bosphorus* (London: Smith, Elder & Co.)

MAHJOUBI, A. 1967 'Découverte d'une nouvelle mosaïque de chasse à Carthage', *CRAI* 1967, 264–77

MANLY, S. (ed.) 2004 *Harrington, Maria Edgeworth* (Peterborough, Plymouth and Sydney: Broadview Editions)

MARSDEN, A. 1971 *British diplomacy and Tunis, 1875–1902: a case study in Mediterranean policy* (Edinburgh and London: Scottish Academic Press)

MARTEL, A. 1967 *À l'arrière-plan des relations franco-maghrébines (1830–1881). Luis-Arnold et Joseph Allegro, consuls du Bey de Tunis à Bône* (Paris: Presses Universitaires de France)

MARTEL, A. and SEBAG, P. (eds) 1966 *Pierre Grandchamp. Études d'histoire tunisienne XVIIe – XXe siècles* (Paris: Presses Universitaires de France)

MAUPASSANT, G. de 1889 'Promenade à travers Tunis', *Le Gaulois*, 12ème février 1889 [= Salinas 1990, 190–1]

MCGOOGAN, K. 2005 *Lady Franklin's revenge. A true story of ambition, obsession and the remaking of Arctic history* (Toronto: Harper Collins Publishers Ltd)

M'CHAREK, A. 1988 'Maghrawa, lieu de provenance des stèles punico-numides dites de la Ghorfa', *MEFRA* 100, 731–60

MELIA, J. 1939 *En Tunisie. Carthage chrétienne d'aujourd'hui* (Paris: Fasquelle)

MENDLESON, C. 2003 *Catalogue of Punic Stelae in the British Museum* [British Museum Occasional Paper 98] (London: The Chameleon Press Ltd)

MERLIN, A. 1921 'La mosaïque du seigneur Julius à Carthage', *BA/BCTH* 1921, 95–114

MILLER, E. 1967 *Prince of librarians: the life and times of Antonio Panizzi of the British Museum* (London: André Deutsch)

MILLER, E. 1973 *That Noble Cabinet: a history of the British Museum* (London: André Deutsch)

MOMMSEN, T. 1881 'Auctorum ad inscriptiones africanas adhibitorum recensus', *CIL* 8, pars prior (Berlin: G. Reimer), xxi–xxxiv

MONTFAUCON, B. de 1719–24 *L'antiquité expliquée et représentée en figures*, 10 volumes and 5 supplements (Paris: Delaulne), translated by the Rev. D. Humphreys as *Antiquity Explained and Represented in Sculptures*, 1725 (London: J. Tonson and J. Watts)

MOORE, J. P. 2000 *Cultural identity in Roman Africa: the 'La Ghorfa' stelae*, unpublished Ph.D. thesis, McMaster University (Hamilton, ON)

MOOREHEAD, C. 1998 *Dunant's dream: war, Switzerland and the history of the Red Cross* (London: Harper Collins Publishers Ltd)

MORGAN, T. 1886 *Romano-British pavements. A history of their discovery and a record and interpretation of their designs* (London: Whiting and Co.)

MORSY, M. 1984 *North Africa 1800-1900: a survey from the Nile Valley to the Atlantic* (London and New York: Longman)

MURCH, A.E. (ed.) 1959 *Tangier to Tunis* (London: Peter Owen Ltd), translated and abridged from A. Dumas, *En véloce*, 4 vols, 1848–1851 (Paris: Cadot)

NAPOLÉON BONAPARTE, C.-L. III 1865–66 *Histoire de Jules César*, 2 vols, with separate atlas (Paris: Imprimerie Nationale)

NEIRA JIMENEZ, M. L. 2000 'Las expediciones de la primera mitad del siglo XIX al Norte de Africa. Su contribución al descubrimiento y estudio de los mosaicos romanos', in Khanoussi, Ruggeri, and Vismara 2000, 797–816

NEWTON, C. T. 1865 *Travels and discoveries in the Levant*, 2 vols (London: Day and Son)

[NEWTON, C. T.] 1876 *Synopsis of the contents of the British Museum Department of Greek and Roman Antiquities. Greco-Roman Sculptures*, part 2, 1876 (London: British Museum)

NEWTON, C. T. 1880 'On the study of archaeology. A discourse read at the Oxford meeting of the Archaeological Institute, June 18th, 1850', *Archaeological Journal* 8, 1–26

NOAH, M. M. 1819 *Travels in England, France, Spain and the Barbary States, in the years 1813–14 and 15* (New York: Kirk and Mercien, and London: John Miller)

NORMAN, N. J. 1988 'The architecture of the circus in the light of the 1982 season', in J. H. Humphrey (ed.), *The circus and a Byzantine cemetery at Carthage*, vol. 1 (Tunis: INAA and Ann Arbor: American Schools of Oriental Research/University of Michigan Press), 7–56

NORMAN, N. J. 1994 'Excavations in the Yasmina necropolis. The 1993 season,' *CEDAC Carthage* 14, 12–14

OSLER, E. 1835 *The life of Admiral Viscount Exmouth* (London and New York: William Jackson)

PARLASCA, K. 1958 'Mosaikfälschungen', *MDAI(R)* 65, 155–85

PARRISH, D. 1984 *Season mosaics of Roman North Africa* (Rome: Giorgio Bretschneider)

PARRISH, D. 1992 'Menses,' *Lexicon Iconographicum Mythologiae Classicae* VI (Zurich and Munich: Artemis Verlag), 479–500

PEDLEY, J. G. (ed.) 1980 *New light on ancient Carthage* (Ann Arbor: University of Michigan Press)

PERKINS, K. J. 1986 *Tunisia: crossroads of the Islamic and European worlds* (Boulder, Colorado: Westview Press, and London and Sydney: Croom Helm)

PERKINS, K. J. 1997 *Historical dictionary of Tunisia* [African Historical Dictionaries 45], second edition (Metuchen, NJ, and London: Scarecrow Press)

PERRY, A. 1869 *Carthage and Tunis, past and present: in two parts* (Providence, Rhode Island: Providence Press Company)

PICARD, C. 1951 *Carthage* (Paris: Les Belles-Lettres)

PICARD, G.-C. 1951–52 'Rapport sur l'archéologie romaine en Tunisie pendant l'année 1951', *BA/BCTH* 1951–52, 191–5

PICARD, G.-C. 1964 'Un palais du IVe siècle à Carthage', *CRAI* 1964, 101–18

PICARD, G.-C. 1965 *La Carthage de Saint Augustin* (Paris: Fayard)

PICARD, G.-C. 1983 'La recherche archéologique en Tunisie des origines à l'indépendance', *CEA* 16 = *Carthage* 6 [Actes du Congrès (première partie)], 11–20

PODANY, J. 2006 'From floor to wall: lifting and exhibition practices applied to ancient floor mosaics', in Ben Abed 2006, 115–27

POINSSOT, L. 1929 *L'autel de la gens Augusta à Carthage* (Paris: Vuibert)

POULSEN, E. 1986 'Tombs of the IVth–Vth centuries A.D. in the Danish sector at Carthage (Falbe, site no. 90)', *CEA* 18 = *Carthage* 8 [Actes du congrès (troisième partie)], 142–59

PRINGLE, D. 1981 *The defence of Byzantine Africa from Justinian to the Arab Conquest. An account of the military history and archaeology of the African provinces in the sixth and seventh centuries*, 2 vols [BAR International Series 99] (Oxford: British Archaeological Reports)

RAKOB, F. 1984 'Deutsche Ausgrabungen in Karthago: die punischen Befunde', *MDAI(R)* 91, 1–22

RAKOB, F. 1986 'Les fouilles allemandes de Carthage: l'état des niveaux puniques', *CEA* 19 = *Carthage* IX [Actes du congrès (quatrième partie)], 1–67

RAKOB, F. 1991a 'Allemagne. Fouilles à Carthage en 1990', *CEDAC Carthage* 12, 7–12

RAKOB, F. 1991b 'Ein punisches Heiligtum in Karthago und sein römischer Nachfolgebau. Erster Bericht', *MDAI(R)* 98, 33–80

RAWNSLEY, W. F. (ed.) 1923 *Life, diaries and correspondence of Jane Lady Franklin, 1792–1875* (London: Erskine MacDonald)

REBUFFAT, R. 1969 'Maisons à péristyle d'Afrique du Nord: répertoire des plans publiés', *MEFRA* 81, 659–724

REBUFFAT, R. 1974 'Catalogue des maisons à péristyle d'Afrique romaine', *MEFRA* 86, 445–99

REINACH, S. 1888 'Une campagne en Tunisie' and 'Les ruines de Carthage', in *Esquisses archéologiques* (Paris: Ernest Leroux), 72–101 [reprinted from *Bulletin hebdomadaire de l'Association Scientifique de France*, 21st February 1886]

REINACH, S. and BABELON, E. 1886 'Recherches archéologiques en Tunisie (1883–1884)' *BA/BCTH* 1886, 5–40

REVAULT, J. 1974 *Palais et résidences d'été de la région de Tunisie (XVIe–XIXe siècles)* [Études d'Antiquités Africaines] (Paris: Éditions CNRS)

REVAULT, J. 1984 *Le fondouk des Français et les consuls de France à Tunis (1660–1860)* (Paris: Éditions CNRS)

RIVES, J. B. 1995 *Religion and authority in Roman Carthage from Augustus to Constantine* (Oxford: Clarendon Press)

ROSSITER, J.J. 1998 'A Roman bath-house at Bir el Djebbana: preliminary report on the excavations (1994–1997)', in Humphrey 1998, 103–15

ROUSSEAU, A. 1850 'Lettre à l'éditeur de la Revue archéologique sur une mosaïque trouvée à Carthage', *Revue Archéologique* 7, 260–1

ROUSSEAU, A. 1864 *Annales tunisiennes ou aperçu historique sur la Régence de Tunis* (Algiers: Bastid, and Paris: Challamel)

SAINTE-MARIE, E. de 1875a 'Notice sur l'emplacement d'un édifice ancien à Carthage (temple de Baal, Curie, couvent de Salomon, Basilique 'restituta' et divers thermes)', *RSAC* 17, 131–40

SAINTE-MARIE, E. de 1875b 'Bibliographie carthaginoise', *RSAC* 17, 69–110

SAINTE-MARIE, E. de 1876 'Les ruines de Carthage', *Explorateur* 1876 (Paris: Aux Bureaux de l'*Explorateur*), 3–36

SAINTE-MARIE, E. de 1878a 'Recherches bibliographiques sur Karthage', *RSAC* 19, 97–186 [corrected version of Sainte-Marie 1875b]

SAINTE-MARIE, E. de 1878b *La Tunisie chrétienne* (Lyons: Bibliothèque Illustrée des Missions Catholiques)

SAINTE-MARIE, E. de 1884 *Mission à Carthage* (Paris: Ernest Leroux) [originally published as a serial in *Journal des Savants*]

SALIES, G. 1974 'Untersuchungen zu den geometrischen Gliederungsschemata römischer Mosaiken', *Bonner Jahrbücher* 174, 1–178

SALINAS, M. (ed.) 1990 *Guy de Maupassant, lettres d'Afrique (Algérie, Tunisie)* (Paris: La Boîte à Documents)

SALOMONSON, J. W. 1965 *La mosaïque aux chevaux de l'antiquarium de Carthage* (The Hague: Imprimerie Nationale)

SALZMAN, M. R. 1990 *On Roman time: the Codex-Calendar of 354 and rhythms of urban life in late antiquity* (Berkeley, Los Angeles and Oxford: University of California Press)

SAUMAGNE, C. 1924 'Notes de topographie carthaginoise. La colline de Saint Louis' *BA/BCTH* 1924, 175–93

SAUMAGNE, C. 1928–1929 'Notes de topographie carthaginoise, I. La *turris aquaria* (d'après les fouilles de 1926)', *BA/BCTH* 1928–1929, 629–47

SAUMAGNE, C. 1931 'Les recherches récentes sur la topographie de Carthage', *Journal des Savants* 1931, 145–57

SAYADI, S. 2007 *À travers les cartes postales: Carthage 1895–1930* (Tunis: Les Éditions de la Mediterranée)

SEBAG, P. 1958 'Une description de Tunis au XIXe siècle', *Cahiers de Tunisie* 6, 161–81

SENAY, P. 2000 'Le rapport préliminaire des fouilles au site de la basilique dite 'Triconque' de *l'Aedes Memoriae* de Carthage (1994, 1996–2000)', in P. Senay (ed.), *Carthage XI; à la basilique dite "triconque" de* l'Aedes Memoriae [= CEA 36], 115–41

SENAY, P. 1996 'Le monument circulaire, l'*aedes memoriae* des testimonia antiques, un monument insigne de la Carthage paléochrétienne', *CEA* 31, 147–63

SHAW, T. 1757 *Travels or observations relating to several parts of Barbary and the Levant* (Oxford: A. Miller and W. Sandby)

SMITH, D. L. (ed.) 2000 *A tour of duty in the Pacific Northwest: E. A. Porcher and H. M. S. Sparrowhawk, 1865–1868* (Fairbanks: University of Alaska Press)

SMITH, R. M. and PORCHER, E. A. 1864 *History of recent discoveries at Cyrene, made during an expedition to the Cyrenaica in 1860–1861, under the auspices of Her Majesty's Government* (London: Day & Son)

SOUMILLE, P. 1992 'Les multiples activités d'un prêtre français au Maghreb: l'Abbé François Bourgade en Algérie et en Tunisie de 1838 à 1858', *Histoire d'Outre-Mer. Mélanges en l'honneur de Jean-Louis Miège*, vol. 1 (Aix-en-Provence: Publications de L'Université de Provence), 233–72

SOUMILLE, P. and PEYRAS, J. 1993 'La mémoire du Protestantisme à Tunis d'après les monuments du cimetière Anglican de Bab-Carthagène (depuis le milieu du XVIIème siècle jusqu'à la fin du XIXème siècle)', in J. Peyras (ed.), *Les monuments et la mémoire* (Paris: Éditions Harmattan), 51–69

SPUFFORD, F. 1997 *I may be some time: ice and the English imagination* (New York: St. Martin's Press)

STAGER, L. E. 1992 'Le tophet et le port commercial', in Ennabli 1992, 73–79

STERN, H. 1953 *Le calendrier de 354. Étude sur son texte et ses illustrations* (Paris: Imprimerie Nationale)

STERN, K. B. 2011 'Keeping the dead in their place: mortuary practices and Jewish cultural identity in Roman North Africa', in E. S. Gruen (ed.), *Cultural identity in the ancient Mediterranean* (Los Angeles: Getty Research Institute), 307–34

STEVENS, S. T., KALINOWSKI, A. V. and VANDERLEEST, H. 2005 *Bir Ftouha: a Pilgrimage Church Complex at Carthage* [Journal of Roman Archaeology Supplementary Series 59], Portsmouth R.I.

STORZ, S. 1991 'Kobbat Bent el-Re: rapport préliminaire sur les recherches effectuées de 1978 à 1989', *CEDAC Carthage* 12, 41–60

STRZYGOWSKI, J. 1888 *Das Calenderbilder des Chronographen vom Jahre 354* [Jahrbuch des Kaiserlichen Deutschen Archäologischen Instituts, Ergänzungsheft I] (Berlin, G. Reimer)

TEMPLE, G. 1835 *Excursions in the Mediterranean. Algiers and Tunis*, 2 vols (London: Saunders and Otley)

THORN, D. M. 2007 *The four seasons of Cyrene. The excavations and explorations in 1861 of Lieutenants R. Murdoch Smith, R. E., and Edwin A. Porcher, R. N.* (Rome: L'Erma di Bretschneider)

TISSOT, C. 1884–1888 *Exploration scientifique de la Tunisie; géographie comparée de la province romaine d'Afrique*, 2 vols (Paris: Imprimerie Nationale), especially 'Topographie de Carthage', Vol. 1, 565–664

TOUTAIN, J. 1915 Untitled note in *BSAF* 1915, 309–16

TRIULZI, A., 1971a 'Una fonte ignorata per la storia della Tunisia: i dispacci dei consoli americani a Tunisi, 1797–1867', *Oriente moderno* 51, 653–78

TRIULZI, A., 1971b 'Italian-speaking communities in early nineteenth century Tunis', *Revue de l'occident musulman et de la Méditerranée* 9, 153–84

TROUSSET, P. 1994 'Les centuriations romaines', in J.-P. Morel (ed.), *La Tunisie, carrefour du monde antique* (Dijon: Éditions Faton), 70–81

TROUSSET, P. 1997 'Les centuriations de Tunisie et l'orientation solaire', *Antiquités africaines* 33, 95–109

TROYAT, H. 1992 *Flaubert*, translated by J. Pinkham (New York: Viking Penguin)

VAN DER KISTE, J. and JORDAAN, B. 1984 *Dearest Affie. . . Alfred, Duke of Edinburgh, Queen Victoria's second son, 1844–1900* (Gloucester: Alan Sutton)

VAUX, W. S. W. 1863a 'On the recent excavations at Carthage', *Transactions of the Royal Society of Literature* n.s. 2, 441–73

VAUX, W. S. W. (ed.) 1863b *Inscriptions in the Phenician character now deposited in the British Museum discovered on the site of Carthage during researches made by Nathan Davis, Esq., at the expense of Her Majesty's Government, in the years 1856, 1857, and 1858* (London: Trustees of the British Museum)

VERCOUTTER, J. 1945 *Les objets égyptiens et égyptisants du mobilier funéraire carthaginois* (Paris: Librairie Paul Geuthner)

VERNAZ, J. 1887 'Notes sur des fouilles à Carthage (1884–1885)', *Revue archéologique* 10, 11–27 and 151–70

VILLIERS, G. 1938 *A vanished Victorian. Being the life of George Villiers, Fourth Earl of Clarendon, 1800–1870* (London: Eyre & Spottiswoode)

VOGUE, C.-J.-M., 1860 *Les églises de la Terre Sainte* (Paris: Librairie de Victor Didron) [reprinted 1973 in Toronto: Presses de l'Université de Toronto]

VON MALTZAN, H. 1870 *Reise in den Regentschaften Tunis und Tripolis*, Vol. 1 (Leipzig: Dyk)

WALFORD, E. (ed.) 1882 [obituary notice for Nathan Davis], *The Antiquarian Magazine* January–June 1882, 152–3

WALL, G. 2001 *Flaubert: a life* (London: Faber and Faber)

WELLS, C. M. 1982 'Excavations at Carthage, Northern Sector, 1981', *EMC/CV* 26, n.s. 1, 206–13

WELLS, C. M. 1992 'Le mur de Théodose et le secteur nord-est de la ville romaine', in Ennabli 1992, 116–23

WELLS, C. M. 1996 'Paul Gauckler et la colline de l'Odéon à Carthage', *Ktema* 21, 157–79

WELLS, C. M., FREED, J. and GALLAGHER, J. 1988 'Houses of the Theodosian period at Carthage', *EMC/CV* 32, n.s. 7, 195–210

WELLS, C. M., CARROLL, M., FREED, J. and GODDEN, D. 1998 'The construction of *decumanus* VI N and the economy of the early colony of Carthage', in Humphrey 1998, 7–63

WERNER, K. E. 1997 'Zur Restaurierung und Verlegung antiker Mosaikpavimente im 18. und 19. Jahrhundert in den Vatikanichen Museen', *MDAI(R)* 104, 477–504

WHITE, J. 1959a 'Hidden stone from ancient Carthage awakes old mysteries at monument', *Washington Post* August 13th 1959, A1 and B6

WHITE, J. 1959b 'Monument's mystery stone identified', *Washington Post* September 20th 1959, A1 and A20

WHITEHOUSE, H. 2001 *Ancient Mosaics and Wall-paintings, Part 1* [in F. Haskell and J. Montagu (eds), *The Paper Museum of Cassiano dal Pozzo. A catalogue raisonné*] (London/Turnhout: Harvey Miller Publishers)

WIGHTMAN, E. M. 1980 'The plan of Roman Carthage: practicalities and politics', in Pedley 1980, 29–46

WILLIAMS, D. F. 1984 'Note on charcoal content in city-wall mortar', in Hurst and Roskams 1984, 81

WILMANNS, G. and MOMMSEN, T. (eds) 1881 *CIL* [Consilio et auctoritate Academiae Litterarum Regiae Borussicae editum] (Berlin: G. Reimer), Vol. 8, Parts 1 and 2

WILSON, A. 1998 'Water supply in ancient Carthage', in Humphrey 1998, 65–102

WILSON, D. M. 1984 *The forgotten collector: Augustus Wollaston Franks of the British Museum* (London: Thames and Hudson)

WILSON, V. 1975 'Punic stelae', in Hurst 1975, 38–9

WOODWARD, F. J. 1951 *Portrait of Jane: A Life of Lady Franklin* (London: Hodder and Stoughton)

YACOUB, M. 1995 *Splendeurs des mosaïques de Tunisie* (Tunis: Agence National du Patrimoine)

V Websites

HOLLOWAY, J. B. with A. BRIGHT-HOLLOWAY, *Cimitero evangelico agli allori, Via Senese, Galluzzo, Firenze, Italia, 1877– /The Modern Protestant Cemetery in Via Senese, Galluzzo, near Florence, Italy, 1877–* http://www.florin.ms/allori.html (created January 6th 2003)

KOESTLER, S. M. *Sally's Family Place* – http://www.sallysfamilyplace.com/wheeler/Porter3.htm (consulted December 26th, 2005)

OUTRESCAUT, P. de 2000 *Le site Pieds-Noirs* http://www.piedsnoirs.org/histoire/tunisie6.htm (list of French consuls at Tunis in the nineteenth century, consulted November 3rd, 2003)

US NAVAL OBSERVATORY, *Sun or Moon Altitude/ Azimuth Table for One Day* http://aa.usno.navy.mil/data/docs/AltAz.html (consulted November 20th and 21st, 2003)

List of illustrations

Author-and-date references are to items in the Bibliography. Those to Davis 1861 refer to the 1861 revised edition with longer pagination; page numbers will differ in other editions.

Figures

Colour Plates

Glossary of Arabic place names

There is no standard transcription for Arabic place names. I have used the following spellings for Arabic place names at Carthage which occur repeatedly in this book, but other versions appear in quotations from other authors.

Bab el-Rih
A monument marked on the plan of Falbe on the north side of the city, the 'Gate of the Wind', which I believe was an arch on the *cardo maximus.* Falbe's site is distinct from the later gate on the Theodosian Wall, but the name may be applied to either site.

Bordj-Djedid
The hill that rises directly from the shore in the north-eastern quarter of the Roman city of Carthage. 'Bordj-Djedid' means 'New Fort', and the summit directly overlooking the sea was the site of a Turkish or Ottoman fort. The summit also has ruins of a huge ancient rectangular double enclosure. The southern slope of Bordj-Djedid is the site of the 'smaller', 'eastern', or 'rainwater' [*sic*] cisterns.

Djebel Bou Kornein
A 'mountain with two peaks' visible across the Gulf of Tunis from Carthage; in Roman times it was the site of a sanctuary of Saturn.

Djebel Khaoui
The catacomb hill south-east of the village of Gammarth. Its name means 'empty mountain.'

Douar ech-Chott
A small village near the Roman circus on the south side of the Roman city of Carthage. Its name means 'village by the salt lake'. The Lake of Tunis may have extended this far in ancient times.

Gammarth
A small village about four miles (six kilometers) north of the Roman city of Carthage. There are ancient underground rock-cut tombs in the hills immediately to the south-east.

Koudiat el-Hobsia
An artificial mound (Falbe no. 74) on the south side of ancient Carthage, just outside the Roman street-grid and west of the merchant port. The Punic *tophet* (the cemetery with burials of babies dedicated to Baal) is on its eastern flank.

La Malga
A small village, now demolished, on the west side of ancient Carthage, within and over the great Roman cisterns of the same name.

La Marsa
An elegant modern suburb of Tunis about two and a half kilometers north of the Roman city of Carthage. Its name means 'the port.'

Sebkha de la Soukra
A shallow salt lake west of Gammarth, also known as the Lake of Ariana, which was open sea in ancient times. With the Lake of Tunis, it made the immediate territory of Carthage a peninsula jutting into the Gulf of Tunis.

Sidi bou-Said
A small village on a high cliff rising directly from the seashore, about two kilometers north-east of the Roman city of Carthage.

Index

References to principal discussions of the indexed items are in bold; italicized numbers refer to illustrations. Topographical references (places and monuments) are to Carthage unless otherwise indicated. *Passim* refers to scattered references throughout the pages indicated. Notes are not indexed except where new material, not signposted in the text, is introduced. Glossary entries and modern authors are not indexed.